The Nature of Love

2

Courtly and Romantic

Books by Irving Singer

The Nature of Love
1. Plato to Luther
2. Courtly and Romantic
3. The Modern World
Mozart and Beethoven: The Concept of Love in Their Operas
The Goals of Human Sexuality
Santayana's Aesthetics
Essays in Literary Criticism by George Santayana (Editor)

The
NATURE
of LOVE

2
Courtly
and Romantic

Irving Singer

The University of Chicago Press
Chicago and London

The University of Chicago Press, Chicago 60637
The University of Chicago Press, Ltd., London

© 1984 by Irving Singer
All rights reserved. Published 1984
Paperback edition 1987
Printed in the United States of America
96 95 94 93 92 91 90 89 88 87   65432

Library of Congress Cataloging in Publication Data

Singer, Irving
     The nature of love.

     Vol. 1 : 2nd ed.
     Includes index.
     Contents: 1. Plato to Luther—2. Courtly and
romantic. 1. Love. I. Title.
BD436.S5 1984   128   84-2554
ISBN 0-226-76094-4 (v. 1, cl.); 0-226-76095-2 (v. 1, pbk.)
        0-226-76096-0 (v. 2, cl.); 0-226-76097-9 (v. 2, pbk.)
        0-226-76098-7 (v. 3)

To
Margaret

Contents

Preface

W<small>E</small> L<small>IVE</small> I<small>N</small> A<small>N</small> A<small>GE</small> O<small>F</small> G<small>REAT</small>
discoveries and, despite the nuclear gloom that hangs over us, hopes
for a new humanity. Muffled as these hopes may be, they are
reinforced by the enormous vitality of contemporary developments
in biology and the life sciences. Within that domain, however, the
most backward region of scientific exploration pertains to problems
about love and sexuality. These affect the moral and personal condition of human beings more immediately than any other; they are
related to aspects of our life in which we all know that we have failed
to some extent; and yet, both science and humanistic research have
neglected the requisite investigations. Government agencies and
professional faculties tend to consider such inquiry too threatening
for them to encourage on any large scale. Even if this attitude can be
explained by reference to basic instincts of privacy wherever sexuality is involved, the fact remains that our communal ignorance creates new and unnecessary hazards, whatever our ethical code may
be.

In some ways, the present inadequacy is most glaring in the field
of historical studies. Though analytic philosophy and academic
psychology have (until recently) ignored human affect, it preoccupied all major thinkers in the West since the Greeks. To my knowledge, however, there exists no systematic history of the subject, no
history of philosophy or psychology or even creative literature that
portrays the magnificent adventure of man's conceptualization in

this field from period to period and from author to author. Nor do I claim to be making up that deficiency myself. In this book, as in the other volumes of my trilogy, I do not attempt to provide the exhaustive account that is needed. The point of view from which I write is limited in its scholarship and somewhat personal in its general orientation. I am particularly interested in discovering the origins of our current ideas about sexual love insofar as they have been determined by works of philosophy and literature. *The Nature of Love: Plato to Luther* dealt mainly with philosophy in the ancient world and the religious concepts of the Middle Ages. The present book focuses on concepts of love between men and women that develop continuously from the eleventh or twelfth centuries through the nineteenth. This temporal span makes a unity within itself. It constitutes the world of ideas we have inherited. The twentieth century overlaps and cannot be understood in isolation from the past, but its own history I leave for the sequel to this volume.

Writing my book in the course of many years, I found that so little had been done along these lines that there were no models for me to emulate or copy. I could draw upon many excellent studies of specific authors or periods in history, but panoramic works by C. S. Lewis, de Rougemont, D'Arcy, and Nygren—just to mention the most prominent—were either too inaccurate or too greatly bounded by their own tendentiousness. They could not tell me what I wanted to know: how man in the twentieth century acquired through the historical development of ideas his ability to think about the nature of love between the sexes. Denis de Rougemont's effort is particularly noteworthy. In works such as *Love in the Western World* and *Love Declared*, de Rougemont treats the concepts of courtly and Romantic love as if they were virtually identical and jointly creative of modern nonreligious attitudes toward sexual passion. De Rougemont sees in the Western world a single, pervasive conflict between passion and orthodoxy, and therefore between courtly and Romantic love, on the one hand, and marriage and established religion on the other. He interprets the legend of Tristan and Iseult as the mythic expression of Western man's quest for passion, which he claims is really a search for death.

De Rougemont's theories have attracted much attention, but

there is very little in historical scholarship to sustain them. As I shall be arguing throughout this book, the medieval and the modern versions of the Tristan legend are greatly different from one another. Concepts of courtly and Romantic love belong to disparate (though intersecting) philosophical traditions, neither of which insists upon a necessary conflict between passion and marriage, and both of which generally identify themselves with affirmative approaches that consider love an ideal completion of life rather than a search or secret hungering for death. In the nineteenth century there does occur the concept of Liebestod, love-death, which I try to explain in relation to what I call "Romantic pessimism." But though it is occasionally foreshadowed even in the ancient world, Liebestod as a fully developed concept of love is less than two hundred years old. In effect, de Rougemont has arbitrarily forced the vast complexity of Western ideas about love into constraining categories drawn from the last two centuries. He has interpreted humanistic thinking about passion as if it all derived from a single type of romanticism. This may make it easier for him to promote the solutions of orthodox Christianity, but it falsifies the facts of history.

The remedy for de Rougemont's kind of propagandistic inaccuracy is sharper philosophical analysis and more precise historical research. The same applies to promising but misleading speculation by Aldous Huxley. I have long admired an essay of his entitled "Fashions in Love." Huxley there suggests that contemporary ideas about love result from a reaction against "the fashionable, Christian-romantic pattern" of the nineteenth century. While he believes the new conception takes love too lightly and therefore needs something like D. H. Lawrence's "mythology of Energy, Life, and Human Personality" as its corrective, Huxley applauds the rejection of nineteenth-century romanticism. He may be right or wrong in this; I myself feel sympathetic toward much of what he recommends. But when Huxley describes the nature of Romantic ideas about love, he distorts the historical data. "Following Rousseau," he says, "the romantics imagined that exclusive passion was the 'natural' mode of love, just as virtue and reasonableness were the 'natural' forms of men's social behavior. Get rid of priests and kings, and men will be for ever good and happy; poor Shelley's faith in this palpable nonsense remained unshaken to the end. He believed also in the complementary paralogism that you have only to get rid of social restraints and erroneous mythology to make the Grand Passion universally chronic."

As always, what Huxley says is imaginative and challenging. But here, at least, it is wildly inaccurate. Rousseau and Shelley are certainly liable to criticism, as is the concept of Romantic love in general—but not in the way that Huxley thinks. The whole endeavor of Rousseau's philosophy was to discover a possible harmonization between passion and virtue, and in general between the natural and the social. He thought this could be done only by purifying passion, not by allowing it to flourish as an exclusive or "natural" mode of love that would make men happy and eliminate the need for priests and kings. On the contrary, Rousseau's idea of purification so thoroughly distills the instinctual out of passion that he ends up with a moral abstraction that has little rapport with what is natural. That will be the basis of my criticism. In the case of Shelley, Huxley's remarks are equally inappropriate. Shelley had no desire to negate the importance of civilization in the growth of man's capacity to love. And he too denies that loving properly merely means doing what comes naturally. Shelley did want to get rid of *harmful* social restraints and *erroneous* mythology, but he never intimates that this can be accomplished through mindless adherence to untrammeled passion. Huxley's account of his views is simply mistaken.

In wishing to rectify faulty interpretations of this sort, I am writing what I call "philosophical history." I use that term because my approach draws upon both of these fields without defining itself as either. I deal with ideas that exist within a historical process, but I make little attempt to show their causal dependence upon one another or to place them within the larger social contexts from which they originate. And although I examine works in philosophy and philosophical literature, I concentrate upon the theme of love in a way that allows me to ignore many of the relevant questions in epistemology, metaphysics, and even ethics. In being philosophical history, the book tries to make sense of its chosen subject by addressing ideas of the past from my own contemporary perspective. This can always issue into new distortions, but my philosophy is pluralistic and that may prevent me from making unwarranted impositions. Moreover, the different chapters are largely autonomous: they may be read as pictures at an exhibition strung together by mere historical continuity.

Love having been a major theme in all of Western literature, I sometimes draw upon the methods of literary criticism. Nevertheless, I generally avoid analyses of formal devices—such as irony or ambiguity—that the authors I discuss use in expressing ideas within their art. Instead I trace the formation of ideals, what I call "idealization," which occurs in both literature and philosophy as part of a constant effort by human beings to resolve basic problems about their affective nature. It is often necessary for me to neglect major works that a literary critic or literary scholar would rightly find worthy of greater attention from his own point of view.

The book is divided into three parts, preceded by an introductory chapter that surveys concepts of love in the West. In the Introduction I demarcate "realist" and "idealist" approaches to love and analyze the latter in terms of the concept of merging. The conflict between the realist and idealist traditions, and the recurrent struggle to harmonize them, establishes a pattern in history that I study throughout the book.

Part I is devoted to humanistic thinking in the Middle Ages, especially in its attempt to overcome the split between human and religious love. Since the term "courtly love" has been the subject of a recent controversy about the utility or even meaningfulness of that phrase, the first chapter in this part offers an analysis designed to give substance to the concept while also distinguishing between different kinds of courtly love.

In Part II, I try to show how medieval humanism's failure to achieve an adequate synthesis between naturalistic and religious love was followed by relatively more successful attempts in later centuries. One of these occurred in the Neoplatonism of the Renaissance, beginning with the philosophy of Marsilio Ficino; another belonged to post-Lutheran, particularly Puritan, thinking as illustrated by the writings of John Milton. Between these two efforts to harmonize the love of nature and the love of God, I find in

Shakespeare's plays a major synthesis of ideas about love that are characteristic of the modern world. The chapter on Shakespeare is the fulcrum of this book. With Shakespeare the earlier humanistic thinking comes together and is unified in ways that prepare us for much that followed in more recent centuries. In Shakespeare the ideal of married love is more completely developed than ever before, while various Romantic concepts appear as if in a preliminary approximation.

In Part III, I approach eighteenth- and nineteenth-century romanticism pluralistically. I suggest that the concept of Romantic love arose as a response to reactions against the Renaissance and Puritan syntheses, which had been attacked by continental Rationalists who argued that sexual love is incompatible with marriage and sometimes claimed that it is pathological by its very nature. In the chapters on Rousseau, Sade, and Stendhal I examine three different attitudes toward passion; and in the subsequent chapters I explore the differences between benign romanticism and Romantic pessimism. The former is optimistic about man's capacity to achieve on earth a heterosexual love that will be comparable to religious love and able to maintain itself in a permanent union such as marriage; the latter finds the world too vile for any such hopes to be realized though it often anticipates a fulfillment of love through death and after death. I analyze these as different but interwoven aspects of the Romantic ideology which creates the background for all twentieth-century thinking about the nature of love.

Among the many philosophers and other writers whom I shall be discussing, very few thought that in their own lives they had found true or satisfying sexual love. We may consider John Donne a shining exception, but Petrarch, Milton, Rousseau, Shelley, Wagner, and others are more eager to confess their inadequacies than to claim much success in this area of life. Even Shakespeare, as I argue, seems to know more about the ideal of married love than about its day-by-day existence; and Stendhal, who considers "l'amour-passion" the only means by which human happiness can be attained, concludes that we must not expect it to last in any one relationship. Cynics may infer from this that these great men spoke beyond their own experience and of things they could not possibly understand.

This, however, ignores the nature of creative genius. The writers I have mentioned imagined possibilities that they themselves may have actualized very imperfectly or for limited periods in their lives but that only great minds such as theirs are able to reveal. What they disclose, through suffering and through personal failure, then seems obvious to the rest of us.

One of my hopes, in tracing the history of these inspired conceptions, is to facilitate the work of future thinkers who will use philosophical and literary insights for scientific investigations based upon verifiable data. Between these different approaches there is no fundamental or necessary chasm. If we are sufficiently pluralistic, we will recognize the potential for beneficial collaboration. After all the centuries of dispute and disagreement, we may soon be in position to reconcile the divergent theories about love, to reach conceptions that will be defensible both as philosophy and as science. That is the opportunity of our present condition as human beings. As Milton says of Adam and Eve at the end of their harrowing experience in Eden, the world is all before us.

My indebtedness to many scholars will be evident to anyone who glances at the references at the end of the book. These notes are mainly citations for passages quoted in the text, but I have also listed other works that were useful to me. For grants that helped to support various stages of my research, I am grateful to the Bollingen, Guggenheim, and Rockefeller Foundations, the Villa I Tatti, and the American Council of Learned Societies. I also wish to thank Josh Cohen, Michael Cull, Herbert Engelhardt, and Norman Rabkin for many helpful comments on particular chapters. I owe special gratitude to the following persons, who read all or much of the manuscript in one or another of its drafts and gave me a vast array of valuable suggestions: Jean H. Hagstrum, Richard A. Macksey, David Perkins, Moreland Perkins, Winthrop Wetherbee, and, above all, my wife Josephine Singer.

I. S.

Introduction
Concepts of Love
in the West

THERE ARE HISTORIANS WHO say that love between men and women, what we would ordinarily think of as sexual love, came into existence only after Western civilization achieved a particular stage of development in the early Middle Ages. Those who have held this view often claim that love was virtually unknown in the ancient world and only a rare occurrence among non-Western societies. Anthropologists, for instance Malinowski in his research with Trobriand Islanders, have documented the fact that Western ideas about love seem to be meaningless in many other cultures, some of them quite advanced; and orientalists have often remarked that before the intrusion of European mores, Eastern thinking about relations between men and women contained little of the West's attempt either to purify sex through love or to make erotic passion into an ideal on its own. This effort, which dominates so much of life in the modern world, is said to have arisen in a particular place—Southern France, or Spain, or Northern Africa—at a particular time in the eleventh or twelfth century, and to have evolved in an uninterrupted manner from then until the twentieth century.

Though this way of thinking about the history of love has often engendered useful scholarship, it is confused in several respects. For one thing, is the view I have been summarizing a theory about behavior or about the history of ideas? Is it claimed that non-Westerners or Europeans in the ancient world did not experience with one another the intimacy, longing, and interpersonal oneness that we associate with sexual love? Even Malinowski notes that while the young Trobrianders defined their relation to one another in terms of sexual interest, easily gratified and generally hedonistic in character, they too experienced strong attachments, emotional dependency, and even occasional jealousy. Surely it is reasonable to assume that people in other lands and in earlier times were not so different from ourselves as to have lived without sexual love until a handful of poets in Provence, or elsewhere, discovered or invented it. It seems much more plausible to think that love, in all its varieties, exists as a complex but common occurrence within human nature as a whole. William James is very persuasive when he says of romantic adoration: "So powerful and instinctive an emotion can never have been recently evolved. But our ideas *about* our emotions, and the esteem in which we hold them, differ very much from one generation to another; and literature . . . is a record of ideas far more than of primordial psychological facts."

In saying this, James correctly implies that the *concept* of sexual love has not existed uniformly and fully developed in all cultures and at all times. There is as little reason to assume a unitary structure in this respect as there would be to think that science or technology has been identical throughout the growth of mankind. What happened in the Middle Ages is important as one among other developments in man's thinking about moral goals, about human possibilities, about sexual ideals that influence his conception of himself whether or not they govern his behavior. Great changes in thought did occur in a particular place, Northern Africa and Southern Europe, at a particular time, around the twelfth century, and very dramatically; and these changes did contribute to a massive flowering that continues into modern consciousness. But the principal events occurred in the history of philosophy and the literary arts. By lending dignity and the sense of rectitude that always comes from conformity to social expectations, ideas about love have also had an effect, sometimes an enormous effect, upon Western behavior. Concepts and, above all, ideals mold and subtly modify our experience of the world. The given is never wholly distinguishable from its interpretation. And though men and women may feign to feel whatever kind of love is approved in their society while really having other interests, the feigning becomes a type of behavior that contributes its own reality. Human nature is itself an interaction between mental constructs acquired through patterns of accumulated experience, individual or communal, and biological mechanisms genetically programmed.

To study the history of love completely, we would have to investigate the ways in which developments of mind—developments in ideation and idealization—are capable of altering behavior while also following a course of evolution within their own domain. That is a task for philosophy and the life sciences, but one in which very little progress has been made as yet. And though I hope my work may be of help in this enterprise, I do not address myself to it in the present book. I wish instead to analyze and clarify the concepts themselves. They diverge considerably, so much so that one may wonder whether there is in the West a common culture or a system of common ideals at any time. The diversities can, however, be systematized to a considerable degree; and I begin by suggesting that Western thinking about sexual love may be categorized in terms of two basic approaches. On the one hand, there is the idealist tradition that Plato codifies for the first time, that Christianity amalgamates with Judaic thought, that courtly love humanizes, and that romanticism redefines in the nineteenth century. On the other hand, there is what I shall call, for want of a better term, the realist tradition that from the very beginnings has rejected the pretensions of idealism as unverifiable, contrary to science, and generally false to what appears in ordinary experience.

In the history of thinking about love, the idealist tradition has always been dominant in the sense that its theories were the most interesting and the most fruitful for later speculation. Early in the development of idealism the concept of love became attached to religious and metaphysical doctrines that sought to penetrate nature's secret mysteries. The realist response took the form of critical disbelief, encouraging reliance upon the verities of sensory experience. Whether as an ideal for changing the world or as a psychological state that mattered to many people, love was to be analyzed in terms of what man could learn about himself through empirical observation. The realist tradition usually turns to the latest science in the hope of attaining accurate insights into nature, including human nature; but only in the twentieth century has science provided the knowledge that realism needed to articulate a vision of its own. In studying realism's past responsiveness to concepts generated by various types of idealism, we can see what realists may finally achieve in the present. We may also find that they can accept more of the idealistic attitude than has often been supposed. Particularly in those areas where idealism furthered humanistic perspectives, an accommodation between the two traditions may now be feasible as never before.

There is one point on which realist and idealist accounts of love tend to agree. They usually begin with the loneliness of man. All animals are aware of otherness; they recognize the possible threat in things that are not themselves. Human beings are especially sensitive to the dangers of isolation. The feeling of separateness is distinctly human. Not that men and women have it on all occasions, but they have it sufficiently often to make the phenomenon a central fact in their experience. Its importance is symbolized in the Book of Genesis by the intimation that only man comes into being without a mate. Only after God realizes that it is not good for Adam to be alone does he create Eve. In Plato's *Symposium* the gods are described as being complete within themselves, self-sufficient, autonomous by virtue of their absolute perfection. But for that reason, Plato insists, it would be absurd to think that the gods love anything but themselves. That is the great difference between the gods and human beings. Ideas about the desirability of loveless self-sufficiency recur throughout Western thought, for instance in Rousseau's belief (renewed in different ways by Thoreau, Ibsen, and others) that man is often happiest when he lives in isolation, freed of the shackles of interpersonal dependency. But more characteristic is that passage in Milton's *Paradise Lost* where Adam, reminding God that a mortal such as himself cannot hope to attain the blessedness of divine solitude, requests the making of a fellow creature with whom he may communicate. Adam suffers through the love which then ensues, but he successfully eliminates the sense of loneliness that belonged to his original condition.

In the tradition of idealistic love, man's primordial loneliness and felt separation provide the impetus to his erotic adventures. The lovers are frequently orphans, like Tristan, or persons cut off from home, like Iseult. When we first meet Romeo, he is out of favor with his lady Rosaline and isolated in his sadness, though surrounded by jovial, admiring friends. The realist tradition recognizes something similar. In Proust, who aspires to a realism relevant to the twentieth century, the long first section of *Remembrance of Things Past* begins with the solitary anguish of the child waiting for his mother's good-night kiss. The entire work consists of a series of attempts to overcome separateness from other people, and from ideals (such as artistic creativity) that matter to the narrator. In psychoanalytic theorists like Fromm and Reik, love is seen not only as the striving to regain oneness with the mother, which Freud emphasized, but also as a healthy means of coping with the necessary separation from her.

Despite the importance it accords the state of isolation, idealist thinking generally considers it surmountable. For the lovers are one, and in some sense always have been. Throughout all possible separations, and despite the blind interference of external forces, they are really indissoluble. How are we to understand the word "really" here? I think it refers to the nature of the oneness itself, the lovers' union, which the idealist refuses to treat as merely a psycho-biological fact about man's existence. According to the realist, people come together for the sake of individual benefit: men and women live with one another as a convenient way of satisfying their needs. This kind of community, whether in society or in the love of man and woman, the realist interprets as an overlapping or wedding of interests rather than a merging of personalities. Yet it is merging through love that the idealist tradition often seeks to glorify. For things only conjoined can be readily separated; they may fit together but they cannot become an essential part of one another, and to that extent the overcoming of separateness remains incomplete. What is merged, on the other hand, contains a common element, an identity that defines the nature of both participants equally well. In finding the beloved, each lover discovers the hidden reality which is himself. In this sense, the lovers have always been united, despite their physical separation, for they have always shared the same self-definition. Just as two heaps of salt may be referred to by the same word because there is some property that both possess, so too—the idealist insists—are lovers joined by a single oneness that is their merged condition.

Though it has always posed difficulties for theologians, the possibility of merging between man and God was affirmed by mystics in the Christian tradition. The idea of a merging between human beings in love with one another develops throughout the Middle Ages as a humanization of the mystical approach. It reaches a peak in Renaissance descriptions, such as John Donne's, of intermingled souls and eye-beams twisted upon one double string, the two lovers being one. In the Romantic era the unity that comes from indissoluble merging is often named as the sole defining attribute of an authentic love between man and woman. A great deal of the idealist tradition could be explicated in terms of the concept of merging alone.

The notion that people can merge with one another is, however, a strange idea, elusive, baffling. In everyday life, we realize that one person's experience may have something in common with another's. We see the same bear and it frightens us in the same way. In our joint fright, a sense of kinship may develop. But we would not ordinarily speak of merging in our personalities, of being or becoming one another. We are distinct individuals, each living his own life, each responsible for what he does. In the idealist conception, however, people lose their individuality, or revert to a profounder oneness that preceded it. They are caught up by, immersed in, something bigger and grander than themselves as separate entities, something that negates and even destroys the boundaries of routine existence. Nor should we dismiss such ideas, however fanciful they may sound. Emotion is always volatile; when sufficiently torrid, it can melt our sense of individuality and possibly wash it away. The idealist lover no longer feels that he belongs to the world of separate selves, and that is why he often loses all concern for former responsibilities. He may lie, he may steal, he may kill—there is nothing a Tristan or Iseult will not do in order to preserve their sense of oneness. In merging with the beloved, lovers in the idealist tradition believe that they have transcended the restraints of ordinary life, even though they cannot escape them entirely.

Let us assume that the concept of merging makes sense. But how could merging possibly occur in the world as we know it? By means of magic. At least, whatever provides the love for which an idealist yearns will seem magical to everyone else. It is magic that violates empirical laws of nature, thereby creating that which cannot be obtained by ordinary means. Magic violates by its very being: it destroys the orderliness and comfortable routine that characterize everyday existence. To merge in the manner of idealistic love is to obliterate the old reality, one's former way of life. Magic tries to accomplish this, and it may well symbolize radical transformations that love can actually institute.

The techniques of magic are familiar to everyone who has studied the concept of love in the Western world. There is the love philter that Tristan and Iseult drink, believing it is cooling wine—in other words, a good that belongs to their normal, civilized world, whereas instead it destroys their capacity to benefit from civilization. There are the arrows of Cupid that rain down upon Dido and Aeneas, arrows being instruments of war that represent the suffering unto death that soon follows. There are more subtle means as well: the sudden exchange of glances that signifies the meeting and mingling of souls, in *Romeo and Juliet* as in hundreds of courtly romances that preceded it; the delicate touching of fingers that communicates the electric charge which is life called forth by love, in Michelangelo's version of God creating Adam as well as in *La Bohème* when Mimi and Rodolfo grope for her key under the table; the ritualistic kiss with which the prince awakens Sleeping Beauty to heightened consciousness through love, and which Leontes in Shakespeare's romance *The Winter's Tale* wishes to bestow upon what he presumes to be the statue of his dead wife.

The Winter's Tale ends with Leontes' realization that love can be a socially acceptable and wholesome magic. For the statue—his wife in her frozen and withdrawn condition, a state of alienation parallel to the former madness of Leontes alienated from himself—comes alive now that he loves her again. As in Greek mythology the statue of Galatea becomes a living woman for Pygmalion thanks to the magical powers of Aphrodite the goddess of love, Leontes feels his wife respond to his embrace. "If this be magic," he says, "let it be an art/Lawful as eating." If it were lawful, however, love would no longer be magic. And if, like eating, it were a commonplace occurrence in ordinary life, it would not interest the idealist. For him, love is always an *extra*ordinary event, an epiphany of the mystical oneness which is the merging with another person. That, as we shall see, is why the mature Shakespeare can never align himself entirely with the idealists.

The idea of love as merging through magic receives one of its earliest expressions in the speech that Plato gives Aristophanes in the *Symposium*. After explaining how present-day men and women are only half of the totalities they originally were, and which the gods bisected, Aristophanes describes love as a yearning for the other half from whom one has been severed, the person who belongs to us "in the strictest sense." He has Hephaestus, the wonder-worker, ask two lovers: "Is the object of your desire to be always together as much as possible, and never to be separated from one another day or night? If that is what you want, I am ready to melt and weld you together, so that, instead of two, you shall be one flesh; as long as you live you shall live a common life, and when you die, you shall suffer a common death, and be still one, not two, even in the next world."

Aristophanes is not Plato's spokesman, of course, and when Socrates delivers the final speech, he says nothing about melting or welding. Instead he depicts true love as the knowing of absolute beauty provided by a special faculty of reason. Absolute beauty, the form or defining principle of beauty (and goodness), is a metaphysical entity the lover contemplates. In the *Symposium* Socrates does not say that men can merge with it, though in the *Republic* he does mention this as a possibility. Nevertheless, his speech at the end of the *Symposium* is basic to all idealistic thinking about love as merging. Where Aristophanes had spoken mainly of unifying bodies, making the lovers into one flesh, Socrates insists that the object of love is not a specific instance of beauty, certainly not this or that beautiful body, but *absolute* beauty—the idea, the essence, the formal character, of beauty wherever it occurs. Since everything is beautiful sub specie aeternitatis, Socrates concludes that absolute beauty is the ground of all being. Aristophanes called love "the pursuit of the whole," meaning the primordial spherical body of man that the gods bisected. For Socrates too, love is the pursuit of the whole—the whole universe seen as a totality and understood by reference to its ideal form, its eternal value.

Plato left the matter there; but Christianity did not. It combined the eroticism of Aristophanes' myth with the spirituality of Plato's conception of an ideal good. The Hebraic God became the object of love, displacing absolute goodness, which served as one of his major attributes. Throughout a long tradition in the West, religious love was defined as a search for union with the supreme reality which was God. For many mystics God was a person with whom one merged as one might with a human lover. It is this strand of mysticism, bristling with physical imagery, that led some realist critics to consider religious love a sublimation of sex. In the religious love of other mystics, however, the independent personality of God—and everything else that might enable one to treat divinity anthropomorphically— vanishes to a point where supreme reality becomes the mystical experience itself. For these mystics, the sense of oneness, the act of merging with all being, contained within itself the religious import that was formerly accorded to an encounter with a separately existent deity.

The differences between these two religious attitudes contribute to the differences between medieval and Romantic mysticism. Both were attacked by Christian orthodoxy, which maintained that man could not merge with God though they might be wedded to one another in a union that retained their ultimate diversity. To the extent that Christian dogma denied the possibility of merging, it has always incorporated some of the realist approach to love. It was mystical beliefs about oneness, however, that enabled concepts of religious and human love to influence each other reciprocally throughout the history of idealistic theorizing. Not only was there a similar emphasis upon indissoluble merging, but also a comparable belief in what is, in effect, magic as a means of initiating it. As the erotic lover is suddenly and madly overcome by love, so too does the religious lover undergo miraculous, usually spontaneous, conversion and revelation. The avowals, commitments, I-love-you's of the one are duplicated by the ritual phrases, prayers, and cabalistic utterances of the other. Even in orthodox religions that deny the possibility of merging with the godhead, elements of magic insinuate themselves in various ways. Thus communion occurs when the believer eats bread that is the body of Christ and drinks wine that is his blood. Christ, himself the merging of man and god, undergoes the Passion—a love that magically enables the world to transcend itself, i.e. to merge with the world beyond. The mystic abstracts this aspect of established doctrine and singlemindedly makes it the principle of his loving aspiration.

Mysticism is not limited to Christianity. But it is largely through the Christian reinterpretation of Greek philosophy that the tradition of idealistic love developed. Aristophanes' myth was probably taken from the Orphic mysteries, and even in Genesis we find the notion of a primordial human whole, Eve having been created from one of Adam's ribs. But only Christian mysticism (abetted by related developments in Judaism and Islam) was able to synthesize ideas about love-as-merging with the cosmic metaphysics of Plato and Aristotle. Though concepts of idealistic love between men and women may have had forerunners in the ancient world, their most inventive expressions occur after Christianity entrenched itself throughout the West. The two major approaches to ideal erotic love—medieval courtliness and modern romanticism—both consist of attempts to humanize the love that Christian mystics had generally reserved for man in relation to God. Whether or not its object is suprahuman, the idealist tradition seeks ultimate oneness through the magic of merging with another person.

Merging, magic, metaphysical import: these terms suggest a unified vision of the world. But when we look closer, we find enormous diversity within idealism despite the unmistakable resemblances among the different members of its conceptual family. There are also general methodological difficulties that must be considered. If we think of history as a succession of unrelated events in response to one or another demand of the immediate environment, we shall not find much continuity or development among the concepts of love. If, on the other hand, we expect to find a systematic meaning or dialectical determination in it all, as Hegel and Marx do, we shall be constantly defeated by the waywardness and inconsistency of historical fact. But possibly we can avoid both extremes. In the eight hundred years that have been dominated by courtly and Romantic concepts, by religious ideas with which they are interwoven, and by the realist attitude that both precedes them and serves as their critique, man would *seem* to be working towards illumination about several fundamental problems in his affective being. History is like a number of rivulets running through the countryside. The path each of them takes is influenced by unpredictable occurrences in the soil, the climate, the amount of rain, etc.; and yet the direction of flow is also a function of the successive movement from their one or many sources. The ideas of love this book seeks to analyze are historical rivulets, rivulets in history, that intersect and freely branch within themselves. In the patterns they make, these conceptions reveal various problems basic to mankind's thinking about human affect. I mention some of them now in order to systematize in advance the diversities that we shall be studying.

First, I detect a long-enduring attempt to see whether love as spiritual aspiration can be harmonized with love as sexual reality. For the Platonist, spirituality takes precedence in the order of being while sexuality is usually first in a person's experience. For the Christian ascetic, the two are implacable enemies and man must choose whether to serve one or the other, God or the devil. Throughout the centuries we are considering, however, we find a frequent search for accommodation—in one manner or another—between the opposing extremes. The prevailing system of thought in the Middle Ages, the caritas-synthesis, provides a reconciliation that worked very well for many Christians. The caritas-synthesis sees all reality under the aspect of spiritual love, originating in God's agapē and returning to him through each creature's natural desire to reciprocate his love. As a striving for man's greatest good and source of happiness, erotic love—whether in sex or in some religious extension of it—finds a legitimate place within the system as long as it too leads toward the love of God. The caritas-synthesis did not explain, however, how persons could love one another as just the human beings that they are, combinations of body and soul, ends in themselves and not merely instrumentalities for loving God.

In its own chaotic way, the cluster of humanistic ideas that scholars have called the concept of courtly love deals with this problem. But no satisfactory solution could be attained, despite the efforts of Dante, until the religious doctrines of the Middle Ages were greatly modified. This happened in the Neoplatonism of the Italian Renaissance and in Luther's attack upon the caritas-synthesis. In Romantic religion, much of which considered itself Christian, the conflict between the spiritual and the sensory, between the "transcendent" and the "immanent" (as it was often called), is eliminated by a divinization of the vital principle that runs through love in nature. To orthodox Christians who considered this a new form of pantheism, the solution was unacceptable as religion; to realists who saw it as a sentimental idealization of sex, it was not adequate to the needs of scientific explanation. The problem for the twentieth century was, and is, whether this or any other Romantic synthesis between spiritual and sexual love could be harmonized with ideas about health or personal growth that were now evolving.

The second of these major problems deals with the relation between marriage and sexual love that is either premarital or extramarital. All the traditions we have discussed recognize that marriage and nonmarital sex can each provide its own kind of love. The friendship that Plato examines in the *Symposium* and the *Phaedrus* begins as sexual love between two persons not married to each other, both of whom happen to be male; but Plato's *Laws* approaches love from a different perspective. For there Plato argues for the social importance of marriage and describes the optimal relationship between husband and wife. Medieval Christianity insisted upon the goodness of married love but tended to consider it a nonpassional affection or working partnership. Though the Protestant Reformation sought to bridge the chasm between sexual passion and Christian marriage, it retained much of the medieval approach.

For many people in the Middle Ages, and later, the religious conception was inadequate, insensitive to human interests. While it held that marriage was a sacrament, it seemed to ignore the possible ideality of sexual love between the spouses; and certainly the church could find no justification for a yearning to merge with another person in ardent bonds that belonged to the core of one's being. But where advocates of courtly love saw this metaphysical oneness as the achievement of men and women who truly loved each other, they often had difficulty applying such ideals to marriage. When married love received its greatest idealization in the late Renaissance and in the Romantic period, massive attempts were made to harmonize marriage and sexual passion, but frequently in ways that had little rapport with the day-to-day necessities of human beings living in the real world.

A third problem overlaps the first two. In the Western world, love has generally been treated as an ideal and not merely as a disposition comparable to attitudes such as fear, ambition, disdain, boredom, or cheerfulness. These readily lend themselves to empirical investigation, but theories about love have generally sounded like exhortations to search for values that may or may not exist. The first problem, about love as sense or love as spirituality, pivots about the difficulty of changing a natural response into an idealistic striving for the infinite. The object of a spiritual love, whether God or the Good, might possibly serve as an ultimate lure for mind and heart, but can it be loved in experiences comparable to what we undergo when we love human beings? We may wish to love another person while also loving God, and we may see no incompatibility between human and religious love, but how are we to understand the idea that each type of love explains the nature of the other? Underlying the conflict between sexual love and marriage there also lingers this apparent split between love as a mundane attitude and love as a transcendental aspiration. For some theorists marriage is merely a worldly institution requiring adherence to the legal bonds it imposes, while passionate love enables men and women to seek ideal values that rise above the routine conventionalities of married life. Others maintain the reverse: they treat conjugal love as the remote and elusive goal that fulfills, ideally, a long process of psychobiological exploration which includes sexual passion between male and female.

This problem has pervasive importance because scientific analysis addresses itself more easily to attitudes or dispositions than to ideals. When a modern psychologist studies love, he investigates a complex system of behavior related to developmental processes and explicable in terms of individual survival, species reproduction, and the acquisition of cultural habits. The psychologist is in no position to adjudicate about ideals: he may recognize that love sometimes involves a search for them, but he cannot distinguish between true love and a deceptive imitation on the grounds that only one ideal object is appropriate while others are not.

The great bulk of Western theorizing about love has, however, sought emotional responses that were uniquely correct, uniquely suitable for the fulfillment of one or another moral aspiration. The problem consists in making sense of these endeavors in view of the possibility that lovers may really be motivated by attitudes that are quite remote from such ideals. Human beings are often self-oriented, possessive and appetitive, frequently manipulative and domineering toward those with whom they share intimacy. How can we reconcile man's self-love with a benevolent concern for other persons, or sexual urgency with a nonappetitive acceptance of another's being, or aggressiveness with a compassionate, tender giving of oneself? Can these be explained in terms of each other? Does love include both polarities, or possibly neither?

For the realist tradition, the problem is solved by reducing the ideal of love to whatever data empirical observation discloses. Love is then seen as a natural phenomenon distorted by man's propensity to formulate idealistic philosophies. From this, it follows that either we find in man an instinct or social aptitude for loving others or else love is just a devious form of selfishness. Theories about an instinct of love or an innate ability to acquire love in society having thus far eluded scientific proof, the realist often concludes by reducing love to reproductive drive, need gratification, or dependence upon parents. He may be right, but still men and women act as if programmed to idealize, to bestow value, to create and cherish objects loved beyond their capacity to satisfy selfish interests. Regardless of our desire to be precise and rigorous in all analyses of human nature, we misrepresent man's affective being if we assume that an ideal such as love can be reduced to something else with which our current science feels more comfortable. For this reason alone, the concepts of courtly and Romantic love are still worth studying—if only for the sake of learning how to move beyond them.

As I mentioned in the Preface, the succeeding chapters may be read as pictures at an exhibition. I have hung them in accordance with my own aesthetic taste, my own moral orientation, and my own intuitive sense of what is real and important in human nature. To this extent, of course, they are more than just a random display. But also they are internally related by having a place within a temporal order, and that alone makes a continuity of historical processes. We use synoptic and largely unsatisfactory terms—"idealization," "courtly love," "Romantic love," "religious love," "idealism," "realism," "naturalism," "humanism"—in order to sharpen the focus of our telescopic lens in ways that are coherent with our own particular perspective. There is nothing wrong in doing so, and much would be lost if we avoided all general terminology in the (mistaken) belief that this affords a greater fidelity to details. At the same time, we must always remember that, suggestive as our thematic analyses may be, they cannot alter the fact that in itself human experience is a flux of largely chaotic and sporadic adventures in the imagination. Historians, like philosophers of love, contribute their own idealizations. That, I am convinced, is unavoidable. But, as Spinoza would say, if only we accept what is necessary, we thereby master it and attain our freedom.

Part I
Humanism in the Middle Ages

1

The Concept of Courtly Love

THE TERM "COURTLY LOVE" DID not originate during the Middle Ages. It was introduced into the language of scholars and laymen only in 1883. In that year a great French medievalist, Gaston Paris, used the words *amour courtois* to characterize an attitude toward love that first manifested itself in French literature of the twelfth century. Paris was primarily interested in the content of poems and legends, but he also thought that courtly love pervaded medieval culture as a social ideal. Under his influence scholars began to talk about a "system" of courtly love, a "code," a "body of rules," and even a "way of life." They often gave the impression that all secular literature written in Europe between the twelfth and fifteenth centuries would somehow be related to this phenomenon, defending or attacking it or at least showing its effect upon cultivated thought. As one might expect, the critical theory became more and more diffuse. In recent years, particularly within the last two decades, several scholars have complained that the term "courtly love" is now too amorphous to be of any use. Some have argued that Paris' original thesis is inherently untenable; others have said that a gradual change in thought and behavior may have occurred in the twelfth and later centuries, but nothing as dramatic as formerly assumed; and one scholar has even denied "that there was any such thing as what is usually called courtly love during the middle ages."

In view of the fact that we are dealing with the thought, the literature, and even the social behavior of several centuries—many people in different countries, dozens of languages, several distinct traditions—it would be remarkable if there were any *single* code or system of rules that could possibly have characterized the European continent as a whole. Human nature rarely lends itself to that kind of uniformity. Communication being as difficult as it was during the Middle Ages, one can be sure that ideas about love varied greatly. Of greater interest, therefore, is the question whether anything ever existed that might properly be called a concept of courtly love in the medieval period. If we can make sense out of the idea, historians and sociologists may then determine to what extent it belonged to literature and philosophy, to what extent it contributed to the thinking of ordinary people in daily life, to what extent it was limited to one or another socioeconomic class, and to what extent it could have affected historical change. In his own approach to the concept of courtly love, the historian Johan Huizinga distinguished between representative ideals and compensatory ideals. The former he thought of as symbols of what actually existed in a culture; the latter as compensations for what did not exist but was considered desirable. Huizinga argued that courtly love was an ideal of the second type. Unfortunately, he made only limited attempts to clarify the meaning of the term.

Gaston Paris believed that the essence of amour courtois could be found in a poetic romance by the twelfth-century author Chrétien de Troyes which recounted the adventures of Lancelot and Guinevere. The romance was called "Le Chevalier de la Charrette" ("The Knight of the Cart"), and it described adultery against a background of knightly adventure in a feudal society which held that marriage is holy and that nothing can justify a violation of the marital vow. Paris defined the new attitude toward love as inherently illicit, furtive, idolatrous, and ennobling. For though the adulterous love ran counter to religious and secular norms, and therefore had to be kept secret, it was treated as something that ennobled the lovers and warranted their total dedication. The lover felt he must devote himself entirely to his lady, accept her authority in every area of life, submit to her demands, and humbly serve her in any way he could.

In glorifying idolatry of this sort, courtly love would have to undermine feudal duties that a knight normally owed his master—in this case, King Arthur—and it would also violate religious commandments about the love of God. Worshiping Guinevere as a goddess, at one point even genuflecting as he leaves her bedchamber, Lancelot could not be said to love the Christian God with all his heart and all his mind and all his soul. According to Paris, the romance weaves its drama out of this inevitable conflict between courtly love, on the one hand, and the established institutions of state and religion on the other.

Though different authors and different societies dealt with the conflict in their own individual ways, Paris thought that the nature of courtly love remained substantially the same. His definition was furthered by an influential book, *The Allegory of Love,* that C. S. Lewis wrote in 1936. Lewis there described courtly love in terms of four characteristics: humility, courtesy, adultery, and the religion of love. He thought they united in a "systematic coherence" that defined a single sentiment, and like Paris, he claimed that most of medieval love-literature could be elucidated by reference to it.

If this is what one means by courtly love, however, one immediately finds reason to doubt that the concept functioned in the Middle Ages as Paris and Lewis believed. Taking Lancelot's relation to Guinevere as the model or paradigmatic case, what are we to say about the common troubadour emphasis upon sexual continence? Lewis blandly states that courtly love manifests itself "throughout the love poetry of the Troubadours as a whole," and by the troubadours he is referring to the poets of Provence who flourished for two or three hundred years beginning at the end of the eleventh century. But they frequently rule out adultery as a part of true love. Sometimes they even exclude the possibility of coveting another man's wife sexually. In its later developments, troubadour poetry often turns into mere paeans of praise that even a jealous husband could find gratifying.

Scholars have also questioned the reliability of some of the other defining attributes. I am convinced that the definition of courtly love formulated by Paris and Lewis is very misleading. But rather than eliminate the term from scholarly discourse, I think it is wiser merely to redefine the concept in a way that will accommodate the great diversity of attitudes toward love in the Middle Ages. No single work of literature can yield the essence of secular love throughout the period, and there is no need to assume that any one concept had the systematic pervasiveness that Paris and Lewis were looking for. And yet, the history of ideas about love did undergo a new development at the end of the eleventh and beginning of the twelfth centuries. A fresh approach to human relations arose in that early renaissance and it continued for hundreds of years, in some respects up to the present, as a recurrent phenomenon that can very well demand to have a title of its own. Lewis oversimplifies matters when he says that the French poets of the eleventh and twelfth centuries invented or discovered or "were the first to express" the romantic passion of nineteenth-century poetry. But certainly there is a kinship between ideas about sexual love in these different periods of history. In various ways, the Romantic concept of love is more closely linked to medieval ideas than to any that preceded them. Something of special significance did happen in the twelfth century, and those who see a continuity—even an evolution of ideas—developing for eight hundred years are not guilty of falsifying the facts.

Since this new phenomenon in thought, in literature, and to some extent in social behavior was nurtured within the medieval courts, as opposed to monasteries or churches, and since it was concerned with attitudes related to courtliness, nothing is lost if we retain the term "courtly love." At the same time, it is important to realize that the concept cannot be defined in terms of fixed and invariable attributes, necessary and sufficient conditions. For that would mean that every love that has been called courtly must satisfy all of these conditions, and vice versa. It seems more reasonable to seek a cluster of ideas that may not *imply* one another on all occasions but often go together in a characteristic manner particularly recognizable during the period we are considering.

Approaching the idea of courtly love in this fashion, we can say that even though it is not the only conception of love between the sexes that belongs to the thinking of the Middle Ages, it influenced many writers in that period and generally involved the following beliefs: (1) sexual love between men and women is *in itself* something splendid, an ideal worth striving for; (2) love ennobles both the lover and the beloved; (3) being an ethical and aesthetic attainment, sexual love cannot be reduced to mere libidinal impulse; (4) love pertains to courtesy and courtship but is not necessarily related to the institution of marriage; (5) love is an intense, passionate relationship that establishes a holy oneness between man and woman. Once we place these beliefs, not always stated overtly, within their medieval context, we discover various kinds of idealization that overlap or resemble one another well enough to bear the same general term. Before we study the different types of courtly love, however, I wish to clarify the five criteria that I have suggested for its definition.

❀

1. Sexual love between men and women is *in itself* something splendid, an ideal worth striving for. This may not seem revolutionary, but in fact it is a radical conception that few thinkers in Europe had seriously entertained before the eleventh century. Plato, for instance, described love as the greatest of all ideals and a key to understanding the nature of reality, but he did not think that love fully showed itself in relationships between men and women. There was something in their biological disparity that made it difficult for members of the different sexes to respond to one another with the kind of love that Plato idealized. The stirrings of true love he found in homosexual friendships of a passionate sort, and even there consummatory interests prevented the ideal from manifesting itself in its final purity. Consequently Plato's philosophy articulates a ladder up which the soul must rise in order to liberate itself from dependence on any one body, any one person, and all particularities of the empirical world, in order to attain that oneness with the Good or the Beautiful which brings us as close to perfect love as is humanly possible.

I mention Plato because he is the greatest philosopher of love in the ancient world, and his influence upon Western culture became a permanent and inexhaustible resource. But Platonism is not the only philosophical movement that found it difficult to believe that love as an ideal possibility could exist between men and women. Christian theology, both orthodox and heretical, institutional and mystical, Platonistic and non-Platonistic, maintained that the only object worthy of love, the only person capable of eliciting an authentic love, was God himself. All love originated with God and ultimately returned to him. God was in fact love itself, that being his supreme attribute. To suggest that men and women could love one another would not have shocked Christian thinkers, but they always interpreted this love as subservient to a love of God without which human attachments could only be sinful and degrading. St. Augustine even defined the word "lust" (*cupiditas*) as any inclination that "aims at enjoying oneself and one's neighbor [i.e. another human being] without reference to God." True love, what he called *caritas*, would involve the enjoyment of God for his own sake and "the enjoyment of oneself and one's neighbor in subordination to God." There could be no love between man and woman that was honorific *in itself*, meritorious because of an ideal goodness to be found in their relationship alone.

Prior to the advent of courtly love, there existed ideals of human conduct that were neither Platonic nor Christian, but in general they did not focus upon the sexual intimacy between men and women. Aristotle, Cicero, and their followers throughout the centuries exalted friendship as a superior virtue and sometimes admitted the possibility that men and women could be friends; but there was nothing in the nature of friendship, as they saw it, that had any particular relevance to human sexuality or to the cravings that unite men and women. Though pagan mythologies recognized sexual love as a controlling force in human nature, they generally depicted the destructiveness that might issue from it; only rarely did they consider an erotic need for union as the basis of a separate or defensible ideal. Love between the sexes could always turn into madness, and though madness could sometimes be divine, it was not to be recommended in the way that hundreds of medieval writers would eventually advocate the passion in courtly love.

For its part, the love that the Bible enjoined upon men and women might well have established itself as an ideal oneness between them; but once the Old Testament was Christianized, it became difficult for anyone in the Western world to emancipate sexual love from the limitations imposed by the love of God. Even the Song of Songs, which seems so modern to us now, so free and naturalistic in its celebration of sexuality, was reinterpreted as the love between Christ and his church. In the Hellenistic period, fables about young and innocent passion captured the imagination of many readers, but it took a thousand years for the essential goodness of such love to assert itself as an ideal to which men and women could devote their lives without necessarily submerging it in the love of God. What had been an inevitable calamity in Greek tragedy, or a base preoccupation to the philosophers, or a sinful deflection of religious love as envisaged by the theologians, now became a goal that men and women could rightly pursue just by loving one another *as* men and women. Having idealized this human potentiality, the proponents of the new conception would then have to determine whether or not it was compatible with the traditional standards of Christianity that most people also accepted in the Middle Ages.

2. Love ennobles both the lover and the beloved. In becoming an ideal for human beings, and possibly the highest of all ideals, the oneness between man and woman was thought to ennoble both of them. Arising out of the male-dominated society that everyone took for granted, courtly love automatically used the active term "lover" for the man and the passive "beloved" for the woman. This alone would constitute a problem for many of its adherents. For all of them, however, it was a matter of belief that lover and beloved both enjoyed a distinctive nobility that could not be reached in any other way. Far from being a misfortune, as the philosophical and theological traditions had maintained, sexual love would make people better, finer, more likely to realize their human nature. Writing at the end of the courtly tradition, and even attacking it as a dangerous illusion, Shakespeare represents love's claim to nobility when he has Antony embrace Cleopatra in public while proclaiming: "The nobleness of life/Is to do thus; when such a mutual pair/And such a twain can do't. . . ."

Does this mean that love could not be nobleness unless it were enacted by a man and a woman who had the qualities of Antony and Cleopatra? Does love make noble those who would otherwise be inferior, or does it derive its value from the prior goodness of the lovers themselves? Different voices within the courtly tradition answer this kind of question in different ways. It is a problem to which we shall return. In all the varying replies, however, it is always assumed that the nobility of love—whatever its origin—makes the lovers better as human beings. Without love, or once it has been lost, their life would lose its savor. Men and women deprived of their beloved would pine away, die of broken hearts, or suffer psychosomatic disorders. Though even successful love could create such pathology, "love's sickness" being a total disorientation that was painful as well as pleasant, lovers were superior people merely in undergoing the amatory experience.

Being the cause, or at least the manifestation, of nobleness, love would have to duplicate the moral virtues that were associated with nobility in general. Since the social structure of the Middle Ages was mainly feudal and hierarchical, men were expected to serve their lords while women were required to show fidelity. In courtly love this was transformed into meaning that the lover would serve his lady and that she would be faithful to him. Courtly love is often said to have placed women on a pedestal and to have made men into knights whose heroic lives would henceforth belong to elevated ladies. The idea arises from the fact that men frequently used the language of chivalry to express their servile relationship to whatever woman they loved, and sometimes they described her as a divinity toward which they might aspire but could never hope to equal. Much of the troubadour poetry rehearses this refrain. But the courtly attitude could also be moderate in its conception of the beloved, recognizing that one might love her even if she was not a goddess. For her part, the woman could manifest through different kinds of fidelity the excellence that love had created in her. She might, for instance, refuse to have sexual relations with anyone other than her lover. But here again the nobility of love could show itself in a less extreme fashion. A married woman might cheerfully submit to her husband's demands without thereby impugning her devotion to the man she loved in a way that she did not love her husband. In that event, her behavior would simply parallel the virtue of a knight who serves his lord and possibly the church as well as the lady he loves. Similarly, he might enjoy the sexuality of other women—his own wife, his mistresses, and even an occasional peasant girl—without confusing the pleasures experienced in such encounters with the special ecstasy to be found in the company of his beloved. His love for her was a spiritual dedication that could not exist in relations with other women; and correspondingly, her fidelity to him would manifest that nothing outweighed the value of his service to her.

Embodying this special kind of ideal affinity between a man and a woman, love could only occur between one particular man and one particular woman. Their mutual nobility of devotion created a unique oneness between them. A man who fell in love with a woman, thereby losing his capacity to love other ladies at the same time and in the same way, would be jealous of all other men because he would realize that if his lady loved them she could not love him with the uniqueness that courtly love requires. And though jealousy was ordinarily considered to be a vice when it appeared in the woman's husband, it was ennobled by association with the ideality of true love. As something lovers experience, jealousy was commendable. Far from revealing possessiveness or brutal domination, it would merely attest to the inescapable bonds of love that linked one and only one man to one and only one woman. Like deeds of valor and superhuman constancy in the face of social opposition, jealousy was needed to defend a love that improves the character of human beings. What in others might have been a fault thus became a sign of virtue.

3. Being an ethical and aesthetic attainment, sexual love cannot be reduced to mere libidinal impulse. One of the reasons the ancient world tended to see love as a calamity was the fact that it was so obviously related to sexual instinct. Since this was purely mechanical, as Lucretius argued, love between the sexes could not be anything more than slavery imposed upon us by our corporeal being. Whether one's interest was oriented toward pleasures of the senses, or was passionate and therefore an emotional excitement, sexual love could hardly involve conditions suitable for the attaining of high ideals. This kind of materialism existed long before Lucretius began to write. Plato attacked it by suggesting that love is not reducible to sex, indeed that sex is reducible to love. In doing so, Plato

initiates the great idealistic tradition which continued not only in the Christian attitude toward love but also in courtly and ultimately Romantic ideas about spiritual unity that provides a goodness sex alone could not equal. Before the beginnings of courtly love, there had been attempts to idealize sexuality by amalgamating it with various religious rituals of the ancient world. But courtly love approaches the sexual in a different way. Like Platonism and other developments within the idealist tradition, it subordinates the physiological and biological mechanism of sexual attraction to an attunement between souls—a bonding whose value cannot be wholly explained in physical terms. Courtly love was explicitly sexual much of the time, though not always, but it was not to be confused with attachments that were merely sexual. To treat another person as simply a sex object was to disregard the nobility of a love that involves more than just a search for direct gratification.

On the other hand, there is no need to minimize the role of sexuality in courtly love. To do so would be to render the concept inapplicable to the great bulk of medieval romance literature, to the teachings of secular moralists, and to most of the troubadour poetry in France (and its equivalents in Germany or Spain). De Rougemont, inspired by Dante Gabriel Rossetti and the mentality of Pre-Raphaelite Victorians, has popularized the notion that courtly love was "really" antisexual, puristic and ascetic, in conformity to its alleged dependence upon the Catharist heresy. But not only does this grossly misrepresent the influence of that heresy, but also it distorts the nature of nonreligious writings about love in the Middle Ages. In most of them, sexual deprivation was not a central or basic principle; and even among the troubadours, whom de Rougemont cites as the proof of his argument, repression and renunciation were only rarely identified with asceticism or a denial of all sexual components in love.

4. Love pertains to courtesy and courtship but is not necessarily related to the institution of marriage. If we think of courtliness as the acquisition of those polite and equilibrating gestures which enable human beings to communicate without intruding upon each other's privacy, to breach the sanctuary of another's separate being

without storming it in the manner of material self-assertiveness, we begin to see the suitability of the word *courtly* in courtly love. Rudiments of the affiliation between courtship, courtesy, and courtliness are apparent even in the behavior of nonhuman species. In the ceremonial rituals of mating birds and animals one often finds those mincing, dance-like gestures of tentative approach and momentary withdrawal that characterize much of what human beings consider to be the politeness of courteous or civilized behavior. As the Middle Ages developed out of darker centuries of ignorance and poverty, they acquired the capacity to enjoy gracious and formal amenities of cultivated society. Men and women could find new and even luxuriant ways of demonstrating their erotic interest in one another. Whether remaining purely verbal or inducing mating possibilities, whether formal or flirtatious, feigned or sincere, fleeting or permanent, this attitude provided a means of enjoying one another's company in a context that was more or less sexual without necessarily being related to an institution such as matrimony.

This is not to say that courtly love was limited to extramarital dalliance or premarital courtship. It was not the same as married love, but only occasionally was it thought to be essentially incompatible with marriage. This important point has been misunderstood by many popularizers, and even scholars, who have wished to treat courtly love as either fanciful yearning or else as a form of adultery. Neither of these is a necessary element within the concept. In some of its versions, courtly love could very well occur between married people, as a supplement to matrimony and as a strengthening of it.

In general, courtly love came into being as a response to the institution of marriage in the Middle Ages, as an attempt to recommend the value of sexual courtesy and individual choice in an area of life that had been controlled by economic, political, and largely impersonal considerations. Courtly love contributed to a way of thinking we easily accept in the modern world: namely, the belief that marriage cannot succeed unless husband and wife have freely chosen one another on the basis of their reciprocal attractiveness and mutual adaptability. Even where courtly love did not lead to marriage, as in the case of the troubadours, it revealed the importance of choice and personal preference in the creation of authentic love between men and women.

The courtly romances of the Middle Ages were especially concerned about the harmonization of love and marriage. In the Hellenistic period there had been a swelling of popular literature devoted to tales about young lovers seeking permanent happiness in each other's arms. Since the audiences were likely to be sentimental rather than rebellious, it was sexual pleasure within the comforts of conventional matrimony that was ordinarily depicted as the appropriate goal. As the Christian era developed, humanistic attitudes toward sex were condemned by the church as a danger to orthodox ideas about conjugality. Medieval romances often tried to reconcile the two, and, as we shall see, a number of possible solutions to the conflict between love and marriage, erotic pleasure and social conformity, were articulated within the boundaries established by the courtly outlook. Though the Middle Ages derived its conceptions of rectitude in marriage from the Christian theologians and philosophers, its sense of marital joy and interpersonal delight came from the new attitude defined by courtly love.

In the development of this humanistic ideal, Ovid plays a special role. His works were widely read throughout the Middle Ages and often accepted as authoritative despite their pagan presuppositions. The cynicism in *The Art of Love* was either misunderstood by medieval authors or discounted as subordinate to Ovid's sympathetic concern about the problems of love between the sexes. His *Metamorphoses* and *Heroides* included several stories about passion that was mutual, sincere, life-enhancing, and permanent. They served as illustrations of sexual love, and even married love, that courtly romances could then embroider in the contemporary manner.

A number of scholars have emphasized the extent to which Ovid contributed to noncourtly, as well as courtly, thinking about love in the Middle Ages. Brooks Otis claims that in Ovid there were really two poets: one the witty libertine who treats marriage or constancy in general as inimical to the pleasures of philandering, the other the West's first champion of true and lasting love between man and woman. Otis finds in the *Metamorphoses* a defense of conjugal love as the highest amatory value, and he insists that this was the most original aspect in Ovid: "nobody in classical or Hellenistic or pre-vious Roman literature really anticipated him." This line of inter-pretation is extended by other scholars who argue that in the Middle Ages Ovid was often thought to have given an "endorsement" to married love.

If we were to consider courtly love as always nonsexual devotion, or else as sexual intimacy irreconcilable with marriage, the claim that Ovid had a pervasive effect would seem ridiculous. And yet, the scholars I have mentioned are right in saying that he did. Through-out all his poetry, Ovid manifests a realistic attitude to human relations that can hardly be equated with the idealistic aspiration of courtly love, but the Ovidian approach nevertheless provided suste-nance in many ways. In creating their own kinds of idealization, advocates of courtly love had no need to spurn Ovid's influence completely. In fact, as I shall try to show, Andreas Capellanus' theory of courtly love is virtually a systematic attempt to synthesize Ovidian realism with idealistic elements that derive from Plato and Christianity.

5. Love is an intense, passionate relationship that establishes a holy oneness between man and woman. Nowadays we tend to take it for granted that love and passion go together and that they contrib-ute to attachments that human beings may justifiably value. Prior to the courtly revolution, however, love between man and woman was usually defined in other ways while the notion of passionate oneness was reserved for religious love. Intense sexual desire has always been recognized as something typically human; in fiction it could even serve as the cause of the Trojan wars. But as the ancient world did not generally conceive of passion as the basis for acceptable conduct, neither was it thought to indicate how ultimate union between men and women could really be attained. In the *Symposium*, Plato has Aristophanes narrate the myth about love as a search for one's other self, one's alter ego, the complementary being without which one could not achieve a sense of wholeness. In the *Phaedrus*, Plato includes descriptions of souls seeking to merge with one another through the molten intensity of sexual emotion. But Aris-tophanes' speech is ironic and the condition described in the *Phae-drus* is made to seem either diseased or preliminary to a higher state.

The "pure love" that Plato advocated would free one from irrational and disturbing interests usually present in sexuality. It would eventuate in ardent oneness but only by enabling the individual soul to merge with abstract principles beyond the body and mind of another human being. The passionate love of God, as described by all the Christian mystics, involved a similar completion, except that now the abstract principles were attributes of a supreme and super-human person.

Courtly love in the Middle Ages had nothing to say about the kind of passionate oneness that the philosophers and the mystics sought. But it did extol the value and desirability of a comparable state that men and women might attain merely in relation to one another. St. Paul had instructed all Christian spouses to love each other, and this maxim was repeated throughout the edicts of the church. But it was always understood that married love meant affection, liking, sympathy, or good will. It was a domestic virtue that enabled husband and wife to perform conjugal duties with a cheerful faith in the goodness of the divine order. What God had brought together, no one would want to put asunder. Christian love between man and woman would therefore be a benign willingness to live in peace and harmony with the person to whom one was yoked through the sacrament of marriage. One's *passion* would be reserved for God; passion toward one's spouse could only be considered inappropriate and even sinful.

In asserting that men and women could justifiably love each other with passion and that ardent desire would provide a supreme joy not to be found elsewhere in life, a oneness that could fully satisfy and even sanctify, courtly love inevitably conflicted with religious dogma. Various attempts were made to synthesize the two, and in the course of centuries both of them progressively changed. Within the idealist tradition, courtly love gave way to other secular attitudes—the Neoplatonism of the Renaissance, the romanticism of the nineteenth century—but the ideas of religious love in the Middle Ages also yielded to later developments, even within Catholicism, and it was the conflict with the humanistic demands of courtly love that helped to make this necessary.

In treating love as a search for passionate oneness with another human being, the courtly notion is also to be contrasted with the idea that love seeks to further the goodness of sensuous pleasure. Whether or not it is reducible to sex, love has sometimes been defined as a prime opportunity to enjoy another person through the senses. In an earlier book I analyzed these different concepts in terms of my distinction between the "sensuous" and the "passionate." Where the passionate involves yearning and intense emotion, the sensuous relies upon superficial but possibly uncloyed pleasures afforded by the senses. As I argued in that other place, the sensuous attitude could accommodate its own kind of love, one that many people find preferable to the dreadful joys of passion. But it was not sensuous love that determined the nature of courtly love. That generally required lovers to be carried away in their erotic need for one another. Though lovers might also enjoy the sensuous, their love would show itself in extreme emotionality as well as in the ability to forgo sexual pleasure if the circumstances of love demanded any such sacrifice. As courtesy and courtliness involved the refined manners of courts and courtiers, the civilized love between men and women could always turn into a sport, a game that depends upon a play of words rather than actual feelings. But by its very character, the game logically presupposed the importance of emotional intensity. And if love-play was sometimes dominated by pretense, it nevertheless consisted in pretending that one's words either masked or intimated the existence of passionate desires that would show themselves clearly in an appropriate setting. A clever seducer, a Don Juan of the Middle Ages, could turn courtly pretense into a new form of sensuousness; but his successes were always parasitic upon the ideals of passion. By developing these ideals in its own way, courtly love went far beyond the sensuous.

At the very outset, I remarked that the five criteria I would be discussing could not provide necessary and sufficient conditions for the concept of courtly love. For no concept of this sort can be that precisely delimited. And neither can a definition exhaust the great diversity among the particulars it unites. To see what courtly love really means, we must turn to the different variations that differently manifest it, each in its own fashion. That courtly ideals were articulated in the eleventh or early twelfth century, at a time when religious love was enjoying official dominance, may well occasion historical wonder. But I shall concern myself less with causal explanations than with the analysis of concepts that structured the new attitude toward love. Courtly love interests me primarily as a development in man's capacity to idealize, and only secondarily as a temporal phenomenon. Even to speak of courtly love occurring at a particular time and expressing a single mode of ideas can be misleading. For that makes it sound like a coherent movement or codified doctrine that univocally represents an era. But such is not the case. The courtly love of Chrétien de Troyes differs enormously from that of Dante. Nor is it merely a matter of dates or national origins: Chrétien differs also from Bernard de Ventadour, his contemporary, just as Dante differs from Petrarch and Cavalcanti.

Elements within the courtly approach were anticipated not only by Plato, Ovid, and the Bible but even by the Egyptians of antiquity. Much of its ideology originates with early Arabic poetry and philosophy, introduced through Spain into Southern France. The first great moment of courtly love culminates with the literature of the troubadours in Provence. This phase often emphasizes the worship of the female, who is to be loved with an unrequited desire that purifies the lover's feelings and transmutes them into verse. The troubadour's lady is usually a particular woman, but one who serves as a generic source of inspiration, a muse who has earned her pedestal by her ability to encourage art at the same time as she reigns over the niceties of civilization. In a later stage, courtly love moves northward to Aquitaine, eventually to England. Here the inequality of the sexes tends to be diminished, the woman being joined on her pedestal by a man of noble heart whom love has helped to elevate. In its northern version, courtly love is sometimes adulterous, generally sexual in its obvious intent, and only rarely interested in the values of unrequited yearning. The mutuality of amorous emotion and the sharing of beneficial pleasure become the norm. The woman ceases to be an object of worship or distant inspiration and instead becomes the beloved who elicits noble actions while also reciprocating her lover's passion. This type of courtly love is so unacceptable to ecclesiastic authority, however, that the church does everything it can to destroy it. Courtly love survives, but with difficulty, and the next great moment derives from the Provençal, not the northern version: in Sicily and then Italy the beloved is once again made an object of poetic adoration, except that she now becomes more and more ethereal. Neoplatonic influences enter more overtly than in the earlier stage, and resolute steps are taken to reconcile courtly attitudes with the demands of religious love. This final effort is not a fulfillment of courtly love, only its culmination within a historical era dominated by the superior forces of the church. Once it has been dematerialized and rendered harmonious with Christian dogma in the Renaissance, courtly love becomes attenuated and disappears. Or rather it goes underground, returning in a totally different form when it is revived by Romantic love at the end of the eighteenth century and forced to serve an ideal it would hardly recognize as its own.

Throughout this diversity (much richer than I have here indicated), the concept of courtly love affirms that love between human beings is in itself authentic and magnificent. It is love based on natural inclinations, such as sexual desire, and yet directed toward highly moral and aesthetic values. The tradition of courtly love is Western man's first great effort to demonstrate that the noble aspirations of idealism need not be incompatible with a joyful acceptance of sexual reality. Where Platonism sought to transcend the ordinary world through an idealization of naturalistic myths about love, and medieval religion merged Platonic (and Aristotelian) ideas with Judaeo-Christian concepts of divinity, courtly love is the naturalization, or humanization, of both Platonism and religion. In that sense it is, within its period of history, the wheel come full circle—but with a difference. By using idealistic concepts to dignify relationships that were demeaned by Greek philosophy and the doctrine of Christianity, it awakens new and exciting possibilities for the erotic imagination.

Having said all this, we may now agree that the Western concept of love (in its heterosexual and humanistic aspects) was—if not "invented" or "discovered"—at least developed in the twelfth century as never before. Only at that late date was man able to begin thinking consecutively about ways of harmonizing sexual impulses with idealistic motives, of justifying amorous intimacy not as a means of preserving the race, or glorifying God, or attaining some ulterior metaphysical object but rather as an end in itself that made life worth living. In the Middle Ages the air all educated men breathed was saturated with Neoplatonism and the Christianization of Aristotle. Without this constant presence, in the multifarious ways of human culture, courtly love could never have arisen. But once it began, it evolved in accordance with its own inner logic, digesting the past as all great idealizations do, pathetically struggling with the realities of its time, creating the future by what it failed to say no less than by what it did say.

2

Troubadour Fin' Amors

I_N *The Nature of Love: Plato to Luther*, I tried to show that the Platonic concept of eros was the major ingredient in Western mysticism though less predominant within orthodox doctrines of religious love. Courtly love, in all its varieties, is similarly dependent upon the eros tradition. Whether courtly love was patterned after mystical love or vice versa, as some believe, need not concern us. In some respects, the two are wholly antagonistic: courtly love being limited to human beings, while mystical love is directed toward God; the courtly cultivating sexual desire while the mystical wishes to eliminate all but the spiritual; the courtly heretical or nonreligious and thus representing worldly attitudes the mystical seeks to renounce. At the same time, courtly and mystical love resemble one another in ways that reveal their Platonic parenthood. This is especially true of the troubadour concept of "fin' amors"—the Provençal term for pure love—which combines Neoplatonic theorizing of the Middle East with elements of Christian mysticism and ends up with an idealization of human love that leads to great poetry even if it eventuates in sexual frustration.

With the occurrence of the cult of Mary in the eleventh century, the close relationship between these different elements of the eros tradition becomes clearly established. When, in the following century, the troubadour Bernard de Ventadour dedicates himself to his Lady ("ma domna"), he is not of course confusing her with the Mother of God. And neither is St. Bernard of Clairvaux espousing courtly love, which he condemned, when he addresses the Madonna as the "fairest among women," adding that God awaits her consent before proceeding with the salvation of the world. Yet both Bernards have in common an idealistic search for goodness and beauty, the upward aspiration of love, and the firm belief that the value of its object is something external to the lover himself.

As most aspects of the eros tradition have their source in Plato's *Symposium*, it would be surprising if one could not find at least the seeds of courtly love in that work. It hardly matters that the manuscript was unknown in Europe until much later: Plato was studied elsewhere and his ideas were thoroughly disseminated throughout the Western world. In fact, one may think of the courtly tradition as a prolonged effort to resolve some of the problems raised by the *Symposium*. For instance, Socrates defines love as the desire for the perpetual possession of the good, and he insists that all men are alike in having this desire. But only the philosopher is able to satisfy it, since only he can rise to the supreme knowledge of absolute beauty in which perpetual possession of goodness consists. Now even if one were to agree that the philosopher's love is the highest form of love, questions would still remain about the love that was available to other people. The courtly tradition appropriates the Platonic mode of analysis but applies it to persons who are not philosophers and cannot hope to attain absolute beauty of the sort that Plato describes. These persons—poets, knights, and others who wish to perfect themselves—ascend the same ladder as Plato's philosopher. From his point of view, they merely belong to a lower level of achievement. To them, however, no love beyond their own is needed for happiness. They do not condemn the philosopher just as they do not scorn the religious mystic (many of the courtly lovers finding no difficulty in considering themselves good Christians); but for all practical purposes the kind of love they seek assumes the character of an absolute. It is a way of life that rivals both philosophical and religious approaches to an ultimate ideal.

When we examine the details of the courtly ideal, it is remarkable to see how many of them are already present in Plato. Explaining what is meant by "perpetual possession of the good," Socrates says that the goal of love is "to procreate and bring forth in beauty." This in turn is related to the universal love of immortality, which men try to satisfy through different pursuits. Leaving aside the philosopher's ascension (the path that truly leads to perpetual possession of the good), Socrates lists three ways in which men have sought immortality. In effect, the first is physical; the second spiritual; and the third a combination of the two. Men whose "creative instinct" is physical try to achieve immortality by begetting beautiful children. They therefore "have recourse to women, and show their love in this way." Others are more interested in conceiving spiritually. Their progeny is wisdom and virtue in general. "Of this all poets and such draftsmen as have found out some new thing may be said to be begetters." Since wisdom also entails justice and noble conduct, these begetters include men of action as well. Finally, there are those who are fortunate enough to find in the physical beauty of another individual a suitable environment for begetting the spiritual beauties in which wisdom and virtue consist. About such men Socrates says the following:

> If in a beautiful body he finds also a beautiful and noble and gracious soul, he welcomes the combination warmly, and finds much to say to such a one about virtue and the qualities and actions which mark a good man, and takes his education in hand. By intimate association with beauty embodied in his friend, and by keeping him always before his mind, he succeeds in bringing to birth the children of which he has been long in labour, and once they are born he shares their upbringing with his friend; the partnership between them will be far closer and the bond of affection far stronger than between ordinary parents, because the children that they share surpass human children by being immortal as well as more beautiful. Everyone would prefer children such as these to children after the flesh.

Now here, in the third kind of imperfect love, there surely appears the underlying pattern in courtly love. Of course, certain adjustments had to be made. Plato assumes that men would show their love to women only for purposes of reproduction. Courtly love, being heterosexual, will have to change that, though possibly less than one might think. Even among the troubadours, who were less likely to emulate Greek society than the Italian Neoplatonists of the Renaissance, one is occasionally surprised to find the lady addressed as "midons," a masculine term meaning lord or master. But putting aside this kind of problem, one is struck by the extent to which the varieties of courtly love seem to issue from this passage in the *Symposium*. Though the troubadours rank the noble and gracious soul of their beloved higher than anything else, they are also sensitive to her physical beauty, which they extol as the greatest inducement for loving her. Treating the lady as an object of devotion, the troubadours might not have described their love as a "partnership"; but in the northern tradition the idea of intimate association on a reciprocal basis becomes an important factor. For its part, the Italian version will emphasize the spiritual aspect of the relationship, the edifying venture of discovering through another person the nature of goodness and beauty as an ultimate reality. Of even greater significance, perhaps, is the fact that all types of courtly love contrast love with marriage as it ordinarily exists, find the spiritual progeny of love superior to merely human children, and in general assert that lovers achieve immortality by bringing forth in beauty. For the troubadours this is done through poetry and music the beloved has divinely inspired; for the northern tradition it comes from deeds of service in a noble cause sanctioned by the lady; for the Italians the offspring are religious sentiments as well as refined conceptions of gentility and graciousness.

Over and above these general considerations, there are also specific details in Plato that anticipate the ideas of courtliness. In some ways Socrates himself, as a complex literary character, is oddly suggestive of the troubadour lover. In the *Symposium* he is often portrayed as a man with interests that are amorous and human as well as philosophical. But notice the variegated structure of these interests. As a philosopher, he is in love with absolute beauty. From whom does he acquire the doctrine that supports this attitude? From a woman, Diotima. He describes her as his "instructor in the art of love," and to illustrate her extraordinary accomplishments he tells us that she postponed a plague in Athens for ten years. In the dialogue she speaks with the clear authority of a sybil. Deferring to her, Socrates presents himself as a sheer ignoramus, eager to learn but unable to question anything she says. There is little distance between the intellectual humility of Socrates and the representative utterances of a troubadour like Peire Vidal, who remarks: "If I know how to say or do anything, she who gave me learning and knowledge should have the thanks."

In relation to other individuals, however, Socrates appears in quite a different light. Alcibiades claims that Socrates always manages to get himself next to the handsomest person in the room, and his erotic interest in fine young men is later alluded to. This is much as we might expect from one who spent his days in the agora as Socrates did. And it is relevant that Socrates never claims to have achieved for himself the philosophical love that Diotima describes. In fact, she even states that his lack of knowledge about absolute beauty results from his love of young men, "the sight of whom at present throws you and many people like you into such an ecstasy that, provided that you could always enjoy the sight and company of your darlings, you would be content to go without food and drink, if that were possible, and to pass your whole time with them in the contemplation of their beauty."

What is particularly revealing is the manner in which Socrates conducts his love affairs. Alcibiades portrays him as a man who is always feigning in his relations with other people. Several young men are listed, Alcibiades among them, with whom Socrates has pretended to be in love, "when in fact he is himself the beloved rather than the lover." And indeed, Socrates often sounds like the pursued, not at all the pursuer. When Alcibiades first enters, Socrates begs the others to protect him from the intensity of the young man's affection. In a way that almost seems coquettish, Socrates says: "From the moment when I first fell in love with him I haven't been able to exchange a glance or a word with a single goodlooking person without his falling into a passion of jealousy and envy, which makes him behave outrageously and abuse me and practically lay violent hands on me." It is as if Socrates were the adored lady of a troubadour who, for some reason, has lapsed from the ideals of courtly love. That Alcibiades thinks in these terms is evident from his self-condemnation as well as his continued reverence for the nobility of Socrates' character—which he calls "divine and precious and beautiful and marvelous." In his attempt to prove that Socrates is "superhuman and wonderful," Alcibiades describes an occasion on which the two slept under the same covers. Despite his prolonged efforts to seduce Socrates, Alcibiades could only put his arms about him, his physical passion remaining unsatisfied throughout the night. As we shall soon discover, this is an archetypal scene for the troubadour version of courtly love. As with the troubadours too, Alcibiades declares himself a helpless servant to one who can behave as Socrates did: "I had no choice but to do whatever Socrates bade me. . . . I was utterly disconcerted, and wandered about in a state of enslavement to the man the like of which has never been known."

In having an ambiguous, and possibly ambivalent, character, Socrates effectively represents that ambiguity toward matter which is always present in Plato. Perfect love would seem to require a dedication to absolute beauty that is wholly spiritual, transcending the body and eventually discarding it as a ladder for which one no longer has any use. But possibly, Plato seems to say, this is too much to expect of men, even the noblest and most philosophic. Living in the world, as perforce he must, perhaps the lover can only hope to subjugate physical desires without eliminating them, using the body as a vehicle to spiritual beauty and thus as an ever-present means of approximating the ideal. It is this compromise that the troubadours make explicit in their poetry. It is fundamental to the ways of thinking that give their work its greatest importance in the history of ideas.

Since the troubadours had no access to the writings of Plato, their acquaintance with his doctrine must have come to them through the Neoplatonism of the Middle East. In Plotinus, the great Neoplatonist of the third century A.D., one finds a concern for the intermediary stages of being that somewhat balances his more prevalent desire to merge with the purely spiritual One. Merely in articulating the steps in the hierarchy of perfection and showing how they demand their own kind of harmonious order, Plotinus prepares the way for the troubadour compromise. It is, however, in the writings of Arab

Neoplatonists of the eleventh century that this development is most fully anticipated. Avicenna's *Treatise on Love* devotes a major chapter to the search for beauty in another human being, a type of love less exalted than devotion to the Good in itself and yet recognized as a great source of value. Like all followers of Plato, Avicenna begins with the idea that everything in nature is determined by love, which consists of a craving for goodness relative to the needs of each being. Within man, he claims, there are innately two orders of love: one belonging to the animal soul, the other to the rational. Prior to Avicenna, Muslim philosophy had generally denied that love deriving from the animal soul could have any value. The Sufis, for instance, insisted that everything related to man's animality had to be suppressed. For them the love of beauty as it occurs in physical nature, or in other persons, inevitably draws man away from the more important love of Pure Good attainable only through spiritual interests. It was this belief that Avicenna sought to undermine.

In order to show how the love of natural beauty may contribute to spiritual growth, Avicenna asserts from the very outset that it is part of the nature of rational beings to covet a beautiful sight. If this is limited to the animal faculty, it leads to vice and is indefensible. If, however, the animal and rational souls cooperate, so that a man loves a beautiful object not with carnal desire but through the intellect, his attitude is "an approximation to nobility and an increase in goodness." For through this mingling of interests, animality is arrested and yet provides familiarity with a beautiful form that will eventually lead a man upward in the hierarchy of love as he progresses toward that which Avicenna calls "the First Source of influence and the Pure Object of love."

In defending the love for beautiful forms in human beings, Avicenna mentions three consequences for the animal soul. The first of these is the urge to embrace the object; the second is the urge to kiss it; and the third is the urge to have sexual intercourse. In a way that reminds us of the nocturnal scene between Socrates and Alcibiades, Avicenna instantly rejects the third consequence as limited to the animal soul and therefore incapable of the needed alliance with reason. Avicenna recognizes that conjugal union may serve a rational purpose, as it does in causing the propagation of the species, but the act itself and the sexual interest that goes with it contain nothing rational. As a result, the love of beautiful forms—though partly animal by its very nature—requires total subjugation of the desire for sexual completion. For the other effects of animality, however, the very opposite is true: "As for embracing and kissing, the purpose in them is to come near to one another and to become united. The soul of the lover desires to reach the object of his love with his senses of touch and sight, and thus he delights in embracing it. And he longs to have the very essence of his soul-faculty, his heart, mingle with that of the object of his love, and thus he desires to kiss it. These actions, then, are not in themselves blameworthy." Indeed, so far is Avicenna from considering such effects to be blameworthy that he concludes the chapter by saying: "Whoever is filled with this type of love is a man of nobility and refinement, and this type of love is an ornament and a source of inner wealth."

Similar ideas are expressed by Ibn Hazm, the Hispano-Arabic contemporary of Avicenna. His treatise *The Ring of the Dove* derives from the same Neoplatonic tradition, but it is written in an anecdotal fashion that must have made the metaphysics more accessible to poets such as the troubadours. Though the usual ideas about an inborn search for the Good are always presupposed in Ibn Hazm, they figure less prominently in the foreground of his design. Instead, he defines love in ways that are reminiscent of Aristophanes' myth about merging in the *Symposium*. Many of the Muslim philosophers had already characterized love as an attempt to merge with the beloved. Avicenna described it in terms of what the Sufis called "unification," and in a footnote his modern translator quotes from the writings of the Brethren of Purity: "Some scholars are of the opinion that love (*'ishq*) is an extremely strong desire toward unification (*ittihâd*). This is of all the discourses the most correct, weighty and profound."

In Ibn Hazm the notion of merging is developed to its fullest, and always in relation to love between human beings. Love, he says, is "a conjunction between scattered parts of souls that have become divided in this physical universe, a union effected within the substance of their original sublime element." As commingling and separation occur in the material world, so too are they processes in the spiritual realm that souls inhabit. Lovers are thus persons whose souls origi- nally belonged to the same substance, from which they have been divided (extracted) and into which they wish to be reconstituted. The very words that Ibn Hazm uses to depict the lover's state could well have appeared in the speech of Aristophanes: "The lover's soul," Ibn Hazm says, "is ever seeking for the other, striving after it, searching it out, yearning to encounter it again, drawing it to itself it might be as a magnet draws the iron." But Ibn Hazm lives in a post- and neo-Platonic era, and though he recognizes that unification begins with sensory experience, he emphasizes "fusion of souls" as love's aspiration to a greater extent than Plato himself did.

When it comes to distinguishing between erotic dispositions, Ibn Hazm more or less duplicates the approach in Avicenna. Since the individual soul is beautiful, it feels an affinity toward all beautiful forms in the physical world. If the soul can find something of itself, a spiritual kinship behind the form, it falls in love with it. If the object is purely physical, as in the case of sexual desire, the soul cannot make contact with another soul, and therefore love does not arise. But this is not to say that love is nonphysical. The state of union, through which love is fulfilled, Ibn Hazm describes in terms of the sensory delights that lovers derive from one another's presence. It is only sexual intercourse that he rules out, both for religious reasons and for the sake of protecting love since it can easily be destroyed by sex. Short of this catastrophe, however, love can feed on all the manifestations of the material world, in particular anything beauti- ful in either male or female: "physical forms have a wonderful faculty of drawing together the scattered parts of men's souls." In fact, for all his idealism, Ibn Hazm seems to assume that the actual beginnings of love must always be physical admiration. Two people meet and are visually enchanted with one another. If their interest remains at the level of sensory attraction, their bond is merely carnal. For love, or passionate love as the translator calls it, to exist, something else must occur. But this too is described in a way that stresses bodily involvement: "When carnal desire moreover becomes so overflowing that it surpasses these bounds, and when such instincts share equally with the soul, the resulting phenomenon is called passionate love."

These ideas enter directly into the poetry of the troubadours as part of a general pattern that belongs to much of their thought. Like many troubadours, Ibn Hazm uses his distinction between love and mere animality to deny that a man may love more than one person at the same time. Like them, he cites the pain of loving an object that must not be possessed if love is to continue. He depicts, in what will become the usual manner, how separation causes a true lover to waste away through love-sickness or else go mad. Chapters are devoted to persons who will take on major importance in the creative literature of the Middle Ages: the messenger, the helpful friend, the spy, the slanderer. In one place, where Ibn Hazm describes the beloved's use of her eyes, we encounter the preoccupation with sight characteristic of courtly love, and the eros tradition in general, but expressed with a wealth of imagination hardly equalled anywhere else: "To make a signal with the corner of the eye is to forbid the lover something; to droop the eye is an indication of consent; to prolong the gaze is a sign of suffering and distress; to break off the gaze is a mark of relief; to make signs of closing the eyes is an indicated threat. To turn the pupil of the eye in a certain direction and then to turn it back swiftly, calls attention to the presence of a person so indicated. A clandestine signal with the corner of both eyes is a question; to turn the pupil rapidly from the middle of the eye to the interior angle is a demonstration of refusal; to flutter the pupils of both eyes this way and that is a general prohibition. The rest of these signals can only be understood by actually seeing them demonstrated."

Of greatest relevance is the manner in which Ibn Hazm portrays the changes that lovers undergo. Like the troubadours, he describes how much a man will do in order to show his good qualities and make himself desirable to the beloved. Some scholars claim that these alterations in the lover are not ennobling effects of love, since they precede its occurrence instead of following it as specified in troubadour theory. Still, the fact remains that Ibn Hazm's lover may change from stingy to generous, gloomy to cheerful, cowardly to brave, stupid to clever, illshaped to handsome. And there is every reason to believe that these newly acquired virtues are supposed to last as long as love does. Moreover, Ibn Hazm devotes a whole chapter to the way in which passionate love causes the lover to submit to his beloved. Stubbornness is replaced by docility, intractability by gentleness, arrogance by subservience. When the beloved is unsympathetic to the lover's suffering, he accuses himself and tries to justify her coolness. Even if the beloved is a slave girl belonging to the lover, he will adjust his character and accept humiliation in order to show the submissiveness that love ordains. For this aspect of courtly love, we need not go any further than Ibn Hazm.

If troubadour thinking is related to Muslim philosophy, however, the one is not reducible to the other. For the troubadours introduced something that neither Avicenna nor Ibn Hazm would ever have countenanced: a kind of autonomy or self-sufficiency of human love, its making a closed trajectory within itself. Avicenna claimed that the love of beautiful persons was a positive value, but he always thought of it as a step that led beyond relations between man and woman or man and man. Though it was desirable as a means of uniting the animal soul with the rational, its greatest utility consisted in preparing us for that spiritual love in which the object was pure beauty or goodness itself. About this more ultimate love the troubadours are remarkably unconcerned. Their beloved is indeed more than just another beautiful form in the external world: she is for them the supreme instance of beauty and that is why they love her. And yet, they do not love her for the sake of beauty, at least not beauty as an absolute or abstract entity. It scarcely occurs to the troubadours that love might be extended beyond the lady. In their thinking, fin' amors has no direct relation to the love of God. The poets may implore God for assistance, and despite the unorthodox character of their woman-worship, they may occasionally suggest that God condones it. But there is nothing in fin' amors that would enable it to issue into a love of divinity, whether Christian or Muslim. On the contrary, fin' amors serves as an *imitation* of religious or philosophic love, which it uses as a theoretical model to be duplicated among human beings.

Instead of fitting into a spiritual development toward God or absolute beauty, fin' amors arrogates to itself a similar ultimacy of dedication and finality of emotional involvement. That is why Ibn Hazm's lovers, however submissive to the beloved, cannot be equated with the troubadours. The lovers Ibn Hazm portrays submit to a beautiful soul with which their own was mingled in all eternity. The practitioner of fin' amors looks elsewhere: he chooses a woman who embodies and objectifies *in herself* beauty, goodness, and all the other goals of human aspiration recognized by the eros tradition.

That the troubadours should have chosen to sing of love for women has long intrigued historians. Was not the medieval, like the ancient, world notorious for its misogyny? Did not the church fathers trace all evil to the sin of Eve, whose daughters were similarly contaminated? Was not the social and legal order of the twelfth century inimical to any conceivable ascendancy of the female? Like all generalizations of this sort, these—whose partial truth one may possibly accept—force scholars into two postures. They may account for troubadour love as a reaction to the ruling ideology, or else they may adduce evidence to show that women were more highly regarded than one generally assumes. Most scholars take the first alternative; a few, like Henry Adams, take the second, emphasizing the pervasive veneration of the Virgin Mary and citing popular documents that maintained women can be intellectually superior to men.

In either event, it is the phenomenon of idealization that historians tend to overlook, though it is precisely here that the troubadours made their most interesting innovation. Their choosing to love women is not remarkable. Men had been doing that ever since Adam bit into the apple, thus aligning himself with Eve instead of God. World literature before the troubadours is filled with stories of men loving women. True, this was not a common theme in the chansons de geste that immediately preceded troubadour poetry in France: in the *Chanson de Roland,* for instance, the hero's fiancée is mentioned in only one stanza and no other woman is even named.

But these were military epics, works that specialized in the exploits of Mars, not Venus, and they were more exclusively masculine than most epics had been. Those of Homer, closer to native myths and larger in scope, weave a fair amount of heterosexual love into their pattern. Nor are we to pretend that Paris did not "really" love Helen, that his involvement was purely sexual or that he merely esteemed her as a valuable possession. Though excellent scholars have suggested this, I see no reason for denying that Paris loved Helen, that the old men of Troy would have done so too—as they confess—if only they had been younger, and that (subject to modifications) this is the same kind of love as other men felt towards other women in Greek and Roman literature: e.g. Daphnis and Chloe, Hero and Leander, or among the poets, Asklepiades and Didyme, Catullus and Lesbia, Propertius and Cynthia. The troubadours may have devoted more verses to the celebration of heterosexual love than anyone else, but they are certainly not the first poets to have sung of a love for a lady. Their distinctiveness lies in their use of idealization for amatory and poetic purposes.

Or perhaps one should say that the originality of the troubadours consists in the way in which they idealize the beloved. A particular woman is treated as the unique instantiation of the highest ideals. She not only captures the lover's heart, as any beautiful woman might, but also she is seen to represent everything of value to the lover. The troubadours elevate women in the sense that they choose one woman as the exemplar of all significant virtues and use that as the reason for loving her. The act of idealization underlies desire in fin' amors, which resembles Platonic and religious love in this respect. If the woman were not the repository of perfection, the lover claims, she would have no lover. He is able to love her because in body and mind, in manner and morality, in birth and social mien she is objectively outstanding. In principle at least, it is not the lover's devotion that renders the lady unique; it is rather the inherent excellence of her total personality that elicits his love, naturally and inevitably, much as a magnet draws an iron object towards it. As we have seen, the image of the magnet appears in Ibn Hazm, but without any idea of spatial relations. For the troubadours the magnet is always on a higher plane, lifting the weighty soul of man upwards as the result of love inspired by a woman who has been idealized.

Actually, there are two things idealized by fin' amors: first, the beloved, the lady supremely beautiful in all respects; second, love itself, as the longing and desire elicited by the goodness and beauty of this particular woman. Thus, on the one hand, Arnaut de Mareuil addresses his beloved: "Good lady, perfect in all good qualities, so worthy are you above all the best women that I know"; Pons de Capdeuil says: "You are so worthy, courteous in true speaking, frank and gentle, gay with humility, beautiful and pleasing, that it is not to be said that you lack any good quality one could wish in a lady"; and Peire Raimon describes the object of his devotion as "the beautiful one who is flower and mirror and light and head and guide of all good breeding." In his own rough way, Guillaume IX, Duke of Aquitaine, the first troubadour, reveals the objective priority of the lady's beauty as well as anyone: "For you are whiter than ivory; that is why I love none other." And in another poem, he enumerates the powers of the beloved as follows: "The joy of her can make the sick man well again,/her wrath can make a well man die,/a wise man turn to childishness,/a beautiful man behold his beauty change;/the courtliest man can become a churl,/and any churl a courtly man."

On the other hand, the troubadours idealized love itself, their own desire, their own condition as lovers. Bernard de Ventadour claims that "no man is of value without love"—meaning, of course, fin' amors since he specifies that "by nothing is man made more excellent than by love and the service of women, for thence arises delight and song and all that pertains to excellence." Elsewhere, Bernard reveals the importance of yearning as an essential element in love: "I crave so noble a love that my longing is already a gain." Guillaume IX, like so many others, assures us that the joy of loving "cannot find its equal, and whoever would praise it properly would not be able to accomplish this task, not if he tried for a year"; and Bernart Marti proudly announces that "so much have I desired love and have put all my mind [into attaining it], that never voluntarily, whilst I live, do I wish to ply any other trade." The wording of Marti's assertion may sound crudely practical—as if love were indeed a trade—but clearly it is intended to glorify fin' amors as the only activity one should follow.

As a way of life based upon its own principles of idealization, the pursuit of fin' amors was more revolutionary than its own adherents realized. The troubadours would have been astounded to learn that they were socially subversive, and they must have found the violence of ecclesiastic attack simply incomprehensible. To them it surely seemed that their ideas buttressed the social order by making its values emotionally accessible. The medieval world was hierarchical, predicated upon fealty and the sense of duty that bound subject to master. The troubadours did not attack this order of things; they merely used it imaginatively, offering to their lady—who sometimes was their legal sovereign—the vows of service and fidelity expected of every lower link within the medieval chain. Marriage being a holy sacrament as well as a device of political power, the troubadours strengthened it by rejecting adulterous relationships. The lover could address his idealized desire towards another man's wife, and that was the customary choice, but he could not express it through sexual intercourse. The concept was flattering not only to the lady, who was loved despite the necessary frustrations built into fin' amors, but also to her husband, whose unique prerogatives were in principle respected, even augmented. Adultery being a sin they officially sought to avoid, the troubadours could well deny that they were flouting social or ecclesiastical authority.

And yet the church was right to suspect that troubadour love was dangerous, even heretical. In failing to define itself as subordinate to the love of God, fin' amors encouraged self-sufficiency among human beings. Moreover, the elevation of the beloved was not always limited to a mere imitation of mystical love. Maurice Valency has pointed out that the lady's salutation, the first reward of fin' amors, took on the full ambiguity of *salut*, meaning salvation as well as greeting. Thus Aimeric de Peguilhan says of his lady's appearance in public: "By reason of your salutation, without more, every man thought himself ennobled and cured of ill." Addressed to God, or Christ, or the Virgin, this could have served as an appropriate tribute to the power of divinity. Addressed to another human

being—particularly a woman, whom the Bible calls the weaker vessel—such adoration would surely have seemed idolatrous to many
devout Christians. It was *as if* the troubadours had despaired of
achieving salvation through religious love, *as if* they sought from
human beings that which only God could provide.

Equally important is the fact that, in glorifying human love and in
elevating the object as they did, the troubadours idealized desire. If
they had been concerned with the mating of human animals, their
poetry would not have been terribly disturbing. Medieval literature
was often devoted to stories about lovers seeking one another's
embraces, before marriage as well as afterwards. This the church
could understand and accept as an effect of nature. Mating interests
are not idealized if they merely conduce to the biological goals of
reproduction. Copulation might well contribute to *uti*, the use that
creatures properly made of one another, without jeopardizing the
frui or final enjoyment that could only be experienced in relation to
God. But the troubadours employed a different mode of thought:
they abstracted desire and then idealized it within itself.

As in Plato, and possibly Plotinus, troubadour desire is eros showing itself through carnal impulse as well as spiritual, upward striving. Guillaume, Bernard de Ventadour, and all the others make it
very clear that they wish to see the beloved's naked body, that they
wish to touch and kiss her, that they yearn for all the solaces of love
short of actual intercourse. But in demanding the frustration of
their sexual instinct, they did not eliminate it: on the contrary, they
intensified its idealization. By imposing restrictions upon itself, fin'
amors turns back the electric charge of physical desire, frames it
within the context of a spiritual quest, employs it as the energy of an
idealizing impulse that finally issues into poetry. It is the grandeur of
this adventure within the life of erotic imagination that the church
did well to fear. For it provides a comsummation that mere sexual
pleasure could never equal, a joy that troubadour poetry constantly
refers to, hopelessly seeks to describe. It is a joy constructed out of
pain and sorrow, as frustration necessitates, but it turns into a more
profound joy than anything afforded by simple achievement of
libidinal desire. That is why Bernard de Ventadour says that "the
love of two pure lovers consists in desire and willing" and then adds:

"And he is indeed truly foolish who rebukes her for [not giving him] what he wants, and requests of her what is not fitting." It is for this reason too that Daude de Pradas and other troubadours say—in a way that is oddly reminiscent of religious writers such as Richard of St. Victor—that they would rather not enter into paradise if it means relinquishing that woman "in whom reigns Beauty and Youth and all that usually gives pleasure to Love."

In this ability to use an idealized object to arouse sexual desire and then to frustrate that desire for the sake of the spiritual ends of pure devotion and the writing of poetry, there may well be something unnatural about fin' amors. In a sense it requires renunciation even more astonishing than the mystic's. For the mystic gives up physical interests in the hope that, if he does it correctly, he will enjoy the eternal good of beatitude. But the troubadour, willing to forgo the traditional paradise of religious bliss as well as the earthly paradise of sexual completion, seems to be denying both God and nature. At least, that is how his conduct appears to a "natural man" like Othello:

IAGO: Or to be naked with her friend in bed
          An hour, or more, not meaning any harm?

OTHELLO: Naked in bed, Iago, and not mean harm?
         It is hypocrisy against the devil.
         They that mean virtuously, and yet do so
         The devil their virtue tempts, and they tempt
         heaven.

In a similar vein, the Catholic scholar Etienne Gilson wonders whether fornication might not actually be "more sane and inoffensive" than the purity of troubadour love based on sexual frustration.

But possibly Gilson and Othello have failed to appreciate the merits of fin' amors. For though it is indeed unnatural in the sense I have mentioned, it is a natural and productive method for enlivening the imagination. It is noteworthy, and not wholly surprising, that with the troubadours nature poetry really begins to flourish in the Western world. In their writings one finds the sensitivity to landscape, the love of nature in all its graphic aspects, which the Romantics revived and which seems to be diminishing only in recent years.

The troubadours were among the first to see the things of this world as objects to be enjoyed in the imagination and not merely used for the glorification of God. They are especially attuned to the beauties of spring, and to the cruelties of months that arouse the joy and sadness of newly awakened love. But at all times of the year, they feel the goodness of nature, appreciated in itself, and then employed to symbolize the glory of human love. Thus, Bernard de Ventadour:

> When tender leafage doth appear,
>   When vernal meads grow gay with flowers,
> And aye with singing loud and clear
>   The nightingale fulfills the hours,
> I joy in him and joy in every flower
>   And in myself, and in my lady more.
> For when joys do inclose me and invest,
>   My joy in her transcendeth all the rest.

Nor is it strange to find in Bernard that combination of eros symbols—the bird soaring toward the sun, the ecstasy of immolation, the experience of fusing or melting with desire—which then became the stock-in-trade of all Romantic poetry about nature as well as love:

> When I behold on eager wing
>   The sky-lark soaring to the sun,
> Till e'en with rapture faltering
>   He sinks in glad oblivion,
> Alas, how fain to seek were I
>   The same ecstatic fate of fire!
> Yea, of a truth I know not why
>   My heart melts not with its desire!

This love of nature, based upon a frank acceptance of bodily desire, is hardly characteristic of religious love in the early Middle Ages. Yet it finds its way into the sensibility of the most lovable of medieval saints. Francis of Assisi, born a hundred years after Guillaume IX, turned away from a youth spent as an ordinary troubadour to give himself to Lady Poverty. Renouncing fin' amors for reasons of religion was not itself uncommon. Even Guillaume had done so, repenting what he took to be the godlessness of his lewd infatuations in years gone by. What distinguishes St. Francis is the fact that he carries troubadour love of nature *into* the religious attitude. Though Christ had come to save the world, one never feels that he—as the personage described in the Gospels, at least—was ever at home in it or wholly at peace in the company of its creatures. With St. Francis, however, there is infinite friendliness between himself and everything in nature and the empirical world. He addresses the birds and the moon as "sister," the wind and the fire as "brother"; but to him they are all "dearly beloved" and he praises them for merely being what they are as elements of existence. This love of nature appears less in Giotto's murals than in the great painting by Giovanni Bellini. In Giotto, St. Francis seems to be acting out a stiff and prearranged role, lecturing the birds rather than conversing with them, living within a landscape too cramped and artificial for his unbounded feelings. In the Bellini, however, St. Francis steps out of his Platonic cave with arms freely outstretched toward Brother Sun, as if this gesture of embrace puts him in loving contact not only with the sun and the sky but also with every thing that resides in the countryside beneath them. Latter-day trouba-dour that he is, his lips intone the "Canticle of the Sun," the Platonic symbol of the Good, the goal of aspiration.

In St. Francis love is no longer fin' amors but only a Christian transformation of it, which also happens in the poetry of orthodox mystics like St. John of the Cross and St. Teresa of Avila three hundred and fifty years later. But even in the early twelfth century the language of sexual love was sometimes used to express religious devotion. Troubadours like Marcabru argue that an acceptable love between men and women must always conform to the dogmas of the church. At times Marcabru sounds like a destructive critic of the new fashion in love, but often he seems to be working towards its synthe-sis with ecclesiastic doctrine. In few of the troubadours do we find a single concept of love to which they subscribe without contradiction. In most of them, love appears as a complex phenomenon they approach from one perspective after another.

For this reason scholars are simpleminded when they speak of troubadour poetry as if it contained no concept of love other than fin' amors. That concept belongs to a large body of troubadour writing, but rarely in poets of this period does it occur as the *only* idea about love. Consider the poem of Guillaume IX about his escapade with Agnes and Ermessen, whom he beguiles by pretending to be a mute and whom, as he says, he "screws" 188 times. There is no courtly love in that poem; but elsewhere in Guillaume it appears definitely as fin' amors, and occasionally as a condition of sexual fulfillment that struggles toward mutual oneness and equality. In defeating the mold of self-imposed frustration, the latter involves an ideal that is not as fully developed in troubadour poetry as the concept of fin' amors. But the fact remains that each of the major troubadours presents us with a panoply of ideas and attitudes about love. Ulrich of Lichtenstein, for instance, wrote many a poem about the beauties of merging with one's beloved, but he could also reveal its total impossibility—at least, on some occasions:

> Lady, let our spirits mingle,
> I in you and you in me;
> Let the two of us in single
> Being both together be,
> Each to other let's be true!
> "Sir, that I will never do.
> I am mine, let yours be you."

In Bernard de Ventadour, possibly the greatest of these poets, one finds the brightest and richest spectrum of approaches to love. Whether they belong to a "dialectic," as some critics have maintained, or merely illustrate a succession of possibilities, the alternative conceptions in Bernard include consummation as well as frustration, adultery as well as chastity, reciprocity and admiration between equals as well as reverence for the distant beloved. If Bernard can prostrate himself, saying "Good lady, I ask you for nothing/but to take me for your servant,/for I will serve you as my good lord,/whatever wages come my way," he can also assert that

"The love of two true lovers lies/in their mutual will and pleasure;/ nothing can be good in it/if they are not equal in desire. . . ."

As the troubadour tradition grew, different writers emphasized different aspects within the spectrum. Later poets, such as Walther von der Vogelweide and Hartmann von Aue, might ridicule the artificialities of fin' amors; but they could also return to it as a basis for their own ideas. Even the *Carmina Burana*, a collection of Latin poems of the thirteenth century, manifests an idealization of longing and a dedication to joyfulness in love that links it to the earliest writings of the troubadours. To suggest that the *Carmina Burana* is concerned only with sex, and therefore is foreign to the spirit of the troubadours, serves only to misinterpret both. The love of nature, almost to the point of pantheism, is more sophisticated in the *Carmina* (and more closely related to Vergil and Ovid), but it is often continuous with troubadour thinking. We do best to consider them as overlapping developments within a humanistic attitude that characterizes much of the literature of the Middle Ages. There is no reason to place them in vastly different categories.

The Crusade against the heretical Albigensians terminated the career of the troubadours in Provence, and of fin' amors as they understood it. Perhaps it is symbolic that the presence of these daring innovators was cut short while their poems lived on and exerted influence. Later centuries, particularly the nineteenth but also our own, could not fail to admire the determination with which they insisted on loving real women with a desire that was explicitly sexual while also doomed to calculated frustration for the sake of benefits to the imagination. A Freudian may well find in this circuitous pattern various traces of infantile regression. He may point out resemblances between, on the one hand, the poet abject before his lady, and on the other, the child yearning for and looking up to a mother he craves sexually but may not seduce. It would be foolhardy to deny such parallels. But what impresses me as more significant is the remarkable insight into human feeling that the troubadours evince. How well they knew what was required for the creation of their kind of poetry! How well they constructed a system of erotic idealizations that could never have existed without the paradoxical acceptance and frustration of desire! And how courageous they were, these frivolous, even flippant, joyful sufferers who dared to sing about a love for women that was meritorious in itself, justified by no superior claims of orthodox religion or transcendental philosophy! Fin' amors has limitations as a concept of love, but it endures as one of the first steps in the modern search for a humanizing relation between men and women.

3

The Courtliness of
Andreas Capellanus

THE TROUBADOURS OF PROVENCE
mainly wrote poetry; and though their verse is often discursive, they
made no efforts to codify their views. Theirs is a conglomeration of
scattered expressions, diverse ideas. Only in its northern version
does French courtly love receive a doctrinal formulation. Even then,
there is only one great text: the *Tractatus amoris & de amoris remedio*,
written by Andreas Capellanus around 1185 and condemned by the
bishop of Paris almost a hundred years later.

Andreas' *Tractatus* is divided into three books: the first, concerned
with the nature of love and its acquisition; the second, with the
retaining of love; the third, with its elimination and rejection. That
Andreas should have ended his treatise by condemning the very
ideas that he himself expounds in the earlier books has caused much
speculation on the part of scholars in the field. Some deny that
Andreas actually wrote the third book. This would save him from
the charge of inconsistency, but there seems to be little if any evidence to support the theory about a second author. Others explain
the structure of the *Tractatus* by saying that Andreas is merely
imitating Ovid, who also wrote a book of remedies. But though
Andreas was clearly influenced by Ovid, their final books are significantly different. Ovid never renounces love. He only wishes to
remedy its more extreme, less beneficial, symptoms. Andreas does
renounce sexual love, attacking it as offensive to God and inimical to
the religious love for which all Christians ought to aspire. It would

seem, then, that Andreas was either insincere—affirming one thing in the first books and then its denial in the third—or else intimidated by the church or else strangely given to self-contradictions. Scholars have held all these positions, but I think they are mistaken.

The most promising solution to the problem comes from the work of Alexander Denomy. In his book *The Heresy of Courtly Love*, he notes that when Andreas' treatise was condemned in 1277 it was grouped with the writings of those "who say that things may be true according to philosophy but not according to Faith, just as if there were two contradictory truths." This view, which the Averroists upheld and Aquinas attacked, is sometimes called the belief in "double truth": natural reason being a means to truths that may indeed contradict the truths available through faith. As a good Christian, one who believed in double truth would reject the truths of reason that oppose those of faith, but he would do so as an act of faith rather than reason—in a sense, renouncing reason as he would also wish to renounce the world itself. On this interpretation, Andreas emerges as neither insincere nor intimidated nor self-contradictory. In the first parts of his *Tractatus*, he would be following natural reason and accounting for love in the courtly manner coherent with the truths of reason. In the final book, he would be recognizing that these truths are incompatible with those of faith and expressing a preference for the latter.

There is much in Andreas to support Denomy's argument, but there are also difficulties. For one thing, Andreas himself never distinguishes between reason and faith, which is not surprising since the Christian Averroists did their work some fifty years after he wrote the *Tractatus*. When Andreas rejects courtly love, he appeals to the teachings of the church but not to faith as opposed to reason. Indeed, he makes an effort to show that the third book does not really contradict the first two. At the outset of his "Rejection of Love," he denies ever having *recommended* love in the earlier books. He says that he was merely providing instructions so that "invigorated by the theory and trained to excite the minds of women to love, you may, by refraining from so doing, win an eternal recompense and thereby deserve a greater reward from God." Andreas explains this by saying that God is more pleased with one who is capable of sinning but does not do so than with a man who has no such opportunity. Andreas does not suggest that good reasons for advocating love are to be supplanted by the faith of Christian dogma, and he explicitly gives reasoned arguments for resisting love which "any wise man" would recognize.

Furthermore, Denomy's interpretation fails to account for the fact that many of Andreas' ultimate objections to courtly love are present in the first book as well as the third. Most of the first book consists of dialogues between men and women, who vary from dialogue to dialogue according to their social status—middle class, simple nobility, higher nobility, and clergy. Within these dialogues, which actually number more than half the pages of the *Tractatus*, questions about courtly love are discussed from different points of view, including those of the church. Although one may seriously doubt that Andreas uses these dialogues simply as vehicles of information and without a desire to recommend the courtly love toward which they are slanted, they often voice condemnation of love. This being so, I believe that one should approach the entire *Tractatus* as a work of dramatic ambivalence, as itself a dialogue between two aspects of the medieval soul, two approaches to life brilliantly elaborated and dialectically confronting one another. Andreas does not alternate between reason and faith, but rather between nature and God or the secular and the holy. Nor does his allegiance to the natural ever free itself from its dialogue with the holy. In the twelfth century a complete separation must surely have been impossible.

In recent years D. W. Robertson Jr. and John F. Benton have suggested that the *Tractatus* can be interpreted as a work of irony and intentional ambiguity. This is true, but it does not follow that Andreas sought to be satirical or "humorous" any more than Plato did—though certainly there are considerable elements of both satire and humor in these as in other philosophers. I see no reason to believe that Andreas pervasively "meant to be funny," as E. Talbot Donaldson claims, and therefore that we need not read him as a serious author. If one requires a suitable model to account for Andreas' ambivalent approach, one should look to the writings of St. Bernard. In the book on *The Love of God* and in the *Sermons on the*

Canticle of Canticles, St. Bernard describes the degrees of love as beginning with man's natural self and slowly, step by step, leading him upward toward the spiritual. On the first step, love is carnal, the heart being attracted to the humanity of Christ. Only later does the soul of man ascend to a purely religious love—"passing through nature to eternity," as Shakespeare was to say. It is this, I think, that sets the pattern for the irony in Andreas, the framework within which he presents his version of courtly love, articulating it as a dramatic voice that may speak its lines here on earth, in nature, but that must finally be silenced for the greater glory of God.

Seen from this perspective, Andreas' book may be read as an attempt to harmonize courtly and religious love. The former will have to be subordinated to the latter, but not until its implications have been fully examined. In exploring the concept of courtly love, Andreas interprets it in a way that combines the various strands within the northern tradition: on the one hand, the troubadours and trouvères with their Platonistic idealism; on the other, Ovid and his sense of sexual reality. The influences of both Plato and Ovid are evident from the very first sentence of the first chapter: "Love is a certain inborn suffering derived from the sight of and excessive meditation upon the beauty of the opposite sex, which causes each one to wish above all things the embraces of the other and by common desire to carry out all of love's precepts in the other's embrace." Andreas resembles Plato in stating that love is an inborn suffering, eros being a function of human insufficiency, man's inevitable lack of goodness. In Plato the love of absolute beauty or goodness (as Diotima describes it, for instance) consists of metaphysical intuition quite different from either sight or meditation, but at various times Plato speaks *poetically* of the "vision" of the Good, as if it were somehow comparable to them. In the allegories of the cave and of the sun, he mentions sight and meditation with the understanding that these are mere symbols for that transcendental faculty which perfect love employs. In a way that duplicates the troubadours' use of Platonic themes, Andreas has obviously dropped the metaphysical reference of the empirical symbols and defined love in terms of them alone. Sight and meditation are thus to be taken at their face value, as the psychological processes with which we are familiar, the beauty of the opposite sex being something apparent to common sense whether or not it also symbolizes absolute goodness. This in turn enables Andreas to avail himself of the Ovidian concern for reciprocity, each lover wanting the embraces of the other as an expression of sexual oneness—"the common desire to carry out all of love's precepts in the other's embrace." So far does Andreas extend in this direction that his description of the actual genesis of love reminds one of Lucretius reducing passion to sexual desire plus erotic imagery: "For when a man sees some woman fit for love and shaped according to his taste," Andreas says, "he begins at once to lust after her in his heart; then the more he thinks about her the more he burns with love, until he comes to a fuller meditation."

In other ways too, Andreas shows the influence of thinkers like Ovid and Lucretius. It is present in his severely limiting love to heterosexual relations, in his deriving the word *amor* from the Latin word for hook—"which means 'to capture' or 'to be captured,' for he who is in love is captured in the chains of desire and wishes to capture someone else with his hook"—in his asserting that everyone capable of performing the act of Venus is subject to Cupid's arrows, in his practical and sometimes cynical advice to men about the flattering words with which to accost a woman, in his assurance that only love got with difficulty is highly prized, in his advocating jealousy and even occasional deception as a means of preserving love, and so on.

For all these Ovidian borrowings, however, Andreas retains his character as a moral philosopher in the idealist tradition. At every point, he recognizes the demands of nature but also wishes to fit them into a system of personal and social morality. Like Ibn Hazm or the troubadours themselves, Andreas praises love for elevating men toward virtuous behavior they could not otherwise attain. It makes the lowborn act with nobility, and the proud man it makes humble. Men in love rise above the meanness of self-interest. They become "accustomed to performing many services gracefully for everyone." Moreover, love is sharply distinguished from mere sexuality. In a manner that he might have acquired from the Platonic tradition but probably not from the Ovidian, Andreas insists that love adorns a man with the virtue of relative chastity. Though love arises from an indiscriminate lust, it fixes upon a single beloved so that "he who shines with the light of one love can hardly think of embracing another woman, even a beautiful one."

Exclusiveness of this sort contravenes Plato's dedication to absolute beauty since the Platonic philosopher emancipates himself from all empirical attachments by loving beautiful objects one after the other, or even all at once, never allowing himself to be ensnared by anything short of the Beautiful itself. But even so, Plato would have recognized that Andreas is showing persons who are not philosophically trained how they too can overcome their carnal inclinations. Through love a man restricts his sexual appetites to a single woman, and in his relationship with her they are made to serve the ends of moral aspiration. Though Andreas is not a Platonist, his ideas about love (as opposed to sex itself, where he seems to permit almost anything) are those of the tradition that derives from Plato.

Andreas' way of subordinating his Ovidian tendencies to others that are more Platonistic also appears when he discusses the five means by which love may be acquired. These are: a beautiful figure, excellence of character, great facility of speech, wealth, and readiness to grant favors. The last two are immediately eliminated as base considerations, and verbal facility is given only secondary importance. Andreas remarks that a man or woman who can speak well makes it easy for love to arise in another person, but he also states that readiness of speech is not enough; and to what I said earlier about his giving men advice on how to praise a woman, I must add the fact that he (unlike Ovid) never confuses these tactical moves with the lineaments of true love. Andreas insists that true love is acquired only through beauty of figure or excellence of character, and of these two he gives the latter the greatest importance. Though a beautiful face or body may elicit love, Andreas deems a courtly relationship inferior unless beauty is accompanied by goodness. In one place he relates the beauty of youth to what he calls "the natural instinct of passion," reserving love of a nobler sort to persons who have knowledge, virtue, and good manners. In general, he cautions the eager lover against the allurements of a beautiful appearance. With respect to men and women alike, it is excellence of character that assures the kind of love Andreas is prepared to defend. Since perfect courtly love involves mutuality of affection, it can only exist between a man and a woman who are both virtuous. Where the lovers are equally praiseworthy, even physical defects will not count as impediments: "A person of good character draws the love of another person of the same kind, for a well-instructed lover, man or woman, does not reject an ugly lover if the character within is good."

A statement of this sort reminds one of Aristotle as well as Plato, of philia as well as eros. The sense of community is there, the idea of goodness at either end of a friendly relationship, and also an implied interest in the welfare of the other. But of course Andreas is not referring to a fraternal bond between philosophers in a Greek city-state. The communion he is thinking of obtains between men and women who wish to direct their indiscriminate lustfulness towards a particular person of the opposite sex whose inherent goodness can serve to dignify the relationship. Where religious love in the Middle Ages distinguishes between cupiditas and caritas, the former being carnal and the latter purely spiritual, Andreas suggests a third alternative. He envisages courtly love as a kind of earthly paradise, a libidinal oneness that is also spiritual, a love that aspires upward (unlike cupiditas) but makes no attempt to approximate caritas, to seek union with the Christian God, or in any way to divest itself of bodily pleasures compatible with moral goodness.

In presenting this alternative, Andreas investigates problems in morality that no one else had really considered. For although he will have to reject courtly love as ultimately irreligious, he first examines the implications—both practical and philosophical—that follow from accepting it as an erotic ideal. In this respect, his *Tractatus* is possibly unique in medieval moral philosophy. One occasionally feels that Andreas was born too early, that humanistic thinking had not yet advanced to a point where his kind of problem could be adequately resolved. But in one way or another, and despite his joking manner at times, he raises most of the questions about love between the sexes that later philosophers were to reexamine so carefully. Had he not preceded them, they might not have been able to do so.

The most interesting problems in Andreas are the ones debated in the dialogues of Book I. In these dialogues, the man tries to convince a woman to take him as her lover. He makes this attempt solely by means of argument, offering reasons to support his plea, reasons that are generally moral though sometimes prudential. To the modern reader, these argumentative dialogues may well appear ludicrous. Who ever heard of a man convincing a woman to love him by means of a philosophical debate? Ovidian flattery, language artfully used to facilitate seduction, subtle appeals to the instincts and the appetites—this we can understand. I can even hear a twentieth-century cynic advising the man to find ways of losing the argument if he wants to win the woman. But the modern reader is often too literal-minded. He easily misconstrues the function of the dialogues. Andreas knows that love is governed by emotion as well as intellect. He knows that reasons merely bring forth other reasons. Why should they not? For his are philosophical dialogues in the manner of Plato or Hume, not speeches to be memorized by aspiring lovers. They are imaginative devices for considering human problems from diverse points of view, and need not be taken as anything else. Andreas lived in an age when Abelard and Guillaume de St.-Thierry had made dialectics into a veritable method for doing theology. Why should he not attempt something similar within the field of erotic morality?

As a rational confrontation between opposites, dialectics often has the form of thesis, antithesis, and synthesis. In Andreas, at least, this is generally the case. For instance, notice how the first dialogue considers what kind of man a woman ought to choose as her lover. From the description of love with which the *Tractatus* begins, it is apparent that true lovers must have excellent character. But does this mean that excellence of character precedes love or issues from it? When a woman takes a lover, should she seek the most worthy man she can find or should she use her love as something that *creates* worthiness in her lover? The troubadours usually chose the second alternative. They typically presented themselves as men who sought the benefits that accrue from loving a "perfect" woman. Compared to her, the troubadour lover considers himself unworthy. But once the concept of reciprocal love displaces fin' amors, all this must change. For now the woman will also want a "perfect" man, one who is antecedently worthy of her love, as she is worthy of his.

Speaking in the different voices of his dialogue, Andreas argues first for one alternative, then for the other, and finally tries to reconcile them within a synthesis. On the one hand, we are told that women should love men as a way of rewarding them for moral excellence, for having "done many praiseworthy deeds, extended many courtesies, offered numberless services to everybody." As in the court of the Heavenly King those who have the greatest merit receive the greatest rewards, so too on earth a woman of character ought to give herself in love to the worthiest man she can find. At least, a man has the *right* to plead for love on the basis of his noble character. Men may not verbalize such pleas, but why else would they strive to distinguish themselves, to shine in a woman's eyes, to inspire in her that admiration without which love cannot occur? On the other hand, we are reminded that love is itself the source of goodness. The man who cannot lay claim to deeds of excellence that would make him worthy of the woman's love is told to argue as follows: "no man could do good deeds unless the persuasion of love impelled him, and you ought to grant me the love I seek, so that men will think you did it to make me do well. . . . For I know that it will be considered more to your credit if out of your grace alone you give me your love, or the hope of it, than if you grant it to me in payment for what I have done; that would be like paying a debt, but the other remains pure generosity."

Against this, the woman claims that the argument is subversive to morality since it puts a premium upon the negligent man instead of rewarding the one who has done good deeds. In giving his reply, the man makes a distinction that enables the dialogue to reach a synthesis. If the lover is a mature person who has opportunities to act well but in fact has not done so, then he ought to be passed over in favor of a more worthy man. If, however, the suitor is still young and has had no such opportunities, he ought to be loved for the sake of the goodness in character that will be created in him. In a way that conflicts, or at least contrasts, with the previous references to heavenly rewards, the speech continues as follows:

> For as the Heavenly King rejoices over the conversion of one sinner more than over ninety-nine just, because of the good that follows therefrom, so a woman does better if she takes a man who is none too good, makes him praiseworthy through her good character, and by her instruction adds him to the court of Love, than if she makes some good man better.

The passage then ends with the claim that society gains more from the improvement of a man who is not good than from the increasing of goodness in one who is already good. Still, the importance of prior excellence is not to be neglected either. Giving the problem its final resolution, the dialogue goes on to establish an integrated series of steps that ought to be followed in choosing a lover. In the first stage, the woman encourages the man, allowing him to hope for her love; in the second, she accords him a kiss; in the third, the superficial contact of an embrace; and only much later, in the fourth stage, "the yielding of the whole person." Since the fourth stage culminates and completes the relationship, it is to be reserved for the man who proves himself worthy. Sexual union thus serves as an incentive to good action on the part of the aspiring lover. Being the last of the four stages, it is a reward that may always be withheld if the man has not succeeded in rendering himself excellent in character and behavior. At the level of the other three stages, however, the woman is free to choose a youth who is none too good. By giving him hope and the lesser delights of physical contact, she will encourage him toward noble action. If he fails, the woman withholds the final consummation and goes in search of someone else who either is already worthy of her or may become so with her assistance.

In reaching this synthesis, the dialogue is harmonizing more than may initially appear. By adding the fourth stage to the first three, the argument combines troubadour fin' amors with Ovidian eros. The goal of love is no longer calculated frustration, but rather sexual fulfillment within an ethical system. In emphasizing the role of moral character, Andreas goes beyond Ovid; and by giving the fourth stage the importance that he does, he goes beyond fin' amors, which limits itself to the first three. Moreover, it is significant that Andreas should be synthesizing the alternatives he considers. Not by chance does he cite heavenly rewards that merit earns and then contrasts them with divine grace extended to the unworthy sinner. For, in effect, his solution to the moral problem is a replica of the caritas-synthesis. As God's agapē is fundamental to religious love, so is the woman's gracious giving of herself the basis of courtly love as he describes it. In both God and the woman, love is the source of goodness, that without which no human goods could possibly exist. It is therefore prior to goodness and may be visited upon the unworthy man as well as one who has earned it. At the same time, love is also the reward for which men strive, the goal of upward aspiration. Andreas has his stages of love just as the medieval theologians had their degrees of salvation. Both hierarchies pertain to love as a striving for goodness, which must combine with love as a free bestowal in order for there to be the harmonious union, the completed circuit of give and take, that medieval Christians wished to institute on earth as well as in heaven.

As the humanization of caritas, Andreas' type of courtly love encounters problems similar to those that faced the religious synthesis. For instance, if love is something freely given—by the woman, as it is by God—then it may also be arbitrarily denied. In religious love such freedom bespeaks the infinite authority of a supernatural being. And yet, outpouring love is said to be the essence of the deity. How then can he withhold it, deny his grace in any manner whatsoever either to the righteous or the sinning? Similarly, how can the courtly lady refuse to love, rejecting lovers regardless of their worth and despite their future promise? Before the awesome character of the religious question, finite man could only humble himself. Not even the church could hope to understand how God is love but also free to limit or control the giving of his goodness. And in the corresponding problem for courtly love, Andreas too reaches no solution. On the one hand, his voices frequently assert that love depends upon the woman's free bestowal of herself, and that nothing avails the lover unless the woman offers love by her own free will. On the other hand, women are threatened with the penalties love reserves for those who refuse to join his army. In one place, the man denies that any good and wise woman would actually withhold herself. Since nothing could be more desirable than love, how can a lady who is not acting out of ignorance or perversity reject an opportunity to love? But the man in this dialogue does not push his advantage, and when the woman insists that she knows what she is doing, he merely laments the choice she has freely made.

In the sixth dialogue Andreas examines this problem systematically. First the man begs the woman not to spurn his love unless she finds him unworthy of her. She replies that, however worthy a suitor may be, the woman is always free to refuse him, and that he has no right to feel injured since the beloved is under no obligation "to give something to someone who asks for it." The man does not agree, however: he tries to prove that the woman cannot properly deprive him of her love. He argues that since no human being can be happy or moral unless he loves, it is always improper to reject a loving heart: "If a person of either sex desires to be considered good or praiseworthy in the world, he or she is bound to love." Consequently, the woman must accept either a man who is bad or one who is worthy. By what is called "Love's precept," the woman is forbidden to love bad men, and therefore she is obligated to love the suitor unless she can show that he is not really good.

To much of this the woman readily acquiesces. She admits that one must not deny love and yet that one must only love those who are good. But she now defends her freedom to accept only a particular person of her choosing, whichever good man she prefers over all others. In general, courtly love attacked promiscuity as the church also attacked polytheism. As there was only one God, so was there only one man and one woman who could satisfy the ideal longings of the other. On this basis, the woman might readily acknowledge the worthiness of a man but still conclude that he is not right for her. That does not please the lady's interlocutor, who engages in a diversionary tactic we may disregard. In answering him, however, the woman confesses to loving another man whom she desires with her heart. However greatly her *head* may incline her toward the suitor we have been listening to, she gives as the final reason for not yielding to him the fact that "I have no fondness or affection in my heart for you."

Andreas leaves the matter there, and perhaps we should not be surprised that he cannot resolve the problems he has been considering. His version of courtly love being an attempt to harmonize vastly different elements, it inevitably struggles with the irreconcilable—as does Christianity itself. Each derives its rational component from the Greeks, ultimately Platonic philosophy, and each seeks to combine it with a vital but unclear acceptance of emotion transmitted through the Roman dispensation—on the one hand, feelings of the heart that belong to passion and Ovidian sexuality; on the other, the sense of mysterious descent and the gratuitous giving of oneself described in the New Testament. Nor is Andreas unmindful of what he is doing. At times he even constructs the dialogues out of a studied conflict between his disparate sources.

The first dialogue has an especially interesting structure in this respect. In it Andreas confronts Platonic beliefs about the objective value of the beloved with other ideas, stemming from Lucretius as well as Ovid, about the delusiveness of love. First, Andreas advises the man to flatter the woman, to commend her in any way he wishes since women delight in being praised. But he also says—and he says it twice in three sentences—that these remarks have nothing to do with love, which shows itself only when the man goes on to tell the woman that God has made her as an exemplar of beauty or good sense and therefore one must marvel to see that she has no lover. This, of course, is what we expect from one who loves in the manner of the Platonic tradition. The object must be loved for the sake of its inherent goodness; to love a woman who is lacking in beauty or character is inconceivable. In this particular dialogue, the woman denies that she is either beautiful or outstanding in any other way. The man then replies that if she does believe she is not beautiful, so much the better! Why? Because it should prove to her that he really loves her, since "to me your beauty excels that of all other women; and love makes even an ugly woman seem very beautiful to her lover."

This is not what Platonism taught, at least not in respect to "true love," and its inclusion makes sense only if we think of Andreas struggling towards a synthesis with the realism of someone like Lucretius or Ovid. That such is indeed his intention appears from one of the speeches in the fourth dialogue. There the man says that love's arrows are not unloosed by the beauty of the beloved, but rather "it is love alone that impels men's hearts to love." The next sentence, however, seems to say something quite different. We are now told that when a man loves a woman, "her beauty is always very pleasing to him even though others find her misshapen and spiritless." This implies that the woman is objectively beautiful, but that love is required as a means of detection. Further down, the speech slips back into the Platonic mold—as if Andreas felt the need to articulate all the alternatives—and the man tells the woman that he loves her "because of your dazzling beauty and the fame of your excellent character."

As a synthesis, this is not much of a success. But the problems have been presented, and not until romanticism dropped the belief in objective goodness prior to love could anyone within the idealistic tradition make much headway with them. Something similar applies to the question of reciprocity. As I have said, Andreas discards the concept of fin' amors inasmuch as he builds mutuality into his verson of courtly love (which the troubadours also did occasionally). But at times Andreas seems to revert to fin' amors, although he feels the need to compensate for this extreme position by ending up with one that contradicts it. When he finally rejects courtly love, he not only knocks women from their pedestal but also debases them in the mire and denies that they could ever reciprocate love. In Andreas one finds more than just a statement of these opposing attitudes but less than a viable synthesis.

Within the structure of the *Tractatus*, subservience to the beloved takes on special interest because it is what the woman herself sometimes demands. To this extent, one might say that the concept of fin' amors has already been modified. In most troubadour poetry, women are not generally represented as expecting anything of their lovers. They are simply *there*, like Mount Everest. They embody ideals which matter to the poets, but which they themselves hardly seem to comprehend. Nor is this too surprising if one remembers that fin' amors developed out of a Hispano-Arabic world in which women were kept uneducated, in which the beloved might even be a slave girl. What a difference, therefore, to see women argue their case in the dialogues of Andreas! A kind of mutuality is achieved just in having men and women *agree* about the supremacy of the beloved: that she has the right to choose her lover; that he must prove himself worthy of her and so advance upward, step by step, toward a culminating union at her level; that everything noble and virtuous, everything that makes life worth living, proceeds from women, who are even described as the source of goodness itself. But though the lady now discourses with her lover, the men frequently cast themselves into the typical posture of fin' amors. On their knees, hands clasped, they beg the beloved to accept their love, their life, their service, and to do with them as she pleases. This mood is especially evident in the third dialogue, where a man of the middle class speaks with a lady of the higher nobility; but social difference alone cannot account for the way in which the man treats the woman like a divinity.

At the same time, troubadour devotion is clearly secondary in Andreas. Most of his women are quite uncomfortable in their role as goddesses. In the seventh dialogue the woman complains against the awkwardness of being praised immoderately. The man has just finished telling her that the whole world extols her virtue, wisdom, beauty, and so on, and that merely to serve her "is to reign over everything in his life." As against this, the beloved points out that praising her so effusively detracts from the worth of other women and that saying he reigns over everything by serving her is actually to insult all other ladies, particularly those who are better than herself. The man gets out of it by promising to serve women in general for the sake of his love toward her in particular. Still, the lady has made her point: she is not wholly pleased with being exalted as the embodiment of an ideal. She is, however, willing to encourage a lover to do good deeds on her behalf. In a relationship of that sort, the woman enjoys a reciprocal love. She participates as a very special human being, not as a goddess being worshiped.

The importance of reciprocity as an ideal of love is emphasized at various places in the *Tractatus*. In the eighth dialogue, both interlocutors seem to agree that no one is properly joined in love if "the character of the man is not as good as that of the woman or when the pure affection of the heart is not equal on both sides." In a later chapter, on how love may come to an end, Andreas goes even further: he explicitly classifies "inequality of love" with "fraudulent and deceitful duplicity of heart," these being things that inevitably destroy true love. A deceitful man cannot really love, he says, regardless of how worthy he may otherwise be. The position is fully summed up when Andreas states: "Love seeks for two persons who are bound together by a mutual trust and an identity of desires, and other people lack all merit in love and are considered strangers to his court."

Unfortunately, this paradise of blissful mutuality is not free of serpents. Although Andreas would seem to be criticizing Ovid's reliance on deceit, his chapter about how to increase love once it has been consummated duplicates this aspect of the Roman poet. He says that the feeling of love, as well as the desire for exchanging solaces, will augment if lovers can be made to meet rarely and with difficulty. He also claims that jealousy increases love, and in fact Andreas calls jealousy "the nurse of love." Both of these points—on jealousy and the cultivation of difficulties—are also discussed in the seventh dialogue. There the man speaks of them as belonging to the very definition of love, so much so that their absence from married life makes it impossible for love to exist between husband and wife. "For what is love," says the man in a line that could have been taken from Ovid's *Art of Love*, "but an inordinate desire to receive passionately a furtive and hidden embrace?" The man goes on to argue that in marriage embraces cannot be furtive, since neither husband nor wife need fear the objections of anyone, and therefore married people cannot be said to love. He concludes that jealousy, which is a disgrace between husband and wife, should be welcomed as a means of helping love to grow.

When the woman objects to this, saying that jealousy is "nothing but a shameful and evil suspicion" and that furtive embraces are less desirable than those that are easily attainable, the man sharpens his argument. He distinguishes between "true" or "real" jealousy and "shameful suspicion." Real jealousy he defines as an "emotion whereby we greatly fear that the substance of our love may be weakened by some defect in serving the desires of our beloved, and it is an anxiety lest our love may not be returned, and it is a suspicion of the beloved, but without any shameful thought." Real jealousy thus consists of three elements: a fear of one's own moral inadequacy, a fear that the woman does not reciprocate one's love, and a fear that she loves someone else. Since the woman is free to love whomever she wishes, the jealous man cannot condemn her in any way. His emotion is therefore different from a suspicion that she has acted shamefully. Andreas seems to use the phrase "shameful suspicion" ambiguously—sometimes referring to the man's shamefulness in suspecting the woman; at other times, the suspicion of shameful conduct by the woman. In either event, shameful suspicion is foreign to love since it presupposes a condition in which the woman has no right to love anyone other than this particular man. For that reason, it must not be confused with (real or true) jealousy. A husband cannot be jealous of his wife, only suspicious in a manner that involves shamefulness either on his part or hers or both, depending on his attitude and the nature of her conduct. Lovers being free in a way that married persons are not, since marriage is contractual, a lover's jealousy need never be shameful suspicion. The latter destroys love; but true jealousy contributes to it.

In making this distinction, Andreas is disassociating himself from Ovid—or rather, from *The Art of Love*. Though Ovid there supplies the notion that love and marriage do not mix, and even the idea that one depends on freedom whereas the other is bound by law, he is too shallow a moralist in that work to recognize the subtle point Andreas makes. Andreas wishes to defend love as a search for mutual goodness. Consequently, he must show that even jealousy, which he, like Ovid, considers integral to love, can be justified on purely moral grounds. It must not be confused with shameful suspicion, or any other failing that pertains to some other way of life. Nevertheless, the character of true jealousy—as Andreas describes it—already contains the seeds of love's own destruction. For jealousy is defined as fear. It is fear of oneself, fear of the beloved, fear of the absence of mutuality. But how can one believe that successful and reciprocated love depends upon emotions of this sort? One may well imagine a critic of love, Lucretius for instance, condemning it as something that ultimately reduces to jealous anxieties. St. Bernard rejected all kinds of love other than religious love on the assumption that they are always predicated upon fear. That Andreas should make this the basis of a courtly love he is advocating, at least presenting sympathetically, seems odd and paradoxical. In its beginnings, Andreas had told us, love is a suffering—"for before the love becomes equally balanced on both sides there is no torment greater"; but once reciprocity has been achieved, can suffering still be the character of love?

Given this dilemma, perhaps we can better understand Andreas' final rejection of courtly love. In addition to the religious reasons, he confounds lovers with an argument internal to courtly love itself: "The mutual love which you seek in women you cannot find, for no woman ever loved a man or could bind herself to a lover in the mutual bonds of love." Further on, he says "no woman is attached to her lover or bound to her husband with such pure devotion that she will not accept another lover, especially if a rich one comes along, which shows the wantonness as well as the great avarice of a woman." Here we have it then: it is all the woman's fault. She is by nature incapable of that mutuality which true love requires. She fails in this because—as Andreas' women themselves seemed to think—it is too absurd to speak of her as the embodiment of goodness. With that misogyny by which the medieval establishment sought to protect itself against humanist ideals, Andreas proclaims:

> Furthermore, not only is every woman by nature a miser, but she is envious and a slanderer of other women, greedy, a slave to her belly, inconstant, fickle in her speech, disobedient and impatient of restraint, spotted with the sin of

pride and desirous of vainglory, a liar, a drunkard, a babbler, no keeper of secrets, too much given to wantonness,
prone to every evil, and never loving any man in her heart.

It only remains for Andreas to quote Solomon (he means Eccle-
siastes): "There is no good woman."

In rejecting courtly love with such vehemence, Andreas reveals
how deeply divided the medieval mind could be. Some writers, de
Rougemont for instance, try to explain this division by arguing that
courtly love was a vastly antisocial movement. I myself find little in
the writings of Andreas to support de Rougemont's opinion. It is
true that in its groping toward reciprocity and sexual philia
Andreas' kind of courtly love envisages a society different from—
though in many ways congruent with—the secular and ecclesiastic
fellowships that ruled the feudal world. It is also true that women in
his dialogues claim social rights previously denied them: the right to
choose their own lovers, for one thing, but also the right to love a
man who belongs to a higher class, and even to make amorous
overtures if this can be done "gracefully and courteously." Finally, it
is true that the Courts of Love, whose decisions Andreas occasionally
cites, enabled women to proclaim their liberation and extend their
social power. What is not true, however, at least not evident from
texts such as Andreas', is the assumption that all this arises from a
rebellious, resentful, hostile attitude toward society at large, particularly the society of the Middle Ages.

In his brief discussion of Andreas in *De l'Amour*, Stendhal focuses
upon the social significance of the Courts of Love. He is fascinated
by the sheer fact that they existed, that ladies in the 1180s could
discuss matters considered taboo in 1822. But he also wonders
whether the Courts of Love had any other importance, for instance
whether public opinion enforced their decisions. Stendhal honestly
confesses that he does not know, but the question he asks as if to
suggest a possible answer is very penetrating: "Was it just as shameful to disregard them as it is in these days to shirk an affair dictated
by honor?" Now this seems to me the right approach. In the
nineteenth century, ideas of Romantic love may often have been
subversive and antisocial, but the code of honor was not. It was a

development *within* society, like a gentleman's club or the senior common room in an English college. Considerations of honor, or of status in club or college, may conflict with other social ideals without tending to undermine society itself. Similarly, courtly love parodies other, more dominant ways of life in the Middle Ages; but it does so from within, as an attempt to take over the society rather than destroy it. Courtly lovers were members of both the feudal order *and* the Army of Love.

The very fact that love is said to have an army, a society to which all lovers belong just by being lovers—as all Christians shared the fellowship of Christ just by believing in him—is itself significant. Romantic love in the nineteenth and twentieth centuries often set a pair of lovers apart from everything and everyone else; they could not belong to an army of lovers because their love was a way of protesting against all societies. Romantic lovers of this sort are "seuls au monde," to use Sartre's phrase—alone in the world and separate from it. But courtly love was different. It straddled, and sought to benefit from, two worlds: the world of medieval society in general and the world of love in particular. These worlds were interdependent, and in many respects one and the same.

It is in this context, I believe, that Andreas lists the Rules of Love. They provide a voluntary code of honor from which the Courts of Love derived whatever social authority they may have had. As a matter of fact, however, the Rules add very little to what Andreas discusses elsewhere. Of greater interest than the Rules is the problem he examines in the second dialogue. There a man of the middle class speaks with a woman of the nobility, who rejects him because of his lower rank. The suitor argues not only that love cuts across the barriers of society, excellence of character being the sole criterion, but also that nobility itself is determined by a man's goodness. Thus when the woman says that every man should seek for love within his own class, the suitor agrees but then claims to be a member of the same nobility as she: "If I have cultivated a character excellent through and through, I think that puts me inside the walls of nobility and gives me the true virtue of rank."

This may seem to be subversive, and in a sense it is egalitarian. Instead of limiting nobility to considerations of birth, the argument relates it to "good character and manly worth and courtesy" of a sort that anyone might conceivably attain. But actually the position is not at all subversive to society, nor foreign to the frequently disorganized character of medieval life. Nowhere does the man cast doubt upon the necessity of class distinctions, nowhere does he say anything to diminish the authority of the nobles. He merely wishes to join them, not because all men are really equal but rather because he—like them—is better than most. As also applies to the troubadours, love is a means of social ascension. The man wants to join the noblewoman on her level; he is not a Mellors trying to take Lady Chatterley "away from all that."

Though Andreas' emphasis upon character does not subvert society, it does force the nobles to prove themselves worthy of the rank to which they were born. In making this demand, the interlocutor is enunciating the moral principles officially proclaimed by every feudal state. At the same time, however, it is interesting to note that the second dialogue ends with the aspiring man's defeat. As if to remind him that reality scarcely conforms to official ideals, the woman continues to refuse the man for reasons of class distinction. In words that sound like those of the troubadours, the lover promises to continue his suit forever, partly in the hope that God will alter the woman's determination, but also for the benefits he derives merely by loving her—fruitless as that may otherwise be.

Having presented these opposing positions so emphatically, Andreas begins the next dialogue by offering a resolution in his own voice. In principle he accepts the idea that love need not be limited to one's own class; and elsewhere he shows how a woman may aspire to a higher rank, while her lover moves downwards because of love. Nevertheless, Andreas thinks that traffic between the social orders can be justified only in exceptional cases. A man of the middle class cannot hope to achieve the love of a noblewoman unless he is a person "with innumerable good things to his credit, one whom uncounted good deeds extol." This makes it sound almost, though not quite, hopeless. If a woman of the nobility chooses a commoner whose virtue is anything less than overwhelming, Andreas considers her behavior shameful. As a general rule, he concludes, a woman of the nobility should not accept a man of the middle class if she can find a nobleman who is more or equally worthy; but if she fails in this endeavor, she may satisfy herself with an extremely outstanding member of the middle class. Needless to say, Andreas never mentions anything lower. The bottom of the social pyramid may be used for purposes of brute sexuality, but not for love.

With some of the other social problems courtly love encounters, Andreas has greater difficulty. Marriage is an institution he wishes to uphold as much as the privileges of nobility; and yet his version of courtly love offers itself as an alternative to the married state. In the dialogue that analyzes jealousy, the woman refuses to believe that love cannot take place between husband and wife. The matter is taken to the Countess of Champagne, whose verdict runs as follows:

> We declare and hold as firmly established that love cannot exert its powers between two people who are married to each other. For lovers give each other everything freely, under no compulsion or necessity, but married people are in duty bound to give in to each other's desires and deny themselves to each other in nothing.

This passage is often quoted but generally misunderstood (by de Rougement, as well as many others). For one thing, it must not be taken as an attack on marriage. Nowhere in Andreas does anyone ever disparage the married state. The verdict just quoted specifically refers to the relationship between husband and wife as one that is governed by correlative obligations. The morality, even the holiness, of marriage is presupposed. In the same dialogue, when the man argues for extramarital love, he goes out of his way to recognize the "affection" that married persons are expected to feel for one another. The woman complains that he is undermining marriage, and in a sense she is right: courtly love competes with married love, offering to husbands and wives emotional possibilities marriage itself may not always afford. Nevertheless, the man makes it very clear that he recognizes the goods that married life does provide. He merely denies that love (as this strand of the courtly tradition defines that term) can exist in marriage itself. Just as father and son may feel great affection for one another without their being *friends*, he says, so too may husband and wife feel "every kind of affection" without their being lovers.

The matter is not a trivial verbal issue. Quite obviously, the man is recommending that marriage be supplemented by courtly love whereas the woman wishes to limit herself to the goods that conjugality can yield. Like many women in the Western world, she opts for the security of marriage rather than the furtiveness of an extramarital attachment. "I ought therefore to choose a man to enjoy my embraces who can be to me both husband and lover." This is a defense not of marriage but of married love that includes courtly love, a combination of ideas that the man would consider contradictory. Presumably, Andreas sides with the man inasmuch as he ends the dialogue with the statement by the Countess of Champagne. She maintains that married people cannot be lovers to each other; but also, she offers to the Caesar of marriage that which belongs to Caesar. Marriage justifies itself as a system of mutual rights and duties, while courtly love entails moral possibilities that go beyond the married state. That, I think, is how we must take the Countess' rhetorical question: "How does it increase a husband's honor if after the manner of lovers he enjoys the embraces of his wife, since the worth of character of neither can be increased thereby, and they seem to have nothing more than they already had a right to?"

Only if marriage claimed to be the single source of goodness, the sole vehicle of love, could these ideas be considered subversive. But few people in the Middle Ages would have thought of making such a claim for marriage. One may even argue that Andreas has idealized married life to the extent that he emphasizes the place of affection in it. When he discusses decisions in cases of love, he goes so far as to deny the appropriateness of saying that greater affection exists between lovers than between married people. He cites the following as a "logical answer" to the problem: "We consider that marital affection and the true love of lovers are wholly different and arise from entirely different sources, and so the ambiguous nature of the word prevents the comparison of the things and we have to place them in different classes."

At the same time, one cannot doubt that Andreas' type of courtly love mimics medieval marriage, just as fin' amors imitated devotion to the Virgin. Why else, in the legend of Tristan, to which one of the dialogues refers, should the beloved have had the same name as the woman the hero later marries? In that legend, love and marriage conflict dramatically, Tristan sleeping with another man's wife and refusing to sleep with his own. But this results not from a subversive intention but rather from the persistent, though in this case hopeless, attempt of courtly love to have the best of both worlds. One of Andreas' Rules of Love ordains that "it is not proper to love any woman whom one would be ashamed to seek to marry." Courtly love is an imaginative play upon the established code of marital society, men and women acting with one another *as if* they were husband and wife but within a context of greater moral potentiality. Without the institution of marriage courtly love could not have existed, anymore than poetry can exist without prose or dreams without reality. In its wilder moments, courtly love may have tried to substitute dreams for reality; but generally it held on to both, in conflict or in harmony, and in the hope that each would purify the other.

Of course, the Andreas type of love is subversive to medieval marriage in merely being adulterous. However much he may recognize the value and authority of married life, Andreas undermines it to the extent that he permits infidelity. And yet, of greater importance, I think, is the fact that adultery poses such a tremendous problem for him. In *The Art of Love*, Ovid sounds as if stealing from another's orchard is half the fun of making love. Not so Andreas, despite his advice about jealousy and the search for difficult or furtive embraces. Though Andreas may prefer that courtly love avoid adultery, he always leaves open its possible occurrence, regretfully perhaps but also with a sense of proud obedience to the realities of nature. In this vein, one of his interlocutors distinguishes between "pure" and "mixed" love. Pure love, the man says, binds the hearts and minds of lovers without leading to sexual intercourse. In words taken from the troubadours, he remarks: "It goes as far as the kiss and the embrace and the modest contact with the nude lover, omitting the final solace, for that is not permitted to those who love purely." Mixed love is different from mere carnality, since that would not be love at all; but unlike pure love, mixed love "gets its effect from every delight of the flesh and culminates in the final act of Venus."

Having made this distinction, the man then goes on to recommend pure love as preferable to the mixed. While mixed love dies out quickly, injures one's neighbor, and offends the Heavenly King, pure love is free of danger or defect. It neither injures nor offends, saves the beloved from the jeopardy of losing her reputation, and increases without end. But obviously, Andreas is making a minimal effort on behalf of pure love. Nowhere do we find him extolling the benefits of frustration, or even suggesting the creative utility of self-denial, as troubadour after troubadour had done. Moreover, the woman's speech roundly ridicules the idea of pure love: "You are saying things that no one ever heard or knew of, things that one can scarcely believe. I wonder if anyone was ever found with such continence that he could resist the promptings of passion and control the actions of his body. Everybody would think it miraculous if a man could be placed in a fire and not be burned." And even the man in the dialogue states that mixed love is not to be condemned. It too "is real love, and it is praiseworthy, and we say that it is the source of all good things, although from it grave dangers threaten."

Andreas himself, in a later chapter where he speaks in his own voice, tells us that pure and mixed love are not really different, though they may seem to be. The substance of love is the same for both; they originate with "the same feeling of the heart," nothing fundamental changing when two persons move from pure to mixed love. Elsewhere, he even encourages women to yield to the solicitation of a lover if he is unrelenting—"for all lovers are bound, when practicing love's solaces, to be mutually obedient to each other's desires." The need for reciprocity of love matters more to Andreas than an arbitrary distinction between partial and total consummation. Whatever he may think about the menaces of adultery, his philosophy has virtually no defense against its likely occurrence.

For this reason alone, Andreas must eventually reject his own teachings. In the final chapter, where he lists many reasons for condemning courtly love, the first one deals with God's hatred of those who propitiate Venus outside of wedlock. But the conflict between the two sides of Andreas goes much deeper. For him the sinfulness of adultery reveals the sinfulness of passion itself. Though marriage was a holy sacrament and adultery a violation of God's law, courtly love might have been tolerated had it not symbolized passionate interest inimical to religious love. The impassioned bestowal of, and search for, value in another human being could not be reconciled with medieval ideas about the love of God that Andreas also accepted. His courtly lovers wish to love each other as the embodiment of goodness, for the sake of excellence in character that each presumably has or will attain. They do not love each other as instruments for ascending the ladder of caritas; they do not try to use one another as the means towards a love beyond their own. At least in Andreas' formulation, courtly love takes the place of that spiritual marriage which Christian dogma reserved for the union with God. Promising its own kind of heaven, courtly love could only be heretical.

Thus, even if it were not extramarital, Andreas would have felt the need to renounce courtly love. Immediately after saying that God hates those engaged in adultery, he adds "or caught in the toils of any sort of passion." That is why he hardly allows the woman who defends the love between husband and wife to pursue the implications of her strange idea. Being a woman and obviously given to the cravings of the body, she can only reason that "love seems to be nothing but a great desire to enjoy carnal pleasure with someone, and nothing prevents this feeling existing between husband and wife." To have her say this is, of course, to give her the weakest possible defense of married love. Her statement not only conflicts with the courtly attempt to distinguish between love and lust, but also with the church's views about the role of sex in marriage. As the man points out in his reply, it is a sin for married people to offer one another solaces that are not inspired "by the desire for offspring or the payment of the marriage debt." What he means by payment of the marriage debt is unclear, but we may infer from his subsequent reference to apostolic law that he wishes to exclude passion: "An ardent lover of his wife is an adulterer." This saying, which is to be found in St. Jerome, typified the church's attitude toward sexual conduct between married persons. There was no attempt to limit married love in the sense of affection—if anything, that was to be increased. Nor was the doctrine intended as a way of encouraging abstinence, a wholly different consideration. "Ardent" is the crucial word. A man could not love his wife with *passion*. For that conflicts with religious devotion. Whether or not the participants were married, the passion that courtly love idealizes necessarily negated the primacy of God.

In *The Allegory of Love*, C. S. Lewis cites various texts to prove that in the Middle Ages the ecclesiastical authorities generally believed that the sex act was inherently innocent. It was only the desire or the pleasure or the intention which accompanied sexual behavior that they considered guilty or sinful. In the case of Aquinas, the matter is more complicated. He says that sexual desire or pleasure are not in themselves blameworthy, but only as they tend to subjugate reason. For our purposes, however, it is sufficient that each of these alternative views would condemn courtly love. It does not advocate desire or pleasure for their own sake, only as elements within a relationship governed by moral principles; yet it treats desire and pleasure as the source of goodness, the basis of love. Even at its coolest, in the playful discourse of lovers for instance, it could not have satisfied the scruples of Aquinas. For he means by reason something other than the mere appraisal or bestowal of excellence. He is referring to a faculty that enables one to appreciate the orderliness of God's creation as well as its dependence upon the reality of God himself. This faculty would be submerged, he thought, in passionate coitus and in every relationship that inflates the importance of desire or pleasure. Nor is the situation changed by substituting pure love for mixed love. Just as St. Jerome had said that the ardent love of one's wife is adultery, so too does Aquinas condemn the kissing and touching of women for reasons of delight, whether or not the activity leads to sexual intercourse. Though he antedates Aquinas, Andreas lived in a world that was dominated by ideas such as these. In his final pages he renounces all sexual love and defends marriage not only as a sacred bond but also because "with a wife we *overcome* our passion." (my emphasis)

Yet even here, at the very end of the dialectic, Andreas seems to be searching for a synthesis. The *Tractatus* ends with the rejection of courtly love, but most of the negative arguments had already been answered in the earlier pages. In the eighth dialogue, for instance, the man denies that God is "seriously offended" by the courtly love he has been proposing. For love is practiced under the compulsion of nature, which means it can be easily expiated; and anyhow, "it does not seem at all proper to class as a sin the thing from which the highest good in this life takes its origin." Nevertheless, the man recognizes that the love of God is a "very great and an extraordinarily good thing," so that one who prefers a wholly religious love acts in a highly commendable way. To love God, however, is to renounce the world; and few people are capable of that. If the woman in question does not wish to devote herself entirely to the Heavenly Country, she ought not to take refuge in the arguments of religious love. Either she relinquishes her natural condition, or else she tolerates her immersion in nature. In the latter event, she must accept her human frailty, admit she is not a saint, and give herself to the highest love of which she is capable—courtly love.

In a similar vein, Andreas later condemns but in a sense condones courtly love on the part of the clergy. He says that a clerk (as he was himself) ought to "renounce absolutely all the delights of the flesh." But immediately afterwards he shrugs his shoulders and gives permissive advice more suitable for men who cannot escape their nature: "since hardly anyone ever lives without carnal sin, and since the life of the clergy is, because of the continual idleness and the great abundance of food, naturally more liable to temptations of the body than that of any other men, if any clerk should wish to enter into the lists of Love," etc., etc.

Within this context, Andreas' renunciation of love need not be taken as either fraud or inconsistency. It is but the otherworldly perspective against which the medieval mind continually tests that love of nature which meant so much to it and which courtly love represents. Ultimately, and for those who can attain it, the religious life must win out. The world must be transcended, and all its creatures. The human will must be abased for the greater glory of God. Andreas is still on Plato's ladder, and he must deny courtly love in order to move higher. Insofar as courtly love conflicts with the love of God, it is guilty love. But the guilt of courtly love, in Andreas as well as the Tristan myth, as we shall see in the following chapter, is always something external to it, something that appears from a rung of the ladder higher than itself. If only for that reason, Andreas' synthesis can never succeed. His philosophy subordinates the courtly to the religious, but finds no way to make them interpenetrate. Their conflict is too strident: the aspiring soul must finally choose between this world and the next. If it chooses this world, it has settled for a lesser good; if it chooses the next one, it has lost its place in nature. For the two realms to be harmonized, either courtly or religious love had to be reconstituted. In the Italian Renaissance, both were. But until that happened, no adequate synthesis was available to the erotic imagination of Western man.

4
Medieval Romance

I<small>T</small> I<small>S</small> O<small>FTEN</small> S<small>AID</small> T<small>HAT</small> T<small>HE</small> romances of the Middle Ages had little to do with the lives that men and women actually lived during that period. Whatever the truth or falsity of this opinion, the most famous medieval romance was lived by two real people in the twelfth century: Abelard and Heloise. Abelard was a philosopher, a dialectician, and one of the originators of what would now be called theology. He wrote poetry and was familiar with the writings of the earliest troubadours. Heloise was renowned for her "literary learning" even before she met Abelard, which occurred when she was sixteen or seventeen. Hired as her tutor, Abelard falls in love with the young girl. He is forty years old, has had little experience with women, and he soon finds that his career as a canon of the church is severely jeopardized. When Heloise becomes pregnant, he offers to marry her. She strenuously resists on the grounds that it would wreck his worldly ambitions. He marries her nevertheless, but tries to keep the marriage secret. Taking this as a sign of betrayal, her uncle hires hoodlums who castrate Abelard. Wounded and publicly shamed, Abelard takes refuge in a succession of monasteries. He spends the rest of his life writing works that the ecclesiastical authorities—St. Bernard in particular—often condemn as misguided or even heretical. Immediately after his castration, Abelard persuades Heloise to take the veil. She eventually becomes the abbess of a nunnery that Abelard helps her to organize. Though she leads a life of confinement, she never ceases to think of Abelard as her husband. She lives and dies as a nun, but also seeks preferment in the world for the son she bore to Abelard as a result of their early love affair.

The story of Abelard and Heloise was known throughout the later Middle Ages; and it entered directly into the history of literature through a remarkable series of letters that Abelard and Heloise wrote to each other long after their separation. She was already an abbess and he was devoting himself to his writing. The letters are preceded by an autobiographical account in which Abelard details the history of his calamities. Taken together, the history and the letters constitute a text that scholars have studied from various points of view. They interest me as an example of erotic concepts creating live mythology. Assuming that most of this material is authentic, we may see it as elucidating ideals that were already operative in the occurrences being described, while also depicting a cardinal reality, the experience of Abelard and Heloise, which later versions of courtly and Romantic love could then idealize in their own way. The twelfth-century documents are works of art, not literal reports. They may be taken as narrating one of the earliest love stories in the modern world, revealing ideas and presuppositions that will recur throughout all subsequent centuries, including our own.

If we approach the history of Abelard and Heloise in this fashion, there is much that has troubled scholars which need not concern us at any length. Are the letters of Heloise authentic, or were they written by Abelard himself, if not someone else? Was Abelard a heretic couching his dangerous thought in orthodox protestations, or was he a devout Christian who occasionally lapsed into heretical statements without being aware of their implications? These are important questions, but we can avoid them. We need only consider the complex of ideas—some orthodox, some heretical, some un-classifiable—that later thinkers would draw upon to create new conceptions of love closer to their own experience.

This approach seems particularly relevant because in their writing we find Abelard and Heloise immersed in a world of diverse ideals which already determines much of their reality. Even as she hastens to the altar and takes the veil, Heloise quotes lines from the

Roman poet Lucan that serve as a commentary to her action. So Abelard tells us, and in him too we must assume that the mythological import of their experience was already operating. They are both living a legend, and, through the literary re-creation of their experience, contributing to the idealization of their love. Actually there are two legends that issue from the history of Abelard and Heloise, two systems of overlapping ideals, two perspectives that often clash with one another. One of these legends I shall call the Catholic; the other, the humanist.

The Catholic legend sees the lovers as sinners who ultimately find God. The humanist legend dates the beginnings of courtly love with their encounter in 1118, treats Abelard as the first modern freethinker, and Heloise as possibly the first Romantic. Each of the legends can cite evidence to prove its case; but it is only when we put the two together, and give up the attempt to prove one or the other, that an accurate picture emerges. Patterns of idealization were too chaotic in the beginning of the twelfth century to lend themselves to either interpretation exclusively. Medieval Catholicism was still developing, having hardly entered the age of scholasticism, for which Abelard is often considered an early and primitive precursor. And the humanism of the Middle Ages was also just beginning. It doubtless received an impetus from the story of Abelard and Heloise, but there is no single doctrine that resulted.

For this reason, commentators like Gilson look in vain for a coherent design within the autobiography of Abelard or the letters that follow it. Gilson divides Abelard's career into two parts: in his earlier life he is aggressive, selfish, the sly seducer who really knows nothing about love; in his later years he writes letters that show him outstripping Heloise in holiness and indicate that he has learned the spiritual significance of their carnal episode. This, of course, is what Abelard explicitly tells us. For he believes in the Catholic legend about himself much as Gilson does eight hundred years later. Abelard begins the history of his calamities by citing the didactic purpose it is supposed to serve: he will write about his life in order to provide an example that may help the reader to mitigate and endure unfortunate "human passions." At the same time, Abelard is also confessing his earlier sinfulness in the manner of Augustine. Like Augustine in the *Confessions*, he looks back at his former interests with a mixture of horror and fascination. As Augustine loved his mistress but then renounced this earthly madness for the love of God, so too is Abelard eager to depict his craving for Heloise as mere animal lust that the religious life has finally taught him to cast out and put aside as a device of the devil. The same is true of his aggressiveness, his combative spirit and arrogant desire for self-assertion.

To a Christian of the Middle Ages willfulness was more sinful than fornication. In making his confession, Abelard will show how both led to calamity in his early life, and how he was eventually redeemed through the miraculous mercy of God: "When, therefore, I was labouring wholly in pride and lechery, the remedy for either malady was by divine grace conferred on me, albeit unwilling. . . . For lechery, indeed, by depriving me of those parts with which I practised it; but for the pride which was born in me from my surpassing knowledge of letters . . . by humiliating me by the burning of that book in which most I gloried." In having him castrated, Heloise's uncle was thus an agency of Providence, and the same applied to the ecclesiastical courts that condemned Abelard's writings.

This makes a pretty picture, dualistic in its structure like a painting by Fra Angelico, and one that assures Abelard of God's abiding kindliness toward him. For though he suffers in the body and the pride of authorship, he has been cleansed on earth in preparation for a blissful eternity. In the fifth letter he writes out the following prayer for Heloise and her nuns to recite on his behalf: "Punish, I beseech Thee, in this world the guilty, that Thou mayest spare them in the world to come. . . . Afflict our flesh, that Thou mayest preserve our souls." And since God chastises those he loves well, all things conspire for the best. We have been reserved for some great end, Abelard assures Heloise; and he piously concludes the history of his calamities with the intimation that God's supreme bounty will not have allowed him to suffer needlessly.

When we examine this picture more minutely, however, serious problems arise. For instance, the book in which Abelard gloried and which was burned (at Soissons in 1121) was an early draft of later books that were also burned (after the Council of Sens in 1141). The autobiography was written in the 1130s, while some of these books were being composed. Abelard may have thought that they were conceived without the willfulness that had now been cleansed from his soul, but the content of these works does not reveal the vast difference that he has led us to expect. Except for his final year at Cluny, after he had been condemned to silence by the pope, Abelard ends where he began: as a master dialectician trying to make sense of the Christian dogmas and in the process encountering the systematic hostility of a church that had not yet learned how to reconcile reason and faith. In his life struggle Abelard appears combative and aggressive at the ending much as he had at the beginning. The sixty-year-old philosopher who angrily stalks out of the Council of Sens is not a different man from the twenty-year-old student who comes to Paris to learn philosophy and confound his teachers. Abelard informs us that his father was a knight who acquired a love of letters and eventually took religious vows (as did Abelard's mother). In the son the parental experience repeats itself. Abelard, both early and late, is a warrior, a feudal knight, a battler against obscurantism within the church as well as false doctrines without. Given this continuity, and the skirmishes with authority to which his self-dedication led, it seems unlikely that the burning of his earlier book could have caused the religious conversion or humility to which he refers.

It is more plausible to think that Abelard—like Augustine and many other Christians of the Middle Ages—was *continually* condemning everything in himself that symbolized resistance to God's order. This attitude would be a living proof that one had conquered pride and been chosen as an example of divine charity. Since the proof appeared more edifying if one's sinfulness was extreme, all faults had to be painted in the blackest colors. Thus, Abelard tells us repeatedly that he felt only lust toward the seventeen-year-old Heloise who had been placed in his charge and to whom he had free access in her uncle's house. He says that one might as easily have entrusted "a tender lamb to a ravening wolf."

But even at seventeen, Heloise was obviously precocious, and the speeches Abelard quotes do not suggest that intellectually she was anyone's tender lamb. Moreover, Abelard reports that he himself was fairly chaste in matters of sex: "I ever abhorred the uncleanness of harlots, and was withheld from the society of noble women by the assiduity of my studies." Though Abelard was almost forty years old at the time, he speaks of being overwhelmed by the joys of love no less than Heloise, and for the same reason: sexual experience was new to him as well as her. Obviously, Abelard was not a wolf in the sense of being an accomplished roué. On the contrary, he was an inexperienced scholar who suddenly discovered the allurements of love in the person of the only girl whose intellect he could fully respect. He does not even describe her as physically very interesting. He says only that "in face she was not inferior to other women," whereas her learning was supreme. His two great passions—in Heloise and in books—subtly intermingle when he portrays the delights of love: "First in one house we are united, then in one mind. So, under the pretext of discipline, we abandoned ourselves utterly to love, and those secret retreats which love demands, the study of our texts afforded us. And so, our books lying open before us, more words of love rose to our lips than of literature, kisses were more frequent than speech. Oftener went our hands to each other's bosom than to the pages; love turned our eyes more frequently to itself than it directed them to the study of the texts. That we might be the less suspected, blows were given at times, by love, not by anger, affection, not indignation, which surpassed all ointments in their sweetness." The scene anticipates Francesca's account, in Dante's *Inferno*, of how she and Paolo put aside their reading in order to make love; and the references to amorous beatings may remind us of Zerlina's aria "Batti, batti, bel Masetto" in Mozart's *Don Giovanni*. Abelard ends up writing love poems to Heloise, songs that were later sung in the streets of Paris—to the infinite joy of Heloise herself, as she wistfully recalls after becoming a nun.

How innocent their love seems to us now! How vapid the word "lust" appears as against the experience of these awakening souls! Once he has been castrated within the dispensation of a God whose benevolence he dare not question, Abelard will have to use ugly words to describe his feelings during that year of passionate love. But there is no reason for anyone else to do so.

Though she too suggests that Abelard did not love her for herself, but only as a sexual prey, the mature Heloise presents us with quite a different perspective upon their former relationship. It is, for her, not at all a cause of self-condemnation. In accepting the natural and normal character of their sexual intimacy, Heloise does indeed appear as a sybil of humanism in the modern world. When she describes her days with Abelard, her frank and honest approval of sex makes her seem enlightened and much more liberated than him. Having become a nun, she is troubled to think of the body intruding upon her spiritual profession, but she is also unwilling to relinquish happy memories that linger although her soul would be quieter if they did not:

> So sweet to me were those delights of lovers which we enjoyed in common that they cannot either displease me nor hardly pass from my memory. Whithersoever I turn, always they bring themselves before my eyes with the desire for them. Nor even when I am asleep do they spare me their illusions. In the very solemnities of the Mass, when prayer ought to be more pure, the obscure phantoms of those delights so thoroughly captivate my wretched soul to themselves that I pay heed to their vileness rather than to my prayers. And when I ought to lament for what I have done I sigh rather for what I have had to forego. Not only the things that we did, but the places also and the times in which we did them are so fixed with thee in my mind that in the same times and places I re-enact them all with thee, nor even when I am asleep have I any rest from them. At times by the very motions of my body the thoughts of my mind are disclosed, nor can I restrain the utterance of unguarded words.

Is Heloise really contrite? Passages such as this make one doubt it. She gives voice to the conventionalities of her new condition, knowing that Abelard expects them of her, but her heart still yearns for that year of love when she was a teenager exploring a brave new world. Though her reference to the "phantoms" of libidinal pleasure sounds like Lucretius denouncing sexual images as harmful and illusory, her self-condemnation is only a lesser part of what she really feels. What seems more authentic is the romantic nostalgia, the harking back to one's youth in dreamlike states both waking and asleep, the vivid remembrance of erotic things past, and the inclination to rebel against an oppressive though inescapable reality in the present. In the next paragraph she piously quotes the words: "Who shall deliver me from the body of this death?" But in her mouth they convey an almost ironic ambiguity. Is the body of her death the compulsion, evil and unwelcome, to revert to carnal memories? Or is it rather her imprisonment in the nunnery of an unnatural and forbidding religion? Without denying both terms of this ambiguity, it is the latter that Alexander Pope emphasizes in his poem "Eloise to Abelard":

> Now warm in love, now with'ring in thy bloom,
> Lost in a convent's solitary gloom!
> There stern religion quench'd th' unwilling flame,
> There dy'd the best of passions, Love and Fame.

In ways that reinforce both the Catholic and the humanist legends, Gilson speaks of "pure love" as the basis of Heloise's entire life. He sees her systematically humiliating, degrading, sacrificing herself for the sake of the man she loves, giving to him what both she and Abelard claim that Abelard could never give to *her*—a love that seeks the welfare of the beloved instead of the satisfaction of the lover's own desires. In his book on St. Bernard, Gilson even suggests that Abelard's thinking about man's love of God makes sense only if we realize that it is the kind of love that Heloise gave to Abelard. Unlike St. Bernard, Abelard had argued that a pure love of God would renounce even an interest in beatitude, and in general any rewards the lover might receive in enacting his love. The love of God would thus be a total self-dedication, a selfless submission to the will of that divine object uniquely worthy of love. St. Bernard found this notion heretical, since God was himself the essence of beatitude, and to love him properly would have to include an interest in attaining beatitude for oneself. What Abelard really described, Gilson argues, was not the love of God but rather the love of another human being—and in particular, the pure love of Heloise for Abelard that enabled her to debase, even to prostitute, herself for the sake of his greater advantage.

Something can be said for Gilson's thesis. It is true that Heloise claims to love Abelard with what she calls an "innocent" and self-denying love, that she submits to his commands time and time again, that she consistently argues for decisions that will benefit him and not necessarily herself. As she says in the first of her letters: "God knows I never wanted anything from you but yourself—*te pure, non tua, concupiscens* [desiring you purely, not what was yours]. It was not marriage, no, nor gain of any kind that I was looking for; it was not my own desires nor my own pleasures, but yours, as you very well know, that I longed to satisfy."

But then one begins to wonder. Abelard is old enough to be her father. At his age and with his degree of intellectual eminence, he is surely a great authority to her. Above all, he represents the very concept of "pure love" that Heloise would have learned from his teachings and that she now applies to him as the loved object instead of God. Abelard's theological doctrines having been formulated long before he met Heloise, there is no reason to believe that his thinking about the love of God was modeled on her attitude. Gilson has reversed the natural order of things; it is *her* love which patterns itself after the dogmas of the man she reveres. Seeking to get him to reciprocate, what better way than to assert that she has always loved him as he himself said everyone should love God. In other words: you are a god to me, and will you not therefore be merciful?

At the same time, one may also question the accuracy of Heloise's claims. In one place, she states that God should have punished her more and Abelard less, and that she is actually the cause of his downfall. Explicitly confessing that she has neglected the love of God, she also intimates that her love for Abelard was not as selfless as she has pretended. When she argues against their marriage, she says that she did not want to be criticized by the world for having taken so illustrious a philosopher away from it. Reminiscing about the man he once was, she reveals what a good he was *to her*:

> For who among kings or philosophers could equal thee in fame? What kingdom or city or village did not burn to see thee? Who, I ask, did not hasten to gaze upon thee when thou appearst in public, nor on thy departure with straining neck and fixed eye follow thee? What wife, what maiden did

not yearn for thee in thine absence, nor burn in thy presence? What queen or powerful lady did not envy me my joys and my bed? There were two things, I confess, in thee especially, wherewith thou couldst at once captivate the heart of any woman; namely the arts of making songs and of singing them. Which we know that other philosophers have seldom followed. . . . It was on this account chiefly that women sighed for love of thee. And as the greater part of thy songs descanted of our love, they spread my fame in a short time through many lands, and inflamed the jealousy of many women against me. For what excellence of mind or body did not adorn thy youth? What woman who envied me then does not my calamity now compel to pity one deprived of such delights? What man or woman, albeit an enemy at first, is not now softened by the compassion due to me?

Thus, when Heloise insists that she loved Abelard only for himself, we should possibly interpret this as meaning that she loved him for those excellences of mind and body that she could enjoy. This is not to say that she used him as a commodity, as a mere instrument to the attaining of what she selfishly desired. In accepting him as he was, she may well have loved him for his own sake as she claims. But even so, her love would have differed from one that renounced all benefits and merely gave itself in the sacrificial manner envisaged by Abelard's thinking about the love of God. On the contrary, the love she describes sounds rather like the love of God as St. Bernard conceives of it: a love that delights in the beloved, appreciating his perfections and eager to share in them, a love that involves the sacrifice of lesser goods but always in a way that makes the lover approach a state of beatitude that all men desire most. It would be foolhardy to suggest that St. Bernard saw and was influenced by the letters of Heloise; but perhaps it was her kind of attitude that contributed to his thinking about love.

Whether one begins with the Catholic or the humanist legend, the story of Heloise and Abelard prefigures most of the problems of love in the medieval world. In both legends the drama of the love affair, and possibly much of the passion within it, results from the conflict between religious and human love. Abelard, Heloise, St. Bernard, and all Christians in general believed that human beings must not love one another with the kind of total devotion that was warranted only in relation to God. The two lovers may suffer in the flesh, he because of castration and she because of sexual deprivation, but their spiritual distress is even greater. He vilifies himself as a ravening wolf in order to convince her that only God can love her with a love that does not reduce to lust. However much he may have loved her, it is only God that he feels he *ought* to have loved. She is tormented by her erotic fantasies because they prove to her that she does not love God as she believes she should. Yet she cannot extirpate the natural interests that belong to the only love she has ever experienced. We may question the desirability of her kind of love, for her self-sacrifice and self-abnegation before Abelard seem pathological, but we cannot deny that this was the great event in her life. She could not enjoy it because of something that goes far beyond Abelard's personality or physical mutilation. And that is the split between loving God and loving another human being which troubled all who were devoutly religious in the Middle Ages.

Though Heloise proclaims that she does not love God properly— "I am sure that up to now I have done nothing out of love for him"—she continually argues that her residual love for Abelard is not merely concupiscence. When they were together, she delighted in erotic pleasures; now that they are apart, she forgoes them except in fantasy. The only constant that she recognizes is her desire to be "yours before everything." As I remarked earlier, the concept of courtly love implies a distinction between sex and love precisely of this sort. In the northern tradition to which most of the literary romances belong, the troubadour attempt to idealize frustration was certainly not prevalent. But like the poetry of fin' amors, the romances presuppose that love that is worthy of the name includes more than mere sexuality. Both in the man and in the woman, it appears as that giving of oneself to which Heloise so often refers.

Heloise knows that her love for Abelard is idolatrous and therefore when she says that she would not have hesitated to follow Abelard "into hell itself," her statement need not be taken as wildly metaphorical. In medieval romances such as *Aucassin and Nicolette* and *The Châtelaine of Vergi* we shall encounter lovers who would be willing to choose hell over paradise provided that they can find their beloved in the former place. But Christ too descended into hell; and in defining her love for Abelard as a self-sacrificial bestowal of herself, Heloise believes (at least in part) that the holiness of love will finally vindicate her attitude. This line of thought will take lovers very far in later generations. In them, as in her, sexual love becomes a means of transcending ordinary life, much as mystical love had always wished to do. To the defenders of orthodoxy, such mimicry could only be heretical; but from the lovers' point of view, it was a merging of sacred and profane, and therefore an elevation of the natural into a superior realm that justifies whatever risks one may have to run.

Within the Catholic legend, Heloise's problem is much as Gilson has stated it: "to find in the passion this man inspires the strength required for a life of sacrifice which is both meaningless and impossible save on the level of the love of God." From the humanist perspective, which dominates both medieval and modern romance, the life of sacrifice becomes meaningful if it belongs to an authentic love between man and woman. Only in this context can one understand Heloise's original refusal to marry Abelard. Their child having been born and their love affair discovered by Heloise's uncle, Abelard offers to marry her despite its effect upon his career in the church. She opposes the idea, insisting that marriage and the life of the intellect are incompatible. She is often ridiculed by scholars who point out that the authority she cites in making her case argued for celibacy rather than the unmarried fornication she has in mind. It was her idea that Abelard's fame and glory could be preserved if only he remained a bachelor, continuing their love affair without the formality of marriage. But far from proving the "hypocrisy of Heloise," as one writer has put it, her speech reveals her willingness to forgo the advantages of a legal bond that would have tied Abelard to her permanently and irrevocably. In the romances of Chrétien de Troyes, as we shall presently see, love—whether accompanied by marriage or not—must always contend with the conflicting aspirations of fame and glory. Like Enid, in Chrétien's story, Heloise sacrifices her possessiveness as a wife in order to free her lover for the pursuit of worldly goods they both value.

Nevertheless, one cannot deny that the reasoning of Heloise

implies an incompatability between love and marriage. Theorists who define all courtly love in these terms are neglecting the many occasions in which medieval literature asserts their harmonization; but Heloise must be counted among those who see marriage as an impediment to love. Abelard depicts her as saying "how much dearer it would be to her, and more honourable to me, to be called mistress than wife, that affection alone might hold me, not any force of the nuptial bond fasten me to her; and that we ourselves being parted for a time should find the joy of meeting all the keener the rarer our meetings were." And in one of her letters to him, Heloise insists that though "the name of wife appears more sacred and more valid, sweeter to me is ever the word friend, or, if thou be not ashamed, concubine or whore. . . . I preferred love to wedlock, freedom to a bond."

Cicero, like Aristotle before him, had taught the Middle Ages that true love consisted in friendship which is benevolent, disinterested; but that was quite different from Heloise's idea. For her, and for her followers in succeeding generations, love is a transcendent consummation, a sacred friendship through sexuality that matrimony alone could not create. In his book on the medieval mind, Henry Osborn Taylor remarks that though marriage was holy in the teachings of Christ, "it did not preserve its holiness through the centuries which saw the rise of monasticism and the priestly celibacy. A way of life is not pure and holy when another way is holier and purer; this is peculiarly true in Christianity, which demands the ideal best with such intensity as to cast reflection on whatever falls below the highest standard." The life of illicit sex that Heloise proposed would have provided Abelard with the very opposite of "priestly celibacy," but to the extent that it was motivated by love, this way of life could also claim participation in an ideal friendship that marriage might not approximate.

On the other hand, Abelard clearly indicates that he does not share Heloise's beliefs about an incompatibility between love and marriage. In one of his later letters, he asks her to recite a prayer for the two of them which begins with a consecration of the marital union. It ends with the hope that oneness between husband and wife—obviously Heloise and himself—will be completed in heaven.

He implores God: "those whom Thou hast parted for a time in this world, unite forever in the next."

In a similar vein, Tristan and Iseult, so thoroughly parted in this world that they never were able to marry one another, might pray to be united after death by a god who sympathizes with the tragedy of their love. And just as the lovers' souls are as closely entwined as the hazel and the honeysuckle, and the briar that rises from Tristan's tomb crosses the chantry to fall upon Iseult's, so too, tradition tells us, when Heloise and Abelard were buried together his corpse threw open its arms and clasped her body in one final, inseparable embrace. In Abelard's cycle of lyrical poems known as *Planctus*, we may read the consoling suggestion that God will accept their union of body and soul and not forever treat them as merely sinful lovers:

> Where love is the moving force
> and reparation is made,
> no judgment in all the world
> could fail to extenuate!...

The harmonization of courtly and religious love, which neither Abelard nor Andreas nor any other philosopher in the Middle Ages could effect, functioned as an ideal of the imagination in much of medieval literature. What orthodox Christianity would not tolerate even as a possibility forced itself into the creative, albeit fanciful, fabric of popular romance. Throughout their sufferings, Tristan and Iseult constantly receive support from the Christian God who recognizes their innocence even though their adulterous behavior renders them guilty and impious. Different versions of the legend present God's attitude in different ways, but Béroul, Thomas of Britain, and Gottfried von Strassburg—whose writings all occur between 1160 and 1210—include scenes in which God directly intervenes to save the lovers from execution or from punishment through the ordeal by burning iron. In this episode, Iseult is spared even though her oath of innocence was a contrived deception. God sees into the hearts of the lovers, knows that their adultery was caused by the potion they mistakenly drank, and therefore protects them against malicious enemies. In doing so, God is also defending the love that pervades their passion. What could have been sinful becomes a spiritual achievement that shows itself in the need for mutual fidelity and the inability to live without each other.

In the version of Gottfried von Strassburg, the relationship between human and religious love becomes a major problem for interpretation. On the one hand, Gottfried mentions God and uses Christian terminology more than any of his predecessors; on the other hand, he presents the love between Tristan and Iseult as a supreme good despite technicalities about adultery. Where earlier versions introduced a hermit who reminds the lovers that their life together in the forest is itself perdition, Gottfried eliminates the hermit and portrays the lovers' isolated condition as an earthly paradise, a return to the purity of nature and a welcome escape from the corruption of life in the court. Critics have disagreed about Gottfried's intention. Some have insisted that his view is definitely heretical since he depicts the love between Tristan and Iseult as the summum bonum, the highest good that men and women can reach. As such, human love, *minne* in the medieval German, would not be subordinate to the love of God but rather a substitute for it. Other critics maintain that Gottfried thinks of minne as a good that symbolizes and fully accepts a superior love, the love between man and God, to which it leads as a means to an end.

On the latter interpretation, Gottfried's conception would not be especially heretical. It would merely incorporate within a graphic and highly imaginative romance the doctrine that the church was developing and that Aquinas would later formulate as the caritas-synthesis. By loving one another for the sake of God, Tristan and Iseult would still belong to the great order of the cosmos in which everything manifested God's love. The trouble with this interpretation is the fact that Gottfried scarcely attempts to place the love between his characters in the context of anything but the human and the natural. The language in which he describes their love may sound religious, even mystical, but it is the religion and the mystery of their mutual bond that principally interests him. The phrase "religion of love" which C. S. Lewis mistakenly applies to all the versions of courtly love fits Gottfried's intuition in a way that does not apply to any of his predecessors. Treating the union of his lovers, particularly its configuration in their forest exile, as the holiness that nothing else on earth can equal, Gottfried employs religious ideas that are very different from those of the church. At the same time, Gottfried never claims to be writing anything anti-Christian and he never argues for dogmas that are explicitly subversive. His frequent references to the Christian God leave open the possibility that he himself may not have recognized how radical his thinking was for the Middle Ages.

The problem about Gottfried's intentions must be left unresolved. We have no way of knowing whether he thought that love between man and woman, even the idealized and fabulous love between his legendary characters, embodied the summum bonum within itself or merely indicated how sexual experience can be subordinated to the orthodox faith. It seems clear, however, that the love between Tristan and Iseult, as Gottfried describes it, is at least a *replica* of man's love of God as conceived by the ecclesiastical tradition. Various scholars have pointed out that Gottfried's approach to love shows the influence of Bernardine mysticism. In his *Sermons on the Canticle of Canticles*, St. Bernard had taken the sexual imagery of the Song of Songs in the Old Testament and interpreted it as a mystical marriage between Christ the bridegroom and his bride the church (or occasionally, the human soul). The biblical garden of love, the reciprocity of love between bride and bridegroom, the oneness of their flesh, and in general all the bodily manifestations of libidinal union within a natural context—this had been for St. Bernard a metaphoric and symbolic representation of mystical beliefs about holy love that the purified spirit might someday attain.

Gottfried begins with St. Bernard, though he never mentions him, and then uses his ideas poetically and for humanistic purposes. Gottfried stands the Bernardine doctrine on its head; or rather, if we begin with a secular and impartial approach to the Song of Songs itself, he puts back on its feet the biblical text that St. Bernard had stood on its head. Duplicating the ecstatic fervor of Bernard's writing, Gottfried suggests that the love which warrants such religious emphasis is sexual love itself. The bride and bridegroom are the man and woman who know the meaning of human love and are capable of devoting themselves to its hardships in a world that opposes its mere existence. Only they can appreciate the beauty of fidelity; only they have learned how to achieve oneness with another person.

In Gottfried's version, the story of Tristan and Iseult is thus designed to illustrate the transcendent goodness of this sanctified love in nature. It flourishes in the wilderness, but arises out of attributes in the lovers that we can recognize as idealizations of traits that were valued in the medieval courts. Though Gottfried's lovers become aware of their affinity only after they have drunk the *minne-trank*, the love potion, they are initially presented to us as manifestations of heroic manhood and womanhood. He is the greatest of all warriors, and she is so uncommonly beautiful that no one but Helen of Troy can be likened to her. In this sense, they are made for one another. And whether the minnetrank is magic or just an aphrodisiac (as the sophisticated Gottfried intimates), it primarily signifies the force of nature that underlies the dynamic search for one's alter ego. In addition to the values of Mars and earthly Venus, the lovers also manifest the attainments of Gottfried himself. For they and only they are presented as artists, inspired musicians whose singing and playing of the harp can effect a supreme oneness, with their audiences when they perform in society and with each other when they finally withdraw to their blissful and all-sufficient isolation. Tristan perfects the art of music in Iseult long before they fall in love. He serves as her tutor, much as Abelard instructed Heloise. What he teaches her is subsumed under the concept of *moraliteit*. Gottfried tells us that this is "the art that teaches good manners"— behavior that puts us "in harmony with God and the world."

The ethics to which Gottfried refers is the morality of courtly love, for he insists that moraliteit serves as the sustenance of the *edelez herzen*, the noble hearts, to whom he dedicates his book in the Prologue. He there describes his ideal readers as men and women who wish to attain the perfection of sexual love, and he remarks that they will always be a small minority, what Stendhal later called the "happy few." Moraliteit separates the edelez herzen from all others by developing in them the fine behavior and delicate sensibility that Tristan inculcates in Iseult. Before he had arrived, she was already an accomplished musician whose sweet singing and wondrous beauty could echo "through the kingdom of the years deep down into the heart"; but it is only under the tutelage of Tristan, who later kills a dragon to conquer her and then arouses her deepest emotions when he hands her over to King Mark, that her song can adequately express the sorrow as well as the joy that belongs to Gottfried's conception of love. For the medieval Christian, life itself is sorrow mingled with joy, as signified by Christ's self-sacrifice and resurrection. For Gottfried it is the intimacy between two exceptional human beings, god-like in their natural perfections though also human in their fallibility, that becomes the epiphany of love as an ultimate joy-in-sorrow.

Gottfried's mysticism of human love asserts itself most vividly in his description of the *minnegrotte*, the Cave of Love in which Tristan and Iseult live during their one period of complete happiness. Vergil too had envisaged the consummation of love between Dido and Aeneas in a grotto to which Venus has lured them. But in Vergil, as in Wagner's opera *Tannhäuser*, the sexual pleasures that one enjoys in the cave of Venus are evil and then destructive. Throughout the Middle Ages, however, the image of a cave or grotto frequently symbolized sexual love that could develop into a benign fulfillment of nature, itself a fruitful womb. This is true of Gottfried's poem, except that the cave now becomes a partly human construction resembling a Christian basilica, even serving as a place of worship. He says that the "cave of lovers" that Tristan discovers had been hewn out by an ancient race of giants, who sealed it with a bronze door to assure privacy and to signify the secrecy of love. They also provided a latch on the inside, since love admits of neither deceit nor force, and built three little windows to symbolize kindness, humility, and breeding.

As an architectural structure, Gottfried's cave has characteristics that his medieval audience could recognize as meaning what they would in any Christian church. "Its roundness inside betokens Love's Simplicity; Simplicity is most fitting for Love which must have no corners, that is, Cunning or Treachery. Breadth signifies Love's

Power, for her Power is without end. Height is Aspiration that mounts aloft to the clouds: nothing is too great for it so long as it means to climb, up and up, to where the molten Crown of the Virtues gathers the vault to the keystone." And so on for the white walls, the green marble floor, and finally the bed of crystal, a broad slab raised high off the ground and set in the middle as a kind of altar on which the rites of Venus could be fully accomplished. In a way that anticipates Rousseau, Gottfried remarks that the bed must be of crystal because love is both "transparent and translucent." It is that which enables the lovers to see into each other's heart, each of them glowing from within. In choosing so hard a surface for the altar of love, Gottfried may also be referring to the suffering that the lovers must endure. Their passion for one another is itself a testament to their fortitude and heroic capacity as opposed to indulgence in the soft and fleshly delights that belong to mere sensuousness.

In their hermitage of love Tristan and Iseult nourish themselves simply by looking at one another. Pure devotion is "the best nourishment" that human beings can find, and it sustains the lovers in the high feast of pleasures that are wholly natural. "Man was there with Woman, Woman there with Man. What else should they be needing? They had what they were meant to have, they had reached the goal of their desire." The lovers entertain each other with love songs that echo through their cave, sometimes sad and sometimes sweet, music obviously being an important part of their erotic ritual. Gottfried tells us that the giants of antiquity who had constructed the grotto used it regularly as a place for carrying out the demands of Venus, but no one previously had ever equalled Tristan and Iseult in their pure and unsullied consummations. Gottfried's religion of love consists in his attestation of the sacred goodness that binds his archetypal heroes to one another. Their relationship is physical—overtly and magnificently sexual—but also moral, artistic, and spiritual within its own dimensions. Its sanctity derives from living in accordance with nature and in total freedom: "They did just as their hearts prompted them . . . what they did was entirely as they pleased, and as they felt inclined."

The character of Gottfried's message becomes evident if we briefly compare his work with previous versions of the Tristan myth.

Béroul, writing in the middle of the twelfth century and therefore just sixty-five years earlier than Gottfried, is scarcely interested in analyzing the concept of love; instead he depicts vivid adventures that the two lovers—neither of whom embodies an ideal—encounter in their difficulties with society. The version of Eilhart shows how a great warrior can fail in his epic mission because of the obstacles created by an illicit passion. For Eilhart the love potion is a destructive poison that creates not ideal harmony but only a temporary madness. The sufferings of love are therefore consequences of its own inadequacy. Once the effect of the potion wears off, Tristan and Iseult regain their senses and yearn for the life in society which is their natural condition.

For his inspiration Eilhart was partly reverting to Vergil's description of the love affair between Aeneas and Dido. There, however, the heroic male is preserved from a tragic ending by watchful gods who do not forget his political destiny even if, under the influence of sex, he himself is willing to jeopardize it. In the twelfth century a compromise was established by the Norman revision of Vergil's work in which Aeneas has a second love affair, this time with the Lavinia he later marries. His passion for Dido is just madness, but his relationship with Lavinia fits into a characteristic mold of courtly love. Eilhart will not, however, accord his protagonist this comforting resolution; and when Gottfried, following the version of Thomas of Britain, gives Tristan's love for Iseult an honorific status superior to anything life in society can provide, he too rejects the possibility of a happy ending.

Gottfried never finished his version of the Tristan legend, but there is little reason to think that he would have written a retraction such as Andreas Capellanus', or even lines about Christian love of the sort that Chaucer added on to his *Troilus and Criseyde*. Having narrated a tragic love affair from a humanistic perspective quite similar to Gottfried's, Chaucer appends an epilogue that renounces courtly love as utterly inferior to the love of God: "And since his love is best beyond compare,/Love of the world deny with all its care." Chaucer implies that he has recounted the love between Troilus and Criseyde merely to provide an entertainment for readers who find something attractive in the idea of a noble but purely human love between the sexes. He obviously wishes to assure us that he himself follows the teaching of the church; he may be guilty of pandering to heretical tastes, he intimates, but he must not be condemned for holding unorthodox beliefs on his own.

Throughout the long text that he succeeded in writing, Gottfried indicates that a maneuver such as Chaucer's cannot be expected from him. Neither is he likely to have completed his story of adulterous love in the manner of Marie de France. In her romance *Eliduc*, written some fifty years before Gottfried, she recounts the history of a knight who is happily married but leaves his wife to seek adventures elsewhere. He falls in love with a beautiful young princess, whom he woos in courtly fashion and also marries. Returning with her, he leads a double life with the two women who love him and whom he loves in return. When the young wife learns about her predecessor's existence, she dies; but the older woman brings her back to life as an act of love for her husband. The first wife then enters a convent. It would appear that courtly love has thus triumphed, but Marie de France carries the story one step further. For though all three characters seem happy in the new arrangement, the knight and his young bride become increasingly penitent as they reflect about their experience. Eventually they too renounce their sexual love and join the first wife in her acceptance of religious orders.

To the mythic mind, the solution of *Eliduc* offers the best of both worlds. Having enjoyed the benefits of love as well as marriage, the characters escape the sufferings of Tristan and Iseult and finally put themselves in position for heavenly rewards. At the opposite extreme, much closer to the spirit of Gottfried, stands the thirteenth-century chantefable *Aucassin and Nicolette*. Here the anonymous narrator allows nothing to counter the ultimate superiority of that sexual love which causes his young lovers to struggle against parental and social interference. They experience the bliss of physical consummation long before the story ends with their happy marriage, and the suggestion that their kind of love can lead to punishment in the next world occasions one of the most remarkable passages to be found in medieval literature (though many variations of it occur in other works). Having been warned that because of his

behavior he will end up in hell and never enter paradise, Aucassin
replies:

> What do I care about paradise? I don't want to enter it. I
> only wish to have Nicolette whom I love so. Nobody goes to
> paradise except such people as I shall name for you. Old
> priests go there, old clodhoppers, and one-arms who all day
> and all night crouch before the altars in old crypts, old
> fellows with threadbare cloaks, and old tattered clothes, all
> naked and shoeless, and tumored old folks who are dying
> anyway of hunger and thirst, cold and disease. All those go
> to paradise, and I don't give a damn about them because I
> myself want to go to hell.
> To hell go the fine intellectuals, and the handsome
> knights dead in tournaments and gallant wars, and good
> soldiers and fine fellows. I want to go with them. And into
> hell go the lovely ladies of courtly life who have had, each
> one of them, two or three lovers along with their own
> barons. And there also go the golden-haired and the silver,
> and the blue-eyed and the gray, and there also go the
> minstrels and the jugglers and the king troubadours of the
> century. I want to go with them, but first let me have
> Nicolette, my very sweetheart, with me.

Aucassin's portrayal of hell resembles its description in George
Bernard Shaw's *Man and Superman*, except for the fact that the
thirteenth-century narrator wants to spend eternity nowhere else.
When Aucassin and Nicolette achieve their happiness at the end,
they do so in the manner of lovers in a Hellenistic fable. They make
no atonement for earthly pleasures, and they mention no God to
whom thanksgiving is due.

In their rejection of the dominant religion, Aucassin's brave
words are obviously extreme and unrepresentative. They should be
balanced with the assertion, in other romances, that the Christian
God has approved courtly love as a legitimate expression of his
intention. In *The Romance of the Châtelain of Coucy*, written in the
thirteenth century, the narrator tells us there is one thing he knows
to be true: it is that love is the "sovereign good" for all persons.
"Never is a man handsomer, more joyous, more laughing and gay
than when he is in love, especially when he loves in the hope of love's

delights. Therefore all people should carefully treasure this rare gift of love and take all pains to deserve it by keeping the faith and by service." The faith here referred to is dedication to the ideals of courtly love, but later in the romance they are merged with the dogmas of Christianity. As he lies dying, the protagonist asserts the belief that love is a god on earth whom he would have served however long he lived. A cardinal of the church assures him that he will attain salvation: "Friend, have no fear, for you die in the work and in the service of Jesus Christ who created us and shaped us."

A similar conception appears in *The Lay of the Little Bird*. This is an anecdotal tale about a clever bird who foils the attempts of a mercenary man to possess him. Like Tristan and Iseult, the bird is a mystical musician whose song not only creates beauty but also heals human sadness and enables love to flow sweetly in the hearts of men and women. Singing in his own language, the bird tells people to accept God's commandments, as opposed to living a life of indiscriminate pleasure, but to rest assured that if men and women love each other in the courtly manner no harm can befall them. "God and Love are one. God loves sense and chivalry; and Love holds them not in despite. God hates pride and false seeming; and Love loveth loyalty. God praiseth honor and courtesy. . . . But courtesy and honor, good sense and loyalty, are the real vassals of Love, and so you hold truly to them, God and the beauty of the world shall be added to you besides."

In the Tristan legend the medieval authors do not go this far. Even Gottfried, who often mentions God, makes little attempt to show how human love can be reconciled with the total dedication demanded by the church. So great is his emphasis upon the sorrow and the suffering inherent in love, so strong is his sense of tragedy, that his references to the eternal oneness of the lovers cannot be taken as meaning they will enjoy the salvation Christianity promised. In one of the other versions, however, the death of the lovers is followed by events that might well signify the possibility of union that persists beyond the grave. For out of Tristan's tomb there springs that briar which climbs across the chantry where he and Iseult have been buried and then roots itself near her tomb. Three times it is cut down by the local peasants and three times it grows again. The number suggests some religious import, and when King Mark forbids any further cutting of the briar we may take him as recognizing the holiness of their mystical, supernatural love.

Even so, this scarcely amounts to harmonization with ecclesiastical doctrine. The greatness of the Tristan legend resides in its delineation of conflicts that *cannot* be harmonized. In all the versions, the most constant of these is the warfare between love and the rest of society—a theme also prominent in romances like *Aucassin and Nicolette*. There the young lovers are thwarted by the fact that she is a Mohammedan slave while he belongs to an aristocratic family that expects him to make a politically advantageous marriage. But in *Aucassin and Nicolette*, as in many stories like it, the ending is a happy one inasmuch as the interests of love and society are mutually satisfied. The girl turns out to be a princess in her own right, and once she and Aucassin get married, their love, far from diminishing, becomes a social as well as a personal triumph.

In the Tristan legend, the lovers tragically fail to harmonize love and society, though the parents of Tristan were successful in this attempt. Gottfried tells the story of the parents' love in great detail as a preliminary to the contrasting one between Tristan and Iseult. Rivalin and Blancheflor, Tristan's father and mother, are courtly lovers of a very typical sort. He is a great warrior but dispossessed of his lands and socially inferior to the young princess, King Mark's sister, with whom he falls in love. Blancheflor is beautiful, pure, and modest, captivated by Rivalin's prowess, but unable to believe that he can truly love her. Their doubts and fears, mingled with their hopes and desires, cause each to undergo the usual lovesickness which enters through the eyes and lodges in the heart. Once they recognize that they are in love, they enjoy the pleasures of physical consummation and declare their total devotion to one another. When Rivalin must leave to reconquer his homeland, Blancheflor accompanies him; and when she realizes that she is pregnant, they get married and take their place in society. Rivalin is killed in battle, however, and Blancheflor dies giving birth to Tristan.

This is a sad ending to the romance of Tristan's parents, but it is not tragic. There are no ideals that conflict, no supervening goods that dramatically oppose one another. Though death and the limitations of mortality impinge upon them, the lovers have solved the major problems of human existence: they have managed to live for love, and Blancheflor, brokenhearted at her husband's death, dies for it. The history of Rivalin and Blancheflor thus serves as an edifying contrast to the tragedy of Tristan and Iseult, a model that these two cannot live up to since there is no way in which they can reconcile the ideals of love with those of society. The good life involves adherence to both, but circumstances make that impossible for them.

In contrast to the harmony of love and society, illustrated in the experience of Rivalin and Blancheflor or the final successes of Aucassin and Nicolette, medieval romance also contains variations in which the lovers reject society instead of returning to it. They generally escape to the land of faery, to enchantments that symbolize the wonderful and imaginative condition of love itself. In the *Lay of Sir Launfal* by Marie de France and in the anonymous *Lay of Graelent*, the pattern is well established. At the outset, the heroes are men who have had no experience of love. They are both out of favor at court for reasons related to their refusing the amatory gestures of the Queen, presumably an older woman. Graelent tells her that he loves no one since he is unworthy of undertaking so high and serious an enterprise. In saying this, he reveals that he understands the idealistic nature of love, unlike the brazen, frivolous, and demanding Queen. Graelent describes love as something that requires "chastity in thought, in word and in deed . . . sweetness, and truth, and measure; yea, loyalty to the loved one and to your word." When he learns of the Queen's interest in him, he shows that he respects the ideals of feudal honor as well as love. He refuses to commit adultery with the wife of his sovereign lord.

Once they escape the problems of the court by venturing into the surrounding countryside, Launfal and Graelent each discovers love, and in a similar fashion. They meet a kind of nymph of the woodland, who satisfies all their desires and gives herself bountifully with only one condition: the knight must preserve the secrecy of his loving relationship. The *Lay of Sir Launfal* intimates that it may all be a happy dream of the young man, and the *Lay of Graelent* describes his experience as if it were a quasi-pornographic wish-fulfillment. Graelent comes upon the beautiful lady while she is bathing in a fountain in the midst of the forest. He seizes her clothing in the hope of enjoying the sight of her naked body when she emerges. After some banter, in the course of which he assures her that violence or abuse is foreign to his being, she comes forth as he requested and he gently begs for her love. She concludes at once that he is indeed "a valiant knight, courteous and wise," and therefore worthy of her affection.

Launfal's meeting with the Fairy Queen, as we quickly realize this embodiment of the natural world must be, is presented more decorously; but his subsequent sojourn with her is equally fanciful. In both stories, the Fairy Queen provides wealth, leisure, pleasure, and all the sensuous delights that any male could possibly desire. Regardless of what Graelent had previously said, the love that he finds in the company of his lady of the forest involves "chastity" only in being an example of perfect courtly love. It is wholly and completely sexual, and yet a source of virtue rather than vice or dishonor. Within the medieval context, we are obviously encountering the distinction, which goes back at least as far as Plato's *Symposium*, between the two types of Venus. Now, however, the heavenly Venus is an incarnation of the goodness in nature itself, and she is being contrasted with a glittering but false product of evil in society as represented by the Queen at court.

The dramatic confrontation between the two Venuses dominates the denouement of both lays. In each of them the hero refuses to participate in the court's adulation of the Queen, and he rejects her husband's claim that she is the most beautiful woman alive. In each story the protagonist is condemned to death after asserting that he has intimate knowledge of one more beautiful than she. In the *Lay of Sir Launfal* the Queen pretends that the young man had sought to seduce her, thereby awakening in the medieval audience reminders of Potiphar's wife in the Bible. This theme is subordinated, however, to the beauty contest which eventuates when the heavenly Venus appears at court to vindicate her lover's preference. Everyone immediately recognizes that she is infinitely more beautiful than the Queen and that her lover cannot be punished or criticized in any way.

The *Lay of Sir Launfal* ends in his riding off with the fairy maiden on a single horse that takes them into a happy land from which they never return. In the case of Graelent, however, there are matters related to the character of courtly love which still needed to be resolved. For even in mentioning his beloved to others, Graelent has violated the courtly rule about secrecy, and the maiden therefore disciplines him by riding off alone. He follows, and when he reaches the stream that is the boundary of her realm he nearly drowns trying to cross over. It is death that separates the two worlds. The heavenly Venus relents, however, and saves her lover from the powerful currents, carrying him off into her land of perpetual delight. As though to symbolize the human soul that longs for this kind of reunion with nature through love, Graelent's horse forever after grieves for his lost master, seeking him in the woods, pawing the ground and neighing loudly throughout the countryside.

In escaping from the corruptions of society, have Launfal, Graelent, and others in medieval romance who undergo similar experiences merely crossed over to the world of death? If so, it is not death as nothingness or Nirvana, as in nineteenth-century romanticism, nor is it a version of orthodox Christian thinking about heaven. The medieval lovers find an earthly paradise, often represented by the image of nature civilized—an enclosed garden or a fountain in the midst of woods, for example. But not infrequently the new Eden is a land of enchantment that only the dead can reach. The love *of* death is not at all basic to medieval ideas about human love, which is why de Rougemont's attempts to explain courtly love along those lines are unacceptable. But a love of life that occurs *beyond* death, a life that lovers may hope to share once they emancipate themselves from the evils of our world—this is a fairly common theme in all the literature of the Middle Ages.

In an early version of the Tristan legend, the relationship between love and death appears in Tristan's assuring Iseult that one day they will travel together "to a fortunate land from which none returns." He goes on to mention "a castle of white marble; at each of its thousand windows burns a lighted candle; at each a minstrel plays and sings a melody without end; the sun does not shine there but none regrets his light." From the allusions to white marble, suggesting a tomb, and the absence of daylight, one might surmise that Tristan is talking about the darkness of death. But his description ends with the assertion that "it is the happy land of the living." Previously Iseult had spoken of an enchanted orchard that minstrels know: "a wall of air girdles it on all sides; there are flowering trees, a balmy soil; here without vigil the hero lives in his friend's arms and no hostile force can shatter the wall of air." If this is death, it must be one that provides all the pleasures of life which lovers seek. That is the function of magic and romantic enchantment. The passage does not express any desire for dissolution or self-destruction. Neither does it idealize a total escape from society. The lovers' imagination peoples the enchanted castle with persons like themselves—harpists, heroes, friends, all enjoying the accoutrements of the courteous life.

The other side of the Tristan legend, its tragic ending and the suffering of its lovers, is, however, equally important in medieval romance. The evil in society often wins out, crushing love without enabling the lovers to recoup their losses on earth or anywhere else. In the *Lay of the Nightingale* by Marie de France the jealous husband terminates his wife's innocent love for her neighbor by killing the nightingale that she claimed to watch from her casement. The lovers stop seeing each other even at a distance and we are left with the sad idea that the beautiful song—signifying the purity of their love—has been forever silenced. In *The Châtelaine of Vergi* the star-crossed lovers fall victim to a malevolent duchess, another Potiphar's wife, and her scheming husband. He extracts the truth about the lovers' secret intimacy, and this enables the duchess to convince the maiden that her lover has betrayed her. Here too the ending is an unhappy one, since the lovers kill themselves. We are left with nothing but a sense of anger and resentment toward a social order that obliterates human love. There is no enchanted land to which the unfortunate lovers may escape, and even their innocence and purity of heart, the qualities that give their love its ideality, have served as instruments that enabled society to destroy them.

Tristan and Iseult are not innocent lovers. After they drink the potion, but also long before, they are treacherous, cunning, and extremely resourceful in the tactics of worldly deceit needed to keep their love (and themselves) alive. They are innocent in the sense that they are true to one another, even though Tristan errs in marrying the second Iseult, but they are totally unscrupulous when it comes to manipulating others in any way their love requires. At the same time, they belong to society as dutiful adherents, accepting whenever possible its conventions and most of its ideals. It is, in fact, their social involvement that prevents them from escaping, or really wanting to. In the forest each laments that the other is being deprived of his or her proper role in society. Though Eilhart explains this by saying that the effects of the love potion have now dissipated, Béroul presents their concern as indicating not only mutual devotion but also a joint awareness that social ideals matter as much as those of love.

This ambivalence between the two sets of ideals gives the Tristan legend its profundity: as Hegel says, it is the conflict between good and good that creates great tragedy. The medieval lovers, as contrasted with Wagner's, want to enjoy both love *and* society. The world makes this impossible, and despite heroic efforts on their part all attempts at harmonization are doomed in advance. The two lions in Iseult's dream, pulling her in different directions, finally tear her apart and annihilate the possibility of a permanent earthly paradise.

Chrétien de Troyes also contributed to the Tristan legend, but his version has been lost and all his other romances take a different approach to the conflict between love and society. Writing about the same time as Andreas Capellanus and under the patronage of the Countess Marie of Champagne, he fills his psychological novels with lengthy descriptions of courtly love—its exhilarations, its vital goodness, and also its kinship to insanity. In this respect Chrétien's writings are not, of course, unique. What gives them their special quality is the way in which each of his romances employs, as a thematic base, different aspects of the relationship between love and society.

As the love in Chrétien is always courtly, so too is the society he considers always chivalric. In his book *Mimesis*, Erich Auerbach complains that courtly romances such as Chrétien's turn away from reality instead of presenting it as it is: they sacrifice realism for the sake of propagating the restricted ideals of an "illusory world of class." Auerbach relates this not only to sociological conditions of feudalism and the aristocracy of knights in the Middle Ages, but also to a "Platonistic" belief that "nobility, greatness, and intrinsic values have nothing in common with everyday reality." While this judgment is fair insofar as Chrétien limits himself to problems experienced by members of the ruling classes, Auerbach neglects the fact that these problems arise out of moral dilemmas that belonged to the reality of life in the Middle Ages as much as social and economic conditions that preoccupy later examples of "realism." If Chrétien is to be considered unrealistic, it is not because of his reliance upon tales of heroic adventure—these are merely fictional devices that get us to think about conflicts between love and society—but rather because each of his works concludes with the harmonization of the contrary ideals in too simplistic and predictable a manner. Life, we feel, does not provide so constant a succession of beautiful sunsets.

For there are no tragedies in the writings of Chrétien that have come down to us. For instance, consider *Cligés*, a work of his that has often been called the anti-*Tristan*. This appellation is accurate, but for reasons that are not always recognized. Working with similar materials, Chrétien never allows the sufferings of the lovers (Cligés and Fenice) to diminish our expectation that sooner or later they will win out. And indeed they do, marrying each other and assuming all the perquisites of royalty once Cligés' uncle, the equivalent of King Mark, conveniently goes mad and dies of grief because he could not capture his traitorous nephew. Like Gottfried von Strassburg, Chrétien begins with a love story that details the courtly emotions of Cligés' parents and ends with his mother dying of a broken heart much as Tristan's had. But where Gottfried presents the parental experience of courtly love eventuating in marital success as a contrast to the adulterous love that destroys Tristan, Chrétien uses the former as a model his lovers finally manage to emulate.

Cligés and Fenice are able to solve the problems of Tristan and Iseult partly because they have decided not to follow their example. In love with Cligés but married to his uncle, Fenice asserts that she could never lead the life that Iseult did: "Such love as hers was far too base; for her body belonged to two, whereas her heart was possessed by one. Thus all her life was spent refusing her favors to neither one. But mine is fixed on one object, and under no circumstances will there be any sharing of my body and heart." Fenice avoids the experience of Iseult by using a kind of antilove potion, which causes her husband to dream that he is possessing her sexually while really their bodies never meet. Her lovemaking with Cligés, which occurs in a secret garden that serves as their earthly paradise, is just as adulterous as in the relationship between Tristan and Iseult; but in having given her body only to the man she loves, Fenice retains a purity (despite her deceptiveness) that Iseult cannot equal. We are led to conclude that the love between Fenice and Cligés has the same natural goodness as the love between Cligés' parents. The couples have not been united by a deadly poison; and once Cligés has proved his knightly valor by fighting for his beloved, the two of them can assume their rightful place in society and enjoy marital bliss for the rest of their lives.

A similar harmonization occurs at the end of *Erec and Enid*, but here Chrétien addresses himself to a different kind of conflict between love and society. Now the two courtly lovers, he a splendid warrior and product of the knightly class, she a maiden described as even more beautiful than Iseult, marry one another toward the beginning of the story. Their love is not adulterous and neither does it end in premature death, as in the case of Tristan's parents and Cligés'. On the contrary, this part of the romance culminates in a bridal night in which the young couple "allow each sense to be gratified" and then enjoy a lengthy honeymoon during which they live only for each other. The conflict with society arises from the fact that Erec wishes to do nothing but fondle his wife; he loses interest in the fighting that a knight must do, or even in entering tournaments.

When Enid learns that her husband's reputation has been impaired by their love, she informs him of this and then supports his resolution to seek new adventures. She convinces Erec to take her along, which he agrees to do provided that she never try to help him, no matter what the danger. She continually fails to live up to her promise, but in the process saves him from death several times. On each occasion he castigates her ferociously, and yet he finally loves her more than ever. In many respects their adventures together serve as a testing of Enid—as if *she* were the courtly lover who had to prove herself worthy of *her* beloved. Through feats of valor comparable to what is usually expected of the male, she succeeds magnificently. Far from being a troubadour lady elevated on a pedestal, she lives in the world alongside the husband she loves and manifests her equality by helping him to survive in the social role he has chosen for himself. When the two of them surmount all the obstacles of their adventures, they return to court and are crowned as king and queen. Never before have they loved each other as much, and never before has their love had as great a capacity to buttress them in society. *Erec and Enid* reveals the message that Chrétien's writings generally seek to convey. As a recent scholar puts it: "The romances of Chrétien say that love properly conceived and followed is the basis of chivalric virtue and true knighthood and, contrariwise, that love falsely conceived and followed is the destruction of knightly society."

The false conception of love is illustrated by the excessive devotion to each other's company that originally separated Erec and Enid from the world, necessitating their search for heroic experience. In the romance *Yvain*, and in the one about Lancelot, Chrétien deals with other mistaken attitudes toward love. Having conquered a nymph of the forest by killing her husband, a knight devoted to guarding her sacred fountain, Yvain marries her himself and assumes a similar office. When he leaves to perform further deeds of heroism, since he fears that love for this lady may undermine his knightly reputation, Yvain promises to return within a year but then fails to keep his promise. Most of the romance deals with his frantic effort to regain the lady's love while also demonstrating his valor. To be a complete man, to enjoy the goods of both love and society, he must prove himself faithful to a single woman as well as courageous in combat. Chrétien arranges for Yvain to win out; but with Lancelot the difficulties are much greater, and perhaps that is why he left his Lancelot romance unfinished. Lancelot's adultery cannot eventuate as Cligés' had, for there is nothing in the Arthurian legend that would permit him to marry the Queen. His relationship to Guinevere must therefore be dominated by his posture as a troubadour-knight who serves her abjectly and with religious dedication worthy of a goddess—except for the fact that he does sleep with her.

But even in the Lancelot romance, Chrétien allows the possibility of reconciliation between love and society. He cannot get rid of King Arthur or arrange for the lovers to marry one another; but he shows how the love between Lancelot and Guinevere bolsters, rather than undermines, the hero's ability to satisfy his chivalric ideals as a great warrior must. This social function had been jeopardized not by Lancelot's adulterous passion for the wife of his sovereign (a consideration that does not interest Chrétien very much, either as something that establishes Lancelot's love or even as a threat to his feudal honor) but only by the Queen's having ordered him to demean himself in public. At the outset, Lancelot had hesitated for a second before riding in a peasant's cart as the condition for being taken to Guinevere. She spurns his love as imperfect because he did hesitate, although she recognizes that it is ignoble for a knight to ride in such a cart. To test his love she then imposes a series of trials, such as ordering him to fight badly and so to lose a tournament. Once again, Lancelot's sense of honor stands in opposition to the purity of his love. At the end, however, he proves himself capable of living up to both ideals, each for the sake of the other. Guinevere takes him back with total acceptance; and the King, whose wife is still deceiving him, rewards Lancelot jubilantly for his knightly successes. The conclusion was written by a different author, but he insists that Chrétien has given his consent.

Many critics have seen Chrétien de Troyes as a master of irony; and possibly one is justified in thinking that Lancelot's genuflection as he leaves Guinevere's bedroom is to be taken as Chrétien's way of ridiculing that much of courtly love which apes religious devotion. But despite the subtlety of Chrétien and his residual ambivalences, we may also read him as an enthusiast of the twelfth century who sees no reason why courteous and ennobling love between men and women should not be condoned by orthodox Christianity as well as feudal society. He does not wish to supplant or even question the institution of marriage: it completes the love between Erec and Enid, Cligés and Fenice, and Yvain and his lady, even though the lovers never define their relationship in terms of it. Far from identifying courtly love with adultery, Chrétien treats the latter as one among several circumstances under which the former may occur. To this extent, his romances may seem naive and unrealistic despite their psychological insights. And possibly that is why they were copied in later centuries but did not create as long a line of transformations as in the case of the Tristan legend. In the Western world, and above all in the Middle Ages, harmonization of the sort that Chrétien presents has not been the most common experience. The tragedy of hopeless love speaks to a level of our being that distrusts the wish-fulfillments of Chrétien's romances. Theorists like de Rougemont are wrong to think that passion inevitably seeks its own destruction, but only an inveterate optimist could fail to recognize the devious ways in which reality destroys love (and sometimes lovers as well). One can only conclude that Chrétien was an inveterate optimist.

Many of the problems of courtly love recur, and possibly reach a culmination, in one of the great best-sellers of thirteenth-century France—*The Romance of the Rose*. It is a romance to end all medieval romances, a long allegorical poem consisting of two parts that seem to move in different directions. Written by Guillaume de Lorris about 1237 and left unfinished, the first part tells us of the poet's dream about the usual garden of love, about love's commandments once the poet falls in love with the woman who is the Rose of that garden, and about his attempts to reach her. Guillaume describes love in language that belongs to most of the varieties we have been considering: "Whoever wishes to make Love his lord/Must courteous be and wholly void of pride,/Gracious and merry, and in giving free. . . . That you may be a lover tried and true,/My wish and will are that your heart be fixed/In one sole place whence it cannot depart/But whole and undivided there remain."

This approach to love could not have surprised any of Guillaume's readers, nor would they have flinched at the speech he then gives to Reason, who seeks without success to convince the lover that his devotion to the Rose is foolish and diseased. Guillaume's allegory of courtly love had a great effect upon Dante, Boccaccio, Chaucer, and many other writers of the later Middle Ages. They saw it as an all-inclusive statement about the nature of human love, and also as a roman d'aventure in which the heroic quest became the pursuit of love itself. When the second part appeared some forty years later, a new conception of love was introduced and the abstract talk about courtliness was transmuted into sexual references that must have shocked many people at the time. It is fitting that the author of this second part was Jean de Meun, the man who first translated the letters of Abelard and Heloise. What Jean learned from Abelard's pre-courtly account of sexual love might well have served as the basis for his revisionist, post-courtly doctrine.

The shift in perspective from the first to the second part has been seen by some critics as indicative of a crisis in the thirteenth century. Henry Adams thinks that in the decades that separate Guillaume and Jean "the Woman and the Rose became bankrupt. Satire took the place of worship. Man, with his usual monkey-like malice, took pleasure in pulling down what he had built up." Others charge Jean not only with malicious satire and cynicism, but also with "obscenity" and "a sexual liberalism which concocts a spicy stew out of erudite tinsel and philistine pruriency." Ernst Robert Curtius, who makes this judgment, associates Jean de Meun with the Averroists whom Aquinas attacked for having spoken against "the good of sexual moderation." As a matter of fact, however, the passage from Aquinas' *Summa contra Gentiles* which Curtius quotes enunciates the same philosophy of love that pervades Jean's part of *The Romance of the Rose*. This is not to deny that Aquinas would have condemned a great deal of Jean's work. Some of it has to be considered heretical, such as his denial that sexual abstinence is in itself a virtue, and much of it raises doubts about the church's interpretation of God's word. But the two thinkers agree with each other, as opposed to Andreas or proponents of fin' amors, in believing that ultimately sexual love must be justified as a means of replenishing the species.

Aquinas would also have relished the ridicule to which Jean subjects the kind of love that Guillaume had sought to promulgate. That women are not superior beings whom the lover must serve and before whom he must abase himself, that they are in fact worthy of Juvenal's misogynist satires, that most of them are deceptive, covetous, and mercenary—all of this renews the church's belief that it is not through courtly types of love that man can hope to find redemption. At the same time, Jean also belongs to a humanistic outlook that separates him from the theology of Aquinas and establishes his work within the tradition of those who hold that the nobleness of life consists in sexual intimacy between man and woman.

Jean retains so much Ovidian unscrupulousness in matters of lovemaking, and so often suggests that sensuous promiscuity is desirable, that we need not do battle with scholars who emphasize the differences between him and those who defend the courtly faith. And yet there is ample reason to say that what matters to Jean can be called love rather than mere sexuality. He makes it very clear that he attacks women only to revile those who have deified them. When his spokesman rehearses Juvenal's antifeminist remarks, he quickly adds that they apply to "evil women." Jean may suggest that most women are liable to condemnation, but he leaves open the possibility that some are not, and he gives to the lover's Friend the following lines that could have occurred in the first part of Andreas' treatise: "This is what you should do if she you love/Is true in heart and innocent in face:/A man who's innocent and debonair—/Who is not careless where he sets his heart—/Will not be too impressed with face and form,/But will assure himself of character/Founded on art and science . . ." I must admit that the chapter ends with advice of a different sort, recommending money as a way of capturing a lady's favor; but then Jean confuses us again by insisting upon equality between the sexes, and above all, the importance of husbands' trusting their wives.

Jean's allegory concludes with a prolonged and even grotesque portrayal of how the male organ of sexuality penetrates the female as the act in which the lover finally wins his Rose. The erect penis appears as the staff with which the lover seeks to enter the narrow passageway that leads into the ivory tower, and coitus is described as a plucking of the sweet bud of the rose tree. Whether we take this account as pornography or the equivalent of sex education, it seems quite remote from the idealized fantasies of men and women in love that fill most courtly romances. As I have emphasized throughout, these often included consummatory sex, but the sexual encounters generally exist within a situation that reaches beyond the mere conjunction of male and female bodies. Jean ends his poem with the moment of fornication (after which the fictional dreamer awakes) because he wants us not to forget that the goal of love is fecundity. But just before his final chapters he narrates the story of Pygmalion, which he takes from Ovid's *Metamorphoses*, telling it in a way that shows his filiation to the ideas of moral refinement that structure courtly romance.

Falling in love with a statue he has created, Jean's Pygmalion undergoes lovesickness like any other courtly lover. Since the frozen female is not a troubadour lady but a mannequin whom he can enjoy within the limits of his imagination, Pygmalion dresses and un-dresses her, even slipping a marriage band upon her ring finger. What he then says, "like loving, loyal spouse," are words that Ovid did not supply but that reverberate instead with the spirit of medi-eval romance: "With this ring I thee wed, and thus become /All thine, as you all mine. Let Hymen here/And Juno heed my vows, and present be/At this our marriage. If they're witnesses/(And they of wedlock are the very gods),/Sufficient are our rites; no priest, or clerk,/Or mitred prelate do I wish, or cross." Like Tristan, Pygma-lion expresses his love in music; and when Venus answers his prayer, giving life to the statue, he experiences with his pure and beautiful maid the reciprocal love portrayed by so many writers of courtly romance: "In loving words they're mutually allied;/Each gives the other thanks for love received;/In mutual embrace they both find joy;/Like turtledoves they mutually exchange/Their kisses, winning mutual delight."

By this reliance upon "loyal love" Jean may rightly claim a place within the idealist tradition. As if to prove that what he has to offer is more than just realism alone, he also presents his doctrine within a

Christian framework. He starts by saying that nature furthers love in its attempt to defeat the works of death by constant reproduction within each species. But then he has Nature remark that by herself she cannot prevent the dissolution of any individual. That depends upon the triune God, whose being she mirrors, and whose incarnation as Christ she describes in fairly orthodox manner. In her speech Nature incorporates the testimony of Plato, but more relevant is the fact that Jean's ideas about natural love derive from the writings of twelfth-century thinkers such as Bernardus Silvestris and Alain de Lille. These philosopher-poets, themselves greatly influenced by Boethius, Peter Lombard, and Hugh of St. Victor, emphasized the oneness between God and nature, the role of cosmic love as a unifying factor within nature itself, and the holiness of procreation as the means by which the will of God and nature could be served. Bernardus celebrates the fertility of the natural world, and Alain, as Winthrop Wetherbee says, "makes healthy sexuality his central metaphor for human perfection." Both poets studied the pagan classics and sought to understand the universe from the point of view of human needs and expectations. Writing at a time when Aristotle had not yet conquered Christian philosophy, they borrowed from the Neoplatonism of Plotinus and other Hellenists whose works had survived the Dark Ages. The school to which they belonged lasted only fifty years, and its major inspiration was finally defeated by the caritas-synthesis, which maintained that the love of nature had to be subordinated to the love of God. But their influence continued as a humanistic and even naturalistic leitmotif that provided an alternate way of thinking in the Middle Ages. In showing nature as an emanation from God, this minority view continued the idea that God himself was present in nature, and therefore that all things natural must be good.

Beliefs such as these seemed pantheistic and were often attacked by ecclesiastical authorities. But in many respects, the twelfth-century tradition that sustained Jean de Meun's thinking could easily feed into the mainstream of thirteenth-century orthodoxy. Like the others in his school, Alain attacks homosexuality as a common but unnatural practice that undermines nature's concern for reproduction. Marriage was a sacrament because it was the sanctified method for carrying out nature's will; and within its holy bond sexual love was to be encouraged provided that it did not degenerate into passionate fervor.

It would be too much to suggest that this alternative tradition within Christianity can account for everything that Jean puts into *The Romance of the Rose*. Some critics have even suggested that his Lover acts in ways that actually contradict the *amor naturalis* which Alain and Bernardus had recommended. But even if this is true, even if Jean's delight in physical pleasure takes him into a love of nature that his philosophical sources would have considered unacceptable, he nevertheless shows how unashamed sexuality can clothe itself in the mystical belief that human and divine love are not really contradictory. It is from this conception that his kinship to courtly thinking develops. Though he fails to see that Jean continues, occasionally at least, this one strand of courtly love while also rejecting the courtliness that Guillaume represents, C. S. Lewis states the matter very well when he remarks: "It is almost true to say that there was nothing in Dante which was not also in Jean de Meun—except Dante himself."

From this perspective, Jean must be counted as a significant antecedent of the Renaissance, as Dante also was. With *The Romance of the Rose* we have touched the roots of much that was to flower in Italy and elsewhere two centuries later, and eventually in the plays of William Shakespeare.

Part II
From Courtly to Romantic

5

Love in Three Italian Poets
Petrarch, Cavalcanti, Dante

I HAVE SPOKEN OF THE CONFLICT between religious and courtly love as a dialectical play within the thinking of the Middle Ages. But if we push the idea of "dialectic" a little further, if we introduce the Hegelian notion of self-transcendence within a synthesis, we discover something that neither Andreas nor Aquinas nor any of their contemporaries could have predicted. By self-transcendence Hegel means the inner change to which both a thesis and its antithesis will submit in order to achieve the stability of a synthesis. As in all of Hegel's philosophy, the concept sounds artificial and even mentalistic: as if the world had decided in advance to arrange itself in neatly dialectical patterns. Once we eliminate all such pretensions, however, and approach Hegel's insight as an occasional tool—sometimes useful, sometimes not—its great utility becomes more evident. Thinking in these terms, we might expect to find both courtly love and medieval religious love resolving their conflict in ways that caused each of them to change. This double self-transcendence is not inevitable. It did not occur in Aquinas, and hardly, if at all, in Andreas. Conceivably, one type of love or the other might have triumphed without a scratch, without a modification of any importance. As a matter of fact—and it is always against matters of fact that the Hegelian dialectic must be tested—both antagonists changed tremendously, just as Hegel would have predicted. They change in ways that reveal their conflict with one another, each appropriates something of the other's principles, neither can ever be the same again. In a sense, each destroys the other; but also, they preserve one another, keeping each alive for some future regeneration under more suitable circumstances.

Religious love being the dominant force within medieval philosophy, one is not surprised to find it modifying all the courtly ideas of poets such as Petrarch and Dante. But the details of these modifications are often unforeseeable, showing inventiveness and daring as well as a need to accommodate to the ruling ideology. By the time one reaches the fifteenth-century Renaissance, courtly love has been vastly transformed. Its libidinal elements are somewhat purged, its rivalry with religion diminished, its intellectual bases undermined. At the same time, however, the submissiveness of courtly love enables it to reform the character of orthodox belief. Philosophers like Ficino and Bembo recast the medieval conception of religious love under the very influence of those courtly ideas the church had rightly feared.

In tracing this development among the Italians, we do best to start with Petrarch. Not that he comes first in point of time: he actually follows Dante, Cavalcanti, Guinizelli, and the other practitioners of the *dolce stil nuovo* (sweet new style). Nor does Petrarch contribute new or profound ideas; there is much truth in Santayana's complaint that Petrarch's art "is greater than his thought." But in Petrarch the fourteenth-century struggle between courtly and religious love is more deeply felt, and more vividly recorded, than in any other writer of his age. He also marks a new departure in making this struggle the major theme of all his writing. Earlier poets had often renounced courtly love for reasons of religion, generally as they grew older or weary of frustration. As we have seen, Guillaume IX started the fashion, and Chaucer's pious conclusion to his *Troilus and Criseyde* reminds one of Andreas' final recantation. In reading Petrarch, however, one encounters a constant alternation between the two loves, an ambivalence of feeling that operates throughout, a rhythmic oscillation, pervasive and productive of his entire genius. It is true that his *Canzoniere*, a sequence of 365 poems (one for each day of the year), ends with a 366th dedicated to the Virgin Mary and pleading for forgiveness. But even the first poem laments the vanity of his courtly love; and the remaining ones, which celebrate his lifelong devotion to a lady he calls Laura, shunt back and forth between the sentiments of a troubadour and those of a devout Christian. Try as he may, Petrarch cannot harmonize the two sides of his nature, and his failure is the cause of painful anxiety. His feelings for Laura are too powerful to be renounced; yet his religious beliefs convince him that this is what he must do. This theme becomes fairly commonplace in later literature. In Petrarch it is fresh and powerful and sadly moving.

In *The Secret Book*, a work of prose that Petrarch may not have intended for publication, the theme is presented through discussions between the author and St. Augustine. Augustine's *Confessions* was a favorite of Petrarch's, and one may well imagine why. For Augustine too defined his life as a constant struggle between the two poles of his dualistic conception—the citadel of nature and the city of God, the cravings of the body and the yearnings of the soul, the love that is based on desire and the one that seeks renunciation. Many hundreds of years separate the two men, and the courtly love for Laura differs tremendously from the carnal appetite that beguiled the saint while also horrifying him, but Petrarch finds it easy to identify with Augustine. They are brothers within the eros tradition.

Despite this kinship between Augustine and Petrarch, the saint does not speak in *The Secret Book* as he does in the *Confessions*. As Petrarch's interlocutor, Augustine expounds the doctrine of the church, with sympathy but also with the strictness of authority, as if he were speaking from beyond the ladder of salvation—no longer struggling to climb it himself. The book is Petrarch's confessional. Time and again he beats his guilty breast, admitting to the sinful stupidity of his courtly passion. Reason, confirmed by Christian faith, assures him that Augustine is right; but Petrarch also knows he is too weak to reform. Moreover, he senses that reason has not done its job properly, that somewhere within the structure of the religious life a place must be found for what he feels toward Laura.

The discussion about love in *The Secret Book* begins with Petrarch's saying that while sexual passion for a "low woman" is madness and folly his love of Laura was nothing like that. Because she herself was "the image and picture of perfect honour" and in her face a divine loveliness shone forth, his love for her could only lead him upward. Hers is "a mind that has no care for things of earth, and burns only with the love of what is heavenly." Since her physical being matters less to him than her soul, his devotion to Laura has nourished his inclinations toward virtue and nobility. To this the voice of Augustine replies that the love for Laura has rather been his ruin: "She has detached your mind from the love of heavenly things and has inclined your heart to love the creature more than the Creator: and that one path alone leads, sooner than any other, to death." When Petrarch protests that Laura has led him to God, Augustine insists that his obsession has prevented him from loving God in the correct manner. "You have admired the Divine Artificer as though in all His works He had made nothing fairer than the object of your love." As for Petrarch's claim that he loved Laura's soul, not her body, Augustine denies that mortal man can love in so pure a fashion. At this point the dialogue anticipates, as we shall see, the central problem in the Italian Renaissance:

> St. Augustine: "Are you mocking me? Do you mean to assert that if the same soul had been lodged in a body ill-formed and poor to look upon you would have taken equal delight therein?"
> Petrarch: "I dare not say that. For the soul itself cannot be discerned, and the image of a body like that would have given no indication of such a soul. But were it possible for the soul to be visible to my gaze, I should most certainly have loved its beauty even though its dwelling-place were poor."
> St. Augustine: "You are relying on mere words; for if you are only able to love that which is visible to your gaze, then what you love is the bodily form."

Having established this, Augustine then goes on to show that Petrarch's love was really an infatuation that deprived him of his reason and created intemperate desires in him. Augustine concludes the argument as follows:

> "Nothing so much leads a man to forget or despise God as the love of things temporal, and most of all this passion that

we call love; and to which, by the greatest of all desecrations, we even gave the name of God, without doubt only that we may throw a heavenly veil over our human follies and make a pretext of divine inspiration when we want to commit an enormous transgression. In the case of the other passions, the sight of the object, the hope of enjoying it, and the ardour of the will take us captive. Love also demands all that, but in addition it asks also a reciprocal passion, without which it will be forced to die away. So, whereas in the other cases one loves singly and alone, in this case we must give love for love, and thus man's heart is stung and stung again. . . . I purposely leave out what Cicero was not ashamed to imitate from Terence when he wrote, 'Wrongs, suspicions, fierce quarrels, jealousies, war, and then again peace—behold the miseries of love.' Do you not recognize at once in his works the madness and, above all, the madness of jealousy which, as one knows too well, is the ruling power in love, as love is the ruling passion among all others?"

After all this, the interlocutor who bears the name of Petrarch can only confess that his love for Laura has indeed led him into the abyss, that it has demeaned him instead of bringing him closer to God. When he begs to find the path of rectitude, Augustine draws upon the Latin poets who describe the remedies of love, the means by which passional madness can be cured prior to a rebirth in religion. To this too the voice of Petrarch finally assents. But is it Petrarch himself who is speaking? Has the poet really changed as much as the dialogue would seem to suggest? That seems unlikely, since Petrarch's love poetry continued for many years after *The Secret Book* was written. By the end of his life, Petrarch may have achieved the kind of religious love that Augustine represents; but throughout his literary history, the poet speaks with the voices of both interlocutors, dividing himself in two and incorporating their antagonistic philosophies within the edifice of his poetry.

To the casual glance, the ambivalence of Petrarch may seem to resemble the dualism of Andreas. Nor is it mere coincidence that each employs the dialogue form. But really the two approach love in ways that are quite distinct. When Andreas defends courtly love, he speaks with a tone that is firm, confident, secure within the dimensions of a growing ideology. By the time of Petrarch—who is sometimes called the last troubadour—courtly love had been thoroughly attacked by the church; Andreas' book had already been burned. Consequently, everything that Petrarch writes evinces moral distress of a sort that is totally absent in Andreas. Petrarch himself describes his condition as "accidie" or depression; in *The Secret Book* Augustine calls it a "terrible plague of the soul—melancholy," as contrasted with the "wholesome dread" religious love instills. He gets Petrarch to admit that he is being destroyed by his devotion to Laura, "this wretched state [in which] everything is harsh, gloomy, frightful." In short, Petrarch's depression results from the madness of courtly love. That, at least, is the argument of *The Secret Book*. But if we stand back from the dialogue, if we reflect upon the fact that both voices in it emanate from the same author, a somewhat different conclusion may recommend itself. Petrarch suffers not because he has forgotten God—as Augustine claims—but because his soul has become a field of battle between the two loves. His depression is mainly a symptom of the exhausting struggle. Andreas describes two ways of life and then leaves it to the reader to choose in accordance with his spiritual aspirations. But Petrarch cannot choose; at least, he keeps vacillating between the alternatives. He both internalizes the struggle and perpetuates it. His depression is moral fatigue, resulting from an inability to identify himself completely with either cause.

If this interpretation is right, one should expect to find in Petrarch a failure of both religious and courtly love. That he has sinned against heaven and slipped off the ladder that leads to caritas, *The Secret Book* freely confesses. But in principle his beliefs about the love for God remain those of the medieval church; he never questions the authority of Augustine in matters that relate to religious love. With respect to courtly love, however, his unquiet soul issues into beliefs as well as feelings significantly different from those of Andreas or the troubadours. He cannot stop loving Laura in ways that resemble fin' amors, but neither can he resist religious accommodations that subtly change the entire character of his love.

For one thing, the very gloominess of Petrarch reveals a basic change in courtly love. In both Andreas and the troubadours, the ruling emotion is joy—joi, jovens. Troubadour poetry is often tinged with sadness, but it generally belongs to a joyful enterprise. It is the sadness of sexual frustration that the poet has cheerfully accepted. He may sigh with longing and beg his lady to gratify his desires, but he also delights in her elevated purity when she continues to frustrate him. The troubadour suffers like an adolescent boy in love for the first time and with an older woman. His spirits may be dampened by her remoteness, but he enjoys his sadness and feels that this is really living. Submitting to his beloved, he may even talk himself into a state of bliss, like the anonymous troubadour who says: "I am joyful: That is her commandment." In Petrarch, however, the melancholy is a disease, a debilitating sorrow. The frustration is moral, not sexual. Unlike the troubadours, he is ashamed of his passion for Laura. As he says in Canzone CCLXIV: "I go thinking in tears and self-pity. . . . I reflect in terror on my state, on the dishonor of my life. . . . I see the better way and choose the worse."

Together with this sense of shame—of guilt and sinfulness in courtly love—Petrarch's poetry often reveals a wish to be punished. And as the wages of sin are death, his love for Laura dissolves into a suicidal fantasy. De Rougemont has popularized the notion that courtly lovers are always in love with death instead of life or one another. In relation to both fin' amors and the northern tradition, de Rougemont is surely wrong, as I have been arguing; but once we get to Petrarch, his suggestion becomes more plausible. For then the courtly attitude toward death begins to undergo changes that bring it closer to de Rougemont's theory.

Prior to the age of Petrarch, poets used the concept of death to symbolize their suffering state, their intermittent loss of hope, and in general all the repressiveness that fin' amors entailed. Bernard de Ventadour is perfectly representative when he says: "Noble lady, full of joy, your lover is dying! I fear that my heart will melt if this endures." The poet obviously has no wish to die; death is not something he is in love with; and however much his love involves frustration, he accepts it as part of the self-sacrifice that all ideals demand. As one could have expected from a troubadour poet, the next line runs: "Lady, for your love I join my hands and adore you!" This alternation between dying and living, despairing and hoping, fearing and adoring is characteristic of fin' amors. Far from identifying love and death, the poet is revealing the precarious existence of noble sentiments in human life—much as Plato does when he speaks of Eros living one moment, dying the next, living again, and so on as the progress of love determines. Likewise, in the northern tradition, death symbolizes the risks that lovers run for the sake of their beloved or to prove the authenticity of love—as when the protagonists in the Tristan legend declare that they would rather die than live without one another. In these earlier versions, death is something foreign to the joyfulness of courtly love, an enemy and a scourge that may intrude upon the ideality of the relationship but cannot subjugate it. In Petrarch, however, love for Laura is itself a kind of spiritual death.

Thus it is that Petrarch speaks of love as a snare: "And so I fell in the net, and was undone." It is a torture of the soul that destroys but does not deliver, a threat more cruel and hateful than death alone: "Oh, I shall always hate the window whence/Love, cruel love, transfixed me with this ray!/Why had it not sufficient force to slay?/It's good to die in youthful vehemence." On the basis of lines such as these, one cannot conclude that the love of Laura is really the love of death. Certainly death has enlarged its domain within Petrarch's love: it fascinates and obsesses him, almost as much as Laura herself; it signifies the terrible dimensions of his passion. But it is not yet the object of his search. What that is Petrarch reveals in the line that immediately follows the ones I have quoted: "No, I must live, in lifelong penitence." In loving Laura as he does, Petrarch forces himself to live a penitential existence. In her he objectifies, and idealizes, his inclinations toward all the good and beautiful things in this world that deflect him from the love of God. She embodies everything he cherishes that thwarts his religious aspiration. It is not death he is in love with, but lifelong punishment for loving sinfully.

This may help us to understand Petrarch's proclaimed enjoyment of suffering. "I am one of those," he says in an early canzone, "who joy in weeping. It even seems that I seek out means to fill my eyes with tears and my heart with pain." It will not surprise us that these lines resemble those of earlier poets, such as Bernard de Ventadour and Chrétien de Troyes; but Petrarch's masochism signifies something very different from theirs. When Bernard de Ventadour says

"I weep because sighs taste better after weeping," he is attesting to the exhilarating magic of being in love. The poem in which this line occurs begins: "So full of joy is my heart that it transfigures everything for me." In other words, even the pain of frustration can serve the lover and is therefore worth pursuing. For it will bring joy once the beloved realizes how strong his feelings are. Thus the poem ends with the lines: "Messenger, go run, tell the Loveliest One of the pain and the sorrow I endure for her sake, and the torment." The sentiment is wholly coherent with the lines in Guillaume de Lorris' part of *The Romance of the Rose* where the God of Love says that "Love brings a very jolly malady/In midst of which one laughs and jokes and plays./Lovers by turns feel torments first, then joys./Lovesickness is a changeable disease:/One hour it bitter is, the next as sweet; . . . "

Even in Chrétien de Troyes, who eventually rejected courtly love as irreligious, a similar attitude accounts for his strange eagerness to suffer. To illustrate the self-destructiveness of courtly love, de Rougemont quotes the following from Chrétien (actually, one of his characters): "From all other ills doth mine differ. It pleaseth me; I rejoice at it; my ill is what I want and my suffering is my health. So I do not see what I am complaining about; for my ill comes to me by my will; it is my willing that becomes my ill; but I am so pleased to want this that I suffer agreeably, and have so much joy in my pain that I am sick with delight." But far from being an indication of self-destructive love, this merely expresses the troubadour dedication to a joy that even sorrow can augment. If Bernard and the character in Chrétien are masochists, theirs is a masochism Petrarch rarely duplicates. For him the pain of love is not a means to greater joy within love itself. He wants to suffer in order to prove that love is *not* joyful, that it is a calamity like all the other lures of empirical nature. Petrarch delights in suffering much as a Christian mystic might—at least, a flagellant like Henry of Suso, or Augustine himself. Petrarch differs from the ordinary ascetic only in punishing himself by means of the anguish of sexual love. The logic in his self-inflicted pain is otherwise the same.

It is for a similar reason that Petrarch's descriptions of nature are remarkably different from what we find in the nature poetry of the troubadours. For both alike, nature is transformed by the poet's love. But there the resemblance ends. Fin' amors being joyful, nature comes alive for the troubadours: whatever the season, it bursts forth in a dance of sensory delight. In Petrarch's poetry, nature is not at all joyful. Lovely though it may be, it reeks of melancholy. Its beauty, like the beauty of Laura, frightens and deceives. In ways that nineteenth-century poets were to cultivate more thoroughly, Petrarch projects his sadness into the landscape itself: "Therefore I think each wood and ragged spot/ and field and river knows how I am tried." If nature is alive in Petrarch, it is only through a weighty wisdom that he himself does not have: "All the wild knows what one knows not." This is no longer the world of the troubadour poets, a panoply of immediate joys and incidental though necessary suffering. We are now in a depressive world where even nature distrusts its moments of sunlight and gaiety.

At the same time, Petrarch often sounds as if he too believes in fin' amors. In some respects Laura resembles many of the former ladies on a pedestal. As we saw in *The Secret Book*, Petrarch gives her credit for having improved his character and directed his soul upward. In the *Canzoniere* there are lines of adoration that could have been written two hundred years earlier. Important as these verses are, however, the figure of Laura that emerges from the totality of Petrarch's poetry sets her apart from almost any other troubadour lady. On the one hand, she is more of an actual individual. She appears as a woman who really lived, a historical personage, not a fictional one. It seems perfectly normal that scholars have investi-gated her family name and the number of children she bore her husband during the years when Petrarch was distantly adoring her. Most of the ladies in troubadour poetry were also real women, but they were not usually presented as such. The physical traits the poets described were often superimposed, not unique to this or that person. The troubadour ladies were realistically portrayed, but generally as concrete illustrations of what the troubadours desired. Laura, however, is a particular woman seen in various situations, living and finally dying like others at the time. In this sense, she is present to us more than any of her predecessors. On the other hand, her features are not delineated with anything like the detail or precision to be found in the poetry of the troubadours. Petrarch may refer to her "ivory hand," but he does not dare anything more specific.

Nor does Laura—in the *Canzoniere*, at least—submit to the fact of Petrarch's love in the way that many troubadour ladies did. Laura not only frustrates his desires, she also disdains the love itself. Augustine says she is innocent of Petrarch's madness, and the truth is that she opposes his infatuation in the same manner as Augustine himself. At times, she even becomes a religious symbol, an angel or blessed damosel: "The radiance of her eyes outdid the sun,/transfiguring the earth in a holy blaze." At other times, she is the "lovely and beloved enemy," cruel, forbidding, the icy snare for Petrarch's ambiguous devotion. After her death, she rises to heaven and spends her time chiding the poet for that "tearful trance" in which he mourns her death and goes on loving as before. As Petrarch himself internalizes religious scruples about courtly love, thereby transforming it into something new, so too does Laura become more ethereal. The idea of coitus with her seems almost blasphemous; and only with the greatest reluctance does Petrarch confess to Augustine that his love is even remotely based upon sexual desire.

To some critics Petrarch's love is not at all ambiguous. They see it as "the progress of a gradual spiritual development." One scholar of the nineteenth century describes the *Canzoniere* as the presentation of "a passion ardent and carnal at the outset, but restrained by the honour and virtue of the lady whom he loved, and which, purified by sorrow at her death, was raised to an ideal love, and this too finally transformed into the love of God." Though this may have been what Petrarch officially intended, it is false to what he actually presents in his major love poetry—both early and late. Almost to the end of the *Canzoniere*, Petrarch's courtly devotion to Laura remains intact; and from the very beginning, it is contrasted with the ordinary carnal affairs that the poet was also engaging in.

Petrarch's famous *Epistle to Posterity* may be useful at this point. He there remarks that "in youth I felt the pains of love, vehement in the extreme, but constant to one object and honourable; and I should have felt them longer had not death—bitter, indeed, but useful—extinguished the flame as it was beginning to subside." He then goes on to discuss "looser indulgences of appetite," clearly distinguishing them from his love for Laura. Though these remarks need not be taken as authoritative with respect to the *Canzoniere*, they sound like a more reliable guide to Petrarch's work than the overly simplified summary of the nineteenth-century critic. Within the *Canzoniere* themselves, it is lines such as the following that best express the Petrarchan attitude toward love, the pervasive sadness caused by conflict between courtly and religious beliefs, and by the poet's inability to find peace through either of them:

> Can it be love that fills my heart and brain?
> If love, dear God, what is its quality?
> If it is good, why does it torture me?
> If evil, why this sweetness in my pain?
> If I burn gladly, why do I complain?
> If I hate burning, why do I never flee?
> O life-in-death, O lovely agony,
> How can you rule me so, if I'm not fain?
> And if I'm willing, why do I suffer so?—
> By such contrary winds I'm blown in terror
> In a frail and rudderless bark on open seas. . . .

Towards the end of his life Petrarch underwent a religious conversion and felt he had now renounced everything but the love of God. In his treatise *Remedies against Good and Evil Fortune*, the man who had once extolled the virtues of the divine Laura shows himself to be a typical misogynist of the Middle Ages. But even in the later period Petrarch keeps adding to the *Canzoniere*, and the cycle of poems called the *Triumphs* seeks to redeem his love for Laura by fitting it into a larger system of salvation. Like Dante's Beatrice, Laura now explains her former coldness as a gesture of love, not scorn. Her heart was never divided from Petrarch's, she tells him from the comfort of her heavenly abode; her remoteness in life was only a device to chastise his passion and thus to save his soul. The harmony of their love, its mutuality within a reciprocal relationship—the one thing that never appears in Petrarch's earlier poetry—she now insists upon and even claims to have been aware of all along. Though she had never admitted this before, "the amorous impulse was almost equal in us two." We are thus left to believe that all is really for the best, in this best of medieval worlds. Petrarch has finally achieved the consolation of knowing that Laura loved him on earth and will soon be his in heaven.

But this is not the side of Petrarch one finds most interesting. Within the poetry of love, the accommodation with religious doctrine is something Dante expresses with greater inventiveness. Petrarch's lasting strength consists in the honest turbulence of his youthful poetry—his moodiness, his doubts about himself as well as Laura, his sense of despair about human love. Whether or not he is the first modern poet, as Benedetto Croce has said, he is surely one of the first to have made "the melancholy of failure" into the dominant theme of love between the sexes. Shelley saw him as a poet who unsealed "the inmost enchanted fountains of the delight which is in the grief of love." To call him a fourteenth-century Romantic, however, as other writers have done, serves only to slur over the differences between courtly and Romantic love that I shall be analyzing throughout this book. Nevertheless we may agree that in Petrarch there does occur an early version of that vaguely sad and self-destroying love which was to be idealized by many pessimistic poets in the Romantic period. Petrarch provides a lineage for this aspect of romanticism. The links are unmistakable.

I began this chapter with Petrarch because in him one sees most clearly the consequences of internalizing the conflict between religious and courtly love. In making that conflict the major theme of his greatest poetry, Petrarch does more than merely idealize the beloved as the troubadours had; and he does more than idealize the cosmic being toward which religious love is directed. He also idealizes the tumultuous state of a lover who allows himself to be divided by the two kinds of love. He presents the misery, not the joy, of longing, the moral degradation in earthly passion, the spiritual death of a soul that continually punishes itself for misdirecting its desires. If Petrarch is in love with the condition of penitence, however, he is also in love with the imaginative possibilities that it affords. This does not mean that Petrarch's inner conflict was merely a literary device. It is real to him, as the ladies of the troubadours were real to them. But in both cases the approach to love is, at least partly, determined by a sense of poetic opportunity. By glorifying his painful obsession, instead of ending it as Augustine recommends, Petrarch finds nutriment for his art. The poetry itself exposes and expresses—more successfully than any that had preceded it—the play of imagination in one who loves neither well nor wisely.

This emphasis upon the woeful imagination of the lover, something that hundreds of later poets were to imitate, does not start with Petrarch. Its character is already manifest in the verse of Guido Cavalcanti, a more philosophical though not a greater poet than Petrarch. Cavalcanti, who died in 1300, four years before Petrarch was born, does not seem to have been troubled by religious problems. In this respect, he is closer to the troubadours than Petrarch was. But the mind of Cavalcanti is more advanced, more learned than the troubadours'. In the so-called *Canzone d'Amore*, the poem that begins with the words *Donna me prega* ("A lady asks me"), he works out an intricate theory of love in accordance with what purports to be medieval science. The troubadours attempted nothing comparable. Nor would they have accepted much of what Cavalcanti says about love. For him love between the sexes is governed by misery, not by joy; it results from absorbed attention, compulsion, not devotion to the good; in a sense, it destroys both lover and beloved. Augustine might have said the same, and one must assume that Cavalcanti felt his influence as much as Petrarch did. But Cavalcanti is deeper than Petrarch, and more original. Where Petrarch presents a very dramatic, but really superficial, struggle between two kinds of love, Cavalcanti penetrates into each. In one he finds not religious devotion, but the search for ideal sexual love; in the other, a sensory desire for some woman he has met. Their interaction results in Cavalcanti's version of courtly love. As a yearning for mutual happiness, this love is necessarily doomed; as an act of the imagination, however, it provides a unique and indispensable fulfillment.

In his day Cavalcanti had the reputation of being a philosopher.

In the *Decameron* Boccaccio calls him "one of the best thinkers [loici] in the world and an accomplished lay philosopher [filosofo naturale]." Boccaccio also repeats the "gossip among the vulgar" which held that Cavalcanti was an atheist. Possibly he was, for his poetry is remarkably free of religious ornamentation. He may occasionally speak of his lady's glory having "risen into heaven"; but he is obviously toying with doctrinal ideas, not espousing them. When he gives an explicit statement about the nature of love, as in the *Canzone d'Amore*, he claims to be offering a scientific demonstration (*natural dimonstramento*). Dante Gabriel Rossetti, who translated many of his poems, complains that Cavalcanti has allowed "the perversity of a logician to prevail in much of his amorous poetry." And elsewhere Rossetti speaks of the *Canzone d'Amore* as "a poem beside the purpose of poetry, filled with metaphysical jargon, and perhaps the worst of Guido's productions . . . I have not translated it, as being of little true interest."

Rossetti's Pre-Raphaelite scorn reveals his own inadequacies, or the limitations of his time. One feels that Ezra Pound comes nearer to the truth when he says of Cavalcanti: "The tone of his mind is infinitely more 'modern' than Dante's." So modern is Cavalcanti that Pound's own translations often seem out-of-date now and sometimes barely intelligible. If any translator can succeed in doing justice to Cavalcanti—those rigorous metaphors, those clean, clear, simple rhythms, those images so sharply focused as to dazzle the imagination—perhaps this poetic soulmate will be an analytic philosopher or empirical scientist of the twentieth (or twenty-first) century.

But even within his own tradition, Cavalcanti was always considered obscure. For three hundred years after its composition the *Canzone d'Amore* was the subject of commentary after commentary, each more ingenious than the last, many differing about the text itself. Some saw in Cavalcanti nothing but the glorification of sensuous appetite. That was the opinion of Giovanni Pico della Mirandola, who maintained that Cavalcanti's subject was merely "amore vulgare"—something Pico himself considered unworthy of being called love. On the other hand, Marsilio Ficino, Pico's teacher, goes to considerable lengths to claim Cavalcanti as a fellow Platonist. In his *Commentary on Plato's Symposium,* Ficino devotes more space to Cavalcanti's *Canzone d'Amore* than to anything else not written by Plato himself. In it Ficino finds the traditional distinction between earthly and heavenly eros: "Guido [Cavalcanti] locates the former love in voluptuousness, the latter in contemplation. He thinks that the former revolves around the particular beauty of one body, the latter around the universal beauty of all mankind."

Other philosophers have interpreted Cavalcanti in a variety of different ways. Santayana sees him as one of those poets who have "souls naturally Platonic," whether or not they declare themselves Platonists in philosophy. But when one examines the textual evidence for this kind of interpretation, one begins to wonder whether Cavalcanti had even a Platonic soul. To prove his point, Santayana cites the following sonnet, "Una giovane donna di Tolosa" ("A Young Lady of Toulouse"), which he translates himself:

> There is a lady in Toulouse so fair,
> So young, so gentle, and so chastely gay,
> She doth a true and living likeness bear
> In her sweet eyes to Love, whom I obey.
> Within my heart my soul, when she appeared,
> Was filled with longing and was fain to flee
> Out of my heart to her, yet was afeared
> To tell the lady who my Love might be.
> She looked upon me with her quiet eyes,
> And under their sweet ray my bosom burned,
> Cheered by Love's image, that within them lies.
> Alas! they shot an arrow as she turned,
> And with a death-wound from the piercing dart
> My soul came sighing back into my heart.

In making his translation, Santayana renders "la donna mia" as "Love" (in the fourth line) instead of "my lady." He justifies this as a minor liberty, but actually it changes the original completely. For if the lady in Toulouse resembles Love, one might possibly speak of her as a "Platonic reminiscence of a fairer ideal." Santayana does so, thinking that the poem reveals a characteristic search for beauty in one imperfect approximation after another: "All beauties attract by suggesting the ideal and then fail to satisfy by not fulfilling it." To bring his revision in line with more usual readings of the sonnet, Santayana allows that "la donna mia" refers to the woman (Giovanna) whom Cavalcanti presumably loved in Florence before leaving for Toulouse. But, of course, this would not prevent a Platonizing poet from using the Florentine lady to symbolize the ideal for which he really aspires.

Santayana's interpretation of Cavalcanti is suggestive, and his insights about Platonic love are often brilliant. But Cavalcanti is not a Platonist, though on occasion he may sound like one. Returning to the original of "Una giovane donna di Tolosa," one is astounded to find how greatly it differs from what Santayana led us to expect. Cavalcanti does not say that his lady bears a resemblance to Love, and he never mentions Giovanna at all. The lady of Toulouse is said to be something similar (*simigliante cosa*) to "la donna mia." The word "donna" occurs in the last line of each stanza, and in a way that indicates a conception of what the beloved either is or ought to be. In the first stanza she must have sweet eyes (*dolci occhi*), and the lady from Toulouse lives up to this requirement; in the second stanza the poet's heart goes out to the lady, but he is afraid to tell her what kind of woman his beloved should be; in the third stanza his soul rejoices because her sweet regard leads him to believe that she is indeed his kind of woman, his rightful lady—"la sua donna dritta"; but finally his heart is wounded by the cold and cutting glance that the Toulousan casts as she turns away from him.

In a sense, the poem does articulate a disparity between the actual and the ideal. And possibly a poet such as Cavalcanti could not have sensed this disparity without Platonistic antecedents—in his society if not in his own thinking. But the fact remains that to interpret Cavalcanti's poem as itself either Platonic or Neoplatonic is to distort it. For in narrating the history of his calamity, Cavalcanti does not use the object of his love to *represent* anything. She is not a symbol of absolute beauty or of beauty in women; she is not a reminiscence of some fair ideal. She is just a young lady of Toulouse, beautiful and noble, and with forthright gaiety—"una giovane donna di Tolosa/ Bella e gentil, d'onesta leggiadria." Her sweet, engaging eyes cause the poet to *think* that she will respond to his love; from her eventual scorn, he sadly discovers that she will not. Cavalcanti is not seeking an ideal of beauty, but rather the experience of love for a particular woman. As a result, his frustrations are not those of the disillusioned Platonist; and for him they serve as a proof and constant reminder that love cannot succeed in any realm of being. If Cavalcanti is an idealist, it is only in refusing to end his search for sexual love. With respect to the outcome of each encounter, he is generally realistic or skeptical—much as Ovid or Lucretius were, though without the crudities of either.

What separates Cavalcanti from the Roman poets, and what gives him his greater delicacy and refinement, is the courtly tradition itself, as it had developed in the two centuries preceding. The differences between Cavalcanti and the troubadours have often been noted: where they are hopeful, he is sad; where they idealize frustration in sex, he uses it to show love's ultimate futility; where they prefer imagery to conceptual analysis, he is probing and intellectual. But the continuities are also present, and several of Cavalcanti's sonnets are paeans of adoration that the earliest troubadours might have written—if they had written in Italian and with the mentality of a philosopher. The entire tradition of French courtly love is summed up, distilled, and clarified in a poem such as this:

> In you reside the flowers and the verdure,
> And that which glows or is beautiful to see,
> Your face is more resplendent than the sun,
> Who sees you not can never value aught.
>
> In this world there is no creature
> So full of beauty or of pleasure,
> And he who dreaded love is reassured
> By your loveliness and can no longer fear.
>
> The ladies who make up your retinue
> Please me merely through your love of them,
> And I beseech them, in their courtliness,
>
> That those who can should honor you still more
> And venerate your true supremacy,
> Since of all women you remain the best.

The lady more resplendent than the sun, the giver of warmth and light and so the standard of value ("chi voi non vede, mai non può valere"); the lady more beautiful and pleasing than any other creature of this world; the lady whose loveliness reassures her suitor about the reality of love and so removes his fears; the lady at the top of a social hierarchy defined by *cortesia*, causing others to pay her homage and inducing the lover to love them for her sake *as if* in imitation of Christian caritas—all this is Provence revisited. At the same time, it is wholly consistent with the northern version of courtly love—which explains why the Neoplatonism of the troubadours contributes only a minor strand within the total complexity of Cavalcanti. For him as for the Tristan legend, the ladder of love leads upward toward a beloved who is in principle accessible, attainable, and sometimes attained. She is the best of women, but the lover may also hope for some reciprocation beyond the limitations of fin' amors. Cavalcanti sings of his beloved as if he were Tristan yearning for Iseult, momentarily forced to adore her at a distance, sustained by her beauty but parted from her as she passes in procession. Compare the poem I have just quoted with the following passage from the Tristan legend:

> The cortege of the Queen now followed. At its head came the laundresses and the chambermaids, then the wives and the daughters of the barons and the counts. These passed in single file, escorted each by a young knight. Finally there advanced a palfrey ridden by the loveliest woman Kaherdin ever had laid eyes on: she was beautifully made of body and face, with falling hips, well-defined eyebrows, laughing eyes and tiny teeth; a gown of red samite covered her; a string of gold and jewels bound her smooth brow.
> "It is the Queen," whispered Kaherdin.
> "The Queen?" said Tristan. "No, that is Camille, her maid."
> There followed on a grey palfrey another lady, whiter than snow in February, redder than roses; her bright eyes sparkled like stars reflected in a fountain.
> "Now I see her, there is the Queen!" said Kaherdin.
> "Ah, no," said Tristan, "that is Brangien the Faithful."
> But at once the road grew bright, as though the sun suddenly had shone out through the foliage of the great trees, and Iseult the Blonde appeared.

For all these resemblances, however, there is one respect in which Cavalcanti differs greatly from the northern tradition. For though he compares the beloved to stars and snow and other conventional symbols of natural beauty, he does not describe her. The medieval romances were fanciful in being wish-fulfillments, but realistic in dealing with persons the reader was to imagine in all their reality. In Cavalcanti there are no longer delineated persons of this sort. His women are generally presented as the abstract occasion for love. Nor is the lover, presumably the poet himself, depicted as a man living at a specific time in a specific place or as part of an actual society. He is merely a bundle of psychological states, which are then classified, analyzed, and ultimately fitted into a philosophical conception about the nature of love. The investigation itself is not especially dramatic. In ways that anticipate Proust, Cavalcanti usually limits himself to what the lover undergoes in the course of his amatory experience. Of all his women, if (as most critics have assumed) there is more than one, only the lady of Toulouse is given a name. Cavalcanti calls her Mandetta, but she has no further identification. As a person she is less recognizable than the shepherdess whom Cavalcanti encounters in the woods on a day in spring that was made for mutual delight. This girl we do see vividly: she has curly blonde hair, eyes full of warmth, a rosy complexion, her feet bare and bathed with dew. When the poet asks her whether she is alone, she frankly admits her desire to have a lover by her side. Cavalcanti gallantly offers his services, and they slip away to make love in the bushes. The ballata ends with the following lines:

> She took my hand with an amorous design,
> And said that she had given me her heart,
> She led me into leafy coolness,
> Wherein I saw all-colored flowers
> And so much joy and sweetness felt
> That the God of Love himself
> I seemed to see there.

The ballata has the typical form of a French pastourelle, and most critics have refused to give it much importance. One scholar speaks of it as "a love episode which seems to have nothing to do with the serious *Amore* of most of the poems"; and he points out that Cavalcanti's brother-in-law ridiculed it in a sonnet of his own. But in some respects the pastoral expresses Cavalcanti's philosophy of love as surely and as beautifully as anything else he wrote. For Cavalcanti's ideal is predicated upon the goodness of sexual pleasure. In the other poems he does not describe the physical dimensions of intimacy as he does in this one, but in various places he indicates that he sings of a love which is carnal. In the *Canzone d'Amore* he says that love belongs to a person's sensory nature; and later on he pointedly repeats himself: "non razionale mà che si sente dicho"—"not rational, but what is felt, I say." The god who appears in the final stanza of the ballata is the same being as the Amore that Cavalcanti investigates throughout the rest of his poetry. The shepherd girl has obviously given Cavalcanti what he wanted all along; and we knew from the very start that she was worth the effort. For the second line of the ballad describes her in the most elevated of courtly language: "Più che la stella/bella al mio parere"—"more beautiful than the stars she seemed to me." Of course, in one respect she is not the typical object of Cavalcanti's love. She is only a shepherdess, not a lady; and though, in his moment of amorous excitement, the poet sees flowers of every color, he does not see them in *her*. In other women, he wants what she can give him, but also more. What then is he looking for?

Though somewhat obliquely, Cavalcanti tells us in the blasphemous sonnet to Guido Orlandi. He there claims that in the church of San Michele in Orto men worship a madonna whose face shows forth the beauty of his lady. For all we know, it may have been Cavalcanti's beloved who sat as model for the statue of the Virgin. What matters in the poem, however, is the fact that Cavalcanti assigns to the young lady—his beloved—all the magic of the idol in the church. She cures the sick, drives devils away, and makes the blind to see again. It is not Christ or the Virgin Mary who performs these miracles, but rather Cavalcanti's mistress. She embodies the power of the Virgin and does not merely depict her. For the woman is now the reality, and the religious aura of the statue symbolizes the infinite goods that come from adoring *her*.

No troubadour would have dared to go this far. Their ladies may have served the same function as the Virgin Mary—bestowing goods, according salvation, revealing an unlimited perfection—but no conflict or inconsistency with church doctrine was ever intended. Later, when the Albigensian Crusade obliged the troubadours to write hymns to the Virgin instead of poems to their ladies, they merely changed the name of the beloved. In their verse Mary often served as a mask for an actual woman, but they never said this overtly. For them it sufficed to speak of the Virgin as if she herself were their lady, as Orlandi does in the conventional madrigal that answers Cavalcanti's sonnet. Mary is there described as a "fair rose, in holy garden set," that being courtly language for talking about a woman except that this one is the Mother of God. For Cavalcanti, however, it is a particular human being, not the Virgin, who is holy. In another sonnet, he specifically excludes a Christian or religious object of love by denying that anyone prior to his beloved has ever led our mind as high as she. She is herself the goddess of beauty, not as a Platonic reminiscence and not as an image of Mary, but as the living incarnation of what all men want.

All men want beauty, but they want it as something that responds to them while they respond to it. The troubadour lady had difficulty responding to her lover: she generally had to stand still and be adored. Even Mary, who descends like God in acts of loving-kindness, does not respond to her many lovers with a love identical to theirs. It is this that Cavalcanti now demands. In the *Canzone d'Amore* he even defines love in terms of a similar aspect, "simil . . . complessione," of the beloved that directs her toward the lover in ways that reciprocate his interest in her. The similarity of their being reveals itself in that unifying glance from which all courtly love originates. Their eyes meet, and the "spirits" of their souls start coursing back and forth. Looking at this beautiful woman, the lover boldly expects to derive pleasure from her. And she feels something similar, for Cavalcanti tells us that timid beauties are incapable of love. But though each is disposed to enjoy the other, their mutual delight is more than just the escapade with the shepherdess. The woman's receptiveness causes no descent, or condescension, of the lover; and neither does it elevate him. Cavalcanti seeks a beautiful woman who will be as noble as himself, indeed another self, one that is kind and not cruel, gracious not forbidding, humble not proud, daring not diffident, ardent not prim, a physical reality and not a theoretical perfection. They are to meet on the human level—he as a sensitive man of imagination, she as the radiant beauty whose very radiance is a kind of divinity—and they are to make love like human beings. The *Canzone d'Amore*, as I read it, is a testament to such love.

But though this is what Cavalcanti wants, alas it is not what he gets. Time after time, he soars and is dashed down again. Without being a Platonist, without a transcendental goal toward which he might aspire, he continually strives for a love he never attains. His is the poetry of failure: not a metaphysical failure, for there is no conflict between this world and some other, but just the fact that life cannot give him what he desires. The beautiful women he adores end up by rejecting him for unknown reasons of their own: this is the "schuro luce" in the *Canzone d'Amore*, the "dark ray" that emanates from Mars (the irascible planet) and eventuates in the lover's despair. The poet learns that the world is not attuned to his search for love. And that is all. Things are that way. As a philosopher, Cavalcanti instructs us in the bitter truth, weeping that it should be so—and who before Leopardi in the nineteenth century has wept more beautifully than Cavalcanti?—but also using his failures as a means of learning about human nature.

In making his investigation, studying the nature of sexual love while undergoing the constant realization that he is failing at it, Cavalcanti begins—if it has a beginning—the long tradition that culminates in Proust. To this extent, he is indeed more modern than Dante or any of his other contemporaries.

In the final section of *La Vita Nuova* (*The New Life*) Dante says that he will someday write of Beatrice things that have never yet been said of any other woman. He carries out this promise in the *Divine Comedy*, but in the *Vita Nuova* itself he develops a conception of the beloved that can hardly be matched in previous literature. For our purposes, it is of greatest interest as a new attempt, in that sense offering the possibility of a "new life," to harmonize human love with religious orthodoxy of the thirteenth century.

The originality of Dante's effort need not concern us at any length. The troubadour Peire Vidal had earlier said "Good Lady, I think I see God when I gaze upon your delicate body"; and as early as Plato's *Phaedrus*, one finds descriptions of lovers prepared to fall down and worship the beloved as if in the presence of a god. But none of these, or other, foreshadowings diminish the grandeur of Dante's achievement. For into his poetry he cast the conflicting ideals of his age in their fullest, most contemporaneous, development, and yet their transfiguration into one another emanates entirely from his own imagination. If Dante's synthesis is not wholly successful, as I shall argue, it nevertheless provides a basis for further syntheses in the Renaissance.

A great tradition of Dante scholarship has maintained that the elements in his synthesis were courtly love and the love for God, and this is correct insofar as Dante did seek to harmonize these opposing types of love. But from the very outset, it is essential to realize how selective he was in what he included within the synthesis.

In particular, there is much of courtly love as we have been studying it that Dante would not tolerate. To see this, we need only consider the canto of the *Divine Comedy* that recounts the history of Paolo and Francesca da Rimini. They are in hell because they committed adultery. They are only in the first circle, however, because theirs is the sin of lust or incontinence rather than the more serious sins of treachery or utter selfishness. Paolo and Francesca were murdered by her husband, and his guilt is punished in a much lower circle of hell. The unfortunate lovers belong to a region populated by Dido, Cleopatra, Tristan, and others who transgressed while seeking to attain mutual love. Their self-indulgence is a sin even though it arises from the power of love which motivates all things in the universe. Dante summons Paolo and Francesca by invoking the love that moves them even in hell, and they float towards him under the influence of the same erotic instinct that causes the dove to return homeward to his mate.

Francesca tells their story while Paolo, inseparably bound to her for all eternity, holds her hand and weeps without a word. In life she had been the aunt of a friend of Dante's. Married for political reasons to a deformed husband, she had fallen in love with his younger brother, who had served as an intermediary; she had been tricked into thinking that he was proposing for himself, only to find too late that he had been acting on behalf of the family. It was, in short, a contemporary case history that duplicated the situation of Tristan and Iseult. Francesca implicates courtly romance as a party to her guilt by relating how she and Paolo had been reading together the story of Lancelot and Guinevere without any thought that harm might result from it. When they reached the kiss that Lancelot first bestows upon Guinevere, they were overcome by passion, and so began their sexual intimacy. Galahad (Galeotto) was the go-between in the Arthurian tale, and Francesca tells Dante that "Galeotto fu il libro e chi lo scrisse"—the book and he who wrote it served as a pander to their lust in the manner of Galahad. At this point Dante faints out of sheer compassion, falling down as if he too were a dead man.

Critics have interpreted this episode in various ways. Some have taken it as evidence of Dante's great tenderness; others have seen it as proof of his recognition that sin may easily conquer those who think they are just dallying in innocent pleasure. Santayana treats the misery of Paolo and Francesca as symbolic of love that has no society to support it, no goal beyond mere possession; their punishment is therefore a self-defeating eternity in each other's arms as the showing forth of their moral failure. "Abandon yourself, Dante would say to us—abandon yourself altogether to a love that is nothing but love, and you are in hell already. Only an inspired poet could be so subtle a moralist. Only a sound moralist could be so tragic a poet."

What Santayana says may well be true, but he ignores what is most poignant in the love of Paolo and Francesca. And that is the fact that in itself it is relatively guiltless. Despite the element of adultery, theirs is the kind of love—as in a courtly romance—for which all human beings yearn. In being adulterous, it causes them to violate social arrangements that can destroy them without affecting their underlying innocence. They are the victims not only of the husband who murders them while they perform the act of lovemaking—a double crime, one might say, since he destroys life at a moment of greatest consummation—but also they suffer at the merciless hands of a theology that casts them into hell for failing to submit to the dictates of their society. Their "self-indulgence" consists in little more than a search for human love, and Dante becomes a party to their tragedy merely through his mode of classification, accepting them as legitimate inhabitants of the infernal whirlwind. With his usual sensitivity, however, at least in matters of love, Dante shows how ambivalent he is in this moral stance. Fainting away, he reveals that he cannot face up to a cosmic reality that imposes such extreme punishment.

In falling as if dead, the state of annihilation that he approximates so often in his love for Beatrice as described by the *Vita Nuova*, Dante is telling us symbolically that whether or not he himself has committed adultery, he cannot pretend to any ultimate superiority that would set him apart from these lovers. Francesca's description of how their eyes and then their bodies met is filled with self-pity, no doubt, but it scarcely suggests that Dante considers Francesca to be a criminal. It would likewise be difficult to imagine Paolo, weeping silently and forever, as a vile seducer or vicious Don Juan. Who then is to blame for the misfortune of the lovers, given the world they live in? Dante implies that it is the literary profession itself, to which he belongs. Those who write about love become responsible for the intimate thoughts and dangerous behavior of their readers. Paolo and Francesca are the ones who have fallen into the darkness of their mutual solitude, but Dante recognizes that they are not the only culprits in the case.

Dante moves beyond this and the other circles of hell by writing what Croce has called a "theological romance." Within its conceptual structure, however, it treats all romance involving erotic consummation as something less than ideal. If Paolo and Francesca must end up in hell because of their adultery, one might expect to find examples of happy and mutual sexual love, albeit nonadulterous, among the blessed in heaven. As a matter of fact, Dante describes nothing like that. In paradise he does meet the chastened souls of men and women who were amorous in life and now joyfully inhabit the planet Venus, but the human love that distinguishes these blessed spirits is left unanalyzed, and those who identify themselves do not really illustrate ideals of sexual love. One is a prince with whom Dante enjoyed a close friendship; another is an old woman whose generosity during her final years in Florence balanced her earlier escapades with two lovers and four husbands; and the third is a famous troubadour, Foulquet of Marseilles, who renounced the world and ended up as a bishop. They all demonstrate that human love finds its greatest fulfillment in the love of God. They do not reveal the ramifications of authentic and satisfying love between man and woman. Similarly, the Earthly Paradise at the summit of Mount Purgatory has no inhabitants, in recognition of man's lost innocence resulting from events in the Garden of Eden. In being empty, it must be contrasted with those flourishing earthly paradises that courtly lovers sought (and sometimes found) in nature itself and in each other's arms.

Just below the Garden of Eden, on the seventh cornice, Dante locates the penitents of natural and unnatural lust. They are closest to paradise because their sexual ardor symbolizes God's overwhelming love, but they must still be purified of their carnal inclinations. On this seventh cornice Dante encounters Guido Guinizelli, the founder of the dolce stil nuovo. Dante refers to him as his father, indeed as the father of all Italians who wrote poetry in the sweet and chivalrous style; and scholars have often suggested that Guinizelli anticipated Dante's synthesis between courtly and religious love. But though he spoke of his beloved as a *donna angelicata* (angelic lady or lady-made-angel), Guinizelli did not dare to treat her as Dante treated Beatrice. Charles Singleton has pointed out that Guinizelli's famous poem "Love and the Gentle Heart Are One" ends in an ambiguity that Dante would turn into affirmation. In Guinizelli, the poet appears before God, who condemns him for having loved a woman as only God himself should be loved. The poet concludes with an apology in which he claims that sin cannot be imputed to him since his beloved had the appearance of an angel and seemed to have descended from the heavenly kingdom. Singleton rightly notes that this provides no resolution to the conflict between human and religious love, though it inspired Dante to go ahead as he does in the *Vita Nuova*. Here in purgatory, Guinizelli is being cleansed, or so we must presume, of imperfections in his imagination that prevented him from reaching Dante's solution to the problem of love.

If I am right, however, Dante effects his solution by excluding all but a very partial aspect of courtly love. That it is not a complete, or satisfying, synthesis appears once we examine some of the details in the *Vita Nuova*. Though the work of his early youth, the *Vita Nuova* shows Dante's great self-consciousness about his place in history. One feels that it could have been written only in Italy, at the very end of the thirteenth century, and by a man who wished to separate himself from much of the love literature of the previous two hundred years. Dante begins by telling us that Beatrice is the "now glorious lady of my mind." The word "glorious" (*gloriosa*) would be taken by his contemporaries as meaning that she was already dead; and the reference to his own mind makes sense once we realize that Dante, who never touches his lady, scarcely intimates what her physical attributes may have been. *Beatrice* means "bestower of blessings," and Dante's approach to the being of his beloved has convinced several critics that she is just a symbol of theology or grace abounding—not a real woman at all. Others remind us that Dante talks about her as if she were real, and there is much authority, including Boccaccio's biography of Dante, for thinking that she is the Beatrice Portinari whom Dante met on May Day 1274, when he was nine years old and she a little younger.

But it does not matter whether the literary Beatrice is based upon the actual one. For the Beatrice that Dante presents to us is a personage who must be taken as both a symbol *and* a reality. Dante identifies her with the number 9, quite suitably since she embodies for him the power of all the muses and since the root of 9 is the number 3 or trinity. She also appears on earth and later in heaven as someone who exists, an extraordinary woman whose beauty a poet would naturally wish to extol. We may therefore think of Beatrice as a real human being who serves to inspire the mind or imagination of a Dante. Nevertheless, Beatrice is not depicted as a concrete or particularized individual. She is an abstract, almost allegorical, embodiment of beauty, goodness, and the other perfections for which Dante loves her.

In portraying the superiority of their lady, many troubadours had also emphasized her remoteness. But the troubadour ladies were generally described with details that enable us to imagine what it would be like to see or hear or touch them. They may have existed only in the poet's mind, but that was a secret of the trade that the poets kept hidden. In Dante the secret takes on new significance. Real as Beatrice may be, we are not to respond to her as if she were an ordinary reality whose physical being we could savor or enjoy. She is not only pure, which Dante continually tells us, believing that this makes her holy, but also she is *purified* and therefore limited to only a fragment of what the courtly tradition had expected to find in a beloved.

In discussing the *Vita Nuova*, T. S. Eliot suggests that the authenticity of Dante's love for Beatrice may be understood in our age better than ever before, accustomed as we are to Freudian theories about childhood sexuality. To have fallen in love at the age of nine and to be obsessed for the rest of one's life with the same girl, even though one sees very little of her in subsequent years, to dote upon her after she dies at an early age, and to use her as the focus of one's theories about love and beauty—all this Eliot sees as true to psychological reality. He even suggests that far from having been precocious, as a lover at age nine, Dante was possibly a little slow in his development since (according to Eliot) his kind of devotion more often occurs in five-year-olds. What Eliot does not consider is the extent to which Dante's world outlook, based upon his childhood obsession, must be regarded as pathological. I am not referring to the fact that a poet whose maturity is dominated by an early cathexis of this sort may *himself* be neurotic. That is another issue; and as the biographies of many artists indicate, such pathology can often be a useful source of motivation for creative work. What concerns me more immediately is the moral ideal that someone like Dante extracts from his fixation. As a concept of love, it seems neither wholesome nor commendable. It involves not only the repression and self-denial that belong to troubadour frustration, and not only the flight from reality as in many courtly romances, but also a refusal to believe that love can be defensible unless the beloved is an angel of some kind. Even in the experience of a five-year-old, one would find this conception bizarre and possibly sick.

Starting with Jungian ideas about archetypal patterns, Maud Bodkin has remarked about the "infantile character" of Dante's love for Beatrice. That would locate the basis for his idealization even earlier than Eliot suggested. But possibly Bodkin does not mean to be taken literally. She is primarily interested in Dante's tendency to present Beatrice as a "mother-image." This does not limit us to a particular stage of development, and it is borne out by the lines in which Dante likens his behavior to that of a child in relation to its mother. These analogies occur in the *Divine Comedy* as well as in the *Vita Nuova*. In purgatory, when Beatrice first appears at the moment that Vergil (whom Dante frequently calls "father") departs, he says she seems to him as formidable as a mother to a little boy. Though he is now a middle-aged man, she scolds him as if he were a wayward child. Since she is the guide to his education in the secrets of divinity, one can also understand Dorothy Sayers' inclination to see her as his "heavenly schoolmistress" rather than as his mother. In either event, she is a reincarnation of those authoritative and otherworldly ladies, the fairy queens in romances such as those of Launfal and Graelent, who rebuke their human lovers for having failed in their fidelity.

For Beatrice, unlike these other supernatural females, such failure does not mean betraying the secrecy of their love. On the contrary, Dante prides himself on his ability to tell the world about it. What Beatrice condemns is his having substituted lesser loves after she had died and disappeared. It is the kind of complaint that a neurotic mother might make. For she alone is irreplaceable, being the only one who has given birth, and she may possibly hope that her unique importance to a child will continue long after her death. When Beatrice finally leaves Dante, near the end of the *Paradiso*, she yields to the spiritual preeminence of the Virgin Mary, i.e., the mother of God. One may interpret Dante's love, together with the conceptual framework upon which it is constructed, as an intricate variety of Mariolatry. It lends itself to this interpretation even more than the approach to love in most of the troubadours, who were influenced by the cult of Mary but rarely treated their beloved like an actual mother.

At the same time, the nature of Dante's love for Beatrice changes as his art evolves. Even in the *Vita Nuova* it undergoes a remarkable development. In the beginning, Beatrice serves as the source of the poet's amatory experience, which Dante describes with an interest in the psychology of emotion quite similar to Cavalcanti's. Like Cavalcanti, he sees love as a search for joy—in his case merely the joy of receiving Beatrice's salutation—that eventuates in a melancholy state related to death and frustration. This is the "dark ray" that pervades all of Cavalcanti's work, and it appears at the beginning of the *Vita Nuova* on several occasions. At one point the young Dante dreams that the god Love is carrying in his arms a sleeping figure "nude except for a scanty, crimson cloth." One of the few things Dante had told us about Beatrice is that she dressed in red. Her sleeping nudity, as she is held by Love itself, now signifies her slumbering emotionality as well as her imminent demise. In the dream Love awakens the lady and forces her to eat Dante's glowing heart. She does so with reluctance. Immediately afterwards Love bursts into tears, enfolds the lady in his arms, rises to the heavens with her, and leaves the poet to his anguish. The sexual metaphors will not be lost on twentieth-century readers, and neither will they fail to recognize the pattern of guilt and self-punishment Dante experiences in having even dreamed of sullying the purity of his beloved.

In the *Vita Nuova* this initial presentation of Dante's love is succeeded by another one, in which he emulates Guinizelli and hopes to find joy merely in praising the angelic lady. Once she dies, the work devotes itself to a final movement in which Beatrice's mystical qualities are depicted and the poet concludes that the true happiness of love lies in a spiritual union to be attained beyond the world of matter. By the time Dante reencounters Beatrice at the end of the *Purgatorio*, her role is fully clarified as both the conveyor of God's love and also the intermediary that elicits love in Dante for the sake of directing it toward the goals of spirituality. Our last sight of her, twinkling in the empyrean like a joyous star, shows her in the company of the celestial hordes, still a person in one sense or another but now wholly etherealized.

Those commentators who insist that Beatrice remains for Dante a real woman even in his journey to paradise call attention to the fact that she gets angry, smiles, and sometimes shows sarcastic wit. Some of them make much of Dante's report that seeing Beatrice for the first time in the *Divine Comedy*, when she replaces Vergil as his guide, he feels again "i segni dell'antica fiamma"—the signs of the former flame. The words are those that Vergil had given Dido to express sexual longing. But here they need only be taken as indicating the power that Beatrice exerts upon Dante, who is similar to Dido in being helpless and totally subjugated by love. There is nothing in the presentation of Beatrice throughout Dante's writings to justify Boccaccio's fanciful conclusion to his *Life of Dante*. In a passage that foreshadows the writings of any number of nineteenth-century Romantics, Boccaccio tells us that when Dante died "he rendered up to his Creator his toil-worn spirit, the which I doubt not was received into the arms of his most noble Beatrice, with whom, in the sight of Him who is the supreme good, the miseries of this present life left behind, he now lives most joyously in that life the felicity of which expects no end."

This picture of heavenly intimacy runs counter to the vision of Dante himself. In paradise as he describes it, love is finally and fully completed, but it never appears as an interpersonal event. Though the blessed souls belong to an enormous community of spirits who recognize their joint proximity to the mystical center of being, each of them directs his love individually towards God. Each experiences love as the ability to worship God within one's own station and from one's own particular perspective. We are not regaled with images of lovers strolling arm-in-arm or spouses enjoying the goodness of love in each other's embrace. Beatrice may someday welcome Dante to his appropriate circle within the empyrean; she will certainly not set up housekeeping with him, however pure and spiritualized.

Boccaccio's idea of what he "doubts not" may also remind us how partial and limited is Dante's conception of love. Whether the object of Dante's devotion is taken as a woman, as a symbol, or as a combination of the two, she does not help us to understand women that men have loved without writing poetry about them—women they have lived with, loved from day to day, shared their lives with throughout long periods of close association, women they have used and possibly abused in the process of raising a family, struggling jointly against a hostile environment, or cooperating in some moral or religious enterprise. Dante had a wife who bore him four children, and at least one commentator suggests that she appears in Beatrice's maternal manner more than Dante himself may have recognized. Even so, Dante tells us nothing at all about married love, and his love for Beatrice cannot be identified with any love he may have had for his own wife. Dante is thought to have had mistresses and possibly sexual exploits of a more casual sort; yet except for obscure references to a lady who entranced him after Beatrice's death—references so vague that many have thought that she merely symbolizes the study of philosophy rather than theology—he imparts very little about all this experience. Even the later poems to the "stone-hearted lady" do not reveal the knowledge about sexual relations that he was doubtless acquiring throughout his life.

Dante's genius as a poet is indistinguishable from his profundity as a moralist, but in questions related to love he draws a veil that cuts off all but a very narrow perspective upon human nature. The love for an angel-like woman is a reality he explored more than any other man who ever lived. He did so, however, at the expense of neglecting a great network of other realities that we in the twentieth century, at least, tend to consider more pertinent. Reverence for the beloved is an important part of some types of love. It protects and preserves the object of one's bestowal from dangers and impurities that belong to ordinary existence. It is a suitable theme for poetry and a natural aspiration for lovers. It is not, nor can it become, the totality of love between men and women.

But possibly Dante can escape—or at least deflect—such criticism if we think of him as primarily a poet of religious love. We would then accentuate those components in his synthesis which duplicate the medieval concept of caritas. And the *Divine Comedy* does pivot upon this doctrine of love as its fundamental axis. The last lines, immediately following Dante's ecstatic vision of the Divine Presence, the highest point of his supernatural voyage, that beyond which his powers of imagination cannot take him, enunciate the motivating source of all his endeavors: "My will and my desire were turned by love,/The love that moves the sun and the other stars." This is the love that Dante had studied in the writings of St. Augustine, St. Thomas, St. Bernard, and the other fathers of the church who greet him in paradise. Dante's views are orthodox insofar as he defines love as God's own essence and maintains that God instills it in all of nature so that his creation may return his goodness to him as the final goal. Equally orthodox is Dante's belief that, through perversion or excess desire or an insufficiency of dedication, man's will may distract him from what he really wants.

All this Dante could have learned from St. Thomas alone. And yet, he is not a Thomist in his theology, as Gilson and other scholars have also remarked. His ideas are quite distinct, even peculiar, given to poetic license in various places where he might have hewed much more closely to the teachings of the church. He finds room in the same circle of paradise not only for St. Thomas and Richard of St. Victor but also for "the eternal light" of Sigier of Brabant, whom St. Thomas had attacked as one who propagates falsehoods of an Averroistic sort. And in general, Dante's conception of religious love includes much that Aquinas would not have approved. In the *Divine Comedy* Dante indicates that all human loves must be arranged in a hierarchy of importance that culminates with the love for God alone. St. Thomas would have agreed to this and he would have recognized the suitability of Beatrice's leaving Dante to the higher guidance of St. Bernard, a devoted servant of the Virgin Mary; but one cannot imagine that the doctrine of caritas, particularly as it is formulated by St. Thomas, would accommodate the figure of Beatrice herself.

Though Dante's notion that a beloved woman is the manifestation of divinity might have been acceptable to Ibn Arabi and other Sufi mystics, this idea had never been a part of the Christian tradition. It was by turning away from all adoration for women, either through the holy bonds of matrimony or by submitting to monastic celibacy, that St. Thomas thought that sinful man could return to his creator. Affection for one's wife might find a niche within the hierarchy of virtues that lead to the love of God, but St. Thomas would have been baffled by Dante's obsessive need for Beatrice and he could very well have considered it a subtle form of "luxuria," the excessive attachment to worldly goods of a sexual nature.

In 1576, the Inquisition refused to allow the *Vita Nuova* to be reprinted until some of the words that describe Beatrice were significantly altered. Where Dante had spoken of her as an emanation of God and even a kind of second coming of Christ, she was now to be characterized in terminology considered less blasphemous. Whether or not Dante was interrogated for possible heresy during his lifetime, as some historians claim, there could have been no ecclesiastical sanction for believing that Beatrice was a "new Creation" intended by God to reveal a level of perfection hitherto unattained by human beings, or that her death was presaged by the kind of cosmic events—earthquake, blackened sky, etc.—that occurred at the time of the crucifixion, or that her earthly mission was carried out with such sanctified holiness as to enable her to rise immediately into the empyrean without abiding first in purgatory. The church taught that saints could go directly to paradise because they had no sins to be cleansed; but the determination of who was or was not a saint was never thought to lie within the power of a single individual, above all a man who had loved the deceased since he was nine years old. Dante takes this prerogative upon himself and with no greater authority than his genius as a poet. His desire to further the Christian message is undeniable and he effectively shows how the love of a particular woman can be harmonized with a profoundly religious approach. But it is not an approach that the followers of St. Augustine would have accepted as wholly congruent with their own.

For this reason, one should not be surprised that, after Dante, Petrarch reopens the entire issue of conflict between human and Christian loves, or that the voice of Augustine convinces him that his love for Laura, and by inference Dante's love for Beatrice, cannot provide the solution that these poets hoped for. It has been argued that Beatrice manifests to Dante the beauty and goodness of God only in the sense that whatever human beings love must reveal the presence of divinity. On this interpretation, Dante's conception would closely approximate the doctrine of caritas. Beatrice would only be one among many objects of love, all capable of being loved by someone or other as a stepping-stone to the final love of God. This, however, is not the vision Dante presents to us. He is speaking literally when he proposes to say of Beatrice what no one else had said of any woman. He does not mean that she is merely unique to him, a manifestation of his own religious experience. That would have involved a subjectivism to which he never admits, and which he would have considered an insult to his lady. Moreover, Dante never portrays Beatrice in the company of other heavenly souls who serve a similar function for other lovers. She has been chosen by God from all eternity to be a saint on earth and one of the elect in paradise; she has a preordained place among the blessed spirits that all Christendom must recognize. She is not rendered perfect by Dante's using her as a vehicle for the love of God. The idea of caritas would have us use everything in that fashion; but Beatrice elicits love as if she were herself divinity.

To this extent, at least, Dante's philosophy cannot succeed in its desire to synthesize the caritas doctrine with the concept of courtly love. Dante has deviated from the former just as he neglected the latter's humanistic intent. He nevertheless encourages further attempts to effect a synthesis between the two. If only by creating great works of art that express a personal conception of love, he awakens vast possibilities for that new life in Italian culture which is the Renaissance. In his supreme and magnificent individuality he is himself the beginning of it.

6

Neoplatonism
and the Renaissance

THOUGH DANTE WAS PHILO-
sophical, he was not a philosopher. He can quote from St. Augustine
and St. Thomas, but he cannot emulate their achievement. Nevertheless, his attempt to harmonize human and religious love stood as
a model that philosophers in the Italian Renaissance could use as a
source of inspiration. The most important of these is Marsilio Ficino, whose writings towards the end of the fifteenth century provided a systematic synthesis that influenced generations of thinkers
and artists. Ficino's mission in life was ostensibly very simple: he
wished to combine the philosophy of Plato with the orthodox dogmas of the Christian faith. In his youth he had done much work on
Lucretius, but having devoted himself to Platonism he then destroyed these earlier writings. He became a parish priest, and possibly that was a comparable gesture of dedication for the part of him
that was typically religious. He aimed to be wholly Platonic and
wholly Christian, mingling the two traditions in a way that would
enable each to strengthen the complementary truths of the other.

As I tried to show in *The Nature of Love: Plato to Luther*, medieval
Christianity cannot be understood apart from its Platonic element.
In even the most orthodox thinkers, primarily St. Augustine but also
St. Bernard and St. Thomas, the caritas-synthesis employed Platonistic ideas about eros in its account of man's desire to possess the
perpetual goodness which is God himself. One could argue, therefore, that Ficino's mission had already been accomplished; and

despite the sense of excitement and discovery that pervades his literary output, Ficino himself may have felt that there was nothing revolutionary in his attempt to merge Plato and Christianity. Throughout the Middle Ages Plato had been subordinated to Aristotle, and Ficino reversed their order of importance, but this alone need not have jeopardized the structure of the caritas-synthesis. For centuries the texts of all but two or three of Plato's dialogues were unknown by scholars in the West, and even Petrarch, who cherished the Platonic manuscripts that his library contained, did not know enough Greek to be able to read them. Ficino changed all this by translating the corpus of Plato's writing into Latin and by appending commentaries that opened up domains of scholarship that would not have existed otherwise. I do not think he suspected that anything basic to the traditional views of medieval Christianity would be affected by what he was doing.

If I am right in this surmise, one can only conclude that Ficino failed to understand the impact of his life's work. In seeking to harmonize human and religious concepts of love through a clarified integration of Platonism and Christianity, he introduced changes in the old theology that constitute a reformation within Catholicism almost as fundamental as Luther's reformation from without. Each marks a redirection of doctrinal perspectives as a response to the conflict between religious and human love that existed throughout the Middle Ages. Luther's approach is more extreme than Ficino's because his refusal to believe that man is natively capable of loving either God or other human beings leads him to reject the caritas-synthesis entirely. Having no such intention, Ficino thought that rediscovering Plato would provide a new defense of the medieval doctrine against skeptics, atheists, and heretics. But in the process Ficino introduces so many Platonistic ideas formerly neglected by the fathers of the church that he inevitably alters the traditional dogma. God's love for man and man's love for other human beings as well as for God are reaffirmed as parts of the cosmic order, but they are described in ways that undermine the usual formulations of the Middle Ages. Had he lived three hundred years earlier, Ficino would have been censured and his writings burned. By the fifteenth century, however, the world of ideas had changed so greatly that his innovations not only survived but also flourished among many who considered themselves wholly orthodox.

In addition to translating Plato, Ficino translated Plotinus, and scholars have often thought it was through the eyes of Plotinus that Ficino studied Plato himself. The school of thought that centered about Ficino in the Italian Renaissance is generally called "Neoplatonic" because it contains so much that goes beyond the writings of Plato. It is, in fact, a fifteenth-century version of Hellenistic Neoplatonism, which includes the Neoplatonism of Plotinus. In his attempt to harmonize Plato with Christianity, Ficino resorts to ideas of Plotinus that even a Platonist like St. Augustine would not have found acceptable.

We see the character of Ficino's new direction by remembering that the Christianity that derives from St. Augustine completely subordinates all human loves to the love of God. While trying to remain orthodox in his theology, Ficino, more than any other great philosopher of his age, nevertheless shows the influence of the humanistic developments we have been discussing in this book. In some respects his world view is comparable to that of Aquinas, who also emphasized how all things human and natural could be loved for the sake of God; but in Ficino the hierarchical ordering within these kinds of love becomes less prominent than their interpenetration. In Ficino, as in Aquinas, all love originates in God's love for his creation, particularly man, whose nature impels him to love God as the source of his being and to love everything else that conduces to loving God. For Ficino, however, as opposed to Aquinas, a proper love of things and persons in the world is *itself* a love for God. The Christian goal on earth now becomes the ability to love "God in everything." The effect of this shift in theology, slight as it may seem, was enormous.

The distance between Aquinas and Ficino is most evident in the new importance that the idea of beauty acquires. Beginning with Plato and continuing throughout the eros tradition, the concept of beauty provides a focus to all theorizing about love. Plato identified the Good and the Beautiful, and he believed that the empirical world was a manifestation of both. But beautiful occurrences in the world are generally appreciated through the senses, and it was this allurement that medieval Christians found most threatening. As I have suggested, it was not sensory pleasure in itself they considered evil, but rather its capacity to ensnare human emotions, to create passions that would deflect one from the love of God. This is a concern that Ficino shares with other Christians, and it was especially pronounced in his greatest disciple, Pico della Mirandola, who became a follower of the puritanical Savonarola. But the philosophy of Ficino himself is pervasively optimistic about man's ability not only to enjoy beauty without undermining the love of God but also to find God through a love of beauty. This basic faith, this confidence in the sacramental goodness of beauty wherever it may occur, serves as the philosophical foundation to those creative achievements in Italy during the fifteenth century that are distinctive of the Renaissance. The ancient world was reborn through the discovery of Greek and Roman masterpieces, in literature and philosophy as well as in the visual arts, but more important still, the search for beauty permeated civilized aspirations to a degree that had not occurred since the Hellenistic period.

The work in which Ficino contributed most toward the reintegration of love and beauty was his *Commentary on Plato's Symposium*. It is often referred to as the *De Amore*, a suitable revision of the original title inasmuch as Ficino's commentary is less of a scholarly exegesis than a philosophical treatise based upon interpretations of the various speeches in the Platonic dialogue. Ficino treats all the speeches as equally authoritative, but he takes from each of them only those ideas that he can use for his own conception. The philosophy of the *De Amore* is consequently different from anything one could find in the *Symposium* itself, however one regards Plato's intentions throughout the ambiguities of that work. While continuing the Platonic, or rather Neoplatonic, tradition, the *De Amore* presents a new approach to love more suitable for the world in which Ficino lived.

Plato had defined love as "desire for the perpetual possession of the good [or beautiful]." Ficino begins with this and never deviates from it, but he accentuates the role of beauty as a vital presence suffusing our experience of reality. It is "the splendor of the divine light shining through bodies." Love is therefore an appetite, indeed a craving, for "lo splendore del divino." That is why the passions of lovers cannot be quenched by seeing or touching the body of their beloved. The restlessness of human love results from the fact that lovers experience in each other an emanation of God's own being. Ficino describes this emanation not only as a splendor of visual beauty but also as "a sweet aroma," "a subtle essence," "an indistinguishable flavor" that pervades physical beauty. To respond to what is beautiful in an object is to experience the captivating glow of divinity. In loving anything, one manifests that ardent search for beauty which both explains human nature and reveals its ability to reach God.

This conception of love, mingling aspects of Platonism with a version of Christianity, does not escape the conflict between loving God and loving nature that weighed upon the mentality of the Middle Ages. But in Ficino, as in the Renaissance generally, the conflict is no longer burdensome. It tends to be minimized and even disregarded. In the Renaissance the love of beauty received a dignity, nobility, and social value that has been equalled in very few moments of human civilization. It was an age that reveled in material appearances—the face, the figure, the bodily grace of human beings; the form and color of buildings, statues, paintings, costumes; the physical display and to some extent the inner workings of surrounding nature. Writing for his select Florentine audience, Ficino both expresses and renews their feelings about the rightness of an ardent attachment to all this.

A familiar question looms before us at this point. If one loves the natural world, given Ficino's definition of love, is one loving nature *itself*, material beings as they seduce and delight us, or is one really loving their derivation from God? Ficino's official intention is unmistakable. In defining love as the search for lo splendore del divino, he refers to something greater than nature, something that infuses it from without and lures one to go beyond it. To this extent his doctrine does not greatly differ from the transcendentalism of Plato or the dualism of Augustine and Aquinas. But Ficino's love of nature is more profound than theirs, and one constantly detects his reluctance to give up earthly pleasures for the sake of spiritual values that may be inimical to them. Ficino's philosophy is inclusive:

he is unwilling to deny the goods of this world in order to exalt those of the next. Though they still belong to a hierarchy of importance, each shows forth divinity in its own way.

In his attempt to characterize the Platonism of the Italian Renaissance, Santayana claimed, as we have seen, that "all beauties attract by suggesting the ideal and then fail to satisfy by not fulfilling it." In Ficino, however, as in Cavalcanti, neither of these propositions holds. Ficino would say that all beauties attract because, in being beautiful, they *embody* and do not merely suggest the ideal. Manifesting its shining splendor, they are more than just resemblances. As a result, they satisfy within their own dimension while also leading on to spiritual possibilities beyond themselves. This acceptance of the natural is fundamental in Ficino's philosophy, as it is in Santayana's, even though Santayana misinterprets his kinship to Ficino.

So eager is Ficino to accommodate the good of mundane pleasure that some scholars have called him a "neo-pagan thinker." Emphasizing Ficino's antiasceticism, Edgar Wind credits him with the "transvaluation of values" that recurs throughout Renaissance efforts to direct Christianity towards a love of life. The truth, however, is more complex. For in Ficino one still feels the tension of divergent views: one can find in his writings the justification for disdaining the material world as well as for enjoying it. In one place in the *De Amore* he speaks of two "daemons" that define the extremes within the five classes of love to which human beings have access. One of these daemons he calls "good" because it enables men to recognize and experience divine beauty through the study of philosophy, the practice of justice, and the dedication to religion. The other daemon is "bad" because it furthers the impulse to generate children and is therefore sexual. Having said this, Ficino immediately adds that in reality both daemons are good: "the creation of offspring is considered just as necessary and honorable as the quest after truth." But the fact remains that he has just called the second of his two daemons a "malevolent spirit," and one cannot believe that he sees in sexual love an authentic opportunity to appreciate lo splendore del divino.

Between the two extremes, Ficino delineates three types of love that he calls "passions" rather than daemons, since they are not psychological dispositions but rather emotional experiences developing in time—beginning, increasing, diminishing, and ending in relation to another person. All of these loves originate with sight: for the visual appearance of a body provides both pleasure in itself and a reminder of the universal type that Ficino, like Plato, thinks we are innately equipped to perceive and perpetuate. If we are inclined to the life of contemplation, our response to the beauty of the beloved immediately ascends from the sight of its physical appearance to an intuition of its spiritual origin. This kind of love is closest to the first of the two daemons, and Ficino calls it *amore divino*. The love that is closest to the other daemon belongs to the sensory or "voluptuous" life, transforming the initial experience of sight into a craving to touch the beloved. This kind of love is called *amore bestiale*.

In the center of this classification of the five loves, there is one that mediates between the extremes and that represents Ficino's attempt to resolve the ambiguity in his approach. For equidistant between the highest and the lowest loves, between the holiness of contemplation and the bestiality of the voluptuous or merely generative, he finds what he calls "human love" (*amore umano*). This is the love that people have in their moral and personal relationships with one another. It is an emotional attachment but it would seem to be neither contemplative nor sexual. As I shall suggest later, it comes closest to our concept of friendship, involving social goods of a mutual and beneficial sort. Ficino insists that its physical bond always remains at the level of sight.

In being the midpoint within the classification of love, amore umano expresses that delicate, but possibly unstable balance that one finds in so many paintings of the Italian Renaissance. It is man's condition depicted as a visual experience, one person looking at another (and in general at the spectacle that all existence affords) as if the object for each were an epiphany of wondrous delight. The friends or lovers are poised somewhere between reverence and carnal admiration. Though awestruck by the divine splendor present in so much beauty, they also seem to be musing about sexual opportunities that lurk behind the screen of propriety. All we *see* in such paintings is the human being looking with rapt attention, but the magnificence of these masterpieces by Botticelli, Donatello,

Piero della Francesca, Raphael, Michelangelo, and many others arises from their ambiguous reference to spiritual and physical possibilities embedded in the visual.

In his desire to resolve this kind of ambiguity, Ficino begins with the idea that beauty must be experienced through mind or sight or hearing. The other senses, such as touch, taste, and smell, serve the ends of material survival, but, according to Ficino, they do not acquaint us with the beautiful. This is an aesthetic principle of the greatest consequence in all art theory since the Renaissance. As a doctrine within the philosophy of love, it is crucial because it enables Ficino to eliminate amore bestiale as an acceptable type of human interest. All love begins with the sight of the beloved, but in amore bestiale it degenerates into a craving for tactile pleasures more suitable to animals than to human beings. Since these are the pleasures of sexuality, culminating in the desire for coitus, Ficino is denigrating erotic love even more than Plato had. Plato thought of sexual passion as a stage one goes through in the process of loving the Good. For Ficino, however, it is merely a misuse of one's natural state. At times he denies that amore bestiale is even to be called love at all. It is a "disease," a form of "insanity."

In effect, this means that for Ficino there are really only two kinds of love—amore divino and amore umano. The two types of Venus, celestial and earthly, as in Plato, correspond to these two kinds of love. Amore umano is the highest love that most ordinary people can achieve. It originates with a sense of visual beauty and does not descend to tactile or other nonvisual interests in the beloved; but neither does it rise beyond an empirical acquaintance with its object. In amore divino the lover recognizes that the splendor which is the beauty of his beloved emanates from a spiritual source, ultimately deriving from God himself. Although both loves provide the experience of beauty as a formal principle, only amore divino enables the lover to emancipate himself from the dangers related to immersion in the body. Only then can he behold ideal beauty through the mind, through the intellect and his powers of contemplation.

The humanism of Ficino consists in his refusal to recognize any incompatibility between amore divino and amore umano. He sees the goodness in them both, and that is why he never condemns earthly Venus. Man seeks through her to perpetuate on earth the beauty he has contemplated as the celestial Venus. Provided his desire to generate beauty does not lead him into the bestiality of carnal passion, it is a natural consequence of contemplating the beautiful. Sexual love itself may be an evil for Ficino, but the creating of beautiful children is not. Like the creation of works of art or harmonious social systems, it helps man to express his love of beauty and thus continue God's mission. Moreover, Ficino and his followers minimize the split between a love of spiritual beauty and a desire to generate it on earth by suggesting that the greatest lover is capable of both. Pico uses the image of two-faced Janus to describe "celestial souls" who are able to live in the body as well as in the mind, using both in a way that reveals that each type of Venus is good. Such superior beings "behold the Ideal Beauty in the Intellect to love it perpetually; and inferiour sensible things, not to desire their Beauty, but to communicate this other to them."

In a similar vein, Ficino gives a higher priority to loving a person who is beautiful in body as well as soul than to loving one who is beautiful in body or soul alone. The beauty of the body must be loved for the sake of the divine beauty that radiates through it, as opposed to any material purpose, but even religious love, Ficino insists, is augmented by a spiritual love of the body. To the modern reader, it may be difficult to understand how loving a body spiritually is to be distinguished from loving it materially. The Freudian would maintain that the former is merely a sublimation or aim-inhibited expression of the latter. For a Neoplatonist such as Ficino, however, Plato's distinction between form and matter enables one to demarcate the two elements in every occurrence of physical beauty. Looking at the beautiful face or body of our beloved, we are to see it under the aspect of its formal properties and not its material embodiment. These formal properties are perfections that Ficino, like Plato, considers to be objective in reality. Through them we formulate the concept of mankind, and thus discover what our nature is. We love bodily beauty not because we love the body but because we love its beauty, and that results from the splendor of those abstract entities which combine to give us our idea of humanity. What Ficino calls "the absolute beauty of the human species" is the concatenation of ideal properties that one or another person may approximate in some respect. People love one another as an expression of their yearning for this ideal. The underlying object is not physical; and since mankind was created in the image of God, it leads one toward the divine love that Ficino thinks everyone innately desires.

If we ask Ficino about the terminus of this instinctual craving, we are once more confronted by ambiguities. Ficino maintains both that man wishes to love himself in the beloved and also that true love requires reciprocity. Love being a search for beauty which is the splendor of God, it causes a mere human being to experience the divine presence and thereby to become divine himself. Men become God by means of love, transforming themselves into the essence of his being. For Aquinas and medieval orthodoxy in general, the idea of merging with the highest good in this fashion would certainly have been considered heretical. Ficino presents the idea with little argument and with calm assurance that, of course, everyone would prefer to be a god. Moreover, he thinks that reciprocal love between human beings reveals the nature of deification. For then lover and beloved are mutually merging with the divine beauty as it exists in each other. But in the human relationship the lovers are using one another as means to loving something *beyond* them both, and we may wonder whether this can truly be a reciprocal love between two people. Ficino does nothing to resolve the problem.

In a way that adumbrates nineteenth-century ideas about the kinship of love and death, Ficino treats reciprocity as a condition in which each lover dies in himself and is reborn in the other. He means that they lose their separate identities, sacrifice themselves for one another, submerge their personalities in each other. Since love aspires to deification, each of the lovers is yearning for oneness with the supreme beauty that will thereby destroy their present humanity. But what seems like an impoverishment of the person, the lovers dying in themselves, becomes an enrichment through reciprocity. Though each lover is lost in the other, each also lives in the beloved. By mutually possessing one another, they regain themselves as well as the other and consequently undergo what Ficino calls a resurrection. Indeed he considers it a double resurrection since each of the lovers is reborn with two selves, the beloved's as well as the lover's own self.

We shall later see how these ideas contribute to Romantic philosophy beginning with Kant on married love, but here it is important to remember that the context of Ficino's philosophy is always Platonistic and Christian. Like Plato he thinks of love as a male enterprise. Women are mentioned only when he argues that the need to propagate beauty explains a man's desire to generate beautiful children by a beautiful woman. But the need to propagate beauty presupposes an ability to contemplate beauty in itself, and that Ficino locates in males rather than females. Since only men are capable of contemplating beauty, those who pursue amore divino "naturally love men more than women." He immediately adds that such love is not homosexual. Like Plato in the *Laws*, Ficino condemns sexual activity between men as the worst kind of bestiality. He clearly wishes to limit the reciprocity of love to the masculine friendship that presumably existed in the Platonic Academy he himself established in Florence. Like-minded men would experience mutual affection based upon their ability to appreciate the beauties of mind, person, soul, and body that they find in each other's company. As philosophers, they would realize that the value in their friend pertains to an idea of humanity that appears beautiful to us because it participates in the divine beauty. As Christians, they would know that the beauty of all persons, and in general of all things on earth, not only derives from, but is also an ingredient within, the beauty of God himself.

This conception of friendship that goes by the name of love because the friends are jointly engaged in a mutual attempt to love God will recur even in the Protestant existentialism of Kierkegaard. Though Ficino emphasizes man's search for deification, and therefore belongs to the eros tradition within Christianity, he also tantalizes us with ideas about agapē. He does not state them as single-mindedly as Luther will, but neither does he subsume them within the caritas-synthesis as Aquinas had. Whether or not he should be classified with the pantheists or religious naturalists, as some scholars have suggested in seeing him as a forerunner of Spinoza, his conception of God's presence in the world prepares us for modern philosophies that would surely have astounded him. Commenting upon Diotima's speech to Socrates in the *Symposium*, he presents the rich complexity of his thought in the following passage: "we shall not only love God without limit, as Diotima is depicted as commanding, but God alone. . . . If we love bodies, the Soul, or the Angelic Mind, we do not really love these, but God in them: the shadow of God in bodies, the likeness of God in the Soul, and the Image of God in the Angelic Mind. So in the present we shall love God in everything, so that in the future we may love everything in God, for so we set out. . . . Joined then, by love, to our own Idea, we shall become whole men . . . and seem, in loving God, to have loved ourselves."

These words may be taken to sum up Ficino's entire philosophy of love. They are words that reverberate throughout the Renaissance, in England and France as well as Italy.

Since I am not writing a history of Neoplatonism, I shall not attempt to trace Ficino's influence. For our purposes it will suffice to show how his followers altered details of his philosophy, and how his realist opponents sought to discredit it. Among his immediate disciples, it was probably Pico della Mirandola who modified the master's doctrine most significantly. In thinking of the human soul as having infinite value, worthy of its aspirations toward divinity, Ficino never doubts that its origin as well as its goal must be God himself. When he describes the completion of man's love, however, he denies that it involves a *total* merging with divinity. If man's destiny is to become godlike, which is to say, one with God, this nevertheless could not mean that man would lose his identity or dissolve into the divine essence. For Pico, all such reasoning was inadequate, and he sees Ficino as guilty of "utter confusion."

Assuming the attitude of radical mystics in the Middle Ages and earlier, Pico attacks Ficino for pretending that the love of God could enable man to establish friendship with him. For that would imply an equality which cannot exist between finite man and infinite divinity. This being impossible, neither could there be reciprocity of love between the soul and God or anything less than absolute merging once love has been consummated. On the contrary, Pico insisted, the goal of man's love for God was total submission, loss of oneself, destruction of all separateness. Ficino thought that man and God could ideally establish a friendship between them that would serve as a model for friendship among human beings, which itself involves the participation of God. As a "third friend," the divine presence would link two human beings to one another. Ficino's philosophy of love being based upon this conception, Pico threatened the entire structure by denying the very possibility of friendship with God.

In seeing self-annihilation as love's fulfillment, Pico was duplicating the kind of heretical doctrine that Abelard had defended hundreds of years earlier in his controversies with St. Bernard. Pico too was censored by the church, but this did not greatly hamper his theorizing. When Giordano Bruno carried Pico's ideas somewhat further, developing Neoplatonism into a doctrine about the merging of finite and infinite not only at the height of love but throughout all being, he was burned at the stake. Though Bruno sought to prove that God's love pervaded everything, which Christians had always maintained, his philosophy was more radical in its pantheism than anything Pico or the other Florentine followers of Ficino envisaged. Considered much less threatening to the church, their ideas were not greatly suppressed.

By denying that man and God could be friends, Pico was counteracting that much of Ficino which emphasizes the goodness in characteristically human virtues. In a similar vein, Pico's ideas about love in general subordinate "vulgar Venus" to "celestial Venus" more thoroughly than Ficino's had. In his commentary on Benivieni's *Canzone d'Amore*, Pico articulates the Neoplatonic ladder of love which reveals "how from sensuous beauty one rises by ordered steps to intelligible beauty," but he thinks the lower reaches can be valuable only as a reflection of celestial Venus. Where Ficino had argued that human love depends upon visual pleasures afforded by the sight of beauty in material objects, Pico insists upon the need to move beyond this stage as quickly as possible since beauty itself could only be spiritual and nonmaterial. As a result, Pico provides us with a less fully developed conception of noncelestial love, and he shows much less concern for material beauty than is to be found in Ficino's philosophy (or Plato's).

Despite this quasi-ascetic element, however, the Neoplatonism of Pico also includes ideas about the grandeur and the greatness of man that go beyond anything Ficino said. Following what he could have discovered in Dante or St. Augustine, Ficino had treated the human soul as a kind of center or pivot within the universe, a link between the world of spirit and the world of matter. Located as he was, man could move in one direction or the other; he belonged to both worlds, and his destiny depended upon his free will, which enabled him to choose one or the other as the object of his love. All this is repeated in Pico but now extended in ways that became particularly important for thinkers in the Renaissance. In his *Oration on the Dignity of Man* (as it came to be called), Pico not only describes man's supreme capacity to move up or down but also he portrays him as heroically separate from both worlds. Man's condition results entirely from his own choice; it is not determined by any necessary function or prior limitation. Man has no fixed and definite place within the cosmic hierarchy. He stands outside, in glorious independence, as if, though Pico does not say this, he were to the natural world what God is to everything in general.

Pico encloses these ideas about the nobility of man in a myth of creation. Having formed heaven and earth and filled them with diverse creatures, God decided to make a being that could appreciate his stupendous achievement, someone who would love its beauty and sense its awe-inspiring immensity. But creation having been virtually finished, God found no place within the different orders of being, no category or function that would distinguish the offspring he now had in mind. He therefore created man as one who would love and admire his work but would do so without any determinate nature of his own. Pico then quotes God as addressing Adam in the following manner:

> "Neither a fixed abode nor a form that is thine alone nor any function peculiar to thyself have we given thee. . . . the Nature of all other things is limited and constrained within

the bounds of laws prescribed by Us. Thou, constrained by no limits, in accordance with thine own free will, in whose hand We have placed thee, shalt ordain for thyself the limits of thy nature. . . . We have made thee neither of heaven nor of earth, neither mortal nor immortal, so that with freedom of choice and with honor, as though the maker and molder of thyself, thou mayest fashion thyself in whatever shape thou shalt prefer. Thou shalt have the power to degenerate into the lower forms of life, which are brutish. Thou shalt have the power, out of thy soul's judgment, to be reborn into the higher forms, which are divine."

Pico goes on to extol the goodness of God in having generously afforded man so felicitous a nature. Animals bring with them from the womb all that they will ever have or be, and spiritual beings have their perfections within them by their very essense. Only man is born with the seeds of all ways of life, and only he can mature into whatever he chooses to cultivate. There is a typically Renaissance flourish in Pico's words when he says, "We can become what we will." It is immediately followed, however, by moralistic cautioning about the dangers this entails: unless we are careful, we can degenerate into "wild animals and senseless beasts." We are finally admonished to "let a certain holy ambition invade our souls, so that, not content with the mediocre, we shall pant after the highest and (since we may if we wish) toil with all our strength to obtain it."

In his *Oration* Pico contents himself with this note of warning, but elsewhere in his writings we find that pessimism about profane love and bodily beauty which distinguishes him from the more serene and optimistic Ficino. Michelangelo, who grew up in the company of both philosophers and remained a Neoplatonist throughout his life, shows the influence of Pico more than of Ficino. Walter Pater characterized Michelangelo's entire productivity as an "effort to tranquillize and sweeten life by idealizing its vehement sentiments." There is much truth in this, particularly if we realize that central among his vehement sentiments was Michelangelo's agonized desire to live in the body as well as in the spirit while directing his ultimate love toward the latter only. From Ficino he could have learned that through idealization one sweetens and tranquillizes the love of matter and thereby prevents amore umano from turning into amore bestiale. But from Pico, who undoubtedly spoke to Michelangelo's experience as a troubled homosexual, he must have derived reinforcement for his constant, though despairing, struggle against physical impulses that frequently subjugated his idealistic aspirations. The power, the dynamism, the striving to liberate spirit from recalcitrant stone or paint or words—in short, the movement, life, and sense of creativity that distinguishes everything Michelangelo did—expresses the Neoplatonic ambivalence as an endless inward combat. Where others might have been satisfied to treat the body as a fortunate recipient of a purified beauty beyond itself, or else as a burden one casts aside in rising to greater glories, Michelangelo retains both of these alternatives, places them in sharpest conflict with one another, and depicts the unremitting grief that results from an inability to choose between them.

In her book *Neoplatonism of the Italian Renaissance*, Nesca Robb emphasizes the extent to which Michelangelo's genius issues from these tensions within himself: "His passion is rooted in an eternal paradox. Visible things must be loved since they alone can recall the vision of pure beauty, but to see that vision and try to reveal it to men is to know that matter is forever at enmity with the spirit." As he got older, Michelangelo increasingly asserted—in his poetry as well as in his visual art—the fervor of his dedication to pure spirit alone. Throughout his life, however, he sought to celebrate the beauty of the human body. His sonnets speak of "the soul imprisoned in her house of clay" but also they tell us that God refuses to show himself "more clearly than in human form sublime, /which, since they image Him, alone I love."

When he was well past sixty, Michelangelo wrote a series of love poems to Vittoria Colonna, a chaste and religious widow renowned for her intellectual powers. Since neither Ficino nor Pico have much to say about the love of women, some scholars see Michelangelo's writings as a new development in Florentine Neoplatonism. Once we examine the poetry, however, it becomes clear that Michelangelo is resorting to conventional attitudes of Dante and Petrarch. Like other Petrarchists of the age, he loads his lines with abstract conceits that make them seem bloodless and impersonal, though always driven by that rough energy which is typically his own. As in Dante, the lady he adores is an emanation of the spiritual realm for which he yearns; she is part of his attempt to free himself from mortal coils. But unlike his more refined predecessors, Michelangelo is too honest to hide the traces of a deeper misogyny that often appears in his work. In his sculpture he frequently used male models for female figures, with the result that they tend to look grotesquely hard and unfeminine. Remarks he made to friends would seem to indicate that female flesh was not a source of allurement to him at any time of life; and there is no evidence of his ever falling in love with a woman. It is therefore relevant to juxtapose his spiritual and elevated poems to Vittoria Colonna with a drawing of her that many experts attribute to Michelangelo. It shows the beloved as an old hag, her sagging breasts hideously exposed, Michelangelo portrayed as staring at her beneath a boar's head in which he is coiffed. Between them in the sketch there appears the "fica" gesture, thumb between fingers, as a vulgar symbol of brutal coitus. The violence of these contrasting perspectives—the strident opposition between earthly and heavenly beauty, human and celestial love, bestiality and pure spirit—must make us wonder about Michelangelo's erotic disposition. It seems unlikely that the love of woman could have belonged to his primary inspiration.

In this regard, as in so many others, Leonardo da Vinci shows us another side of the Renaissance. A little older than Michelangelo, a fellow Florentine and also homosexual, he too leaves behind drawings of grotesque females, but they are no more hideous (or numerous) than the grotesque males he drew. Moreover, Leonardo's paintings often depict the female figure and personality in delicate, mysterious nuances that bespeak a reverence for what distinguishes women from men. The difference between Leonardo and Michelangelo is evident in their respective portrayals of Leda and the Swan. Michelangelo depicts the brutality of rape, the twisted torso of the hapless woman indicating that the strange creature between her legs may be a god but to her it is a hostile force imposing itself for purposes she can neither understand nor enjoy. In Leonardo's painting, we see the swan as the bringer of glad tidings, as the messenger and joyous symbol of love—whether in the service of the

Holy Ghost or of beneficent nature, as in those medieval poems about birds that I discussed in earlier chapters. Leda's gestures are now relaxed and wholesomely receptive, her sexual intercourse serving as a welcome opportunity for diverse kinds of consummation.

In his scientific work, Leonardo investigates the details of sexuality with an interest and fascination that only rarely seems to be prurient. He claimed to be an opponent of Neoplatonism, and he tried to cultivate in himself so great a love of nature that everything natural would yield its inherent beauty. In his treatise on painting, he encourages young artists to study things in the world that are easily overlooked because custom has taught us to consider them ugly: e.g., cracks in the plaster of walls or puddles in the street. Properly observed, and accepted for what they are by a love that all nature merits, they would finally disclose their own type of beauty.

Despite his official denial, one might see in Leonardo's attitude an influence of Neoplatonism at its more pantheistic pole. But even so, his thinking reaches beyond the ideas that Neoplatonism may have brought to it. When he talks about love, he seems quite content to take our sensory experience as the model for explication. "The lover is moved by the beloved object as the senses are by the sensible object and they unite and become one and the same thing." In general, one finds in Leonardo so plastic and comfortable an appreciation of the material world that the need to transcend it, which characterizes the Neoplatonists, no longer has much meaning for him. The greatest desire of Michelangelo was, as he says in one of his sonnets, "Ascender vivo fra gli spiriti eletti"—to soar alive among the chosen spirits. This is the upward finger of Plato as he converses with Aristotle in Raphael's painting of *The School of Athens*. In Leonardo one intuits everywhere the gesture that Aristotle makes, his hand open, receptive, horizonal, as if to symbolize the vast and ever-increasing possibilities in the natural world around us.

Though Michelangelo illustrates how the inherent violence within the polar opposites of Neoplatonic love can generate the greatest art in the Renaissance, we must turn elsewhere for more successful efforts at harmonization. Lorenzo de' Medici does not approximate the genius of Michelangelo, unless one counts his ability to rule Florentines, but his poetry shows how Ficino's teachings could be molded for naturalistic as well as religious purposes. Lorenzo's grandfather Cosimo had first established the Platonic Academy of Ficino, and Lorenzo in his youth was as much immersed in its Neoplatonism as was Michelangelo. But as he matured, he obviously learned that philosophical doctrines had to be altered when they no longer satisfied human needs. Critics have often condemned Lorenzo for being insincere in his espousal of Neoplatonism, and basically irreligious despite the many religious poems he wrote. He is even seen as a "sensualist" using whatever ploy was needed to mask his real interests. However these disputes are resolved, there is no doubt that Lorenzo was extremely versatile. His poetic imagination ranged through the gamut of everything to be learned from Dante, Petrarch, Cavalcanti, as well as from the newer Italian poets who spoke of ideal beauty. When he wrote carnival songs, he found no difficulty in using the language of peasants, and he saw no point in pretending that their love of beauty was particularly idealistic. When he wrote religious poetry, he made little effort to deviate from orthodox conventions that still formed the traditional backbone of the state.

Since Neoplatonism was in the air, a kind of lingua franca for the more cultivated of his countrymen, Lorenzo naturally employs it in his personal love poetry. The *Symposium*'s ladder of love intrigues him, but he is capable of orienting it in directions that Pico would have found scandalous. For Lorenzo it could lead not only from sight to spiritual attainment but also from sight to tactile pleasures. Where other Neoplatonists first encountered beauty in the mind or imagination and then rose to contemplate its perfection in the realm of spirit, Lorenzo frequently ends his quest with the beauty of a particular and very erotic woman. In one sequence his initial inspiration is the supremely beautiful Simonetta, who has died and left the poet with the ideal of her beauty which he now seeks to rediscover in some living lady whose qualities can emulate hers. Lorenzo often talks in the fashion of Platonistic philosophy; but he always modifies it to suit his own experience. His beautiful beloved is not an abstraction; she is not a symbol or even an emanation from the divine like Dante's Beatrice. She is instead a real woman he meets at a ball and woos as a worthy reminder of the departed Simonetta. This idea of a new love renewing one's access to an idealized person now dead will recur in the Romantic period, in Poe as well as Goethe's Werther. The difference is that Lorenzo encases it within an attitude that strives for explicit enjoyment rather than nostalgia.

In his commentary on some of his sonnets, Lorenzo reveals that he knew perfectly well what he was doing. While recognizing that sexual love may not be what Plato advocates, he nevertheless defends it because "it contains in itself so many goods and avoids so many evils that according to the common usage of human life it occupies the place of good." This is especially so, Lorenzo continues, when the two conditions for true love are satisfied: "First, that one love only one object; second, that this object be loved always."

For Lorenzo sexual love is merely what is "natural," and therefore he fails to see how it could be worthy of blame. Being "l'appetito di bellezza"—the appetite for beauty—it manifests a desire to unite with a beautiful object. Since that conduces to the propagation of the species, Lorenzo insists that "nothing is more natural." He concludes by describing love in terms reminiscent of the courtly traditions of the Middle Ages. It is a true sign of "gentilezza," nobility, and it leads to a refinement in human relations. Its goal is happiness; but Lorenzo realizes that the lover's lot is more often filled with misery. Throughout his poetry there lingers a melancholy aura and a pessimism about the attainment of human aspirations, not unlike the mood in Cavalcanti. Like the earlier poet, Lorenzo may have felt the oppressiveness of religious hostility toward sexual love; and he too expresses the poignancy of living in the moment, grasping for pleasures one is created to enjoy and yet doomed to savor only briefly. It was Pater who noticed, if not first at least with the greatest understanding, the Renaissance sensitivity to the sadness of life. In people less vibrant with the new and joyful hope that flourished in the fifteenth century, this capacity for melancholy may not have been as acute. Lorenzo, so thoroughly a man of his times, voices this facet of the Renaissance in lines that are probably his best known nowadays:

Quant'è bella giovinezza
Che si fugge tuttavia!
Chi vuol esser lieto, sia:
Di doman non c'è certezza.

(How beautiful is youth,
Which flees forevermore.
Let him who will, be happy!
Tomorrow nothing's sure.)

The worldliness in Lorenzo's modifications of Platonistic teachings is matched by Castiglione's *Book of the Courtier*. This handbook and guide to the perfect gentleman of the early sixteenth century exerted enormous influence upon social manners throughout Europe. Its philosophical content has usually been denigrated as a mere dilution of ideas drawn from Ficino and his Neoplatonic followers. A recent scholar remarks: "It is obvious . . . that from the doctrinal standpoint Castiglione offered nothing that had not already been said by Ficino, his primary source, and by Bembo." This, however, misreads and undervalues Castiglione's achievement: it neglects the originality of the synthesis he proposes throughout his work. We may well agree that Castiglione's account of the six-stage ladder of love in Plato's *Symposium* comes mainly from Ficino's translation, and also that the presentation is clothed in the ecstatic style of Pietro Bembo—a Neoplatonic poet, philosopher, and cardinal of the church whom Castiglione introduces as a character in his book along with other prominent Italians. Bembo's description of a final merging with an abstract beauty which is God appears, at the very end of *The Courtier*, as a terminating statement of irreproachable truth. But if we study Castiglione's book in its entirety, it soon becomes evident that Bembo's authoritative voice is not the only one we are expected to take seriously. The moral doctrine in Castiglione contains much that Bembo does not say. Castiglione's originality lies in the artfulness with which he fits

Bembo and Ficino into a philosophical vision quite different from their own.

To see this, we need to remember that *The Courtier* consists of dialogues or conversations among the elegant aristocrats in the court of Urbino. Their discussion deals with the attributes that would go to make up a "perfect courtier," in other words, what in their stratum of life would be an ideal man. One of the four books deals with the manners, the humor, and in general the social virtue needed to be a good courtier in that society; another book considers what the "perfect lady," the counterpart of the ideal gentleman, would have to be. Of particular interest to us in the twentieth century is the open and unrestrained way in which the quality of women is defended—by gentlemen in the court as well as by the ladies. While those who consider women to be weaker in intellect and ability to control their passions are given ample opportunity to express this point of view, we are left with the definite impression not only that women are capable of symbolizing ethereal beauties from another world but also that they can attain a moral stature in this world equal to the male's.

This way of thinking about women Castiglione could not have found in Ficino or Bembo. And in depicting how love between men and women contributes to an ideal life at court, Castiglione takes us far beyond Ficino's academy of friendly men-philosophers. In *Gli Asolani*, Bembo had written an imitation of Plato's *Symposium* in which women take the place of the handsome youths whose beauty was designed to lead the true lover toward his transcendental goal. But in Castiglione we find something more—an integrated society of cultured men and women speculating about models of perfection who belong to either sex. In this enlightened community the ladies who elicit and reward love have an active role more extensive than the ones that Platonic philosophy ordinarily permitted them.

The goal of love, as Bembo portrays it in his speech, is not matrimony; Castiglione's final conception of the courtier in love includes nothing about marriage. The ideal gentleman uses his love for a lady as a stepping-stone to the higher calling of metaphysics and religion. But what is most crucial here is the fact that Castiglione presents this as a portrait of the courtier in his maturity and even old age. The question being discussed is whether he should hope for love of any sort in view of his inability to experience it as he might have in earlier years. The relationship between a courtier and a lady when each of them is young follows quite a different pattern. The earlier passages dealing with such matters often resemble the dialogues in Andreas Capellanus. Indeed, the doctrine that generally emerges from these parts of *The Courtier* is very similar to medieval courtly love, but now revised to accentuate the importance of marriage as a suitable outcome. If the court lady is married to a husband who does not love her, she is advised to reciprocate the feelings of someone who does, although a fear of scandal or dishonor requires her to avoid sexual consummation. If the woman is unmarried, she is encouraged to direct her love toward someone she will be able to marry. Castiglione makes none of Andreas' attempts to distinguish courtly love from married love, but like him he recommends courtliness in love as that which ennobles men and women, leading them to social and moral improvement.

So strong is this humanistic, and one might say anti-platonistic, theme in Castiglione's writing that even Bembo's moralizing discourse manages to include an apology for "sensual love" among the young. The elderly courtier will be able to enjoy love inasmuch as he can still seek perfection in the beauty of a woman's face, but Bembo remarks that young people are too greatly enmeshed in their libidinal needs for them to be satisfied in this fashion. Human frailty being what it is, sensual love in the young "deserves to be excused, and in some sense is perhaps permitted . . . provided that in such love they show gentleness, courtesy, and worth and the other noble qualities."

Bembo does go to considerable lengths to warn young people about the afflictions and unhappiness, even unto the longing for death, that all sexual love creates by virtue of its impurity; he extols as virtually "divine" those who control their appetites; and he insists that persons who have reached the age of maturity can truly love only by ascending the ladder that enables them to rise above sexuality. All this we could have expected from a Neoplatonist of the Renaissance. But in recognizing that the lowest rung, the level of fully savored sense experience, is one on which young men and women may linger without being particularly blameworthy, Bembo-Castiglione sounds more like Plato in the *Phaedrus* or the *Symposium* than Ficino in his Christianized revision of Platonism.

On the other hand, one always feels that in Castiglione civilization subjugates biology. The refined ladies and gentlemen conversing in the court of Urbino cultivate a rarified and somewhat artificial manner quite remote from either life in nature or the more naturalistic side of Plato's thinking. They illustrate what is nowadays called "Platonic love." This term (*amore platonico*) was first used by Ficino, offhandedly in a letter to one of his friends, to signify his own Neoplatonic conception. Since the Renaissance it has often connoted a bloodless, effete relationship vaguely based upon courtesy and cool friendship that has little in common with Platonic philosophy. *Amore platonico* easily merged with the abstract conceits of seventeenth-century love poetry, what the English poet Suckling referred to as "this new religion of love," and it became institutionalized in polite but sometimes vacuous practices at various courts: precious use of language that had no rapport with the behavior of love, and even the role of "cicisbeo" or humble escort by which men could show their devotion to ladies they did not dare (or did not wish) to approach more intimately. It is the kind of love that Stendhal calls, with a certain amount of derision, "l'amour goût," usually translated as "mannered" or "sympathy" love, a device by which "good taste" displaces normal heterosexual passion.

This aerated approach to love is typified by the famous remarks about kisses that Castiglione puts into Bembo's speech. Having argued that rational or spiritual love is more conducive to happiness than love that involves the senses, Bembo nevertheless admits that sometimes the same thing—a kiss, for instance—may be acceptable in one context even though it is forbidden in the other. Where the love between a man and woman is nonsexual, a kiss serves as a unifying of souls. It enables the lovers to "pour themselves each into the other's body by turn and mingle so together that each of them has two souls; and a single soul, composed thus of these two, rules as it were over two bodies."

The modern reader may find this idea contrived and even bogus, and there were those in the Renaissance who would have agreed.

For while similar notions reappear in many Neoplatonic treatises, some of which are impressive philosophical works such as Leone Ebreo's *Dialogues on Love,* realist critics refused to interpret lovers' kisses in so idealistic a fashion. As we shall presently see, John Donne delights in the image of intermingling souls which Castiglione and Bembo present him with, but still he sides with those who denied that even the noblest of lovers kiss in a way that eliminates the body or defeats its natural pleasures.

Doubts about the authenticity of the love that Castiglione describes were not uncommon in the Renaissance. They were awakened not only by a refusal to accept Neoplatonic premises, but also by suspicion that systematic self-delusion was being encouraged. In his speech Bembo says of the amorous courtier that "by the force of his own imagination" he will make his beloved's beauty "much more beautiful than in reality it is." Comparable statements can be found in Ficino's *Commentary* and elsewhere in the Neoplatonic literature. In all these sources we are left with the impression that love is a creative means of subsuming reality within the imagination, enhancing beauty rather than merely discovering it in another person. To this extent the Renaissance doctrine differs significantly from its original Platonism. To this extent, too, it anticipates Stendhal's ideas about crystallization and even the concept of bestowal as I have analyzed it. But Bembo's remark may also be interpreted as an admission that the love he is describing falsifies reality, augments it in the way that lies and seductive untruths of polished courtiers might.

The traits of character that Castiglione finds ideal in his lovers are "sprezzatura" and "una certa mediocrità." The former is nonchalance, grace, kindly disdain; the latter is a charming balance or even-tempered equanimity that was particularly prized in women. There has always been something in the Italian spirit that both elicits and admires these characteristics, but critics like Machiavelli systematically argued that sound principles of conduct cannot be constructed upon such ideals. In *The Prince*, Machiavelli insists that he writes about how men live, not how one might imagine they ought to, and that he does so because acting in accordance with elevated standards inevitably leads to catastrophe in the real world. Though Machiavelli barely discusses the nature of love, his play *La Mandragola*—generally recognized to be the greatest comic drama of the Renaissance—deals with human intimacy in the same deflationary manner. His protagonist Callimaco sings about his love in words that seem idealistic, but his motivation is shown to be mainly sexual. Eager to commit adultery with a virtuous wife who eventually acquiesces with no regrets, Callimaco reasons like Aucassin when he says that the worst to fear from such behavior is "that you'll die and go to Hell. But how many others have died! And in Hell how many worthy men there are." If only he can retain his erotic prize, Callimaco claims that he will be "more blissful than the blessed, happier than the saints above." Accepting him as her rightful husband, the lady uses the same words that Dante had addressed to Vergil: "my lord, my master, and my guide." The entire idealist tradition—Christian as well as Neoplatonic—is thus reviled as a massive distortion of how lovers really behave, and of how they have to, the world being what it is.

Machiavelli's realism was a response to ideas prevalent in his own period, but a similar reaction had occurred in the writings of Boccaccio almost 150 years earlier. Despite his reverence for Dante, Boccaccio treated sexual love as a human enterprise based upon laws of biology. Compared to Shakespeare's or even Chaucer's version of the Troilus and Cressida story, Boccaccio's may seem courtly and polite, but more often he considers love as a sexual excursion to be governed by ethical principles needed for the maximization of pleasure. In the *Decameron*, the cardinal sins are those of repressiveness, cruelty, or the selling of love for money. Sex is accepted as a natural appetite whose pleasurable goodness can and should be enjoyed by women as well as men, equally, unashamedly.

Later in life, possibly under the influence of the religiosity that prevailed in Florence after the black plague, Boccaccio rejected his earlier ideas about sexual love. He even called Dante's adoration of Beatrice a "violent and insufferable passion." But despite these changes in the soul of Boccaccio, he generally portrays the human condition not as a progress up Plato's ladder but rather as a series of experiments, sometimes radically opposed to one another, in learning how to cope with the vicissitudes of erotic pleasure. And though it would be misleading to identify Boccaccio with the moral in any one of his works, the *Amorosa Visione* stands out in particular as an expression of naturalistic faith that neither Dante nor Petrarch nor any of their admirers in the Renaissance would have found commendable. In that book the amorous vision shows sex to be the deity in life. Boccaccio's god of love is the fact of sexual impulse alone, civilized and possibly refined, though often crude or vulgar, which he worships even at moments when he strenuously renounces it.

In the fifteenth and sixteenth centuries, the hedonism of Boccaccio was digested by thinkers such as Lorenzo Valla and Mario Equicola. Valla harmonizes Epicurean love of pleasure with Christianity and ends up repudiating the orthodox emphasis upon asceticism, celibacy, and virginity. If five senses give so much pleasure to human beings, how much better would people be if they had fifty and could enjoy them fully! And since everything nature has created is "holy and laudable," Valla ranks courtesans and prostitutes as morally superior to women who become nuns or remain virgins and thereby deny their natural inclinations. As for the beautiful, Valla concludes that even the vision of heaven can hardly exceed the beauty to be found in a woman's face. In his book about the nature of love, which was read as a kind of encyclopedia on the subject, Equicola carries the message further. With Neoplatonists in mind, he ridicules any conception of love that does not give the body its proper importance:

> There are people who suffer from a new kind of madness. They seek to ignore the body's beauty, and to be kindled only by spiritual beauty, to be satisfied by sight and hearing alone, forgetting that human desire is fulfilled only when the mind has nothing more to desire, when it is totally satisfied. . . . To love truly is to love body and soul together, necessarily to love vigorously both the one and the other; and I affirm that in such love one may not be separated from the other. The lover seeks both sensual enjoyment, and to be loved in return. Therefore the lover wants two things:

from his lady's soul, love; and from her body, the fruit of love. . . .

The conclusion is obvious. As a follower of Equicola states: "he is blind to love who does not care for sex but as though he were a pure intelligence, seeks to satisfy his mind alone." Equicola justifies his concern for "the great friendship and union" between body and soul by citing as his authority not Plato or Plotinus but Aristotle. For the Aristotelians of Northern Italy, whose influence increased throughout the sixteenth century, it was axiomatic that "love is of soul and body, and the operations of the soul depend on the body."

In the essays of Montaigne, the realist response to the Neoplatonism of the Renaissance receives its strongest formulation. Though Montaigne's ideas vary considerably throughout his life, he consistently attacks the idealism of Platonists such as Ficino and Pico. In his "Apology for Raymond Sebond," he argues that man is no better than the animals. Not only is human nature lodged at the lower reaches of the universe, man being one among other animals that walk rather than fly or swim, but also human beings manifest their inferiority through the vain assumption that they can equal God, rise to heaven, or discover divine attributes in themselves. "We are neither above nor below the rest," Montaigne asserts; those who maintain that man can raise himself merely lead him to the abyss. As if with Pico in mind, Montaigne says about idealists: "They want to get out of themselves and escape from the man. That is madness: instead of changing into angels, they change into beasts." The arrogance and vanity of self-glorifying imagination is the moral failing that Montaigne exposes at every turn. It deludes human beings into believing that they stand outside the limits of nature; and it fools them into thinking that spiritual perfection is something they need only choose in order for it to become a reality. Above all, imagination misrepresents the nature of love.

In a later chapter I shall return to Montaigne's ideas about marriage, but here we may consider what he says about friendship and sexual love. They are for him largely unrelated to one another, and of the two, only the former is described as an unalloyed good. Though Montaigne approves of Cicero's suggestion that "love is the attempt to form a friendship inspired by beauty," he does not take it to mean that men are likely to become friends with women whose beauty they appreciate nor even with other men if the beauty is bodily or external. Like Ficino and Pico, Montaigne wishes to extol masculine friendship as intimacy that unites people in ways that are not at all physical. It is a union that Montaigne describes in the language of mystical merging—"our souls mingle and blend with each other so completely that they efface the seam that joined them, and cannot find it again"—and he appears to become speechless when he tries to explain the love that bound him to his great friend Etienne de la Boétie. All he can say is: "Because it was he, because it was I."

In contrast to this ineffable state of brotherly affection, sexual love is for Montaigne a natural phenomenon that belongs to a wholly separate category. As against Plato, Aristotle, Ficino, Bembo, Leone Ebreo, and Equicola—all of whom he mentions—Montaigne insists that "love is nothing else but thirst for sexual enjoyment in a desired object, and Venus nothing else but the pleasure of discharging our vessels." He recommends sexual love for reasons that establish him as possibly the first modern man. For he sees it as the avenue to *health*, and for Montaigne that seems to be sufficient justification for this problematic condition. In general, Montaigne claims that previous thinkers have neglected the importance, to our souls as well as our bodies, of health itself—what he calls "ebullient, vigorous, full, lazy health, such as in the past my green years and security supplied me with now and then . . . vivid, bright flashes beyond our natural capacity, and some of the lustiest, if not the most extravagant, enthusiasms."

We have long since been prepared for Montaigne's doubts about the "extravagant," for that is what he condemns as fanciful vanity that causes men to reach erroneously beyond their grasp. But what is equally interesting is his reference to the "lustiest" enthusiasms. The wording makes Montaigne sound like a staunch advocate of sexual passion. As a matter of fact, however, his attitude is much more circumspect. When he discusses the pleasures of sexual love, he usually prefers those that belong to the "lazy" rather than to the vigorous or ebullient. He boasts that no man has been "more impertinently genital in his approaches" than he himself; and yet he admits that even in his youth he never let himself go, he never forgot himself, "entirely." In one place he says of sexual intercourse that "the whole movement of the world resolves itself into and leads to this coupling . . . it is a center to which all things look"; but elsewhere he remarks that Venus herself must have introduced obstacles and impediments to lovemaking since she best realized "how insipid a pleasure it is unless it is given value by imagination and a high cost."

What one may conclude from these ambivalent statements is either that they were written at a time of life when Montaigne's sexual drives had lost their earlier urgency, or else that his temperament was predominantly sensuous and playful rather than strongly libidinal. The evidence indicates that both alternatives are correct. In writing about sex, Montaigne freely admits to problems of impotence and a predilection in his later years to observe the phenomenon of love as it occurs in other, younger persons rather than an eagerness to compete with them. At the same time, he constantly muses about the importance of learning how to prolong the pleasures of sex, to turn sexual occasions into delectable feasts at which one slowly samples every conceivable delight instead of gulping down whatever comes to hand. He frequently quotes from Ovid, whom he resembles in his attitude toward women. In the essays they are always "the other," as if Montaigne could not imagine that any woman would read these confessions written for men like himself. He generally sees the female as the creature that flees, and thereby stimulates masculine appetites—"their role is to suffer, obey, consent." But at times he recognizes that love is "a relationship that needs mutuality and reciprocity."

When Ovid spoke in this fashion, he was mainly articulating the need for a responsive partner to play with, although his humanitarian desire to maximize pleasure for women as well as men need not be denied. In Montaigne the same is also true, but now the Ovidian message occurs within a context that seems wiser or, at least, more insightful. Except for upbringing, Montaigne insists, males and females are not very different. In their sexual animosities, they easily accuse one another; but they are motivated by similar laws of nature. To the extent that men or women strive for absurd spirituality in their love for each other, they violate their humanity and suffer the consequences. If, however, they treat sexual love as a civilized means of satisfying the body's needs without afflicting the soul unduly, they can avoid the sorrows of passion and may even enjoy the well-being that comes from healthy-mindedness.

Montaigne's philosophy of love completes the reaction against Neoplatonic idealism. But it is not a stable or wholly coherent conception within itself. While encouraging man to accept his place among the animals with intelligence and goodwill, Montaigne fails to show us how lustiness can be rendered acceptable without destroying the primordial power that nature normally vests in it. The difficulties in his approach are revealed when Montaigne tells us that "Love is sprightly, lively, and gay agitation; I was neither troubled nor afflicted by it, but I was heated and moreover made thirsty by it. A man should stop there; it is hurtful only to fools."

But, as Shakespeare's Puck would say, albeit cynically: "What fools these mortals be!"

Thus far in this chapter I have been describing the career of Neoplatonic love in the Renaissance in terms of its governing ambiguity: things and persons in the world are to be loved only for the sake of a spiritual beauty that transcends them, and yet the beautiful cannot be appreciated unless we love its manifestations in matter. Opposing philosophers, such as Pico and Montaigne, gravitate within the same field of force. If we feel that their individual contributions are somewhat unsatisfying, it is because they fail to provide an adequate synthesis of the extremes that define the Renaissance ambivalence. Some scholars have claimed that Leone Ebreo or even Mario Equicola succeeded in this attempt, one from a Platonic, the other from an Aristotelian, point of view. But though these, like other thinkers of the sixteenth century, systematically sought a "coincidentia oppositorum" (reconciling of opposites) that unified everything in the cosmos, the most exciting effort toward synthesis occurs in the poetry of John Donne.

Writing in the last decade of the sixteenth century and then into the beginnings of the seventeenth, starting as a Catholic and ending as an Anglican prelate, in his youth an adventuresome Don Juan and in his maturity a devoted husband, Donne was singularly equipped to appreciate the contrasting attitudes toward love. In the revaluations that his work has undergone in the twentieth century, Donne is sometimes ranked as a philosophical poet of the first order and sometimes as little more than a thieving magpie. We need not try to adjudicate this dispute. Certainly there is no divine comedy to be extracted from Donne's writings; but his intellectual authenticity does not suffer as a result. With his usual insight, Dr. Johnson was right when he suggested that wit in the metaphysical poets, of whom Donne is the greatest, consists in "a kind of *discordia concors*; a combination of dissimilar images, or discovery of occult resemblances in things apparently unlike." But with an equally characteristic obtuseness, motivated one feels by doctrinal bigotry, Dr. Johnson ignores the text when he slurringly remarks that the efforts of Donne and his followers "were always analytic; they broke every image into fragments." Johnson concludes that the "slender conceits and laboured particularities" of these poets could scarcely represent "the prospects of nature, or the scenes of life." With respect to Donne, at least, nothing could have been further from the truth. More than almost any other poet who has ever lived, his analysis was always directed toward syntheses that would reveal concors and coincidentia in the most vivid fashion possible.

At the same time, and this may have occasioned Johnson's critique, Donne's love poetry does not speak with a single voice despite its syntheses. His *Songs and Sonnets*, a collection drawn from different periods in his early life, contains examples of all the Renaissance philosophies that Donne's scholarship yielded as raw material. To begin with, there are libertine poems that belong to an Ovidian tradition that continued into the Renaissance. This tradition was renewed by writers like Chapman and Marlowe, and it served as part of the naturalistic reaction to Neoplatonic theorizing about love. The neo-Ovidian poets are often artificial and self-conscious in their defense of sexual pleasures; they have little of Ovid's sunny insouciance and carefree sensuousness. Like the Neoplatonists themselves, their ideas are weighted by the accretion of centuries, a load that Ovid never had to bear. In Donne's libertine poems, this aspect of Ovid shows itself in the doubts about the permanence of love, about the likelihood of achieving reciprocity, and about the value of fidelity. But within the same collection and presumably written at a similar time, neighboring poems assert the preeminence of soul over body, the distinction between love and lust, and the goodness of striving for perfection through devotion to a woman's beauty—all of which would seem to align Donne with Petrarch, Dante, Bembo, and others in the Neoplatonic lineage.

Donne's Ovidian insights structure poems such as "Love's Alchemy," "Community," "The Indifferent," and the song that begins with the lines "Go and catch a falling star,/Get with child a mandrake root." The mandrake root is Machiavelli's mandragola, and in this poem as in the others I have mentioned, Donne portrays love as a fickle appetite that may have relevance to reproduction but little, if any, spiritual import. His Platonistic and religious leanings appear in poems such as "The Undertaking," "A Valediction: Forbidding Mourning," "The Relic," and "Negative Love." As the last title suggests, Donne borrows from the negative theology that tries to reveal the oneness of divinity by negating all the things of this world. In his libertine voice, Donne tells us that "Changed loves are but changed sorts of meat/And when he hath the kernel eat,/Who doth not fling away the shell?" In his Neoplatonic vein he depicts so purely spiritual a union between the lovers that their physical separation creates "not yet/A breach, but an expansion,/Like gold to airy thinness beat." This is something that cannot be equalled by "dull sublunary lovers' love/(Whose soul is sense)."

To have felt and formulated the conflicting power of these alternatives would have been in Donne no great distinction; we have seen the same in other writers of the Middle Ages and the Renaissance. His greatness consists in his ability to *fuse* the two alternatives. Because he thought that Donne, like the other metaphysical poets, failed in this attempt, Dr. Johnson said that heterogeneous ideas were being "yoked by violence together." Coleridge had a better understanding of Donne. He recognized and responded to the concept of merging that underlies Donne's mode of synthesizing the extremes. Discussing "The Canonization," Coleridge says that you must learn how to read it in such a way that "you merge yourself in the author, you *become He*"; and Cleanth Brooks has pointed out that Donne's emphasis upon the fusing and welding of apparent contradictions is reborn in Coleridge's own description of imagination in general as that which "reveals itself in the balance or reconcilement of opposite or discordant qualities: of sameness, with difference; . . . a more than usual state of emotion, with more than usual order." As we shall see, these ideas about merging and the imagination structure the nineteenth-century concept of Romantic love. In Donne the notion of merging provides a philosophical basis for those poems that are neither Platonic nor libertine but somehow both at once, each perspective uniting with the other in a way that requires stereoscopic comprehension.

In poems such as "The Good-Morrow," "Love's Infiniteness," "Air and Angels," "The Ecstasy," "The Anniversary," "The Canonization," and "To His Mistress Going to Bed," Donne uses the language of spiritualization to manifest the goodness of wholly sexual love between man and woman. He transcends libertine interests in the body by denying that love can be reduced to lust alone. In "The Ecstasy" we are first presented with the difference between the merging of bodies and the merging of souls. The former consists in hands being "firmly cemented" and eye-beams "twisted . . . upon one double string." The merging of souls, however, is the creation of a "new concoction"—a super-soul more perfect than the individual souls that have been mixed within it. This mingling of the souls is for Donne love's ecstasy and he tells us: "We see by this it was not sex."

Having established the difference between love and mere sexuality, Donne then goes on to insist that there is nothing in sexuality itself to prevent it from embodying the spirituality of love. "The Ecstasy" ends with the lover's claim that when the unified souls descend into the affections and faculties that only sense experience can apprehend, nothing in the purity of love will have been lost. Among true lovers there is "Small change, when we're to bodies gone." Indeed, the purity of love itself requires the soul's descent into the body—"Else a great Prince in prison lies."

This final image tells the whole story and reveals the depth of Donne's inventiveness. For all the Platonists, beginning with Plato

himself, had maintained that the soul was a sovereign entity imprisoned by its immersion in the body—its primordial descent at birth or
at the creation of the universe being a tragic decline from the purity
of its spiritual origin. Donne reverses all this. The great prince that
in prison lies is for him still the soul, particularly the soul of an
authentic lover, but now its imprisonment results from the *repression*
of bodily interests, and that is caused by everything—including
Neoplatonic philosophies—that would prevent it from descending
to sensory consummations without which its love can only be incomplete. Even in Donne's later life, after he had become the dean of St.
Paul's, he begs the Lord to deliver men "From thinking us all soul,
neglecting thus/Our mutual duties." Though it is ours, the body is
not us, and lust is not the same as love; but the human soul cannot
experience love without the satisfactions of the body.

In merging Ovidian and Platonic concepts, Donne wishes to unify
more than just body and soul. He also seeks to overcome, or in-
teranimate (to use the word he coins), traditional distinctions between time and eternity and between microcosm and macrocosm.
Ovid had never promised an eternity of pleasure, only a succession
of happy moments while time endures. The Platonists wished to step
out of time in their search for an eternal goodness. But Donne insists
that when lovers remain faithful to each other, the temporal mixing
of their souls creates a love that is itself eternal: "Whatever dies was
not mixed equally;/If our two loves be one, or, thou and I/Love so
alike that none do slacken, none can die." In space as well as time, all
contradictories are abolished through the occurrence of love. For
love "makes one little room an everywhere." The lovers "possess one
world," but it is the macrocosm, the great world, as well as the
microcosm. The little place of each person's individuality becomes
the everywhere of infinite space once it merges with the being of the
beloved.

When this happens, the lovers attain a unity even more extensive
than what Ficino envisaged: "But we will have a way more liberal/
Than changing hearts, to join them, so we shall/Be one, and one
another's All." And if each lover is the other's all, their love defies the
usual laws of nature. "All other things to their destruction draw,/
Only our love hath no decay." This makes the lovers monarchs

within their own domain, and uniquely secure: "Who is so safe as we, where none can do/Treason to us, except one of us two?" Furthermore, love consists in the mere fact of oneness between two lovers rather than a oneness with the beauty in either. Donne generally associates beauty with pleasures of the body. These are to be enjoyed fully and the beautiful may serve as "a convenient type" to represent "the heaven where love doth sit"; but that heaven is identified with "mind," and the oneness of properly mingled minds is what Donne recognizes as the basic category in love. In one of his sermons he speaks of love as a "transmutatory Affection, it changes him that loves, into the very nature of that that he loves, and he is nothing else."

In "The Canonization" Donne employs the symbol of the phoenix to express this mysterious merging through love:

> The phoenix riddle hath more wit
> By us; we two being one, are it.
> So, to one neutral thing both sexes fit.
> We die and rise the same, and prove
> Mysterious by this love.

In mythology the phoenix dies and is reborn in a literal, physical manner. It is consumed in fire, but rises from its own ashes. In Donne's poem, the metaphor is also physical. Writers in the Renaissance often used the verb "to die" to signify the completing of sexual intercourse. Consumed by that consummation, Donne's passionate lovers do not find that lovemaking has shortened their lives, as some contemporaries thought, but rather that it leads to new possibilities for enjoyment. From a religious perspective these could only be spiritual consummations that await a soul after the death of the body, but for Donne they are present in the rejuvenated goodness— equally spiritual—that consists in being reborn to sexual life. The lovers "rise the same," for they live again as lovers for each other, in the flesh and with the suggestion of renewed risings or erections through which their love may be physically continued again and again. In the Renaissance the oneness of lovers was frequently symbolized in the image of the hermaphrodite. This is the "one neutral thing" to which Donne refers. It is both the greater body that includes male and female, "both sexes fit," and also the merging of alter egos, complementary souls, as in Plato. Proving "mysterious" by this love (i.e. filled with the mystery of holiness), the lovers assert the sanctity of their union.

In speaking of a "canonization," Donne alerts us to the fact that the Ovidian tradition has been synthesized with one that is not merely Platonistic but also Christian. The lovers become saints by virtue of their love. We are told that they can "die by it," be approved through hymns, and be invoked by those who "beg from above" a pattern of their love. But though the metaphor is transparently religious, neither orthodox nor mystical Christianity supports it. The lovers are not sanctified by anything that Catholic or Protestant doctrine could easily have recognized. At the same time, it would be erroneous to suggest that Donne has in mind a "religion of love" independent of Christianity. He plays upon the inherited dogmas of the church because he wishes to reform them, to suggest through his radical poetry that sacred love is not limited to oneness between a mystic and his God. The lovers have not denied the flesh—on the contrary—but like the more usual Christian saints they have renounced the secular world.

"The Canonization" begins with the line, "For God's sake, hold your tongue, and let me love." We are to take the invocation of the deity literally, not merely as a colloquial interjection, for the lover behaves as he does in a holy quest. The lady must hold her tongue because his love is a blessed communion that goes beyond language; and his critic within the poem must withdraw his condemnatory words because the lover has already withdrawn himself from the mundane pursuits that this critic represents. Merchants, soldiers, lawyers: these are mentioned as people who inhabit a domain distinct from the world of lovers. They are not injured by what lovers do, and therefore have no reason to complain. The lovers will not be buried in half-acre tombs, but their wealth of feeling will show itself in "a well-wrought urn" that contains their mortal remains. In pagan rites, funereal urns were used as objects of devotion, in part perhaps because they resembled a rounded womb, the natural consequence of lovemaking. In Donne the image signifies an aesthetic function as well. Not only are pagan and Christian merged with one another, but also both are fused with art forms—Donne mentions verse, "sonnets" (i.e. his own)—that will keep alive the legend of the lovers.

In "The Ecstasy" Donne carries his religious symbolism even further. For the word *ecstasy* refers to the "Mystic Experience" in which God takes the devout believer unto himself. Donne is clearly suggesting that something comparable, and possibly the same thing, happens on earth when lovers merge in moments of orgasmic satisfaction. In Elegy XIX, "To His Mistress Going to Bed," the metaphor occurs in the description of a woman's undressing prior to making love with the poet who eagerly awaits her in bed. The "fanciful argument," as a recent critic puts it, consists in maintaining that "since the Beatific Vision is like taking off your clothes to experience full joy, then taking off your clothes to experience full joy is like the Beatific Vision."

In depicting lovers who stand before God in their nakedness, saintly by virtue of their innocent love, indeed sanctified by love itself, Donne reminds us of Titian's painting "Sacred and Profane Love," as it has been called for the last three hundred years. Despite conventional expectations, Titian represents sacred love in the figure of a female nude, while a woman sumptuously clothed portrays the profane. As Panofsky and Wind have pointed out, these are the iconographic embodiments of the two Venuses in Plato, amore celeste and amore umano in Pico or Ficino. Sacred love is shown as more than just a beautiful nude; she is also exuberant in her self-revelation. She spreads her arms, one of which holds aloft a lamp as if to illuminate the mysterious, and she makes no effort to hide her naked beauty. Behind her a red cloak suggests vivid possibilities and even emotional ecstasy. By contrast, the clothed Venus seems sedate and almost squat in her earthbound limitations.

I said that Donne's Elegy XIX, and in general his conception of sexual ecstasy as both profane and sacred, reminded one of Titian's painting. But there is a difference. Donne does not claim that sacred love is like a beautiful nude who has nothing to hide in the face of divinity. He is arguing, instead, that profane love is *itself* sacred, that love is holy wherever it appears and most obviously in sexual consummation. Titian's conception is typically Platonistic, just as the philosophy of love in St. John of the Cross and St. Teresa of Avila is typically Catholic. These orthodox writers also use the language of sexual love to describe the ecstasies of mystical union. They were steeped in medieval romance and the poetry of courtly love, and they were quite sophisticated about the worldly bases of their religious metaphors—as St. Bernard also was, centuries before. But like St. Bernard, they use the language of earthly love in order to enliven our imagination to the infinitely superior values of ecstatic oneness with the divine. They resemble Donne, belonging more or less to the same period of time, in treating the symbolism of sex as a device for understanding the extrasexual; but unlike him, they deny the possibility of merging sacred and profane. Bernini's statue of St. Teresa seized by divine rapture, her eyes sunken and her body in lordosis, the arms outstretched in utter receptivity, may well suggest the posture of a woman in postorgasmic bliss. St. Teresa herself would probably have accepted this way of portraying religious ecstasy. But she would have spurned Donne's belief that the orgasmic is in itself holy. For her it could be nothing more than a symbol of spiritual oneness that transcends all sensory experience.

Some of the differences between Donne and these Spanish mystics may be related to differences between Protestant and Catholic theology. Though Luther's ideas about God's agapē descending to earth and showing itself in ardent embraces of men and women required centuries of further development, their first fruits appear in Donne's poetry. Nevertheless, Donne does not neglect the older religion. There is only a progression in thought between the synthesizing love-poetry of his youth, which often sounds Catholic as well as Protestant, and his later devotional verse. In Holy Sonnet XIV, where Donne implores the three-person God to batter his heart, the words could very well have come from St. Teresa or St. John of the Cross:

> Take me to You, imprison me, for I,
> Except You enthrall me, never shall be free,
> Nor ever chaste, except You ravish me.

If we read these lines in the context of Donne's earlier work, they attain a richness that exceeds the limits of conventional mysticism: the ravishment for which the religious soul now yearns takes on heightened significance once we remember how great a value passion had in the sexual love to which Donne previously devoted himself. In Holy Sonnet XVII Donne reveals the harmony between the two great loves in his life. The poem was written after the death of his wife, "she whom I loved," and Donne begins by lamenting that now "my good is dead." But if one is a Christian, as Donne always said he was, how can the good be localized in another mortal? How can it be dead when she dies, particularly if her soul has been "into heaven ravished"? Donne does not address himself to this enigma. His faith in the merging of human and divine, due to the presence of God's love mysteriously working its way among his creatures, will not brook further analysis. In this sonnet about the wife he loved so much, he can only say that "Here the admiring her my mind did whet/To seek thee, God; so streams do show the head."

The suggestion that one's love of God is "whetted" by the love of a woman may sound like Dante, and the image of streams merging with their source may recall the final vision of Beatrice as a ray of light mingled in the celestial brilliance of the godhead. But Donne is also writing about the woman he married and lived with until she died, the mother of his twelve children. Anne Donne is not the symbol of theology or even of aspiring spirituality. She is a woman like any other—except that she is the one he loved passionately, the one whose father had him imprisoned for daring to marry her as the outcome of their sexual love.

In the Introduction to his edition of Donne's poems, Herbert J. C. Grierson interprets Donne's philosophy as "a justification of love as a natural passion in the human heart the meaning and end of which is marriage." As a general statement this is far superior to C. S. Lewis' assertion that " 'the love of hatred and the hate of love' is the main, though not the only, theme of the *Songs and Sonnets*." Lewis considers "contempt for love itself" to be one of Donne's principal themes. He calls Elegy XIX "a pornographic poem" and claims that "The Ecstasy" is an even "nastier" one.

Lewis has been thoroughly and rightly criticized for these absurdities. But one must also remark that Grierson's emphasis upon marriage as the burden of Donne's philosophy is somewhat inaccurate. Though sexual love as Donne describes it is wholly compatible with marriage, he scarcely develops the concept of married love itself. For that we shall have to turn to others.

While various critics have considered Donne a poet whose virtue is wit but not clear thinking, I have been presenting him as one who synthesizes, with some success, contrasting philosophies of love in the Renaissance. Similar efforts need not be made for Edmund Spenser. It is widely recognized that his poetry combines, and at its best amalgamates, Christian, courtly, and Neoplatonic ideas of love. In the *Four Hymns*, Spenser balances hymns in honor of earthly love and earthly beauty with hymns to love and beauty that are heavenly or divine. In a manner that medieval proponents of the caritas-synthesis would have admired, he depicts earthly love rising through the levels of aspiring eros "out of the lowly dust . . . to the purest sky" while heavenly love descends in God's agapē and teaches man how to love his brethren. Though eros here is sexual, it distinguishes itself from lust by its ability to participate in this circuit of love.

In terms of his immediate inspiration, Spenser starts with ideas, such as those of Bembo and Castiglione, about the elevating goodness of a man's love for beauty in the lady. But unlike these Italian writers, Spenser wishes to retain all the earthly benefits of sexual love once it has been purified through Platonistic spirituality. His lovers return to the world with a glow of religious sanctity and complete their union in the bonds of matrimony. As we have seen in earlier chapters, medieval romance often presents marriage as the goal of love; and in Chaucer, whom Spenser thanks for having "taught me, homely as I can, to make," he could have found paeans to married love in "The Franklin's Tale" and elsewhere. Spenser weaves these idealistic elements into a design that is explicitly Christian. For him marriage signifies, and embodies, the knitting together of natural inclinations as an essential part of the cosmic plan. Nature thus becomes not an arena for delectable sport, as so often in Ovid, or simply the agency for procreation in accordance with God's will, as in Bernardus Silvestris and Alain de Lille, but rather a life-giving sustenance that shows itself in sexual love. Men and women find the meaning of their joint existence in the joys of marital affection. In the *Areopagitica* John Milton calls Spenser "a better teacher than Scotus or Aquinas" because only he understood how "true temperance" depends upon experience of the pleasures and perils in human intimacy. Nor is it hard to see why Milton should have said this. No one in the Middle Ages could have helped a seventeenth-century man like him to harmonize Renaissance versions of Platonism with Christian ideas about conjugal love. However sparse his reasoning may be, and despite his pervasive reliance upon sweet-flowing rhetoric, Spenser provides that service.

The Spenserian ideal of marital love had an effect on Shakespeare as well as Milton, as we shall see in the following chapter. It becomes for Shakespeare a touchstone of the truly natural, and its deterioration in one dramatic circumstance or another generally indicates a catastrophe in human nature. We may also see Shakespeare, in particular facets of his genius, as a synthesis between Donne and Spenser. In "The Phoenix and Turtle," a poem published about the same time *Hamlet* was written, Shakespeare reminds us of both poets at once. Hamlet tells Ophelia that "We will have no more marriage," and that play (like others we shall be considering) largely concerns itself with the failure of married love. Its success, manifested in an ideal merging of the sort that Donne conceived, appears in "The Phoenix and Turtle." As in "The Canonization," Shakespeare's phoenix symbolizes sexual passion consumed by its own ardor and then restored to life. The turtle(dove) represents true love. It was a dove that led Noah to a new and better world, and throughout the Middle Ages this bird portrayed the Holy Ghost descending as God's agapē. Here the mythological pair belong to nature, though also transcending it. They are creatures united by that "love and constancy" which Shakespeare calls "a mutual flame." The poem depicts the concordant oneness between lovers suitably matched and devoted to one another within a permanent relationship.

Above all, "The Phoenix and Turtle" celebrates the amorous union itself, playing upon its ambiguous nature as either a merging or a wedding. First we are told that "So they loved as love in twain/Had the essence but in one;/Two distincts, division none:/Number there in love was slain." Since the two remain distinct though also one, this might imply a wedding. As the subsequent stanza paradoxically says, "distance, and no space was seen." That defeats number, arithmetic, because we cannot clearly describe the unified couple as either one or two. Later, however, the lovers are said to have merged with one another: "Reason, in itself confounded,/Saw division grow together,/To themselves yet either neither,/Simple were so well compounded."

In *Midsummer Night's Dream* the idea of reason being confounded by mysterious truths beyond its reach is the burden of Hippolyta's reply to Theseus' hardheaded speech on the morning after. In the poem Shakespeare sides with Hippolyta as against those who rely upon rationality alone. The union of the phoenix and the turtle signifies love's mystical being, which reason cannot understand but must accept as reality rather than illusion. Shakespeare incorporates all this in the line, "Love hath reason, reason none." Dying, the phoenix and the turtledove are consumed in cinders within an urn, as in Donne, but when they return to life, it is not as birds that live in nature. The "beauty, truth, and rarity," which their love contains, no longer exists on earth since it is buried with them. It now exists "to eternity."

The eternity in which Shakespeare's couple find their rest has often been interpreted as a Platonic or Neoplatonic transcendence of the body. This view is supported by the following stanza:

> Leaving no posterity:
> 'Twas not their infirmity,
> It was married chastity.

Is Shakespeare referring to a marriage that is sexually unconsummated? Is it possibly an intimate attachment between two men that consists in the chastity of a pure friendship? One or another reading of this sort would be needed to justify the Neoplatonic interpretation. And perhaps that is how we should read "The Phoenix and Turtle." But we may also take Shakespeare's wording as an enunciation of the Spenserian ideal of married love, of love between married men and women so pure as to be chastity in itself even though it includes sexual intercourse and whether or not it leads to progeny. Throughout his life as a playwright, this remains the supreme concept of love for Shakespeare. It beguiles his reverberating imagination and draws it into explorations that no one else has ever matched.

7

William Shakespeare
Philosopher of Love

What is love? 'tis not hereafter;
Present mirth hath present laughter;
  What's to come is still unsure:
In delay there lies no plenty;
Then come kiss me, sweet-and-twenty,
  Youth's a stuff will not endure.

T HESE LINES FROM *Twelfth
Night* belong to the Clown's song in Act II, scene 3; they are followed
in the next scene by stanzas that link the "innocence of love" to death
resulting from rejection by one's beloved. She may be sweet-and-
twenty but she can also be a "fair cruel maid." If we put the two songs
together, we may see in Shakespeare a kinship with the realistic
strand of Renaissance love theory. The first song even sounds like an
elaboration of Lorenzo de' Medici's poem about youth and beauty
that flee forevermore. And like Lorenzo in that place, Shakespeare
would seem to have no faith in religious concepts that promise a
superior consummation of love in the "hereafter." The subtitle of
Twelfth Night is "What You Will," and Shakespeare presupposes that
extensive enjoyment, here, now, and however long nature allows, is
what everyone really wills as the outcome of sexual love.

Despite the problematic nature of this assumption, Shakespeare—in *Twelfth Night*, at least—scarcely deliberates about it and
never subjects it to scrutiny. That being a frequent stance of his,
some critics have found Shakespeare's philosophic scope meager

and even inadequate. Santayana in particular lamented the lack of theological insight or metaphysical feeling in Shakespeare. Hazlitt too remarks, though not disapprovingly, that "Shakespeare discovers in his writings little religious enthusiasm." Certainly Shakespeare is not doctrinal in the sense that Lucretius or Dante was; and it is only with difficulty that one could extrapolate from his thinking a perspective that might possibly be considered theological. He is, as Santayana perceives, a supremely secular poet, able to understand the importance of religious issues for others but not driven by an urgent need to resolve them for himself.

On the other hand, we misread Shakespeare's drama if we take it as merely the play of ideas and attitudes belonging to the characters in each work and never to the dramatist. Though Keats may be right in seeing Shakespeare as the exemplar of "negative capability"— through sympathetic imagination he identifies with each view of the world as it contributes to a human experience, himself avoiding tendentious resolutions—Shakespeare's thought is inwardly motivated and by no means random. The conflict in each dramatic situation expresses the mind of a moralist as well as a methodology. If Shakespeare has no comprehensive ideology, no all-embracing metaphysics, his perspective nevertheless encompasses every aspect of speculation about man and nature.

In many respects the Shakespearean plays are all post-Ficino and post-Luther; they show the influence of what was in the air during the Elizabethan and Jacobean periods. But they also follow a development that defies traditional categories and must be studied as stages in Shakespeare's individual, even idiosyncratic, thinking. At the beginning, in the *Sonnets* and *Love's Labour's Lost*, the language is often Platonistic; at the end, in *The Winter's Tale, Cymbeline, The Tempest*, the prevailing mood is naturalistic and not at all like Plato's. It would be quite misleading, however, to say that Shakespeare himself was a Platonist in his first plays who turns into a naturalist by the end of his career. Both voices recur throughout his work, often side by side, as if they were primary colors that he could mix on his palette to achieve whatever effect he needed at the moment. He is less interested in their particular pigmentation than in the dramatic and dialectical brilliance of their interaction.

For instance, consider the setting of *Love's Labour's Lost*. It is Ficino's Academy translated to a French court, since royalty catches the theatrical imagination more vividly than a community of mere philosophers. Or better yet, it is noblemen pretending to seek the intellectual joys that Florentine Neoplatonists cultivated. Within this context we learn very little about Ficino on the nature of beauty or the essence of good, but we immediately encounter Castiglione's revision of Ficino's teachings. Shakespeare's noblemen have foresworn all female company and yet they quickly fall in love with ladies who are for each of them the showing forth of that ideal realm they have presumably been seeking. For Castiglione "the lady" could eventually become a spouse, but her main function was the embodiment in herself of ultimate beauty. Following the lead of Edmund Spenser, who succeeded in combining Neoplatonism with traditional ideas about matrimony, Shakespeare sees the beloved as a woman to be married.

In *Love's Labour's Lost* ideal love is thus transmuted into marital love, and this remains constant throughout the succeeding plays. It is a norm from which Shakespeare does not deviate. If his tone sounds increasingly naturalistic, that is surely due to the fact that Neoplatonism has so little to tell us about married love. To explore the dramatic problems in this ideal, Shakespeare had to develop a conceptual language more capable than Platonism of analyzing the condition of human beings as they exist in the ordinary world, a world in which people yearn for one another, get married, participate in society, and belong to the natural order of things. He duplicates, in effect, the trajectory of courtly romance, which amalgamates aristocratic concepts of courtly love with the everyday interests of boys and girls, men and women, all bursting with erotic passion that religion in the Middle Ages tried to repress. But since Shakespeare lived in a world no longer dominated by the caritas-synthesis, the conflict between sexual love and a hostile environment had to show itself through other ideologies of repression. Shakespeare easily found suitable substitutes for medieval religion. Repression can be symbolized in many ways.

In some of Shakespeare's plays, eliminating the Christian element scarcely altered the affirmative quality of his marital ideal. But in others, the avoidance of religious criteria was also accompanied by a cynical approach towards everything that might idealize sexual love. This is most apparent in *Troilus and Cressida*, particularly if we contrast it with Chaucer's *Troilus and Criseyde*. Beginning with Boccaccio's story of a Trojan warrior who has had much erotic experience but never truly loved a woman until he undergoes the misfortune of giving himself to a faithless one, Chaucer depicts both characters as noble star-crossed lovers. His Criseyde is the equal of Troilus in purity of heart; and when she unaccountably betrays him, Chaucer merely tells us that he is following the report of an earlier author. Speaking in his own voice in the first book, Chaucer insists that love between man and woman is "a thing so virtuous" that the worthier a man becomes the more deeply he must have loved. In one place he gives Troilus a paean to the god of love that uses all the language of medieval religion; and elsewhere Chaucer indicates that the joy these courtly lovers experience in each other's arms is part of the divine plan, a consummation in no way inimical to the love of God. It is only at the end, after Criseyde acts disgracefully, that Chaucer writes his quasi-recantation. Having been killed by Achilles, Troilus ascends to heaven and there perceives the vanity and worthlessness of all those earthly joys that time destroys sooner or later. To avoid the sorrows of human love, and its ultimate futility, Chaucer now advocates religious love as something that will never risk betrayal or diminution. At the end of *The Canterbury Tales* he likewise retracts the sinful ideas about love to be found in *Troilus and Criseyde*, which he places on a par with "many a lecherous lay" that he had written and for which he hopes Christ will now forgive him.

In Chaucer, as in Andreas Capellanus, it is hard to know how this contradiction or ambivalence about love is to be interpreted. What is more relevant, however, is the fact that it exists because *both* courtly and religious ideals are so emphatically, even didactically, presented by Chaucer as goals worth pursuing. In Shakespeare there can be no similar conflict between them, since neither of these ideals works for him as they had for Chaucer two hundred years before. In a sense Shakespeare is closer to Boccaccio, who ends his account with nothing but a warning to men about the women they fall in love with. At the same time, Shakespeare's interests go beyond the writing of a cautionary tale. Though he resolves our doubts about Cressida's character by having Ulysses comment on the "wanton spirits [that] look out at every joint and motive of her body," her faithlessness is not his principal concern. Writing in the seventeenth century, he could take it for granted that his audience would identify Cressida—as she herself predicts in the play—with woman's frailty and infidelity. Instead, the question that Shakespeare raises and carefully explores throughout the work is deeper, at least more analytical, than anything he could have received from his antecedents. Assuming that Cressida is morally inferior, he seems to say, how is it possible that so excellent a man as Troilus could have been misled into loving her?

In part, Shakespeare's reply is psychological: youth is an impulsive time of life, love is blind, passions often destroy reason. This kind of answer, which is central to the comedy of *Twelfth Night* and was platitudinous by the time Shakespeare wrote, becomes dramatically explosive in *Troilus and Cressida* because there Shakespeare encloses it within a systematic investigation about the nature of love. What does it mean to love not just a woman like Cressida but any human being, or, for that matter, anything at all? The entire play revolves about the different responses Shakespeare articulates. Though they are presented dialectically, they also indicate an approach that is wholly Shakespeare's.

By its plot alone, *Troilus and Cressida* deals with two different phenomena: war and sexual love. The two do not exist independently, however; the Trojan War will end if Paris returns Helen, and Troilus loses Cressida once her father defects to the Greeks. This much Shakespeare inherits from tradition, but the analysis of the interrelationship between war and love he contributes himself, from his own point of view. Helen and Cressida are beautiful women, desirable both as sexual objects and as manifestations of the beautiful. Beginning with this fact, Shakespeare then asks what can truly justify the sacrifices that loving them entails. Paris' love for Helen embroils all the Greeks and Trojans whereas Troilus' love for Cressida involves only him and Diomedes, his rival among the Greeks. Nevertheless, the social and the personal situations are alike, for

they arouse the same problems about valuation. Is the beauty of
Helen or Cressida, or any other beloved, worth the terrible cost of
loving them? Since love is a valuing of something, what kind of
valuation is it?

Shakespeare explicitly examines these questions in Act II, scene 2,
where the Trojans are deliberating about the continuance of the war
they are fighting in order to retain Helen. Hector, the hero of the
Trojans both morally and militarily, insists that "she is not worth
what she doth cost the keeping." To which Troilus asks: "What's
aught but as 'tis valued?" Hector's reply expresses a belief in objective order that reason can discern as the grounds for valuation:

> "But value dwells not in particular will;
> It holds his estimate and dignity
> As well wherein 'tis precious of itself
> As in the prizer. 'Tis mad idolatry
> To make the service greater than the god; . . ."

In answering this, Troilus argues in effect that Hector has forgotten that valuing something means committing oneself to it, and
commitment depends upon individual will as well as objective judgment. Honor consists in recognizing and accepting the nature of
one's commitment. It is significant that Troilus illustrates this point
by reference to a hypothetical marriage:

> "I take to-day a wife, and my election
> Is led on in the conduct of my will—
> My will enkindled by mine eyes and ears,
> Two traded pilots 'twixt the dangerous shores
> Of will and judgment. How may I avoid,
> Although my will distaste what it elected,
> The wife I chose? . . ."

Thus far the debate has proceeded on the level of philosophical
disputation. It is interrupted by the outburst of Cassandra, whose
divinations put her in touch with reality in a manner that reason
cannot accept. She is therefore dismissed as a madwoman, and her
brothers continue as before. In making his final statement, Hector
appeals to a principle of order in nature, comparable to what Ulysses

has also been lecturing his fellow Greeks about in Act I. Just as Ulysses claims that the physical universe observes "degree, priority . . . proportion, season, form," so too does Hector maintain that "Nature craves all dues be rend'red to their owners." Since there is no "nearer debt in all humanity than wife is to the husband," he concludes that the laws of nature itself demand that Helen be returned. Given the fact that Hector and Ulysses provide a consensus of wise opinion, and that the Trojans will be destroyed once they have decided to keep Helen despite nature's law, there is every reason to think that Shakespeare himself sides with Hector's objectivist ideas about valuation. But Hector does not prevail; he yields when Troilus asserts that Helen is for all the Trojans "a theme of honor and renown,/A spur to valiant and magnanimous deeds."

In saying this, Troilus has transferred the discussion to a different, somewhat extraneous level. He is now appealing not to Hector's sense of right or wrong, good or bad, but rather to his professional ideals as a warrior. To one who fights in pursuit of fame and glory, it may not matter that the cause of contention is hardly worth the struggle. What matters most is one's dedication and heroic self-sacrifice, even if the object for which one fights is worthless. This renews Troilus' emphasis upon the importance of commitment, but it is now cast into a mold of military idealism that Hector cannot resist. In allowing Troilus to win the argument, he manifests a moral and intellectual flaw that later costs him his life when he foolishly expects Achilles to abide by principles of chivalric honor (as he and Troilus do) instead of acting deceitfully for reasons of self-preservation. In a sense, Achilles enacts retribution by nature's laws for Hector's having succumbed to the reasoning of Troilus. But this functions as irony in the play: for if nature truly embodied objective laws of honor and rectitude, how could it possibly choose the unscrupulous Achilles as its representative?

The debates about the nature of valuation recur throughout *Troilus and Cressida*, within the Greek camp as well as the Trojan, and in their exchanges with one another. They underlie the competition between Ajax and Achilles, each of whom is finally shown to "over-hold his price." Both are easily manipulated by leaders like Ulysses who understand the willfulness in their overestimations of themselves. Diomedes taunts Paris for having diminished his own value in stealing so valueless a woman as Helen, and he assures Troilus that Cressida will be prized in accordance with "her own worth." When she betrays him with Diomedes, whose moral value we must distrust in view of his reputation as a sly seducer, we are forced to conclude with Troilus that Cressida's worth is nothing much. Reading her letter from her new residence among the Greeks but thinking of her former promises of devotion, his final comment on her character is: "Words, words, mere words, no matter from the heart." The line is similar to Hamlet's when he informs Polonius that he is reading only words, as if the contents of his perusal are as valueless as Cressida's protestations.

Shakespeare could have left us with the suggestion that another type of woman might have honored her commitment more than Cressida did. The moral Boccaccio ends with implies as much, his story offering itself as advice about the choosing of the right kind of woman to love. Shakespeare makes no such effort because it is the nature of love itself he is bringing into question. He even repeats Chaucer's conclusion about the value of all human love being doubtful simply because it is subject to the ravages of time. That is part of the message in Ulysses' great speech about envious and calumniating time which infects "beauty, wit, high birth, vigor of bone, desert in service, love, friendship, charity." These are the medieval virtues of man in nature that Chaucer subordinates to a more permanent love of God. Without mentioning any religious alternative, Shakespeare suggests that the passage of time is enough to debase values, to create inconstancy and betrayal by one's beloved. "One touch of nature makes the whole world kin," Ulysses says, not meaning that Rousseau is right and that brotherly love results from a return to nature, but rather that all of mankind exists in a temporal flux which inclines everyone towards what is new or merely different. We are all alike in having a natural propensity to both overvaluation and infidelity. Whether or not there exist more permanent values, that alone explains why love in general, and Cressida's in particular, must be liable to faithlessness.

This is the lesson that Troilus learns, but even at the height of passion he recognized the dangers he was courting. He tells Cressida that "the monstruosity in love" consists in the fact "that the will is infinite and the execution confined; that the desire is boundless and the act a slave to limit." In effect he is repeating the earlier argument of Hector, who distrusts "particular will" and wishes to prevent its overextension beyond the limits of nature. Whatever lovers swear and actually believe, they delude one another, and themselves, about their abilities. Troilus knows that even though he and Cressida would like to continue their love forever, they may not have the fortitude. At least he knows this to be true of lovers in general. But then he exempts himself and Cressida—"Such are not we"—and the rest of the play serves to prove that they too are kin to the one disastrous touch.

In *Troilus and Cressida*, Shakespeare would seem to be arguing both that love is a freely given bestowal of value which may seem magnificent at the time but ultimately wreaks havoc, and also that it is a complex of delusory appraisals about the beloved's character and one's own capacities. In either event, nature is shown to be cunning in its ability to hide from man the realities that are actually motivating him. Such is the explicit belief of two characters in the play: Pandarus and Thersites. The act in which Troilus and Cressida declare their love for one another begins with Pandarus' bawdy conversation with Helen and Paris. Picking up Paris' remark that "hot blood begets hot thoughts, and hot thoughts beget hot deeds, and hot deeds is love," Pandarus concludes by wondering whether love is not therefore a generation of vipers. For if love is generated merely by hot blood, hot thoughts, and hot deeds, it cannot be a noble and honorific aspiration as Troilus foolishly believes. It is merely a generating of something ignoble—vipers in the metaphor—whose nature pertains to sex rather than love. Courtly lovers must therefore be misguided, just as noble Hector is in relying upon the principles of chivalry. Neither in war nor in love can idealistic attitudes be justified.

The same reductive approach is expressed throughout by Thersites, who tells us early on that "all the argument [of the Trojan War] is a whore and a cuckold" and later explains the scene where Troilus frantically observes Cressida with Diomedes by saying it is merely lechery "with his fat rump and potato finger [that] tickles these together." We may rightly insist, as many critics have, that Shakespeare is not to be identified with Pandarus and Thersites. But except for a suggestion, never developed to any degree, that Hector himself must be a loving husband whose example provides affirmative possibilities to the imagination, Shakespeare gives all the strength in his analysis to the deflationary voices in this play. He himself has pandered to the audience's eagerness to observe love in action and like Thersites he too is an outsider to the events being depicted, a player not a doer, one who entertains as an Elizabethan clown, giving pleasure while arrogating to himself the right to utter painful truths that men of action dare not speak. There is much more to Shakespeare than this, but surely part of him vents itself in the negative sentiments about love that linger as the residual outcome of the play.

If we think of *Troilus and Cressida* as a quasi-tragedy whose premise is the inconstancy of women, it may readily be seen as a companion to *Much Ado About Nothing*, written a year or two earlier. That work is a comedy and it ends with joyous weddings, but it too begins with the fact of inconstancy: this time in the male. At the very beginning, Benedick prides himself on being the kind of man who loves no woman, though presumably he frequents many, and therefore he will not consider marriage as a suitable goal. To take this attitude is already to presuppose an inner logic between love and marriage, which Shakespeare will develop elsewhere, but in *Much Ado About Nothing* he is primarily concerned with the idealistic pretensions of courtship itself. As in *Troilus and Cressida*, he concludes that idealized love is not to be trusted. For though Hero, the beloved whom Claudio professes to adore, remains constant to him, Claudio does not—in another sense—remain constant to her. His inconstancy consists in refusing to believe that she is innocent of the charges against her. When Benedick and Beatrice resolve their mutual aggressiveness, perceiving in it the fact that they need each other, their relationship manifests a type of oneness far superior to the courtly love that had bound Claudio to Hero.

Instead of issuing from a search for an ideal female whose perfection turns the lover into an ideal male, the love between Beatrice and Benedick originates in recognized facts about human nature. The conflict between man and woman must be overcome, as Beatrice and Benedick finally do, but in itself it is presented as a foreseeable consequence of natural differences between the sexes. Feeling the exhilaration of a love that supplants sexual animosity, Benedick espouses marriage and justifies his new attitude by an argument from nature that no one would have contested in Shakespeare's day: "The world must be peopled." Benedick's ultimate conclusion occurs in the final scene, first when he stops Beatrice's bantering mouth by kissing her, and then when he defends his own inconstancy as a thinker by assuring us that "Man is a giddy thing." From this we may wonder how long his love for Beatrice will continue after the curtain has dropped, for one who believes in the fickleness of man, and himself can fall in love so quickly, may easily return to his earlier feelings. But that is not what Shakespeare had in mind. For him, man is giddy because of his immersion in time—just as Ulysses had said in *Troilus and Cressida*—and the solidity of the love between Beatrice and Benedick results from their wise adjustment to each other's temporal nature. In remarking that "there is no staff more reverent than one tipped with horn," Benedick even implies that his love for Beatrice would be able to surmount her sexual infidelity. To Troilus or Claudio this would be unthinkable and possibly that is why their kind of love, beautiful as a courtly ideal but fragile in the real world, is one that Shakespeare wishes to supplant.

In *Much Ado About Nothing* we come very close to the moral demonstrated in Mozart's *Così fan tutte*: you cannot love truly if you expect too much of either yourself or your beloved. Throughout his maturity, Shakespeare repeats this truth unendingly, sometimes with cynicism but often with resignation and a sympathetic sadness as if to remind us that he too, as a poet, is one who idealizes beyond nature and does so at his peril.

In saying previously that Shakespeare hardly sees life from a religious point of view, I did not mean to suggest that religious categories were of no importance to him. He is particularly intrigued by the possibility that love between men and women might itself become a religion. Just before his friends trick Benedick into thinking Beatrice loves him, he muses about the opposite sex in a way that prepares us for Shakespeare's ideas about love as a religion. Though one woman is fair, another wise, another virtuous, Benedick tells us that no woman will come into his "grace" until all graces are to be found in a single woman. He has been asking whether he might possibly be "converted" to love, and it is clear that the woman who combines all graces must be an emanation from, or embodiment of, divinity in the manner of Dante's Beatrice. To show the absurdity of the enterprise, Benedick proceeds to list rather mundane goods that the ideal female must also possess: she must be rich, mild, noble, of good discourse, an excellent musician, etc.; and then, as if to prove how modest are his demands for nothing less than perfection, he allows God to decide what color her hair may be. The scene concludes with Benedick having made a total about-face. For he ends up revering his own Beatrice, not as an impossible goddess but merely as a woman who loves him like a fellow human being. His earlier prediction comes true in the sense that he finds no perfect woman worthy of being worshiped. Yet he loves Beatrice inasmuch as he feels compassion and concern for her. Though he declares that he will be "horribly" in love, there is no question of either him or Beatrice turning their love into a religion.

The idea of love as a religion had preoccupied Shakespeare as early as *Romeo and Juliet*. There we are presented with the two types of Venus: earthly as in Rosaline, whom Romeo loves with a carnal passion at the beginning, and heavenly in the person of Juliet, who leads him into a realm that the other characters cannot penetrate. The lovers turn to Friar Laurence as one who is also detached from the material values of the ordinary world. They escape from it much as Aucassin and Nicolette did. And though the ghostly father marries them in order to legitimize their elopement, they live and die in a union that exists by transcending the normal interests of society. Once their death brings peace among those who had felt only hatred for one another, Romeo and Juliet become saints to their countrymen. Within the dramatic structure of the play, the suffering of the young couple serves as a Christ-like sacrifice eliminating evil by means of love.

Playing upon the religious imagination in this way, Shakespeare constructs the initial conversation between Romeo and Juliet, the interweaving sonnet which first unites them, out of conceits about pilgrims, saints, and a holy shrine. It follows upon Romeo's description of Juliet as "true beauty," "beauty too rich for use, for earth too dear"; and it adumbrates the speech in which she reveals herself as an incarnation of agapē: "My bounty is as boundless as the sea,/My love as deep; the more I give to thee,/The more I have, for both are infinite." In the *Purgatorio*, Dante had discussed the nature of divine love as an infinite renewal of this sort; but even he had not suggested that a mere woman could effect the miracle on her own. Juliet belongs to the secular tradition of courtly romance in ascribing her mystical powers to love alone. She later reminds us of Iseult in Gottfried von Strassburg's poem, welcoming the night as the time when she will find in Romeo not darkness or oblivion but rather "day in night." In refusing to worship the garish sun, she alludes to a mansion of love bright and festive with stars that shine with the kind of gaiety that Tristan and Iseult expected to find in their enchanted castle.

In general, the purity and infinite perfection of Juliet's love, in which there is no "monstruosity" despite its boundless desires, sustains the religious character of this play. Where Cressida is morally infirm and subject to prevailing winds, Juliet is constant unto death. Both she and Cressida note that obstacles engender love, but only her love is able to surmount them. She prepares us for even more heroic females in Shakespeare such as Imogen-Fidele, the antecedent of Beethoven's Fidelio and the model of womanly fortitude. In questing for Juliet, Romeo ascends like the bird of eros but continually falls. He is impulsive, foolish, and emotionally unstable. His adolescent behavior does not drag Juliet down or diminish the ideality of their love, but it eventuates in a death that benefits only the survivors.

Nor does Shakespeare intimate that these lovers will find each other on the other side of death. For though they are made for one another and the language of religion attests to their sacred oneness, Shakespeare uses the tragedy more as a condemnation of society than as a revelation of love triumphant in the next world. Romeo and Juliet are passionate lovers in a sense in which Beatrice and Benedick can never be, but we are meant to see them as equal candidates for marital love. Indeed, Shakespeare in this early period would seem to treat their passion as the only suitable introduction to married love. The hatred that separates their families cannot keep them from loving each other—if anything, as a psychoanalytic reading would maintain, it augments the fervor and the urgency in their need for one another. But the social conflict can and does prevent them from getting married in the conventional manner and with the approval of their people. Their death enacts a human failing, on the part of others if not themselves. It is not a prelude to heavenly bliss but only an example of how the administration of worldly power can destroy that in life which makes it holy.

Ten years later, towards the end of his relatively short career as a writer, Shakespeare returns to similar problems in *Antony and Cleopatra*. The tragedy he there presents arises from a dualism that he exploits fully for dramatic purposes. On the one hand, there is a political and military struggle for the world in its entirety. Antony and Cleopatra are not merely incomparable lovers but also a would-be emperor of Rome and a queen of Egypt aspiring to unite the civilizations of East and West. On the other hand, the civilization of the East, as represented by the erotic nature of Cleopatra, is devoted to principles that negate those of Rome. Cleopatra embodies sexual love as a religion that transcends the military ideals of the Roman empire while Antony wavers between the two systems of value. In Cleopatra's embrace, finding nobleness in doing thus when such a mutual pair can do it, he may rant about letting Rome in Tiber melt "and the wide arch of the ranged empire fall." But the subsequent action shows this mutual pair sending men to their death, and eventually dying themselves, in an effort to wrest dominion over Rome from an Octavius Caesar who scorns the religion of love in which they are immersed.

Several critics have seen in Shakespeare's careful delineation of this dualism an ambiguity or ambivalence that he makes no attempt to resolve. The play then appears as an integrated counterpoint of West against East, Octavius against Cleopatra, with Antony hopelessly trying to combine the two. I think this approach is more or less correct. Shakespeare distributes his strongest and most convincing poetry in this work so evenhandedly that neither side can claim ultimate adherence. Antony is rightly condemned as a doting mallard, a general who has squandered his virility to cool a gypsy's lust, a ruler who has cast away a kingdom "for a mirth," and Octavius has the final word not only in capturing all power to himself but also in trumpeting the supremacy of his ideology when he commands, in the last line, "High order in this great solemnity." At the same time, Octavius' appearance at the end follows upon the scene in which Cleopatra kills herself with the dignity and mystical beauty of a goddess returning to her native divinity. Octavius is preoccupied with questions about how she died, at first assuming that she was poisoned by figs in the Roman manner, but all this merely reveals his relative pettiness: he has no comprehension of the spiritual circumstances that Shakespeare has woven into Cleopatra's death. Though order and rationality win out in political terms, the passionate realm in which the lovers live and die asserts itself, more fully than anywhere else in Shakespeare, as a reality that cannot be rendered subordinate.

In fashioning so finely tuned an ambiguity, Shakespeare need not be taken as a technician who merely portrays different modes of life. It seems clear to me that the ideal for him would be a harmonization, at least a reconciliation, between the values of love and society, sex and reason, passion and orderly administration. But like the authors of the Tristan legend, he knows that reality is rarely conducive to such ideal accomplishments. Like them, he is writing a tragedy that forces us to experience the split between real and ideal by depicting opposing interests in their most extreme opposition.

There are two respects, however, in which Shakespeare had material more advantageous than the Tristan legend. First, he could draw upon, and often hew quite closely to, the facts of history as reported in Plutarch's *Lives*. Second, Plutarch provides, at least in one place, a mythological framework that Shakespeare could employ in the poetic process of accentuation. Describing Cleopatra's visit to Antony, in her barge on the river Cydnus, Plutarch presents most of the magnificent detail Shakespeare uses for the speech of Enobarbus. Plutarch's account concludes: "And then went a rumor in the people's mouths that the goddess Venus was come to play with the god Bacchus for the general good of all Asia."

In his usual fashion, Shakespeare takes this elegant prose of Plutarch and turns it into a revelation. In Enobarbus' speech the sexual implications are embellished to the maximum. Where Plutarch had merely told us that the silver oars of Cleopatra's barge kept time to the sound of music, Shakespeare adds that the water they beat followed faster "as amorous of their strokes"; where Plutarch speaks of a sweet savor of perfumes issuing from the barge, Shakespeare insists that "the winds were lovesick with them"; where Plutarch mentions pretty boys who fan the queen, Shakespeare tells us they are "dimpled" and that by fanning Cleopatra's delicate cheeks they seem to make them glow while cooling them. This remarkable phenomenon alerts us to the suggestion in Shakespeare that Cleopatra is indeed a goddess of love, more than just a queen. The idea is completed when Enobarbus subsequently states that "other women cloy/The appetites they feed, but she makes hungry/ Where most she satisfies." That is not a normal capacity. It is magic, a mystery of the erotic life, or else so great a sexual talent that for most people it may well seem god-like. In the case of Cleopatra, we are instantly informed that her ability to awaken appetites despite satiety, comparable to the restoring of life to what has died, takes on religious import: "For vilest things/Become themselves in her, that the holy priests/Bless her when she is riggish."

In most civilized societies the genitals, male as well as female, have been considered the "vilest things." In the mentality, and in the body, of Cleopatra they become holy, and that is why even priests bless her lecherous inclinations. Throughout the play, Shakespeare never swerves from an accurate presentation of Cleopatra as a scheming and lascivious female; but her mystical role as a love goddess enables her to assert that she is fire and air, her other elements belonging to the baser life she leaves in dying. Shakespeare avails himself richly of the fact that Cleopatra is Egyptian and therefore symbolic of the barbarian religions in which rulers are thought literally to be gods who participate in fertility rites that nature itself demands. Since gods do not die, death for these monarchs must be the entry into a better life in which their libidinal function is carried out more successfully than on earth.

Approaching the intimate history of Antony and Cleopatra in this way, Shakespeare turns it into a variant within the myth of Dido and Aeneas. Vergil had depicted Aeneas' love affair with the Carthaginian queen as a mere distraction, an interlude that precedes the hero's founding of Rome. In Chaucer, Dido and Aeneas were transformed into courtly lovers: Dido dies as a manifestation of the heroic nobility in love, and Aeneas' political mission pales before the quasireligious erotic ideals that his departure is now seen as having betrayed. Christopher Marlowe, writing just before Shakespeare, alters the legend by making Dido into a raging monster whom Aeneas must escape in order to preserve his manhood. In Shakespeare's play, all these elements are combined and reconstituted. His Cleopatra is a regal African like the Dido of Vergil, a woman who understands and appreciates the holiness of love as in Chaucer, and yet a competitor with the male, whom she finally leads to destruction. But since she is also Egyptian, it is the continuance of her love life after death that particularly fascinates Shakespeare. When Antony prepares to die, he foresees his life in eternity as an endless frolic with Cleopatra: "Where souls do couch on flowers, we'll hand in hand,/And with our sprightly port make the ghosts gaze:/Dido and her Aeneas shall want troops,/And all the haunt be ours."

It is, however, in the demise of Cleopatra that Shakespeare most develops the idea of love surviving death. In the first scene of the play Antony and Cleopatra had bantered about the quantification of love, he claiming there is beggary in the love that can be reckoned, while she coquettishly pretends that she will limit how much he can love her. Antony concludes the argument by insisting "Then must thou needs find out new heaven, new earth." He means that by its very nature their love is boundless. The subsequent action shows not only the definition, the precise configuration, of the love between these two but also its bounded limitation within the world. In dying as she does, Cleopatra foresees a new heaven and a new earth closer to the biblical significance of these words, a life beyond death in which love shall have no limit. It will even partake of material goods associated with bodily existence. "I am again for Cydnus," she says, to remind us of the earthly and consummatory splendor in her first meeting with Mark Antony. She hastens to her death in order to reach Antony before he can kiss her servant Iras, who has just died. And this continuance of life will also be a new beginning in marriage. Antony will no longer be the husband of Octavia but hers instead. If not in this world, then in the next one, marriage sanctifies the love that could not be legitimized previously. "Husband, I come," she calls soon after announcing that she has immortal longings in her. In the afterlife she expects to merge the roles of wife and mistress, an aspiration similar to Juliet's when she names Romeo "husband-friend." Nothing that Octavius Caesar acquires through his victory would seem to equal this epiphany of sexual love transcending the temporal order, flourishing in death beyond anything life could offer.

Yet Shakespeare never encourages us to believe that death is preferable to life or that the lovers have succeeded rather than failed. In loving as they have, they achieve a great good, but it is partial and incomplete. The rest of what they wanted in their venture has been lost through love, destroyed by it, the virile male swallowed up by the libidinal female who may provide mystical benefits in another world but cannot help him to survive in this one. Antony's early comment about the nobleness of life takes on a new meaning by the end of the work. It consisted in the embrace between a man and a woman such as himself and Cleopatra "when such a mutual pair/And such a twain can do't." The play demonstrates that they cannot do it, or rather that they cannot get away with it, and for objective reasons that leave open the possibility that far from being an epiphany their love is merely an illusion.

The nineteenth-century conception of Liebestod, love-death, is anticipated in *Antony and Cleopatra* more than in almost any prior work of art. Shakespeare differs from the later Romantics, however, in the calculated distance that his ambivalence poses between the concept and even the most susceptible audience. In *Midsummer Night's Dream* he employs a similar tactic. Here love is associated less with death than with sleep and dreaming, those kinsmen of death that likewise belong to night and the mysteries surrounding our everyday consciousness. The joy and suffering, fulfillment and frustration, insight and absurdity that we observe in the exploits of the lovers throughout *Midsummer Night's Dream* are digested in Theseus' commentary in the final scene. Hearing about the miraculous occurrences we ourselves have been watching, he can only conclude that they are "more strange than true." He likens lovers to madmen and lumps together the lunatic, the lover, and the poet. They are all compacted of imaginings that may create a new religion but cannot make it worthy of acceptance.

Shakespeare's thoughts about the lovers do not end, however, with the speech of Theseus. It functions as a dialectical moment immediately followed by Hippolyta's assertion that what has happened to these young people must itself reveal "something of great constancy;/But howsoever, strange and admirable." The beauty of this play about love pivots upon the discrepancy, and also the responsiveness, between these two points of view. The word "admirable" means "wonderful" in this context, and it is the wonder of love as a transcending experience that Shakespeare balances against the cool reason which Theseus represents. Shakespeare does not worship in the religion of love, or if he does, it is not as one who is blinded by his faith. Much of what is required of the true believer seems ludicrous, false, and revolting to him. But he nevertheless takes his place among the congregation, as one who wishes to revise and reformulate their creed.

In his speech Theseus does not say the lover, the lunatic, and the poet are identical; he only finds them similar. In several plays, however, Shakespeare treats love as if it were a kind of lunacy giving rise to its own type of inferior verse. That lovers often write bad poetry is to Shakespeare a constant source of merriment. We are regaled with the limp stanzas written by Benedick, by Orlando in *As You Like It*, and even by Hamlet when the amatory fit is on him. Benedick and Hamlet recognize that they cannot write good poetry, but Orlando proudly displays his creations on trees in the forest of Arden. This is itself an aberration from civilized behavior and so a form of madness. When his beloved Rosalind, masquerading as a young man, taunts Orlando for misusing the trees, she remarks that "love is merely a madness, and I tell you, deserves as well a dark house and a whip as madmen do; and the reason why they are not so punished and cured is that the lunacy is so ordinary that the whippers are in love too."

The madness in love, as Shakespeare sees it, consists primarily in overvaluation of the object. This was the basic moral in *Troilus and Cressida*, and it is crucial to the ambiguity in *Antony and Cleopatra*. As if he already had both those stories in mind, Shakespeare has Theseus describe love's frantic delusion as the seeing of "Helen's beauty in a brow of Egypt." In *Romeo and Juliet*, the railing Mercutio characterizes all ardent lovers as would-be poets who seek to outdo Petrarch by claiming that neither his nor anyone else's beloved could equal theirs. By comparison, "Laura . . . was a kitchen wench (marry, she had a better love to berhyme her), Dido a dowdy, Cleopatra a gypsy, Helen and Hero hildings and harlots." And just as the lover's will exceeds his capacity, which Troilus had pointed out, so too does a man in love exaggerate the importance of being incapacitated, spurned or otherwise defeated in his choice. In educating Orlando about the absurdities of love, Rosalind tells him that the old chroniclers lie when they say that rejected lovers drop dead: it was not Cressida's infidelity but only a "Grecian club" that ended Troilus' life, and Leander drowned in the Hellespont because he was taken with cramps. "Men have died from time to time, and worms have eaten them, but not for love."

To state that love is prone to self-delusion and overvaluation of the object does not mean that it can never escape these disabilities. Shakespeare gives us examples of men who love ardently but in a manner more defensible. When Henry V woos Katherine of France, he approaches her not only as her conqueror but also as one who loves her truly. That, at least, is what he continually maintains, while also confessing that he knows no ways to mince it in love, that he cannot rhyme himself into a lady's favor, and that he will not pretend that he will die if she rejects his love. He recommends himself as "a fellow of plain and uncoined constancy," a man of good heart, a soldier who bluntly speaks the truth. Though this is their first meeting, Shakespeare expects us to believe that Henry really does love Katherine. Troilus too had praised himself for being unable to sing lovesongs or sweeten his amorous discourse like the clever Greeks. He describes himself, and therefore his ability to love, as "plain and true." As Brutus says in *Julius Caesar*, "there are no tricks in plain and simple faith." Benedick might have said the same, and possibly it is this attitude that explains the simple devotion of Ferdinand to Miranda in *The Tempest* and Florizel to Perdita in *The Winter's Tale*. In Sonnet 130, Shakespeare takes pride in loving a mistress whose "eyes are nothing like the sun." He refuses to depict her features with the inflated language so common in the poetry of lovers, and he concludes this sonnet with an affirmation of love that is strengthened by its capacity to overcome falsifications and a feverish imagination: "I grant I never saw a goddess go;/My mistress, when she walks, treads on the ground./And yet, by heaven, I think my love as rare/As any she belied with false compare."

It is now that we may begin to perceive the ideal of love that Shakespeare holds before him as the touchstone of erotic success. Comedy and romance being media that reveal how consummation may occur in human experience, the Shakespearean comedies and romances end with the achievement of ideal love. It involves marriage, and therefore differs from most Neoplatonic conceptions; but even more important, its basic realism, its resistance to overvaluation, provides a new orientation. While recognizing that the lover sees the beloved as beautiful in one sense or another, Shakespeare identifies love with an attitude that goes far beyond the search for beauty itself. What distinguishes his true or successful lovers is their fidelity to a beloved whose beauty may accompany but does not account for the relationship of love. Instead, love draws upon virtues such as loyalty and becomes an ethical principle that can no longer be submerged in the aesthetic. For the Platonist, goodness and beauty cannot be severed since they both define the highest form and that is the ultimate goal of all desire. Shakespeare, however, is sensitive to the ways in which the two diverge. To contemplate beauty is for him no guarantee that one will act beautifully or even resist an evil temptation to use the beautiful for ugly purposes. A villain like Iago can and does appreciate the beauty in

Desdemona, but it arouses malicious hatred in him which stifles whatever love may also be involved. Moreover, the beautiful as Shakespeare perceives it, in his refusal to think like a metaphysician or theologian, is not eternal. It occurs as a happy accident in nature and lasts within a sharply delimited period of time. Love is an ideal for him not in discovering a beauty that never dies but rather in awakening a constancy of attachment that survives despite the inevitable loss of beauty.

Having made this shift in perspective, we can see why Shakespeare ridicules the bad poetry of lovers. The constancy or fidelity in which love consists must be shown in action. Love defines itself by what the lovers do rather than by their ability to express in words whatever beauty the beloved may already possess. Benedick turns out to be a true and authentic lover because he can unite with Beatrice in concerted action to save their friend Hero. Even if he could write beautiful lines about the charms of Beatrice, his love would not have shown itself in that so much as in his willingness to accept Beatrice as his companion despite her imperfections, all of which he previously delighted in exposing. In Sonnet 116 Shakespeare argues that love involves constancy in two respects: first, in remaining faithful although the beauties of youth—"rosy lips and cheeks"—are cut down by time's destroying sickle; and second, in not altering even when alteration has occurred in the beloved's affection. This is the sonnet that begins with the words "Let me not to the marriage of true minds admit impediments" and ends with the idea of love that "bears it out even to the edge of doom." A love of this sort, surmounting changes in the conduct as well as the physical appearance of the beloved, depends upon endurance through time rather than its transcendence. Showing itself more properly in moral behavior than in poetic excellence, Shakespeare's ideal requires the longevity of an institution like matrimony. Though Sonnet 116 does not deal with married love as such, it is quite appropriate for its opening line to reverberate with language taken from the marriage service.

The second type of constancy described in Sonnet 116 also helps us to understand those instances of love's failure which dominate

Othello, The Winter's Tale, Cymbeline, and *Much Ado About Nothing.* In each of these plays the possibility of married love is defeated, permanently in *Othello* though temporarily in the others, by the fact that the lover alters when he thinks he has found alteration in the beloved. In each play the husband (or betrothed, in the case of Claudio) reacts violently and with a kind of madness to the fear of having been betrayed by his wife. Even in the comedies, where Shakespeare frequently makes light of the cuckolded state he assures men that they will probably experience at some time or other, it is mainly the *idea* of adultery that preoccupies him rather than its actuality. In the plays I have mentioned, the drama arises not from anything the wives have done, none of them being guilty, but rather from the behavior of men tormented by the sheer possibility that their wives may have been unfaithful. Othello, Leontes, Posthumus, and Claudio are husbands who fail in love not merely because they are so easily convinced of the infidelity of their wives, but also because they are unable to remain constant themselves when challenged by this threat to their sense of manliness. Their wild and destructive response to meager evidence enlarged by their jealous imagination is itself an alteration in the face of supposed alteration, and therefore a lack of love. The same might be said of Troilus, but his erotic tragedy belongs to a different category. For one thing, his jealousy is based upon very solid data—even "ocular proof"; also, he has never married Cressida. Their love affair exists in a context of wartime chaos as opposed to the institutional circumstances of domesticity. Its problems are therefore unlike those of marriage.

In depicting wives who are faithful, and in *All's Well That Ends Well* and *The Taming of the Shrew,* wives who are not only faithful but also extremely constant in relation to a cruel husband, Shakespeare would seem to ascribe a greater capacity for marital love to women than to men. At least the women know instinctively what the men have to learn by experience that is painful both for others and themselves. But even in *Othello,* where the enraged husband finally realizes that loving wisely is not the same as loving "too well," the men sometimes succeed in their needed education. In the totality of

the drama, their former jealousy then appears—as Andreas Capellanus would also have said—as an essential part of love, albeit a part
that can destroy the loving relationship itself.

If Shakespeare's jealous husbands fail or falter in their married
love because they delude themselves about their wives, the ones who
succeed are usually those who made a realistic choice from the very
outset. The King of France takes Cordelia, after Lear has disowned
her, because he rightly reasons that her virtues are as great without a
dowry as they would have been with it. He does not claim to bestow
value in loving Cordelia, only to recognize her intrinsic worth; but
this is sufficient for marital harmony.

We learn the same from the three caskets in *The Merchant of Venice*.
The gold and silver caskets do not give access to Portia's love because
they symbolize worldly values (and even beauty itself) that do not
pertain to her inner being. Gold is "what many men desire," and for
each of them silver is "as much as he deserves." The suitors who
choose these caskets are motivated by greed or arrogance, thinking
that the goods they want or the preferment they merit will guarantee success in marriage. They are rejected because their attitude is
purely egocentric: they do not bestow value upon the woman as she
is or accept her in herself. The third casket yields the secret of love
inasmuch as it has no outward show of excellence. Being made of
lead, it is "plain and true." It threatens more than it promises and
therefore requires the lover to "give and hazard all he hath." Portia
immediately reveals that the hazard and the threat in loving her
result from the fact that she is fallible, imperfect, a mortal rather
than a goddess. Despite her heroic achievements in the play, she
presents herself as "an unlessoned girl, unschooled, unpractised."
She knows that this is not exactly true, but it signifies limitations in
her as a human being (and as a lover) that may prevent the suitor
from getting everything he desires or deserves unless he is capable
of taking her as is, faults and all.

Offering herself on these terms, as a base metal rather than a
precious one, Portia illustrates that female submissiveness which
Shakespeare considers the modest virtue required of a good wife.
For all the quality of intellect, independence of spirit, and transves-
tite liberties that he accords the women in his plays, Shakespeare

generally relegates them to a secondary role in the order of command. Those who assert themselves against male dominance, or seek to emulate the male too precisely, are presented as vixens or termagants. Katherine the Shrew is tamed in the way that dogs are trained because a condition considered unnatural has to be driven out of her. Lady Macbeth is herself the "damned spot" that must be purged because she has succeeded in unsexing herself as she originally demanded. Katherine and Lady Macbeth are morally no worse than Petruchio and Macbeth, the males being similar to the females in violence or evil, but as women they bear an additional burden within Shakespeare's morality. They transgress the laws of nature not only in what they do but also in the mere conception of themselves as quasi-males. The crimes of Lady Macbeth are too great for her to be reeducated; but when Katherine's willfulness has been domesticated, transformed into the canine virtues of obedience to one's master and hostility towards everyone else, Shakespeare assures us that she and Petruchio will have a happy life together. Certainly he has shown that they are made for one another. That is not nothing, but neither is it very much. I find it hard to believe, despite some modern interpretations of this play, that the ideal of married love is compatible with the sadomasochism these two have established as the basis of their well-run marriage.

Fortunately, Katherine and Petruchio are not representative of the men and women who show forth Shakespeare's ideas about conjugal love. The harmony that is finally established between them occurs only *after* they have been married. For most Shakespearean couples, the work of accommodation and adjustment between the sexes takes place during the period of courtship prior to marriage. By the time each play ends, hostility has turned into concord, ignorance of erotic reality into well-earned sophistication, love into matrimony. The comedies and romances leave us with the assurance that the marriages will succeed because we have seen the elimination of all the major impediments. In the romances, these impediments are usually external to the lovers. Florizel-Perdita and Ferdinand-Miranda are never in conflict with one another; they are inwardly united from beginning to end, like Romeo and Juliet. And like these two, the lovers in Shakespeare's romances reunite the previous, warring generation, teaching their parents—through the example of inner oneness—the meaning and the efficacy of love. Having overcome external interference from the world at large, the lovers enter into a marital bliss whose magnitude will be even greater than it could have been if the environment had not imposed hurdles to be cleared. Knowing this, in his role as seer of the human heart, Prospero creates obstacles to the "swift business" of union between his daughter and Ferdinand, "lest too light winning make the prize light."

In the comedies, the barriers that initially separate the lovers are internal as well as external, and more often the former rather than the latter. Beatrice and Benedick, Rosalind and Orlando, Helena and Demetrius must first overcome the doubt and diffidence that separate them from each other. Once they have reached agreement between themselves, the world affords no opposition to their union. In their emphasis upon everything in men and women that divides them until the process of accommodation is completed, the comedies are psychologically more realistic than the romances. They are equally idealistic and even fanciful, however, in their comforting assurance that now all will be well.

If we turn to the few places in which Shakespeare deals with the actual content of marriage, as opposed to the ideal of married love, we find little to make us think that all is indeed well. Leaving aside the failed marriages in *Macbeth, King Lear, Hamlet, Othello*, and some of the other tragedies, the marital condition is generally presented as the occasion for bickering, animosity, and constant jockeying for power within the family. Where we encounter husband and wife who do love each other, such as Brutus and Portia in *Julius Caesar* or Macduff and his wife in *Macbeth*, we are told very little about the details of their intimacy. In no place do we see husband and wife learning from one another in the course of their married relationship, and rarely do we see them cooperating in a common cause that matters to them both.

In this regard, consider *All's Well That Ends Well*. Shakespeare there deals with the theme of the wayward husband reconciled to his wife through the resourcefulness of her constant love. It is the same theme as in *The Marriage of Figaro*, both play and opera; but in

Shakespeare, as opposed to these later works of art, the husband does not develop or grow in his attachment to his wife. At the end, having been trapped by her in a definitive manner, he merely submits to the fact of his marriage. Bertram does promise that henceforth he will love his wife "dearly—ever, ever dearly." But nothing in him has changed, and we cannot be expected to believe him. For one thing, we have never seen him living as a married man. In *Cymbeline* the final conversion of Posthumus to repentant, loving husband seems more convincing in view of the suffering he has had to undergo. But there too the married life itself is not presented. The marriages we do see in Shakespeare more often fall between the extremes represented by Titania and Oberon on the one hand, and Hotspur and his wife on the other. The former is the archetype for those screwball Hollywood comedies in the 1930s where a divorced couple play nasty tricks on one another, experiment with extramarital partners who turn out to be as unsuitable a mate as a donkey for the Fairy Queen, and finally realize that imperfect as their love for each other may be, it is preferable (for some unknown reason) to any of the alternatives. At the opposite extreme, the relationship between Hotspur and Lady Percy brooks no possibility of divorce, but neither is it entirely harmonious. It is structured by a constant ambivalence: playfulness and genuine affection mingling with distrust, scorn, and gratuitous insult by a husband whose behavior his wife can scarcely understand.

In the *Sonnets* Shakespeare recommends marriage as an accepted means for procreation. Through it men can reproduce themselves, which is why he urges his beautiful and self-regarding friend to get married, while also continuing the species. The marital condition belongs to that order in nature which Ulysses, Berowne, and other spokesmen for Shakespeare hold up as a blueprint for human emulation. In *The Winter's Tale, As You Like It,* and *The Tempest* nature in a pastoral setting is able to bring man closer to his authentic being. Where life at court is corrupt and even murderous, the countryside reveals human nature at its best. But in all these plays, nature is always shown to be most benign when refined by goods that derive from civilization. Properly employed, these artifices of cultivation are themselves a part of what is natural. In this vein, Polixenes in *The*

Winter's Tale, who must himself learn what is natural to fathers and to sons, remarks that "nature is made better by no mean/But nature makes that mean. So over that art/Which you say adds to nature, is an art/That nature makes." Polixenes' speech is ironic since he is arguing for cross-fertilization even though he wishes to prevent his well-born son from marrying the shepherdess Perdita. In an equally ironic way—tempered by the fact, unknown to her, that she too is of royal blood—Perdita argues against the planting of flowers bred out of different strains. They both see nature as an ordering principle in which civilized and noncivilized forces combine to mutual advantage.

In a similar fashion, marriage itself appears in Shakespeare as the domestication of nature, a humane control upon the primitive instincts that are needed for survival. That is the difference between kind or happy nature in *As You Like It,* which ends in the achievement of multiple marriage, and the raw, unbearable miseries of nature in *King Lear,* where married love has been destroyed by the evil sisters. In *As You Like It* Shakespeare introduces a hymn to marriage which extols "high wedlock" as a "blessed bond of board and bed." What happens at the board and in the bed, eating and copulating, results from civilization no less than instinct. Shakespeare idealizes married love because it satisfies social as well as biological need. The mystic goodness of married love, a consummation as natural as the ingesting of wholesome food, he celebrates in *The Winter's Tale* when Leontes receives a second chance to love his wife, who is thereby resurrected: "O, she's warm! [*Embracing her.*] If this be magic, let it be an art/Lawful as eating."

As a corollary to his idealization of married love, Shakespeare attacks unsanctioned lust as well as sacramental virginity. In *Measure for Measure* he puts these two in direct conflict with one another as a way of suggesting that neither is finally acceptable. The passion of Angelo for Isabella is condemned as sexual turpitude not only because it is forced upon her through threats to her brother, but also because it has no place within a prospective marriage. Isabella rejects this opportunity to save her brother's life because she is convinced that her honor as a virgin has greater value. When the Duke proposes marriage to her, however, she is given a more suitable opportunity to renounce virginity.

In *Measure for Measure*, marriage is held in such great esteem as to be able to cleanse the illicit behavior of Claudio and Juliet, which becomes legitimate by means of it, and even to provide an adequate mechanism for Angelo's reformation. By marrying the woman with whom he too has had premarital relations, Angelo makes amends to society and need not be punished for his misuse of power. Lucio, who openly advocates licentiousness, is dealt with much more severely than the high-principled Angelo. Lucio is forced to marry a prostitute, in retribution for his sexual philosophy as much as for his slandering of the Duke. One feels that Angelo, that fallen angel, has been spared because he had the right ideas about love and marriage, though he could not resist the temptation of Isabella's flesh. Angelo will doubtless prove an unsatisfactory husband, but here again Shakespeare shows it is the ideal of married love that interests him more than the actual conditions under which it is likely to occur. Within the broad flowering of his genius, the latter would seem to be one of the realms in which his imagination was least developed. Married love as a day-by-day experience was possibly an aspect of human nature he knew very little about.

But though Shakespeare would seem to know less about the ramifications of married love than about other forms of life, he often studies marriage in relation to institutions that threaten it. As the domestication of nature by means of a civilized convention, Shakespearean marriage is always in danger of being undermined by the rest of society. Not only is there opposition from one or another family, as in *Romeo and Juliet* or *The Merry Wives of Windsor*, and political difficulties, as in *Antony and Cleopatra*, but also there runs through much of Shakespeare's work a dramatic contrast between the goods of marital love and those of friendship.

In the *Sonnets* the friendship between the poet and the man he is addressing may well be taken to be a kind of homosexual love.

Unless the "dark lady" is another man or else a feminine component within the beloved friend, both of which are possibilities for interpretation, she represents a woman for whom they vie though they would not marry her. In *The Two Gentlemen of Verona* the values of friendship and marriage are more clearly pitted against each other. First friendship is demolished by love, when one of the men neglects his own sweetheart and tries to steal the other's lady. Then friendship conquers love once the traitor confesses his guilt and refuses his friend's magnanimous offer to let him have the woman. Finally the two ideals are merged, the friends returning to one another's affection and each marrying the lady he originally loved. Like the *Sonnets*, the play is primarily concerned with the problems of friendship or love between men; but it concludes with a double marriage affording the complex pleasures of a ménage à quatre— "one feast, one house, one mutual happiness," as the final lines proclaim. *The Merchant of Venice* ends with a similar arrangement, Antonio being rewarded for his friendship by the opportunity to live with Bassanio and Portia.

In *Romeo and Juliet* it is Romeo's friendship for dead Mercutio that leads him to fight Tybalt and thus to be exiled from the love of Juliet. In *Midsummer Night's Dream* love and friendship conflict at first and then are harmonized when friends and spouses set up housekeeping together; but in this play Shakespeare concentrates on the question of love's irrationality and we do not see friendship in action. In *Othello* the ideals of love and friendship have both been so greatly debased that no reconciliation is possible. The intimacy that binds Iago to Othello is a false and malignant friendship based upon Othello's mistaken belief that Iago is "full of love and honesty" towards him. They discuss Desdemona with the freedom of soldiers united by male bonding to which all women must be subordinate. Real as it may be, Othello's love for Desdemona is not strong enough to protect him from his friend's treachery. Chaos is come again when he loves her not, because then he behaves like Iago, who says he suspects his own wife of infidelity (with Othello).

Assuming the manner of the typically despotic husband, generally much older than his wife, Othello portrays the odious behavior that folk and courtly literature presented as justifiable grounds for adultery. His jealousy is therefore a way of eliciting punishment upon himself for his failure as a husband. The curse of marriage, he insists, is the fact that men possess women—"We can call these delicate creatures ours"—and yet they cannot totally control their wives' appetitive nature. In Act I, Othello said he wished to live with Desdemona "not/To please the palate of my appetite,/Not to comply with heat—the young affects/In me defunct—and proper satisfaction;/But to be free and bounteous to her mind." This intention cannot be carried out, however, if one assumes that a husband can possess or even govern a wife's desires. It is also possible that Othello would have felt no jealousy for Desdemona's innocent friendship with Cassio if the "young affects" had not been defunct in him throughout their marriage.

I am not suggesting that *Othello* be read as a study in the horrors of the male menopause. But one cannot fail to notice that Shakespeare prevents us from imagining Othello and Desdemona in any happy sexual consummation of their marriage. At the beginning of the play, and then again on Cyprus—as if to make sure we do not miss the point—their lovemaking is interrupted by Iago and a world that disprizes love. To speculate, as some recent critics have, about whether Desdemona remained a virgin, or whether Othello insanely feels that he must chastise her for no longer being one now that they are married, seems to me unwarranted, beyond substantiation. What Shakespeare does imply, however, is that the matrimonial bed is not a scene of spousal joys for this married couple. It is finally presented to us, on stage, as a place in which the violence that springs from hatred and frustration is performed.

Desdemona originally told us that she saw Othello's visage "in his mind." This balances his desire to be bounteous to her mind, as if they both had no other faculty. But if that is how they perceive one another, she cannot be expected to have rejuvenated the palate of his appetite—at least, not for long. Though she wishes to accompany Othello to Cyprus lest she be bereft of "the rites for which I love him," her father has already described her as "A maiden never bold;/Of spirit so still and quiet, that her motion/Blush'd at herself." It was for her mildness, and for her wondrous pity towards him, that Othello claims to have loved her. Had she succeeded in reawakening his sexuality, he—who finally taunts her for being "obedient," i.e. compliant to men's desires—would have reasoned, in his madness, that she is indeed a "cunning whore of Venice."

Othello reveals what happens when a man fails in friendship as well as in love, trusting a friend who acts maliciously and distrusting a wife whose conduct is irreproachable. This is the same theme as in Molière's *Tartuffe*. Elmire, the wife in *Tartuffe*, can prove herself to her husband because she enjoys the powers of erotic intelligence that belong to several of Shakespeare's women in the comedies. She understands her husband's feelings and is well experienced in the vicissitudes of marital sexuality. Desdemona lacks these natural talents. In her "monumental alabaster," she appears as a latter-day replica of Dante's Beatrice, but one whose spiritual beauty is now besmirched by conjugal matters beyond her comprehension. In portraying her marriage as her undoing, as well as her husband's, Shakespeare never doubts the ideality of married love. He merely shows, as in so many of his plays, how rare and difficult it is for human beings to live in accordance with this ideal.

8
Puritans and Rationalists

In The Thinking Of Post-Neoplatonists such as Spenser and Donne, married love establishes itself as an ideal possibility in human nature. In Shakespeare's work it serves as the supreme goal for which true lovers yearn. It is only in the following generation, however, that the conjugal ideal becomes a concept that is relevant to the everyday lives of ordinary people. Among the Puritans in England and America the ideal of married love takes on social as well as religious importance. In John Milton it finds its greatest exponent and, in a sense, its greatest critic. For Milton, as for other Puritans, marriage was the highest bond that could exist between man and woman on earth, but also it was the root of their greatest misery and degradation.

Writing in the mid-seventeenth century, Milton inherits ideas about married love that ultimately derive from the beginnings of the Reformation about a hundred and thirty years earlier. These ideas contained within them a conflict that becomes agonized in Milton more than in any other writer, though as I shall argue later in this chapter, something comparable occurred in the Rationalism that succeeded the Catholic Counter-Reformation on the Continent. The conflict was already present in the tension between two of the directions taken by Luther as his thinking about love developed. On the one hand, Luther justified marriage for priests as well as laymen on the grounds that neither celibacy nor virginity was to be equated with chastity of soul. Where marriage included conjugal love, sexual behavior was redeemed by the presence of love itself. Marriage was ordained in part for the gratification of sexual need, and for Luther as for his medieval forebears this meant that marriage was the appointed means of regulating a natural appetite, like hunger or thirst, that man could not escape. But, on the other hand, Luther insisted that no special value or preeminence should be attached to sex. It was not to be idealized or even dignified as something that might be enjoyed for its own sake. It was still original sin, though acceptable if it occurred within marriage, and therefore no type of sexual love would in itself enable man to rise above his fallen state.

This ambivalence within Luther's outlook was complicated by his firm belief that God's agapē could descend upon a married couple, sanctify their love, and thereby cleanse their moments of closest contact—sexual as well as nonsexual—of all impurity. Their union would then become a vessel and a manifestation of divine love as it works its goodness through the world. From this point of view, sexual love in marriage was itself a holy communion with the godhead.

All these strands recur throughout Puritan writings of the subsequent generations, though doubt about the spirituality of sexual love often prevailed. This is not to say that the Puritans were "puritanical." Even John Calvin, whose theocracy in Geneva legislated death as the punishment for adultery and strictly limited public demonstrations of affection, proclaimed the importance of sex within marriage and allowed divorce on the grounds of impotence. The Puritans in England and America thought of sexual love as part of the natural integument that held together the family unit. For them, married love was not a passionate or extravagantly emotional oneness but rather a constant, enduring fellowship between a man and a woman who create a beneficial society within the wilderness of nature. Though it was the greatest unity that human beings could achieve among themselves, conjugal love included respect as opposed to adoration, friendliness instead of rapture, a wedding of compatible interests (financial as well as personal) and not the merging of spiritual atoms.

This ideal of marriage as the manifestation of "heterosexual friendship" and what would later be called "esteem enliven'd by desire" predominates in Milton's work, but always in a dialectical struggle with the belief that married love involves a oneness more intimate than mere friendship or esteem. The two conceptions structure the human drama in *Paradise Lost*. For there the nature of marriage is studied by reference to a man and a woman who were originally merged, since one of them was fashioned out of the rib of the other. This is the "one flesh" of which the Bible spoke. But Milton, making the bond between Adam and Eve an archetype for all marital unions, presents their relationship as more than just a physical merging. When Adam first sees the new companion God has created for him, he describes her as:

> "Bone of my bone, flesh of my flesh, my Self
> Before me. Woman is her name, of Man
> Extracted; for this cause he shall forego
> Father and mother, and to his Wife adhere;
> And they shall be one flesh, one heart, one soul."

This merged condition is essential to Milton's epic because it explains how Adam could fall from grace. When Eve offers him the forbidden fruit, he is not beguiled. Eve does not seduce him and neither does she deceive him in any way. She accurately describes her encounter with a serpent who claims that eating this fruit has given him the power of speech and therefore is not harmful. Adam instantly realizes that Eve has transgressed, that she is doomed, and that she will die. He freely joins her in her fate, with full knowledge of its implications, as an expression of what Eve herself calls "exceeding love,/Illustrious evidence, example high!" In his polemical writings Milton argued for the legitimacy of divorce, but that solution never occurs to Adam. On the contrary, Adam says that even if God now creates another Eve to take the place of this one who has violated the great command, he could never bear the loss of his original wife. Having to decide between identification with her as against continued rectitude in the eyes of the Lord, Adam chooses the former:

" . . . I with thee have fixed my lot,
Certain to undergo like doom. If death
Consort with thee, death is to me as life;
So forcible within my heart I feel
The bond of Nature draw me to my own—
My own in thee; for what thou art is mine.
Our state cannot be severed; we are one,
One flesh; to lose thee were to lose myself."

Eve weeps tenderly and for joy at the suggestion that Adam loves her enough to commit what may be a crime, to risk God's displeasure, to face the possibility of death; but what surely moves her most is this proof of their inseparability, "the link of nature," as Adam calls it. Though Milton states that Adam eats the forbidden fruit "Against his better knowledge, not deceived,/But fondly overcome with female charm," he nevertheless treats Adam's act of love as a development in his spiritual capability. Here, before he partakes of the Tree of the Knowledge of Good and Evil, Adam has already recognized and accepted his nature as a human being, as a man who feels the love that merges him with woman. Such awareness could not have existed previously. Eve speaks the truth when she tells Adam that this was the "happy trial of thy love, which else/So eminently never had been known." His growth, in self-knowledge as well as sensibility, Adam dare not admit to God's messengers. When the Son of God descends to judge him, Adam conceals the love that motivated his transgression. He puts the blame on Eve: "Her doing seemed to justify the deed." He is condemned for having obeyed her instead of God and for being led by her instead of guiding her himself. But the facts, as we have seen them, are somewhat different.

That Adam should have hidden his actual motivation in this fashion may be taken as evidence of his ultimate cowardice. God is not so easily fooled, however, and it is significant that the Divine Presence makes no reference to what Milton knew to be the character of Adam's guilt. His offense consists not in obedience to the woman, but in putting his love of her before his love of God, in giving the link of nature priority over submission to God's commandment. And possibly the fact that Milton fails to draw this implication should alert us to the great importance of what he is unconsciously avoiding. That is the sin of narcissism, the improper love of self. In being merged indissolubly, Adam and Eve are, in effect, a single androgynous being and their greatest crime consists in acting as if they were complete within their totality. In Plato's *Symposium*, it was the arrogance of the hermaphroditic creatures, secure within their spherical oneness, that caused the gods to split them into the two sexes of male and female. In Milton, narcissistic love of oneself—what in Christian doctrine would be called the sin of pride—issues from the first experiences of Eve, who admires her image in a stream before she has been introduced to Adam. She quickly realizes how much better it is to love him than to love herself alone or any image of herself. But since she is part of him, their oneness merely creates a larger, and more dangerous, narcissism in them both.

Only God properly loves himself—for Milton that was incontestable. Having eaten the fruit of the forbidden tree, Adam and Eve wish to be "equal with gods," i.e. self-sufficient and therefore capable of expressing their love entirely within themselves. When Adam had originally requested a companion with whom he might converse, he remarked that he was incapable of enjoying solitude like God, who is alone from all eternity but perfect in himself. In seeking now the communal and "collateral" love of another being, Adam is striving for a closer emulation of the divine sufficiency. His fall would not have been as poignant had he not been venturing toward a condition that Milton sees (paradoxically) as both ideal and sinful.

In the attempt to approximate divinity through a process of merging, we may recognize the influence of Neoplatonism as well as Lutheran ideas about agapē. When God's emissary, Raphael, satisfies Adam's curiosity about love among the heavenly spirits—whether they "mix/Irradiance, virtual or immediate touch?"—we learn that they experience total merging. They are, as Rousseau would later say about the saints in his firmament, completely transparent to one another. "Easier than air with air, if Spirits embrace,/ Total they mix, union of pure with pure/Desiring...." This exceeds human nature, for the angels are not restrained by either flesh or mortal soul; but in some respects their love is similar to Adam's:

"Whatever pure thou in the body enjoy'st/ . . . we enjoy/In eminence."

Something similar was the goal to which the lovers in Donne's
poetry aspired, a mingling of spirits that does not eliminate bodily
enjoyment though it transcends the body itself. Milton's Neoplatonic sources also reverberate in the serpent's suggestion to Eve that
death can only mean a blissful putting off of the human in order to
put on the divine. And finally, there is Adam's perception of Eve, at
the moment of creation, as "so lovely fair,/That what seemed fair in
all the world seemed now/Mean, or in her summed up." In this most
beautiful paradise, Eve is the highest beauty and therefore worthy
of inspiring love in Adam. She is also a Rose among roses, that being
the circumstance in which the serpent discovers her. He seduces her
in a corrupted reenactment of the *Romance of the Rose*. Adam himself
has woven a garland of roses for her; but when he learns what she
has done, he drops it and all the roses instantly fade. Never again will
she be for him a Renaissance embodiment of beauty.

Despite these intimations of Neoplatonism, the ruling ideology in
Milton's epic remains Lutheran and Puritan. The contrary values
within Protestantism operate upon the dilemma that Adam experiences as a loving husband. Before the fall, he appeals to Raphael for
help. As if Raphael were a celestial therapist, Adam tells him of a
marital problem that lies athwart his love for Eve. Though Adam
realizes that she was created as a being secondary to himself, inferior
in mind and less capable of asserting God-given dominion over
other creatures, her extraordinary beauty and completeness in herself makes everything she says seem "wisest, virtuousest, discreetest,
best." Raphael perceives in this situation what Freud (or
Shakespeare) would consider an "overvaluation of the object." He
encourages Adam to assert his own self-esteem, to employ his
reason, and to recognize that true love involves a realistic appreciation of beauty. If Eve's loveliness of appearance transports Adam, it
is well worth cherishing and admiring, but his feelings must not turn
into abject subjugation. Neither can Eve's ability to arouse his sexual
appetite, the sense of touch and "dear delight" that leads to propagation, justify Adam's overestimation. Adam must remember that

passion is common to all the animals and therefore cannot reveal the great potential in human love. Raphael tells him to love Eve for what is "higher in her society."

This sounds like the conventional wisdom that one can expect of a visiting angel instructing an innocent and newly created man. But Adam surprises us by insisting that Raphael has not really understood his problem. It is not Eve's physical beauty or sexual attractiveness that he is referring to. These do awaken in him "mysterious reverence," but they delight him less than a kind of behavior that Raphael does not seem to comprehend:

> " . . . those graceful acts,
> Those thousand decencies, that daily flow
> From all her words and actions, mixed with love
> And sweet compliance, which declare unfeigned
> Union of mind, or in us both one soul—
> Harmony to behold in wedded pair
> More grateful than harmonious sound to the ear."

Adam shrewdly remarks that in itself delight cannot cause subjection and that Raphael himself has told him that love is both the way and the guide to heaven. Why then does Adam experience this problem about decision and command, this unwelcome willingness to accede to Eve's persuasion? It is here that he asks Raphael about the nature of angelic merging. Raphael answers with a smile that glows "Celestial rosy-red, Love's proper hue." But he does not resolve Adam's difficulty. For Adam and Eve are not pure spirits and their oneness can never be achieved in the manner of angels. Raphael has succeeded in warning Adam of the dangers that lurk in the grassy goodness of Eden, but he has failed to show him how to cope with the intricacies of married love. This is where Adam needed help most of all, and possibly he is forced to undergo his painful course of education because it is an area in which the celestial hordes are too inexperienced or confused to give advice.

Though Adam is perplexed in his relationship to Eve, most critics have assumed that Milton himself believed in male superiority. His comparison of Adam and Eve seems unequivocal:

Not equal, as their sex not equal seemed;
For contemplation he and valour formed,
For softness she and sweet attractive grace;
He for God only, she for God in him.
His fair large front and eye sublime declared
Absolute rule; . . .

Milton's prose as well as his poetry frequently asserts that the woman resembles God's image less than the man does, that she stands on a lower level in the cosmic hierarchy, and that she can never pretend to equality of intellect or practical judgment. In his *Life of Milton* Dr. Johnson remarks that "there appears in his books something like a Turkish contempt of females, as subordinate and inferior beings." Adam himself gleans the following as the moral of his embittering experience: "Thus it shall befall/Him who, to worth in women overtrusting,/Lets her will rule."

Adam says this when Eve blames him for weakly having yielded to her desire to work alone despite his fears that Satan could thus get at her more easily. But at this point the fallen couple are bickering about responsibility and their remarks mainly reflect the state of their anxiety. Of greater relevance, I think, are the various modifications to the principle of inequality that occur not only in *Paradise Lost* but also in Milton's other writings. In *Tetracordon*, where Milton argues that in general the male must govern the female, he also states that "particular exceptions may have place, if she exceed her husband in prudence and dexterity, and he contentedly yield, for then a superior and more natural law comes in, that the wiser should govern the less wise, whether male or female." In *Paradise Lost*, as one of the first effects of eating the forbidden fruit, Eve consciously aspires to greater equality with Adam. "Inferior, who is free?" she asks herself, wondering whether she should withhold her newly acquired knowledge from him in order to elicit his love more effectively and to render herself "more equal, and perhaps—/A thing not undesirable—sometime/Superior." When she nevertheless shares her knowledge and Adam shows his devotion by identifying with her fate, she weeps in the realization that his love, the link of nature, is itself an equalizing force.

In judging Adam and Eve, the Son of God condemns the woman to a marital condition in which she shall submit to her husband's will and he shall rule over her. This, however, had been presented as their life in Eden. What has been eliminated in the fallen state that Milton now envisages is any final equalization between man and wife. Yet it was Adam's request for an equal that led to Eve's creation in the first place. Soon after he comes into being, Adam complains that his life in Eden is solitary and incomplete since the other creatures are not his equals. Arguing with the Lord, he speaks of fellowship or philia which has thus far been denied to him: "Among unequals what society/Can sort, what harmony or true delight?/Which must be mutual, in proportion due/Given and received."

The mutuality of delight that Adam seeks includes the give-and-take of sexual pleasure. Immediately after he acquires a wife, he leads her to the nuptial bower. She had been created out of him while he slept, the product of an erotic dream. Though she now blushes and shows virgin modesty, she follows him in the mysterious rite of sexual consummation. As early as St. Augustine, Christian orthodoxy had maintained that there was no sexual desire in Eden prior to the fall. Augustine also wondered why God had given Adam a woman to eliminate his loneliness when it would have been much preferable to have created another man as the friend and equal that he required.

In his prose writings Milton ridicules this suggestion, but in *Paradise Lost* he capitalizes upon Augustine's surmise that sexual intercourse would have been necessary even before the fall since that was the method of propagation God had prescribed. Augustine insisted that coitus occurred without passion, without libidinal impulse, without desire of any sort—merely as an agency of free will: "those parts, like all the rest, would be set in motion at the command of the will; and without the seductive stimulus of passion, with calmness of mind . . . the male semen could have been introduced into the womb of the wife with the integrity of the female genital organ being preserved." To Milton this obviously made no sense at all. His Adam and Eve are created as fully sexual beings, luxuriant in their instinctual drive, ecstatically gratified by erotic consummation, utterly unaware that voluptuous pleasures can be anything but pure and wholesome. With his Puritan denial that virginity is a more spiritual condition than married love, Milton consistently argues that there can be nothing sinful in sexuality itself.

At the same time, the unfallen Adam recognizes that sexual goodness, "the sum of earthly bliss/Which I enjoy," lies at the root of the problem he had hoped Raphael would help him to understand. It is because she is so satisfying in her sexuality, so perfect as a means of gratifying his turbulent passion, that Eve seems absolute and awesome to him. After the fall Adam condemns his former attitude as one in which sensual appetite usurped the prerogatives of sovereign reason. In depicting the earlier state, however, Milton portrays it in his freshest and loveliest poetry as totally innocent, untainted by anything guilty, shameful, or disordered.

With the eating of the forbidden fruit, the nature of human sexuality changes. In a sense, it becomes less consummatory. It is now an intoxication that excites beyond its ability to satisfy. The eaten fruit is thus equivalent to the love potion that Tristan and Iseult drink. It resembles the passion flower whose juice infects Titania's dreams. First when Eve eats and then again when Adam does, the earth trembles and nature groans—as when the high seas rose in torment around Tristan's boat and the order of things suffered a violation when Titania chose a donkey as her beloved. Because they are inebriated by this poisonous kind of love, Adam and Eve feel as if they have indeed ascended to the gods. What previously had been pure and sinless in their sexuality, though fully sensuous and wholly passionate, now turns into "lust."

The debased condition created by the eating of the fruit Milton characterizes with words such as "lascivious," "wanton," "carnal," "inflaming." Not only does Eve show lack of modesty and Adam greater urgency than ever before, but also they are "wearied" by their amorous play and eventually fall into a "grosser sleep/Bred of unkindly fumes." But though these new experiences presumably result from the change in Adam and Eve's sexuality, what that change might be is not immediately clear. In treating unfallen sex as "purity" and "innocence," Milton had never denied that it included the intensity that we normally associate with libidinal drive. On the contrary, Adam describes his original sexuality as different from the delicate enjoyment of taste or sight, or the smelling of flowers, or hearing the melody of birds. From the very beginning, sexual impulse is for him "vehement desire," "transported touch," "commotion strange." How, then, does unfallen sexuality differ from the lust and lasciviousness of the later state?

To answer this question, we must return to the scene in which Eve, discovering her own water image before meeting Adam, narcissistically dotes upon it. She is then directed towards another human being, albeit one organically linked to her, in the hope that she can overcome the dangers of fixation upon herself. Eating the forbidden fruit, however, she acquires knowledge of good and evil. This entails awareness of one's inadequacies, and therefore creates anxieties of self-consciousness that belong to all morality. Fallen sex is no longer innocent inasmuch as it arises not spontaneously but rather as an expression of needs (both physical and interpersonal) that one is consciously, *self-consciously*, trying to satisfy. That is how Milton describes the later responses of Adam and Eve, emphasizing their lack of carefree pleasurability. This in turn is related to the fact that sex now becomes something they find shameful. They are even ashamed of their nudity. The Son of God shows his compassion by giving them their first suit of clothes, but he does nothing to lighten the burden of moral self-consciousness, the superego, which they have acquired in eating the forbidden fruit.

But still, one may ask, what is it that makes nudity shameful, or sexuality in general? Since their naked pleasures in the flesh involved no shame before the fall, why should they do so now? I think Milton would reply that Adam and Eve are ashamed because they have violated God's law. Since God is love, they have sinned against love itself and therefore contaminated the core of their most intimate union. Milton consistently portrays the later sexuality as a condition in which Adam and Eve use one another in a calculated effort to satisfy their appetites, instead of achieving sexual consummation in the process of loving one another. Where sex had formerly been the expression of love, it is now limited to mutual self-gratification. Adam and Eve are united by their joint participation in guilt, but the guilt itself divides them in a way that creates shame as well as the pained self-consciousness of their new sexuality.

Milton thus confronts us with a distinction between two types of sexual ontology. It is a dualism that recurs throughout his writing and helps to explain how he could have repeatedly condemned "sensual enjoyment" while idealizing the sexual pleasures of conjugal love. On the one hand, he unleashes an endless diatribe against carnal lust when it causes a man and a woman to "fadge together" in a loveless sexual union. A recent author has extracted the following phrases from Milton's prose descriptions of this kind of sexuality: "the quintessence of an excrement," "the prescribed satisfaction of an irrational heat," "a beastial necessity," "beastial burning," "animal or beastish meetings," "a brutish congress," "the sting of a brute desire," "the promiscuous draining of a carnal rage." On the other hand, Milton never ceases to extol the "rites/Mysterious of connubial love." It is, as Milton says in an image whose sexual import he must have intended, a "Perpetual fountain of domestic sweets." As a mechanism of creation, sexual intercourse within the bonds of marital oneness cannot be impure:

> Our Maker bids increase; who bids abstain
> But our destroyer, foe to God and Man?
> Hail, wedded Love, mysterious law, true source
> Of human offspring, sole propriety
> In Paradise of all things common else!
> By thee adulterous lust was driven from men. . . .

The contrast Milton draws is clear enough, but its fidelity to the myth of Adam and Eve seems less apparent. Wedded love is ranked as infinitely superior to the pleasures of prostitution ("the bought smile/Of harlots"), or the joys of promiscuity ("Casual fruition"), or even the elevated flights of courtly love ("court amours . . . which the starved lover sings/To his proud fair, best quitted with disdain"). But is the superior goodness of marital sex to be found in the world outside of Eden, or only in Adam and Eve's unfallen bliss? Milton, like Luther and Calvin, accepts the orthodox belief in original sin. On this view, mankind as it now exists is fundamentally depraved, having inherited the sinfulness that resulted from the great transgression. That would mean that after the fall all natural responses are corrupt and therefore all sexuality is one or another version of lust. Yet Milton refuses to accept any such conclusion. He persists in believing that wedded love, whenever it occurs, reinstates the purity and innocence that characterized the sexuality of Adam and Eve before the fall.

That marriage can effect this miracle serves as an article of faith in all Puritan theology. It recurs throughout Protestant thought, from the beginnings to the present. Since man is sinful by nature, he cannot escape postlapsarian sexuality through any efforts of his own. Through agapē, however, God may descend into a particular wedded union and bestow upon it connubial love that restores the blissful sexuality for which man was created before he fell. The institution of marriage provides a context in which this may happen. Without it, sexual behavior can never attain the inherent innocence that God intended; but where there is married love, sex is purified by the presence of God.

So firmly does Milton believe in the sanctity of married love that he argues against the continuance of any marriage in which it no longer exists. His writings on divorce advocate the legality of dissolving a marriage whenever love has disappeared, for the married condition is desecrated if couples stay together once they no longer love each other. In *Samson Agonistes*, where Milton portrays Delilah as the faithless wife of Samson, he describes their marriage as a bondage that should be ended out of respect for the holiness of married love itself. As Samson, eyeless and demeaned, grinds at the mill with slaves, so too does Milton elsewhere remark that laws of marriage that prevent divorce condemn men and women to "grind in the mill of an undelighted and servile copulation."

But though Milton argues for divorce as the remedy to loveless sex, and in a similar vein minimizes the sinfulness of adultery, he does not identify married love with the purity or innocence of its sexuality. That was for him only a secondary part of matrimony. The Book of Common Prayer had defined the purposes of marriage as procreation of children, avoidance of fornication among those who lack "the gift of continence," and formation of a "mutual society, help, and comfort" that man and wife should have for one another in prosperity as well as adversity. While interpreting procreation and the avoidance of fornication in such a way that continence no longer has the virtue of a special gift, Milton makes the creation of a mutual society the first and principal purpose of marriage. In *The Doctrine and Discipline of Divorce* he stresses the "peculiar comfort," the "fitness of mind and disposition," the "apt and cheerful conversation" that truly unite a married couple. He uses the word "conversation" to mean companionship, solace, mutual concern, and the friendly communication of feelings and ideas. By considering this function more important than even the return to purified sexuality, Milton reinforces the Puritan approach to love between man and wife. He talks about "free and lightsome conversation" in a way that may seem foreign to the stolidity and dullness of some of the more puritanical Puritans, and certainly his acceptance of the sexual element in marriage went beyond anything that could be tolerated by fellow religionists who reviled him as a "libertine," but his doctrine nevertheless begins and ends as an explication of how heterosexual friendship, the Puritan ideal of marriage, could be defended as a human virtue.

Within the realm of Milton's imagination, the true libertine is, of course, Satan. When he first watches the wedded bliss of Adam and Eve as they embrace, he burns with the same jealousy and anger that Molière's Dom Juan experiences while observing the happy and authentic love that binds a newly married pair. Dom Juan vows to destroy their happiness by seducing the bride. Satan invades the mind of Eve with a libidinal dream, presumably of an adulterous sort, and finally completes his seduction when the serpent rises to the clouds with Eve in an ecstasy of exhilaration that follows her eating the forbidden fruit, both the rising and the eating being symbolic of illicit sexual pleasure.

To oppose the Satanic influence, Milton proposes the human capacity for "conversation." The most moving and profound conversation between Adam and Eve occurs, though this is only intimated by Milton, in their postlapsarian state. For they learn to live together, surviving in a hostile environment and with full awareness of their limitations. In a sense, the serpent did not deceive them. He promised that they would be as gods through their knowledge of good and evil, and indeed they achieve a maturity of love, a mutual and superior oneness in the face of sin, guilt, and perpetual exile, that they could never have experienced in their childlike innocence. Their progress leads them not only into distrust of one another, not only into hatred and tormented sexuality, but also into an abiding love that enables them to rise above their imperfections. In the world in which *we* live, the love they finally achieve stands as a meaningful possibility. It is true to our reality, whereas their earlier love seems like an imagined wish-fulfillment, a dream of how things *might* have been.

The genius of Milton consists in his ability to recognize and describe the goodness of love in both dimensions: the benign utility of realistic married love as well as the joy and poetic simplicity of its idealistic counterpart. In the experience of young men and women, a brief period of innocent courtship often precedes the marital routine of intimacy with a spouse burdened like oneself by daily necessities. Throughout the history of a marriage one experiences elements of both types of love. Each is predicated upon the communicative companionship that Milton considers uppermost and that he encourages us to harmonize with consummatory sex. For despite the sadness of it all, Milton's vision of the world remains optimistic. Though he realizes how difficult it is to combine the contrary modes of love and sexuality within an institution such as marriage, he never wavers in his belief that married love enables God to carry out on earth his providential mission. The final passage in *Paradise Lost* may fill us with commiseration for Adam and Eve, and pity for ourselves who know too well the world into which they are now wandering, but the lines do not depress or dismay us:

> Some natural tears they dropped, but wiped them soon;
> The world was all before them, where to choose
> Their place of rest, and Providence their guide.
> They, hand in hand, with wandering steps and slow,
> Through Eden took their solitary way.

When first they made love, "into their inmost bower/Handed they went." Now that they are going into the great and frightening world, they hold hands again. On both occasions they are joined by a similar bond, but stumbling together into our own reality they experience a love that seems to us more thoroughly human than before—closer, at least, to what we recognize as human nature.

In offering his optimistic myth, Milton nowhere pretends that the harmonization of married love and passion, of marriage and sexual love, can often or consistently occur in the real world. When Adam berates his fallen spouse, he laments God's decision to generate mankind bisexually. It is a sentiment one might have expected from Plato or Augustine, who thought it would have been preferable for human beings to propagate by fertilization outside the body in the manner of fish. But even Luther remarks that, if he had been consulted, he would have recommended that God continue the process of creation by making each person himself, as he did with Adam. In Milton, Adam's plea for asexual propagation serves as the immediate prelude to his account of why man will rarely find a happy marriage in the brave new world outside of Eden:

> " . . . For either
> He never shall find out fit mate, but such
> As some misfortune brings him, or mistake;
> Or whom he wishes most shall seldom gain,
> Through her perverseness, but shall see her gained
> By a far worse, or if she love, withheld
> By parents; or his happiest choice too late
> Shall meet, already linked and wedlock-bound
> To a fell adversary, his hate or shame:
> Which infinite calamity shall cause
> To human life, and household peace confound."

In the context of his total vision, Milton is merely detailing the dangers that married love must overcome. The harmonization of sex and friendship through marriage may be uncommon, but Milton sees it as a viable hope for man's redemption on earth. Despite his own personal failures, married love remains for him a basic and attainable goal in human nature.

The prevailing view among seventeenth-century philosophers was, however, much more pessimistic. Particularly in the great school of Rationalism, which developed mainly on the Continent and often reflected attitudes of the Counter-Reformation, the conflict between sexual and marital interests was seen as inevitable in man's condition. In its broadest outlines, this idea was the traditional and orthodox view that existed in Plato and Aristotle, the Stoics, and the fathers of the Christian church, as well as in secular moralists like Andreas Capellanus and Montaigne. Andreas Capellanus belongs on this list to the extent that his interlocutors deny that courtly love can exist within a marriage. The latter might include conjugal affection but it excluded sexual passion while the former burned with an erotic intensity that could always jeopardize the comfort and stability of married love. Except for the fact that Augustine and Aquinas condemn courtly love precisely on these grounds, they distinguish between sexual and marital love in a similar fashion.

In the line of historical influence, however, it may have been Montaigne who had a more immediate effect upon the seventeenth-century Rationalists. Speaking as one who recognizes the goodness of both marriage and sexual love, Montaigne argues that each must exclude the other. A good marriage tries to create between the sexes a bond similar to friendship. It is "a sweet association in life, full of constancy, trust, and an infinite number of useful and solid services and mutual obligations." Though he relishes the pleasures of sex and knows that women also do, Montaigne insists that no woman who has savored the excellence of married love would want to give it up in order to change places with her husband's mistress. Nowhere does he seriously consider the possibility of combining and harmonizing the two systems of value within a single relationship. Far from considering how contemporary marriage could be modified or reformed in order to increase libidinal satisfaction among spouses, Montaigne finds the institution inherently inimical to the wanton and voluptuous interests of sexual love. Marriage is for him a "sober contract" in which the appetites must become "dull" and "blunted," and its sacred intimacy turns into a kind of incest when sexual pleasure intrudes too massively.

It is a sign of Montaigne's limitations as a thinker that he scarcely explores the paradox in advocating equality between the sexes as far as sexual need is concerned while also denying to happily married women the erotic gratifications their husbands may freely experience with other women. He does say that a husband's honor should not be made to depend on his wife's fidelity, and more than once he implies that women may have to seek the goodness of sexual love outside of marriage. But he never develops these intimations. In conformity to his goal of revealing himself "tout entier et tout nud," he always writes from his own point of view, which is to say, as a man addressing other men who also benefit from the double standard. He wishes primarily to establish the undesirability of marrying for love, as well as the hopelessness of finding love of the sexual sort even in the best of marriages. "I see no marriages that sooner are troubled and fail than those that progress by means of beauty and amorous desires. It [marriage] needs more solid and stable foundations, and we need to go at it circumspectly; this ebullient ardor is no good for it. . . . Few men have married their mistresses who have not repented it—even in the other world: what a bad match Jupiter made with his wife, whom he had first frequented and enjoyed in love affairs! It is the old saying:'Shit in your hat and then put it on your head.' "

In the philosophy of Descartes we find a comparable dualism despite the many doctrinal differences that separate him from Montaigne. Descartes says very little about marriage per se, but the structure of his thoughts about the passions indicates no way in which marital love can be harmonized with sexual love. For Descartes love itself must be distinguished into two types as different from one another as the categories of mind and body in his metaphysics. "I distinguish," he says, "between love that is purely intellectual or reasonable [rational] and love that is a passion." The first kind of love belongs to the essence of mind or soul and would exist even if there were no body. It consists in the soul realizing that something it perceives is a good for it. Judging the object to be valuable, the soul identifies itself as part of a desirable whole that results from the union between itself and the object. Rational love consists in an act of will based upon knowledge about objects that are valuable to oneself and therefore suitable as members of the new totality.

In this world, however, the soul is always joined to the body, which generally makes it necessary for rational love to be accompanied by love as a passion. For Descartes this only means that the body is disposed to further those interests of the soul which constitute intellectual love. At no point does Descartes suggest that the impulses or instincts of the body *contribute* to such love. It is in this vein that he distinguishes between love and "delight." Through delight we experience bodily enjoyment of "that which pleases us as the greatest of all the goods that belong to man," which occurs when we find someone of the opposite sex who may become "another self" to us, a person whose pleasing features lead us to think that he or she may be a desirable other half within a totality consisting only of us two.

Though this may resemble the union love always seeks, Descartes insists that love and delight are not to be identified with one another. Human beings desire the enjoyment that delight promises, and Descartes recognizes that this phenomenon "serves as the principal material for novelists and poets"; but he argues that it is merely a confused representation instilled by nature alone. We must remember that for Descartes everything related to man's bodily substance is experienced in the soul as a "confused" thought. Feelings or sensations are just a confused presentation of what the soul can perceive as a clear and distinct idea existing in its own mental essence. Delight is not really love because the pleasures of the former derive from physical impulses, as in sex, that involve no clarified intelligence or rational awareness.

In effect, Descartes is saying that love truly belongs to the mind rather than the body, its defining attributes pertaining to a knowledge about goodness and an eagerness to unite with what is good for the mind rather than anything the body may independently crave. This is not to imply that Descartes proposes an ascetic ideal, or even that he is duplicating the medieval distinction between caritas and cupiditas. As we shall see, his conception of love does seem to be based upon the priority he gives to the love of God, but he never suggests that this prevents one from enjoying the goods of the body. On the contrary, he claims that intellectual love will enable us to experience all the "licit pleasures" that one can enjoy in this life. But for him this must depend upon knowledge of the truth, as required by our being as rational creatures, and that involves considerable detachment from the senses. How such detachment is compatible with the experiencing of all licit pleasures Descartes does not explain. He stops short in the face of this kind of problem, and one may easily dismiss his philosophy as simply inadequate in this respect.

On the other hand, Descartes offers something more substantial when he relates both intellectual love and passionate love to benevolence. In all love, as he conceives of it, one enters into a unified whole with the beloved object. It is in the nature of love to further this totality by doing whatever is beneficial for the object. The desire to possess the beloved as a good we wish to appropriate to ourselves is "one of the commonest effects of love," but a desire of that sort does not belong to the essence of love. When we love something, either through reason alone or through the passions, we are evaluating the goodness in the object and considering what our union with it requires of us. If we esteem the object as less valuable than ourselves—as when we love "a flower, a bird or a horse"—we undergo what Descartes calls simple affection. Loving the object of our affection, we have created a new whole; but when it becomes necessary to sacrifice the lesser part of this whole, we immediately recognize that we can and should prefer ourselves to what we love. Where we esteem the object as much as ourselves, our love is friendship with an equal. The love that is friendship, Descartes says, can be experienced only with human beings, and he extends it to all men in general. Presumably this includes women, but Descartes does not investigate the implications of heterosexual friendship. In one place he remarks that friends esteem each other more than themselves and therefore, to preserve the totality which their love has created, each is willing to sacrifice himself rather than his friend. This may not contradict the idea that friendship involves equals, but it makes it difficult to imagine how the relationship could be extended to mankind as a whole, to all men indiscriminately.

Love as affection and love as friendship are for Descartes important elements in a life worth living. Whether experienced through the purity of the intellect or through the confused thoughts that passion generates, they illustrate how it is that love creates the transfer of interests from a selfish will to one that cares about the welfare of the new totality. At the same time, affection and friendship are subordinate to a love in which the object we esteem is recognized as having a value greater than ourselves. This occurs when a man loves his prince or his country, but Descartes also gives the example of a good father whose love for his children is so pure that he seeks their good with even greater care than he seeks his own: "Considering that he and they form a whole of which he is not the best part, he often places their interests before his and is not afraid of losing himself in order to save them." Descartes suggests that a man's love for his mistress may be similar, but he also intimates that it involves possessiveness and is therefore a lesser instance of this kind of love.

The strongest example of love for an object one esteems more highly than oneself, "devotion" as opposed to friendship or simple affection, Descartes finds in man's love of God. For the sake of the union with the supreme goodness which is God, we then desire only that God's will be done even if this requires our own destruction. Descartes is quite orthodox in asserting that man's love of God is "the most ravishing and most useful passion we can have," and as a good Catholic he insists that we can love God "by the sole force of our nature." But then he skirts the difficult problems that Luther and the Reformation had raised for all Christians in the seventeenth century: "I do not assert that this love is meritorious without grace—I leave it to the theologians to disentangle that matter."

In his usual manner, Descartes justifies on purely rationalistic grounds his notion that the love of God is superior to all other love. Not only is God most worthy of esteem, but also God must be considered as a perfect mind or thinking entity. The human mind aspires to the infinite knowledge that God already possesses and therefore loves God as its supreme good. Joy and feelings of grandeur attend this love for a being that gives our mind the possibility of attaining the infinite knowledge it inherently desires, but these feelings do not define the nature of love. In principle, Descartes maintains, love is purely intellectual, or rather the acceptance of a purely intellectual possibility.

To this extent, Descartes idealizes a type of love that often resembles amore divino in Ficino. He differs from Ficino, however, in saying that the desire to become a god through love—the inclination to merge with God—is a dangerous "extravagance." He treats it as the very great error of craving divinity for oneself instead of loving God. As a Rationalist, Descartes sees the mind as an organ of clear and distinct thought, not as an agency of metabiological transformation. Furthermore, he distinguishes between the good and the beautiful in a way that implies a critique of Ficino and of all Renaissance Platonism. Since beauty depends upon our external senses, particularly sight, Descartes cannot dignify it with the cognitive clarity of goods perceived by means of reason alone. He recognizes that beauty coming through sensory experience usually affects the soul more strongly than goodness intuited through reason, but from this he concludes that the passions related to the beautiful "are the ones which deceive the most, and against which we should guard ourselves most carefully."

Descartes agrees with Ficino in one crucial matter: he too claims that intellectual pleasures must always have far greater value than pleasures of the senses. Most philosophers since Plato have held this conviction, and understandably so: it articulates that love of reasoning for which they have a professional predilection. Pleasures of the senses can easily distract one from the concentration that philosophy requires, and therefore they have readily been categorized as disordered passions. As a bulwark of the grand tradition that even Freud belongs to, Descartes also assures us that "love for an object that does not merit it can render us worse than hate for another we ought to love." This, he says, is generally the case with sexual love that is prone to sacrifice everything for the sake of its object. Descartes does not say that all sexual love must be harmful in this way; and he recognizes that, however distorted it may be, any love that provides pleasure must be good to that extent. He even believes that "disordered and frivolous" love can sometimes improve a person's character. Nevertheless, he leaves us with the impression that sexual love runs so great a risk of being disproportionate to the value of its object that one does well to avoid it on most occasions.

As the rational alternative to sexual passion, Descartes recommends contentment, stability, repose. These are the goods afforded by intellectual love, and in promising them Descartes was speaking to the demands of many people in the seventeenth century who were not themselves philosophers. Without necessarily accepting his metaphysical speculations, they could use his ideas to justify the sacrifice of sexual love in order to find a reasonable and contented marriage that, they thought, would enable them to retain their composure as well as their sense of moral rectitude.

In the writings of Spinoza, a philosopher who differs from Descartes in many ways, we find a similar dualism with respect to love. For Spinoza the goal of philosophy is to provide a guide for those who wish to escape human bondage through a rational love that yields the greatest self-contentment of which man is capable. As in Descartes, the ideal is equilibrium which transcends libidinal cravings. In his book *On the Improvement of the Understanding*, Spinoza remarks that most men seek their highest good through riches, fame, or the pleasures of sense. He assures us that these interests do not create happiness and that sensory pleasure in particular enslaves the mind, preventing it from thinking of any other objective, indeed leading to "extreme melancholy" even when gratified. Spinoza concludes that sexual passion—like the search for riches or fame—fails because it arises from the love of something ephemeral, something mutable and perishable through time.

This assurance that pleasures of the flesh are vain and inconsequential because their objects do not last has always characterized Western moralists who desired oneness with some infinite and eternal being that would never change or disappoint. That is the basis of Pascal's skepticism about all love for human beings. Writing at the same time as Descartes and Spinoza, Pascal portrays everything in life other than the love of God as unending restlessness caused by a perverse refusal to realize wherein true happiness lies. All human loves being selfish, man cannot love another person for what he is in himself, but only for what he can provide as a good to be possessed. "We never, then, love a person, but only qualities." For Pascal sexual love epitomizes human vanity. The cause of love is a "*je ne sais quoi*, so small an object that we cannot recognize it"; the effects are "dreadful . . . [upsetting] a whole country, princes, armies, the entire world. Cleopatra's nose: had it been shorter, the whole aspect of the world would have been altered." Obviously Pascal lent no credence to those who claimed to have found in sexual love something more than just an obsession with a woman's features.

Spinoza differs from Descartes as well as Pascal inasmuch as he reaches conclusions comparable to those of the orthodox moralists by means that are radically heterodox and even naturalistic in their implications. Where Descartes believes in free will as the basis of all morality, Spinoza insists that the mind is determined by laws of nature exactly as the body is; where Descartes thinks of God as pure and eternal thought outside the finite universe, Spinoza identifies him with nature: not "natura naturata"—things as they occur empirically, one after the other—but rather "natura naturans"—nature as itself an infinite totality, an organic whole operating harmoniously in accordance with immutable laws internal to itself. Despite his frequent references to God and the intellectual love of God, Spinoza was often criticized in his own day as a "hideous atheist." Even if we see him as a pantheist or panpsychist (more accurate descriptions of his philosophical attitude), his theological ideas seem almost diametrically opposed to those of Descartes. Yet his conclusions about the nature of love, ambiguous as they may be, are not entirely dissimilar. They seem equally rationalistic, and are in fact more hostile to the suggestion that sexual love may be harmonized with marriage or the dictates of reason.

In criticizing Descartes, Spinoza denies that love is to be defined in terms of the lover's wish to unite himself to something. This merely describes a property of love, he says, and not its essence. That consists in our ability to enjoy an object while being aware of it as the object of our enjoyment. Spinoza offers the following as his definition: "*Love* is pleasure, accompanied by the idea of an external cause." It is this definition that Schopenhauer was later to ridicule as virtually worthless without, however, understanding its function within Spinoza's philosophy. For Spinoza, pleasure is more than just a titillation of the senses. It is the means by which an organism completes its being and realizes its potential. Pleasure is defined as "the transition of a man from a less to a greater perfection." Pleasure is not perfection itself, since that would be a final completeness that man will never attain, but only an increase in being that manifests itself in the positive character of our experience. For pleasure to be love, it must contribute to a state of awareness in which the lover recognizes the object that has elicited his pleasure. The lover wants the object of his love not in the Cartesian sense of freely willing to unite with it but rather in enjoying its presence, finding "contentment" in its mere association with him.

In terms of later psychological theory, words like "satisfaction" or "self-fulfillment" might serve as a more accurate translation than "contentment." It is fundamental in Spinoza's thinking that all creatures seek to maintain their existence and to enjoy their potentialities to the maximum degree. Schopenhauer could very well have accepted this notion as a forerunner of his own ideas about the "will to life"; and Nietzsche did see it as similar to what he meant by the "will to power." Spinoza says that desire in general is "the essence of a man" because it is the effort by which all men seek to persist and flourish in their individual being. Nor is this a matter of choice, he says. Everyone tries to preserve his being since the laws of his own nature determine him to do so. These laws of self-fulfillment are the fundamental reality in which we live.

Given metaphysical beliefs of this sort, Spinoza proceeds to formulate a theory of value that many naturalists in succeeding centuries have found attractive. Contrary to Platonists and Christians alike who believe that goodness exists as an objective goal, external to man but systematically eliciting his desire, Spinoza argues that good is merely that which people do desire. In a definition that underlies all philosophical hedonism, utilitarianism, and pragmatism in the modern world, Spinoza states: "By *good* I here mean every kind of pleasure, and all that conduces thereto, especially that which satisfies our longings, whatsoever they may be. By *evil* I mean every kind of pain, especially that which frustrates our longings. . . . We in no case desire a thing because we deem it good, but, contrariwise, we deem a thing good because we desire it."

With this as his conception of good, Spinoza has no difficulty in arguing against the idealization of humility. Since reason and virtue can disclose no moral imperative greater than the laws of one's own nature, they require that every man love himself to the best of his ability, as one who naturally wishes the greatest perfection of his being. When Spinoza says that virtue is to be desired for its own sake, he merely means that virtue encourages us to preserve our being and that this alone constitutes happiness. Suicides are "weak-minded" persons, intellectually confused about human reality, who foolishly allow themselves to be dominated by external causes that happen to be repugnant to their nature.

Having taken us this far, Spinoza insists that each man augments his ability to preserve his being by acting in such a way as to strengthen the being of all other men. His doctrine of enlightened selfishness thus turns into humanitarian faith that is crucial to his philosophy. He says that men are useful to one another and that united they are individually more powerful than each alone, but what really underlies his belief that rational men will always be concerned about other people is his assumption that the best possible condition occurs when human beings as a whole become "as it were, one single mind and one single body." Though Spinoza finds in this premise nothing but the dictates of reason, he is expressing a dogma that is as unverifiable as any in the traditional religions. Including as it does all mankind, the unity of mind and body that he describes is in principle the same community of love that Christianity sought to establish on earth.

As in Christianity, this idea of love is based upon a conception of humanity as a pinnacle within nature's hierarchy. Spinoza goes to considerable lengths not only to argue that a rational man will desire for others the same goods he desires for himself, but also that these others with whom he shares his love cannot include animals. Being lower in the order of rationality, animals may be used in any way that suits our human needs. Spinoza sees no possibility of fellowship with them, and he considers prohibitions against slaughtering other creatures as merely "womanish pity." Unlike Descartes, who held similar views, Spinoza does not deny that animals have feelings. Nevertheless, he renews the biblical authorization for man to rule over everything in nature, defending such domination with mystical beliefs about the supremacy of reason.

Plotinus, whose conception of God as a oneness in nature often resembles Spinoza's pantheism, eliminated all such ideas of man's dominion over less rational beings by asserting that each higher link within the universal chain bestows love upon the lower ones. This conception is not to be found in Spinoza. In a sense, his humanism has taken him beyond it. For him mankind is an endangered species that must huddle together against everything in nature that threatens its existence. For Spinoza, reason at its best includes the ability to acquire scientific knowledge and to understand the universal laws that determine each particular occurrence. This being man's supreme achievement, he need extend his love only to those who participate equally in the goods that reason recognizes. Not until Schopenhauer do we reach a great philosopher who integrates Spinoza's naturalism with a sense of compassion towards everything that lives, particularly sentient creatures less rational than ourselves, all struggling to exist while being determined by the same immutable laws of nature.

Like Schopenhauer, Spinoza has no doubts about the pettiness of man. He criticizes both Descartes and the Stoics for assuming that man need only exercise his will in order to govern his emotions. Not being free, the will could have none of the independent power these philosophers ascribed to it. But then, we may ask, how can man attain the kind of love in which Spinoza found the possibility of salvation? To this, he replies that man's weakness being a product of diseased passions, his moral strength requires their emancipation from everything in the world that corrupts them. Since it is always "excessive love" for something we cannot master that creates spiritual infirmity, we must use the deterministic laws to develop in ourselves a faculty that prevents the enslavement of our natural impulses. "For no one is solicitous or anxious about anything, unless he loves it; neither do wrongs, suspicions, etc. arise, except in regard to things whereof no one can be really master."

It is here that reason provides the solution for Spinoza. It does not destroy or subjugate the passions, but it harnesses their power by creating an intellectual love that transforms them into an activity of the mind. As he had dignified nature by treating it as God, so too does Spinoza find man's salvation in what he calls "the intellectual love of God." By this he means joyful acquisition of clear and distinct knowledge about the world, knowledge that shows how every event has been determined by the laws of nature. God being the totality of these natural determinants, the love of God is based upon recognition of that which cannot alter. This kind of love affords possession of something that is not subject to variations; it blossoms when our reason is properly employed and therefore fully gratified. The intellectual love of God enables us to escape the sorrows that attend ordinary love for individual things or persons. Their being will change and elude our search for total mastery; but God, natura naturans, is "immutable and eternal."

Through the intellectual love of God, the Spinozistic philosopher-saint attains the only kind of freedom Spinoza considers possible. Understanding the deterministic order of things, he accepts it as a whole, which is God, and thereby acquiesces in everything, much as the Stoics had recommended. The idea that all the pain and suffering of life will thus take on a meaning that washes away its misery may well seem overly simplistic to us. But this part of Spinoza is hardly different from the religious orthodoxy he shares with so many centuries of thought before him. What is novel is his refusal to believe that the ideal involves a mutual love between kindred spirits. His God is not a person, but only an infinite substance, and no one who understands God and the nature of love could want (or expect) him to love us in return. For that, as Spinoza says, would mean that God would have to be an entity that passes to a greater perfection, which is absurd since God feels no pleasure and is subject to no emotion.

Avoiding the traditional faith that God is a person who reciprocates our love, Spinoza nevertheless accepts the mystical belief in a love that identifies man and God. For though he is not a person of any sort that we can recognize, God loves himself with an infinite intellectual love. Spinoza does little to explain how this can be, but he claims that God "rejoices" in the infinite perfection that he knows to be himself. As a result, "the intellectual love of the mind towards God is that very love of God whereby God loves himself." Since man's intellectual love of God is the essence of the human mind regarded under the aspect of eternity, it reveals how man is one with God and also, in this sense, how God (insofar as he loves himself) loves man as well.

This much of Spinoza may seem to return to views that even Ficino might have found suggestive of man's divinity, but Spinoza never wavers in his Rationalistic belief that beauty and goodness are not the same and that the former is always tainted by its dependence upon sense experience. While he encourages the wise man to "refresh and invigorate himself with moderate and pleasant eating and drinking, with sweet scents . . . with music, with sports, with the theater, and with all things of this kind which one man can enjoy without hurting another," he insists that bodily beauty generates discord, hatred, and even madness. The man who loves God properly knows that loving the beautiful—particularly as it appears in a woman one passionately desires—cannot bring about the ultimate power that everyone seeks.

In his brief reference to marriage, Spinoza admits that it may possibly exist in harmony with reason, but only if love is caused by something more than beauty of the body. For husband and wife to live joyfully together, each must attain the intellectual freedom in which human blessedness consists. There may be great wisdom in this idea of Spinoza; had he wished to do so, he might have developed it into a useful conception of married love. But, as a matter of fact, he does not tell us much about the harmonization of reason and the marital state. Nor does he try to show how the ideal of sexual love could be integrated with both. His anxiety about the perils of libidinal passion precludes his making that attempt. His philosophy has not resolved the problem. It merely perpetuates it within a new and splendid reformulation.

The split between marriage and sex, which was also a split between reason and emotion, and social order and passion, is remedied in the seventeenth century by a literary tradition that is now ignored by all but the scholars who specialize in this period. In contrast to the philosophical doubts about man's ability to harmonize these different aspects of his being, there existed a "romanesque" convention in popular novels that generally assumed a happy outcome. After many episodes in which heroic men and beautiful women undergo the trials and misadventures occasioned by forces in society that are hostile to sexual passion, the fated lovers finally win out, marry one another, and live happily ever after in ways that are usually left to the reader's imagination. Particularly on the Continent, these benign romances became the stock-in-trade of popular dramas. In the history of literature, the romanesque productions on the stage constitute a development beyond their counterparts in medieval romance; but the continuity with tales such as *Aucassin and Nicolette*, or even the works of Chrétien de Troyes, is evident.

The romanesque literature of the seventeenth century is neglected in the contemporary world because its aesthetic quality was generally so low. One has to keep it in mind, however, because it helps us to understand the differences between two of the greatest tragedians of the age, Corneille and Racine. Both are concerned about the conflict between reason and passion, which they categorize in similar ways. For each, reason includes social values, order in the state, military and political glory, duty, honor, and marriage between people who respect and esteem one another, while passion involves instinctual gratification, oneness with nature, and the craving for happiness that has always been associated with the concept of love. Here, however, the similarities between Corneille and Racine end. Though they study the same kind of problem and, being tragedians, conclude with unhappy resolutions, the philosophic roots of the suffering they depict are as different as the doctrines of Descartes and Spinoza.

Like Descartes, but also in conformity with the romanesque tradition, Corneille assumes that man's free will enables him to choose what is truly valuable. Without the ability to exert his will in the pursuit of goodness and virtue, the tragic hero could not have had the fortitude or devotion needed for him to be a lover in the first place. He must show himself worthy of the supremely noble and beautiful females who regularly elicit masculine love in the plays of Corneille. These in turn would not have been the ideal women for whom the men are prepared to dedicate their being unless they too recognized that honor and social rectitude must take priority over passion. As the seventeenth-century English poet Richard Lovelace put it: "I could not love thee, Dear, so much,/Loved I not honour more." In Corneille's tragedies this means that an inner harmony already governs the relation between sex and reason. The sufferings of the individual lovers result from conditions that require them to give up their hopes for personal happiness in order to satisfy the greater demands of rationality. But this, as Descartes would argue, manifests a higher love which they appreciate *because* they are heroic lovers. Corneille's heroes and heroines find themselves in situations where reason and personal love cannot both be satisfied; but in their hierarchical ordering, the two aspects of human nature combine to make it possible for lovers to achieve a more sublime love through the joint acceptance of their tragic circumstance.

Racine, on the other hand, is closer to Spinoza: his dramas show sex and virtue as mutually destructive, deadly enemies, if only because passionate love cannot be made, under any conditions, to subserve the demands of reason. The tragic characters in Racine are either lacking in a faculty of free will, as Spinoza would have said of all things in the world, or else they are gripped by libidinal drive so powerful that it overcomes virtuous resistance in even the most courageous and well-intentioned human beings. Sexual love is no longer portrayed as a complement to rational estimations of value and social order, but rather as a blind, stupid, violent force of nature closer to hatred than to kindliness. Passion does not reward the Racinian lover; it uses him for ends that have nothing to do with happiness. It is a wild, generative power of the sort that Lucretius described.

Racinian tragedy seeks to demonstrate that even the most honorable and heroic men and women cannot control the instinctive tide that drags them to their destruction. In Corneille there is nothing in the independent being of reason or passion to explain the weakness and futility of man. In Racine this is shown to follow from the very nature of each. Reason is incapable of controlling passion, and passion is so voracious that it will not accept the restraints reason tries to impose. Man is inherently split, his needs cannot be fulfilled on earth or in any possible harmony of natural faculties—just as Pascal had also said, under the influence of the same Jansenism to which Racine finally succumbed.

This demonstration of the unremitting warfare between reason and passion, and in general the insufficiency of human nature, is the hallmark of Racine's genius. It appears most brilliantly in *Phèdre*, which he adapted from Euripides with significant changes. Racine's Hippolyte, the son of Theseus and stepson of Phèdre, is no longer a man who offends Venus by devoting himself only to hunting and military prowess. He pursues a princess, Aricie, whom he loves with the same passionate ardor that Phèdre feels towards him. But just as Phèdre's love is a guilty one, being quasi-incestuous, so too is Hippolyte's marred by the fact that Aricie is his father's enemy. Phèdre and Hippolyte each recognize that, from the point of view of social values, their passions are misplaced. Each of them struggles to do the right thing, both in relation to one another and to Theseus, but passion fixed upon its prey—Vénus tout entière à sa proie attachée—will not release them from an outcome that can only lead to death. At the end, Theseus and Aricie are reconciled to one another, in a political arrangement; but otherwise, nothing overcomes the dualism that Racine has carried to its extreme conclusion.

In discussing the medieval legend of Tristan and Iseult, I suggested that there lingered throughout a pervasive ambiguity about the love potion, and about passion as a whole. On the one hand, the potion symbolized the fact that the lovers are mystically made for one another, he as the great warrior and she as the beautiful woman who can be matched only by the most heroic male, their passion not being inherently hostile to society but rather a completing of its highest aspirations. On the other hand, the philter is also a poison that represents nature at its most violent, a force that undermines the bases of honor and society, a disease that culminates in the death of the unfortunate lovers. In the transition from Corneille to Racine, who often speaks of passion as a disease that people contract unwillingly, seventeenth-century literature manifests a development from one pole of the Tristanian ambiguity to the other. In neither alternative does one find the relative optimism of Milton and the Puritans. Corneille's protagonists are prevented from enjoying both love and marriage; and in Racine, conflict is presented in a way that makes harmonization impossible for all human beings.

The most profound expression of this split occurs in the work of a woman novelist whose psychological analysis cannot be equalled by any other writer of the period. In *La Princesse de Clèves* Madame de Lafayette carries the struggle between marital and sexual love even further than Corneille and Racine. Her great novel is often compared to the plays of Corneille inasmuch as it culminates in duty overcoming passion for a man whom the Princesse de Clèves loves but feels she ought not to marry. Though this similarity exists, the thinking of Madame de Lafayette is actually much richer than its Corneillian element. In the dedication of one of his plays Corneille says that a decent man's love will always spring up in response to his will and that "a person beloved is under far greater obligation to our love when this results from our choice and her qualities than when it arises from a blind attraction." Madame de Lafayette begins with this dictum but then the experiences of her characters lead them far beyond it. The Princesse de Clèves is preeminently decent and constantly wishes to love her husband with the same passion that he feels for her and that she feels *unwillingly* for Monsieur de Nemours. But her wish avails her nothing: though she has chosen the worthy Prince de Clèves as her husband, this fails to bring happiness to either of them since it cannot bring into being the passionate love she would like to bestow upon him. Clèves' love for his wife includes choice based upon esteem as well as passion for her, and to this extent Corneille's generalization is borne out by the sense of obligation that contributes to the Princesse de Clèves' rejection of Monsieur de Nemours. But in refusing him, she is also curing herself of passion interpreted not as just a "blind attraction" but as a Racinian disease.

At the same time, Madame de Lafayette is even more devastating in her pessimism than Racine ever was. For her critique extends to the ideal of married love itself. At the outset, the Princesse de Clèves assumes that a good marriage is one in which husband and wife are not only suitably paired with respect to the moral and human qualities recognized as virtues in their society but are also in love with one another. Her mother enunciates this benign principle when she tells her young daughter about "the only thing that can bring happiness to a woman—which is to love her husband and to be loved by him." But then her mother fails her at a crucial moment: she allows her to marry a man she respects but for whom she feels no sexual interest. When the Princesse de Clèves is overwhelmed by her passionate yearning for Monsieur de Nemours, she fights it with the same guilt-ridden ambivalence that Phèdre shows, except that she succeeds in mastering it. In the process she does something considered unprecedented, and incredibly naive, by contemporary readers of the novel as well as representative characters within it: she tells her husband about her passion, though she does not name the man she loves and does everything possible to keep Monsieur de Nemours from knowing about her feelings for him. Her husband's love turns to jealousy, even hatred, and he dies of a mysterious illness occasioned by his mistaken assumption that his wife has been unfaithful.

It is this heroic, though hapless, rectitude on the part of her protagonist that enables Madame de Lafayette to apply Racinian pessimism about sexual love to the morality of marriage itself. The Princesse de Clèves suffers not merely because she has been infected by passion but also because there is something in the nature of married love, which she experienced with her husband, that cannot coexist with passion. Free to marry Monsieur de Nemours once her husband dies, the Princesse de Clèves rejects him and withdraws from society.

This final act of renunciation is clearly the epiphany toward which the entire novel has been tending. To make the decision reasonable, we are presented with very good arguments in its favor: the Princesse feels a sense of duty towards her husband's memory, his death having been occasioned by her innocent but calamitous attachment to another man; Monsieur de Nemours has had many love affairs, and he may possibly love her less than he himself believes. On the other hand, she cannot help recognizing that he is her only hope for happiness, and she sees him "as a man worthy of undivided love, whom she loved so deeply that she would have loved him even if he did not love her." They are perfectly matched with respect to social status and there is nothing in the standards of propriety to keep them apart. Despite the contrary arguments, reason as well as nature would seem to recommend their marrying. Why then does the Princesse de Clèves choose renunciation?

Madame de Lafayette's protagonist gives up her last chance for happiness because she is now convinced that marriage and passionate love are by their very nature irreconcilable. She tells Monsieur de Nemours that her experience of passion has proved to her that marriage with him would lead to agony rather than bliss. For she has learned that passion engenders fears and jealousies that would not exist if she were married to someone she did not love as desperately as she loves Monsieur de Nemours. She speculates that he loves her now as passionately as he does largely because of the obstacles that have separated them thus far. If these were eliminated through the accessibility in marriage, he would eventually lose interest and revert to his old habits as a Don Juan. Her renunciation is finally depicted less in terms of duty or virtue than as a search for "repos"— peace of mind. Loving Monsieur de Nemours as she does, she is certain that she can find contentment only by *not* marrying him.

In an earlier novel, *Zaïde*, Mme de Lafayette reaches equally negative conclusions from another point of view. She there defends the contentions of a character who maintains that "passions that come only with time cannot be called true passions." Since passionate love occurs as a spontaneous event, a thunderclap without warning, a sudden invasion or affliction, permanent relationships such as marriage destroy it through the mere passage of time. The supreme happiness promised by the romanesque tradition is thus a delusion: one has to choose between marriage and sexual love, just as Montaigne had said. One cannot have both, however intense or mutual the passionate love may be, and however much society may support the marriage.

In opting for peace of mind (or peace of soul, as *repos* is often translated), the Princesse de Clèves carries out the teachings of both Spinoza and Pascal. Renouncing Monsieur de Nemours, she also renounces "the passions and entanglements of this world." In the closing paragraphs, her judgment would seem to be vindicated since we are told that eventually Monsieur de Nemours found ways to mitigate his sorrow and that the short life remaining to the Princesse was filled with examples of virtue, even holiness.

In the years when she was writing *La Princesse de Clèves*, Madame de Lafayette enjoyed the friendship of the Duc de La Rochefoucauld. Some scholars have suggested that his cynical maxims about love influenced the conceptual structure of her masterpiece. In La Rochefoucauld, however, there is a healthy-minded attitude quite foreign to the self-defeating dualism that pervades Madame de Lafayette's thinking. In one place he remarks, "We defy inclination oftener from vanity than from reason," and, as if he were musing about the Princesse de Clèves, he says, "Virtuousness in women is often a love of their reputations and their peace of mind." Madame de Lafayette's heroine thinks it is reason, virtue, and a wise concern for peace of mind that justifies her act of renunciation; but one can see in it a fear of risking the goods of vanity and reputation. If she loved Monsieur de Nemours with the purity of motive that she pretends, and if she found him as lovable as she claims, would she not have run the risks of marriage as he begs her to? And is her peace of mind really threatened by the possibility that Monsieur de Nemours may someday redirect his passion; or is it rather endangered by the full sexuality that would be required of her if she married him? These alternatives are not mutually exclusive; and we may even give an affirmative answer to both, since her difficulty in responding sexually to his passionate love could lead to infidelities on his part. In raising these questions, we are mentioning realities of love that Madame de Lafayette ignores. La Rochefoucauld investigates them very carefully.

Emphasizing, as he does, the extent to which people delude themselves in matters of love, La Rochefoucauld is no more optimistic about marriage than the others of his period whom we have been considering. He settles the issue in one of his shortest utterances: "There are successful marriages, but no blissful ones." This is what the Princesse de Clèves might have said, at the end of her experience, as rebuttal of her mother's promises about marital happiness.

But La Rochefoucauld writes with a more constructive intent. He wishes to expose the vanity and self-interest that dominate so much of our social experience, including love and marriage, because he wants to teach people how to be honest in their behavior. For him the cardinal sin in life is hypocrisy. People pretend to be motivated by virtue or selfless love even if they are acting for reasons of personal interest. Since their selfish motives are too subtle for them to detect, the moralist must force them to see the disquieting truth. He must make lovers recognize the actual springs of conduct, its origin in psychological forces natural to the human condition but quite remote from the idealistic appearances in which hypocrisy clothes everything.

In performing this service, La Rochefoucauld is easily misread as a man who believes in none of the usual virtues—and certainly not in love between human beings. He is often cited as having said that no one would fall in love who had not heard it spoken about, and that true love is like ghosts, everyone talking about it but no one actually seeing it. If we study his maxims closely, however, we find that his cynicism often presupposes an ideal that has been violated in prac-tice but that he is trying to defend. He does not ridicule the ideal—only those who delude themselves into thinking they are living up to it. Thus, when he compares true love to ghosts, he does not say that *no one* has seen it but only that "few of us" have; and similarly it is only "some people" who would never have fallen in love if they had not heard about it. A love that amounts to more than selfishness or vanity may be rare—and La Rochefoucauld says the same about friendship and generosity—but he does not conclude that true love cannot occur. On the contrary, he credits it with the ability to overcome coquettishness, just as "true friendship" can destroy envy. If the manifestations of unselfish love and friendship are not fre-quently seen, that is because La Rochefoucauld's ideals are hard to attain—which is not the same as saying that he considers them futile or unrealistic.

Most people are deceived about love, La Rochefoucauld insists, because they lack knowledge of themselves. "If a pure love, untar-nished by our other passions, exists, it exists at the bottom of our hearts unknown even to ourselves." In assuming the task of enlightening lovers about their misconstrued passions, La Rochefoucauld does not, however, align himself with the Rationalists. For they thought of reason as a separate faculty that discovered ideals that were independent of the passions and for which the will might strive. The moral perspective that La Rochefoucauld offers is quite different. Though true love is not reducible to self-interest, neither is it wholly distinct from it. Only by understanding and *accepting* the selfishness in our nature are we able to overcome it through an authentic concern for someone else's welfare. Nor can good and evil be separated from one another as the Rationalists had maintained. In a way that anticipates the Nietzschean transvaluation of values, La Rochefoucauld claims that "Evil results from good, and good from evil." He also finds the Rationalists mistaken in thinking that reason can be counted upon to control our inclinations; more often this happens because of vanity, even when the consequences are beneficial. And though passion may seize a person with the virulence of an infection, and frequently resemble hatred more than friendship, it nevertheless can lead to fidelity that consists in "forever finding new things to love in the loved one."

The portraiture of love in La Rochefoucauld is a study in chiaroscuro, the ideal appearing as a remote but attainable refinement of natural impulses related to human self-interest. In the *Maximes* La Rochefoucauld defines love as "in the soul . . . a thirst for mastery; in the mind a harmony of thought [dans les esprits c'est une sympathie]; in the body, nothing but a delicately hidden desire to possess, after many mysteries, whatsoever one loves." In the *Justification de l'amour*, written a little earlier, this ambivalent conception of love receives a more positive formulation. The possibility of true love is defended as a valid goal for "honnêtes gens," people who are honest, genuine. *L'honnêteté*, the authenticity that enables lovers to rise above self-deception about their motives, establishes a relationship in which men and women communicate with one another while keeping their intimacy hidden from everyone else. Through their secret understanding of what unites them, La Rochefoucauld's lovers satisfy their passionate interests while also expressing in delicate language the esteem they feel for one another. La Rochefoucauld wishes to help love survive in a society that is eager to vilify it despite hypocritical professions to the contrary. The lovers must learn a secret language, just as the adherents to courtly love did, because they know that few people can appreciate the ideals for which they strive. La Rochefoucauld scarcely describes the harmonization of goods, social as well as personal, for which the lovers yearn in their secret communications, and he himself offers little hope that—given what the world is like—many people can succeed in this quest for an honest love; but he staunchly defends it as the foundation of the moral life.

In the work of Molière one finds a similar mixture of hope and cynicism about the possibilities of love. His plays often end with the marriage of young lovers who have had to surmount the stupid and materialistic obstacles of their society before they could consummate their oneness. And like La Rochefoucauld, Molière is fascinated by the spectacle of men and women who think they are in love but who really illustrate its failure. The shadow of Dom Juan that falls across Molière's final period demarcates a gallery of men who are por-trayed as pathologically unable to love anyone, including them-selves. Dom Juan can see the beauty in each of the women he seduces, even marries, but he systematically fails to love any of them. In *The Misanthrope*, Alceste suffers the indignities of his hopeless passion because he is incapable of love, though he himself thinks that he loves Célimène and wishes only to marry her. It is fitting for him to seek a desert island at the end. For he cannot live in any ordinary society, as shown by his inability to control his feelings or to harmonize them with social ideals such as married love. The same disability underlies the character of Tartuffe, who passionately de-sires Elmire but has no means of getting her to reciprocate since she knows that if he truly loved her he would respect the ideals of marriage that matter most to her.

If we wish, we can identify Molière's major talent either with the brighter or with the less optimistic side of his genius. We may read him as the friend of the romanesque lovers who finally beat the system and enjoy happiness in each other's arms; or else, as the saddened analyst observing erotic failure. Molière's conception of human nature is big enough to encompass both perspectives. But even when he is pessimistic, there resides in him a deep-rooted faith in the possibility of reconciling passion and reason, love and marriage, however difficult that may be. His version of the Amphitryon myth contains various changes and additions that reveal his basic belief in harmonization. When Jupiter succeeds in seducing Alcmène by assuming the bodily appearance of her husband Amphitryon, he feels that his conquest is incomplete. For he realizes that Alcmène has submitted only because she thinks he is Amphitryon. Wishing to be loved for himself alone, he asks Alcmène to distinguish the lover in him from the husband. She refuses to do so; and she emerges from her seduction, of which she is unaware since she does not know that he is not her husband, as one whose value remains unsullied. She says that she cannot and will not distinguish between lover and husband: her husband is her proper lover and her lover must provide not only the pleasures of their mutual passion but also the goods of a married life in common.

In the moral victory of Alcmène, that madonna of nature whose experience with the god results in her giving birth to Hercules the savior of mankind, Molière finds a way out of seventeenth-century dualism. He offers his solution in the form of a myth, however, because—like Milton—he knows that even if reality sustains the underlying faith, most of life is probably unwilling or unable to make the necessary commitment.

Part III
Types of Romantic Love

9

The Concept of
Romantic Love

THE CONCEPT OF THE ROMANTIC
has been even more controversial than the concept of the courtly.
On the one hand, great scholars such as A. O. Lovejoy have argued
in the last sixty years that no one system of ideas can define everything in literature or culture that has been called Romantic: "The
word 'romantic' has come to mean so many things that, by itself, it
means nothing." Lovejoy saw that what has passed as romanticism in
one or another European country has often had little in common
with romanticism elsewhere. He concluded that there existed "a
plurality of Romanticisms," some of them antithetical to one
another. On the other hand, scholars like René Wellek and Morse
Peckham emphasize the extent to which the history of ideas underwent a dramatic new development at the turn of the nineteenth
century, in various respects more revolutionary for European culture than anything that had preceded it. Wellek claims that "identical or very similar views of nature, of the imagination and of symbol
and myth pervade all European literature . . . of that time and . . .
these ideas have a profound coherence and mutual implication."
Peckham modifies Wellek's views, partly duplicating Lovejoy's plu-
ralism while also tracing the importance of what Peckham calls
"organic dynamism" within romanticism as a whole.

I shall not be offering a definition of romanticism, though I
recognize that seeking one can be a worthy pursuit for scholars. Like
other portmanteau words—the Renaissance, for instance—the term

can be useful for demarcating a major occurrence in history; but no definition will ever encompass the complexity of similarities and differences that constitute so massive a phenomenon. To this extent Lovejoy's cautionary influence is salutary. It need not, however, prevent us from discerning major changes in European thought that began to appear towards the end of the eighteenth century. The word "Romantic" was introduced by German poets and philosophers around 1800 to signify the world view they were in the process of creating. Though the term did not catch on in England for some time, Romantic concepts had an immediate effect there. In France Stendhal seems to have been the first writer who called himself a Romantic, but he did so almost twenty years later and his ideas were often quite different from those of the English and German Romantics. For many of them, the philosophy of Rousseau and the literature of Goethe pointed in the direction to be taken, but Rousseau and Goethe were so idiosyncratic that one could very well argue that they should be classified as precursors rather than typical Romantics. Among those who might be characterized as clearly representative—Novalis and Shelley, let us say—it is a family resemblance, and not a single doctrine, that unites them. In describing similarities among the Romantics, we must always remember that the differences are equally relevant, as the subsequent chapters will continually demonstrate.

With respect to the concept of love, we must further recognize that not everyone who has been considered a Romantic, or an exponent of romanticism, believed in Romantic love. Byron, for instance, is often called a Romantic, and for good reason. In his willingness to expose and to dramatize his own experience, in his grandiose rejection of conventional standards, and in other ways too, he resembles Romantics like Shelley or even Novalis and may well be linked to them by the same term. But Byron also belongs to what I have called the realist tradition, and that sets him apart from these Romantics. To accommodate such differences, we may, as some scholars have, call him a "Romantic realist." But this is largely a terminological issue, and for our purposes we need only note that, except on isolated occasions, Byron did not believe in the concept of love that distinguishes most Romantics. By means of this concept, romanticism continues the idealistic tradition that sees a meaning-fulness in nature, that treats this meaningfulness as basic to spiritual longings definitive of man, that finds love to be their greatest ex-emplar, and that considers the pursuit of love worthier than any other interest. Byron scorned these Romantic beliefs while Shelley desperately sought to defend them. That is the crucial difference between the two, whether or not we call them both Romantics.

As advocates of idealism in the nineteenth century, the propo-nents of Romantic love reawakened interest in Platonism, medieval Christianity, the Neoplatonism of the Renaissance, courtly love in its diverse aspects, and also the erotic literature of more recent centu-ries. From Plato and the Neoplatonists they inherited the search for purity in love that transcended ordinary sexual experience, true love being an ideal relationship that rarely appeared in the empirical world. From Christianity—particularly the ecstatic mysticism of writers like St. John of the Cross, St. Teresa, Ruysbroeck, Eckhart, Boehme, and others—they appropriated the notion of an interper-sonal love that enabled the lover to partake of divinity. In courtly love they saw an attempt to justify an intimacy between men and women that would be comparable to religious love. These various influences did not have the same effect upon all who believed in Romantic love: some were Christians, but others were not, and many who were inspired by their discovery of Platonic or courtly idealism remained faithful to such teachings only when they suited their own needs as nineteenth-century thinkers.

When scholars ask what it is that distinguishes romanticism from earlier forms of idealism, they often point to the extraordinary importance that was given to feeling rather than reason—in contrast to the Rationalism of Descartes or Spinoza or Leibniz, for instance. David Hume had argued in the middle of the eighteenth century that reason is and ought to be the slave of the passions. His entire epistemology was designed to show that our experience of the world, even the knowledge we could rightly claim, depended upon a kind of animal faith that derived from feeling rather than reason. Hume considered sympathy, benevolent concern, or what he called "fellow-feeling" as the basis for moral conduct. His ethical philoso-phy appeared at a time when many authors were recommending "sensibility" as a virtue in sexual relations. To a large extent the concept of Romantic love issues from this moment in English thought, together with similar developments on the Continent. Fielding, Richardson, Prévost, Marivaux, and others treat the ideal lover as one who experiences, as Fielding puts it, "a tenderness joined with a sensibility inexpressible." The lover is for them supremely moral since his attitude reveals human feeling at its best, sympathy for another person reaching into his or her innermost being. Romanticism goes beyond its eighteenth-century origins, as we shall see, but its emphasis upon feeling is partly an effort to combine Humean empiricism and the concept of sensibility with the idealistic traditions we have been studying.

It is not the case that Romantics believed "feeling is all," as some commentators have suggested, but only that feeling is primary, both in morals and in the acquisition of knowledge about the world. Though at the very outset A. W. Schlegel called Romantic literature "the poetry of longing," Coleridge is a better guide to the movement when he says, more moderately, that "deep thinking is attainable only by a man of deep feeling." Even in the "theology of feeling" of Schleiermacher or Chateaubriand, infinite desire was expected to awaken our appetite for, and eventually to put us in touch with, ultimate truths that reason would later validate. Most Romantics thought that love enabled us to know and appropriate the universe by means of endless yearning for oneness with another person, or with humanity, or with the cosmos as a whole. That is why Wordsworth spoke of poetry as "the most philosophic of all writing." He meant his own kind of poetry, with its effort to express a love of nature, whose being he wished to represent "not standing upon external testimony, but carried alive into the heart by passion." Through passion, and above all through love, one discovered what reason also sought—truths about the world that reason could only approximate but that feeling would establish as revelatory of the reality in which one lived.

It is in this vein that Keats says "I am certain of nothing but the holiness of the Heart's affections and the truth of the Imagination." In linking the heart and the imagination in this fashion, Keats reflects an eighteenth-century train of thought that became axiomatic for Romantic theory. While treating sympathy as fundamental in ethics, Hume—and then followers of his such as Adam Smith— had argued that fellow-feeling can operate only through an act of imagination. We could not appreciate another's pleasure or pain through our own sensations, and neither could our intellect make us experience them in the way that sympathy requires. Imagination was needed for that. In England and Germany there developed a concept of "sympathetic identification" elicited by means of the imagination. This idea belongs to all varieties of Romantic love in the nineteenth century, but it originates much earlier and in a different context. For instance, Dr. Johnson, who would have condemned most of romanticism, says in the middle of the eighteenth century that "all joy or sorrow for the happiness or calamities of others is produced by an act of the imagination, that realizes the event . . . by placing us, for a time, in the condition of him whose fortune we contemplate; so that we feel . . . whatever emotions would be excited by the same good or evil happening to ourselves."

As Walter Jackson Bate points out, Johnson thought that sympathy of this sort merely corroborates what reason can also tell us. According to Romantics such as William Blake, however, the imagination has within itself a power that accomplishes what Johnson refers to but does so by *exceeding* everything rational. Blake describes the human imagination as the faculty that reveals God's own creativity; it is the means by which the world becomes a unity instead of a system of unrelated objects. Through the imagination, Blake maintains, we participate in God's being as the creator of such unity. We thereby identify with him, with nature, and with all men and women.

In Blake, this conception of sympathetic identification through the imagination belongs to a religious perspective that he sums up by saying that "God is Man & exists in us & we in him." Imagination is thought to effect this union and thus to make religious love a possibility for human beings. Romantic versions of Christianity generally affirm that love not only unites the human and the divine, but also that it derives from acts of the imagination causing us to appreciate, through sympathetic identification, the oneness in all being. Blake believed that through imaginative love man learns to experience God as a vital presence pervading the world, and that only this enables him to overcome his alienation from the rest of nature. When that happens, one perceives humanity as a single entity that survives by mutual interpenetration, men and women transcending their differences joyfully in sex as well as in society. In the Romantics as a whole, love is a metaphysical craving for unity, for oneness that eliminates all sense of separation between man and his environment, between one person and another, and within each individual.

Scholars often explain this Romantic preoccupation with oneness as a reaction against the dualisms of the seventeenth and early eighteenth centuries. Imagination assumed its central importance because it seemed, by its very nature, to unify the categories of sense and intellect, passion and rationality, matter and mind. It showed how their interests are ultimately inseparable. In the writings of Coleridge, who stands as an intellectual father to much of subsequent romanticism, we frequently encounter the attempt to reunite what previous philosophy had dissected. When he defines love between the sexes, Coleridge describes a condition of sheer unity while also rejecting all ideas of dissociation between love and marriage. The definition itself reads as follows: "Love is a desire of the whole being to be united to some thing, or some being, felt necessary to its completeness, by the most perfect means that nature permits, and reason dictates."

Coleridge begins his analysis by saying that he will avoid both "the extravagance of pretended Platonism" and also its materialistic alternative. He is, in fact, reflecting the influence of the new German philosophy—which we shall be studying in greater detail later in this book—and repeating its idealization of ever-increasing totalities. Though he speaks of the "perfect means" that nature permits, he does not really share Plato's belief in the prior and objective being of perfection. The "completeness" for which love aspires results from love itself. It is true that Coleridge mentions a ladder of love that he claims to have derived from Plato: "we rise from sensuality to affection, from affection to love, and from love to the pure intellectual delight by which we become worthy to conceive . . . our marriage with the Redeemer of mankind." But even if this looks and sounds

Platonistic, i.e. Christian Neoplatonistic, it already belongs to a different dispensation. For Coleridge uses his ladder to illustrate how all ideals, even religious ones, issue from a search for union between male and female. "From this union arise the paternal, filial, brotherly and sisterly relations of life; and every state is but a family magnified. All the operations of mind, in short, all that distinguishes us from brutes, originate in the more perfect state of domestic life." This is something Plato did not believe; nor did many of his followers.

Some of the later Neoplatonists might have agreed with Coleridge when he then goes on to say that "one infallible criterion in forming an opinion of a man is the reverence in which he holds women," but he explains a man's need for a woman in ways that are foreign to the interests of Neoplatonism. He begins with the assertion that every sensitive person feels imperfect as well as inadequate, and therefore requires a mate who will complement his own deficiencies. Married love is a union of men and women each of whom possesses "qualities which the other has not." For Coleridge this kind of union represents an ideal that underlies whatever human beings can achieve: "In everything the blending of the similar with the dissimilar is the secret of all pure delight. Who shall dare to stand alone, and vaunt himself, in himself, sufficient? In poetry it is the blending of passion with order that constitutes perfection: This is still more the case in morals, and more than all in the exclusive attachment of the sexes."

Coleridge concludes his discussion with the usual assertions of the idealist tradition about love's capacity to raise the body to the level of mind instead of allowing the mind to "sink" in the body. In saying this, however, he remarks that love differs from bodily appetites such as hunger in having "an associative quality." He means that love not only unifies complementary opposites but also that it does so through an imaginative process that invests everything in nature with the lover's joyous response: "the very skies smile in unison with the feeling of true and pure love. It gives to every object in nature a power of the heart, without which it would indeed be spiritless."

We may, if we wish, read this as an instance of the pathetic fallacy in lovers who project their own feelings upon a nature that nevertheless operates through wholly different principles. But the later

Romantics interpreted Coleridge as a guide to something much more pantheistic. Nature could not really be spiritless because it manifested in its dynamic and organic unity a constant impulse of love, a power of the heart. Moreover, the associative quality to which Coleridge refers would have to be a "blending," as he himself suggests. Not just a blending of similar with dissimilar, or of passion with order, but also a total merging between lover and beloved. As he says in one place: "Each strives to be the other." Coleridge does little to clarify his meaning but, in the romanticism to which he contributed, the notion of merging becomes increasingly important. It structures the ideas about love in Romantic theorists of every kind, whether or not they were acquainted with Coleridge's writings. It appears in the thinking of Friedrich Schlegel as well as Shelley, in Novalis as well as Wagner. For philosophers such as Hegel or Schopenhauer, it poses problems that finally lead them to reject one or another aspect of romanticism.

In subsequent chapters we shall see the concept of merging at work within the speculation of various Romantics. Here it is only necessary to remark that A. W. Schlegel, writing at the beginning of the nineteenth century, defines Romantic poetry as literature that perceives the cosmos as "all in all at one and the same time." In a similar fashion, Novalis idealizes the poet who "blends himself with all the creatures of nature, one might say feels himself into them." This blending or merging is what Wordsworth has in mind when, in *Tintern Abbey*, he encourages man to seek "a sense sublime/Of something far more deeply interfused." In the 1800 Preface to the *Lyrical Ballads*, Wordsworth defends rustic life on the assumption that it alone enables human passions to be "incorporated with the beautiful and permanent forms of nature." In Shelley and Keats, the conception of merging as the ground of universal love reappears and is explicitly applied to relations between the sexes. Like Wordsworth, Shelley insists that "The spirit of the worm beneath the sod/In love and worship blends itself with God!" But Shelley says this in a poem to a woman, Emilia Viviani, with whom he himself wishes to merge. In other poems Shelley speaks of lovers who attain "one soul of interwoven flame," who "mingle into" one another and "interpenetrate" through love. In *Endymion*, Keats begins with the suggestion that man is nurtured by love—"until in the end/Melting into its radiance, we blend,/Mingle, and so become a part of it"—but the narrative itself recounts a quest for "eternity of passion" consummated between a man and woman who wish only to "melt into" one another.

Though Shelley harmonizes Romantic ideas about merging with eighteenth-century hedonism and utilitarianism, neither he nor Keats nor any of their followers identifies love with a search for pleasure alone. In being a mystical process, merging can be painful and frightening. Romantic love often articulates a sense, and sometimes a shriek, of terror. It appears when Shelley says to Emilia, in a piercing tone, "I am not thine: I am a part of *thee*." The fearful wonder of this transfiguration resounds throughout the Romantic literature of the nineteenth century. In *Wuthering Heights*, in many respects a quintessence of all Romantic novels, Catherine reveals the nature of her horrible love when she says: "I *am* Heathcliff—he's always, always in my mind—not as a pleasure, any more than I am always a pleasure to myself—but as my own being."

Painful as well as pleasurable, merging could occur with almost any object. This idea reached the Romantics from multiple sources, but the derivation out of Spinoza is particularly striking. By identifying God with nature taken as a whole, Spinoza radically altered traditional beliefs about the love of God. For now everything could be loved, not merely as God's handiwork as the caritas-synthesis maintained, or even as an emanation of his being as Neoplatonism thought, but rather as part of the infinite totality which he was. Whatever one loved was equally a mode of God or nature, in itself the only real individual and the only true perfection. According to Spinoza, all of reality is present in each object since the existence of anything involves its relations to everything else. In the concept of Romantic love these ideas about the cosmos flourished as never before. If God and nature were the same, and if every object contained all reality within it, romanticism could easily conclude that all occurrences of love were good, and perhaps equally good. Regardless of what the beloved might be—however imperfect or even sinful—to love her was to love God. In merging with anything, one inevitably merged with the totality of everything. Love retained its metaphysical import but emancipated itself from the search for prior perfection that had dominated ancient and medieval philosophy. Love did not require the pursuit of an ideal that was separate from, or logically independent of, experience: for the very act of merging brought out the ideality in everything that exists.

It followed that the Romantic lover had only to seek love itself, which is to say that the experience of love meant more to him than the attributes of any specific object. Faust drops dead when he loses faith in the mere process of striving, when he wants to arrest and examine the passing moment; he is awarded eternal salvation for having kept going as long as he did. To love for the sake of love, to love in order to have the inherent goodness of love itself, to seek and to aspire but without a unique or determinate object in mind, is well expressed by the idea of pursuing an unknown. Throughout the Platonic tradition the highest form—or whatever substituted for it—was thought to elicit love precisely by being known, or at least, by being knowable. With one grand stroke, the Romantic philosopher Fichte annihilates all this when he defines love as a desire for something *unknown*, something for which we feel a need while remaining "unaware of whence fulfillment may come." In other words, love is blind—not in the sense of being dazzled by splendors in the beloved, as the courtly tradition would say, or deluded about objective facts, as realist critics claimed, but only because there is no goodness prior to love and therefore nothing for it to see or contemplate until it creates its own perfections.

At this point we may return to the two types of mysticism I mentioned in the first chapter of this book. For one of them, religious love leads to union with an autonomous deity whose being elicits the experience of merging and cannot be altered by it; for the other, religious love reveals a divinity whose very nature belongs to, is even defined by, the mystical merging itself. Both conceptions of merging have been present in most world religions. Traditional theism as well as the primitive religions that preceded it favored ideas about God's independent existence: they portray him as living a private life, like a king in his palace, though he also pays occasional visits to his people. The Bible generally depicts these visits as physical manifestations—God appearing to Moses as a burning bush and to the wandering congregation as a pillar of fire. The culminating appearance is in the form of Christ, God showing himself as man in order to signify his unremitting concern for human salvation.

The mystic who belongs to this tradition may eliminate the physical imagery but he is likely to concentrate upon the fact of visitation. When he tries to tell others about the divine visit, however, he may find himself unable to describe his visitor with any clarity. Since every adjective that might be used borrows its meaning from the empirical world which God transcends absolutely, "the negative theology" argued that none of them can really apply to him. Negative theology denied that God's attributes could ever be known in an affirmative manner. From this, the Romantics concluded that the divinity one could actually love was not something antecedent to, or independent of, the mystical experience. Apart from his merging with the mystic, God was unknowable; and only as God appeared within this experience could he even be conceived. In merging with the deity, mystics were helping to create God as a reality in human experience. Ideas of this sort had limited importance in the Middle Ages, though they were defended by Eckhart, Boehme, and others, but they influenced many Romantic thinkers in the nineteenth century who felt that the spirit of Christianity demanded reinterpretation along these lines.

In Luther we may also see a forerunner of romanticism. Though human nature was innately depraved, Luther believed that in his infinite bestowal God would use two or more individuals as the vehicle for agapē. Joined by holy matrimony, a married couple could—if God so ordained—experience sexual love for one another that would be purified by the fact that agapē was uniting them within its passage back to God. If we now eliminate the concept of a supernatural being who exists apart from man's experience of love, we are left with a humanization of Lutheranism that Luther would have rejected as atheistic but that Romantic thinkers found very attractive. In general, Romantic love—whether it is religious or secular, involving man and God or just human beings—finds its divinity in the act of loving. The descent of agapē, or its return to an independent source, no longer made sense as once it had, but its sanctity and godliness as that which unifies, purifies, and redeems human nature, using frail mortals as intermediaries within its cosmic journey, became the fundamental principle in the concept of Romantic love. For medieval Christianity, God is love; for the Romantic ideology, love is God.

As I suggested in earlier chapters, the idea of merging presupposes a conception of the world as magical. It is not surprising, therefore, that the Romantic period returns to medieval romance and its reliance upon magic. As in those legends of the Middle Ages where a knight falls in love with a maiden who turns out to be the Fairy Queen, the magic in romanticism effects the fusion between human and superhuman, natural and divine, real and ideal. In *Endymion* the youth who succeeds in melting into the radiance of love does so once the two females he adores—one a goddess and the other a mortal woman—merge with one another, becoming a single object for his devotion. Something similar occurs in *Lamia*, and generally throughout Keats' fantasies of love. Though the world impedes the harmonization of sense and spirit, Keats continually shows how they participate in one another—at least ideally, under the aspect of an authentic love between man and woman.

This reconciliation, through sexual love, of the spiritual and the naturalistic had been the goal of medieval romance, and of medieval humanism as a whole. In reviving that tradition, nineteenth-century romanticism benefits from sophistication and enlightenment that could never have existed in the Middle Ages. Even Gottfried von Strassburg, who used the language of Christian mysticism to talk about love, would not have said, as Keats does in one of his letters, that "Love is my religion—I could die for that." And though Gottfried, like many other writers of the thirteenth century, treats sexual exploits as an appropriate illustration of love in action, his attempt to divinize sex could not draw upon the historical consciousness to which the Romantics had access, living in the shadow of a thousand years of conflict between Christianity and its humanistic opponents. When Keats says that "the mere commingling of passionate breath" can—through love—produce an ideal consummation, he continues the synthesizing work of Gottfried in the more favorable intellectual climate that permeated the nineteenth century.

I do not mean to suggest that everyone who believed in Romantic love shared Keats' attitude toward sex. He was criticized for it, even by Shelley as we shall see, and Wordsworth (whose prudishness Shelley ridiculed) generally thought of love as a quasi-maternal, nonsexual bond. But though he did not live to develop his approach in a systematic theory, Keats represents the pervasive eroticism, however subtle, that belongs to all Romantic theory. In its emotional power and blurring of a separate consciousness, sex is the clearest form of merging that most people can understand. If God is present in the world, not as an antecedent being that descends but as a unifying force that creatively emerges in the world's continuous dynamism, sexual metaphors are needed to express this proto-biological process. Romantic love is a search for a new, unknown, infinitely alluring but inherently imperfect object of desire which becomes less and less imperfect as we progressively, and successfully, merge with it. To think in these terms is to think erotically, even if—for largely doctrinal reasons—we couch our affective motivation in language that is abstract or in concepts that accentuate the spiritual. The words of mystic Blake, in his poem "The Question Answer'd," are proof enough:

> What is it men in women do require?
> The lineaments of Gratified Desire.
> What is it women do in men require?
> The lineaments of Gratified Desire.

The Romantic concept of love has been attacked by many authors and from many points of view. The critiques by Irving Babbitt, de Rougemont, and José Ortega y Gasset have received considerable attention, particularly among literary scholars. Though I shall examine their arguments only briefly, they may be useful in delineating difficulties for the Romantic philosophy.

First, there is the problem about objectivity. Since the Romantics denied that love is the search for a known or knowable object whose prior perfection elicits love, critics such as Babbitt conclude that they were merely expressing an egoistic attitude. In *Rousseau and Roman-*

ticism, Babbitt argues that the Romantic "is in love not with a particular person but with his own dream." Hazlitt is the lover he here describes, but he uses similar phrases in talking about Rousseau, Shelley, Novalis, and others. He sees the "romanticist" as one who does not "wish to transcend his own ego. . . . There is in fact no object in the romantic universe—only subject."

Babbitt's prime example in relation to this criticism is a brief theater work by Rousseau entitled *Pygmalion*, subtitled "scène lyrique." Babbitt calls attention to the fact that Pygmalion, falling in love with Galatea (the statue he has just completed), is principally enamored of his own genius as an artist. This suggestion is not without merit. Rousseau's little drama begins with Pygmalion's fears that his genius has been exhausted, his talent dissipated; it ends with an ecstatic surmounting of all doubt and depression once the artistic product of his hands and heart comes to life, descending from her pedestal and touching him as a real woman might. There is no reason, however, to infer from this that the object of love "is not in any proper sense an object at all." Even if we take Rousseau's dramatization of the Greek myth as symbolic of Romantic love in general, our conclusion can only be that for the Romantics love depends upon imaginative processes, which is quite different from saying that it is covert egoism. Galatea as a statue is indeed Pygmalion's creation; but as one who comes to life, as one who begins to live her own life—thanks to Venus, whom Pygmalion has invoked so that he can love Galatea as *more* than just a statue—she becomes the beloved with whom he now can merge. Being a woman, she represents that other person with whom the lover experiences sympathetic identification.

Babbitt is certainly justified in recognizing that the danger of love reducing to egoism confronted Rousseau and all later Romantics; but it was for them a danger to be examined and overcome. Babbitt fails to realize the extent to which the Romantics idealized love as something that transforms primordial selfishness into unselfish oneness with other persons. As we shall see in the following chapter, Rousseau analyzes this process in relation to his distinction between "amour-propre" and "amour de soi." In *Pygmalion* the sculptor begins with the former condition, which is vanity and self-glorification, but achieves a more wholesome state of being after the gods have given him a woman to love. "Je m'enivre d'amour-propre; je m'adore dans ce que j'ai fait" ("I am intoxicated with self-love; I adore myself in what I have done"). This is how he speaks when, in his initial depression, he comes upon the statue he has created. Once it begins to elicit his erotic interest, however, he senses a desire to animate it with his own soul, even to die in order to live in Galatea. We recognize this as the Neoplatonic suggestion that the lover lives in the beloved, but for Rousseau the idea immediately turns into a problem about the nature of merging. Pygmalion argues that "if I were she, I would not see her, I would not be the one who loves her." In his prayer he asks that Galatea live and that he "forever be another, in order always to want to be her, to see her, to love her, to be loved by her."

Pygmalion's request is granted insofar as Galatea becomes a person to love and be loved, attaining an identity of her own signified by the fact that each of the four times she speaks she refers to her own selfhood. Touching herself, she first says, "Me," and then "This is me." Touching a piece of marble, she remarks, "This is not me." But when she finally touches Pygmalion, she sighs "Me again" ("encore moi"). The scene ends with Pygmalion resolving his former doubts about merging: "it is you, it is you only: I have given you my entire being; I will no longer live except through you." Far from being just an egoistic intoxication, love in Rousseau's drama appears as the search through imagination for a living creature with whom one can merge in order to escape from egoism. Galatea the woman is still Pygmalion, but no longer as merely a thing he has created. The miracle Venus effects makes it equally true to say that he is she, since henceforth his love for Galatea as a real person will cause him to live his life only by means of her.

Implicit in Babbitt's critique of Romantic love is the assumption that it must always involve delusion about the beloved. Shelley's "desire of the moth for the star" and Chateaubriand's confession that his imagination instilled love for "a phantom" Babbitt cites as proof of Romantic self-delusion. As we shall see, Ortega criticizes Stendhal's approach to love in a similar manner. This line of attack is, however, unconvincing for the simple reason that these and most other Romantics are as much concerned about the risk of self-delusion as are their critics. When they speak of its occurrence in their experience, they are either admitting that they have failed to live up to the ideal or else they are describing love's precarious though beneficial dependence upon the imagination. Stendhal differs from some of the other Romantics inasmuch as he seems, at times, to justify self-delusion in love on the premise that human beings cannot obtain happiness in any other way. But even he is primarily interested in the imagination as a creative faculty that enables us to bestow value upon other people without falsifying their reality. We shall have to examine the details of Stendhal's theory in order to see whether it is tenable, but nothing is gained by assuming in advance that he or the others are idealizing sheer irrationality.

In his prolonged foray against romanticism, de Rougemont argues that its principal delusion turns out to be the belief that Romantic love is oriented toward life. De Rougemont claims that "really" the Romantic lover is seeking his own destruction, that passion eliminates barriers between persons for the sake of achieving symbolic annihilation of oneself. As I have suggested, de Rougemont is naive in his belief that the concept of death functions in the Middle Ages as it does in the Romantic period. But also he misrepresents its relevance to ideas about Romantic love as they developed in the nineteenth century. Within romanticism as a whole there were two major strands: the benign or healthy-minded and the pessimistic. The latter often defined love in terms of a quest for desired nothingness, as in Wagner's notion of love-death, but the former sees love as a means of eliminating what is negative or destructive in oneself, thereby attaining on earth a maximum joyfulness of life. These two facets of Romantic love are not unrelated to one another, but they move in different directions and must not be lumped together as if either characterizes all of romanticism. As we shall see, even the despairing mode of Romantic love is more than *just* "a search for death."

A similar superficiality belongs to Babbitt's complaint that Romantic love is largely indiscriminate, and therefore unethical in its conception of the beloved. He cites Alfred de Musset's remark that "To love is the great point. What matters the mistress? What matters the flagon provided one have the intoxication?" Babbitt can find in this nothing but a cloak for "every manner of vileness" that the Romantic tries to glorify as a sublime oneness between human beings. He may be right about some Romantics, but it is significant that Babbitt does not extend his argument and likewise ridicule the Christian saint who wishes to bestow love upon all creatures indiscriminately. Like the saint, the lover de Musset idealizes is not deluded about the nature of his affective interest. Each of them finds an infinite value in love itself, as an embodiment of holiness whether or not the object merits it. They are colleagues within the idealist tradition, and thus equally subject to realist critiques of idealism in general. One can prefer the nonsexual and ultimately otherworldly love of the saint as opposed to de Musset's faith in benign promiscuity; but such preference, which can also go the other way, depends upon individual choice. There is no objective reason to assume some necessary immorality or perversion on the part of those who cultivate the Romantic ideal.

Finally, the critics of Romantic love have insisted that it is antisocial and destructive to the institution of marriage. De Rougemont in particular sees the Romantic attitude toward passionate love as a rejection of marital fidelity, an attempt to ascribe superior value to adultery or extramarital fantasies. And for many Romantics, in relation to much of what they said, this is quite true. Throughout his tendentious argument, however, de Rougment neglects the Romantic desire—sometimes muted but often explicit—to find love within, and by means of, marriage. As in the medieval romances, Romantic idealization of love between the sexes is frequently directed toward the attainment of a permanent and stable union. Moreover, the subversiveness of Romantic love is often an attack on conventional or forced marriages that were still common in the nineteenth century, marriages arranged for reasons other than love. When the Romantics encouraged adultery, they generally did so because it could serve as an alternative to loveless marriage.

With respect to all these problems, the critics of romanticism tend to make it seem more uniform than is actually warranted. In the succeeding chapters I shall have ample occasion to emphasize the diversity among different theorists of Romantic love; but here I should remark that on one important topic, the status of women, there were at least three different points of view. Shelley and Stendhal stand in the vanguard of the feminist movement as we know it today. Their desire to provide women maximum opportunities for intellectual and personal development directly stems from Romantic ideas about love. For sexual love to succeed, they are convinced, there must be equality at a high cultural level between men and women. They demand political action that will prohibit unfair treatment of women, thus giving them greater access to love between the sexes which makes life valuable for all human beings. Other advocates of Romantic love, such as Schlegel and followers of Rousseau, insisted upon differences between the sexes that prevent women from wandering beyond their traditional roles within the family. Still others, Alfred Tennyson for instance, recommended a compromise that afforded women a kind of equal but separate status, allowing them to be helpmates and companions for the Romantic lover but only if they were satisfied to be angels in his household. While fulfilling the demands of domesticity, they would also have a sense of equality with the male and enjoy Romantic oneness with him.

I mention these varieties of opinion in order to show that it would be a mistake to define Romantic love in terms of any single conception. That is why our pluralistic methodology is needed: to savor and appreciate the rich complexity in this, as in all other, concepts of love.

In the chapter on the concept of courtly love, I listed five tenets that could serve as criteria for its definition. Being a later form of erotic idealism, formulated by thinkers who were conscious of their indebtedness to humanism in the Middle Ages, the concept of Romantic love renews these five conditions within its own context. It too implies that sexual love between men and women is in itself an ideal worth striving for, that love ennobles both lover and beloved, that it is a spiritual attainment that cannot be reduced to sex alone, that it pertains to courtship (though not always courtesy), and that it is passion creating a special oneness. But in relation to each of these, Romantic love also reflects the many intellectual developments since the Middle Ages. While defending courtly love against unsympathetic critics, the Romantics realized that a new kind of humanism was required. Unifying the split between sense and spirit, and between love and marriage, they sought to accomplish the goals of courtly love by making them more suitable to a world no longer supporting the older form of Christianity or the feudal institution of matrimony.

Some of the new and exciting concepts in romanticism were rediscoveries from a neglected past. De Rougemont points out that it was Plutarch, writing only a few centuries after Plato, who said: "The physical union with one's wife is a source of friendship; it is like sharing a great mystery together." Similar statements can be found in Renaissance revisions of Platonism, Protestant attempts to dignify marriage as heterosexual friendship showing forth God's agapē, and even Rationalist ideas about the friendliness of marriage as opposed to the evils of passion. The Romantics inherit all this and put it to their own use.

For most Romantics, passion retains within itself the mystical and miraculous power to establish love's special unity between men and women. For some of them, as we shall see when we turn to Rousseau, it is the purification of passion that effects the miracle. But for others, the Romantic search for oneness involved not only beliefs about the universality of passional yearning but often a preoccupation with sexual details that no previous literature had ever expressed so fully. It is not just the fact that romanticism focuses upon personal experience whereas courtly writings deal with exploits and adventures without describing the intimacies to which they lead. There is also the explicit desire, on the part of many Romantic writers, to awaken their audiences to the intrinsic goodness of human consummation whenever it can be obtained or even imagined. From this facet of romanticism, together with the scientific aspirations of nineteenth-century realism, modern sexology arose.

All this occurs at a time when social rigidities were being softened and then undermined at the end of the eighteenth century. The

French Revolution and its aftermath accelerated demands for individual liberties, including the rights of men and women to marry for love regardless of what their families wanted. Some scholars trace the beginnings of Romantic theory to mid-eighteenth-century England because there more than anywhere else women were able to choose their husbands and determine the nature of their married life. Throughout Europe in the Romantic period many thinkers insisted on the value of each person as a unique being who must be allowed to develop toward his or her maximum potentiality. For Romantic theorists, the growth of personhood in all mankind, and in every individual, is itself the basis of human spirituality.

Particularly in its benign and optimistic varieties, but possibly in its pessimistic aspects as well, the concept of Romantic love contributes to the nineteenth-century faith in the sanctity of both self-fulfillment and interpersonal harmony. The Romantic ideology represents, in fact, the highest level to which man's thinking about the love of persons had thus far reached. In some respects, it is a level that has not yet been exceeded.

10

Rousseau
The Attempt to Purify Passion

IN THE HISTORY OF IDEAS ABOUT love, Jean-Jacques Rousseau is unique in one important respect: he combines the roles of philosopher, novelist, and analyst of his own experience. He speculates about love as a philosopher and moralist; he writes an 800-page novel that uses the concept within its narrative structure; and then he leaves posthumous memoirs that exhibit the problems of his own love-life. Among the great writers in the Western world, only Proust approximates his ability to analyze love on the three diverse levels of philosophy, literature, and autobiography. But despite his greatness as a philosophical novelist, Proust was not a complete philosopher; he felt no need to deal with problems of theology, political theory, or ethics in a detailed manner such as Rousseau's. Moreover, Proust merges the three levels: they intermingle and occur simultaneously, *A la recherche du temps perdu* explicitly defying neat classification. Is it fictional autobiography? A psychosociological novel? Or the most vivid and concrete form of *moralité*? Such questions may also be relevant to Rousseau's writings, but they arise in a different way. When we read *La Nouvelle Héloïse*, we tend to approach it as we would a novel by Richardson or Prévost. When we study *The Social Contract* or *Emile*, we expect to find moral philosophy as in Hobbes, Locke, or Montesquieu. When we open the *Confessions*, we immediately associate it with the self-revelations of St. Augustine and Montaigne. It is only after we have come to live with the individual works of Rousseau that we begin to see how subtly the three levels interpenetrate in everything he writes.

In one place Rousseau forestalls some possible objection on the part of the reader by querulously remarking that he cannot say everything at once and therefore will deal with the objection later. And in fact he constantly returns, in what seems to be a haphazard manner, to ideas from an earlier moment in his writing that now come to mind and that he squeezes in as best he can, regardless of the subject matter or form of discourse. Eventually we realize that Rousseau is systematically telling us about himself as a writer, and thereby revealing his way of solving problems about human nature. He often sounds like a breathless child who has a message to convey but does not feel it can be separated from information about himself, about his own experiences as the messenger and means of conveyance. Like the child, Rousseau merges the different types of communication because he has difficulty detaching himself from his subject matter or separating his own personality from the independent world he pretends to describe but actually reveals in its unseparated condition.

This lack of distance from one's inner self was to become the core of nineteenth-century romanticism. In Rousseau, who did most of his writing during the years preceding the French Revolution of 1789, it was a trait that shocked his contemporaries. Even advanced thinkers like Voltaire felt a need to keep their personalities out of their more serious writings. Rousseau shows and even exhibits himself—not always, not equally in all his works, but on many occasions. To us looking back from a post-Romantic period, he may often seem like a typical man of the eighteenth century, and in some respects he conforms to the traditions of his time more than either Voltaire or Diderot. But his writing straddles both past and future, the post-Renaissance rationalism in seventeenth- and eighteenth-century French thought as well as the postrevolutionary Romantic philosophy that drew from Rousseau elements it required. What romanticism took from him, out of context and (ironically) disregarding his personality or intention, would have horrified Rousseau.

No single book provides a preferential entry into Rousseau's thinking about love. *La Nouvelle Héloïse* is, however, a suitable place to begin. It is a sentimental romance resembling any number of others in the eighteenth century, filled with rhetoric that present-day readers can hardly tolerate. It was a best-seller in its time for the same sensationalistic reasons that make novels best-sellers in our own day, and it was immediately rejected by moralists like Voltaire as little more than vulgar trash. Nevertheless it incorporates virtually every aspect of Rousseau's philosophy and many of his most important ideas.

The plot is very simple. Saint-Preux falls in love with Julie. He is nineteen and she is seventeen. They have a natural affinity for one another which they recognize almost at first sight and identify as an eternal bond. Though he has entered her home as a tutor, like Abelard with the original Heloise, he is lowborn and therefore ineligible as a suitor. Through a number of stages their love becomes more passionate. It eventuates in sexual consummation, and a wealthy friend tries to convince Julie's father to allow them to marry one another. Money is not an issue since the friend will bestow a fortune upon Saint-Preux. But Julie's father rejects him because he is not an aristocrat. Julie submits to her father's domination, banishes Saint-Preux from her presence, marries a rich nobleman who has been chosen for her as a worthy and suitable mate. This is M. de Wolmar, a man of intellect who has never experienced passion towards anyone. He is, however, devoted to Julie, becomes a model husband and father, and installs her as the queen of a utopian community he creates on his country estate. Having learned of Julie's passionate love for Saint-Preux, he invites the younger man to join them in a ménage à trois governed by strict rules of conduct. Not only are the former lovers to live as friends rather than as sexual companions, but also Julie tries to convince Saint-Preux that the harmony and stability of her married life is a condition superior to the passionate love that preceded it. After a course of education or therapy, Saint-Preux eventually agrees with her. Accepting their present life as a state of virtue that could never have been attained through passion, he surmounts all the temptations that might have reinstated the earlier relationship. But when Julie dies, having contracted pneumonia while saving her child from drowning, she leaves behind letters indicating that she still belongs to Saint-Preux and hopes to be united with him in heaven as her rightful husband.

In the last two hundred years, critics have generally held one or another of two contrary interpretations of this novel. On one view it is to be taken as a defense of virtue against the seductive dangers of human passion. Being the pure-hearted heroine, Julie embodies natural goodness that approximates divinity. She is always motivated by moral sentiments of the highest order, remains faithful to her husband, and sustains him in the good works of their ideal society. Prior to her marriage she renounces her love for Saint-Preux in accordance with demands of filial devotion that Rousseau had extolled in his moral treatises. In this interpretation, Saint-Preux represents pleasures of the flesh in their most dangerous form precisely because he is not a seducer, not an aggressive Don Juan, but rather an innocent man of feeling who merely desires total oneness with his beloved. And he too finally recognizes that virtue represented by Julie's happy and conventional marriage is preferable to the passionate love they had formerly experienced.

The other interpretation is a little more complicated, but possibly closer to the truth about this confusing novel. It emphasizes an apparent reorientation that takes place after the second of the six volumes. For though the author cannot speak with his own voice in a novel made up entirely of letters written by the characters, Rousseau is thought to be glorifying the magnificence of reciprocal sexual love throughout the first two volumes, and then contrasting it with an inimical ideal of marital rectitude in the subsequent volumes. On this view neither ideal is able to triumph, since Rousseau cannot or will not give either one a final preference. Inasmuch as he is writing a novel, he freely creates a dramatic ambiguity that forces the reader to reach his own conclusions about the nature of love. Slender as it is, the narrative would then engross us by the mere fact of thematic conflict between two ideals that matter to everyone, while also augmenting the suspense that leads us from page to page in the hope of finding an ultimate resolution. When Julie reveals at the end that even she—the paragon of human goodness—will never be able to eradicate the love she and Saint-Preux originally considered eternal, we are left with a pervasive ambiguity that has been built into the dramatic structure of the novel. Since neither love nor virtue can be preferred over the other, Rousseau's thought remains dialectical to the very end. Those who consider this a fault conclude that Rousseau was too divided in himself to reach a final and coherent system of thought; but others claim that this division in Rousseau enables him to express the ambiguous character of human existence.

Over and above these interpretations, there is another that seems to me more plausible than either of them. Unlike the first interpretation, this one denies that Rousseau subordinates love to virtue. Unlike the second interpretation, it sees no reason to think that Rousseau's approach was ambiguous. On this reading, the bond between Julie and Saint-Preux cannot be treated as merely an ephemeral or unworthy condition that virtue must transcend; but neither can Rousseau be taken as arguing for a preferential goodness in passion. On the contrary, he is seen as trying to integrate the passionate life with a moral system that will make it amenable to the needs of society. For Rousseau the principal issue was to find the kind of relationship between men and women that will satisfy *both* love and virtue. The novel is thus an attempt to synthesize the two ideals, as opposed to leaving them in dialectical conflict.

If this third interpretation is right, the drama in the novel does not result from any inherent incompatibility between love and virtue, but rather from the discrepancy between Rousseau's conception of how things ought to be and his realization of how they actually are. Under ideal conditions Julie would marry her lover, and together they would acquire the wisdom that Wolmar represents. The good or virtuous life would belong to the young couple as a consequence of their merged condition itself, their being joined by the eternal unity of passion that links their pure and wholly transparent hearts. But the actual world, which Rousseau condemns here as he does in all his other writings, defeats the ideal. The drama of the work results from the stupidity of Julie's father, who will not countenance marriage between his daughter and an untitled suitor. Had he done so, there would have been no need for a novel. The book would have turned into a treatise along the lines of *Emile*, the right man marrying the right woman and the two of them learning how to live in harmony with nature.

In support of this interpretation, one can cite a crucial passage in the second volume that shows Julie's despair at the moment she has to make the greatest decision of her life. Lord Bomston, the devoted friend of the lovers, has offered them an estate in England and half his wealth in order for them to elope, to marry despite the refusal of Julie's father, and to live in a state of permanent domesticity congruent with the perfect oneness between their souls. Julie will finally reject this magnanimous offer, but her despair is occasioned by the awareness that she will be guilty of a crime against nature however she decides. Her love for Saint-Preux is neither more nor less ultimate than her devotion to her parents and her desire to spare them unnecessary suffering. Both issue from the order of nature, and as principles of morality enabling one to live in nature as one should they are considered equally binding. If this is so, however, the conflict exists not between love and virtue, or passion and marriage, but rather between sexual and filial love. Julie suffers because her father wilfully misuses her love for him. He is tyrannical in refusing to recognize the importance of her amorous interests. He represents the arbitrary use of power by a parent who blindly adheres to conventional social standards—all of which needs to be reformed or even destroyed. On this interpretation, Rousseau's novel is a work that calls for radical changes in society, although it becomes reactionary when he favorably describes the authoritarian utopia on Wolmar's estate.

Each of these interpretations has much to recommend it, but all three may be accommodated within a structural perspective that overrides their differences. As if anticipating Kierkegaard, Rousseau presents the lovers' progress throughout the novel as stages of development that correspond to the aesthetic, the ethical, and the religious. In his final note Rousseau prides himself on having written a story that is "pure and not mixed with unpleasantness." He means that his protagonists are exemplars of sensibility, lovers of the good, persons defined by their pursuit of ideals. The same applies to all the major characters in the novel with the possible exception of

Julie's father. The three who participate in the marital triangle that dominates the plot were conceived as the embodiment of aspirations that Rousseau valued very highly. Saint-Preux begins as the representative of an aesthetic attitude toward love—not promiscuous, as Kierkegaard was later to define the aesthetic, but responsive to its immediate goodness. Being a person in love, he manifests sexual passion as a source of vitality and human well-being. He and Julie move to a condition higher than the aesthetic when they fall under the influence of Wolmar, who represents the ethical stage. Julie finally attains the highest level of human development in her pantheistic love of nature. This supplants the aesthetic and the ethical as ultimate values without denying the ideality in each.

The entire burden of the novel is summed up in the last letter that Julie writes to Saint-Preux, just before the accident that leads to her death. It is a final expression of joy and achievement, the completion of all their struggles; and though her death is sad, her words provide a happy ending: "What a delightful sentiment I am experiencing as I begin this letter! This is the first time in my life that I have been able to write you without fear and without shame. I pride myself in the friendship which unites us, for it is the result of an unparalleled victory. People stifle great passions; rarely do they purify them. To forget a dear one when honor requires it is the effort of an honorable and ordinary soul; but after having been what we were, to be what we are today—that is a real triumph of virtue."

In referring to a triumph that goes beyond the dictates of honor alone, Julie is implying a contrast between herself and the Princesse de Clèves, or heroines in the plays of Racine and Corneille. They too are forced to choose between passion and a variety of moral imperatives incorporated in the concept of honor, and they are heroines because they subjugate their natural inclinations for the sake of a moral good that either lies beyond passion or happens to be incompatible with it under the circumstances. But unlike Julie, they find no way of benefiting from them both within their own experience. The Princesse de Clèves must first choose between her marriage to a loving husband for whom she feels no passion and adultery with the man she loves passionately and who passionately loves her. She honorably renounces illicit passion, but after the death of her husband she is psychologically incapable of retaining the best in each relationship by marrying her passionate lover. A similar dilemma had occurred in hundreds of romances by the time Rousseau wrote his novel. His solution is based upon the belief that neither passion nor even honorable marriage is an acceptable end in itself. Both must be *purified*, as Julie stresses in her final letter, which is to say that each must be experienced in a way that divests it of claims to an exclusive or highest ideality.

In thinking of true or ultimate love as a transcending of both marriage and sexual love, and in general of all moral possibilities that people encounter in their natural relations to one another, Rousseau identifies himself with the Platonic element in the idealistic tradition. In one place, he adds a footnote that tells us "the true philosophy of lovers is that of Plato; while the passion lasts, they never have any other. A sensitive man cannot forsake this philosopher; a cold reader cannot endure him." This comment occurs in Part 2 of the novel, long before the lovers have reached their final stage of perfection. But I think we may take it as a commentary upon the novel as a whole. In Rousseau, as in Plato, the search for goodness causes passion to arise and then takes the ideal lovers beyond passion, beyond marriage, and beyond the limits of ordinary life.

But how can human beings purify passion without destroying sexuality itself? This must always be a dilemma, for Rousseau's philosophy as it is for Plato's. And in fact, Rousseau's attempt to define the highest levels of love as a purification that transcends what the passionate lovers initially desired exemplifies the split between love and sexuality that characterizes the Platonic tradition as a whole. Rousseau himself is aware of the difficulty; he recognizes the split as a problem and even a paradox. More than any of his predecessors, he realizes that a separation between love and lust may actually be pathological. That is what Freud would later maintain on the basis of his clinical experience, but an analysis of the moral dangers had already been provided by Rousseau. In the *Confessions* he describes two kinds of intimacy that he attained with different women. Toward some he felt emotional subservience that cast him into the posture of a stereotypic troubadour, lovesick, devoted, even reverential, but without pronounced libidinal impulse. Towards others he felt strong sexual passions that rendered him "jealous as a Turk, and as savage as a tiger." The *Confessions* reverberate with his inability to harmonize these contrary attitudes. "I know two distinct sorts of love," he says, "both real but with practically nothing in common except that they are alike extremely violent and different in every way from a mere friendly affection. The whole course of my life has been divided between these two quite separate emotions, and I have even experienced them both simultaneously."

Rousseau means that he has experienced each for a different woman at the same time. So too, as we have seen, did Platonic and courtly lovers such as Dante feel toward the beloved a spiritualized love they celebrate in poetry while also enjoying sexual passion for other women and marital devotion to a faithful wife. Beatrice may castigate Dante for his lack of total fidelity, but in general the Platonistic tradition was scarcely troubled by the possibility that the lover's dualistic approach was unwholesome by its very nature. What makes Rousseau distinctly modern, or rather what in him helps create the modern world, is his constant awareness of the problematic character within the split. To the extent that he is indeed a Platonist, he can extol the infinite superiority of love over lust, but he also senses an incompleteness that results from their separation within his own experience.

At the time he began writing *La Nouvelle Héloïse*, Rousseau was forty-five years old and afflicted by the fear that he would die without having truly loved anyone, without ever finding a particular person with whom he could satisfy his need for passionate love. "How could it be," he reports in the *Confessions*, "that with such inflammable feelings, with a heart entirely moulded for love, I had not at least once burned with love for a definite object? Devoured by a need to love that I had never been able to satisfy, I saw myself coming to the gates of old age and dying without having lived."

One may take this as a prelude to the purified love that Rousseau subsequently experienced in his relationship with Mme d'Houdetot, but the immediate consequence of his despair is the writing of *La Nouvelle Héloïse*. For he goes on to say that "the impossibility of attaining the real persons precipitated me into the land of chimeras; and seeing nothing that existed worthy of my exalted feelings, I fostered them in an ideal world which my creative imagination soon peopled with beings after my own heart." These beings are not, however, Platonic essences; and their greatest happiness is depicted as occurring only during the period in which the two kinds of love merge with one another. Though the carnal must eventually fall away, it remains throughout not only as a constant temptation but also as the reminder of a time in their relationship when purification was less important than completeness. The ultimate drama in Rousseau's novel issues from the conflict between the traditional and the revolutionary aspects in his own personality, the former looking back to Platonic or religious idealizations of amorous emotion while the latter demands total harmony with the need for sexual consummation.

Because of this ambivalence, Rousseau often characterizes love between the sexes in ways that modify the idealistic tradition to which he belongs, subtly preparing it for the extensive reinterpretations that romanticism would later introduce. To begin with, one encounters an emphasis upon imagination rather than enjoyment. This distinction was not new, many medieval love poems having been constructed out of the aesthetic advantages of imagining the beauties of the beloved instead of enjoying them directly. But in Rousseau the differences become strident, life in the imagination often asserting itself as a warranted escape from mere actuality, and even as the unique access to truly authentic pleasures of loving. In one of the letters that describe the "intoxicating favors" Julie has bestowed upon Saint-Preux in their sexual intercourse, the young man insists that the act of enjoyment means less to him than the hour they subsequently spent together peacefully talking about their love. Rousseau appends a footnote saying "Oh love! If I miss the age at which you are enjoyed, it is not for the hour of possession; it is for the hour which follows it." In the *Confessions* he tells us more than once that he is a man who was made to imagine rather than to enjoy, and that is why the happiest moments of his life occur when he is by himself meditating in solitude.

In minimizing the value of sexual satisfaction, Rousseau is criticizing Voltaire, Diderot, and others among the Encyclopedists who defined love as primarily an impulse to enjoy another person's sexuality. Although Voltaire speaks of love as "the stuff of nature embroidered by imagination," most of his description deals with stuff and not embroidery. If you want an idea of what love is like, he says, "look at this proud horse which two of your grooms lead to the quiet mare awaiting him; she draws aside her tail to welcome him; see how her eyes sparkle; hark to the neighing; watch the prancing, curvetting, the ears pricked, the mouth opening with little convulsions, the swelling nostrils, the fiery breath, the manes rising and floating, the impetuous movement with which he hurls himself on the object which nature has destined for him." Voltaire recognizes that love among human beings includes other elements; and when he deliberates about the medieval Heloise's love for Abelard, he concludes that she must have lived on "illusions and memories." But the problem arises in the first place because Voltaire wonders how any woman could possibly love a man once he has been castrated and can no longer pleasure her. We seem to be in a different world from the one that is inhabited by the characters in Rousseau's novel.

For his part, Diderot deals with the nature of love in an *Encyclopedia* entry entitled "Jouissance," i.e. enjoyment. He defines "to enjoy" as "to know, to experience, to feel the advantages of possession," and it is in the enjoyment of another human being that he discovers the most noble passion available to man: "Among the objects that nature everywhere offers to our desires, you who have a soul, tell me if there is anything more worthy of your pursuit, anything that can make us happier than the possession and enjoyment of a being who thinks and feels as you do, who has the same ideas, who experiences the same sensations, the same ecstasies, who brings her affectionate and sensitive arms towards yours, who embraces you, whose caresses will be followed with the existence of a new being who will resemble one of you."

Diderot then goes on to extol the elements of pleasure in love and its function as a mechanism for propagation. At the first stage there is mere sexual attraction: "the heart palpitates; the limbs tremble; voluptuous images wander through the mind; a flood of spirits runs through the nerves, excites them . . . sight is troubled, delirium is born; reason, the slave of instinct, limits itself to serving the latter, and nature is satisfied." At a further stage, discrimination supervenes upon sexual excitement, enjoyment occurring once a woman prefers one particular man, who may then consider pleasure as the recompense for some merit in himself. Like Rousseau, Diderot recognizes that love involves "an inflamed imagination," "the most delicate of illusions," and "an almost divine enthusiasm which eventuates in vows of eternal fidelity"; but for him, these are all components within a biological phenomenon that enables individuals to possess each other in the most thorough and enjoyable manner that nature can afford. For Rousseau, imagination is not just a part of enjoyment but rather a substitute for it, an alternative that unites the lovers within a nonphysical dimension and takes them beyond the mandates of biological necessity. When Stendhal later employs the concept of imagination in his analysis of love, he draws more heavily upon Rousseau than upon Diderot. Or rather, he seeks to combine their divergent views while giving priority to Rousseau's.

The love Diderot talks about in this article, and which he describes at length in essays like "The Supplement to Bougainville's Voyages," is a mutual love that enables man and woman to reciprocate their enjoyment of one another. In Rousseau, however, mutuality becomes an end in itself, the sense of oneness having greater importance than any conceivable enjoyment. Love, as he defines it, allows soulmates to unite and to merge independently of sensory pleasure. In being made for each other, his lovers are eternally bound in a metaphysical adventure beyond the limits of sexual experience. Where Diderot refers to happiness of the moment and preference based upon an estimate of merit, Rousseau's lovers speak of perfect union between souls that reach an entire congruence with one another, touching at all points, henceforth destined to have identical feelings even at a distance. "Where are those gross men," Saint-Preux writes Julie in one place, "who represent the transports of love as only a fever of the senses, as a desire of a debased instinct? Let them come, let them observe, let them feel what is taking place in my inmost heart."

To readers of the eighteenth century, Rousseau's idealistic way of describing mutuality could easily sound absurd. When *La Nouvelle Héloïse* first appeared, the Philosophes identified Saint-Preux's love with ridiculous attitudes of self-abasement revealing a desire to suffer needlessly. When Saint-Preux says it is "one of the miracles of love to make us find pleasure in suffering," contemporary eudaimonists could only conclude that he was harking back to the diseased condition of medieval masochists. If happiness was the goal of all human endeavor, which enlightened men in the eighteenth century accepted as a fundamental premise in moral philosophy, what could possibly justify the declarations of a lover who savored the pain of separation and relished the frustration of those very impulses that propelled him toward the beloved in the first place? Even Stendhal, writing some sixty years later and willing to defend Saint-Preux's ideas against those of Don Juan, chooses Goethe's Werther as an exemplar because he finds Saint-Preux himself "such an insipid creature": "He was a true poet, an irresolute babbler, who had to rouse his own feelings by peroration and was, moreover, a stupid fellow."

At the same time, Stendhal finds in Saint-Preux's attitude the potentiality for a greater happiness than anything provided by all other kinds of existence, including direct enjoyment such as Diderot describes. What Rousseau's contemporaries found backward and reactionary could appear to nineteenth-century Romantics as the basis for the only life worth living.

When he defines love as "crystallization," Stendhal also shows the influence of Rousseau more than one might have expected. Having distinguished between imagination and enjoyment, Rousseau readily concludes that even true love is illusion. In one of his letters he says that "the love which I conceive, and have been able to feel, is fired by the illusory image of the loved one's perfection; and it is this very illusion which leads it to enthusiasm for virtue, for this idea always forms part of a perfect woman." Stendhal has a different conception of virtue and that enables him to end up with quite a different philosophy of love; but his idea of crystallization as a perception of perfection in the beloved which is also a happy illusion derives directly from Rousseau. Not only in the text of *La Nouvelle Héloïse*, but also in Rousseau's second Preface, the love between Julie and Saint-Preux is described as an illusion in which the lovers create for themselves an image of beauty and goodness that exceeds anything reality can actually encompass.

But therein lies another paradox. If love is illusory, how can it be a mutual oneness destined for all eternity? If the lovers are merely enamored of images of one another, how can their souls be congruent at every point? If love is just a play of the imagination, it cannot be a "perception of perfection" such as Plato envisaged. In *Emile* Rousseau argues against the dangers of imagination, which is capable of awakening in the child unhealthy sexual interests that do not arise from nature alone; yet he also defends it as the mechanism for transforming the sexual into the spiritual. He says that "true love, whatever is said of it, will always be honored by men; for although its transports lead us astray, although it does not exclude odious qualities from the heart that feels it—and even produces them—it nevertheless always presupposes estimable qualities without which one would not be in a condition to feel it."

Is it, then, "estimable" to live in illusion? In the Introduction to his translation of *Emile*, Allan Bloom claims that the concept of "sublimation as the source of the soul's higher expressions . . . was introduced to the world by Rousseau." But even if this is correct, neither Bloom nor Rousseau shows how imagination can sublimate sex into a love that is objectively justifiable while also being based on illusions.

Stendhal resolves these problems by treating crystallization as a subjective phenomenon that can be defended simply because it leads to happiness. For Stendhal the value of love consists less in the creation of virtuous attributes than in the exhilarating attunement between imaginative faculties. For Rousseau, however, the deceptiveness of love must always be the canker in the rose, as it also is for Proust, who carefully analyzes the inherent paradox. Rousseau does not, but its presence in his thinking leads to his eventual rejection of sexual passion. Wolmar feels no passions, unless one counts his Proustian passion for observation, and he is never deluded by anything. Presumably he makes an error of judgment in remaining an atheist until the end of the novel, but even in that area he is not living in illusion. He is the model husband and a worthy successor to Saint-Preux because his nonillusory dedication to social welfare puts him in touch with reality in a way that Saint-Preux can appreciate only after he and Julie have ceased to be lovers. Rousseau wants to eliminate the delusiveness of passion, and he proposes to do this by sacrificing it to the superior demands of communal service and finally religion. But if passion is delusory, we may ask, how could he have extolled it in the first place?

To the extent that passionate love is merely a figment, it will have to be transcended, Rousseau seems to say, but since it fosters and develops social feelings, it must be recognized as potentially of great value. Almost every character in *La Nouvelle Héloïse* defends passion as the source of beneficial enthusiasm. In a way that reminds us of Plato identifying eros with the dynamism that causes all things in the universe to seek their proper goal, Rousseau repeatedly describes passion as a complex of ardent emotions that elevate the sensitive and questing soul above the realm of reason. The Encyclopedists, going back to Descartes and before him to a long tradition of rationalism, had idealized clarity of mind, precision of thought, scientific and mathematical accuracy. These were not only the means of acquiring knowledge, but also the key to happiness. Without their dominance man could only be passion's slave. Rousseau reverses all this. Uncertain as he is about passionate love, particularly in its striving for consummation, he nevertheless thinks that passion itself is essential to the good life. Lord Bomston, who serves as a philosophical voice, claims that "the highest reason is only attained through the same power of soul which gives rise to great passions, and we serve philosophy worthily only with the same ardor that we feel for a mistress." Even Wolmar is made to recognize his own disabilities. He says: "It is only passionate souls who are capable of struggling and conquering. All great efforts, all sublime actions are their doing. Cold reason has never achieved anything illustrious, and we triumph over passions only by opposing one to another. When the passion of virtue comes to the fore, it alone dominates and keeps all the rest in a state of equilibrium."

In the case of Saint-Preux, we may wonder whether any passions endure beyond the period of ardent love for Julie. He is indoctrinated into a mode of existence that demands their repression for the sake of a supervening morality. Saint-Preux does establish a binding friendship with Wolmar, however, and possibly this may serve as an equilibrating cathexis. In the *Confessions*, Rousseau often speaks of his need for friendship as well as love; and throughout his writings (as in his life) he constantly experiments with the possibility that one or another ménage à trois could satisfy both needs simultaneously. Several commentators have pointed out that the triangular relationship between Saint-Preux, Wolmar, and Julie parallels what Rousseau himself experienced with Saint-Lambert and Mme d'Houdetot. In each of these arrangements the passionate male turns his sexual desire for the woman into a Platonic ecstasy while also attaining an ardent friendship with a man who has more total access to her. Whether the pattern is oedipal or latently homosexual, and to what extent love and friendship in it result from the obstacles that structure each relationship, need not concern us at the moment. What matters most—for our investigation, at least—is the attempt to perpetuate passion as a vivifying force underlying the highest of human ideals while also redirecting it into channels of greatest utility to a newly created society.

In the case of Julie, who embodies the ideal of love more completely than the other characters, we are to assume the existence of passions that Saint-Preux will never equal. As if she were indeed a second Beatrice, Julie achieves cosmic feelings that are religious as well as social and personal. She is a *new* Héloïse not only in having a "heart made for love," as Saint-Preux says about the original Heloise, but also in reaching goals of love that her predecessor could not attain. It is worth noting that in his reference to Heloise and Abelard, Saint-Preux vilifies Abelard as a miserable seducer who experienced neither love nor virtue. This, of course, is what Abelard also says, his letters to Heloise being attempts to help them substitute the love of God for their sinful love of one another. Beset by the erotic memories that fuel her uncontrollable imagination, the medieval nun believes that religious love perpetually eludes her. Yet in Julie the love of God is the great reality that dominates the ending of the novel. But now religious love has been rendered compatible with a love of nature that includes an acceptance of passion as the appropriate response to the cosmos as a whole. Julie worships the God of love whose presence in all things makes nature as sacred as himself. In one place Saint-Preux compares her to St. Teresa, whose mysticism he considers less valid because it addresses itself to God while excluding his creatures. Julie's devotion originates in so great a need to love that it returns to its heavenly source only after proceeding through everything it encounters on earth.

Julie is, in other words, a saint for that new religion of love that romanticism was to propagate throughout the beginning of the nineteenth century. Even if Rousseau's novel had no other value, this alone would assure its greatness.

In its general outline *La Nouvelle Héloïse* is mainly a series of vignettes, passion showing itself in the various stages that lead to ultimate purification in the lives of Rousseau's idealized characters. In *Emile* and *The Social Contract*, both written during the same period that the novel was being composed, Rousseau investigates the philosophical and psychological principles that provide the intellectual bases for this trajectory in human feelings. Saint-Preux had served as a fictionalized self-portrait, revealing Rousseau's sense of his own struggle against personal defects and unmanageable emotions. Abstract and unreal as Saint-Preux may seem to us, Rousseau must have thought of him as a sensitive young man acquiring an education of feeling needed for the contemporary world as Rousseau knew it. In this respect, he anticipates all those nineteenth-century heroes—Julien Sorel, young Werther, Eugène de Rastignac, and many others—who rise from provincial obscurity, sometimes from the lower classes, and learn the realities of life through affective adventures at a level of society beyond their earlier experience.

In *Emile*, however, Rousseau creates two characters who are neither contemporary nor intended as realistic portrayals. They are each a facet of himself, presented together as complementary representatives of what is needed for moral development. One of the characters, Jean-Jacques, is the first-person narrator writing an account of his creative role as Emile's sole and virtually omnipotent tutor. He is Rousseau, not literally but only as the embodiment of a dream of power and rectitude that pervades Rousseau's imagination. In life his imagination issued forth as a stream of words, sentences, books; but in the dream a wise and wholly untainted human being appears. The other character, Emile, is the ideal flowering of the innocence and purity of motive that Rousseau felt within himself and that he blamed the world for having stifled or corrupted. Taken together, the two characters show Rousseau re-making himself, like one of those gods Hume mentions as having realized they had botched their earlier attempts at creating the universe and thus began afresh using some of the old material.

In this respect, Emile is much more than just a "natural man," as most commentators have thought. Rousseau believed that present-day society had so thoroughly disfigured human nature, which contained an underlying program ordained by God, that mankind now required a kind of "denaturing" in order to restore whatever purity might still be possible. I shall not go through the different senses of the word "nature" as it was used by Rousseau and others in the eighteenth century except to remark that when he called for a *return* to nature on the grounds that "the first impulses of nature are always right" he was not advocating an indiscriminate regression to primitive emotions. Like others at the time, he was combating the notion of original sin, which started with an all-powerful and loving deity but then culminated in each person being considered guilty of innate depravity from the moment of conception. Perhaps as a reaction against his upbringing in Calvinist Geneva, perhaps because he felt a residual sense of worthlessness more terrifying than anything experienced by earlier theologians who believed in origi-nal sin while also having faith in the benevolence of God's adminis-tration, Rousseau could not tolerate the idea that man might possi-bly be evil by nature. The current degradation of humanity must, therefore, result from the way in which man has subverted his natural talents in the course of social development. Civilization contained within itself all causes of corruption.

Rousseau could not eliminate society, but he thought he could educate a man in a way that would render him immune to its infectious influence. One might also reconstitute society in the hope of rendering it less inimical to the God-given determinants of hu-man nature. *The Social Contract* devotes itself to the principles upon which society is to be reconstructed, but these in turn depend upon the affective concepts to which *Emile* is dedicated. Another way of putting Rousseau's problem is to say, as he does more or less: Man cannot live in a primitive state of nature because he needs other people; neither can he live in society as we know it because then his relations with others destroy his natural goodness. Consequently, both he and society must be greatly altered in order for him to fulfill his nature. *Emile* and *The Social Contract* address themselves to this double necessity.

As a fundamental axiom about man's natural condition, Rousseau asserts that all behavior is motivated by self-love ("amour de soi"). He thereby aligns himself with a long philosophical tradition that goes back to the Greeks and is manifest in everything Plato and Aristotle wrote. Plato maintained that enlightened self-love would cause one to love the Good, for that gives a man the most that life can possibly yield, even if such love means sacrificing many of one's vital interests, and sometimes life itself. It is in this vein that Rousseau argues that self-love is unavoidable, that it is good and not evil, and that moralists should encourage its development in fruitful directions rather than seeking to eradicate it entirely. For reasons of self-love alone, man has to live in society with other human beings. As Rousseau states in one of his *Dialogues*: "For such is the nature of man in this life, that he can never truly enjoy his self-hood without the help of others."

In *Emile* Rousseau remarks that if self-love is a child's first sentiment, his second one is love for those about him without whom he could not survive in his weak and threatened condition. The creation of society and the love of other persons are thus derivative from one's own self-love. But as his social relations expand, the child begins to compare himself with others and soon he insists that they should prefer him to themselves. He then becomes liable to the greatest of all social diseases, the one that preoccupies Rousseau most of all and that makes life a hell on earth in his estimation. He calls it "amour-propre," which is variously translated as vanity, pride, emulation, self-preference, selfishness, or self-interest. The moral problem for each human being consists in learning how to satisfy amour de soi, thus loving oneself with all the benefits that social intercourse can provide, without allowing self-love and the love for others to degenerate into amour-propre.

This problem governs all the stages of Emile's education but it is most relevant to his emotional and sexual development. In *La Nouvelle Héloïse* one of Rousseau's voices states that all authentic passions begin in solitude; and in many of his writings Rousseau claims that it is only in the isolation of the countryside or of mountainous retreats, or rather in those psychological recesses which these places symbolize for him as they do for the Christian mystics he so greatly resembles, that natural (unadulterated) passions can truly show themselves. But when a man reaches the age of adolescence, nature propels him towards a member of the opposite sex in a way that makes isolation much less feasible. From this circumstance arises the basic dilemma in sexual morality. How can one possibly retain the innocence of self-love, which requires isolation, while also seeking preferment in the eyes of a woman whose company one passionately desires?

In that brief article on "Jouissance" to which I previously referred, Diderot had also recognized that sexual love must be intimately related to something like amour-propre. According to Diderot, a woman who is desired by several men would need to discriminate among them. The one she chooses will inevitably feel that he is superior to the others, that he is *worthy* of being preferred, and that his own self-esteem has been vindicated. For Diderot this was merely part of the mechanism of enjoyment, and in fact a prelude to that happy "forgetfulness of self" which accompanies sexual ecstasy. He thought that the preliminary self-preferment belonged to the condition of people who have "sensitive and young organs, a tender heart, and an innocent soul unacquainted with either mistrust or remorse." That is not a possibility that Rousseau seriously considers; it does not belong to a world that he could recognize. For him the intimacy, the excitement, the emotional necessity of social involvement with a desired person of the opposite sex inevitably leads to pride and vanity of a self-defeating sort— amour-propre in the most pejorative sense. As a result, sexuality contains for him irresolvable difficulties that never appear in Diderot's philosophy.

Given this sensitivity to the inherent dangers of sex (and of all society), it is not surprising that the tutor in *Emile* approaches the need for love with great ambivalence. Though he knows the reproductive instinct is "the impulse of nature," he considers love as something that does not spring from nature. Instead, it functions as a beneficial device for restraining and regulating natural desires. Love performs this important service by directing our libidinal appetite towards a single beloved, thereby causing us to lose interest in other members of his or her sex. Being unnatural in this sense, the phenomenon of love depends upon "enlightenment, prejudice, and habit"; but since these always retain a certain degree of selfish motivation, even *true* love cannot entirely escape the evil of amour-propre. Love is held in honor by mankind because it serves as an ideal search for virtue or beauty, without which all men and women would be nothing but sex objects. But in creating the elevated standards that human nature needs, love always participates in the vanity and pride that lurk beneath the surface of all intimate relations. While recognizing the goodness of sexual love, as opposed to libertinism or mere sexuality, Rousseau finds no way in which it can avoid the snare of social depravity; and so, by this circuitous route, he would seem to have ended up with conclusions that virtually reinstate the belief in original sin.

The two poles of this antinomy are felt by Rousseau with an acuteness that no other writer in the eighteenth century approximates. "One wants to obtain," he says, "the preference that one grants. Love must be reciprocal. To be loved, one has to make oneself lovable. To be preferred, one has to make oneself more lovable than another, more lovable than every other, at least in the eyes of the beloved object. This is the source of the first glances at one's fellows; this is the source of the first comparisons with them; this is the source of emulations, rivalries, and jealousy."

Out of this need for a beloved, Rousseau tells us, "there soon springs" the need of a friend—an interesting juxtaposition in view of Rousseau's continual attempts to solve his erotic problems by means of one or another ménage à trois. Here, however, he speaks of "dissensions, enmity, and hate" as the consequences of both love and friendship. These affective states put us into the control of other persons, make us dependent upon their opinions, enslave us within the empire of people without whom one feels that life would be impossible. Such passions have no basis in the self-love that the child naturally feels. They must therefore be modified, by training as well as constraints within the society for which the child has been educated. The last two books of *Emile*, almost two-thirds of the entire work, concern themselves with the maneuvers the tutor makes in order to control, with this in mind, every detail of his pupil's emotional development.

The enterprise consists in organizing Emile's education in ways that enable him to love other persons, particularly some future wife, while also avoiding the dangers of amour-propre. In effect, this too will be the project that Stendhal undertakes in *De l'Amour*. But where Stendhal begins with a distinction between "passion-love" and "vanity-love," Rousseau's merging the two from the very start introduces a negative or pessimistic outlook that one does not find in Stendhal. One might say that Rousseau is more realistic, more in tune with how things are, or else that he has set himself an impossible task about which he feels defeated in advance. Certainly one senses throughout this segment of Rousseau's writings that desperate measures are constantly being advocated for the sake of paradoxical and even hopeless goals.

For instance, Rousseau recognizes that man's double being, partly natural and partly social, makes it essential for him to achieve interdependence with other people. Rousseau even traces this necessity to early childhood. Aware of both his own weakness and the parental affection that nature provides to help him survive, the child will quickly appreciate the personal advantages in mutual dependence. This condition must occur, however, in a context that is compatible with what Rousseau calls his "fundamental maxim": "freedom, not power, is the greatest good. That man is truly free who desires what he is able to perform, and does what he desires." Throughout the argument, we are thus confronted with a tension between freedom and dependence which Rousseau can hardly manage and which leads him to extreme conclusions.

Assuming that no one wants to be dependent, Rousseau states that our inability to dispense with the help of other people renders us "weak and wretched." If we had sufficient strength, we would all live apart from one another, self-sufficient, independent, wholly free in our personal autonomy. This is similar to Plato's idea about the perfection of the gods, and Aristotle's about the blessed imperturbability of his prime mover. But Rousseau knows, with a painful sense of loss, that it is a state of being for which human nature can only yearn, without ever attaining. He has no doubts about its desirability, and therefore his efforts to combine individual freedom with the unavoidable interdependency that reality demands must always seem joyless, halfhearted, and despairing. Far from being the epitome of happiness, love for another person can only be a compromise between what we really want and what our empirical destiny requires.

Since reliance upon other persons is something that Rousseau finds so unpalatable, the tutor frequently employs a hidden hand, "la main cachée," in guiding Emile's education. Dependence on things being the work of nature while dependence on people is a product of society, Rousseau insists that the child will not experience the former as defeating his fundamental need for freedom in the way that the latter does. We do not feel coerced by a natural constraint—a tree that blocks our path or a storm that chills our body— but we feel an injury to our sense of liberty when another person imposes his will upon us. Consequently, the tutor must always keep his own dominating personality hidden. He must arrange for the child to learn about the world as a result of a dependency upon things, not persons, even when it is other persons upon whom he is dependent. When he is punished, it must be done in an impersonal manner that seems to issue from the requirements of life among material objects. He must learn to act not from obedience but from the necessities imposed by a hostile environment. In his political philosophy, as we shall see, this emphasis upon things rather than persons takes on special importance, since Rousseau's ideal society creates a love of the law, i.e. the "general will" that cannot and should not be identified as the will of any single person.

This means, however, that the child grows up with a most imperfect conception of other people. Not only is his freedom being regulated by a hidden puppeteer beyond his awareness, but also he is continually being deceived about the source and nature of the many dependencies that others continually impose upon him and that he imposes upon them. The tutor would seem to think that the need for other people, which renders our self-love into a need to love them as well, is so intolerable that it must never be allowed to show itself to the unformed child. But to this extent Emile's development is necessarily inauthentic, pervaded by basic lies and fundamental deceptions; and one can hardly believe that it will lead to a knowledge of other persons, to say nothing of the ability to love them through an acceptance of mutual dependency.

Nevertheless, as often happens in the study of Rousseau, one finds that he has already anticipated this kind of problem. He argues that, far from thwarting Emile's capacity for love, he is preventing it from being fostered prematurely. Rousseau believes that until a child reaches the age of puberty, he will not be able to experience the emotions that are needed for love to exist. In general, he maintains that human growth occurs in a number of stages corresponding to levels of social development. There is the animal stage up to five years old, the savage stage from five to twelve, the rational stage from twelve to puberty, and finally the social stage from puberty to maturity. It is only in the social stage that the child is able to feel appropriate sentiments of either sexuality or interpersonal love. Before puberty, he must be shielded from affective experiences that can only distort and misdirect his normal development.

At this point, one need only remark that Rousseau was speculating without the benefit of much scientific data. Leaving aside his implied assumption that ontogeny recapitulates phylogeny, his theory of education seems thoroughly vitiated by errors in the child psychology of his time. We now know that later stages of development, however they are distinguished from one another, overlap significantly with earlier ones. Above all, we have every reason to believe that persons who are deprived of love as children will have great difficulty in becoming loving adults. It is for this reason that so many recent commentators have felt that Emile is, as one of them puts it, "a child without a soul . . . who . . . if we met him in life would make us shudder." He is, in fact, a monster created by an eighteenth-century equivalent of Frankenstein. Rousseau prepares us for all the scientists in Romantic fiction who seek to create pure and loving creatures without realizing that their mode of creation itself defeats the intended purpose.

Rousseau tries to justify the emotional insensibility with which Emile will have grown up by saying that actually all children are indifferent to everyone else, that they take no interest in other persons, and therefore that his model youth is merely less deceitful. Even with respect to sexual impulse, Rousseau claims that not only does it arise late in puberty, but also that it is not "natural" in the way that amour de soi and the need for freedom are. He insists that people who grew up without society (and without its artificial arousal of the imagination) would feel no sexual interest of the usual sort. Since Rousseau has also told us that love has the beneficial capacity of restricting natural inclinations, one should assume that he wishes to distinguish between sexuality and a need to propagate the species. Though he considers the latter an instinct belonging to man's innate structure, he sees the former as largely a result of invidious social arrangements and contrived expectancies.

Similarly, Rousseau maintains that both puberty and its unwholesome preoccupation with sex occur at an earlier age among civilized peoples than among those who are closer to nature. He therefore encourages a delaying of sexual activity, keeping the child away from seductive influences as well as early sex education. Ignorance of sex is to be prolonged for as many years as possible. Since it is not a part of self-love, sexuality can only belong to the realm of amour-propre, and so it is liable to the same perils as the love for another person.

Being a product of vanity, libidinal behavior is for Rousseau basically aggressive and even sadistic. When the Marquis de Sade wrote *Justine or the Misfortunes of Virtue*, he was parodying *La Nouvelle Héloïse* in order to prove that all love reduces to sexuality, and that all sexuality reduces to aggression. The germ for Sade's belief is already present in Rousseau. They both derive the identification of sex and sadism from philosophers, Platonistic as well as Christian, who argued that physical intimacy could not provide either moral goods or innocent pleasures. From this it would follow that *all* sexuality must really be corrupt or vicious. One is shocked to see that when Rousseau discusses sexual precociousness he illustrates the harmful consequences he considers likely by citing the experience of licentious and obviously debased individuals. He speaks of childhood sex as if it could only result in eventually making young men vindictive and wild: "Their imaginations, filled by a single object, rejected all the rest. They knew neither pity nor mercy. They would have sacrificed fathers, mothers, and the whole universe to the least of their pleasures."

Since Emile must be raised without these faults, he looks for a wife on the basis of no sexual experience at all. With the help and connivance of the tutor, he meets an equally innocent and pure-minded girl named Sophie. She has a good heart, but she is not a ravishing beauty. Rousseau thinks that in looking for a wife one should scorn beautiful features. The wife who has them is sure to be vain; and in any event, her husband will hardly notice them after several weeks of marriage. In saying this, Rousseau reveals—what we could have inferred from *La Nouvelle Héloïse*—that for him married love is by its nature quite different from passionate sexual love. Considering whom Emile should marry, he says that "a pleasant and attractive face, which inspires kindly feelings rather than love, is what we should prefer." Elsewhere he speaks of "liking which takes the place of love" as the sentiment that enables a marriage to succeed. Further on, he describes "the gentle habit" that binds husband and wife as something totally distinct from romantic feelings that delude people into expecting fanciful charms while also inducing unbridled passions. Though he recognizes that passionate love can involve mutual desire based upon a kind of equity, "bestowing as much as it demands," Rousseau amalgamates it with the rest of amour-propre inasmuch as it involves exclusions, preferences, and uncontrollable jealousy. He scarcely entertains the possibility of an ardent sexual bond which husband and wife could enjoy—on many occasions, if not continuously—without its degenerating into the state of delusion and virtual madness that Rousseau finds so threatening. As a result, he fails to harmonize—offers no idea of harmonization between—the friendly feelings that marriage requires and the passional excitement that married people cherish as much as lovers.

In suggesting that a happy marriage depends on kindliness rather than romance, Rousseau is obviously returning to the relationship between Wolmar and Julie as opposed to the ecstatic oneness she had previously experienced with Saint-Preux. Emile has been reared in such fashion that we cannot imagine him being filled with the transports of emotion that cause the joys and sorrows of a Saint-Preux. Rousseau does tell us that, in the period of courtship, Emile's feelings are just like those of any other impassioned lover; but the account does not ring true. Emile's emotionality reads like a pastiche, stuck in to round out his character, whereas Saint-Preux's could have been taken from life. As Rousseau describes them, both characters seem weak and passive before the sensible and resolute women they love, but they are nevertheless different kinds of men. Possibly they are the different and contrary personalities that Rousseau felt within himself.

Basically innocent, as he continually insists that he remained despite the acts of turpitude to which he willingly (eagerly) confesses, Rousseau uses Emile and Saint-Preux to represent his own inclinations toward reason or virtue, on the one hand, and feeling or imagination, on the other. But nowhere—except in his writing itself, in his being as an author—does he show these properties coalescing. Emile and Saint-Preux pursue modes of life that are simply incompatible until such time as Saint-Preux has been cleansed of emotional imperfections that Emile has been reared not to experience. The possibility that sexual love may provide happiness and that it can sometimes combine Saint-Preux's kind of passion with Emile's pure-mindedness is something Rousseau will not countenance within his philosophy. This alone makes Stendhal and other Romantic theorists of the nineteenth century feel the need to go beyond him.

In Rousseau's defense, one must admit that he has the tutor give Sophie advice that does acknowledge the importance of increasing Emile's appetite for sex. Before their marriage, Emile and Sophie are taught that sexual activity should be based upon mutual desire, and therefore that a wife must have the unquestioned right to refuse her husband's overtures whenever she does not feel a corresponding impulse. On the wedding night Sophie promptly invokes this right, which Emile accepts as legitimate self-determination on her part even though it means the frustration of his own needs. The tutor then talks to Sophie in private. He encourages her not to be capricious or too severe in the exercise of her power, not to deprive either herself or her husband of possible enjoyment. He also remarks that sometimes the thwarting of desire can lead to increased passion in marriage. By occasionally keeping her husband at a distance, Sophie may get him to value her caresses more than she could by indiscriminate compliance.

But even this concession to the necessity for remaining lovers while also being married is uttered with a sense of pessimism. "Whatever precautions anyone may take," Jean-Jacques says, "enjoyment wears out pleasures, and love is worn out before all others." He assures Sophie that confidence, friendliness, and the gentle habit of companionship will replace the joys of passion in a good marriage, and that the bond children effect can become stronger than love itself. When that happens, the married couple may achieve the fullest type of intimacy and discover the greatest happiness marriage can provide. But Rousseau does not elaborate about this idyllic condition. I take his mention of it as just a sentimental image of the young couple walking off into the sunset.

In making mutual desire the basis of marital sex, Rousseau could be seen as offering a solution to the dilemmas of courtly love. Where the Countess of Champagne insisted upon an incompatibility between conjugal duties and sexual love, Rousseau would seem to be advocating their confluence within the kind of marriage that he establishes for Emile and Sophie. But in fact that is not what he is doing. Not only does he require an extreme purification of passion, almost to a point where it ceases to exist, but also his attitude toward sex in general expresses a fear of consummation that makes one suspect that the ultimate intimacies he promises will not be very enjoyable. The split between yearning for a person one esteems and desiring her in a frankly sexual way remains unresolved, and one intuits that this must always undermine the possibilities of enjoyment. Satisfaction, if it occurs at all, will be experienced in a diminished fashion. Emile may be too purified to feel the kind of guilt that accompanied Rousseau's own sexual pleasures, but neither will he be able to savor erotic opportunities with freedom and a joyful acceptance of one's instinctive being. He will not know how to give or take pleasure, and he may not even realize that he is suffering from a personal deficiency. He will not be truly innocent, just badly educated. Powerful as it is in some directions, Rousseau's imagination cannot (or will not) penetrate into this region of human potentiality.

Shortly after finishing *Emile*, Rousseau began a novel called *Emile and Sophie* which was to narrate what happens once the tutor departs. Though this work remained unfinished, it reveals the doubts that Rousseau himself must have had about the marital advice in the previous book. Despite the great erotic secrets Jean-Jacques has imparted to them, despite the excellence of their personal characters, despite the care with which they have been chosen as well-matched components of a domestic unit, despite the simple virtues on which their newly created family depends, Emile and Sophie soon find that their life together is almost unbearable. She withholds herself totally from her husband, who does not realize she is committing adultery. When he learns she is pregnant by another man, he leaves her and sets forth upon a series of picaresque adventures. Rousseau planned to end the novel with scenes of reconciliation after both spouses have eliminated their individual and collective guilt through an adequate amount of suffering. Once again, they would accept the inherent goodness in each other and walk into a cooler but equally radiant sunset. Be this as it may, what Rousseau actually wrote suffices to indicate the inadequacies of his erotic philosophy. In the *Confessions* he remarks that *Emile and Sophie* was designed to teach that a good marriage would have to avoid temptations; and indeed it is the seductiveness of life in pleasure-loving Paris that leads the unsophisticated couple astray. But how their union could have survived in any real society, replete with the perils and pitfalls that Rousseau himself knew so well, he does not say.

If one's emotional life is governed by mere imagination, and if the fear of consummation outweighs one's ability to enjoy, it does make sense to avoid temptation. Whether or not Rousseau was a madman, as many of his contemporaries thought, his thinking is always consistent with this principle. It underlies his attack on the theater, in the *Letter to d'Alembert*, which is primarily motivated by the belief that harm done by the drama is greater than any aesthetic good it may provide. Rousseau was distressed by the idea of a passive audience watching actors carry out the illusion that they were feeling one or another emotion. Not only would the spectators be diverted, i.e. turned away, from their own emotional concerns, but also they would be endangered as moral agents. Rousseau rejects the notion that tragedy can provide the catharsis of feeling which may help to improve a spectator's character; and he insists that both tragedy and comedy flourish by demeaning or ridiculing precisely those virtuous persons who successfully struggle against their passions. Above all, he condemns the fact that all French drama thrives upon the vicissitudes of young lovers. This obsession with love he blames upon the power of women, and he considers their dominance in such matters an example of the unnatural corruption of values which belongs to civilized life in the big cities.

While the *Letter to d'Alembert* reads like a Puritan tract, advocating that theaters in Geneva be kept closed for the sake of perpetuating wholesome habits and encouraging the pleasures of family life, it describes the expressive potentialities of drama so vividly as to help initiate the revolution in aesthetics that romanticism carried even further. In condemning the importance of love in the modern theater, Rousseau argues that even though each play ends with the triumph of virtue, this has less effect upon the audience than the exciting spectacle of the very passions virtue struggles against. He criticizes Racine's tragedies for having unwittingly glamorized the erotic illusions that Racine himself sought to combat. Rousseau was to suffer the same fate himself, romanticism from his own day to the present using him as the apostle of passion without realizing that he wished only to purify it in the name of higher ideals. And in the case of Molière, whom he recognizes as the greatest of all comic writers, Rousseau concludes that even he panders to the sentiments of his public, playing to their prejudices instead of correcting them. Rousseau emphasizes the extent to which dramatic art can infuse an audience's mentality with strong emotions—above all, sexual passion—that no amount of moralizing in the plot will be able to control. The drama cannot inculcate maxims of virtue that the spectators will not tolerate, and, worst of all, the audience participates in the theatrical experience only as passive recipients whose low taste nevertheless determines the difference between success and failure. Despite his fascination with its capacity for expressiveness, Rousseau denounces the entire art form as an example of passive consumption leading to alienation or even immorality.

What, then, does Rousseau recommend? Where does he think that one could find an acceptable pattern of love? He establishes himself as a critic of sexual love, he ultimately doubts the feasibility of the benign marital affections that Emile's tutor has prescribed, and he considers aesthetic presentations in the theater neither cathartic nor commendable. He himself affirms that the love of mankind is what he has constantly advocated: a civic love, a love of country, a love that merges with a sense of moral dedication to one's fellow man. He claims that a passion for goodness of this sort has motivated his aspirations throughout life. Can we believe him? Or is he beating his breast in the hope of capturing our sympathies? Much has been made of Rousseau's exhibitionism; and his professed need to reveal himself to a reading public that will forgive his transgressions while confirming his sense of basic innocence may well be pathological. But even so, one does Rousseau an injustice unless one realizes that there also burned within him a humanitarian love whose purified passion he describes in the final pages of the *Letter to d'Alembert*. As a substitute for dramatic performances in the theater, he recommends festivals of the entire populace, grand celebrations in which people will join together in a collective burst of oneness and communal feeling. In a footnote he describes a boyhood episode that may be taken as the nostalgic touchstone for all his utopian theorizing:

> I remember having been struck in my childhood by a rather simple entertainment, the impression of which has nevertheless always stayed with me in spite of time and variety of experience. The regiment of Saint-Gervais had done its exercises, and according to the custom, they had supped by companies; most of those who formed them gathered after

supper in the St. Gervais square and started dancing all together, officers and soldiers, around the fountain, to the basin of which the drummers, the fifers and the torch bearers had mounted. A dance of men, cheered by a long meal, would seem to present nothing very interesting to see; however, the harmony of five or six hundred men in uniform, holding one another by the hand and forming a long ribbon which wound around, serpent-like, in cadence and without confusion, with countless turns and returns, countless sorts of figured evolutions, the excellence of the tunes which animated them, the sound of the drums, the glare of the torches, a certain military pomp in the midst of pleasure, all this created a very lively sensation that could not be experienced coldly. It was late; the women were in bed; all of them got up. Soon the windows were full of female spectators who gave a new zeal to the actors; they could not long confine themselves to their windows and they came down; the wives came to their husbands, the servants brought wine; even the children, awakened by the noise, ran half-clothed amidst their fathers and mothers. The dance was suspended; now there were only embraces, laughs, healths, and caresses. There resulted from all this a general emotion that I could not describe but which, in universal gaiety, is quite naturally felt in the midst of all that is dear to us. My father, embracing me, was seized with trembling which I think I still feel and share. "Jean-Jacques," he said to me, "love your country. Do you see these good Genevans? They are all friends, they are all brothers; joy and concord reign in their midst. You are a Genevan; one day you will see other peoples; but even if you should travel as much as your father, you will not find their likes." ... I am well aware that this entertainment, which moved me so, would be without appeal for countless others; one must have eyes made for seeing it and a heart made for feeling it. No, the only pure joy is public joy.

Even if Rousseau's report is accurate, we should note that this event took place during his childhood. Nothing like it seems to have happened in his years of maturity; and given the persecutions he suffered in later life at the hands of his fellow Genevans, as well as others, it seems doubtful that he could have had much access to the sense of communal oneness that he describes. His account must therefore be seen as an expression of the need to return to an idealized image of one's homeland, one's organic and primordial roots. What Rousseau may have experienced in this moment of his past he also ascribes to the civic life of the Spartans and Romans. Throughout his writings they are cited as people who enjoyed a collective and communal love that civilization proceeded to destroy over a period of centuries in the West. In order to restore the simple life in which this kind of love could once again be possible, modern civilization would have to be thoroughly changed.

The goal of Rousseau's political philosophy thus becomes the reorganization of society in a way that purifies passionate love between individuals and curtails the search for sensuous pleasure— each of these being products of the unnatural circumstances that man has forced upon himself. They must be subordinated to, and partly replaced by, the nonlibidinal love of one's fellow human beings within a civic-minded community. Rousseau sometimes sounds as if this collective love could not occur beyond a small city-state such as Geneva, but at other times he seems to think it might extend throughout a nation. Ideally it would encompass mankind in general, though Rousseau doubts that anyone could succeed in loving humanity as a whole. When he talks about love of virtue or of the good, he may be taken as meaning an enthusiastic interest in the welfare of men and women considered as fellow human beings. If a social order were established in accordance with humanitarian love of this sort, the problems that Emile and Sophie encounter would not exist. Having been reared with the simplicity of mind and character that natural goodness entails, they could not be tempted by the corrupting influences of a decadent world. On the contrary, they would be able to create their idyllic family, with its concern for friendliness and mutual cooperation, within a commonwealth of people whose self-love could now effectively merge with a purified love for all other members of the group.

The splendors of this ideal condition were to inspire later theorists, some of whom (Robespierre, for instance) used it as a blueprint for revolutionary action. But for many others, in Rousseau's lifetime as well as in the present, his utopian rhetoric is marred by ideas about the relationship between men and women that seem offensively chauvinistic. The Encyclopedists had argued for women's rights, and the relaxed morality of the eighteenth century had encouraged women to search for personal love and sexual completion with the kind of freedom men had always enjoyed. Rousseau opposes all this as contrary to nature. He insists that men must be allowed to rule the body politic even though women will find ways of controlling the men—mainly by capturing their hearts. For reasons of modesty as well as happiness, women should restrict their activities to domestic duties, to the rearing of children, and to preservation of the conjugal bond. This may be part of Rousseau that his admirers in the twentieth century will want to discard as unfortunate or inappropriate. But Rousseau's solution to the woman problem is not so easily detached from the rest of his social philosophy. Repressiveness in one area inevitably leads to repression elsewhere.

To see this more clearly, let me return to the passage illustrating the sense of communal oneness from which I have just quoted. Its ebullient tone can very well beguile a casual reader, who may imagine that Rousseau is depicting a society of interpersonal love. From his moral and philosophical writings, however, we know that he has something quite different in mind. The meaning of the event, the basis for the sense of civic oneness, is to be found in the notion of the "general will," upon which Rousseau's political theory depends. The general will differs from the will of all citizens in being that part of each man's self-love (amour de soi) which harmoniously coincides with the self-love of everyone else. It is therefore the will of the entire community acting as a single entity and concerning itself only with that which furthers the interests of the group as a whole. Since lesser associations within the state, for example economic unions and various personal or religious affiliations, would interfere with the expression of the general will, Rousseau says that either they must be forbidden or else multiplied to the point where they prevent each other from exercising political power.

Some commentators have interpreted Rousseau's suggestion as a defense of pluralistic democracy; but others have seen it as a forerunner of modern totalitarianism, which does not mean that Rousseau would necessarily subscribe to any of the forms totalitarianism has taken in the twentieth century. For our purposes, what is more relevant is the fact that his emphasis upon communal oneness leads him to denigrate affective relationships that individuals establish in their particularized experience of one another. Far from being interpersonal, Rousseau's concept of ideal love minimizes the importance of attachments between people in society in order to maximize the goodness of a totalistic (and rather nebulous) commitment to society itself. In one place Rousseau says that "good social institutions are those that best know how to denature man, to take his absolute existence from him in order to give him a relative one and transport the *I* into the common unity, with the result that each individual believes himself no longer one but a part of the unity and no longer feels except within the whole [i.e. no longer has any self-identity apart from the whole]." To say this, however, is to undermine the value of even amour de soi—at least as it exists in each person by himself. What looks like a love of humanity emanating from acceptance of each man's love of self thus turns into an anti-self philosophy both dubious in principle and perilous in practice.

The differences between Rousseau's political ideas and those of Locke or Hobbes are extremely instructive in this respect. While all three hold some form of contract theory, Locke assumes that man's gregariousness and natural sociability would provide motivation for establishing a political order. Describing the conditions under which men in the state of nature join to create a civil government, he says that "the love and want of society, no sooner brought any number of them together, but they presently united and incorporated." Rousseau starts with a totally opposite assumption. He resembles Locke in thinking that man has an innate propensity for social behavior, but he agrees with Hobbes in arguing that it is only self-love in the sense of selfishness (amour-propre) that explains the formation of society. He refuses to say that man is wicked, vicious, and warlike by nature, as Hobbes believed; but he thinks that the mutual agreements in which man's social contract consists must all derive from the fact that each individual expects to benefit from them in some selfish way or other.

In *The Social Contract*, Rousseau remarks that everyone wills the happiness of each individual within the ideal state (and so expresses the general will that binds them into a unity) because everyone applies the word "each" to himself, voting for the good of all but actually thinking of his own personal advantage as a member of the totality. This not only contradicts the notion about submerging the self in the whole but also gives us reason to suspect that amour de soi (as Rousseau conceives of it) is itself contaminated by selfishness and, to that extent, is inseparable from amour-propre. In *Emile* Rousseau insists that we identify with others not by observing their happiness, which creates envy in us rather than sympathy or fellow-feeling, but only by seeing them suffer as we might too. We imagine ourselves in their situation, feeling compassion for those who undergo misfortunes only because we know that the same could have happened to us. Once again, the love of humanity seems to reduce to an invidious love of self.

Rousseau's emphasis upon man's selfishness at the roots of even a utopian society tends to be obscured if one treats some of his earlier writings in isolation. In the *Discourse on Inequality*, for instance, he speaks of "natural pity" as the feeling that unites primitive man with other human beings. He describes its efficacy in "transporting ourselves outside ourselves and identifying ourself with the suffering creature," pity alone creating an "expansive soul" that enables us to identify with our fellow man. There, too, Rousseau ascribes this development in human sensibility to the agency of imagination, as a result of which one is able to enter into the consciousness of another person. His description is similar to his portrayal of love as a mutual affection that cannot be explained in terms of mere sexuality. But as in the case of love, Rousseau denies that natural pity accounts for moral feelings that belong to reconstructed human beings living a life of virtue within an ideal society. On the contrary, he stresses the importance of negating our sense of pity for the sake of moral principles that are not limited to one or another individual. Not only must we guard against the possibility that some particular feeling will cause us to be unfair to other persons more worthy of our concern, but also we must recognize that equity involves judgment which does not consider individual relations so much as those that can be universalized.

This aspect of Rousseau's thinking leads directly to Kant's ideas about morality, and more recently to John Rawls' theory of justice. "The love of men derived from the love of self is the principle of human justice." With this line from *Emile*, Rousseau sums up the entire tradition he has so greatly influenced. He differs from Kant, and also from Rawls, in underlining the role of love as an enthusiastic and even passionate dedication to society, but like them he thinks of justice as an impersonal arbiter that men accept merely as a means of protecting their own interests.

To my way of thinking, this branch of the contractarian philosophy suffers from a serious flaw that Locke's approach tends to escape. For in predicating the principle of justice upon a rational estimate of how to secure one's own good, Rousseau and his followers neglect prior, though inchoate, emotive bonds without which one could hardly understand life in society. It is because we do care about other human beings, at least those we can enjoy and identify with, that we are willing to cooperate in one or another social order. If we were not inherently loving as well as selfish, delighting in others as well as realizing that we need them to survive, our self-love would always lead us to avoid involvements whose restraints so often militate against our personal advantage. We are willing to endure the impositions of society because we *enjoy* the presence of other people, and sometimes like them for themselves, without any awareness of how our other interests may or may not be implicated. We instinctively bestow value upon persons who share experience with us regardless of their utility to ourselves. The love of others, though not necessarily of many others or of all mankind, is no less fundamental in our nature than self-love. Individuals who enter into a social contract can be considered human only if they already have affectional ties to persons whose welfare matters to them in some degree and for its own sake. Having felt this mutual concern, which is also a mutual need for one another as the counterpart of their concern, citizens may then agree to surrender certain freedoms and to distribute the goods of their joint enterprise with the maximum fairness. There then arises both the institution and the sentiment of justice. But neither would make any sense unless the contracting parties already felt some desire to benefit one another while also benefiting themselves. In short, the rudiments of interpersonal love must be logically, and temporally, prior to the concept of justice. Locke's view of human nature seems to recognize this; Rousseau's does not.

This is not the place to develop these ideas further, but they may serve to indicate difficulties in Rousseau's philosophy. His thinking involves a mystical devotion to nature but it often reveals distrust of the concrete and specific phenomena that go to make up the natural world as we ordinarily know it. What remains from this process of abstraction and purification is a residual enthusiasm plus a vague conception of humanitarian virtue and cosmic piety. He defends the institution of a "civil religion" that would be based on little more than generalized feelings of oneness. In his final writings, he idealizes a sense of merging with being as a whole rather than any particular part of it; and though he asserts that God is unknowable, he affirms his existence as something one's heart alone intuits. In subordinating and even rejecting the material instances of ordinary passion, Rousseau leaves us with little more than a sentimental belief in the goodness of passion itself. In the *Confessions* he says: "My passions have made me live and my passions have killed me." His philosophy takes its revenge by advocating purified passion that results from discarding the erotic, personal, and merely temporal interests that passions usually involve. Nature would be fulfilled but only in being emptied of all the actual ingredients of emotion. Though Rousseau may have tried to justify this approach as a superior love of nature, one could equally well interpret it as the same mixture of fear and subtle hatred that underlies medieval asceticism. In both cases, we are misled if we take the official theology of love at its face value.

In his critique of Molière, Rousseau defends the character Alceste by saying he is a misanthrope only in his hatred for the evil that human beings are capable of doing. Rousseau obviously identifies himself with Alceste, and indeed he resembles him in vilifying the hypocrisy of ordinary social life. Both suffer because they cannot find men and women who will give them what they consider authentic love or friendship; and both resort to a utopia or desert island as the solution to their problems. The only book that Rousseau permits the youthful Emile is *Robinson Crusoe*, and he himself seems to have been happy only in the mountains or other isolated places. What Rousseau does not realize is that people like Alceste and himself have never learned *how* to love another person—despite their eagerness to do so, their good intentions, their noble aspirations, and even their willingness to sacrifice themselves. Rousseau provides the clue to Alceste's character as well as his own when he advocates self-sufficiency as the sole means of escaping dependence upon other people. To love another human being, however, one must create a vast network of mutual and reciprocal interdependence. If people could indeed attain a state of self-sufficiency, they would destroy the very conditions under which love occurs.

In the idealized relationship between persons that Rousseau holds before us as a perpetual guide, the souls of men and women are said to be "transparent" to one another. This idea recurs throughout his writings; and in the *Letter to d'Alembert* he says that when spectators at the communal festivals become actors themselves and serve as entertainment for one another, "each sees and loves himself in the others so that all will be better united." Through open and total involvement of himself, each would reveal his thoughts and inner feelings, his desires and his emotions; only this unfeigned acting out of what one is and hopes to be could lead to a free society of communicating spirits. Through recognition of his own self-love as well as his need for others, each person's mere transparency would thus eventuate in love. In other words, purified passion occurs only among people who are completely transparent to each other.

But this conception of love seems foreign to the actuality of human beings, as either nature or society is able to fashion them. Only angels have no opacity in their being. The love of real persons involves a different attitude from any that Rousseau is willing to countenance. It requires an acceptance of human fallibility, an acknowledgement of momentary needs and inclinations to be satisfied in oneself as well as others, a bestowal of value in addition to an appraisal of the idiosyncracies in another person, and finally an affirmative allegiance to the relationship itself. Love does not demand transparency. It respects the privacy of the other and protects him from affections that can easily degenerate into tyranny and possessiveness. It establishes a community among human interests without pretending that anyone can fully reveal himself or wholly penetrate into all the recesses of those he wishes to love.

Rousseau, like Luther, did not believe that man was truly capable of interpersonal love in his present, unregenerate condition. What Rousseau's philosophy offers us is, however, an inferior substitute. It promotes enthusiastic affirmation and a passionate longing for oneness in ourselves and in the world, but it fails to help us undergo those daily experiences with other people, those minute and often petty interactions, through which love must show itself. In Rousseau's religion the saints are men and women who no longer deceive each other. They have attained an utter sincerity that Rousseau sought to express in all his writings. But even if these ideal creatures of his imagination did succeed in this attempt, even if they were supremely transparent and totally honest with one another, would they be capable of accepting the humanity in themselves as just the persons that they are? I do not think so. Learning how to love involves a talent they would not have acquired, despite their communal ecstasies and regardless of their general goodwill.

And yet, I cannot leave the matter there. In the all-inclusive richness of his mind, Rousseau seems to recognize at times that sexual love can provide a good he has not fully accommodated within his philosophy. At the very end of his last book, *The Reveries of the Solitary Walker*, written after he withdrew from the world and began to savor "le sentiment de l'existence," he reminisces about his youthful attachment to Mme de Warens. What he now describes may partly be a distortion of memory; but even so, his final statement expresses an appreciation of love between the sexes that few other philosophers have ever equalled:

For a period of four or five years, I enjoyed a century of life and a pure and full happiness which covers with its charm everything dreadful in my present lot. I needed a friend suited to my heart; I possessed her. I had longed for the country; I obtained it. I could not bear subjection; I was perfectly free and better than free, for bound only by my affections, I did only what I wanted to do. All my time was filled with loving concerns or rustic occupations. I desired nothing but the continuation of such an enjoyable situation.

In the *Confessions*, Rousseau describes his relationship with Mme de Warens, whom he used to call "Mamma," as a quasi-incestuous union whose sexual component left him with a feeling of sadness. He even denies that his attitude was truly passionate. But he also insists that their intimacy depended on "everything by which one is oneself, and which one cannot lose except by ceasing to be." We may therefore believe him when he says, in the *Reveries*: "No day passes but what I recall with joy and tenderness this unique and brief time of my life when I was myself, fully, without admixture and without obstacle, and when I can truly say that I lived." These words might have been uttered by Stendhal, or by a Stendhalian hero. With them, we are already in the nineteenth century.

11
Sade and Stendhal

I<small>N</small> O<small>NE</small> O<small>F</small> H<small>IS</small> L<small>ETTERS</small> F<small>ROM</small>
prison, the Marquis de Sade complains to his wife because her
servants have refused to send him a copy of Rousseau's *Confessions*.
"While Rousseau may represent a threat for dull-witted bigots of
your species," he says, "he is a salutary author for me. Jean-Jacques
is to me what the *Imitation of Christ* is for you. Rousseau's ethics and
religion are strict and severe to me, I read them when I feel the need
to improve myself." Keeping in mind the pathological irony that
dominates so much of Sade's writing, one could easily interpret his
words as merely a desperate attempt to get the book he wanted to
read. His philosophy would seem to have no continuity with Rousseau's and his claim to be a devotee of the same religion may be taken
as purely farcical. Yet his ideas were indeed inspired by Rousseau's,
though they derive from a logical progression that Rousseau would
have rejected as insane. Stendhal too uses the inspiration of Rousseau in ways that the philosopher would never have tolerated. But
Stendhal has Sade in mind as well as Rousseau and must be studied
in relation to both.

Rousseau had begun with self-love (amour de soi) as the fundamental fact about human nature. From this he then developed
the social ethic that justified unselfish behavior and legitimate controls upon conduct that would otherwise turn into selfishness
(amour-propre). Sade accepts similar premises but he reaches conclusions diametrically opposite from Rousseau's. The nature that

ordains the ultimacy of self-love is not for him a benign or sentimental being. Having read Sade, we see how greatly Rousseau has presupposed a world order of the sort that the medieval theologians took for granted. Though Rousseau's concept of the "state of nature" resembles Hobbes' in some respects, Rousseau assumes that nature itself is harmonious, peaceable, benevolent. That is why he can use it as the pattern for constructing his utopian ideals. The medieval God may no longer serve as the object of devotion, but nature remains as the perfect illustration of divine goodness. Reject this idea and everything else in Rousseau falls apart. Sade affirms his allegiance to nature and then causes chaos in Rousseau's philosophy by rejecting all assumptions about the benevolence of nature.

Starting with traditional conceptions of virtue and vice, Sade asserts that nature uses both for its inscrutable destiny. Neither is unnatural, and in fact the violent destructiveness of all life reveals that acts of aggressive self-preferment put one in closest rapport with how things really are. For the most part, Sade tells us, nature is simply evil. If morals are to be generated from an axiom of natural self-love, they must point in directions quite different from anything Rousseau imagined.

As we have seen, Rousseau's Romantic puritanism had led him to extol the goodness of passion once it was cleansed of imperfections. It was faith in the value, even sanctity, of purified passion that enabled Rousseau to envisage an ideal society in which everyone would give himself to the state while avoiding irrational attachments to mere individuals. Sade seeks to be more consistent. He argues that if one were truly faithful to the idea of self-love, one would eradicate passion entirely: it is inimical to the search for pleasure, it undermines the purposive means by which one ordinarily satisfies oneself, and it leads to fanaticism in politics. Sade maintains that passionate love is always a form of madness, passion being infinitely harmful whether it occurs between two individuals or throughout the social order. The character Dolmance, who surely speaks for Sade in *Philosophy in the Bedroom,* warns his pupil against the dangers of love: "What is love? One can only consider it, so it seems to me, as the effect upon us of a beautiful object's qualities; these effects distract us; they inflame us; were we to possess this object, all would be well with us; if 'tis impossible to have it, we are in despair. But what is the foundation of this sentiment? desire. What are this sentiment's consequences? madness."

Much of this could have been taken verbatim out of Rousseau. Sade differs from Rousseau, however, in finding no redeeming social value in love. He does not wish to perpetuate its influence, either extending or sublimating its properties in any way, because he considers it an absurd aberration. It is caused by a desire to possess some object, and that he considers both natural and commendable. But then instead of facilitating the sexual completion of our desire, it puts us into a state of intoxication that prevents us from recognizing what we really want. As his pornographic writing indicates, Sade has no conception of a love that would be compatible with sexual fulfillment. Instead he describes love as merely "a burning fever which devours, consumes us, without affording us other than metaphysical joys." He says that he would find this excusable if one never needed to quit the adored object. That, however, rarely happens, and instead of creating deathless union, love generally disappears after a short period of infatuation. It lacks the one thing that Sade finds constant and predictable in human nature: namely, pleasure derived from the proper stimulation of one's own sex organs. This usually requires the help of other people, even a large number of them, as in the orgiastic scenes that Sade orchestrates so carefully, but the goal always remains individual pleasure selfishly sought in cool and clever maneuvers that have nothing to do with passionate love.

Rousseau believed that love arose as a response to man's awareness that he needs the help of other people. Eugénie, the neophyte being educated by Dolmance, paraphrases Rousseau's conception when she says that a human being's needs, having caused him to give up his original independence and to live with other people, "must necessarily have established some ties between them; whence blood relationships, ties of love too, of friendship, of gratitude." But Dolmance denies that any human need, particularly the need for coition, can cause authentic feelings unless they are directly self-serving. Once the immediate benefits of sexual or social intercourse disappear, nature bids us to look elsewhere. To live in accordance with nature, we must always seek pleasure for ourselves.

If Sade had said nothing but this, he would merely have been one of those libertine thinkers who derive from Thrasymachus, Callicles, and other hedonists Plato had attacked. He differs from them, and even from their equivalents in the eighteenth century, in openly asserting that the greatest pleasures are intimately associated with pain. By causing pain in others, indulging in cruel and even criminal practices, one duplicates the major bent of nature itself. What we call "sadism" is therefore behavior that puts us in touch with reality. And since our own experience of pain leads to excitement and heightened sensitivity, it too occasions the most intense sexual pleasures. Sade tends to emphasize the *giving* of pain, though this sometimes involves the inflicting of pleasure, as Simone de Beauvoir puts it, but he also insists upon the exquisite joy of receiving pain oneself. Freud's claim that all sadists are also masochists is borne out by the contents of Sade's fantasies. In effect, his philosophy amounts to an idealization of sadomasochism.

One might say that this too was not particularly new in the history of Western thought. But what Sade did introduce, which was more or less new and extremely important for Romantic thinkers of the nineteenth century, was a virulent hatred of precisely that foul and destructive nature which created him as an aggressive being who yearns for sadomasochistic pleasures. In Sade nature appears as pure negativity, an inversion of Plato's Good or the Christian God, drawing everything toward itself for reasons of cosmic horror rather than love, a kind of black hole sucking in all reality. Sade's character Almani presents this aspect of his philosophy when he says:

> "[Nature's] barbarous hand can only nourish evil; evil is her entertainment. Should I love such a mother? No; but I will imitate her, all the while detesting her. I shall copy her, as she wishes, but I shall curse her unceasingly . . ."

From this, one might assume that Sade was simply incapable of enjoying the simple pleasures of life. We know from his biography that such was not the case, and we also know that his philosophy was mainly written during long years of imprisonment and persecution. He might very well have felt an all-consuming hatred toward a nature that had ordained this kind of fate for him. But from Rousseau he had learned the utility of imagination as a mechanism of escape. "The pleasure of the senses," Sade remarks, "is always regulated in accordance with the imagination. Man can aspire to felicity only by sensing all the whims of his imagination." For Sade, as for Rousseau, this did not mean that anyone would wish to carry out these whims. His grotesque fantasies, as well as his violent hatred of nature, are not only the products of incarceration, but also the successful means of enduring it. Sade differs from others, who could easily have deteriorated into mere madmen, in using his mode of survival as a technique for artistic productivity. Beauvoir is quite right when she says, "It was not murder that fulfilled Sade's erotic nature; it was literature." Through acts of creative imagination, he could separate himself from the odious reality he would never escape. He could stand back and assume a pose of nonchalance or pure observation, watching the hideous spectacle of life even if he had no way of undoing its catastrophes. It is a philosophical posture similar to what Schopenhauer later recommends: aesthetic and contemplative detachment enabling one to rise above the voracious cruelty of nature.

This is not to say that Sade would have accepted Schopenhauer's defense of asceticism. Sade wished to free himself of nature in the process of satisfying his own instincts, even though he knew that they came directly from nature itself. This too required a rejection of Rousseauistic passion. One's liberation would consist in performing sexual activities with frozen calculation, and even mathematical abstraction, devising combinations and configurations that provide exquisite pleasures accompanied by no emotions whatsoever. Sade recommends a kind of latter-day sprezzatura, though it withholds us from other people and in that sense is the very opposite of what Castiglione intended. Sade calls the requisite disposition "apétie," in imitation of the ancient Stoic concept. The term is usually translated as "apathy," but it means something closer to affectlessness or coolness of heart. The proper state of soul he describes as "unconcern, stoicism, solitude within oneself." When a libertine succeeds in attaining this condition, he finds that his sense of detachment "is soon metamorphosed into pleasures a thousand times more exquisite than those which weakness and self-indulgence would procure for them." Even violent deeds will be performed in cold blood, so that one's revenge against nature cannot be sullied by sentiment or enthusiasm.

This psychopathic refusal to communicate through emotion, to express feelings that would attach one to other human beings, also has its origins in Rousseau. In his hatred of contemporary civilization, Rousseau had idealized the need to withdraw into isolation and solitude. Even if imagination enabled him to overcome his sense of separateness from other people, Rousseau knew that he could never live the kind of social life to which he aspired. As a fellow victim of persecution, but one who moldered in prison instead of running from country to country to avoid imprisonment, Sade saw no virtue in idealizing unobtainable alternatives to isolation. Instead he conceives of "unique beings," as he calls them, who accept the fact of separateness and, whenever possible, try to make the world suffer for it by acting out their natural aggressiveness.

Sade thus appears as an outsider who will no longer play the game of society, a pariah who will not accept the myth of a social contract or any other excuse for the miseries to which he has been condemned. In all his deformity of character, he stands erect although his head must bow beneath the ceiling of his prison. He is a criminal outcast of a sort that many Romantics would soon revere. He is confined to the pitiful domain of his own imagination, but within it he asserts his dignity as a philosopher-king.

Despite his hatred of the world, and despite his claims to being an immoralist, Sade could not refrain from offering mankind the outlines of a social program to reform and improve human nature. It is most fully articulated in a segment of *Philosophy in the Bedroom* that begins with the words, "Yet another effort, Frenchmen, if you would become republicans." Fifty years later, Sade's call to action was distributed as a pamphlet during the revolution of 1848. It enunciates the philosophy of anarchism, particularly in the area of sexual morality. Rousseau thought that freedom was so precious that, if necessary, the citizens of his ideal state would be "forced to be free." This occurs through the acceptance of laws that caused one to pursue virtuous behavior, as one really wanted to regardless of momentary inclinations. One was free in living up to the general will, which included one's own, that would infallibly create these liberating laws. Sade was convinced that the result could only be the establishment of a despotic state; and in fact, it was attempts to apply Rousseau's philosophy that led to Sade's incarceration after the Revolution. From his cell in prison he could watch the guillotine forcing so many other compatriots to be free. It is not surprising that Sade advocates a republic in which the laws have as little power as possible. The crimes that libertines might possibly perpetrate should not, he says, be punished by any legal authority, since laws and those who administer them are generally guilty of more cruelty than the violators themselves. If a man commits murder, he runs the risk of being murdered by the family of his victim; and that is an adequate deterrent. Sade assumes that personal revenge will be a strong enough motive to control abuses whereas interference by the laws generally multiplies social evils while depriving man of his natural freedom.

In proposing his anarchistic solutions, Sade would seem to have more faith in the viability of the Hobbesian state of nature than either Hobbes or Rousseau did. Without denying that some laws may be necessary, he wants them to be as lenient and as few as possible because he believes in the ability of ruthless nature to enforce communal peace within herself. Officials in the state are dangerous since there is no way of controlling their viciousness, and Christian morals will never bring about a change in the human condition. But through a tolerance of individual appetites, Sade insists, a republic may achieve at least a modicum of humanity and fraternity. The highest reaches of his philosophy occur in the following lines: "The point is not at all to love one's brethren as oneself, since that is in defiance of all the laws of Nature, and since hers is the sole voice which must direct all the actions in our life; it is only a question of loving others as brothers, as friends given us by Nature, and with whom we should be able to live much better in a republican

State, wherein the disappearance of distances must necessarily tighten the bonds."

These words are uttered by the character Le Chevalier, who seeks to thwart Dolmance's power over Eugénie by encouraging her to follow her heart instead of allowing it to freeze into the hardness of insensibility. His efforts come to nought: *Philosophy in the Bedroom* ends with Eugénie proclaiming the total victory of Dolmance and his teaching. Nevertheless, the more humane version of libertinism that Le Chevalier represents establishes a point of reference within Sade's philosophy. Its pluralistic attempt to create a vehicle for human collaboration, fraternity, and even love, expresses the modicum of sanity within his total perspective. Sade's humanism cannot win out against the psychopathic darkness in his soul; but perhaps he is not entirely responsible for that. In the world around him as well as in himself, nature had often revealed, to his dismay, how easily it could defeat virtually all ideals of well-intentioned human beings.

If one thinks of Rousseau's faith in passion as a thesis that Sade counters with his paradoxically passionate insistence upon an antithetical coldness in sexual matters, one may approach Stendhal's writings as one long attempt to effect a synthesis between these two extremes. In *De l'Amour*, the book about love he wrote in 1822, prior to the great novels of his later life, Stendhal dismisses Sade's unique beings as men who "cannot obtain any sensual pleasure unless it is accompanied by circumstances which flatter their pride abnormally." But in other places he states what Sade might well have taught him: that the search for happiness must be predicated upon a realization that pleasure has much less effect on us than pain. Like Sade, Stendhal takes this as proof that men were not created by a benevolent deity. For Stendhal, however, pain has importance not as a sadomasochistic spur to sensory excitation, but only as an element within the passionate love that Sade dismissed as madness and that Stendhal now defends as the only thing that gives meaning to life. The turmoil and suffering a passionate lover undergoes will cause a greater impression upon his being, Stendhal insists, than all the pleasures for which a libertine might hope. Far from proving the undesirability of passion, this convinces Stendhal of its superiority to anything Sade could have imagined.

At the same time, it would be misleading to overemphasize the presence of Sade in Stendhal's thinking. Even the reference to pain as a more striking phenomenon of human nature than pleasure occurs in that part of *Emile* where Rousseau suggests that fellow-feeling more often results from watching scenes of suffering in other people than in seeing them live happy lives. The vanity and coldness of Sade's protagonists may intrigue Stendhal but he wishes to incorporate into his philosophy merely their analytical acuity and refusal to be deflected from rational awareness of personal benefits. To admit only this much, however, would seem to eliminate Sade's influence except insofar as he repeats what Stendhal was also reading in eighteenth-century moralists such as Helvétius.

Still it is important to begin with Sade because of the shadow he casts across important chapters of *De l'Amour*, particularly the one on "Werther and Don Juan." Contrasting the characters of Goethe's novel and Mozart's opera, Stendhal obviously favors Werther. He symbolizes the man of feeling who, although he may end up badly, sustains a passionate love that increases one hundred-fold the enjoyment to be had from intimacy with another person. Stendhal's is a Romantic interpretation of Werther, idealizing his ability to respond emotionally even if it involves suicidal tendencies based upon an infantile fixation. In Werther's experience there is so little enjoyment and so much tumultuous suffering that it seems odd to consider him as one who manifests the goodness of passionate love. On the other hand, the Don Juan that Stendhal depicts could well have appeared in the pages of Sade. He is not only a libertine but also a defiant criminal; not only a man who spurns the idea of virtue that Werther accepts, but also a sadist who expresses his sexuality through cruelty and a lust for power.

Stendhal believes that Don Juan's cruelty is "only a diseased form of sympathy," that men seek power because they think it will enable them to "command sympathy," and that while Werther's sorrowful love involves imaginative pleasures that reverberate throughout adversities, Don Juan must eventually become bored by his succession of conquests. As Stendhal says in another place, what matters in love is not possession but passionate involvement with another human being. He tells us that all the fools and erotic cowards belong to the camp of Don Juan, and that modern "physiologists" can prove that suspicion, emptiness, and unhappiness result from "injustice in the relationships of social life." But as one who aspires to scientific impartiality, Stendhal must also pretend to unbiased acceptance of alternative life-styles. He ends his chapter on Werther and Don Juan in a relativistic manner: "But after all, every man, if he will only take the trouble to study himself, has his own ideal of perfection." Are we really expected to take this profession of relativism as a statement of Stendhal's belief? If we did, his grandiose defense of passion, his claim that it is man's sole opportunity for happiness, would not make sense.

Stendhal's philosophy of love pivots upon his insights about four types of love between men and women: "l'amour-passion" (passion-love); "l'amour-goût" (sympathy-love, sometimes translated as "mannered-love"); "l'amour-vanité" (vanity-love); "l'amour-physique" (physical love). In a standard English translation this last appears as "sensual-love," but that rendering is unfortunate since it would seem to prejudge the physical. Repeatedly throughout his book Stendhal asserts that passion-love between man and woman is the only real, the only authentic kind of love. He defends it against its critics, whether they be followers of Rousseau, Encyclopedists of the eighteenth century, Ideologues of the nineteenth, or libertines like Sade. Yet he never tells us explicitly what is or ought to be the relationship between passion-love and the three other kinds of love.

Since so much of *De l'Amour*, and for that matter Stendhal's later writing as well, makes negative comments about vanity-love, one can imagine his having eliminated it immediately. That would have put his theories into perfect alignment with Rousseau's, for the concept of vanity-love overlaps with the notion of amour-propre. Rousseau's attempt to purify passion is based on the belief, as we have seen, that without purification it cannot be free of vanity. Stendhal follows a different line of reasoning. He begins by distinguishing between passion-love and vanity-love, but then proceeds to investigate their interrelation. In vanity-love one uses another person for reasons of pride or ambition, the beloved being desired as a means of obtaining something else that the vanity-lover wants. In passion-love, the beloved has become a person with whom one seeks total intimacy and mutual enjoyment. Though they are different attitudes, Stendhal also shows how vanity may turn into passion-love. This happens in the history of Julien Sorel, the hero of *The Red and the Black*. After trying to seduce Mme de Rênal as a would-be Don Juan, he ends up as the most passionate of lovers.

Wishing to further passion-love, Stendhal recognizes and accepts the role of vanity-love as an instigator or psychological prod. The two types of love establish a dialectic in the relationships between the lovers in all his novels. Passion and vanity often merge in such a way that neither the protagonists nor the narrator can ever be certain that a particular response issues from one rather than the other kind of love. They are nevertheless distinct as categories of analysis. Even if André Gide was right when he said that "of ten moments of joy, Stendhal owed nine to satisfied vanity," Stendhal himself leaves open the possibility of passionate experience that might originate in vanity but would not be reducible to it. He realizes that all love runs the risk of degenerating into vanity-love; and yet he consistently supports the idea that passion-love can be a separate goal to be striven for and sometimes attained in itself.

The relationship between passion-love and physical love has often caused difficulty for Stendhalian scholars. At times Stendhal sounds as if passion-love must be distinguished from libidinal or consummatory interests. He even says that the more love is based upon physical desire the more it is likely to be inconstant and subject to infidelity. He does not define physical love, assuming that "everyone knows the love founded on pleasures of this kind." At the age of sixteen one's amatory experience begins with the merely physical, he says, and savages do not have leisure or imagination to get beyond it. In all this, Stendhal is possibly copying what he had read in Rousseau and the Platonistic tradition. Illustrating physical love as he does—"whilst out shooting, to meet a fresh, pretty country girl who darts away into the wood"—he would even seem to be repeating Andreas Capellanus' remark about uses to which peasant women may be put without there being any question of truly feeling love for them. But Stendhal also talks about passion-love in ways that do not wholly separate it from the physical. Some of the anecdotes he recounts involve passionate lovers who enjoy sexual completeness with each other. There is no suggestion, in anything Stendhal writes, that physical lovemaking impairs the quality of passion-love. They are not reducible to one another, and much of passion-love relies upon acts of the imagination rather than sexual instinct, but they are in no way incompatible.

In one place, Stendhal says that "some virtuous and affectionate women have almost no idea at all of sensual [i.e. physical] pleasure; they have only rarely laid themselves open to it, if I may put it so, and even then the raptures of passion-love have almost made them forget the pleasures of the body." Is Stendhal saying that these virtuous and affectionate women are wrong to have neglected the physical? In his quasi-scientific manner he may merely be describing an occasional consequence of passion-love; but he might also mean that by its nature it deprives women of pleasures they should be having. Reading the English translation, one hardly knows what to think. He could even be praising women who manage to go beyond the pleasures of the body. In the previous paragraph the translator has him saying that physical love "only holds a very low place in the eyes of tender and passionate beings." But this misrepresents Stendhal's intention. He states that "le plaisir physique . . . n'a qu'un rang subordonné aux yeux des âmes tendres et passionnées." In other words, tender and passionate souls consider physical pleasure subordinate to the goals of perfect intimacy toward which they aspire. To say this is to say that mere sexuality is not the same as passion-love. It does not exclude all or any physical pleasure from the total experience that passionate lovers seek; and neither does it rank the physical at "a very low place."

The fourth type of love, l'amour-goût, would seem to be the hardest to reconcile with the ideal of passion-love. "Sympathy-love" is adequate as an English translation, but it fails to convey the idea of bored companionship that Stendhal has in mind. He thinks of l'amour-goût as a mildly sentimental attitude that provides no surprises and no excitement since its emotional bond is limited and relatively feeble. While retaining kind and friendly regard for each other, the participants in this relationship expect little more than tepid affection. Sympathy-love is more refined than passion-love in the sense of being more conventional; it conforms more readily to the demands of society and politesse. It presents the *appearance* of an emotional attachment, without any of the unpleasantness that often accompanies the real thing. Stendhal believes that without the vanity that always lurks beneath it, this kind of love could scarcely survive; but he also contrasts it to vanity-love since l'amour-goût puts the lover into a submissive, self-denying, and abjectly passive state. To this extent, however, it takes on some of the characteristics of passion-love itself.

If even sympathy-love can merge with passion-love, perhaps one does best to see the total Stendhalian conception as a kind of vector analysis. The four loves interact with one another dynamically, each being capable of turning into the other though in principle always remaining distinct. If this interpretation is right, one could argue that Stendhal's ideal consists in the ultimate harmonization of what is best in all four types of love.

I present this as a tentative hypothesis, Stendhal's writing being anything but systematic. His book is pseudo-scientific and largely a polemical affirmation of the goodness in passion-love. This type rises above the others as an attitude that creates their greatest value whenever it can be harmonized with them; and when it cannot be, passion-love preempts the rights of any alternative. Even by itself, it is to be considered supreme. Stendhal had been greatly influenced by the utilitarianism of Helvétius, but the latter's approach to love he found utterly inferior since it ignored the desirability of passion. Stendhal was convinced that Helvétius, and the rising bourgeoisie for whom he spoke, had no understanding of the emotions, overwhelming but also beneficial, that truly define the nature of love: "People of this kind are not susceptible to *passion-love*; it would disturb their splendid equanimity; I believe they would consider its transports a calamity; in any case they would feel humiliated by its timidity."

Stendhal's mention of timidity alerts us to his kinship with the courtly tradition, which he discusses in various places in *De l'Amour*, even including bits of medieval romance and "the 12th-century code of love" he copies out of Andreas Capellanus. Like the troubadours, Stendhal emphasizes the extent to which passion-love involves a combination of fear and respect for the beloved. The greater a man's love, the more he treats a woman like a superior being, even a divinity, whose affections he dare not alienate. Where sympathy-love may involve meekness and a desire to ingratiate oneself which Stendhal relates to frailty of spirit, the fear in passion-love arises from the inner conflict of wanting the maximum intimacy without being able to know whether the other person may find it annoying and presumptuous. In a way that anticipates modern sexology, Stendhal perceives that this fearfulness towards a revered woman who is passionately desired can lead to sexual impotence. In his famous chapter entitled "Failures" he begins with a long quotation from Montaigne on this "scabrous subject." Like many therapists today, Montaigne ascribes "these inexplicable failures of our power" to "the impressions of apprehension and effects of fear." But Stendhal has at hand a more sophisticated system of concepts than Montaigne could muster, and he accounts for the lover's dismay in terms of the dynamics of passion-love. He argues that apprehension is produced by the powerful desire for a person one values highly, someone who is more than just a sex object. In l'amour-physique, dealing for instance with a chambermaid or some other woman "of no consequence," Stendhal precludes the likelihood of such difficulties. But once passionate love exists, the imagination begins to operate in a manner that makes it possible for one to experience sexual fiasco (to use Stendhal's word).

Rousseau had also recognized that without imagination there could be no passionate love, and he too realized that imagination has interests that can be vastly different from those of enjoyment or sexual satisfaction. But Stendhal goes beyond Rousseau inasmuch as he argues that imagination can lead to a superior kind of enjoyment that only passion-love affords. It takes imagination, Stendhal insists, to develop a relationship of oneness and equality with another person. The savage does not have access to such love because his mind cannot rise above the constant pressure of physical needs that impinge upon him. Only a cultivated lover can experience the reciprocal bond that creates the joys of passion-love. Where Rousseau expresses scorn and suspicion about the corrupting influence of civilization, Stendhal remarks that the imaginative capacity for love develops only as civilized behavior evolves. Once that happens, men begin to see women as fascinating creatures who are nevertheless equal to themselves and therefore suitable as objects of passionate devotion.

In *The Second Sex*, Simone de Beauvoir pays homage to the authentic feminism of Stendhal. She points out the many places in *De l'Amour* where he ridicules the idea that women are inferior to men, or that they should be treated like domestic appurtenances, or that education is wasted on them. In the brave new world Stendhal foresees for the twentieth century, he predicts that educated women will make achievements matching anything men had ever attained. What Beauvoir tends to neglect, however, is the fact that female emancipation matters so much to Stendhal because he sees it as a precondition for passion-love. Similarly, it is his concern about equality that enables him to go beyond the troubadour concept of fin' amors. For him the (heterosexual) lover can be a woman as well as a man, and the beloved a man as well as a woman. His examples of passion-love show women idealizing men and undergoing a search for happiness comparable to what is usually depicted for a man. Stendhal believes in fundamental differences between the sexes, and I shall return to that, but he conceives of passion-love as love that precludes domination and must therefore be based upon actual as well as theoretical equality.

Sade also proclaims a kind of equality for women, and like Stendhal he extends it to matters of sexual practice. In the anarchic republic he envisages, Sade demands that women be given the ability to frequent brothels comparable to those that men have always used. Every woman should have access to every man, he says, and vice versa. With what looks like apparent impartiality, he insists that no one has a right to deny the sexual interests of anyone else. As a matter of fact, however, Sade is the very opposite of a feminist. He does not want to keep women within the traditional limits that Rousseau, for instance, thinks nature ordained, but he wishes to liberate women mainly to make them more thoroughly available to the needs of male sexuality. Though women will now be free to enjoy excruciating pleasures that were previously reserved to libertine men, they are thrust back upon their mere physical being and tyrannized by sexual politics that, assuming might makes right, deprive them of the usual protections of society. Sade justifies aggression and even violence toward females, above all though not exclusively in the course of sexual activity, on the grounds that the male has a natural right to assert his superiority in size and muscular strength by any means that satisfies him. Presumably, Sade would have had to allow stronger women to maltreat weaker men, and possibly his masochistic side reveled in the idea, but what he regularly shows us is men venting their cosmic and sexual hatred upon women, torturing and sometimes murdering them under the guise of mutual liberation. He does not believe in true equality between the sexes. For him this conception must have belonged to that miasma of passionate love which he considers foreign to anything that human beings can actually achieve or really desire.

Not only does Stendhal believe that passion-love is attainable by men and women, jointly, and that it produces the greatest happiness available to them, but also he thinks it develops in a natural progression and through a predictable series of stages. As a student of the human heart, a developmental psychologist or even psychoanalyst before the creation of these subjects, he assigns himself the task of analyzing the seven stages out of which passion-love systematically arises.

About the first four stages, Stendhal has little to say. In the chapter called "The Birth of Love" (was he, perhaps, thinking of Botticelli's painting?) he describes the first stage with a single phrase: "l'admiration." He is referring to the initial glance, the perception of some trait or physical feature that gives pleasure to the eye. In beginning this way, Stendhal would seem to find the origin of love in the search for beauty, an appraisal and not a bestowal. It is a man looking at a woman's face or body and finding it very satisfying aesthetically or sexually or in some other manner that interests him. The word "admiration" combines the sense both of looking and evaluating in the appraisive mode. This leads one to say to oneself: "How delightful to kiss her, to be kissed in return." That is Stendhal's second stage, and he tells us nothing further about it. It is presumably the awakening or focusing of sexual desire. It merges with the third stage, which Stendhal calls "hope" and which often requires little encouragement from the other person. If a woman wants to achieve the greatest sexual pleasure, Stendhal says, she should yield at precisely this point. If she does so, however, her feelings will not yet belong to love itself. For that occurs only in the fourth stage. Here Stendhal gives us what purports to be a definition: "To love is to derive pleasure from seeing, touching and feeling through all one's senses and as closely as possible, a lovable person who loves us."

As a definition, this is almost worthless. It does, however, suggest that passion-love, as Stendhal sees it, must be physical to some extent, and that reciprocity is essential to it. But perhaps one should not expect too much from Stendhal's definition. It mainly prepares us for the next three stages, in which Stendhal articulates the theory of "crystallization" for which he became famous. It is here that his most interesting ideas about love are to be found.

The concept of crystallization presents itself as a very simple idea. Actually it is quite complex. "I call crystallization," Stendhal tells us, "that process of the mind which discovers fresh perfections in its beloved at every turn of events." Taken at their face value, these words would relegate Stendhal to the long tradition in the philosophy of love that begins with Plato and considers love to be a striving toward perfect goodness. The notion that we *discover* perfections in the beloved makes crystallization appear to have the same basis in external reality that the Platonic approach always finds essential for understanding true love. And like Plato, Stendhal would seem to think that crystallization comes from objective nature, which commands us to seek pleasures we can recognize through the intellect and also arranges for pleasures to increase in proportion to the goodness of a desired object.

Stendhal's theory of crystallization is, however, very different from Plato's philosophy of love. The "discoveries" are not really discoveries, but rather creations, and far from relying upon the intellect, the entire process turns out to be a product of the imagination. Those "perfections" in the beloved which cause such delight in the Stendhalian lover have come into being through the act of love itself. Since Stendhal believes in the "coup de foudre," the bolt out of the blue which may or may not cause love at first sight but which symbolizes how the onset of passion lies beyond one's control, he claims that the creativity in love does not involve an act of decision or choice. Stendhal describes love as a fever, just as Proust was later to compare it to an infection brought on by a kind of bacillus. For Stendhal love is the result of a spontaneous and unwilled occurrence in the creative imagination which leads one person to see in another a cluster of perfections that are not there.

The usual terms we use for this kind of experience are words like "illusion," "delusion," "falsification," "exaggeration," or even "delirium." Stendhal employs similar language on occasion, and he has often been interpreted as presenting a highly inconsistent theory of love. For on the one hand, his entire book is a defense of passion-love; but on the other hand, he would seem to be portraying it as an aberration caused by an illusory act of the imagination. Not only does he call passion-love a fever, but also he repeatedly refers to it as a sickness of the soul, a form of madness; and he appears to mean by this more than just the vague perturbations so many poets had described as "lovesickness." But then what exactly is he recommending? Is he idealizing a self-destroying illness, much as the Christian mystics advocated death to worldly interests for the sake of superior joys to be found beyond nature? Nothing of the sort! Stendhal insists that love as crystallization belongs to man's biological being. It brings about the only true or lasting joys that men and women can experience on earth because it enables them to fulfill their natural propensities, as persons whose temporal concerns matter more than all the priestly promises of eternity.

But if this is what Stendhal does believe, his idea must surely be untenable. How can he think that a disease will bring about permanent happiness? To the extent that his philosophy lends itself to this difficulty, I think it is simply indefensible. At the same time, one must also recognize that Stendhal's writings include frequent use of irony, hyperbole, and dialectical posturing. When he characterizes love as a madness or disease, he is often talking metaphorically, tweaking the nose of that bourgeois world he and other Romantics scorned in their condition of aloofness and alienation. To you, *hypocrite lecteur*, as Baudelaire would say, the discovery of nonexistent perfections can only seem like mental aberration, but in fact it manifests an emotional development that human beings require if they are to achieve their greatest happiness. Such a view is not at all indefensible.

Interpreting Stendhal this way, however, we encounter new and possibly greater problems. Throughout his works, above all in the novels, Stendhal always prides himself on being a realist whose methods of analysis resemble those of a scientist. In specializing in psychology, the human heart, he aspires to an expertise comparable to that of medicine or physiology. This may have been one of the reasons Freud and Reik admired him so much. In his voice as analyst and quasi-scientist, Stendhal constantly points out the immaturity, the blindness, and the incredible stupidity of the lovers in all his novels. Though their experiences are vibrant and exhilarating, and though Stendhal always sympathizes with his characters, even to the point of identifying with the vital surge that impels them through their erotic adventures, he also stands back and mercilessly depicts their deviations from reality. This complex talent is conducive to the writing of great novels, since that profits from the dramatic tension, and even ricochet, between the two perspectives. But in a work like *De l'Amour*, which claims to be philosophical and wholly scientific, one has a right to expect greater consistency.

Let us put this problem in abeyance for a moment. It may prove more manageable once we have a better idea of what Stendhal means by "crystallization." He gets the word from a natural phenomenon that occurs in the salt mines of Salzburg. A leafless bough left in the mines during the winter will gradually acquire a brilliant covering of glittering crystals, so much so that the original twigs are no longer visible. The analogy to states of love is fairly straightforward: the untreated bough is what the beloved is like objectively, and the crystalline diamonds are the "perfections" that the lover imagines; they are a consequence of passion. Unfortunately, Stendhal's analogy fails in one important respect. For the salt crystals really do cover the bough. They result from a chemical process and are not subjective or imagined in any way. The beloved's perfections, on the other hand, are said to appear only to the eyes of the lover; and their individual character is determined by the ideals he carries about with him. One of the women Stendhal quotes in *De l'Amour* summarizes his position when she says: "The moment you begin to be interested in a woman, you no longer see her *as she really is*, but as you want her to be, and you are comparing the favorable illusions which this dawning interest produces to these pretty diamonds which hide the hornbeam twig stripped of its leaves by winter, and which are only seen, let us remember, by the eyes of this young man who is falling in love." But surely crystallization, in the case of the salt, is there for everyone to see. Since the perfection of the beloved is not, erotic crystallization can hardly be analogous.

Leaving aside this flaw in Stendhal's presentation, one could take him as meaning that the beauties of the crystalline formations created by the lover's passion—itself a kind of chemistry of the mind—are so great a source of pleasure that it really does not matter how they are produced. As an analyst, Stendhal realizes that they result from the lover's imagination rather than the beloved's attributes. But of greater importance, he thinks, is the fact that nowhere else in life can one attain pleasures comparable to those that crystallization provides. One therefore has to choose between a strict dedication to objective truth, which prevents the occurrence of passion-love, and the lover's act of imagination, which involves illusory perceptions about another person. If this is what Stendhal maintains, there is no inconsistency in his argument. But then it may be attacked on other grounds.

In his book on love, Ortega y Gasset sneeringly condemns Stendhal as a man who was merely in love with love and whose theory of crystallization is false to the nature of love itself. Ortega distinguishes between being in love and falling in love, and he accuses Stendhal of talking about the latter without realizing its differences from the former. Ortega considers falling in love to be a quasi-hypnotic state that causes immature persons to delude themselves about the value of some beloved, and he insists that this is only a pathological substitute for truly being in love. He sees Stendhal as one who confounds the two, treating the frantic violence of falling in love as if it were the emphatic affirmation that constitutes being in love. Ortega rejects Stendhalian crystallization because the idea of imagination creating nonexistent perfections indicates to him that passionate love has not been recognized as a genuine communication between two people. Only falling in love is illusory, Ortega says; being in love enables one to detect what another person is really like. Ortega defines authentic love as an awareness or discovery of the beloved's objective being combined with a total acceptance of that person.

Ortega's distinction between the two kinds of love is very much worth making, but I think Stendhal would be shocked to learn that he has been accused of identifying passion-love with the condition of falling in love. For in talking about passionate love, Stendhal puts great emphasis upon the lover's concern for the welfare of the beloved, his eagerness to share his most valued experiences with her, his belief that only in her company can he obtain total intimacy with another person, and his desire for the equalization of goods that occurs through reciprocity. Much of this exceeds the boundaries of falling in love, and none of it implies the hypnotized submergence of oneself that Ortega identifies with falling in love. In the novels, Stendhal's lovers often begin their amorous adventures by falling in love but they generally go far beyond it.

In *De l'Amour*, the distinction between the two ways of loving is already implied, though not clearly delineated. Stendhal shows how imagination functions not only in making the lover find perfections that would not be there apart from his love, but also in keeping the beloved present—through his affirmative attitude—even when she is absent: "For instance, should a traveller speak of the coolness of Genoese orange groves by the seashore on a scorching summer day, you immediately think how delightful it would be to enjoy this coolness in her company!" There is in this play of the imagination nothing that necessarily limits the relationship to falling in love rather than being in love, nothing that necessarily involves the irrationality and occasional pathology of the former. Moreover, Stendhal often presents the theory of crystallization in ways that Ortega would have approved. In the chapters that deal with love in relation to beauty, he frequently sounds as if the passionate lover's act of imagination consists in bestowing value upon attributes of the beloved that he *knows* are not beautiful. To this extent the lover is not deluding himself or mistakenly finding beauty where none exists. Stendhal remarks that a man who has experienced strong emotions in the presence of a facial defect will cherish it and eventually cease to consider it ugly. He explains the process as follows: "If one arrives thus at preferring and loving what is in itself ugly, it is because in this case ugliness becomes beauty."

In saying this, Stendhal is referring to a change in the lover's valuational response. He is not suggesting that lovers delude themselves in the way that a person does when he considers an ugly woman objectively beautiful, i.e. beautiful as a matter of objective appraisal. On the contrary, Stendhal distinguishes between "true beauty" and the beauty that lovers find. The latter is a result of crystallization, and, as he describes it in this context, only those who have no conception of what love is like would think the lover deluded. The lover experiences no illusion in the sense of mistaken judgment: he merely refuses to limit his appreciative responses to what the rest of the world declares beautiful.

If we interpret Stendhal in this manner, his theory of crystallization begins to look rather similar to the concept of bestowal as I have formulated it. I think Stendhal is confused inasmuch as sometimes he does talk about crystallization as if it were indeed a kind of self-delusion. At other times, however, he is definitely referring to a change in attitude which love engenders, a creative act of acceptance rather than the erroneous fabrication of nonexistent perfections. Loving another person may cause us to ignore any number of defects, and so to treat the beloved *as if* she were perfect as she is; but in this there is madness only for those who do not understand the nature of love. Being an example of bestowal, crystallization would consist in seeing a woman as perfect for oneself, accepting her as someone who has absolute beauty in that sense even though we know she does not have it in any other.

On this interpretation, the Stendhalian theory of crystallization need not be limited to falling in love. Nevertheless, Stendhal's ideas are often remote from what Ortega says about being in love. Ortega claims it is "essential for true love to be born suddenly and never to die." Whatever he may mean by this, he is not depicting anything like the passionate love Stendhal describes. Although the characters in his novels are linked through emotive bonds that they themselves cannot control, only rarely does their love come into being suddenly. He also thinks that passion-love exists in a precarious condition that always precludes the possibility of knowing how long it will last.

In this respect Stendhal may actually be less of a Romantic than Ortega. While he believes in love as the greatest of human values, and recognizes that passion-love involves a search for permanent joy with one other person from whom the lover would never part, Stendhal finds nothing in love itself to assure us that it will blossom as the lover hopes, or even continue to exist for very long. In the novels, his lovers go through many oscillations, changing greatly in relation to one another, and these alterations are not always explicable in terms of vanity or external interference. The search for a completely satisfying and wholly reciprocal passion-love is by its very nature hazardous and uncertain. Stendhal has no doubts about its magnificence as an ideal, but he is not convinced that many human beings have the capacity to live up to this ideal. Ortega accounts for Stendhal's pervasive skepticism by claiming that in his personal life Stendhal was himself "a man who never truly loved nor, above all, was ever truly loved." Stendhal's biographers have sometimes made similar judgments, and a few have interpreted his succession of unhappy love affairs as proof of infantile dependence upon his mother, overvaluation of women leading to inevitable frustration, latent homosexuality, and so forth. There may be some truth in these allegations; but if they are adduced as criticism of his theories about love, their value is rather meager.

It is because Stendhal recognizes the uncertainties in love, better perhaps than anyone else before Proust, that he lists two stages after the occurrence of crystallization. Following the first crystallization, there is a period of doubt, which then leads to a second crystallization. Doubt is needed because even the most perfect happiness can turn into boredom that comes from monotony. Women who are light or too accessible fail to stimulate their lover's imagination. If the relationship is purely sensuous, it will not develop further, and the man will soon move on to another conquest. If vanity-love is added to this syndrome, one ends up with the personality of a Don Juan who never experiences passion-love for anyone. Women who are capable of passion-love know how to awaken doubts that force their lovers to continue crystallizing. An initial act of crystallization is not enough for passion-love to reach fruition.

Stendhal associates the stage of doubting with the feeling of jealousy. Like Andreas Capellanus, he considers jealousy conducive to love though also painful. But it is interesting that Stendhal ignores the distinction in Andreas between "shameful suspicion" and true jealousy. With his greater, and more typically Romantic, interest in powerful emotions, Stendhal sees the lover's jealousy as part of an effort to intensify and prolong the imaginative processes that have created passion in the first place. Stendhal does not seem to care whether the lover's suspicions are shameful either to himself or to the woman whose behavior has awakened them.

In taking this approach, is Stendhal merely being factual, quasi-scientific? Describing the function, and even necessity, of jealousy, he makes us wonder about his intention. Though his book is addressed to tender and idealistic readers of the nineteenth century, he often sounds like Ovid giving instructions about successful promiscuity. He says that each lover must make the other anxious about fidelity, create fears and apprehension. They must even play upon one another's vanity in order to achieve a higher pitch of passion. There are so many maneuvers Stendhal recommends that one marvels at his expecting them all to eventuate in the ardor and unpretentious intimacy for which passion-love aspires. On the one hand, he tells us that "the only crime at which one can take offense in love is want of candor; one should always reveal the exact state of one's heart." This sounds like Rousseau on the importance of transparency. But he also says: "Always some little doubt to calm, that is what keeps one ever eager, that is what keeps alive the spark of happy love. Since it is never devoid of fear, its joys can never pall." These last remarks occur immediately after the chapter entitled "Intimacy," in which Stendhal argues that the greatest happiness between two people can exist only when they are joined by spontaneous and natural responses that preclude all affectation. Somehow he fails to see the contradiction between the two types of advice.

Within the dimensions of his theory this conflict in Stendhal duplicates the tension between pride and passion that characterizes all the lovers in his novels. But the fictional writing always centers about individuals whose narrative experience will reveal whether their basic orientation is vanity-love or passion-love. As I have suggested, they are generally motivated by both, and the greatness of Stendhal the novelist consists in his ability to show the moment-by-moment interaction between the two. Julien Sorel forces himself into the bedroom of Madame de Rênal as the culmination of his vanity-driven campaign to seduce her. When she rejects him, he bursts into tears, submits to her moral superiority, and thereby enters into a passionate love that creates candor and spontaneity in both of them. To the extent that doubt, fear, and jealousy are devices that one uses to retain another's interest, they must belong to vanity-love. They result from calculated efforts to control the affections of the other person. But this would seem quite foreign to passion-love.

In answer, Stendhal can point out that not all moments of fear or jealousy result from conscious maneuvers. He shrewdly remarks that love does not progress in two people at the same rate, regardless of what they themselves may wish. And for all his egalitarianism, he insists that women have a natural tendency to modesty, and therefore they increase their lover's doubts merely by being more reserved than he is. Moreover, jealousy can arise from the lover's feverish need for his beloved, rather than from deliberate coquetry on her part. On some occasions at least, the Stendhalian stage of doubting may occur without the presence of vanity.

Whatever its origins, the insecurity of the lover not only keeps his imagination alive but also it leads on to what Stendhal calls the "second crystallization." This is what insures the duration of love. It induces the sense of mutuality which Proustian lovers never experience and which makes Stendhal's theory supremely benign and wholly Romantic. For now the man or woman sees another person as the source of endless joys and total reciprocity. Although the lover can never be certain that love will last forever, his belief that he has found a special person who will both receive his love and also return it creates the renewed acts of bestowal that constitute the second crystallization. In the first crystallization, a man sees a woman as perfect regardless of her actual properties; in the second crystallization, he sees her as a perfect being who will reciprocate his affirmative attitude. This too depends upon the imagination, and that is why Stendhal cannot envisage a second crystallization with women who surrender themselves too quickly. But love as second crystallization is a rare occurrence, reserved for the "happy few." When it exists, however, the lover feels that he has no other reason for living: "at every moment one realizes that one must either be loved or perish. How, with this conviction ever present in one's mind, and grown into a habit by several months of love, can one bear even the thought of ceasing to love?"

And yet, thoughts about the cessation of love preoccupy Stendhal as well as the ardent lovers in his novels. In *De l'Amour* he includes two chapters on "antidotes to love," perhaps in imitation of Ovid's remedies. Elsewhere he speaks of the crystals of passion decomposing once the lover realizes that he was mistaken in thinking the woman reciprocated his affection. The Stendhalian belief that even true love can die convinced Ortega that Stendhal's theories are inappropriate to anything but falling in love. Being in love, Ortega insists, can only mean a permanent oneness that does not lend itself to processes of decay. Stendhal's remarks about the destructibility of love must therefore prove that his conception applies only to falling in love.

Taken literally, Ortega's criticism cannot carry much weight. Stendhal's account is true to reality inasmuch as it treats love like any other occurrence in nature: capable of growth, development, and glorious efflorescence, but also subject to decline, deterioration, and eventual death. At the same time, Ortega's critique does turn obliquely upon a problem of considerable importance that looms within Stendhal's approach. For though his preoccupation with circumstances under which love may (or ought to) disappear seems reasonable, Stendhal does not show us how love can persevere. Only rarely does he mention the possibility of love continuing throughout a lifetime. In one place in *De l'Amour* he says that wanting to witness "eternal love" he obtained an introduction to a man and his mistress who had lived together for fifty-four years. He left them with tears in his eyes, "for they had mastered the art of happiness." But Stendhal tells us nothing else about their love, and when he talks of marital pleasure he has little to offer. On the contrary, in what he calls his "metaphysic musings," he insists that anyone who has experienced great passions will inevitably despise the joys of a happy marriage. He asks the reader to imagine "a charming country house in picturesque surroundings, all the comforts of life, a good wife, pretty children, plenty of pleasant friends," and then he dismisses it all because "a mind made for passion feels in the first place that this happy life irks him, and perhaps also, that it only gives him a few very commonplace ideas." It is here that Stendhal says that pleasure makes so much less of an impression upon us than pain.

Stendhal's doubts about the value of married life can be traced back as far as his early manhood. In 1807 he writes in a letter to his sister: "When love truly exists in marriage, it is a fire which goes out more rapidly than it was lit." At that time, Stendhal was studying the philosophy of Destutt de Tracy, who emphasized the extent to which habit could have a deadening effect upon sensation. A number of years later Destutt wrote a *De l'Amour* that Stendhal read just before undertaking his own, but there one finds an approach to married love very different from Stendhal's. Beginning with the idea that love derives from reproductive instincts, Destutt shows how its complete development involves man's social nature as well:

> Love is not only a physical need. It is a passion, a feeling, an attachment of one individual to another. Even in beings whose moral capacity is least developed, and among many animals, it is a matter of choice. It is not always determined by beauty alone; the pleasure of loving and being loved is to a large and even greatest extent different from merely enjoying another. The proof is that enjoyment [jouissance]

is very imperfect when forcibly imposed; it is even physically painful; and enjoyment that is too massive or too easily attained is without savor since it does not involve sentiment. Mutual acquiescence is thus one of the charms of love, and *sympathy* one of its greatest pleasures. . . . Love is friendship embellished by pleasure; it is the perfection of friendship. It is the supreme sentiment that focuses all our behavior, that employs all our faculties, that satisfies all our desires, that combines all our pleasures. It is the masterpiece of our being.

With this as his definition of love, Destutt then argues that its ideal fulfillment occurs only in marriage. For only then can the needs of reproduction be integrated with the mutual benefits of sympathy, heterosexual friendship, and harmonious family life. The family being the basis of all society, Tracy concludes that nothing can be more essential to the welfare of mankind than the furtherance of married love.

Eager as Stendhal was to use Destutt's "ideological" method of analysis in order to "de-Rousseauize" his own thinking, he found no way of accommodating this plea for a reconciliation between marriage and passion-love. What he duplicates from Destutt's *De l'Amour* is mainly the philosopher's attack on existing social institutions. While condemning marriages of convenience or self-interest as the cause of widespread unhappiness, Destutt recognizes that most marriages based on passionate love are also unsuccessful. Once the initial excitement dissipates, the lovers often realize that they should never have married one another. With his faith in the inherent goodness of married love, Destutt infers from this that Western society is to blame in its refusal to give young people access to the truths of erotic experience. He suggests that girls be allowed the same opportunities as boys to learn about the world, to experiment with sexual inclinations, to have love affairs freely and, if they lead to unfortunate consequences, without disgrace. In order to eliminate bad marriages, Destutt recommends a return to the French Revolution's acceptance of divorce "pur et simple," legal separation being granted for no reason other than joint testimonial of incompatibility.

Similar ideas reappear in Stendhal's short chapter on marriage, in which he says: "There is only one way of securing more fidelity in marriage on the part of women, and that is to give young girls more liberty and married persons divorce." But when Stendhal describes the liberties he would accord young girls, he is—compared to Destutt—much less radical (or forward-thinking, given the history of the modern world). Stendhal's hesitancy about freedom in the young may reflect his belief that passion-love requires obstacles; but even so, he lacks Destutt's assurance that early education in sexuality can teach people how to preserve their passionate love within a subsequent marriage. For Destutt both are equally natural, and therefore neither should be subjected to much, if any, social restraint.

Believing in married love as he does, Destutt criticizes courtly as well as Greek or Platonic love. He considers the latter an idealization of male friendship which destroys the possibility of family joys ordained by nature. Courtly love, which he associates with all the follies of "galanterie chevaleresque," Destutt rejects because he thinks it always treats women as divine or elevated spirits instead of allowing them to become what he calls in another place "happy companions of husbands of their choice, and the respectable mothers of a tender family raised by their care."

Stendhal's appreciation of all this in Destutt is very limited. What matters most to him is the experience of powerful emotions, strong passions that stimulate the mind and launch us into one imaginative activity after another. As a result, however, he sees in courtly love positive virtues that escaped Destutt. He defends it and even quotes the passage in Andreas Capellanus where the Countess of Champagne rules upon the incompatibility between love and marriage. But Stendhal's attitude toward matrimony is actually more complicated than that. For him passionate love belongs to man's search for enduring happiness, and the lovers he portrays usually do wish to marry one another, to live together and enjoy the pleasures of successful and permanent oneness. At least in principle, neither he nor they would seem to consider love and marriage incompatible. Stendhal condemns marriages that are not based upon passionate love on the grounds that they should never have been made in the first place. In his novels adultery occurs because of a lack of love between spouses rather than an inherent conflict between love and marriage. And yet, he has virtually no conception of what a happy marriage would be like, or how elements of passion-love might survive in the everyday world of married people.

There are several ways in which we might interpret this failure of Stendhal's thought. We could say that his vision is permanently fixed upon the period of courtship in which men and women establish their sexual bond. He has nothing to tell us about the ideal potentialities of marriage because they belong to a later condition. But Stendhal defeats this interpretation, for he explicitly extols the pleasures of courtship as the *highest* good that human beings can know. Only at that stage of life can the happiness of passion-love be truly experienced. To this extent his thinking is simply truncated, cut short by limitations within himself, and possibly his critics are right when they claim that his philosophy is an arrested expression of adolescent emotions that may last a long time in some neurotics but that most adults soon outlive.

Others have thought that Stendhal really favors something like the renunciation of pleasure which I ascribed to Rousseau. As an extreme version of this view, Victor Brombert suggests that "this renouncement is all the more total as all has been consummated. It is when Stendhal's heroes are granted that which secretly they had renounced from the very start, that they turn aside from this gift with the greatest sense of self-denial." But this interpretation casts Stendhal into a philosophical posture that suits him very poorly. For unlike Rousseau, he has no desire to transcend passion-love. He does not wish to use it for the sake of any higher good. Indeed, he does not believe that a higher good exists. As he says in *De l'Amour*, his theme is the study of that "folly called love, which folly nevertheless procures for mankind the greatest pleasures that their species is given to enjoy on earth." He nowhere manifests a desire to renounce such joyfulness or to exclude its sexual components. His impassioned lovers may give up the joy of living together in a happy marriage, the peace and comfort of respectable life in society, and everything else that does not conduce to passion; but passion itself they hold onto regardless of its consequences. If they suffer at the end, as they often do, it is not because they have renounced the pleasures of love from the very start but only because they have found no way of prolonging them.

The first edition of *De l'Amour* ends with a romance entitled "Ernestine, or the Birth of Love." It is a case history of passion-love, presumably showing how it progresses through the seven stages in Stendhal's analysis. It concludes with Ernestine achieving ecstatic happiness when she realizes that her love is reciprocated. The lovers have never shared physical pleasures, however, and Ernestine rejects her beloved because she cannot forgive him for having thrown over an old mistress for her sake. She leaves him in a state of utter despair and the following year marries a rich nobleman she does not love. Is Stendhal merely being perverse, as some critics have suggested, in refusing to allow the lovers to enjoy what each of them wants more than anything else? I think not. For this story, like all his novels, is a parable that illustrates the one great human potentiality that Stendhal understood and wished to idealize, namely that part of our nature which strives for the sheer exhilaration of striving, which recognizes no goal other than happiness but finds its greatest happiness in the imaginative pleasures of searching for happiness. His lovers may obtain one another on occasion, and sometimes permanently as in the case of Mosca and la Sanseverina, but Stendhal knows that if he were to lavish attention upon their married life, he would be detracting from the grandeur of their preliminary struggles. Their greatest moments belong to their passionate love alone, abstracted and portrayed in isolation as a way of revealing its life-enhancing uniqueness. From this point of view, the demonstration is more graphic, more convincing, if Ernestine (like so many others in Stendhalian fiction) does not marry her true beloved.

Believing in none of the dogmas of religion, none of the utopian dreams of social harmony, none of the platitudes that allowed his contemporaries to accept the status quo, none of the promises of libertine delight or sadistic mastery, Stendhal clings to the imaginative creativity in passion-love as the only thing that gives life the intensity without which it is not worth living. Throughout his writings he continually contrasts the vitality of what is unforeseen ("l'imprévu") with the dreariness of disappointing actuality. The latter is marked by the recurring phrase, "Ce n'est que ça?" ("Is that all it is?"). These are the words that Lamiel utters after she brings about her brutish initiation into sexuality. They are the words that Fabrizio uses after participating in the Battle of Waterloo. There is only one area of man's existence to which Stendhal finds them inapplicable: the birth and growth of passionate love. For then everything is poised at the edge of joy and infinite peril, and the outcome is always unforeseeable. In passion-love, experience becomes incandescent, vibrant, magnificently new, even for one who seeks to analyze it as minutely as Stendhal does. For him no other justification of love is needed.

12
Benign Romanticism
Kant, Schlegel, Hegel, Shelley, Byron

IN TURNING NOW TO THE BE-
nign and optimistic aspects of German and English romanticism, we
begin by recognizing that here too the diversity of ideas must always
defeat a search for monolithic uniformity. Though I shall argue that
Kant provides an origin for much of the Romantic concept of love, I
do not wish to minimize the extent to which his thinking is also alien
to it. And though Hegel attacked Kant in ways that reveal the
ontological bases of romanticism as it developed in the nineteenth
century, Hegel frequently claimed that he himself was no Romantic.
Shelley and the early Schlegel may not have rejected that label, but
their ideas about love are often idiosyncratic to themselves and only
partly representative of others in the Romantic movement. And
finally, Byron, concluding this chapter as one who illustrates a realist
reaction to benign romanticism, is quite as Romantic in what he
sometimes says about love as those whose optimism he repudiates.

In some respects, Kant's ideas are the most challenging. They
would warrant examination even if they had no importance for
Romantic or any other subsequent philosophy. As in so many areas
of modern thought, it is essential to use Kant as a point of departure.

The continuity between Rousseau and Kant has been recognized by
various scholars, but little has been written about the Kantian response to Rousseau's ideas about sexual love. As we have seen,

Rousseau starts with an affirmation of the goodness in sexual love, which he then seeks to harmonize with the superior virtue of a rational marriage. Rousseau advocates a purification of passion such that Saint-Preux can finally be united with Julie in some kind of heaven for lovers, while her relationship with her husband manifests the sense of communal oneness that sustains an ideal republic. In Kant's philosophy similar elements occur, but they are now organized into a characteristic dialectic where thesis and antithesis transcend each other for the sake of an idealistic resolution.

As his thesis, or the first premise in his argument, Kant repeats (in effect) what Rousseau had said about the evil or inherent sinfulness of mere sexuality. Wanting to believe that human nature is innately good, Rousseau had argued that sexual desire was not really natural but rather an acquired interest reflecting the corruption in developed societies. In his more pietistic moments, Kant seems to accept Lutheran ideas about original sin, ideas that Rousseau found intolerable; but Kant and Rousseau resemble one another in their assumption that by its very nature sexuality is bad. They both consider it an appetite that reduces other persons to the status of material objects. Sexual desire being an attempt to possess the body of another, Kant tells us, it treats that person as if he or she were only a thing, and therefore just a means instead of an end. For Kant immorality consists in treating people as merely means. That violates their essential freedom, their basic dignity as persons worthy of respect because they serve as ends for themselves.

At the same time, Kant does not want to deny the possibility of sexual love. On the contrary, his philosophy is, in a sense, even more Romantic that Rousseau's. He explicitly searches for the conditions that enable sex and love to be combined, the circumstances under which sexual impulse can be satisfied while also enabling love between human beings to be realized. Love itself Kant defines as "good-will, affection, promoting the happiness of others and finding joy in their happiness." The problem is to find a relationship in which love and sex can be harmonized or, at least, rendered compatible. Kant concludes that this happens only in legal matrimony of a monogamous sort. All other sexual possibilities must therefore be immoral for one reason or another.

A conclusion of this sort may not seem revolutionary and its special role in the history of ideas can easily be misconstrued. But its significance becomes obvious once we compare Kant's attitude toward marriage with that of an eighteenth-century utilitarian such as David Hume. Hume also defended what he calls "our present European practice with regard to marriage," but Hume advocated monogamy only because it seemed to satisfy pervasive human needs better than other social arrangements between the sexes. A priori, Hume considers no sexual adjustment inherently better than any other. He does say that men are bound "by all the ties of nature and humanity" to support the children they beget; but he finds nothing in either nature or humanity to require any *particular* relationship between mother and father or between parents and their offspring. Laws that vary from culture to culture determine how people can or should organize their sexual, reproductive, and familial responsibilities. In advocating monogamy, going so far as to oppose the possibility of divorce, Hume makes no special claims for its preferability. He simply argues that, on the whole, Western-style marriage accommodates the diverse interests of male and female while also encouraging friendship between the sexes, and between the generations, better than any of the usual alternatives.

To Hume the idea of friendship as the basis of marriage is so important that he generally downgrades passionate love. While friendship is a "calm and sedate affection, conducted by reason and cemented by habit," love is a feverish state involving jealousies, fears, and torments that may be fascinating and in some sense agreeable but neither stable nor conducive to social permanence. "Love is a restless and impatient passion," Hume tells us, "full of caprices and variations; arising in a moment from a feature, from an air, from nothing, and suddenly extinguishing after the same manner." He quotes from a place in Pope's poem about Heloise and Abelard where Heloise's passion leads her to reject marriage on the grounds that love requires an inimical type of liberty. Matrimony, particularly monogamy, can be defended, Hume believes, but only if one recognizes that it conduces to serene friendliness rather than anything as frantic and unbridled as sexual love.

In Kant the situation is totally, and paradoxically, different. Despite his underlying puritanism and apparent coldness, despite the rigidity of the moral commandments that serve as a virtual divinity for him, Kant's ideas belong to the idealistic tradition in a way that Hume's, or for that matter Pope's, do not. When Pope depicts the burning desires of Heloise and describes the torment of Abelard, his poetry may seem Romantic because his language is so intense. But Pope does not accept, indeed he ridicules, the idea that this kind of love can provide a solution to the moral problems of human beings. In this sense he, and Hume as well, still adhered to the same traditional orthodoxy that motivated Abelard himself when he wrote out the history of his calamities. Kant belongs to another dispensation, though he himself may not have known that he did. For though he is more extreme in his attack upon mere sexuality than either of these other eighteenth-century thinkers, his ultimate defense of sexual love is so emphatic and so idealistic as to make him one of the founders of nineteenth-century romanticism. The details of his argument are worth the most careful examination.

By its very nature, Kant believes, sexual impulse is an "appetite for enjoying another human being." It is the only means by which one person can be made "an object of indulgence" for another; as such, it may even be considered a sixth sense. In one of his later works, Kant says that sexual inclination "is truly the greatest sensuous pleasure that can be taken in an object: it is not merely sensible pleasure taken in objects that please in the mere act of contemplating them . . . but pleasure from the enjoyment of another person." As an appetite, sexuality involves no desire for the welfare of its object, and consequently a love that arises from sex alone cannot be what Kant calls "real human love." Sexual appetite may possibly be combined with human love, and that is the entire burden of his moral theory in this area, but Kant insists that *in itself* sex can only be a degradation of human nature. Appetites are designed to possess something that furthers our own organic needs; they cannot concern themselves with the object as a separate end whose interests may be different from our own. But only *things* may rightly be subjected to one's own selfish desire. Being appetitive, sexual impulse treats other persons as if they were things; and therefore, Kant maintains, sexuality is inherently immoral. It divests persons of the dignity that all human beings deserve insofar as it is in their nature to be free and autonomous ends. How, then, is sexual love possible? How can the immorality of sex be transmuted, negated and somehow transformed, into the morality of love? The Kantian argument begins with these questions.

In thinking of sexuality as just an appetite, Kant considers it a desire for another that takes upon itself no interest in his or her humanity. That is why it is ethically wrong. It is immoral not only to engage in prostitution, where a woman rents her body as if it were property although in fact one's body is part of one's humanity, but also it is immoral to enter into any relationship that concerns itself only with sexual gratification. In that case, there may be no question of monetary gain, neither participant hiring out the body to another person; but since each is interested in the other as merely a sexual creature, as just a means of satisfying one's own sexual needs, both are surrendering a part of themselves as human beings, and that is a violation of their dignity as persons. Kant believes that persons, unlike things, cannot be split into independent parts. A human being makes a unity, each part of him being integral to the rest. Therefore one must not use the sexuality of another person unless one relates it to that person as a whole. But this is precluded by an activity that seeks to be purely sexual whether or not it involves prostitution. For then both parties dispose of the other as if he or she were nothing but an agency of sex. Each of them inescapably neglects the humanity of the other, treating the whole as if it could be broken into parts, and therefore reducing a person to the condition of a thing.

It follows from Kant's argument that only in one circumstance is sexual desire not immoral. That is a situation in which one person has rights to another person *as a whole*, his sexuality together with all the other parts of his being. But for one person to obtain such rights over another, he must give the other person the same rights over himself. And therein lies Kant's defense of marriage: "Matrimony is an agreement between two persons by which they grant each other equal reciprocal rights, each of them undertaking to surrender the whole of their person to the other with a complete right of disposal over it." Only in marriage does Kant find the mutual give-and-take of rights to every aspect of one's person, and therefore only in marriage does he believe that one can enjoy another's sexuality (or one's own) without committing an immorality. In words that remind us of Ficino, Kant insists that the autonomy which defines the freedom of a human being is not lost through this mutual giving of rights and privileges: "If I yield myself completely to another and obtain the person of another in return, I win myself back. I have given myself up as the property of another, but in turn I take that other as my property, and so win myself back again in winning the person whose property I have become."

By this line of argument Kant claims to prove that sexuality may become moral, though in itself it never would be. It attains its morality derivatively, through the morality of marriage. In that condition two persons share in the humanity of one another; they are equal participants in each other without either suffering a loss to the ultimate freedom that defines their human nature. "In this way the two persons become a unity of will. Whatever good or ill, joy or sorrow befall either of them, the other will share in it. Thus sexuality leads to a union of human beings."

Kant's approach also enables him to show why monogamy is superior to polygamy, for in the latter circumstance each wife gives herself totally but gets back only a fraction of her husband. Hume had criticized polygamy on the grounds that it led to jealousy among the wives, paternal deprivation for the children, each of whom would have too little access to the single father, and hostility among patriarchs, who would have to guard their wives against each other as marauding interlopers. Kant avails himself of no such reasoning. For him monogamy is justifiable by principles much stronger than considerations that are merely pragmatic or prudential. It is a means of fulfilling the ends of humanity, a moral exchange that overcomes the immorality of sexual impulse, an institution that creates a spiritual oneness between human beings of the opposite sex. Without monogamous marriage, sexual love would not be love at all. With it, sexual love becomes a uniquely valuable consummation that shows forth the character of human ideality. Marriage is for Kant a holy bond, a sacramental union that sanctifies passion. Both marriage and sexual love reveal a reality that reason alone could never ascertain.

The shortcomings, and even dangers, in this conception of sexual love are too glaring for us to ignore. Kant's argument is entirely predicated upon the assumption that in itself sexuality is nothing but an appetite for some other person. If this were so, one might agree with his belief in its inherent immorality. As a desire merely to possess, sexuality would just be a selfish attempt of one human being to use another, who is then "cast aside as one casts away a lemon which has been sucked dry." Kant's metaphor should, however, alert us to the likelihood that sexuality was not a cultivated or pervasive enjoyment for him. If it had been, he might have recognized that it cannot be thought of as *merely* or *wholly* appetitive. For though sexual interest resembles an appetite in some respects, it differs from hunger or thirst in being an *interpersonal* sensitivity, one that enables us to delight in the mind and character of other persons as well as in their flesh. Though at times people may be used as sexual objects and cast aside once their utility has been exhausted, this is no more definitive of sexual desire than its responsiveness to those bodily manifestations without which human beings could not be perceived as just the persons that they are. By awakening us to the living presence of someone else, sexuality can enable us to treat this other being as just the person he or she happens to be. Even where a man desires a woman for her sexuality alone, it would be erroneous to think that he cannot be responding to her as a person. For her personality reveals itself in the kind of sexual entity she is for him. In all areas of life, it can happen that people are treated as a means merely, but there is nothing in the nature of sexuality as such that necessarily brings that about or reduces persons to things. On the contrary, sex may be seen as an instinctual agency by which persons respond to one another *through* their bodies.

This aspect of sexuality, its ability to effect intimate communication among persons, is completely ignored by Kant. He sees sex only in its capacity to appropriate, and therefore he must cleanse it through an external principle that will "redeem" its immorality. If one considered sexual experience a continuum that ranges between the appetitive and the interpersonal, one would end up with a stronger—though a much less idealistic—defense of sexuality as well as marriage. Having no reason to denigrate the former or deny its frequent goodness, neither would we seek to glorify the latter or accord it so extravagant an idealization. Kant gives marriage an almost magical power to effect the desired "unity of will." One wonders why he assumes that a mere legality, albeit a mutual self-legislation and exchange of rights, can create a condition he deems tantamount to holiness, the love through sexuality of another person. Yet that is what his theory entails. From one extreme, his thinking has, one might say, romantically burst through to an opposite that is equally dubious. Beginning with unacceptable premises, he inevitably reaches insupportable conclusions.

Kant's initial distinction between love and sex is characteristic of the dualism that pervades his philosophy: duty is to be separated from inclination, just as the noumenal realm of ultimate but unknowable reality is different from the phenomenal world that nature presents and science investigates. The Romantic philosophers of the following generation in Germany—the later Fichte, Friedrich Schlegel, Schleiermacher, Schelling, and Hegel—sought various means of overcoming Kantian dualism. They affirmed the importance of human personality while also unifying it with the rest of life and with a cosmic spirituality that underlay the apparent materialism of nature. This idea of spirit was described in different ways throughout the nineteenth century, but it tended to serve the same function as the concept of God in the Middle Ages. It provided an absolute basis for knowledge, and as the totality of being it eventually came to be called the Absolute. Like the God of the Middle Ages, the Absolute was sometimes treated like an abstract principle and sometimes like a person whose spiritual properties resembled those of human beings at their best. Through a sense of oneness with this cosmic unity, man could hope to obtain the benefits of Western religion whether or not he still believed in the Bible.

Though German romanticism went through different phases and

its adherents disagreed about many points of doctrine, there is one book that incorporates most of the Romantic ideas on love that became prominent in the early nineteenth century. It is a quasi-novel entitled *Lucinde*, written by Friedrich Schlegel in 1799. In saying that it presents the new ideas that recur throughout German philosophy of the period, I do not mean to suggest that all or even most of the major thinkers agreed with its every detail. On the contrary, the book was immediately condemned as pornography, and throughout the nineteenth century it was often attacked as romanticism at its worst. In his essay on the Romantic school, Heine reviles the book as simply ridiculous; Kierkegaard rejected it for being immoral; Dilthey, towards the end of the century, considered it contemptible; and in his history of philosophy, Windelband dismisses it as "sensual though polished vulgarity." Twenty-four years after it was written, Schlegel omitted the work from his own edition of his complete writings. By then he had disavowed much of his earlier thinking, having converted to Catholicism and become a conservative diplomat in Metternich's Austria. Nevertheless, in this one little book, partly fictional and partly essayistic, one finds most of the ideas that belong to the concept of Romantic love as it was eventually formulated in Europe and America. Soon after the publication of *Lucinde*, Fichte hailed the book as a work of genius, and Schleiermacher published a collection of "confidential letters" to defend it from philosophical as well as theological attack. In the twentieth century its importance has been recognized by scholars who see it as the single most important expression of Romantic ideas about love, marriage, and sex.

It is one of the clichés of literary criticism to remark that *Lucinde* articulates a "religion of love." Julius, Schlegel's autobiographical protagonist, addresses Lucinde as a priestess and even a goddess. He appears as a devotee at her shrine, a miserable creature searching for the beatitude he can find only by loving her. The new religion involves two rituals, one that leads to purification through confession and another that attains spiritual consummation through sexual intercourse. There are dogmas within this religion and cosmic perspectives to which I shall presently return. From the very outset, however, one has to emphasize the fact that this is a radical religion, having little rapport with the varieties of Christian belief that preceded it. However one interprets the concept of love that dominates Rousseau's thinking, for example, the religion of love to which his fictional characters devote themselves always eventuates in a version of Christianity. The early Schlegel is quite different. In *Lucinde* human love becomes autonomous, religious within itself and no longer seeking for the sanction of any established creed.

While Schlegel clearly intended to separate love from the traditional religion, his book nevertheless had an influence upon Christian thinking that he could not have foreseen. This is largely due to Schleiermacher's defense of *Lucinde*. Schleiermacher maintained that Schlegel's ideas were not only consistent with Protestant theology, but also that they fulfilled its original intention. Schleiermacher praised the novel for showing how everything could be "human yet divine," and he formulated its message in two theses that seemed to him basic to that much of Christianity which men of the nineteenth century could still find acceptable:

"1. I believe in a divine humanity, which was before it assumed the form of man and woman.
2. I believe that I do not live to follow the will of another, nor for mere pleasure, but in order to be and to become; and I believe that, through the powers of my own will and my perfectability, I shall again come near to the infinite, shall free myself from the bonds of imperfection, and become freed from the limitations of sex."

The idea that love frees us from the limitations of sex sounds like something that could have been derived from Kantian philosophy. As a matter of fact, however, Schlegel and Schleiermacher were now going beyond the restrictions in Kant. In ways that duplicate the myth of Aristophanes in Plato's *Symposium* (which Schleiermacher translated into German), Schlegel returns to the notion of bisexual totality as the primordial form of human nature. The oneness between man and woman does not issue from a legal contract that overcomes the sinfulness of sex, but rather from sexual union and mutual enjoyment itself. Love is the culmination of physical oneness between inherently androgynous beings whose attunement eventuates in spiritual harmony. While Kant still belongs to the older types of Christianity inasmuch as he considers marriage to be a sacrament, both religious and contractual, that enables sex to attain legitimacy it could never achieve otherwise, Schlegel and Schleiermacher formulate a Romantic faith that interprets sexual appetite as part of man's striving for "divine humanity." This divinity results from the joyful, harmonious merging between men and women, whose being as free and autonomous persons completes itself by means of sexual love. Each is mirrored in the other, reflecting and acquiring one another's traits, and thereby fulfilling within themselves as well as through their union mankind's fundamental androgyny.

The revolutionary character of the new religion will be evident if we briefly compare it with the Lutheran doctrines from which Schlegel and Schleiermacher diverge. When Schlegel says that through love "human nature returns to its original state of divinity," he makes no allusion to a Godhead; but he does refer to the purity that Luther thought man possessed before the fall. Given the fall and the sinfulness it entails, Luther saw no way in which human nature could be redeemed through its own efforts. If, in his unfathomable grace, God descended as agapē and filled a man or woman with love, this was a miracle that no one could foresee and only God could effect. Once it happened, everything in human relations—including sexual pleasure—became worthy and even sanctified, but the married couple was only the funnel through which God bestowed his love upon the world and enabled mankind to love him in return.

If we extract the underlying structure from these Lutheran ideas, Schlegel's religion of love may well appear as a variation upon them. Now, however, the concept of love is being used for an un-Christian, even anti-Christian, philosophy that Luther would never have accepted. Though Schlegel is playing imaginatively with Protestant dogma, and though he uses the language of theology, his ideas are too humanistic and too naturalistic to be considered Lutheran. "In the solitary embrace of lovers," he says, "sensual pleasure becomes once more what it basically is—the holiest miracle of nature." This is far from anything Luther believed. The Lutheran idea of sex being sinful until it becomes redeemed through God's agapē is exactly what Schlegel wishes to attack: "What for others is only something about which they're justifiably ashamed becomes for us again what it is in and of itself: the pure flame of the noblest life force." Once he has eliminated Luther's conception of God, the only divinity that remains for Schlegel is love itself, sexual love both physical and spiritual, appetitive and interpersonal at the same time.

Though Schlegel begins with the beauty and holiness of the sexual embrace, he does not limit love to the relationship between the lovers. In his novel a new illumination occurs when Lucinde becomes pregnant, for now she and Julius are able to extend their oneness to include the next generation. And beyond the dimensions of the family, they see their sexual love as a unifying force that gives them a "citizenship" in nature. From having been depressed and demoralized in his earlier life, Julius finds himself capable of heroic deeds for the good of mankind. Feeling for the first time that he is at home on this earth, he intuits a oneness between himself and everything that lives in nature.

The most consecutive development of this Romantic idea that love enables a human being to attain oneness with all nature occurs in Schelling's *Naturphilosophie*. Schelling continues Spinoza's pantheistic belief that God is nature in its totality (natura naturans), but he enriches it by insisting that God is also a separate entity who expresses his being in creating and pervading all of nature. Divinity is thus the spirit of the One and the All, the omnipresent "Ein-und-Allheit." Though independent of the world, God creates himself by continuously infusing nature with his own being as love. Similarly, human beings merge with nature and overcome their alienation from it by means of love—not just a love of nature, but, to some degree, through love of any sort. By loving anything, they participate in "the world's holy, eternal creating primal energy, which engenders and actively brings forth all things out of itself." For nature is, as Schelling puts it, "drenched" with God's love.

Despite these continuities, however, Schlegel's concept of love lends itself to humanistic interpretation that Schelling avoids in his reliance upon religious and transcendental philosophy. Schlegel writes *Lucinde* to show how the ability to love all things results from a developmental growth within human nature itself. Before meeting Lucinde, Julius has sexual adventures that Schlegel never condemns. His failure to do so offended many critics in his society; but it is integral to Schlegel's ideas about love that the impulses of sex and even what he calls "unbridled lust" are not necessarily unwholesome. The novel is subtitled "Confessions of a Blunderer" because it takes Julius so long to discover the woman who enables him to merge sense and spirituality. When he finds her, however, none of his earlier libidinal interests are sacrificed or sublimated. Instead they are satisfied in a way and to a degree that he had never previously been able to approximate. Without them, he could not have reached his final oneness with nature.

Though Schlegel does not provide a formal definition of love, he describes it as a blending of three components: sensuous appetite, passionate longing, and friendship. In one place he also mentions "pleasant society," but it is unclear whether he means the society that is created by the friendship of the lovers or by the larger world beyond themselves that the lovers build up around them. By passion Schlegel means physical and spiritual intensity, what he calls "a feeling for warmth of every sort" which women have instinctively but men need to acquire. It is related to a capacity to undergo erotic sufferings ("Leidenschaft," the word he uses for passion, includes within itself the notion of suffering), and he thinks that nature has equipped women with superior capacity in this domain. For that reason, he believes there are in women no levels or stages of development comparable to what men experience in their attempt to transform the purely sexual into the heightened achievement that love entails. Women are driven by sensory impulse just as men are; but whether or not they have been initiated into sexual experience, women contain within themselves a prior conception of the goal that men must discover empirically. It sometimes happens, however, that middle-class women lose their native innocence with respect to the sensuous "and so purchase every pleasure with remorse." These are presumably those repressed though passionate ladies whose inability to open themselves to the sensuous Stendhal considered so lamentable, as we have seen, in the France that he knew thirty years later. Though they understand the passionate better than men, such women need more time to learn the goodness of the sensuous.

Schlegel sees nature as having compensated men for their slowness in understanding the importance of love: it gives them a superior ability to experience friendship. Friendship presupposes fixed limits that a woman's passionate nature continually destroys. Women feel things too strongly and love too completely to be able to maintain the civilities that contribute to masculine friendship. Men can have with one another a kind of community, Schlegel thinks, that women will never tolerate with another woman or in relation to a man. Through the miracle of sexual love, however, the union between man and woman includes much of what men find in friendships among themselves. Not only do the lovers share comparable inclinations in their sensuous appetites and passionate yearnings, but also they achieve an equality of intellect and mutual respect that prevents either person from dominating completely.

The implications of Schlegel's ideas about friendship between man and woman are scarcely developed in *Lucinde*. On the one hand, he insists that it is absurd to think that a man and a woman can have a relationship that includes nothing but pure friendship; on the other hand, he recognizes that the element of friendship contributes to the spirituality of heterosexual love. Friendship itself he thinks of as either a moral condition that causes men to join together in a "great brotherhood of united heroes," or else as a bonding in which soulmates complement each other's personal attributes. The latter type of friendship goes beyond the needs of heroic action, or even action in general. In this relationship, the friends find that "all their thoughts and feelings grow companionable through the mutual stimulation and development of what is wholly in them." Far from depending upon aspirations of a practical sort, such "internal" friendship can be experienced only by "someone who has achieved complete inner composure and knows how to honor humbly the godlike quality of the other."

In giving this description of internal friendship, Schlegel is depicting an interpersonal ideal that all people can strive for in their relations with one another. Whether limited to nonsexual relations among men or including a heterosexual bond, as in the case of Julius and Lucinde, it involves a complementary appreciation of what is holiest in each person. Its character becomes clearer if we compare it with the Kantian ideas Schlegel must have had in mind. Kant thought of friendship as a condition in which self-love is superseded by a mutual concern about the welfare of the other. If friendship is perfect, each of the friends looks after the other's happiness, loving the other as he loves himself, and thereby restoring to himself the practical benefits he would have acquired through the self-love he has now sacrificed. In choosing mutual friendship, the participants give up some of the goods that self-love would have provided; but since they have a joint concern for each other's welfare, Kant sees them as experiencing a total restoration.

This way of balancing ethical values and selfish goods seems somewhat remote from Schlegel's belief in a mystical complementarity between godlike qualities. Kant does talk about a higher friendship in which "complete communion" can occur between two persons. But he characteristically thinks of it as a state of self-disclosure, a relationship of confidential intimacy that enables people to reveal many of their secrets and communicate their "whole self." There is no suggestion in Kant that even an ideal friendship, remote and unlikely as Kant recognizes it to be, could provide anything like the merging of personalities toward which Schlegel and the other Romantics aspire.

The traits that result from the merging of men and women in love, as Schlegel conceives of it, are also different from those that Kant described. Schlegel thinks that nature has endowed women with a temperamental passivity foreign to the dynamic activism of men. Unlike others who have insisted upon this type of distinction between the sexes, he thinks that woman's passivity is her source of strength. He associates it with vegetative aspects of nature that men fail to understand. The intuitive ability to love which he ascribes to women results from their greater kinship to the organic principle that underlies all creativity. In being passive, they know how to submit to nature and therefore can enjoy the virtues of idleness and quiescent love. By merging with them, men learn that striving and doing are less important than being, and masculine determination less valuable than feminine self-abnegation. Restless activity, which Schlegel calls "nordic barbarity," changes through the process of loving into "the sacred tranquility of true passivity." In words that none of the eighteenth-century philosophers would have fully appreciated, with the possible exception of Rousseau, Schlegel claims that "the more divine a man or a work of man is, the more it resembles a plant; of all the forms of nature, this form is the most moral and the most beautiful. And so the highest, most perfect mode of life would actually be nothing more than pure vegetating."

There is in all romanticism a restless, driven element that would seem to run counter to this emphasis upon passivity. Even Schlegel, as we have seen, finds a place for heroism in both friendship and sexual love. But the activism that characterizes many Romantics has in it a motive similar to the one that Schlegel is here emphasizing. It is one thing to act prudentially, in a rational and purposive manner, taking steps that lead to some practical goal; but our attitude is not the same if in taking action we give ourselves to impulses beyond our control. In the latter disposition, which romanticism often encouraged, man attains a kind of passivity with respect to natural forces that determine behavior and lie hidden beyond the reach of reason. In the Romantic concept of love, this kind of passivity becomes idealized to a degree that previously had never been attempted. What established the value of loving another person was more than just a reasoned harmony between male and female, or any sensible and enlightened arrangement of mutual advantages, but rather the ability to experience organic growth. And that required a willing duplication in oneself of the passivity in vegetative processes. The governing image of Romantic love such as Schlegel's is the reed or strand of kelp forever bending in response to ocean waves, to currents that create its natural and developmental rhythm.

Since he thinks that women have an intuitive understanding of love, it is not surprising that Schlegel should identify them with the vegetative principle from which men have become alienated prior to learning how to love. In taking this view, Schlegel is of course renewing the long tradition that considers nature and growth itself as inherently feminine. Within these primordial ways of thinking, women are also identified with nighttime. As a blurring of the clarity of consciousness, passion is easily associated with things of darkness. And as the moon was often thought to be a goddess, so too does Schlegel's Julius address Lucinde as the "priestess of the night." As if by magic, the values of the Enlightenment have now been eclipsed. In Mozart's *Magic Flute*, written scarcely ten years earlier than *Lucinde*, the Queen of the Night is willful, irrational, and evil. She signifies the destructiveness of sex, and her coloratura music expresses a kind of insanity to which passion may lead. The opera ends with the forces of Day annihilating the cohorts of the Night who had sought to invade Sarastro's holy Temple of Reason. Now, however, nighttime is seen as the occasion for a love that originates in passion and goes on to spiritual attainments that could never have been achieved through a faculty, such as reason, that purports to exist independently of passion. In the darkness of the night, as in the molten intensity of sexual intimacy, entities merge with one another, objects lose their distinctness, individuals no longer sense a difference between what they are and what they want, opposites fuse into a new combination of disparate elements, and all this occurs through feelings rather than clear and distinct ideas. For Schlegel and the Romantics in general, the goodness of life consists in the ability to give oneself to these possibilities.

About the same time that Schlegel was writing *Lucinde*, Novalis was composing the six *Hymns to the Night* that I shall discuss in the following chapter. Novalis writes his poems as a way of communing with his dead beloved beyond the grave. He finds that she remains alive to him only in the night; for only then can he attain a spiritual, though also passionate, love. In the day, reason and sensory interests enable man to act purposively within the empirical world, and Novalis himself devoted much of his productive life to administrative duties that he offered mankind during his daytime existence. But ultimate goodness he could apprehend only through the experiences of the night. Only they put him in contact with the woman he had loved and lost.

In being a goddess of the night, the woman one loves in this fashion is, for Schlegel as well as Novalis, a divinity who survives the mortal limitations of human nature. Through her, death is defeated, and she herself symbolizes the idea that death can be a consummation of life rather than its disappearance. In loving her, the man thus finds oneness not only with this particular woman but also with the spirituality that underlies all being. In Schlegel and Novalis, we already encounter the concept of love-death that Richard Wagner was to develop in his own way some fifty years later. As we shall see, Wagner's treatment of this theme embodies elements of pessimism and despair that descended upon German romanticism in its final phases. In Schlegel and Novalis, the prevailing concept of Romantic love is still fresh and buoyant. They identify love with an endless yearning, but they find peace in the fact of yearning itself. They have in them hardly any sense of nihilism or desperation; and though they realize that the mundane world will never understand the sexual love of their protagonists, they describe the alliance between love and death in language that seems wildly optimistic. Of his mystical marriage to Lucinde, Julius says that it is "the timeless union and conjunction of our spirits, not simply for what we call this world or the world beyond death, but for the one, true, indivisible, nameless, unending world, for our whole eternal life and being." On the basis of this assurance, he claims that if he thought the time had come he would drink a cup of poison with Lucinde "as gladly and easily" as a glass of champagne taken in pursuit of mutual pleasure. This is not a love of death per se; but the course of history was soon to change it into one.

Before we study that development, however, we must first consider some of the other varieties of benign and optimistic romanticism. In Hegel's philosophy they are bound together in a doctrine that dominated some of the most productive thinking of the nineteenth century.

It is sometimes said that Hegel's philosophy stands as a synthesis of Kant and Romantics like Schlegel. Hegel himself thought in these terms; in fact he believed in an evolutionary development that linked the ideas of his predecessors directly to his own. He was right to the extent that one cannot understand Hegel's achievement apart from the thinking of various German philosophers—Schiller, Fichte, Schelling, and others—who sought to go beyond Kant and the Romantics while taking ideas from both.

Schiller, for instance, was one of the first to be troubled by Kant's implicit belief in original sin, by his dualistic approach to ethics, and by his legalistic attitude toward love. In the *Critique of Practical Reason*, Kant had insisted that morality required one to act not merely in accordance with duty but also from a sense of duty alone, regardless of one's inclinations and independently of them. The morality of actions would be found, he said, "in their necessitation *from duty* and from respect for the law, not from love and sympathy for that which the actions should bring about." Kant held this view because he believed that morality derived from nothing but rationality alone; and he was criticizing philosophers like Shaftesbury and Hume who thought it was only the innate sympathy between one human being and another that accounted for the possibility of moral behavior.

Schiller felt the need to overcome this Kantian dualism between reason and inclination. In the *Aesthetic Education of Man* he depicted a society in which the two would be so harmoniously attuned to one another that morality could not be defined by either apart from the other. The harmonization of reason and impulse was basic to all of Schiller's thinking, at least as an indication of how man ought to live. But Schiller also recognized that the moral synthesis between sense and rationality, between one's drives and a reasoned estimate of how to satisfy them, might be only a utopian aspiration forever exceeding the capabilities of human nature. His dramas as well as his philosophic writing bristle with the refusal to accept any facile assurance that harmony was a realistic expectation. In this respect Schiller differed from both Goethe and Schlegel, who felt that a well-ordered life would inevitably lead to reconciliation between the different aspects of man's nature. Hegel agrees with this latter, more optimistic, view, which he seeks to defend by constructing a philosophical doctrine that answers Schiller's doubts from within its own dimensions.

As a way of seeing this, we must remember that Kant too had felt that somehow, somewhere, the divergent faculties of man must be reconciled. He believed that a selfless dedication to duty would be rewarded even though morality itself did not depend upon such rewards. Since adherence to moral law would not necessarily, or often, lead to the satisfaction of inclinations in the natural world, Kant thought one must assume the existence of a deity who rewards the virtuous with happiness in an afterlife. This blessed state of transcendent consummation could never be established by reason, however, and therefore it was something that man had to posit through an act of faith and unverifiable feeling. But this means that Kant, like Schiller, must always entertain the real possibility that harmonization between sense and reason might not occur. However much he may claim that the moral life presupposes a oneness in principle, Kant's philosophy continues to suffer from its initial dualism. Reason indicates the nature of morality; sense craves a happiness that the moral life need not afford; faith unites the two but only in a surge of "rational" feeling that may be delusory and absurd—an affirmation supported by what could well be nothing but wish-fulfillment.

Hegel's solution to this problem is simple: eliminate the dualistic approach and the Kantian difficulties disappear. The ethical life, which includes the ability to love, Hegel interprets as neither inclination nor reason separated from one another but rather the two as a fundamental unity. In no other way could he account for man's dedication to duty on earth, or anywhere else. The rewards of virtue were not transcendent goods to be obtained in another life, but rather they were built into the fabric of morality as its exists in the actual world.

Hegel could make this claim because his philosophy enabled him to eradicate other dualistic doctrines that Kant and his followers had always presupposed. With a pantheistic faith that went beyond anything earlier Romantics had dared to affirm, Hegel denied that it made any sense to speak of a God who was not present in nature itself. Since the God (or absolute spirit) Hegel believed in was pure goodness like the Christian God, the divine being would exclude the possibility of ultimate evil in the world or original sin in man. At its basic level, reality would therefore accommodate the human desire for happiness while also supporting the demands of conscience and duty. The ethical life was grounded in man's condition here on earth, and vice versa. The empirical self that craved the satisfaction of its egocentric desires at the expense of society failed to realize that what it really wanted was oneness with other persons within a moral community. No one can exist as a human being apart from the social group in which he finds his true identity, and therefore what one truly wants cannot conflict with one's ethical nature. Duty toward the group determines the configurations of personal happiness; apart from morality as reason reveals it, the idea of happiness makes no sense at all. Dualism was thus impossible.

While answering the doubts of Kant and Schiller in this fashion, Hegel also leads Fichte's philosophy into a stage beyond itself. Kant had maintained that nothing was good other than a good will, that the goodness of a good will consisted in its absolute freedom, and that freedom involved self-legislation in accordance with the ethical demands that arose from the nature of mere rationality. Starting with this, Fichte had concluded that the need for a good will would explain the being of everything that constitutes the world for man. What man perceived as a physical object and what he sought as a goal of appetite was already a product of his ethical being. He needed the material world as an external inducement to moral behavior; it existed for man as that which provides obstacles his will could overcome for the sake of establishing the goodness of freedom itself. In its later development, Fichte's philosophy came to treat striving alone as the fundamental principle of human nature: man manifests his spiritual being by the fact that he is one who strives, and he approximates the potentialities of spirit only as long as he continues to do so.

This emphasis upon action had been present in German philosophy for many years. In Fichte it becomes the basis for a new conception of love. As far back as Plato, philosophers and theologians had defined human nature as a constant striving; but they always insisted that it was a striving for a good beyond and prior to the act of striving. Whether this objective was God or the Good, its being transcended the world of experience. In Fichte the two worlds coalesce, and striving loses all awareness of an independent goal.

Ethical behavior, and the nature of love, was now perceived as a search without a goal, a yearning for the unknown. To appreciate the goodness of life and the fullness of love, one had only to give oneself to the joys of striving, overcoming external opposition freely and through a spontaneity of will. God was in the world, but not as either the origin or the terminus of love. He was not the preexistent source of one's activism but rather the holiness and spiritual goodness in it.

In its final development, Fichtean philosophy reverts to Christianity, claiming that "the blessed life" eventuates in passivity, even deterministic submission, as the divine spirit destroys the independence of the human will. That was the end of love, a culmination that took one beyond the empirical world. Prior to this supernatural occurrence, however, man could experience the goodness of God's loving nature only through acts of freedom while seeking to establish the divine kingdom on earth. For God was always present in the striving itself.

These ideas about action and about love reappear in Hegel's philosophy. Not only was man a social creature in the sense that the good of others was presupposed by his own self-love, but also his entire history could be explained as a constant search for goals that emanated from an ontological need to struggle. Man strove as a way of surmounting obstacles that existed in order to reveal his own being to himself. In its ultimate condition, his being was free and therefore his history revealed the stages in his own development through which his essential freedom manifested itself. His struggling had no goal other than the awareness or recognition of what its nature was.

Hegel calls this achievement "Bewusstsein," which is usually translated as "self-consciousness." We may retain that as an English equivalent, but actually Hegel means something closer to self-knowledge, self-awareness, or self-comprehension. Far from implying anxiety, concern, or doubt about oneself, Bewusstsein refers to a total understanding of what it is to be conscious, and of all the ramifications present in one's conscious being. Spirit is defined as self-consciousness only in this sense, and absolute spirit—the maximum in conscious awareness—is therefore the ideal of all human endeavor. God remains as that for which all men strive; but now he is wholly present in the world, revealing himself as the evolution of consciousness seeking to attain the fullest self-awareness. Fichte had frequently spoken about striving taking the form of thesis, antithesis, and a synthesis that then becomes the thesis for a new antithesis. Hegel rarely uses this terminology, despite popular misconceptions, but he works out a similar dialectic by which the striving in everything could manifest an orderly and integrated progression. Through its stages of self-consciousness the Absolute comes into being, realizing itself in the world and through the passage of time.

Hegel devoted a great many pages to showing that human history evolves in accordance with this necessity of spirit. He also thought, however, that there was no dualism, whether Platonic or Cartesian, that could separate consciousness from matter or man from the rest of nature. Into his synthesizing philosophy he introduced many of the ideas of Schelling and other philosophers who formalized Romantic notions about the oneness of all nature. By arguing that spirit was always present in nature, indeed striving to express itself through natural events, Schelling thought he had defeated the idea of separation between the self and its environment. They were in some sense interanimated, organically related. Both were part of the struggle by which spirit could reach its self-knowledge at the level of human consciousness. Man and the rest of nature were thus essentially one, explicable in terms of the same principles that enabled the latter to evolve into the former. The whole of nature led up to man, and man at his highest expressed the spiritual striving that activated everything in nature.

This aspect of nature-philosophy, which Schelling inherited from German Romantic poets such as Hölderlin and which found its way into the thinking of English Romantics such as Coleridge and Wordsworth, was taken over by Hegel in a modified form. In asserting the oneness in everything, Schelling had begun with the idea of a prior and ultimate Being that he called "absolute indifference." Like the Godhead in the negative theology of the Middle Ages, the Indifferent could not be characterized in any particular way. For that would limit its infinite and indefinable being. Spirit progressed by differentiating out of the Indifferent, thereby creating opposites that dynamically generated everything that evolved in the realms of mind and matter. The Indifferent itself remained unknowable and beyond all characterization; and that is what Hegel rejected. For him the Absolute would have to show itself in the process of generation and differentiation. The spirit in man must be linked to the spirit in nature, and both must show forth the absolute spirit that was the evolutionary being of everything; but apart from this process, it would make no sense to talk about any ultimate that could explain the nature of reality. Hegel said that Schelling's Indifferent was the night in which all cows were black. For Hegel the ground of being would have to be that which manifested itself by rising through nature and reaching Bewusstsein in the kind of self-knowledge that human reason best exemplified.

To account for the progression from the Indifferent into the world we know, Schelling suggested that it was required by the nature of love. For without division, there could not be reunion; and without a oneness that comes from reuniting separated beings, there could not be love. For Schelling, then, as for the other Romantics, and of course the long Platonic and Christian tradition that preceded them, love turns out to be the basic and primordial category of being.

Hegel's philosophy maintains something similar, though love at work within the world is what he believes in rather than love as the emanation from a prior Indifferent. In the final pages of *The Phenomenology of Mind* Hegel aligns himself with revealed religion which claims it is God's self-love that accounts for the existence of everything. As the Christian God descends into the world in an outpouring of love and then returns to himself as the only object worthy of love, so too does the Hegelian Absolute infuse its spiritual being into all particulars and then progressively return to itself through the evolutionary growth of self-knowledge.

This formal pattern, which recurs as a linking thread through most of Hegel's writings, is explicitly articulated in an early fragment entitled "Love." As a principle applying to all reality, love is there described as a process that occurs in three stages: unity, separation of opposites, reunion. Whether it is the relationship between being and becoming or parents and their child, Hegel says, everything begins with a unity which then separates into opposing elements that are finally reconciled in a loving totality that restores the original oneness. Love is the model for all reality because reality, like love, is reciprocal, communal, and dialectical in its need to overcome separateness through an expanding process of seeking oneness. Hegel calls the stage of separation "alienation," and he thinks of love as a cosmic principle that systematically eliminates alienation of every sort. Through love, isolated individuals overcome their alienation by giving themselves completely to the new union they jointly create by means of love alone. Hegel insists this union will be a "complete surrender" if love is actually present. If there is a "still subsisting independence," the union feels itself to be incomplete. When love is wholly realized, each participant finds himself in the process of giving himself to the new totality. For then he has contributed to the ongoing development. He surmounts his sense of alienation by seeing himself as merely an organ in a larger, living whole. "In love," Hegel tells us, "the separate does still remain, but as something united and no longer as something separate; life [in the subject] senses life [in the object]."

Hegel's closest friend in early life had been Hölderlin, who speaks of the dissonances of the world as similar to a lover's quarrel, since "reconciliation is in the midst of strife and all that is divided becomes united again." This emphasis upon struggle leading to ultimate harmony, division eventuating in a more fundamental union whose significance could not be appreciated apart from its ability to destroy divisiveness, characterizes the many stages through which Hegel's thinking progressed. It reveals the importance in all his philosophy of these ideas about love, and the reason why he thought that love was a symbol or analogy of being itself. Though Hegel's works, voluminous as they are, contain relatively few words about the ideas he had presented in the essay "Love," the lectures on aesthetics that were given late in life and published only posthumously show his thoughts on the matter quite fully. The basic approach is fairly similar in both places, and it is safe to assume that whatever changes may have occurred throughout Hegel's career as a philosopher, he did not greatly alter his youthful theories about love.

The early fragment belonged to the period in which Hegel first wished to supplant Kantian ethics with ideas about a concern for other persons that would harmonize reason and sentiment in such a way that the life of virtue would not exist at the expense of happiness or instinctual gratification. This harmonization occurs, Hegel says, when people respond to one another with love rather than an abstract sense of obligation. That was the message of Jesus, and Hegel interprets what he calls "the spirit of Christianity" as the capacity to effect the oneness of true morality by means of love. In his later thinking, Hegel's Christianity yielded to the abstract theology of his ideas about the Absolute, to a rationalistic doctrine that may be modeled upon the earlier theology but is not as clearly Christian. Hegel's early concept of love nevertheless remains constant. As in Kant, the point of departure is always the idea that lovers give themselves to one another in a mutual exchange that establishes a union through which each gets back what has been given to the other. To this, however, Hegel adds an ontology of love, an analysis of its being, which takes him far beyond Kant.

To begin with, he maintains that true love exists only between equals. There can be no love between masters and slaves, or in sexual relations that enable one person to assert dominance over the other. Being alike in power, each of the lovers sees the other as a manifestation of life itself. As Hegel says, "In no respect is either dead for the other," preparing us for his final epigrammatic statement about love: it is the condition in which "life senses life." Through love, that which constitutes the totality of life in one person senses the living totality in another, and what results from their union is a totality that Hegel considers greater than its elements. He thinks of all reality as conflict between opposites, but in love opposition is defeated by the supervening oneness that binds the individuals within it. He distinguishes love from both *Verstand* and *Vernunft*, the two aspects of rationality that Kant had analyzed, inasmuch as love involves the *sensing* of life and is therefore feeling. It is not a specific or "isolated" feeling, but rather a feeling for the totality of another living being. This other being, whether a man or a woman, or nature itself, ceases to exist as something from which one feels alienated, something whose properties can be set in opposition to one's own, something foreign to the life one perceives in oneself, or something one would be able to treat as merely an object. Instead, the lover and what is loved become "a living whole."

This ontology of love may seem hopelessly abstract, but it enables Hegel to formulate substantive notions about various other conditions. For instance, it allows him to regard death as the separateness that lovers transcend through their inner oneness. Since lovers constitute a living whole, he says, there is no materiality in their being as lovers. Their separability from one another means only that, as different individuals, they can and will die some day. But love includes the idea of immortality within itself inasmuch as love strives to nullify death through the destruction of separability. In his *Lectures on the Philosophy of Religion*, written much later than the fragment on love we are here discussing, not only is love seen as a striving to overcome death, but also death is seen as the revelation of absolute love. Through death one finally relinquishes one's separate being, one's narrow and mortal constitution, in order to achieve a more perfect union with the spiritual order that Hegel considers fundamental in the cosmos. Through death, Hegel says, God "reconciles" the world with his own being. In this respect, "death is love itself."

It is through a similar approach, in the early essay, that Hegel reaches his new and daring conception about the nature of shame. He insists that shame cannot be seen as an attempt to protect the privacy of one's body or personality, since the lover's real fear is that he is withholding himself. The pure heart is thus ashamed if it has failed to give itself completely, if it has retained its separateness instead of negating it in the total union of love. Through love a human being transcends the feeling of shame as well as the fear of death. The reference to the infinite bounty of Juliet's love, in *Romeo and Juliet*, Hegel interprets as meaning that "the more the lover gives, the more he has, since the new totality his love effects will now exceed any richness that a mere individual could possess." He then explains this as follows: "What in the first instance is most the individual's own is united into the whole in the lovers' touch and contact; consciousness of a separate self disappears, and all distinction between the lovers is annulled."

What Hegel means by saying that love annuls all distinction be- tween the lovers is not at all clear, even though similar remarks recur in his later writings about the nature of love. In the book on aes- thetics, for instance, his section on "the concept of love" includes the following lines about the lover's phenomenology: "I penetrate the consciousness of another as this individual I was, am, and will be, and constitute the other's real willing and knowing, striving and possessing. In that event this other lives only in me, just as I am present to myself only in her; in this accomplished unity both are self-aware for the first time and they place their whole soul and world in this identity." But elsewhere Hegel insists that the elements in the higher unity of love do *not* lose their identity, that they continue to interact as separable individuals, and even that their union is a function of their dynamic interaction as different persons. In that place in the early fragment on love where he speaks of life sensing life, Hegel explicitly tells us that "in love the separate does still remain"; but he immediately adds that it continues to exist as "something united and no longer as something separate."

If Hegel distinguished between the lover's feeling and the reality of the lover's condition, perhaps the difficulty could be avoided. For one could then say that the lover himself senses no separation from his beloved, although in reality they are always separable as distinct individuals. This, however, is not what Hegel believes. On the con- trary, he wishes to assert that the oneness lovers feel is indeed their true reality. Through it they become self-aware for the first time and consequently transcend the metaphysical alienation that prevented them from being in touch with their ultimate being. The same applies to the universe as a whole, to all reality. The Absolute is simply the totality of all being, considered *as* totality. Hegelian reconciliation must occur by means of strife, division, separation; but in itself reconciliation would seem to be a state in which all distinctions are finally annulled. Though Hegel had criticized Schelling's "philosophy of identity" because it failed to recognize the way in which unity presupposes and even incorporates division, he himself leaves us with no clear conception of how love can be a merging rather than a wedding of disparate elements.

Hegel stands on more secure ground when he approaches the oneness of love as the product of a dialectical movement through time. The earlier separateness of lovers having yielded to the consummatory union of love itself, their oneness issues into a new creation of life—a living child, which Hegel depicts as a "seed of immortality" since it perpetuates the "eternally self-developing and self-generating" species. The child therefore originates in the parents' unity; but since it continues the self-development of the species, its growth as a mature individual consists in stages of separation that force it to oppose itself to the oneness from which it arose. In doing so, the child is motivated by a desire to attain for itself a further union of the sort that the parents enjoyed. Though this union involves another person, and dialectically propels the species beyond the level of development at which the parents existed, it enables the child to return symbolically to the original state of unity. Thus, as we have seen, the process is always "unity, separated opposites, reunion."

The basis of this conception is obviously organic and possibly anthropomorphic. But that is precisely what Hegel intends. As he sees it, reality can be understood only as a developmental process that begins with unity, dynamically issues into strife or opposition, and then attains a higher oneness that will itself be transcended in the course of time. In its fundamental structure, love is the principle that underlies all being. Nevertheless, Hegel does very little to show how this schematic ontology explains the lives of people who love one another. He frequently talks about organic wholes and the harmony of opposites—what in the Middle Ages would have been called *coincidentia oppositorum*—but he rarely returns to an analysis of the concept of love.

In the lectures on aesthetics, however, Hegel finds that his ideas about "romantic art" would be incomplete without further reference to love. He contrasts it with honor and fidelity. He approaches all three in terms of feelings through which an individual attains knowledge of himself by having his "infinity" as a person recognized and accepted in another human being. Honor makes the attempt through a sense of social distinction; fidelity through devotion to someone higher in rank. Only love enables two individuals to recognize the infinity of themselves as *persons*. This happens through the mutual surrender to one another of their separate and differing types of consciousness, each being a person of the opposite sex. While honor and fidelity are based upon social and intellectual considerations, love originates in feeling. At the same time, Hegel immediately asserts, love involves a *totalistic* feeling that pertains to "spiritualized nature." It is a natural phenomenon inasmuch as it is a relationship between the sexes, but also spiritual since it is the means by which a person finds the roots of his being through that other subjectivity in which he loses all consciousness of his independent self and to which he devotes his entire life in a "splendour of disinterestedness."

Hegel introduces this discussion into his lectures about Romantic art because he claims that classical art, and the ancient world in general, had no conception of a spiritual love between the sexes that would show lovers becoming aware of themselves as infinite persons through acts of mutual self-surrender. Though he does not say so in the lectures on aesthetics, he undoubtedly thought that his idealistic conception of love originated with Christianity. He contrasts Greek tragedy, where he finds no examples of love in the sense he has described, with the erotic idealizations of Petrarch, Dante, and German love poetry in the Middle Ages. In the latter he finds the beginnings of Romantic art, for only there does love appear as the means by which an individual realizes his infinity as a person through submission to the infinity of a person of the opposite sex.

Although he discerns this spiritual significance in sexual and romantic love, Hegel insists upon the need to go beyond it. He calls romantic love a "secular religion" that can justify itself only through the irrationality of subjective passion. He finds it tyrannical in its attempt to sacrifice all other interests to its own imperious demands. Because it ignores, even denies, the objective necessities of social and political life, it is incapable of satisfying the totality of human nature. Consequently, it fails to attain what Hegel calls "absolute universality." Being only the personal feeling of an individual subject, romantic love inevitably conflicts not only with ideals—such as honor—that share its striving for infinity, but also with the requirements of family, marriage, duty, the state, and religion of the traditional sort.

In romantic love, Hegel says, "everything turns on the fact that *this* man loves precisely *this* woman, and she him. The sole reason why it is just this man or this individual woman alone is grounded in the person's own private character, in the contingency of caprice." Later on, he characterizes this contingent and essentially subjective predilection in love between the sexes as "an endless caprice of fate . . . an idiosyncracy and a pertinacity of personal caprice." While Hegel admits that the human heart longs for romantic love and that everyone has a "right" to the happiness it can provide, he refuses to believe there is any objective justification for the exclusiveness by which its infinite idealism chooses just one or another person as its object. If more universal considerations, those related to the needs of the family or of society at large, prevent the lover from getting just the woman he has taken a fancy to, that may be unfortunate but according to Hegel "no wrong has occurred."

This insistence upon the limitations of love between the sexes gives credibility to the assertion by many commentators that the mature Hegel differed radically from those poets and philosophers of romanticism who influenced him in his youth. By the time he wrote the *Phenomenology of Mind* in his middle years, Hegel had already concluded that sexual passion could not provide the final self-awareness that it sought. In a way that is congruent with the remarks in his lectures on aesthetics, the *Phenomenology of Mind* deals with sexual love as a development in human consciousness which must be superseded by affective bonds that provide organic unities of a different sort. Within the family, for instance, Hegel finds basic contradictions between the relationships of husband-wife, parent-child, and brother-sister. Precisely because it is "natural," i.e. founded upon sexual and reproductive realities, the relation between husband and wife ranks as a lower development of the spirit than the other two. Marital union being the ethical goal of romantic love, it enables one consciousness to recognize itself in another. To that extent, it reveals the dynamic search of absolute spirit seeking to attain knowledge about itself. But since this kind of self-knowledge is predicated upon natural necessities rather than the ethical life alone, it is not a *realization* of the spirit. Within the hierarchical order that governs Hegel's phenomenological cosmos, sexual and marital union must find its ultimate being in something other than itself. Its fulfillment as a spiritual entity occurs only in the child that arises out of it.

The relation between parents and children, however, is also incomplete. Regardless of how greatly devoted parents and children may be towards one another, their oneness is contaminated by an element of nature that diminishes its spiritual content. For though he refuses to admit any sharp demarcation between nature and spirit, or feeling and reason, Hegel insists that the Absolute struggles towards its spiritual and purely rational self-awareness by overcoming all feelings and emotions that mere nature generates. Consequently, the natural ties that underlie a love between parents and children prevent their relationship—like the bond between husband and wife—from being purely or thoroughly spiritual.

Within the family, Hegel detects a higher type of love in the unity of brother and sister. Belonging to different sexes, each sibling represents a different aspect of humanity as well as a different element in the ethical life of man; and yet the two are not bound by any natural emotions. Unlike husband and wife, they are not motivated by sexual desire, nor have they surrendered the independence of their infinite personalities to one another. They retain their freedom, Hegel says, and can treat each other with a purity of impulse based upon the recognition that theirs is a moral oneness rather than a relationship that involves organic needs. Theirs is the highest love that can be attained within the family.

But the family is just an element within society, and therefore it cannot be fully realized within itself. Spirit finds a higher totality in the bonds that unify the community at large: the nation, the state, the Volk. Particularly in the twentieth century, Hegel has been much criticized for what appears to be an idealization of the state at the expense of the rights of individuals. Though recently some scholars have attempted to defend him against the charge of statism or crude totalitarianism, no one can deny that his philosophy lends itself to various interpretations. But throughout his diverse statements about political entities, there remains a pervasive search for conditions that create communal oneness and the love of one's society. In this respect, his approach is similar to Rousseau's. And like Rousseau, he thinks of each unity within the state as an affective link to religious love, in his case the love that manifests the highest and furthest reaches of the Absolute striving for a purely spiritual knowledge of itself.

This concept of religious love as the archetype and fountainhead for which all other loves must be sacrificed, transcended, and finally superseded was—as I have been suggesting—present in Hegel's thinking from the start. It serves as a continuous theme not only in the long and tortuous trajectory of his philosophical development, but also in Hegel's derivation out of his Protestant origins. His indebtedness to Luther seems particularly noteworthy. For Luther too had been struck by the fact of alienation in man's primordial state. He interpreted this as original sin preventing human nature from attaining the oneness with God that all men desire and that earlier Christian doctrines promised as the beatific reward for religious conduct. Though he denied that man could do anything to reach his theological goal, Luther insisted that God's agapē would create, through its constant stream of love, sanctified communities on earth. In Hegel, too, the major emphasis in his philosophy falls upon the immanent presence of divine love within the world. Despite his desire to resuscitate Christianity, to make it acceptable to the nineteenth century, one may question whether the mature Hegel is a Christian in any sense that Luther would have recognized. Luther could well have condemned Hegel's ideas about the Absolute as Pelagianism or pantheistic heresy. But this detail—relevant as it is—seems to me less important than the fact that Hegel follows Luther's lead by claiming that only in relation to the world itself, only in man's imperfect struggle to overcome his basic alienation, can human beings begin to understand how divinity may be present to us all.

In other ways too, Hegel resembles Luther. For all their concern about the individual soul seeking to find unity through action, they both have little sympathy with anyone's refusal to submit to institutional demands. As married love includes but also transcends sexual love, so too does Hegel insist that matrimony becomes trivialized if one thinks of it as a mechanism for gratifying personal needs. Through marriage individuals may legitimately satisfy their sexual interests, but marriage as an institution is an embodiment of universal reason and this takes priority over inclinations of the individuals who participate in it. In his *Philosophy of Right*, Hegel argues that far from being a civil contract that might be dissolved by agreement among the parties, marriage is an ethical entity that the state must preserve whenever possible. Though divorce may be permitted under special circumstances, it is not to be given simply because a married couple no longer find their union satisfying. The institution has a higher function than the maintenance of individual happiness. Matrimony is a stage within the hierarchy of spirit that manifests the Godhead. One cannot dissolve it for reasons of personal welfare.

It is this continuity with pietistic Protestantism that Karl Marx attacks in his *Critique of Hegel's Philosophy of Right*. Marx points out that, regardless of the theological veneer, Hegel's ideas perpetuate the bourgeois status quo in which the family unit systematically represses an individual's efforts to overcome his sense of alienation. Far from bringing about a universal love, the Hegelian doctrine could only bolster conventional, i.e., reactionary attitudes toward the possession of material goods. Marx makes this criticism with Hegel as his target, but there is nothing in it that would not have applied to Luther as well.

Despite these similarities, Hegel and Luther are temperamentally not alike. Though they are both muscular activists who nevertheless doubt the spiritual strength of mere individuals, or even their ultimate value, they themselves are psychologically different types of men. In all his writings, Luther shows himself to be one who is certain that nothing human beings do can alter their inherent sinfulness. When Luther feels at home within the world, that alone convinces him of how far he has fallen from grace by accommodating himself to material nature. In Hegel, however, one finds perpetual buoyancy throughout his attitude toward nature and the world, and above all toward man's active role in each. In one place he speaks about the "guilt of guiltlessness." He uses the phrase to condemn the "beautiful soul" that withdraws from the world in order to remain pure but thereby commits the greater sin of isolation and futility. As the Romantics continually assert, man cannot escape his endless need to strive for perfection. Hegel sees the suffering in this, but he also affirms that it can be remedied by accepting the rationality of man's condition. All of history and all of human experience he considers a dynamic and therefore passionate struggle for ideals that may be unattainable and even in opposition to one another, but—through the struggle itself—capable of leading on to higher syntheses.

For Luther as well as Hegel, life is fundamentally tragic. They differ, however, in their conception of tragedy. In his *Aesthetics*, Hegel defines it as a deep conflict not between good and evil but between good and good. Though one of the goods must be destroyed, and eventually both, we become reconciled to this misfortune once we realize that the conflict is meaningful inasmuch as it belongs to a rational and benign process. Throughout each moment of agonized opposition, the Absolute is continuing its work of self-awareness, creating through its immanence within the world that love for itself which harmonizes and justifies all the elements of reality.

This basic trust and optimistic predilection motivates what Hegel called "the logic of passion" within his philosophy. It also explains his insistence upon impulse, and even impulsiveness, as the very life blood of all action: "Nothing great has been and nothing great can be accomplished without passion." In this respect, Hegel's roots go back to Platonism and to the mythological origins of Plato's thinking. The search for wholeness which Plato inherited from the pre-Socratics underlies everything in Hegel. Though he differs from Plato in denying that the Good can be thought of as a logically prior principle transcending the world in its totality, Hegel resembles him in seeing eros as a universal striving for the perpetual possession of goodness; and like Plato, he claims that all ideals are ultimately grounded in reason.

The differences between Hegel and Plato are enormous: in a sense they distinguish the modern world from the ancient and medieval. But throughout the differences, Hegel retains the Platonic belief in love as the force that drives all process and therefore all reality. Where Hegel, unlike Schlegel and many of the other Romantics, refuses to consider each type of love as an extension and culmination of sexual love, which he wishes to subjugate for the sake of a more spiritual oneness that will impose its own demands upon it, there too he is following Plato. Both Hegel and Plato articulate a perspective rich in its complexity and subtle in its design but finally unacceptable to the humanist imagination. For in his own way, each of them creates idealizations that demean our sensory experience in order to glorify reason and spirituality. They both *deny* nature, seeking to move beyond it through dialectical philosophy instead of teaching us how to live within it and in joyful affirmation.

The conceptions of Romantic love that developed in the growth of German philosophy from Kant to Hegel permeated European culture in the early nineteenth century. Among the English Romantics the idealist approach reaches its highest and noblest expression in the thinking of Percy Bysshe Shelley. Neither Coleridge nor Wordsworth nor Keats nor Byron would have agreed with everything Shelley said about love, but throughout his writing he proclaims many of the ideas—particularly about love as merging—that these different men all presupposed. As I have suggested, the concept of merging is basic to much of Hegel's thinking. It is what links him most of all to the English Romantics. Josiah Royce saw this connection very clearly. Discussing Hegel's belief in the organic interpenetration of all moments of consciousness, Royce remarks that it is what Shelley means when he speaks in *Prometheus Unbound* of:

> . . . one harmonious soul of many a soul,
> Whose nature is its own divine control,
> Where all things flow to all, as rivers to the sea;

And Royce could well have added the next line, which is equally Hegelian: "Familiar acts are beautiful through love."

Shelley's ability to express the concept of universal merging in vivid and compelling poetry strikes me as possibly his greatest creative achievement. In a famous essay, T.S. Eliot foolishly condemned Shelley's ideas as not only "repellent" but also "so puerile that I cannot enjoy the poems in which they occur." Eliot even uses words like "childish" and "adolescent" to characterize Shelley's poetry. If he was ascribing the fundamental theme in Shelley to the pre-adult stage of human development, Eliot may well have been right. It is quite likely that merging, as Shelley portrays it, is desired most strongly and most poignantly by young people; but in Shelley's poetry and prose it speaks, or rather sings, with the voice of mature and comprehensive genius. Even if the concept of merging is adolescent, the mentality that informs its expression in Shelley belongs to no one period of life but rather to the timelessness of aesthetic imagination.

Nevertheless, the idea of merging in Shelley is not pellucid, and even sympathetic critics have often disagreed in their interpretation of his erotic poetry. In the Victorian period his images of union were generally taken to signify "spiritual oneness." In more recent years various writers, not all of whom are Freudian, have insisted that the imagery becomes more meaningful once it is subsumed under the category of physical sexuality. For instance, consider the following lines from a lyric entitled "Love's Philosophy":

> The fountains mingle with the river
> And the rivers with the Ocean,
> The winds of Heaven melt together
> With a sweet emotion:
> Nothing in the world is single:
> All things by a law divine
> In one another's being mingle,
> Why not I with thine?

These lines are richly suggestive. They do not preclude the possibility that the mingling may be libidinal, but neither do they require it to be anything but spiritual. Those critics who have stressed the former interpretation feel that the plausibility of their reading is strengthened by the fact that the original publisher deleted a subsequent stanza which commended the lovers as they "sink to intermingle" among the violets in the deep woods. The same type of reasoning is also used for passages in *Epipsychidion* that include lines such as these:

> Our breath shall intermix, our bosoms bound,
> And our veins beat together; and our lips
> With other eloquence than words, eclipse
> The soul that burns between them, and the wells
> Which boil under our being's inmost cells,
> The fountains of our deepest life, shall be
> Confused in passion's golden purity
> As mountain-springs under the morning Sun.
> We shall become the same, we shall be one
> Spirit within two frames, oh! wherefore two?

These poems certainly depict circumstances in which love originates from sexual interest. But even within love that is sexual, Shelley never suggests that sex itself explains very much about the relationship. And when we turn to his essays about love, we also find that his thinking was too complex, too subtle, to warrant either of the alternatives that have been imposed upon him by most commentators.

The most daring of these essays is entitled "A Discourse on the Manners of the Ancient Greeks Relative to the Subject of Love." Shelley wrote it in 1818 as a preface to his translation of Plato's *Symposium*, which he calls *The Banquet*. A few years earlier Schleiermacher, some of whose thinking Shelley occasionally parallels, had translated this and other Platonic dialogues into German, and he too added an introduction. But neither in Schleiermacher nor in any other writer of that period does one encounter the kind of honest and explicit attempt to understand Greek ideas about love that one finds in Shelley's brief essay. None of it was published during his lifetime, and despite what he calls his "delicate caution" in writing about homosexuality, the complete text was published only in 1931. Even then it had to be "privately printed."

In this essay, Shelley is primarily concerned to prevent moral scruples from intruding upon the reader's appreciation of Plato. Within homosexuality he distinguishes between emotional attachments and the physical acts of a sexual sort that often accompany them. The latter Shelley considers unacceptable because they are not "according to nature." In ways that sound like Freud as well as many others, he speaks of an innate structure of sexuality such that homosexual acts violate "the indestructible laws of human nature." This of course is part of the traditional thinking about sex. The Marquis de Sade rejected it, but few others would have done so before the twentieth century. Having put himself on the side of the angels, however, Shelley than proceeds to speculate about the nature of sexual love with candor and originality.

For one thing, he denies that homosexual behavior among the Greeks was characteristically licentious in the way that it became under the Roman hegemony or in the age of Charles II. He thinks of the Greeks as men whose affection for other men admitted few of the excesses that appeal to less refined peoples. Shelley does not deny that Greek love may sometimes have issued into acts that he considers brutal and obscene, but he wishes to emphasize the extent to which physical expression may have consisted only in responses— such as nocturnal emissions—that he thinks his own contemporaries would be less likely to condemn. He suggests that the homosexual lovers often engaged in no explicit sexual behavior with one another, possibly reserving that for their relations with a wife or concubine. But since Shelley recognizes that love among the males in Greece was more than merely friendship, that it was indeed a form of homosexuality, the problem he raises for himself is how anything so unnatural could be compatible with the cultivation and spiritual beauty that he detects in this way of life.

In accounting for the anomaly, Shelley describes ideal love as a combination of sexual and intellectual values that presuppose a heterosexual bond. To the extent that libidinal activities are simply mechanical, he sees that they can be performed with persons of either sex; but he claims that the intellectual component in love searches for a beloved whose traits complement one's own *because* they are sexually different. That is what Coleridge had also said, in the passage on love from which I quoted. The erotic quest can succeed, Shelley argues, only if the beloved possesses the mental acuity and moral refinement that comes from proper education. Since Greek society treated women as household servants, it kept them uneducated and thus prevented men from finding them admirable or even beautiful. As Shelley describes the Greek women, they inevitably became "devoid of that moral and intellectual loveliness with which the acquisition of knowledge and the cultivation of sentiment animates as with another life of overpowering grace the lineaments and the gestures of every form which it inhabits." Deprived of intellectual loveliness, Shelley concludes, women among the Greeks could not have had any physical beauty: at least, none that the men (or they themselves) would have been able to appreciate.

In saying this, Shelley is more radical than Plato, and he puts himself in the vanguard of nineteenth-century feminism. Greek homosexuality was to be rejected not only because it sometimes condoned "unnatural" behavior, but also because it issued from a social order that unjustly reduced half the populace to a condition of degradation, thereby forcing the other half to seek "a compensation and a substitute" among themselves. The ideal of love, heterosexual merging, could become feasible only through "the more equal cultivation of the two sexes." It has often been suggested that Greek culture, including Plato's philosophy, is worthy of criticism for having denied women access to the supremely honorific relationship of love, thereby excluding them from the highest ideals of their society. But Shelley's argument is more insightful, more penetrating. Though he too attacks Greek mores because they prevented women from enjoying the idealizations of love, he perceives that this alone made women *unlovable*. In the Europe of his day, Shelley thought, the sexual situation was less pernicious since men were now encouraged to find in their more natural objects of desire the values that pertain to love. At the same time, he recognized how much the world still prevented women from attaining the beauty of soul and intellect that comes only from total equality.

With respect to love itself, Shelley briefly summarizes in this place the analysis he had given in his earlier "Essay on Love." At first reading, his theory looks vaguely Platonistic, or possibly prophetic of Stendhal's ideas about crystallization (which it antedates by a few years). Actually Shelley is saying something very different from both Plato and Stendhal, even though he too identifies love with a search for perfection. Like Plato, he thinks that the mind is innately programmed with an "ideal prototype of everything excellent or lovely

that we are capable of conceiving as belonging to the nature of man."
Presumably this is an essence or eternal form, but Shelley makes no
claims about its objectivity and he does not ascribe to it the kind of
ontological significance that Plato intended. He does not say that the
prototype is detected by pure reason, though he thinks we see it
"within our intellectual nature," and he advocates no process of
dialectic or philosophic intuition by which it can be discovered. It is
simply present to the mind as an image or conception of whatever in
human beings delights through beauty and goodness. When our
sensory experience acquaints us with a real person in the world who
resembles the prototype in some respect, our imagination is eager to
"refer" all actual sensations to this perfection for which we instinctively yearn.

In his reliance upon imagination, Shelley changes Platonism into
a Romantic idealism quite remote from the earlier philosophy. For
he interprets imagination as acting in ways that belong to revery,
fantasy, and the inner needs of personal emotion rather than abet-
ting the transcendental function of reason. Shelley finds this aspect
of imagination comparable to the process by which one sees the
outline of an animal or a house in clouds or in the fire. Imagination
"moulds and completes the shapes," going beyond them in order to
create a total image that does not correspond to anything objectively
present. That is not at all what Plato meant.

On the other hand, neither is Shelley anticipating Stendhal.
Though love as Shelley sees it partly resembles Stendhalian crystallization, Shelley never suggests that the beloved is thought to embody perfections she does not have. On the contrary, for him the
object of love elicits the imaginative reconstruction of the ideal by
approximating perfections that the lover knows to be nonexistent in
the world. The beloved is an "antitype" that corresponds to, or
merely intimates, the prototype. As a real person, she represents the
ideal that has been created in the imagination of the lover; but she
herself need not be considered perfect.

It is because Shelley thinks of love as imagination subsuming
imperfect creatures under an inborn image of nonexistent perfection that his poetry is able to express such heart-rending lamenta-
tions about the world. His soaring soul suffers as it does because it

cannot understand how nature could have provided him with a prototype of beauty and goodness while systematically preventing any reality from living up to it. Since the perfect image also includes what the poet would like to be himself, and since that involves a capacity to sympathize with other persons, Shelley accommodates his philosophy of love to ideas about human feeling which, as we shall see, he assimilated from Hume and other thinkers of the eighteenth century but which he could not have found in Plato. Like the other Romantics we have been studying, Shelley considers love in its ultimate dimension to be a craving for unity with other people. He believes this occurs only when our instinctual need to sympathize makes us eager to promote their good as well as our own, to eliminate their suffering, and even to load it upon ourselves. We thereby create the oneness of communion. Through love, we become them.

This Romantic concept of merging is fully articulated in those lines that make up the bulk of Shelley's brief "Essay on Love." They need only be quoted directly:

> *Thou* demandest, What is Love? It is that powerful attraction towards all that we conceive, or fear, or hope beyond ourselves, when we find within our own thoughts the chasm of an insufficient void and seek to awaken in all things that are a community with what we experience within ourselves. If we reason, we would be understood; if we imagine, we would that the airy children of our brain were born anew within another's; if we feel, we would that another's nerves should vibrate to our own, that the beams of their eyes should kindle at once and mix and melt into our own, that lips of motionless ice should not reply to lips quivering and burning with the heart's best blood. This is Love. This is the bond and the sanction which connects not only man with man but with everything which exists. We are born into the world, and there is something within us which, from the instant that we live, more and more thirsts after its likeness. It is probably in correspondence with this law that the infant drains milk from the bosom of its mother; this propensity develops itself with the development of our nature. We dimly see within our intellectual nature a miniature as it were of our entire self, yet deprived of all that we condemn or despise, the ideal prototype of everything excellent or

lovely that we are capable of conceiving as belonging to the nature of man. Not only the portrait of our external being but an assemblage of the minutest particles of which our nature is composed; a mirror whose surface reflects only the forms of purity and brightness; a soul within our soul that describes a circle around its proper paradise which pain, and sorrow, and evil dare not overleap. To this we eagerly refer all sensations, thirsting that they should resemble or correspond with it. The discovery of its antitype; the meeting with an understanding capable of clearly estimating our own; an imagination which should enter into and seize upon the subtle and delicate peculiarities which we have delighted to cherish and unfold in secret; with a frame whose nerves, like the chords of two exquisite lyres, strung to the accompaniment of one delightful voice, vibrate with the vibrations of our own; and of a combination of all these in such proportion as the type within demands; this is the invisible and unattainable point to which Love tends; and to attain which, it urges forth the powers of man to arrest the faintest shadow of that without the possession of which there is no rest nor respite to the heart over which it rules.

Various critics, even those who write in defense of Shelley, have taken these words as an expression of narcissism, a desire to use other persons selfishly. Herbert Read relates this "narcissistic attitude" to tendencies toward autoeroticism, immature daydreaming, and latent homosexuality in Shelley. In Shelley's poetry and prose, as well as in his life, Read finds evidence of self-centered preoccupations that seem to him more or less psychotic. It is conceivable that such diagnoses could be defended, but I do not think that they are supported in any significant way by Shelley's writings about love. For though it may be pathological to use others as vehicles for our own personal gratification, there is nothing psychologically abnormal in presenting this as a theory about the nature of love. If Shelley offered an account of that sort, he would merely belong to the company of Hobbes, Voltaire, and others whose psychological stability has rarely been questioned.

As a matter of fact, however, Shelley's thinking includes much more than is dreamt of in the philosophy of Hobbes or Voltaire. Indeed, his theory explicitly contradicts their ideas about the ultimacy of self-love. He enunciates the principle of like attracting like (which even Aristotle maintained) as only one of the poles that dialectically define the communion between human beings for which he thinks we all instinctively yearn. The other pole he describes in "A Defence of Poetry." In that essay, he affirms that "the great secret of morals is love; or a going out of our own nature, and an identification of ourselves with the beautiful which exists in thought, action, or persons, not our own." Far from being narcissistic, this part of love requires an imaginative bestowal of interest in another's well-being: "A man, to be greatly good, must imagine intensely and comprehensively; he must put himself in the place of another and of many others; the pains and pleasures of his species must become his own. The great instrument of moral good is the imagination; and poetry administers to the effect by acting upon the cause."

Only in this context can Shelley's theories about love be understood. He continues the Coleridgean emphasis upon poetic imagination as a cognitive device that can be superior to reason, but he goes beyond Coleridge in seeing more clearly its connection with the affective structure of human nature. Coleridge, like Schelling, had already broken away from Kant's belief that ethical acts were impure to the extent that they were motivated by sympathy or loving feelings (or inclination of any sort) rather than by reason alone. And Coleridge too had recognized the great utility of imagination in providing a sense of oneness with everything in nature. This much belonged to the religious perspectives that he shared with Wordsworth, on the one hand, and Schelling, on the other. Shelley presupposes their point of view but carries it further.

Shelley's writings integrate Coleridge's ideas about imagination with his own thinking about love between the sexes. What matters most for Shelley is the fact that men and women in love use the imagination to commune with one another, to merge their personalities through acts of identification and common interest. Even in poems like *Epipsychidion, Adonais,* and the *Hymn to Intellectual Beauty* —all of which bear a thin veneer of Platonic-sounding rhetoric—he interprets sexual love as an interpersonal communication that need not, cannot, be transformed into a purely spiritual condition.

However much he may wish to soar beyond our dark vale of tears, he always thinks of the beauty for which the poet strives as a "messenger of sympathies,/That wax and wane in lovers' eyes." It is because Shelley gives such great importance to the universal thirst for communion, which involves our entire being rather than isolated components of sense or intellect (or mere imagination), that he presents the sexual impulse as only a small part of the motivation underlying the need to love. In the *Discourse* he says that in itself sex is "nothing." But he also sees that "the sexual impulse, which is only one, and often a small part . . . serves, from its obvious and external nature, as a kind of type or expression of the rest, a common basis, an acknowledged and visible link." For Shelley love is not contaminated by sex, but neither can the sexual be allowed to operate as it would for the libertine—"frozen, unimpassioned, spiritless," as he says in *Queen Mab*. Sex turns into love only as it establishes through physical consummation the satisfaction of our need for heterosexual communality.

For Shelley this need is native to human beings, even though different societies may distort and repress it—as in the ancient world. On the one hand, he insists that the desire for amorous oneness precedes all cultural determinants of our thinking; and therefore the existence of love cannot be explained in terms of developments in the Middle Ages or in modern sentimental literature. But on the other hand, he suggests that civilization creates a sensitivity to interpersonal realities which enables men and women to communicate effectively through love. Not only does civilization enrich the imaginative powers that lovers use to subsume one another under an image of beauty or goodness to which they are attuned, but also it leads them into relationships—such as marriage—that only society can sustain.

In saying this, I am aware that Shelley has often been categorized as a dreamy-eyed devotee of "free love." In the nineteenth century that term was loosely applied to all ideas about human intimacy that questioned traditional restraints. Nowadays we are better able to appreciate Shelley's actual beliefs, as we can understand more sympathetically the tragedy of his unfortunate marriage in adolescence, the needless suffering to which it led, and his courageous attempt in later years to find a proper mate. We are no longer shocked by the lines in *Epipsychidion* that Babbitt and T. S. Eliot found so repulsive. In saying that he never was attached to the great sect of those who think of marriage as an indissoluble bond, such that man or woman "With one chained friend, perhaps a jealous foe,/ The dreariest and the longest journey go," Shelley can now be understood to mean that the search for love must not be impeded by taboos about divorce or extramarital experimentation. He does not deny that true love can be found in marriage. In the essay "Even Love Is Sold," he attacks conventional marriage as it then existed in England but he does so by contrasting it with the "generosity and self-devotion" of enduring unions between "congenial" men and women. When love occurs, he says in many places, it broadens and does not narrow the heart, enabling the lovers—whether or not they are married—to see their oneness as evidence of the inherent communion that links them to everything in the universe. This may be unbearably optimistic, but it is not puerile, as Eliot thinks, and neither is it an unsuitable theme for great poetry.

At the same time, one must admit that Shelley's poetry (and his prose) remains eternally ambiguous. That love which extends beyond one's spouse, creating an ever-greater society of persons and joining us with reality as a whole, just what does it entail? Is love at its further reaches sexual in the same sense as the original intimacy between man and wife? Neither in his prose nor in his poetry does Shelley give a definitive answer. He captivates us with the suggestion that love can and must be free, but he scarcely indicates the dimensions of this desirable freedom. How much is body, and how much spirit? How are the two related? And to whom?

Shelley does not tell us. The truth is that he gives less thought to details about the attainment of love than about the unending search for it. The idea of yearning recurs in all his writings as a motif that he elaborates through endless variations. In some ways it makes him more typically Romantic than any of the other great poets of the nineteenth century. Byron and Keats also take sexual completion as a basis for more extensive ideas about human love—as I shall presently argue, the relationship between Byron's Don Juan and Haidée may even serve as a model for that earthly paradise of interpersonal communion that Shelley sought; and all of *Endymion* shows Keats seeking to rise through quasi-Platonic stages up the ladder of love and into the realm of perfect oneness that Shelley idealized. But there is in Byron a worldliness, and in Keats a sensory alertness and craving for material pleasures, that Shelley does not share. In his Preface to *Adonais*, written in lament for the death of Keats, he begins by repeating his "known repugnance to the narrow principles of taste" present in some of Keats' early works. He found them too sensationalistic, too greatly focused upon direct or obvious goods of sense experience. And indeed one always feels that Shelley's all-pervasive yearning was something he experienced more vividly than any other aspect of love. It is as if he was searching for an unattainable merging that would always defeat the possibility of enjoyment, at least of any that he could savor very long.

Santayana saw in Shelley's genius nothing but a longing for abstract ideas. He therefore concluded that Shelley's poetry could not express historical reality or human nature in general. "What he unrolls before us . . . is a series of landscapes, passions, and cataclysms such as never were on earth, and never will be." But this interpretation, which puts too great an emphasis upon Neoplatonic elements in Shelley's thinking, neglects his constant preoccupation with the need to act, to strive within the world. That is what makes Shelley so characteristic a product of his times. He uses the language of idealistic transcendence much as Schelling and Hegel did; but like them he also seeks a oneness that will be the embodiment in concrete experience of spiritual development that need not have any being elsewhere.

Santayana suggests that Shelley was a panpsychist rather than a pantheist, since he thought that everything was alive, and therefore available for sympathetic identification, but did not believe that mind or inherent divinity required all things to be as they are. I think this is right, and that it enables us to see vast differences between Shelley and much of the Hegelian tradition. Nevertheless, Santayana's insight ignores the side of Shelley which optimistically felt that the world was improving all the time and would continue to do so as long as enlightened critics like himself revealed its nature and furthered its efforts toward self-improvement. Through acts of the imagination the poet-philosopher might create organic totalities that showed forth consummatory values in the universe, values that reason alone could not appreciate. One did not attain the merging which is love by standing back from the world and contemplating mankind's failures with respect to moral ideals, as Santayana would have us think that Shelley intended. Instead, one had to immerse oneself in the bitter struggle and strive for naturalistic goals that achieve their spiritual character once our motivation becomes sufficiently heroic. Santayana thought that Shelley betrayed his vision and the high calling of his poetic talent by seeking for love through actual experience, by having love affairs and getting married rather than being content to write about the beauty of love's sheer possibility. But Santayana misconstrues the greatness of Shelley. Unlike Santayana, and contrary to Platonism in general, Shelley knew that marriage would join him to vital forces that fed his creativity. Like other Romantics of his age, he was an activist—albeit a wounded and unsuccessful one. The beautiful was to be found in emotional encounters; it was not something to be contemplated in the abstract. In this respect, Shelley is not at all Platonistic. For him, as for Hegel, communion within concrete existence was the meaning of love.

Santayana gives only a partial reading of Shelley's philosophy because he neglects the influence that eighteenth- and nineteenth-century utilitarianism had upon it. From the writings of Hume, Adam Smith, and William Godwin, Shelley acquired ideas about sympathy that he could never have gleaned from Plato. In the *Treatise of Human Nature* as well as in the *Enquiries*, Hume devotes himself to two major theses with respect to sympathy: first, that it is an innate disposition in all human beings and therefore not explicable in terms of selfishness alone, as Hobbes had argued; second, that it provides the fundamental principle of morals by causing all men to approve of pleasure or utility wherever it occurs, in others as well as in themselves, and to condemn pain and harmfulness regardless of who it is that suffers from them. Hume defends the first thesis on the grounds that human beings are so greatly alike that one man's pleasure or pain can register upon another's perception of it with sufficient force for the observer virtually to feel the pleasure or pain as if it were his own: "nor can any one be actuated by any affection, of which all others are not, in some degree, susceptible."

From this Humean perspective Shelley derives his conception of love as the bonding within a community of likeness. Since people are different and each can directly experience only his own sensations, Hume mentions that "a great effort of imagination" is needed for one person to feel the sentiments of another. Shelley develops this suggestion to its fullest. In the section on "Benevolence" in his "Speculations on Morals," Shelley not only emphasizes the importance of imagination as a means of overcoming selfishness but also he immediately applies the analysis to understanding the nature of love: "Love possesses so extraordinary a power over the human heart, only because disinterestedness is united with the natural propensities. These propensities themselves are comparatively impotent in cases where the imagination of pleasure to be given, as well as to be received, does not enter into the account." Though compatible with Hume's philosophy, this goes beyond it; and the same is true of Shelley's conclusion to his speculations on morals. He there maintains that "moral knowledge" may arise from awareness of resemblances between ourselves and others but "it is in the [appreciation of the] differences that it actually consists."

This tension between likeness and difference in the dynamics of sympathy Hume had sought to illuminate by saying that "the minds of men are mirrors to one another, not only because they reflect each other's emotions, but also because those rays of passions, sentiments and opinions may be often reverberated, and may decay away by insensible degrees." Elsewhere Hume speaks of affections passing from person to person and begetting "correspondent movements" on the analogy of "strings equally wound up, the motion of one communicates itself to the rest." All this recurs in Shelley's poetry and theory but now elaborated into beautiful and infinitely varied images of reverberation, of resonating harmonics within the soul and between the passions, of complex interactions that unite not just human beings but also everything man can recognize as kindred spirit. And, once again, it is love—not just sympathy—that becomes the basic category of analysis. In the Preface to *The Revolt of*

Islam, Shelley insists that love is "the sole law which should govern the moral world."

In this romanticizing of Hume's doctrine and the tradition in English philosophy that developed from it, Shelley applies the early utilitarianism to an age that had now been influenced by Rousseau and the German idealists. As if with Rousseau in mind, Hume's *Enquiry Concerning the Principles of Morals* suggests that the self-sufficiency of the isolated man could not bring happiness since his innate need for sympathetic identification would be thwarted in that condition: "Reduce a person to solitude, and he loses all enjoyment, except either of the sensual or speculative kind: and that because the movements of his heart are not forwarded by correspondent movements in his fellow-creatures." In Hume's conception, sympathy causes us to share the pleasures that others experience, whereas Rousseau assumed that they would make us envious and that only fear of suffering pains similar to another's would cause a person to achieve fellow-feeling. Shelley continues Hume's argument, relating the capacity of love to an escape from solitude and isolation by means of amelioristic civilization, society being essential in a way that Rousseau did not fully believe. At the same time, Shelley appropriates Rousseau's faith in passionate enthusiasm, in purified love that breaks down barriers and enables us to commune with all of nature. In Shelley, Hume's ideas about man's innate sociability are synthesized with Rousseau's reliance upon the goodness of abstract passion as a unifying force.

We thus return to the notion of merging, since that is the Romantic propellant that launches Shelley beyond the utilitarian cause to which he nevertheless remains faithful. In his discussion of "the amorous passion, or love betwixt the sexes," Hume lists three components: "the pleasing sensation arising from beauty; the bodily appetite for generation; and a generous kindness or good-will." These are all present in Shelley's analysis but he subordinates each of them to the need for imaginative merging with another person. In doing so, Shelley completely accepts Hume's healthy-minded belief that normally the three elements cooperate instead of opposing one another. Where Kant's problem about sexual love arises from his assumption that love and sex are basically contradictory,

Hume affirms that kindness, bodily appetite, and the sense of beauty are "in a manner inseparable . . . any of them is almost sure to be attended with the [other] related affections."

Hume does recognize that kindness, "the most refin'd passion of the soul," and sexual appetite, "the most gross and vulgar," are too remote from one another "to unite easily together"; but he is more interested in showing how all the elements are related among themselves: "one, who is inflam'd with lust, feels at least a momentary kindness towards the object of it, and at the same time fancies her more beautiful than ordinary; as there are many, who begin with kindness and esteem for the wit and merit of the person, and advance from that to the other passions." Moreover, he sees that the sense of beauty plays a special role in uniting kindness and lust, love and sex. Hume suggests that beauty partakes of both of these affections and that "the most common species of love" arises from the beautiful, which then "diffuses" through the other two.

In Kant's philosophy of love, the sense of beauty is given no comparable importance. But for Shelley, as for Hume, it is the linchpin that binds sex and fellow-feeling into a harmonious unity. Shelley may have been, surely was, inspired by Plato's ideas about the ultimacy of beauty, as he was also influenced by Renaissance theorizing about *l'appetito di bellezza*; but his own philosophy is Humean. Beauty is not to be split into spiritual and sensory compartments, each at war with the other. It is instead the integument that unites loving-kindness with sexual impulse through imaginative and sympathetic identification that is itself a search for beauty in another person.

Hume's philosophy of love is thoroughly humanistic inasmuch as it limits itself to relations between human beings (and some domestic animals). Shelley extends the argument to creation as a whole. When he says to the West Wind, which symbolizes all generative processes in nature, "Be thou, Spirit fierce,/ My spirit! Be thou me, impetuous one!", he expresses the craving for a universal love in which concrete beings not himself may communicate with his own aspirations and elicit his concern for their vital needs. In this poem, as in *Alastor* and others, he draws upon the image of a lyre that vibrates sympathetically, through no self-activating effort, with the infinite cosmos to which it belongs. In his *Essay on Christianity*, Shelley calls God that "Power by which we are surrounded like the atmosphere in which some motionless lyre is suspended, which visits with its breath our silent chords, at will." The lyre is the instrument of Orpheus, merged man-god of poets and musicians. Through him the voice of Shelley merges with the suffering and sometimes joyful sound of everything that exists. Through love Shelley becomes "the trumpet of a prophecy" that originates with, and proclaims the nature of, divinity. What is prophesied is the awakening of earth to its own eternal capacity for love.

The benign optimism of Shelley's idealistic conception was soured, as we shall see in the next chapter, by an eventual despair that seized him in the last year of his life. Some scholars have ascribed it to his ambivalent hatred and envy for the failures and successes of Byron. Though this aspect of their relationship is not entirely clear, there can be no doubt that Byron's negative response seems to have had some effect upon Shelley's thinking in his final days.

Previously, Shelley had influenced Byron at a crucial moment in Byron's development. In the six Clarens stanzas of *Childe Harold's Pilgrimage*, Canto II, Byron gravitated within the orbit of Shelley's philosophy as closely as he was ever to come. The stanzas express a love of nature in the locale where Rousseau's Julie experiences it in *La Nouvelle Héloïse*. At the time he was writing this poetry, Byron was having lengthy discussions with Shelley; and in a footnote, he says in words that could have been written by Shelley himself: "the feeling with which all around Clarens . . . is invested . . . is a sense of the existence of love in its most extended and sublime capacity, and of our own participation of its good and of its glory: it is the great principle of the universe . . . of which, though knowing ourselves apart, we lose our individuality, and mingle in the beauty of the whole." In the next canto, however, Byron rejects all vestiges of metaphysical idealism, which he calls the product of "desiring phantasy," i.e. wish-fulfillment: "Of its own beauty is the mind diseased,/ And fevers into false creation."

In reacting against the idea of love as benign merging, Byron emphasizes the sickness in human nature which creates such "phantom lures." With a voice that speaks from experience and observation, he says "Few—none—find what they love or could have loved;" and he goes on to explain this in terms of an irreconcilable difference between how things are and how, in our longing for oneness, we would like them to be: "Our life is a false nature; 'tis not in/ The harmony of things." In the defiant theatricality with which Byron expresses this belief, accompanied by unrelenting self-pity, he strikes a pose that is characteristic of the Romantic movement and belongs to what critics call "the Byronic hero." But as Byron matured, his realism became more profound, albeit more caustic, and in *Don Juan* he used it not merely to demolish foolish idealism while also soliciting commiseration, but more particularly, as a means of investigating the diversities of erotic experience.

Critics often say that Byron's Don Juan resembles his predecessors in name only, for in Byron he is neither a libertine nor a seducer of many women. This is true, and it is also true that Byron sides with his protagonist rather than condemning him, as did Tirso, Molière, and even Mozart. In effect, Byron's Don Juan is the hero of a Romantic Bildungsroman, a young man whose faults are easily forgiven because we see him developing as a human being throughout his misadventures. At the same time, there is one respect in which Byron definitely belongs to the tradition that Tirso began and may rightly give his protagonist the name that identifies that tradition. Though his Don Juan is fundamentally innocent, whereas Tirso's has to be seen as more or less evil, both authors are primarily concerned to deflate idealistic pretensions about sexual love. Writing during the Spanish Counter-Reformation, Tirso was attacking humanist ideas that masked sinful inclinations and deflected man from an authentic love of God. Byron has no religious interests of that sort, but he too wishes to portray love in a way that will prevent it from being treated as a likely path to salvation. He and Tirso are brother-realists under the skin, fellow doubters of those who think that sex can be purified or otherwise rendered amenable to social principles.

Byron differs from Tirso in his wholehearted acceptance of nature in the cantos that recount Don Juan's joyful life with Haidée. Tirso also depicts a love affair between Don Juan and a fisherman's daughter who, finding him on the strand after a shipwreck, nurses him back to health; but Tirso's protagonist seduces her and then burns down her hut as a final act of malice. In Byron, the relationship between Juan and Haidée becomes the epiphany of what sexual love can possibly attain. It is not a permanent achievement, since Byron (like Tirso) believes that hypocrisy and corruption in society will eventually undermine this, and all other, types of intimacy between human beings. Nevertheless, the love that Byron describes is an indication of what men and women could experience if only they were as innocent and as fully natural as the two young people who find happiness in each other's arms, beguiled by no conventional expectations, no artificial restraints, and no philosophical ideals.

In one place Byron compares Juan and Haidée with Adam and Eve in the Garden. He is thinking of Milton's account rather than Augustine's, for his natural man and woman are totally and ecstatically libidinal. Of equal importance, however, is the fact that Byron intimates that never since Adam and Eve had any couple loved in so pure a manner. Juan's relationship with Haidée follows upon a boyish escapade with a married woman whose husband catches him hiding in her bed—a variation of Cherubino's plight in Beaumarchais and in Mozart. After he is driven from the loving arms of Haidée by her repressive father, Juan has other adventures with other women, but none that ever reestablishes the beauty of his one encounter with true love. On the contrary, the rest of *Don Juan* reveals that love is ordinarily licentious, selfish, calculating, fashionable (and therefore a form of vanity), or else a pretense that one goes through for the benefits of a useful marriage. The relationship with Haidée thus appears as a rarity of nature that life in society can never duplicate, and also a nostalgic basis for legitimate anger in the Byronic hero.

In order to make this devastating contrast between nature and society, Byron had only to insist upon the hopelessness and even fatality (for the woman, at least) of the authentic love between Juan and Haidée. But he does more than that: he claims that no love, not even theirs, could survive the shipwreck of an actual marriage to one another. In a way that reminds us of Stendhal, he finds "in domestic doings . . . true love's antithesis"; and in lines that must have influenced Schopenhauer, as we shall see, he asks: "Think you, if Laura had been Petrarch's wife,/ He would have written sonnets all his life?"

In Stendhal, as in one or another of the courtly lovers in Andreas Capellanus, this attitude toward marriage serves to illustrate the superiority of love. In Byron, however, it mainly reinforces his denial that love as it is likely to exist will create harmonious unity in this or any other world. In one of his letters he speaks of love as "utter nonsense, a mere jargon of compliments, romance, and deceit." This is the part of Byron that reflects his unhappy experiments with homosexuality and his periods of compulsive promiscuity with women, more than two hundred of whom he boasts of having had during eighteen months in Venice.

Unlike Stendhal and Shelley, who hoped to emancipate women through education and equality, Byron has little sympathy with feminist aspirations. At times he shows compassion for the suffering of women; occasionally he writes poetry that exalts their purity of soul; but usually he voices traditional fears about female dominance in sex or society. With greater astuteness than many of his contemporaries, he recognizes that sexual love of an idealistic sort is one of the mechanisms by which women have always managed to alter the status quo. His perspective may be distorted, but it enables him to study the history of literature with a clarity that was lacking in many others. At a time when the troubadours were being revered as poets who appreciated the spiritual values in womanhood, Byron found their poems "not more decent, and certainly . . . much less refined, than those of Ovid." He is also more realistic, than Shelley for instance, about courtliness as it actually existed in medieval society, which he characterizes as "barbarism of the chivalric and feudal ages—artificial and unnatural."

Without Byron, the soaring flights of idealists like Shelley might have lacked the restraint of realistic correction. When he became merely cynical and even facetious, Byron's worldly wisdom could easily be discounted as perversion of his poetic talents. But with the cleverness of genius, Byron knew how to disarm such criticism by revealing (when he wished) that he too understood, even if he despaired of finding it very often, the goodness in that natural love between man and woman which Shelley constantly sought. Though he makes little attempt to synthesize the idealist and the realist approaches, Byron surprises us by showing how close he sometimes comes to combining them within his own naturalistic point of view—as in the lines where he remarks that Juan and Haidée should have "lived together deep in woods,/Unseen as sings the nightingale." The lovers are "unfit" to live in the vicious haunts of society, as Emile and Sophie also were, but still, Byron sadly insists, "the sweetest song-birds nestle in a pair."

13
Romantic Pessimism
Goethe, Novalis,
Schopenhauer, Wagner

IN THE PREVIOUS CHAPTER WE studied romantic concepts that were optimistic inasmuch as they considered love an ideal consummation that can be achieved, in one way or another and however imperfectly, within the lives of men and women. Whatever the differences among themselves, Kant, Hegel, Schlegel, and Shelley are alike in believing that happiness in love, including married love, is not only worth attaining but also attainable on earth. Throughout the period of romanticism, from the ending of the eighteenth century through most of the nineteenth, this benign, affirmative, even healthy-minded approach towards human possibilities is countered by a pessimistic attitude that questions the nature and the likelihood of happy love between the sexes. In many Romantics the two perspectives both appear— sometimes as manifestations of ambivalence, sometimes as simple inconsistency, but often in a dialectical opposition that eludes any facile resolution.

Despite his eagerness to change the world in ways that would further the humanistic love for which his soul pitifully yearns, Shelley often expresses a lamenting despair that borders on a love of death. In *Adonais* he mourns the loss of Keats but also portrays death as a condition superior to anything one can hope for in this life, this vale of tears. Oneness with nature and the desired participation in all being, which Shelley had seen as the outcome or metaphysical completion of the loving union between man and woman, he now ascribes to the release from ordinary existence: "No more let Life divide what Death can join together." Not through sexual love but through death alone is Keats "made one with Nature: there is heard/His voice in all her music, from the moan/Of thunder, to the song of night's sweet bird." Keats himself had identified the nightingale's broken music with a consummation that only death can offer. For both Keats and Shelley, the pessimistic alternative provided a second line of defense. If the world would not yield to the changes their concept of earthly love demands, then an equivalent for erotic harmony had to be found in a total negation of the world itself.

In Shelley's writing, the pessimism that became so prominent just before his own death occurs in different forms. In *Adonais* it is the denial that eternity (cosmic love) can really show itself in the temporal world. On the contrary, "Life, like a dome of many-coloured glass,/ Stains the white radiance of Eternity." In his more transcendental moments, Plato might have said this, but not Hegel or the earlier Shelley. In *The Triumph of Life* Shelley's pessimism is similar to what one could have expected from a realist like Byron. There death is depicted as a purgatorial gloom that provides neither repose nor consummatory oneness. The shades of Rousseau and Plato appear in the poem as souls that suffer, the former because in life his spirit lacked "purer nutriment," the latter because his search for beauty and for love was conquered by the realities of life.

In a letter that clarifies the pessimism of *The Triumph of Life*, though it does not mention that work, Shelley remarks: "I think one is always in love with something or other . . . the error, and I confess it is not easy for spirits cased in flesh and blood to avoid it, consists in seeking in a mortal image the likeness of what is perhaps eternal." This contradicts, or would seem to renounce, Shelley's former idealization of love as the discovery in the world of an antitype that approximates the "ideal prototype . . . that we are capable of conceiving as belonging to the nature of man." But even in the essay on love, Shelley had already bewailed his outcast state, being one who "everywhere sought sympathy and . . . found repulse and disappointment." In the poems, we are constantly confronted by his attestations of weakness and incapacity to live and love as he would: "I fall upon the thorns of life! I bleed!"

Within this gamut of pessimistic alternatives, the final part of *Epipsychidion* has particular importance for much of what I shall be discussing in this chapter. After the lines that reveal, more beautifully than ever, how sexual merging creates the spiritual oneness of perfect community, Shelley alerts us to the impossibility of attaining love on earth. Even in utopia, love must "point to Heaven":

> One hope within two wills, one will beneath
> Two overshadowing minds, one life, one death,
> One Heaven, one Hell, one immortality,
> And one annihilation. Woe is me!

And finally:

> . . . 'Love's very pain is sweet,
> But its reward is in the world divine
> Which, if not here, it builds beyond the grave.'

With these words, Shelley expresses the concept of love-death to which Romantic pessimism often resorts. For him, however, it functions within an ambivalence that might have led into new areas of exploration if only he had lived past his thirtieth year. In Schlegel's *Lucinde* one encounters a similiar ambiguity about love and death. Beyond the many stages of union that Julius and Lucinde reach as their intimacy develops, there remains a permanent union they can achieve only after death. In part this idea manifests Schlegel's belief that love is too great a good to disappear once life is ended. To that extent he is being optimistic about the capacity of love to conquer all impediments, including death. But also he is voicing doubts about the willingness of nature, particularly human nature as it exists in all conceivable societies, to tolerate an ideal sexual love between man and woman. What cannot be attained on earth, what the world maliciously prohibits, will therefore have to be found beyond the grave. In later life, after Schlegel renounced his Romantic philosophy as a youthful aberration, he looked forward to the life after death that Catholicism had always promised; but even in his earlier phase he was prepared to believe that the ultimate merging in love transcends the limits of life as we ordinarily know it.

Later in this chapter I shall consider how the concept of love-death was explicitly formulated in the middle of the nineteenth century, for instance by Richard Wagner. Here it is worth emphasizing that the ingredients of this idea were present in Romantic thought from the very start. The conflict between the optimistic and pessimistic poles within romanticism became a structural element as early as 1774, when Goethe first published *The Sorrows of Young Werther*—a book that exerted an influence upon European culture even greater than Rousseau's *Nouvelle Héloïse*. *Werther* not only led to a contagious wave of suicides throughout Europe, but also it created endless controversies about the authenticity of the protagonist's self-destroying love. For some critics, including W. H. Auden in our day, Werther is just a neurotic or possibly psychotic young man who kills himself for reasons he himself scarcely recognizes: he dies not because Charlotte spurns his love, but because his psychological disabilities prevent him from truly loving anyone or anything. For other critics, however, Werther's death is a tragedy of love thwarted by interferences, such as those resulting from conventional marriage, that the world stupidly rears against a romantic passion whose value it neither understands nor tolerates. In his subsequent writings, Goethe himself seemed to be willing to entertain both interpretations. Though there is reason to think he may originally have favored the former, and in fact that he wrote the novel at the age of twenty-five in order to exorcise suicidal inclinations within himself, the later Goethe occasionally remarks that Werther's love cannot be explained in terms of psychological failure. In his "Reflections on Werther," Goethe goes so far as to remark about the man who served as the model for his character: "If, as they say, our greatest happiness rests in our longings, and if true longing may have only what is unattainable as its goal, then all things certainly had come together to make our young man, whom we are accompanying on his erratic journey, the happiest of mortals." Goethe then suggests it was the frustrating of these benign longings that broke the young man's heart.

However this problem of critical interpretation is resolved, one must recognize that it arises because Goethe has used his protagonist as a vehicle for expressing the conflict between optimistic and pessimistic aspects of Romantic love. Though Werther commits suicide after he is unable to get the woman he loves or, failing in that, to cure himself of his obsessional dependency upon her, his interest in Charlotte occurs within a context defined by problems that go beyond their relationship alone. From the outset Werther is presented as a sensitive youth whose capacity for strong and deep emotion exceeds his ability to *use* his feelings, to do with them what he wishes as an artist. He is a painter, but he lacks the talent or technique needed to express on canvas the feelings that matter most to him. These initially involve a sense of cosmic love, an intuition of the presence of God appearing in the beauty of nature. Because nature is so pervasively beautiful to Werther in the beginning of the novel, it manifests a loving presence in all things while also reminding him of a woman somewhat older than himself whom he had previously loved, in whose company he had developed his feeling for nature, and who was now lost to him through death. This typically Romantic nostalgia for the departed mother-figure, the broken link to one's natural source, takes on special significance in Werther's case. For his attachment to Charlotte originates in his identifying himself with the children for whom she serves as a substitute mother.

Initially, Werther's friendship with Charlotte is a happy one for both of them. As if he really were her child, and as if she embodied some natural divinity, Werther feels that she is "sacred" to him; and he tells us that "all passion is silenced in her presence." Moreover, his inability to express his feelings through artistic activity seems to disappear as he starts to do a little work. He soon realizes, however, that his creative powers have actually diminished. On the one hand, he feels that he has never been happier and has never understood nature better; on the other hand, he concludes that he cannot express himself adequately through his art. Previously he and Charlotte had experienced a mystic communion as they watched the rain one evening and simultaneously thought of the same poet, Klopstock, whose writings had stirred them both. On that occasion Werther was overcome by "a flood of emotion," perhaps because he realized that Klopstock had succeeded in expressing *his* feelings about nature through works of art. Despite, or because of, his love for Charlotte, Werther finds that he cannot do anything comparable.

Being unable to use nature creatively or even to enjoy it passively, Werther's happiness turns to despair. Nature as a whole begins to lose its benevolent appearance. Werther's final crisis takes place after his interest in Charlotte becomes possessive, demanding, and explicitly sexual. But it is preceded by his growing fear that nature is neither loving nor interested in sustaining love. What he had called the source of human happiness he now senses as a fountain of misery. In a passage that is reminiscent of Rousseau, Goethe has Werther describe nature in terms of huge mountains, yawning abysses, and headlong falling cataracts. In this wild immensity, Werther sees a sign of man's contrasting pettiness and insignificance. Using words that could have come from Sade, who was writing about the same time, Werther characterizes nature as both ruthless and pervasively destructive:

> There is not a moment but consumes you and yours—not a moment in which you do not destroy something. The most innocent walk costs thousands of poor insects their lives. . . . My heart is wasted by the thought of that destructive power which lies latent in every part of universal Nature. Nature has formed nothing that does not destroy itself, and everything near it. . . . The universe to me is an ever-devouring, ever-ruminating monster.

While Goethe retains his aesthetic distance throughout the novel and neither condemns nor extols Werther's attitude, allowing his readers to decide for themselves whether it is sublime or merely pathological, he introduces the possibility that true love cannot occur within the imperfect conditions of this world. Werther dies with the assurance that after death, after he has freed himself of nature's inner corruption, he will eventually attain oneness with the woman he loves. Though Charlotte does not die with him, he thinks that she will soon join him in some transcendent union. In death, she will be more totally his than she could ever have been in life.

A similar ambiguity about love in relation to death pervades Goethe's later writings. His productive output spans so many decades—he worked on the two parts of *Faust*, for instance, for more than sixty years—that it inevitably reflects winds of doctrine that blew in more than one direction. In his hedonistic acceptance of the senses, his attempt to cultivate ways of enjoying each moment as it passes, he becomes in German literature a symbol of classical or pagan humanism. There is also, within his many-sided personality, a basic faith in the redemptive value of constant striving; and in this respect he anticipates the systematic activism of Hegel. In a letter he wrote towards the end of his life he compliments his friend Zelter for having discovered "permanence in the transitory and thus [satisfying] not only me but also the spirit of Hegel insofar as I understand it." But in Goethe one also finds ideas that align him with many of the despairing young Romantics whose works he (like Hegel) often criticized.

This darker side of Goethe has sometimes led to confusion and misinterpretation by his more pietistic readers. For instance, consider the ending of *Faust*, Part II. The scene takes place in heaven, where a Penitent Soul begs Mary the Mater Gloriosa for permission to instruct Faust in the ways of eternity now that he has died and risen to paradise. Despite Faust's sinful life and his refusal to accept God's grace, his soul has been snatched from the devil and welcomed among the blessed simply because on earth it never ceased to struggle. The Penitent Soul is Gretchen, the innocent girl whom Faust seduced and abandoned in Part I. Though she erred in yielding to his deception, she has been pardoned and is now allowed to take charge of Faust's purification beyond the grave. The final Chorus Mysticus asserts that everything transitory is but an appearance whose being is fully realized and finally completed here in heaven, where "Das Ewig-Weibliche/Zieht uns hinan" ("The eternal feminine draws us upward").

For many commentators this conclusion makes sense only as a reversion to Dante. And certainly Gretchen, despite her sexual experiences on earth, would seem to duplicate the role of Beatrice, luring Dante's soul to herself in paradise, thereby revealing the beauty of divine love. But at a time when Romantics like the later Schlegel were embracing the Catholic faith and rediscovering medieval values, Goethe consistently condemned Catholicism and possibly all other forms of Christianity. The year before he died, the same year in which he finished *Faust*, he speaks of the cross as "the most disgusting thing under the sun [which] no reasonable human being should strive to exhume."

In view of this self-conscious paganism, the echoes of Dante in Goethe must be taken as a literary device, as a mythological contrivance rather than a doctrinal affirmation of the sort that pervades the *Divine Comedy*. There is, in fact, scarcely any theology in *Faust*; and Goethe prided himself on the fact that there was no one grand doctrine or supervening concept that could serve as the foundation to his Gothic drama. Throughout his life he strongly leaned toward a Spinozistic pantheism that would enable his poetic soul to appreciate the diverse and possibly irreconcilable strivings that made up the dynamism in nature. He wished to "love the love in everything." He admired Schelling's philosophy as a continuation of Spinoza's view of nature, but then attacked Schelling for having combined it with Christianity.

What remains, therefore, as the ideological content of the final scene in *Faust* is merely the idea of love-death, not fully elaborated as in other Romantics, but nevertheless present as a partial corroboration of this element in their thinking. In Part I Faust seduces Gretchen by claiming to feel for her something inexpressible: a yearning to give himself completely which must, he thinks, be sacred. Since his behavior shows him to be little more than an egoistic adventurer, a pleasure-seeking Don Juan, we are free to take these words as pure deception, a sprynge to catch woodcocks. But in the previous scene, Faust had sought to convince Mephistopheles that his nameless feeling for Gretchen was a noble impulse that could only be characterized as "infinite, eternal." Mephistopheles implies, and in this place he may speak the truth, that Faust's idealistic ardor is merely a self-deceiving illusion by which the devil uses him to corrupt Gretchen, and thereby turn goodness into evil. But the culmination in heaven reaffirms the element of ideality in Faust's love for Gretchen. It is that which enables her, as a pure-hearted woman, to carry him with her through eternity. This ideal consummation occurs only after death, however, and there is nothing in *Faust*—not even the mutual devotion between Baucis and Philemon—to suggest that Goethe thinks a comparable love can be attained in life itself.

In *Elective Affinities*, finished in 1809 when he was sixty years old, Goethe develops the concept of love-death within the framework of a symbolistic novel about marriage and adultery. Nature appears as a deterministic mechanism that unites men and women as if they were chemical elements bonded to one another regardless of marital commitments that seek to keep them apart. Marriage itself is represented as a humane, moral, and wholly admirable attempt to find happiness through the use of reason and free will. There are even two characters, the Count and the Baroness, who live together in a marital relationship that seems to provide them with happiness they have learned to cultivate through experiences with previous spouses as well as with each other. For legalistic reasons they are not actually married to one another and are therefore committing adultery, but Goethe indicates that their life together embodies most of the goals of enlightened matrimony. The marital ideal is not, however, capable of revealing the deepest secrets of nature.

The protagonists in the novel, who illustrate the ultimate character of love, do not commit adultery; but their passions are extramarital and it is here that nature shows its innermost process. The rational but unimpassioned marriage that Eduard and Charlotte enjoy is wrecked by the chemical affinity that binds Eduard to Charlotte's foster-child Ottilie. Charlotte herself feels love for Eduard's friend, the Captain, but renounces it with determination and self-control. The Captain, who reciprocates Charlotte's passion, acts in a similar manner throughout the novel. Eduard, however, cannot master his emotional need for Ottilie; nor can she extinguish her reciprocal longing for him. Their love ends in tragedy. They suffer, not merely through frustration, but with a sense of guilt, as if in retribution for even having adulterous feelings.

Though the Captain and Charlotte survive the history of torment that descends upon all four of these characters, the passionate lovers are destroyed by their love. They die without having consummated their passion, without having gained a modicum of happiness through it. Ottilie reaches a state of spiritual clarification once she accepts the fact that her yearning for Eduard is guilty, even sinful. Through acts of ascetic self-denial she renounces the world and resigns herself to the destiny that has been chosen for her. Her death, which results in effect from self-imposed starvation, is followed by an apparent miracle that the touching of her corpse elicits. Goethe does not present the event as truly miraculous, but he uses it to symbolize the holiness that Ottilie's love for Eduard achieves once she has defeated her natural interests by means of resignation. Through the freely willed renunciation of sexual desire, she embraces both death and an eternal love. Eduard soon follows her and Charlotte has him buried at Ottilie's side. The novel ends with the following lines in the narrator's voice: "Thus the lovers lie sleeping side by side; peace hovers above their resting place . . . and what happiness is in store for them at the moment of their common awakening!"

In a speech to the Captain earlier in the novel, Charlotte had remarked that neither reason, virtue, duty, nor conventional religion can prevent destiny from controlling our life in nature. For Goethe this is the tragedy in human existence, since natural destinies are not concerned about the welfare of individuals. Much of his greatest poetry expresses the hopelessness of seeking for happy love as opposed to love in death or love through death. In *Selige Sehnsucht* ("Holy Yearning"), he praises the man who "Thirsts for fire/Thirsts for death, and dies in gladness." Goethe's final solace to the aspiring soul consists in the injunction to "stirb und werde!" The word *werde* literally means "become," but Goethe uses it to signify a spiritual growth that makes the lovers' yearning holy. His exhortation is thus to "die and grow!", the idea being that death enables one to undergo an ideal transformation.

Goethe's ambiguity, or rather ambivalence, about the possibility of love on earth is shared by many of the German Romantic poets who wrote during the first decade of the nineteenth century— Hölderlin, Tieck, Kleist, and Novalis among others. Kleist died in a suicide pact with a woman he may have loved; but each had previously chosen death independently of the other, and they killed themselves at the same time as an act of fellowship more than anything else. If theirs was not an actual love-death, it was nevertheless related to one in Kleist's imagination. In his last letters, Kleist speaks of death and love jointly beautifying his final moments "with heavenly and earthly roses." He declares himself supremely happy and refers to his as "the most voluptuous of deaths."

The truly profound and moving voluptuary of death throughout this period was, however, a poet who celebrated the beauties of life as well as the mystical ecstasies that lay beyond. Friedrich von Hardenberg, whose pseudonym was Novalis, saw everything in nature, and everything that man could sensuously experience, as a manifestation of divine love even though he himself experienced a personal tragedy that became legendary throughout the nineteenth century. In his early twenties he fell in love with Sophie, a thirteen-year-old girl who died two years later. For Novalis she became the equivalent of Dante's Beatrice in the *Vita Nuova*. In his *Hymns to the Night* Novalis portrays Sophie as an emanation from God, and he celebrates the phenomenon of death as the goal for which all life has been created. Life was capable of infinite joys that are valuable in themselves, apart from their terminus in death, but it was only death that could reveal the spiritual import of man's encounter with reality.

Novalis formulates this antithesis in his contrast between Day and Night. The world of Day provided the glorious goods of happiness and well-being, whose source was God's unending bestowal. The world of Night, however, was "holy, ineffable, mysterious." The ecstasies of earthly existence, particularly those of marriage and sexual consummation, were all to be taken as symbolic anticipations of the spiritual promise of the Night. For the Night was the state of sanctified death, specifically the death of Christ, and therefore the ultimate meaning of the Christian message. Night was not only the occasion on which Novalis visits the grave of Sophie, feeling himself drawn into it by her ever-present love, but also it was the infinite Mother, Mary as the virgin who bears Christ, and therefore the way to the godhead with which mystical aspiration seeks to merge.

Though the *Hymns to the Night* were written in the last months of the enlightened eighteenth century, we seem to have entered a new realm of feeling, a romantico-psychedelic world that even Goethe found shocking and somewhat obscene. For Novalis, Sophie combines both Day and Night; she is the "Sun of the Night" whose death, innocent as Christ's, is the beginning of the true life. Novalis' love for her is presented as both sexual and spiritual at the same time, and therefore even Rousseau would have considered it an absurd and largely undesirable sentiment. For the philosophical sources of his new approach, Novalis goes back to Christian mystics such as Jacob Boehme, who deified a woman whom he too loved not only as Wisdom (her name is Sophia) but also as the bride of a spiritual marriage depicted in sexual language.

What distinguishes Novalis from his predecessors among the Christian mystics is both his relative freedom from orthodox dogma—not that the mystics themselves were always bound by it—and also his belief that the highest and purest love that religion could afford was in no way jeopardized by, or even separable from, completely passionate love between man and woman. In his *Spiritual Saturnalia*, where he says that "life is for the sake of dying," he states with equal emphasis that marriage is the greatest of all mysteries. He saw no paradox in these utterances, for he believed that love explained both life and death. But since love in life is for him only a symbol of the consummation that occurs after death, his poetic philosophizing often seems morbid, even pathological. And in fact it sometimes is.

If by the concept of love-death we mean the idea that two lovers will consummate their love for one another after death in a way that nothing on earth can equal, we can readily show that the writings of Arthur Schopenhauer support no such idealization. Yet in ways that many scholars have failed to realize, Schopenhauer's philosophy is pervaded by Romantic beliefs not wholly different from those that Goethe and Novalis also held. His pessimistic approach proclaims itself as the antithesis of Hegelian optimism, which he reviles on almost every page. But at the distance of the 120-odd years that separate us from the death of Schopenhauer, we may perceive similarities between him and Hegel that were not apparent to either of them at the time. And often these similarities are explicable in terms of Romantic concepts that link them, each in his own fashion, to thinkers such as Goethe and Novalis.

This kinship to which I am referring is present in the ideas of Hegel and Schopenhauer about the nature of death. For both, death is a total loss of individual identity. Despite a person's desire to continue in existence as a separate entity, he simply disappears. The two philosophers deny that individuality as such has any ultimate significance. Like all other organisms, human beings are merely replaceable parts within a cosmic process which uses them for ends that transcend their personal interests.

Hegel does not consider this tragic condition to be a source of despair. On the contrary, he thinks of death as the best illustration of that "dialectic of love" through which the spirit communes with itself. For the death of every individual is in principle a giving of oneself that not only enables the Absolute to continue its dynamic search for self-comprehension, but also it affords an opportunity for each person to live on by contributing to this meaningful process. In his *Lectures on the Philosophy of Religion,* Hegel amalgamates his conception of death with the Christian notion of incarnation. Though Hegelian philosophy lent itself to various forms of nineteenth-century atheism, orthodox thinkers could find sustenance in Hegel's belief that "death is love itself. . . . Through death God has reconciled the world and reconciles Himself eternally with Himself."

As opposed to religious speculation of this sort, Schopenhauer insists that there is no cosmic order, no divine love, to explain the destruction of individuality. For him the person is insignificant because in reality he has no separate existence. People who fear death think that it involves the annihilation of themselves as independent beings; but, Schopenhauer assures us, this conception is

simply an illusion of the intellect. Each bit of life is just a manifestation of life in general. It is an "objectification" of the underlying
force or dynamic impulse that flows through nature, what
Schopenhauer calls "the will" or "will-to-life." The will is ultimate
reality, knowable because we experience it directly throughout our
lives: we are all volitional creatures immediately aware of ourselves
struggling to satisfy desire, express emotions, and survive as biological entities. Previous philosophers had identified the being of man,
as well as the nature of reality, in terms of either sensation or pure
rationality. Schopenhauer attacks them by arguing that only in our
will do we make contact with underlying reality. In our ultimate
being, we *are* the will. Since the will in human beings is not different
from the will in general, we cannot be wholly separate individuals.
Personal immortality is therefore absurd as well as physically impossible. When we die, we merely lose an illusion created by our
imperfect intellect.

The intellect itself, and reason as a whole, Schopenhauer considers one among other instruments that the will develops in certain
species to enable them to adapt successfully to their environment.
This aspect of his philosophy unites Schopenhauer with eighteenth-
century utilitarians such as Hume as well as twentieth-century prag-
matists, vitalists, and psychoanalytic theorists. He differs from these
thinkers, even from Hume whom he admired so much, in his continual insistence upon the pain and horror of life. The philosophers
I have mentioned are sensitive to the pervasiveness of suffering, but
they do not minimize the importance of the many pleasures life can
often provide. Schopenhauer finds such goods minimal in human
nature, tiny islands within enormous oceans of misery and in no way
representative of man's condition. He therefore sees death as the
desirable end of temporal existence not only in the sense that it
eliminates the illusion of individual separateness, but also because it
terminates a pitiful condition that has nothing to justify its continuation.

Schopenhauer prided himself on the pessimistic caste of his philosophy; but the fact remains that he offers his ideas about death in
the hope of bringing comfort and reassuring clarity to people who
feared their own eventual annihilation. Though the individual con-

sciousness that human beings cherish cannot endure beyond the grave, Schopenhauer believes that the will in everything remains indestructible. At the level of unconscious volition, which mere intellect does not reach, every person's being merges with—or rather emanates from—the universal will that animates all things in nature. Death is the mechanism through which each species, and nature as a whole, goes on living by discarding unneeded instantiations of itself. The species does not die; and since the individual by his essence *is* that species, his true being is not destroyed when death occurs. Human beings succeed one another, Schopenhauer says, like leaves that appear on a tree in different years. In effect they are all the same, for in their vital functions successive generations do not differ, even if the illusion of separateness misleads individuals into thinking they are unique.

Who is likely to be consoled by Schopenhauer's doctrine? Not someone who puts his trust in reason; nor someone who thinks that each person has an eternal soul created especially by God; but possibly someone who believes that nature alone, in its totality, natura naturans, contains the source of all being and of all value. In fact, Schopenhauer's views are a latter-day, but typically Romantic, extension of pantheistic concepts that were attractive to many people in the nineteenth century. But though Schopenhauer relies upon romanticism of this sort, he does not accept it at face value. He attacks the traditional theories of pantheism on the grounds that they impart to nature a humane, even anthropomorphic, concern that is wholly foreign to it. The will is blind; its actions are often random, even confused; and from the point of view of the helpless organisms that objectify its subconscious impulses it acts in ways that can only appear cruel, stupid, vicious, and utterly devoid of those ideal principles that usually structure pantheistic philosophies. In relation to them, Schopenhauer's thinking establishes itself as a divergent form of naturalism. His critique of traditional idealism is halfhearted inasmuch as he thinks that fears of death can be quieted by the belief that human beings are products of an eternal will-to-life; but he is uncompromisingly firm in maintaining that this will cannot be characterized as a striving for spiritual goodness or happiness or anything else that human beings desire for themselves.

As we shall presently see, the bleak comfort that Schopenhauer offers originates in a sense of revulsion toward nature. Not only does the will operate through illusions that mask its ruthlessness, but also its lack of purpose signifies that there is basically no reason why anything at all should exist. As in Platonism, Buddhism, primitive Christianity—parts of which he incorporates into his own philosophy—Schopenhauer sees nothing to justify the fact of existence itself. Original sin consists in acting to perpetuate nature instead of rising above it, and death is "the great reprimand" by which the will to live is punished in all its existent manifestations. Death serves to destroy "the fundamental error of our true nature. . . . At bottom, we are something that ought not to be; therefore we cease to be." In dying, we attain what Schopenhauer calls "the great opportunity no longer to be I." He means not only the opportunity to lose our mistaken sense of individuality but also to give up our concern for existence as we know it.

At this point Schopenhauer employs the ambiguous notion of Nirvana. It is ambiguous because in him, as in Buddhism, it seems to involve more than just the overcoming of separateness. Nirvana is the mystical state in which the enlightened soul finally denies the will to live and thereby effects the partial destruction of the will. But how it is that one can will *not* to will—this Schopenhauer does not tell us, and indeed he claims that all such matters transcend human understanding.

Let us leave it at that for the moment, but now at least we have a foundation for examining Schopenhauer's metaphysics of sexual love. If the individual is really nothing, if each person is little more than the manifestation in appearance of an underlying reality that has neither spirituality in itself nor any desire to promote the welfare of persons, if human beings systematically delude themselves about their goals in life, their objects of desire, and their very being as temporal phenomena, if death serves to liberate one from an illusory and inherently tragic existence, if, in short, the consummations that enable people to continue as affective entities are minor events that cannot explain why human beings act as they do, if all this is the case, one can see why Schopenhauer maintains that earlier philosophies of love have always failed to understand its true character. He begins his discussion by remarking that he has no predecessors either to attack or defend and that he is, in effect, the first philosopher to have studied the subject thoroughly. He says that Plato limited himself to homosexuality and to myth-making, that Rousseau's utterances are "false and inadequate," that Kant's discussion is "very superficial and without special knowledge," and so on. He feels that only his metaphysics of the will can provide the key to the great enigma of love. It is not a function of spirit, of divine agapē, of instinctual yearning for oneness, or of anything else that the idealist tradition considered paramount in human striving. Instead love is the most ingenious of nature's devices for carrying out the demands of the will.

Since the will is merely a force or vital energy that perpetuates animate existence, since it is a *species'* will to live, it shows itself most clearly in the form of sexual demand. Our desire to possess another person in coitus best reveals the will. This being so, Schopenhauer reduces all types of love to mere sexuality—or rather, to the reproductive instinct that motivates sexual response. Though he may be a little inaccurate in denying that he has any philosophical predecessors, he is right in thinking that hardly anyone before him had fully accepted the implications of this naturalistic thesis. It is the basis for his entire philosophy of love. "For all amorousness," he claims, "is rooted in the sexual impulse alone, is in fact absolutely only a more closely determined, specialized, and indeed, in the strictest sense, individualized sexual impulse, however ethereally it may deport itself."

In saying this, Schopenhauer is not denying the importance of love as a force in human affairs. On the contrary, he criticizes La Rochefoucauld for having suggested that romantic love is something of which everyone speaks though no one has actually seen it. No, Schopenhauer insists, love is real and powerful. The erotic emotions described by all the poets, novelists, and playwrights occur in everyday life; people do behave like Goethe's Werther and Rousseau's fictional characters; and therefore the significance of passionate love must be emphasized rather than doubted or disregarded. In arising out of libidinal impulse, love manifests the workings of the will more explicitly than anything else in human nature.

Schopenhauer can make this assertion because he believes that sexual passion is itself an appearance in the individual's consciousness, indeed an epiphany, of the metaphysical will that surges through the universe. Nothing else that happens to human beings can have greater importance; nothing else reveals reality more directly.

In the passage I have been discussing, Schopenhauer would seem to be ridiculing pretensions to the ethereal that lovers (and idealistic philosophers) may use to mask the sexual basis of the amorous emotion. But Schopenhauer's argument is more enterprising than that alone would suggest. For he interprets the pretentiousness in love as part of the devious workings of the will, its subtlety, comparable to what Hegel called "the cunning of reason." In itself, sexual impulse is purely subjective; it can be satisfied with any number of objects regardless of their actual properties. But when sex turns into passionate love, it appears as "objective admiration"—as appreciation or positive evaluation of attributes in the beloved that the lover considers admirable apart from the subjective need that his sexual instincts have created. To this extent all passionate love is illusory; and the greater the passion, the greater the illusion. At the same time, however, there is an objective basis to these delusions of love. They constitute a biological "strategem," as Schopenhauer calls it, by which nature attains its ends. For the will acts as it does, deceiving the lover's consciousness with respect to the objectivity of goodness or perfection in the beloved, in order to direct his sexual appetite towards a mate that is suitable, even optimal, for the goals of reproduction. Therein lies the cunning and the purposefulness of passionate love.

Nature and the will are primarily concerned about the preservation of the species, Schopenhauer tells us, and consequently all amorousness is really directed toward the propagation of the next generation, which also involves the determination of its properties. The objectivity in passionate love consists in the bonding of two persons of the opposite sex who are needed to create precisely the kind of child that the will requires at this time. In itself their sexual instinct, being random and subjective, could not have guaranteed that just these two individuals would mate. By causing them to fall passionately in love with one another, to delude themselves into thinking there is a unique and incomparable value that each possesses, the will arranges for their sexual drive to be directed toward just the outcome that *it* desires.

This is what Schopenhauer meant in saying that amorousness is sexual impulse "more closely determined," "specialized," and "individualized." For the next generation to have a definite and determinate composition, it is necessary that this particular man and that particular woman take an interest in one another, find each other worthy of their obsessive attention, feel sexual excitement, and unite in the making of children. Passionate love is the agency by which the will carries out this goal, and in one way or another all types of love or mutual attraction are related to it.

Schopenhauer's philosophy of love leads him to various conclusions about human intimacy that we shall have to consider in detail. But from the outset it is worth noting how his theory mingles divergent elements in the history of ideas. Since Plato's *Symposium*, in which Aristophanes recounts the myth of the alter ego, the idealist tradition had maintained that lovers were made for each other and that their union signified a metaphysical mission that was greater than anything else they could desire. With its faith in the value of persons, romanticism took this to mean that lovers could fulfill themselves only in the interpersonal oneness that their love created. In a sense, Schopenhauer says the same. But now the concept of the person as an ultimate category has been eliminated, and merging with the alter ego is explained as physical union serving biological ends that neither lover recognizes. In general, the metaphysical striving that Plato interpreted as a search for the Good, and that benign Romantics envisaged as spirit in the process of ennobling carnal impulse, Schopenhauer considers a clever pattern of illusions through which the will establishes our subservience to reproductive necessity.

Alternatively, one can read the historical affiliation from the other end: Schopenhauer inherits the ideas of former realists who reduced love to sex, but then he clothes this deflationary perspective in the garb he has acquired from Romantics of the early nineteenth century. Like these Romantics, Schopenhauer assumes a teleology in love, for its operation is determined by a goal that lures the will into one future configuration or another. Schopenhauer does not think this goal can be known in advance; and in saying that the will is blind, he would seem to deny that it is providential in its evolution. But this too he could have learned from Fichte and others who thought of natural process in general, and human love in particular, as a search for unknown and even unknowable possibilities. For Plato and for Christianity there was a transcendental entity that defined the direction of love—the Good or God as the terminating object of desire. Schopenhauer agrees with the Romantics in denying that any object, at least any knowable object, can reveal the goal or destination of love. He says that the "precise determination" of characteristics in the next generation is "a much higher and worthier aim" than the fanciful notions that fill the minds of people who love each other; but he also insists that until a man and a woman have been thrown together in the violent urgency of passionate love, no one could have realized that their union was needed by the will. Once each generation comes into being, we can say that this was what the will required. But we cannot predict anything about future stages in its trajectory, and therefore the object of love must always be unknown and unforeseeable. Except for the elimination of spirit as a fundamental category, this is what Fichte had also said.

In explaining love as the yearning for a future condition rather than the fulfillment of a prior essence, Schopenhauer's ideas resemble those of Hegel. Though Schopenhauer takes every opportunity to revile Hegel, whom he called a Caliban of modern philosophy, he could very well have been quoting him when he says that lovers long for "fusion into a single being, in order then to go on living only as this being; and this longing receives its fulfilment in the child they produce." Schopenhauer differs from Hegel, however, in denying that the fulfillment of the lovers' longing brings happiness to them. Hegel believed that the process of self-sacrifice for the sake of a new creation reveals the being of each organism; to participate successfully in that process must therefore provide the happiness that every individual seeks. This is what Schopenhauer emphatically denies. For the process, as he sees it, operates in a way that defeats all possibilities of happiness.

According to Schopenhauer, the will is not interested in the well-being of any individual. As long as they are passionately hungering for one another, striving for the oneness they consider to be spiritual or nonmaterial although it is really sexual, lovers are incapable of experiencing happiness. They suffer from that sickness of soul, that tormented restlessness and even madness, which poets have described in endless detail. Once they come together in a coital embrace, they may satisfy the need for propagation but they will find that their passion immediately dissipates without bringing them lasting joy. On the contrary, Schopenhauer repeats and indeed insists upon the cynical commonplace about love disappearing as soon as sexual intercourse has occurred. His metaphysical doctrine about the will enables him to avoid the crudity of suggesting that lovers (particularly the male) are *merely* interested in seduction, deluding one another about their real intentions. For, according to Schopenhauer, they have no way of knowing what they really do intend. They are themselves deluded and cannot possibly realize that their intellect (which includes their own thinking about the love that controls them) is just a superstructure. Nature is using them as instrumentalities, luring them into the requisite attitude by promising an impossible happiness. Once they have planted the seed for a new generation, they come to realize that they have been duped and that nothing in love can make them happy. Eventually their passion disappears; but by then, the will has had its victory and can tolerate disintoxication on the part of the lovers. Each succeeding generation will be enmeshed in similar delusions; for, in this sense, love never dies.

Schopenhauer's pessimism about the human condition in its closest linkage with the will is a corollary of his pessimism about life in general. Human beings are doomed to misery not only because they are the pawns of an unconscious, instinctive force that has no concern for their personal welfare, but also because the innate structure of human affect inherently defeats that search for happiness which the eighteenth-century philosophers considered basic in man's nature. Like Augustine, Pascal, and any number of Christian moralists, Schopenhauer thinks man searches for happiness in vain. It is a quest that reveals human vanity because nothing on earth will ever bring about the condition people seek. When a man is trying to satisfy a desire, he lacks something and is unhappy to that extent. His attempt to get what he wants means struggling with obstacles and often leads to frustration; the search for happiness is not itself a state of happiness. But if we attain the object of our desire, we quickly lose interest in it, find ourselves satiated, deprived of our original appetite, and so end up with boredom that also prevents us from being happy. This is, in effect, the concept of ennui or *noia*, which recurs in all Romantic literature. For Schopenhauer boredom is the inevitable outcome of success, including sexual success, proving that even at this pole of the affective process happiness is not to be expected.

With pessimism as his general ideology, we should expect Schopenhauer to be a critic of the institution of matrimony. Not at all. Though he himself was never married, he recognizes that marriage offers security for each new generation. He also allows for the existence of relatively happy marriages. What he denies is the likelihood that they can result from passionate love, as so many writers in the nineteenth century thought. For a marriage to be happy, it must provide benefits to the man and woman who are united by it; it must satisfy their individual needs and conscious desires. This is less likely to happen, Schopenhauer claims, if they have been thrown together by a passionate impulse created for instinctual purposes beyond themselves than if they have chosen one another coolly and with careful deliberation about selfish interests. In short, the happy marriage is a marriage of convenience, particularly if it has been arranged by parents or others who are not themselves controlled by sexual passion.

So here too, Schopenhauer confronts us with a pessimistic dilemma. If one wishes to be happy, one must marry for reasons other than love—solid considerations of social, economic, even political advantage that enable one to enjoy the companionship of another human being and the pleasures of family life. This, however, runs counter to the necessities of the will, which must be paramount and which manifest themselves in the sexual love for which all young people yearn, against their best interests. As a philosopher, Schopenhauer stands back and observes the spectacle with serenity and resignation. He does not tell young men and women to accept the sage advice of their worldly-wise parents, and neither does he encourage lovers to follow the instinctive drive regardless of danger to their own happiness. If passionate lovers studied his philosophy, Schopenhauer thinks they might profit from its metaphysical insights; but he reconciles himself to the fact that theirs is not a rational state and thus cannot easily be altered by reasoning. Moreover, in one of his pithy and epigrammatic utterances he suggests that possibly civilization as well as nature benefits from the creative delusions that love instills. Happiness requires the satisfaction of sexual desire, but since that destroys passionate love, it also quiets those longings that make all lovers into poets: "If Petrarch's passion had been satisfied, his song would have been silenced from that moment, just as is that of the bird, as soon as the eggs are laid." All of Freud's book *Civilization and Its Discontents* derives from this Schopenhauerian insight into the discrepancy between the goods of biological nature and those of culture.

Schopenhauer himself addresses the problem from a point of view slightly different from Freud's. Since individuals are insignificant in themselves, man's essence being identical with the will-to-life of the species, he claims that we all recognize that bonds based upon passionate love are deeper and more compelling than marriages of convenience. Even when sexual love is adulterous or dishonorable, it is justified in advancing the interests of the species regardless of the suffering it causes to individuals or society. He quotes with approbation Chamfort's remark that, regardless of obstacles created by husbands and parents, passionate lovers "belong to each other *by nature* and *by divine right*, in spite of laws and human conventions." It is this priority of the species over the individual that theater audiences sense when they applaud comedies that culminate in what is called a happy ending. The ending is a happy one only for the will. The fictional lovers will go on to marry one another and be miserable. But this is something the audience does not care to think about. Like the lovers themselves, the delighted spectators have been fooled into thinking that passional satisfactions lead to individual happiness. The metaphysical truth that Schopenhauer detects in the audience's response is the fact that by sacrificing their welfare for the sake of the will the lovers achieve a kind of biological sublimity. They are closer to nature than men and women who, marrying for reasons other than love, are more likely to be happy in later life. "In making a marriage, either the individual or the interest of the species must come off badly."

For the most part, the interest of the species prevails, as it must if the species is to survive. But, of course, we cannot know what that interest is. Men and women are driven into each other's arms by a sexual instinct that the will manipulates for the sake of generating offspring only they can produce; but why the will, or nature in general, should need just these children rather than others that could survive equally well, this is a question to which Schopenhauer claims to have no answer. He does say that each new individual is, to some extent, a new Platonic form striving to come into existence through the vehemence of the parents' passion. But since passion results from causal patterns within the will itself, its occurrence must always be incomprehensible even to the philosopher.

At the same time, Schopenhauer also believes that one can generalize about the conditions under which passionate love normally exists. Sexual impulse being largely indiscriminate, all men and women have a certain amount of desire for someone of the opposite sex. But this is not to be confused with love. As we saw, sexual drive becomes passionate longing only when the man and woman have an *individualized* need for each other as the parent of the child they can produce. To show the nature of individual needs of this sort, Schopenhauer embarks upon a series of empirical generalizations that tend to make the modern reader squirm. Written before the science of genetics existed, his speculations about inherited characteristics are often simplistic and based on superstition. For instance, he thinks that the suitability of two parents, and therefore the corresponding intensity of their passion for one another, is related to the level of intelligence in the female and to the strength of character in the male. Since children inherit their character from their fathers and their intelligence from their mothers, Schopenhauer says, passion will be most intense when a man of strong character encounters a woman of high intelligence. In general, he believes that the will unites persons who make up one another's deficiencies in terms of the needs of whatever children are to be generated.

The details of these grossly unscientific remarks need not detain us very long. If he were alive today, Schopenhauer would probably insist that theories of gene determinism, as formulated by many of the sociobiologists, vindicate and extend the insights of his general metaphysics; and he would recognize that the will operates through Darwinian evolution and natural selection in ways that no one in his period could possibly have imagined. Having only classical philosophy and his own experience to fall back on, Schopenhauer tells us that each person loves what he himself lacks. He observes that the strongest passions are not elicited by those who have the most regular features or the greatest beauty of a conventional sort. But this, he thinks, is due to the fact that passion is more definitely related to the overcoming of biological extremes in each individual. Though a short man would not realize why he has such feelings, the advantages to his offspring will cause him to long for a tall woman; a "manly man" would likewise seek a "womanly woman"; and so forth. Schopenhauer even thinks that a man may fall in love with an extremely ugly woman, provided that "the whole of her abnormalities are precisely the opposite to, and thus the corrective of, his own."

Behind these primitive generalizations there lurks a kind of realism that is still defended by many thinkers in the present. Not only is love thought to be reducible to genetic forces beyond the lovers' awareness, but also the biological differences between men and women are used as a basis for distinguishing between male and female passion. Since love is a passionate urge to beget and the male has the capacity for propagating many children every year, Schopenhauer argues that this explains why men easily fall in love with one woman after another. Being limited in the number of children that she can produce, a woman will have a contrary inclination to constancy or fidelity. She senses an instinctive need to hold onto the father of her future offspring, the one man who would be most likely to protect and care for them. It is therefore understandable, Schopenhauer concludes, that all societies have condemned adultery in women much more than in men.

Schopenhauer himself obviously agrees with this differential attitude toward the sexes. He is often charged with being a misogynist, largely because of comments that he makes in his celebrated essay "Of Women." There he asserts that by their very nature women lack rationality and are intuitive rather than intellectual. He also finds them incapable of developing a sense of justice: for they are designed to bear children and nourish the next generation rather than to rise above nature, to think or adjudicate, as a man might do. How Schopenhauer reconciles his low opinion of woman's intellect with the notion that intelligence is inherited from the female, I do not know; but even in the area of beauty, his essay insists that only a man whose mind has been befuddled by sexual desire for women could think that there is anything aesthetically valuable in "that under-sized, narrow-shouldered, broad-hipped, and short-legged race." In one of his letters he even denies that the faces of these "teat-bedecked creatures" can compare in beauty with those of handsome youths.

If this is not misogyny, what is? At the same time, I think one does Schopenhauer an injustice if one magnifies the importance of these malicious utterances. And neither does it help to ascribe them to latent homosexuality, as recent psychoanalysts have done. For in his essay, as in his philosophy as a whole, Schopenhauer is not primarily interested in condemning women or putting them in their place as the *sexus sequior*, the second sex. What he really wishes to attack is the concept of "the lady." Schopenhauer is particularly revolted by Western notions of gallantry or adoration of the female, and in general what he calls "our preposterous system of reverence—that highest product of Teutonico-Christian stupidity." Above all, he wants to abolish the social consequences of medieval courtly love. Not only does it put women in a false position, he says, but also it elevates a few women of the upper classes at the expense of the great majority of females who become drudges and are rendered needlessly unhappy by an unnatural social system. Through the institution of monogamy, the lady receives, for no good reason, honors and privileges denied to all those others who are relegated to the status of old maid, working woman, and whore. The 80,000 prostitutes in the London of his day Schopenhauer cites as the "human sacrifices offered up on the altar of monogamy." Their suffering is caused by the fact that bourgeois marriage excludes them from a condition of respectability while fostering in married women the arrogance that belongs to the archaic notion of the lady. This idealistic conception of a superior female allows, indeed encourages, society as a whole to ignore its unjust and cruel subjugation of all other women.

In giving his solution, Schopenhauer advocates polygamy as it existed in the Orient. Under that arrangement, no woman is treated as a lady, for none of them receives disproportionate reverence. Moreover, every woman is taken care of on a more or less equal basis; consequently, the majority are not forced to suffer for the sake of a favored few. Schopenhauer's discussion of polygamy is especially interesting if one compares it with Hume's essay on the different types of marital institutions. Hume criticizes polygamy not only because it leads to jealousy among the males and prevents the children from having access to parental intimacy of a sort that naturally occurs in a small monogamous family, but also because it enables one man to become the barbarous ruler of many women.

None of these considerations seem to enter into Schopenhauer's thinking, which is always guided by the metaphysics of sexual love that we have been discussing. If intimacy between male and female is primarily determined by biological considerations relevant to the continuance of the species, society can hardly be justified in favoring some women over others unless there is a genetic advantage in doing so. The concept of the lady arrogates superiority not to those who would be the best mothers but only to those who are born into wealthy or famous families. Schopenhauer prefers polygamy because it gives all women an equal opportunity to bear children. That being his primary concern, he neglects the many other inequalities, particularly in relation to the dominant patriarch, that polygamy necessarily involves and that the concept of the lady seeks to rectify. Nor does he consider the plight of the peripheral males who are excluded from fatherhood in polygamous societies, and in general he has only the vaguest ideas about who might or might not be a suitable parent. Discussing male homosexuality in an appendix to his metaphysical speculations, he suggests that it may exist as a device by which the will eliminates undesirable fathers without having to resort to the more difficult process of destroying their sexual impulses. His argument is not very plausible inasmuch as it is based on the assumption that pederasty mainly occurs in older men whose genetic contribution would be harmful.

There are other difficulties in Schopenhauer's ideas about men and women. The most glaring defect, I believe, is his inability to recognize how greatly nongenetic factors influence marital and sexual relations among human beings. For him, passion is always a fever in the blood, and imagination, as an element within it, operates merely in an epiphenomenal way, masking the reality of the situation rather than contributing directly to it. What Stendhal and Shelley found so crucial for understanding the nature of love, Schopenhauer ignores almost completely.

To a large extent, Schopenhauer's philosophy of love is limited, and therefore distorted, by the fact that the instinctual forces upon which he focuses his entire analysis must operate at an unconscious level. This not only makes his argument reductivistic in the extreme, relying at every point upon a dubious distinction between appearance and reality, but also it precludes an adequate understanding of the role of consummation. When Hume, for instance, talks about marriage, or intimate relations as a whole, he constantly considers what may or may not satisfy, given the multifarious desires that motivate persons under different circumstances. The paramount question always is: what will help people to *enjoy* life, the conditions of their existence being what they are? To Schopenhauer this kind of approach seems superficial, and that is why he constructs a universal metaphysics to explain the dynamics of sex. But nowhere does he show how affective responses are related to one another in a coherent pattern based upon the consummatory goods that they afford.

In Hegel every synthesis or higher oneness operates as a realization of the dialectical units that belong to it. For Hegel, as for Schopenhauer, no consummation is permanent and therefore each must yield to the demands of some future possibility. But Hegel takes this as proof that all life, far from alternating between frustration and boredom, is pervasively an ongoing search for new and richer values. That is the basis of his optimism, and possibly Schopenhauer is justified in reviling it as wish-fulfillment on the part of a deluded philosopher. Even if Schopenhauer is right about Hegel, however, one constantly intuits that Schopenhauer himself has no awareness of how people feel when they are actually fulfilling their nature. Enjoyment, consummation, as a constructive and consecutive element in life, he makes little effort to analyze or understand.

For all his emphasis upon the will, Schopenhauer scarcely mentions the joy to be felt in gratifying it, the satisfaction and delight that animate creatures experience when they do get what they want, when they fully express their instincts and carry through their vital impulses with a sense of completion. There is in Schopenhauer virtually no idea of what it would be like to accept and *affirm* the order of things in nature. I shall presently turn to his attempt to achieve salvation by negating the will, but first I wish to point out that one cannot truly reject something unless one knows what it is to accept it. Schopenhauer assumes that those who talk or philosophize about accepting their role in nature are duped by an illusion of the intellect that the will has created for reasons of its own. The truth is that his own experience is simply deficient at this point. He cannot perceive that the comfort and security creatures feel when they are enjoying their natural condition, satisfying basic drives and savoring whatever benefits these may provide, is an authentic response that runs through all existence like a voiceless Hosanna.

Schopenhauer would reply to this criticism by claiming that I am referring to a rare and insignificant aspect of life. He wisely hedges his pessimism by leaving open the possibility of occasional but very infrequent moments of happiness. After reminding us that happy marriages are uncommon, he then remarks—in a sarcastic passage written "for the consolation of tender and loving natures"—that sometimes sexual passion accompanies real friendship between man and woman. In such a case, a truly happy marriage would be possible since the needs of the individuals could be satisfied as well as the demands of the species. But Schopenhauer is obviously throwing this out as a straw for those desperate optimists who require something to cling to. He gives us no reason to think that the harmonious dispositions needed for friendship are anything but a freak occurrence in passional lovers; and he is quick to point out that harmony is more likely to occur after sexual passion has disappeared. We are left with the impression that somewhere there might exist a man and a woman who are able to love each other passionately while also enjoying each other's company as friends, but the odds of their meeting and living together are hardly worth the wager. In other words, even if Schlegel and Shelley were right in characterizing love as a confluence of heterosexual passion and interpersonal friendship, it almost never happens among real men and women.

Having so little hope of ever finding a durable combination of friendship and passion, Schopenhauer does not waste time trying to delineate the nature of love in marriage. For him the effort would be similar to describing the happiness of Siamese twins—it is something that may occur, but it cannot tell us much about man's reality. He compensates for this shortcoming in his erotic imagination by the careful attention he lavishes upon the phenomenon of compassion. In his book *On the Basis of Morality* he directly attacks Kant's attempt to locate the groundwork of ethics in rationalistic criteria such as the categorical imperative. Continuing Schiller's belief that in morality feelings must be fundamental, Schopenhauer claims that only the compassion human beings feel for one another's suffering can provide a basis for ethics: "Only insofar as an action has sprung from compassion does it have moral value." Through compassion man surmounts the egoism that naturally leads him to desire goods only for himself. Compassion causes an individual to want for others whatever will be good for them, as a way of alleviating their suffering, regardless of who they are or how they came to suffer. Not only does Schopenhauer think of compassion as "an immediate participation" in the suffering of other people, but also he recognizes that it can occur apart from any ulterior motives. He calls compassion an "everyday phenomenon" and describes it as the origin of "all satisfaction and all well-being and happiness." He thereby unifies duty and inclination, ethical obligation and the search for personal welfare, in a way that Kant deemed utterly impossible. Not since Rousseau had any philosopher argued so persuasively that human feeling independent of reason could thus accommodate both the right and the good.

Schopenhauer does not say how it is that men are capable of experiencing compassion for one another. He calls this occurrence an astonishing mystery, since the intellect cannot explain it. Through compassion the barrier between ego and non-ego is momentarily breached; people then identify with each other in the sense that one person shares the suffering in another and is moved to act as if it were present in himself. Since the will is identical in all living creatures, Schopenhauer wonders whether compassion may not have the metaphysical function of breaking down the intellect's mistaken belief about separate individuality. But Schopenhauer can take this step only with great difficulty. If he accepted any such doctrine, it would undermine his official pessimism. For though compassion would still be a response to universal suffering, it would be seen as belonging to the core of man's being. In other words, the will would have to be considered moral, at least to the extent that it provides the mysterious source for our capacity to participate in other people and to find our own happiness by acting for their welfare.

From this facet of Schopenhauer's philosophy, one could go on to construct a progressive, healthy-minded, and even optimistic attitude toward life. As I have been emphasizing throughout, Schopenhauer is often less remote from the tradition represented by Hegel than he likes to think, and despite his scorn for the rationalism of idealistic philosophy. Schopenhauer's ideas about compassion also align him with Christian ethics more than one might have expected. He argues that the two principal virtues in ethics are justice and loving-kindness. Both derive from the phenomenon of compassion; but while justice is negative insofar as it prevents us from hurting others for our own benefit, loving-kindness acts as a positive identification that makes us want to eliminate whatever distresses the other person. Schopenhauer points out that ancient philosophy did not think of loving-kindness as a virtue, Plato having limited his analysis to justice and related concepts. Only with the advent of Christianity, he says, does love of one's fellow man become the basic virtue in Western ethics. Schopenhauer claims that Hinduism and Buddhism had long since formulated the moral teachings of Christianity, but in the Western world he thinks that ideas about brotherly love begin with the Gospels and that the great merit of Christianity consists in disseminating these concepts as ethical mandates.

Leaving aside the historical inaccuracies in these generalizations about the history of religion, particularly with respect to Judaism—which Schopenhauer misrepresents wildly and sometimes to the point of anti-Semitism—it is much to his credit that he never ignores the cruelties Christians have often inflicted upon one another, and collectively upon everyone else. He argues at length against slavery, condemning it as inconsistent with Christian teachings about compassion. He even defends the rights of animals on the grounds that they manifest the same will-to-life as human beings and therefore ought to be treated with similar compassion.

From this benign and wholesome side of his philosophy, Schopenhauer might have reached conclusions that mitigate his vision of cosmic horror. It would not have been necessary for him to turn his dramatic mask upside down or to pretend that life is a divine comedy. He had only to develop the implications for happiness and personal fulfillment in experiencing a sense of oneness with other creatures. He could even have explored the possibility of harmonization between passion and compassion. For there is nothing in the instinctive yearning for a sexual partner that necessarily prevents the lover from sympathizing with him or her as a fellow participant in the sufferings of life. Yet Schopenhauer minimizes the likelihood of any such harmonization, just as he denies the occurrence of friendship between all (or virtually all) passionate lovers. In both cases, he would probably defend himself by citing statistical frequencies. But of course, he had little access to the requisite data, and the truth is that everything in his own temperament closed off his understanding in these areas. His hatred of the world is so great that he prefers to believe—"for the beauty of it," as Molière's misanthrope says—that feelings of humanity cannot be expected to occur in ordinary human beings, particularly those who are possessed by sexual passion.

It is not surprising, therefore, that the final reaches of Schopenhauer's philosophy take one into an ascetic denial of life. Here too his thinking shows its derivation from both Eastern and Western religions. Though he recognizes that the idea of loving one's neighbor belongs to the essence of Christianity, as well as Hinduism and Buddhism, he gives his ultimate allegiance only to the part of these religions that wishes to transcend morality. What interests him most is their teaching that the purpose of life is renunciation, which he interprets as the negating of the will in all its forms. Renunciation is for Schopenhauer the opposite of what it was for Hegel. It involves not an acquiescence in the greater mission of the Absolute, but rather a dying in oneself that symbolically represents the destruction everywhere of everything's will to live. To prove that his nay-saying has a long history in Western thought, Schopenhauer cites the writings of traditional moralists, of theologians like St. Augustine, and of various mystics who believed that the total annihilation of life would be the fulfillment of God's intention. He claims that the Old Testament is absurdly optimistic, but that the New Testament enunciates the spirit of true pessimism. He condemns modern versions of both Catholicism and Protestantism, calling the former "disgracefully abused" Christianity and the latter a "degenerate" variation. He remarks that Protestantism may be suitable for comfortably married parsons, but that it has led to naive rationalism (e.g. Hegel's) and neglected Christianity's authentic awareness of the guilt and sinfulness in existence as a whole.

Traditional asceticism transcends morality for the sake of religious advantages, heavenly bliss and a reciprocal love of God, but for Schopenhauer the denial of life is itself salvation. The Schopenhauerian saint feels no religious love and hopes for no rewards in heaven. He merely wishes to enter into the Nirvana which is total nothingness, the complete negation of the will. Schopenhauer relies upon this Buddhist concept as the one that most perfectly articulates the paradox of nonbeing. We cannot imagine what it would be like for the whole world, or even ourselves, to be nothing; and yet our sense of total guilt and sinfulness, together with our revulsion at the universal suffering that belongs to the nature of being, convinces us that it would be better if there were nothing at all. The will cannot conceive its own destruction; and since we are all manifestations of the will, it is incomprehensible how we can actually will the termination of will. This is the paradox I mentioned earlier. In a chapter on Schopenhauer's philosophy, Bertrand Russell cites it as a basic flaw; but Schopenhauer himself had already pointed out the difficulty. He defends the idea of willing not to will by saying it is an act of salvation that the intellect can never understand, for it encloses a great mystery that our minds are unable to fathom. He rightly insists that there will always be problems that no philosophy can solve; and yet, everything he has learned from life assures him that only in saying no to the will, asserting our essential dignity and refusing as best we can to contribute to the tragedy of existence, do we attain a sense of spiritual freedom.

Rather than attack Schopenhauer because the idea of Nirvana and the notion of nothingness are baffling to us, we may find it more fruitful to see how Schopenhauer's doctrine contributes in its own way to the concept of love-death. At the end of his discussion about the metaphysics of sexual love, Schopenhauer remarks that his analysis has confirmed two fundamental truths: first, that man's true being is indestructible since it renews itself in the next generation through the mechanism of sexual instinct; and second, that this enduring kernel of human nature is simply the species' will-to-life and therefore the immortal part in each of the lovers. This, however, is similar to what Schopenhauer said about death. It too enabled an individual to rise above his mere individuality for the sake of merging with the immortal and indestructible kernel of his being. The acceptance of death and the affirmation of sexual love are thus comparable modes of submitting to the will.

Schopenhauer's philosophy is, however, more extreme than this. For he wishes to argue that love and death are not only similar but also identical in certain aspects. Nor is it simply a question of sexual lovers dying in their separate interests in order to merge with the necessities of nature. Since the will expresses itself most distinctly in coitus, and since all passionate love is just a circuitous device of the will, it is the act of sexual intercourse that truly shows forth the character of love. But that act Schopenhauer sees as itself a kind of death. Though he does not say so overtly, he sides with all the ascetics in history who found something self-destructive in the physical process of lovemaking. For Schopenhauer as well as the ascetics, the brute materiality in reproductive behavior could only appear as the death of something nobler in us all. Liebestod, love-death, is thus a reality, though not to be considered a benign consummation as the idealistic Romantics thought.

In this vein, Schopenhauer suggests that people are ashamed of the sexual act because they know it is the archetypal affirmation of the will, and therefore that which creates this life of pain and misery. He claims that coitus is indeed original sin, in the sense of fundamental guilt for the evils of existence, since man could not exist without it. We emancipate ourselves by denying life in general and by rejecting passionate love, that being a false kind of death since it is really part of the will's struggle for immortality. We attain salvation by refusing to acquiesce in this debasing conspiracy of love and death. We stand back with a proud gesture of disdain, approximating the apétie that Sade idealized. Sade thought this could be achieved by carrying out in cold obedience the demands of sexual nature. Schopenhauer approves of the coldness, for that eliminates deceitful passion, but he finds the greatest liberation in not acting at all, in exorcising sex itself.

As we shall see in the volume that follows this one, Nietzsche correctly diagnosed this ascetic way of thinking as just another manifestation of the will to live—one that enabled Schopenhauer himself to survive, quite cheerfully, as a nay-saying pessimistic philosopher. More than he chose to admit, Schopenhauer resembles those Christian mystics who wished to die in the body in order to live in the spirit. They did not renounce all being unequivocally, as Schopenhauer recommends, but his kind of renunciation is motivated by a similar detachment from nature and the world in general. It is a detachment that nevertheless reattaches the individual, for in the process of renunciation one expresses and asserts oneself as a creature that turns its mind and heart against the vital forces that actually sustain it. The link to nature is forged, for Schopenhauer and the religious ascetics, by the fact that rejecting the world provides its own kind of serenity and possibly happiness. As against

Nietzsche, Schopenhauer might have insisted that therein lies the strength of his philosophy: by being a pessimist, he could have said, and thus remaining in touch with reality, one achieves the salvation of living in the world, and enjoying it, while also rising above it. But then, we may ask, has the pessimist really renounced anything?

Whatever we think of this dilemma, there is no point in amassing arguments against Schopenhauer and the other ascetics. One cannot reason them out of their condemnation of the world. There is no way of proving that a physical process such as coitus can have supreme value, or that life is worth living. But even if we agree with Schopenhauer's judgments about the tragedy of existence, we may yet assert that the mere enjoyment of life—that being the outcome for which our instincts seem to have been created—constitutes a good beyond denial. In refusing to accept the will and therefore rejecting the entire phenomenon of sexual passion, Schopenhauer is free to define his being as one who has not chosen this mode of existence, as one whose intellect rebels against it. But he is hoist with his own petard, for in realizing that the intellect (and what else does a philosopher use in formulating his view of the world?) is only a precarious guide to the truth, he can hardly hope to convince anyone who has opted for a different way of life. Schopenhauer's rebellion—giving back the ticket to the universe, as Ivan Karamazov says in Dostoyevsky's novel—may be justified as a defense against the disruptiveness of love. Had he devoted himself to passion, or even compassion, Schopenhauer might not have experienced those calm, contemplative moments that he cherished and that provided his insights into aesthetics and morality. And certainly he is right to idealize what looms the largest in himself, to deflate love in his philosophy as a way of negating aspects of the world in which he does not wish to participate. But nature keeps on going, the universe being enriched by his thought though altered very little by his teachings.

What remains from Schopenhauer's philosophy is the notion that love takes us beyond the shallow interests of everyday existence, that it puts us in contact with something close to the core of being which, however, is not spiritual and cannot be enjoyed fully in this or any other life. By his long way round to Nirvana, Schopenhauer transmutes the concept of love-death into a doctrine the earlier Romantics could hardly have imagined or developed. He nevertheless ignores questions they raised for which he himself has no solution, questions about the love of persons and the stages one must go through in order to attain healthy and harmonious sexuality. His honesty, his sharp, ruthless insight, and his compassion for universal suffering are undeniable. But as a philosopher of love, he fails us where we need him most.

In a famous letter to Franz Liszt written in 1854, Richard Wagner describes the "gift from Heaven" that has come to him in the reading of Schopenhauer's philosophy: "All the Hegels, etc. are charlatans by the side of him. His chief idea, the final negation of the desire of life, is terribly serious, but it shows the only salvation possible. . . . This is the genuine, ardent, longing for death, for absolute unconsciousness, total nonexistence." The letter ends with the following indication of what would be the basic theme in Wagner's as-yet unwritten opera *Tristan and Isolde*: "As I have never in life felt the real bliss of love, I must erect a monument to the most beautiful of all my dreams, in which, from beginning to end, that love shall be thoroughly satiated. I have in my head *Tristan and Isolde*, the simplest but most full-blooded musical conception; with the 'black flag' which floats at the end of it I shall cover myself to die."

These words were written shortly after Wagner had gone through a period of six years in which he wrote his major theoretical works but no music. It was also a period of political involvement related to the revolutions of 1848, in which Wagner actively sided with the radicals. From having been a militant advocate of socialism, firm in his belief that the brotherhood of man would result from the uprooting of tyrannical institutions, he became more and more disillusioned after the revolutions failed. By the time he read Schopenhauer, he had convinced himself that his earlier optimism was thoroughly unrealistic.

In his autobiographical writings, Wagner reports not only that his failure to write music during these six years was largely caused by his changing attitude, but also that his new philosophy revealed to him a dilemma that was present in his previous work. In a letter written in 1856, he gives the Schopenhauerian approach credit for having shown him a contradiction that had pervaded his creative life. In all his intellectual ideas and in all his reasoning about the human condition, he had concluded with the optimists that the world progressed toward betterment; but now he saw that his earlier operas—*The Flying Dutchman, Tannhäuser,* and *Lohengrin*—expressed his deeper feelings of pessimism through their emphasis upon the need for self-renunciation. Wagner resolved his inner contradiction by consciously revising the dramatic structure of the *Ring* cycle, which was to engage him for another eighteen years. Instead of ending with a humanistic speech in which Brünnhilde declares that "in love alone is blessedness to be found," he allows the gods to be destroyed without hope for redemption by anything other than sheer nothingness.

Wagner's overt espousal of Schopenhauer's philosophy during his middle period has been subjected to much critical scrutiny. In an essay entitled "Sufferings and Greatness of Richard Wagner," the novelist Thomas Mann rebukes "official works on Wagner" that deny Schopenhauerian influences upon *Tristan*. Mann argues that Wagner is Schopenhauer's ideological "next of kin," and that *Tristan* specifically embodies Schopenhauer's thought. Against the critics' claim that Schopenhauer was concerned to deny the will whereas *Tristan* affirms it merely in remaining throughout a love drama, Mann insists that Schopenhauer's doctrine is "fundamentally" erotic and basically devoted to the same kind of yearning that *Tristan* articulates in the music.

I think that Mann is mistaken in his interpretation of Schopenhauer. Nowhere does Schopenhauer suggest that sexual passion, or the erotic life in general, is anything but subjugation to impersonal instinct. That is why he insists upon renunciation as the only path to salvation. At the same time, Mann's argument can very well show the greatness, the aesthetic profundity, of Wagner's music drama. For its success as a work of art results from Wagner's ability to exploit his ambivalence toward the two poles of nineteenth-century romanticism—the optimistic and the pessimistic approaches to sexual love. Both are present in *Tristan*, and both are given their proper importance. The writers Mann criticizes are correct in emphasizing the fact that *Tristan* is a love drama, but they are shortsighted in failing to see that it idealizes renunciation and the blessings of death. In no other way can we adequately explain Tristan's wild and suicidal excitement as he tears off his bandages in Act III after learning that Isolde's ship has arrived. In Act II the lovers had agreed that only in death would they finally be able to merge, and that when Tristan embarked for the journey beyond life, Isolde would come to join him. This is the event now presented in Act III. It is not a tragic occurrence because, as Schopenhauer would have said, death is merely a loss of the illusory sense of individual identity, a return to the true nature of one's being, which is what the lovers have been seeking from the start.

On the other hand, it is equally essential to recognize that the oneness between the lovers, their final merging, is not at all the Nirvana of nothingness that Schopenhauer thought death provides. The Wagnerian lovers find their true nature in each other, in each as the alter ego of the other. Death is not for them a total loss of identity but rather the attaining of a *new identity* through eternal oneness and permanent inseparability. This concept of love-death (Liebestod) pervades *Tristan* more completely perhaps than any other great work of art, but its idealistic elements derive from Novalis as much as its pessimistic background bespeaks Schopenhauer. Mann too mentions Novalis as a source of inspiration for Wagner, and he even suggests that Schlegel's *Lucinde* contributed to Wagner's thinking. To this extent, however, the Schopenhauerian elements are countered, even contradicted, by the presence of an optimistic attitude that Wagner could never eliminate from his creations.

In speaking of Novalis as one who reinforced Wagner's optimism, I have not forgotten that Novalis denies the possibility of love's true consummation this side of the grave. That is certainly a form of pessimism; but in comparison to Schopenhauer, Novalis is optimistic merely in believing that love provides the solution to all human problems. It is faith of this sort that remains as an ultimate residue in the Wagner operas. In *Tristan* the mysticism of night which Wagner appropriates from Novalis reveals how sexual passion transcends

political obligations, moral responsibilities, and in general everything that defines daytime consciousness. The love potion is a poison
that Tristan and Isolde drink in a self-destructive gesture of mutual
hatred. Through it they find not only love and death, but also a love
that cannot exist apart from death. The optimism, the underlying
affirmation, rises from the promise that all the sufferings of their
poisoned existence are redeemed, cleansed, and rendered eternally
valid in the transfiguration that occurs once they are reunited
through Liebestod. In a bold but significant revision of the legend,
Wagner has King Marke state that if he had known about the love
potion he would have given Isolde her freedom so that she could
marry Tristan and live happily ever after. If only because so much of
the opera is submerged in the Schopenhauerian mood of gloom and
hopeless desire, we know that any such solution would have been
unthinkable. On the other hand, all Wagnerian lovers anticipate
apotheosis through love, a rebirth in eternity of their oneness, a kind
of second marriage after death. This is something Schopenhauer
would surely have considered ludicrous.

Wagner's ambivalence about optimistic and pessimistic attitudes is
accompanied by a pervasive ambiguity about sex itself. There has
never been opera music more overtly sexual than the score of
Tristan. Act II in particular can be heard as a lengthy presentation of
lovemaking in the most physical sense of the word, terminating in a
kind of coitus interruptus when the king intrudes upon the inter-
twined lovers and Tristan allows himself to be wounded in recognition of his carnal guilt. And yet the dramaturgy of the entire work
denies the libidinal suggestiveness in the music. Unlike its medieval
sources, the opera does not depict the lovers meeting and consum-
mating their love on many occasions. As far as one can tell in merely
reading the libretto, nothing beyond talk and preliminary courtship
occurs between the lovers. We cannot explain this discrepancy by
saying that a theatrical performance in the nineteenth century could
hardly have been more explicit—in *Tannhäuser* it is both essential
and inescapable for us to see that the relationship between Venus
and the protagonist is thoroughly physical.

The plot of *Tristan and Isolde* makes the lovers appear virginal, and
that is because they, unlike Tannhäuser, are to be considered inno-

cent rather than sinful. As embodiments of true love, they express spiritual implications that go beyond the flesh and therefore beyond the sexual pulsations that course throughout the music. In other words, Wagner wanted the best of both worlds: he wished to benefit from naturalistic as well as nonnaturalistic approaches to the nature of love. The motif of *Sehnsucht*, desperate yearning, which structures everything in this masterpiece could thus be taken as either the natural impulse of sexual desire or else as a longing for spiritual oneness that life itself cannot encompass. Both interact throughout the opera incessantly, in an unrelenting counterpoint that enriches the total expressiveness of the work.

Despite Wagner's scornful remark in the letter I have quoted, much of the optimistic ingredient in his thinking comes from Hegel. The contemporary philosopher who had the greatest effect upon Wagner prior to Schopenhauer was Ludwig Feuerbach, a neo-Hegelian who also influenced Karl Marx. Wagner dedicated his early book *The Art Work of the Future* to Feuerbach, whose *Thoughts on Death* he had read. Feuerbach there argues that man's nature consists in a need to love which is most fully revealed in the phenomenon of death. Since love is man overcoming selfishness and sacrificing his willful existence in order to benefit others, it was through death as the complete destruction of oneself that love appears in its purest manifestation. Given the nature of being, one died so that other elements of reality could exist; by accepting the necessity of this self-sacrifice, one fulfilled the universal need to love. In his later philosophy, Feuerbach modified and rejected the idealistic assumptions of his Hegelian origins, but the early operas of Wagner—and possibly all of them—retain Feuerbach's initial ideas about love and death. In varying degrees they assert themselves throughout the ten music dramas that make up the major corpus of Wagner's work.

In *The Flying Dutchman, Tannhäuser*, and *Lohengrin* the Wagnerian myth involves a sinful but extraordinary male whose fate depends upon self-surrendering love that only a pure-hearted woman can experience. Senta provides the requisite *Treue*, devotion, to the Dutchman and thereby liberates him from the misery of wandering without purpose through the world; they are then united in a oneness after death. Tannhäuser is finally purged of the impurities that come from lusting after Venus by the sacrificial intervention of Elisabeth, who resembles Senta in revealing the female capacity for purified love. Elsa fails Lohengrin in that respect, for she intrudes upon his mystical being, asking forbidden questions about his identity instead of accepting him as he is. Lohengrin resembles Tannhäuser and the Dutchman inasmuch as he too is a transgressor, in his case because he loves Elsa more than God. She dies and Lohengrin returns to the service of the Grail, but the nature of love as self-sacrifice cleansing sin or willfulness remains constant.

The continuity between these three operas was clearly recognized by Wagner. Taking the figure of the Flying Dutchman from Heinrich Heine's fable about the Wandering Jew, he merged the idea of yearning for death with the search for the "infinitely womanly woman"—whom Wagner identifies as "a woman who, of very love, shall sacrifice herself." Of *Tannhäuser* he tells us that the legend appealed to him because it manifested an "unapproachable ideal of love." He characterizes the striving for this ideal as "a longing for release from the present, for absorption into an element of endless love, a love denied to earth and reachable through the gates of death alone." He claims to have needed his medieval source because such a love could never be realized "on the loathsome soil of modern sentience." In similar fashion, Wagner considered Lohengrin to be a mythological embodiment of the yearning for human happiness that Zeus experienced in his love for the woman Semele. This love, Wagner states, is the longing for a total physical oneness, which can only cause the god to "dissolve and disappear" and the mortal who yearns for God to be "undone, annulled." That is what Wagner calls "the necessity of love . . . love's truest, highest essence."

In *Tristan* and the *Ring* cycle Wagner abandons very little of his previous attitude toward love. In *Tristan* the loss of self through love becomes an exclusive theme that eliminates the lovers' episodic struggles to survive, which had dominated the original thirteenth-century text of Gottfried von Strassburg. Wagner accounts for this fundamental change by describing his opera as an exposition of the inner turmoil of love, as opposed to a narrative about its conflict with the external world. In the *Ring*, the magic of the Tristanian love potion recurs in the sorcery that causes hostility between Siegfried and Brünnhilde. The evil effects of such magic are overcome by Brünnhilde's expiating suicide. The lovers are reunited when Brünnhilde immolates herself on Siegfried's funeral pyre and then joins him in a bliss after death. The gods, and the totality of meaningless existence they represent, go up in smoke; but the final measures of the music enunciate the theme of "redemption through love." This is all that remains after the tortuous intrigue and endless misery that propelled world-history to its cataclysmic end.

In writing about *Tristan* and the *Ring*, Wagner points out that the idea of "death through stress of love" is identical in both, though elaborated in different ways. He defines love in *Tristan* as "desire without attainment; for each fruition sows the seeds of fresh desire, till in its final lassitude the breaking eye beholds a glimmer of the highest bliss; it is the bliss of quitting life, of being no more, of last redemption." In a letter about the *Ring*, Wagner begins his commentary by saying that "We must learn *to die*, and to die in the fullest sense of the word. The fear of the end is the source of all lovelessness, and this fear is generated only when love itself begins to wane." He describes his work as a revelation of how the human race lost its capacity for love, which nevertheless shows itself in the character of Siegfried. But Siegfried alone is only half complete: "It is only along with Brünnhilde that he becomes the redeemer." Consequently, "it is woman, suffering and willing to sacrifice herself, who becomes at last the real, conscious redeemer: for what is love itself but the 'eternal feminine' (*das ewig Weibliche*)." Thus we return to Goethe, except that now the ideas of renunciation and Liebestod have been accentuated as never before.

In the two remaining operas—*The Mastersingers of Nuremberg* and *Parsifal*—some critics have seen a resolution of the problems about love posed in the other works. In a sense they are right. Both dramas end with the prospect of successful achievement on earth. Though the music and the myth in each are vehicles for expressing constant striving, they now include positive solutions and even happy endings. The *Mastersingers* is a human comedy in which the young lovers marry one another after proving themselves worthy in the eyes of their society. *Parsifal* is basically a folktale in which the innocent simpleton acquires knowledge through experience and then redeems his fellow man as well as himself through acts of sympathy.

At the same time, one must also recognize that Wagner's earlier despair about satisfying sexual passion in life reappears throughout these works. Though Walther von Stolzing wins Eva by singing a prize song that transfers her "morning dream song" into an expression of his love, Wagner shows greater insight in depicting Hans Sachs' resignation to an existence without sexual fulfillment. Similarly, it is only once he has risen above temptations of the flesh that Parsifal can avoid the fate of Amfortas. Without his sexual purity, i.e. renunciation of passionate love, Parsifal's capacity for sympathy could not alone have enabled him to become a redeemer.

The word Wagner uses to define the power of sympathy in Parsifal is *Mitleid*, literally "suffering with." It is a term that recurs throughout Wagner's work. It is used to refer to Senta's identification with the plight of the Dutchman, and it serves as the cause of Brünnhilde's intervention on behalf of Siegfried's parents. While working on *Tristan*, Wagner writes in a letter that Mitleid is "the strongest fiber of my moral being, and it is undoubtedly this which is also the fountainhead of my art." Wagner then describes Mitleid as the suffering that he himself undergoes when he knows someone else is suffering. As such, it is an identification with another person's being, precisely of the sort that Schopenhauer's book on the foundations of morality analyzes as the nature of compassion in general.

It is understandable, therefore, that scholars have sometimes interpreted Mitleid in Wagner as if it were indeed Schopenhauerian. In the first volume of *The World as Will and Representation*, Schopenhauer says that "all love . . . is compassion or sympathy"; and this has been taken as a forerunner of Wagner's idea. But Schopenhauer's thinking about love is much more complex than Wagner's. When Schopenhauer refers to "all love" in this quotation, he has in mind only love that could be defined as fellow-feeling or loving-kindness. Though he sees this saintly identification with the suffering of others as a recognition that the will in oneself is not to be preferred over the will in others, and in fact that the will is the same in all alike, Schopenhauer makes no attempt to reduce the oneness of sexual passion to the oneness in compassion. For him they are both modes of living in the world, and are thus inferior to the attaining of salvation through the denial of life.

As a result, the concept of Mitleid functions in Schopenhauer's philosophy in ways that are unrelated to what Wagner says. For Schopenhauer, compassion is a moral category, not a religious one. It indicates the foundation of ethical judgment, which arises from a felt concern for others, but it is not the same as renunciation, which entails the rejecting not only of one's own selfish interests but also of being as a whole. Despite the fact that Wagner frequently repeats Schopenhauerian phrases about denying the will, his concept of Mitleid belongs to a mysticism quite different from anything in Schopenhauer. For Wagner, Mitleid is a religious as well as an ethical concept. It involves faith in spiritual possibilities and thus reaches beyond a search for mere nothingness.

It is for this reason that so much of Wagnerian drama looks to us now like Christianity transformed by nineteenth-century romanticism. The concept of love that radiates from Wagner's works is largely an attempt to transmute Christian yearning into an earthly longing for something that cannot be attained on earth itself. Wagner denied that *Tannhäuser, Lohengrin*, and even *Parsifal* were pietistic in any narrow sense; and certainly the orthodox elements in them are freely intermingled with others that are heretical or even pagan. *Tannhäuser* and *Lohengrin* have recourse to folk magic just as *Parsifal* includes significant bits of Hinduism and Buddhism. Like Feuerbach before him, Wagner thought that questions about the literal truth of religion must always be subordinate to its metaphorical truthfulness, and he always sought to express the "mythos" that would reveal eternal absolutes underlying all types of religious devotion. As a matter of fact, however, the Christian faith predominates—in one way or another—throughout Wagner's mythmaking. It is most apparent in the Protestant sensibility that pervades each scene of *The Mastersingers of Nuremberg*, but one can show its supervening presence in all the other works as well.

In one of his letters to Liszt, Wagner claims that he can hardly understand the *Paradiso* part of Dante's *Divine Comedy*, though he greatly appreciates the *Inferno* and *Purgatorio*. Perhaps that is why the mystical realm ("night's wonderworld," he sometimes calls it) in which the love-death eventuates remains for Wagner an unknown, though somehow real, domain of being. It is not the Schopenhauerian Nirvana of total annihilation, but neither is it the paradise of Western theology. Instead, the supernatural state his lovers finally reach seems like a dreamy, sentimentalized, and greatly attenuated conception of oneness between man and woman. One always feels that Wagner dared not move too far beyond the escapist mentality of his audiences in the theater. He wished to involve them fully, to engage them in a Rousseauistic participation in the communal spirit. He knew this was the function of myth, and he thought it was the basis of Greek tragedy's ability to merge aesthetic and religious effects. But in seeking to attain this participatory emotional response, Wagner constructed his dramas out of concepts that were often maudlin, even commonplace.

In his embittered rejection of Wagner (after having originally idolized him), Nietzsche frequently condemns his "theatricality." I think it is Wagner's willingness to make a conventional compromise for the sake of reaching an audience and having a dramatic effect that Nietzsche resented most of all. He felt that Wagner was thereby false to his own aesthetic principles, acting as if a work of art could not express the absolute truth. Nietzsche also criticizes Schopenhauer in book after book, but he always respects him in a way that he finally could not respect Wagner. Schopenhauer may have been wrong, Nietzsche seems to say, but at least he was an honest thinker. Of course, Wagner was a man of the theater who had to make decisions that no philosopher need ever face, but this could not exonerate him in Nietzsche's eyes.

Even if Nietzsche was right, however, the contrived equilibration in Wagner's thinking did not prevent him from making statements as extreme as anything Schopenhauer may have said. In one place Mann quotes the following words of Wagner: "Love in fullest reality is only possible within sex; only as man and woman can human beings love most genuinely, all other love is derivative, having reference to this or artificially modelled upon it. It is false to think of this love (the sexual) as only one manifestation of love in general, other and perhaps higher manifestations being presumed beside it." This takes us beyond Schopenhauer's philosophy. It is more radical and prepares us more directly for the reductivistic side of Freudianism. It represents an aspect of Wagner's mind that cannot be ignored, though he makes no effort to develop it fully. Had he done so, he would have created music dramas of a different sort—not greater as music or as drama, perhaps, and not necessarily more moving or engrossing, but possibly closer in their mythic import to the spirit of later generations.

Wagner wished to create a new religion of love. He did not succeed in that attempt, and Nietzsche may have been right when he complained that Wagner's music expresses the genius of a sick and degenerate soul. Nietzsche meant that Wagner encourages unhealthy attitudes and debases ideals inherited from more authentic Christians and Romantics. What Nietzsche fails to realize is that in Wagner's art their ideas are amalgamated into a new experience that gives each of them immediate access to one's feelings as well as one's intellect. Even if there were nothing else involved, this alone would justify the Wagnerian enterprise.

Romanticism does not terminate in Wagner. But we need not trace the optimistic and pessimistic aspects of Romantic love any further. In Wagner's thinking they are combined with a type of Christianity that was repulsive to many thinkers in the nineteenth century who were religious, and many in the twentieth who were not. Studying Wagner's mythology, one detects the differences as well as the continuities between courtly and Romantic approaches to love. For one thing, we see how inaccurate is de Rougemont's assertion that the two attitudes were alike in being subversive, equally hostile to authority in their struggles with institutions like marriage. What de Rougemont says about the destructiveness of passion may possibly apply to Wagner's *Tristan and Isolde*, but even there it encounters difficulties in view of King Marke's willingness to grant his wife a divorce so that she can marry her lover. But over and above this consideration, the many differences between the medieval and the Wagnerian versions of the Tristan myth show us why de Rougemont's generalizations cannot be upheld.

As a way of concluding this part of my discussion, I need only elaborate the point a little further. I have been arguing that the concept of courtly love introduced moral ideals that supplemented and finally altered orthodox opinion in the Middle Ages, and that the concept of Romantic love contributed to a new approach that departed from traditional religions while also employing some of the ideas of courtly love. Courtly and Romantic differ from one another in the degree to which they rebel against social mores. In becoming lovers, the medieval Tristan and Iseult lose their rightful place in society, and that is a cause of distress to each of them separately as well as in relation to one another. They both recognize their ties to the ruling dispensation and constantly wish to renew them. Tristan has an oath of fealty to Mark, his king and uncle, that he tries to honor. Iseult yearns throughout for the goodness and security of being an admired queen who has not violated her marriage vows. Far from being a subversive document, the legend—in all its medieval versions—hardly questions the basis of authority. In most of its variants, the king is represented as a great-hearted man devoted to both Tristan and Iseult, a kind of God-on-earth who bestows agapē upon them whether or not they merit it by their own behavior. Occasional versions in the Middle Ages do reduce the figure of the king to the debased condition of the vicious husband who defeats natural interests of a young wife he should never have married in the first place. But even then, the legend merely changes from tragedy into melodrama without showing hostility to the social order.

The medieval legend of Tristan and Iseult expresses two contradictory attitudes: one is adherence to a particular type of courtly love idealized in Northern France; the other is submission to feudal rectitude. Each theme mutes the other; neither is completely dominant. As lovers who have drunk the potion by mistake, Tristan and Iseult are not really guilty. Yet each commits treason and must be punished. At first the king nobly refuses to believe they could be treacherous, and generally it is not he who wishes to harm them. Since the king embodies divine goodness in the state, the hateful job of tracking down the criminal pair is given to the felon knights. From the feudal point of view, these barons are loyal, devoted subjects; but the narrators vilify them mercilessly. Why? Because it is essential that they should draw the blame for the king's repressive acts. In that way, the idea of love is protected while the symbol of authority remains intact. Although Tristan and Iseult are the two highest-ranking people in the realm, after the king, and one of them is exiled from the land to which he has been named the heir apparent while the other suffers the indignity of having been taken from her native country as a kind of ransom, neither expresses resentment toward the king. They do not try to unseat him, though they are murderous with the felon knights and with everyone else who thwarts their unlawful passion. However disruptive their courtly love may be in idealizing adultery between a queen and her husband's prime lieutenant (the same applies to Guinevere and Lancelot), its influence is always balanced by an idealization of the established order.

In nineteenth-century romanticism the bivalence between love and orthodoxy often disappears. In Wagner the two oppose each other as systems of value that are basically irreconcilable or, rather, capable of an accommodation only after society is transformed and made conducive to Romantic love. The king in Wagner's opera is more humane than in some of the medieval versions, and he appears no less worthy of his prerogatives; but the scope of his legitimate authority has been delimited as never before. The Wagnerian lovers live in a realm of their own: though they are noble like the king, they do not belong to the same world as he. Their relationship is defined by a ring of mystical fire that cuts them off from the ordinary duties of a lieutenant or a wife. Where courtly love resembled a faction that wants the state to remain strong but with power transferred to itself, Romantic love is more deeply disloyal. It either renounces political ambition and emigrates to a new world of passionate adventure or else it undermines the status quo by presenting it as an inauthentic shadow of some transcendental state that will eventually recognize the majesty of love. Since reality is to be judged and even explained in terms of passionate experience, there is no reason for lovers to submit themselves to anything else.

In the medieval versions of the legend, Tristan kills Iseult's uncle,

Morold, and shares her sexually with his own uncle but never sleeps with the wife he himself marries. In the Wagnerian text there is no other wife, Marke announces that he has never consummated his marriage to Isolde, and Morold turns into a suitor whose death augments Isolde's initial hatred for Tristan. Wagner eliminates the felon knights, condensing them into Melot, who uses Tristan's loving friendship as a means of betraying him. Wagner makes these changes in order to treat passion as the sole governing force in human affairs while diminishing the importance of social ties that contravene the supremacy of Liebestod. Nothingness, the land from which Tristan came and to which the ancient tune, "die alte Weise," recalls him in Act III, is for Wagner a something—the unknowable state of oneness—in which love-death fulfills itself. Only in this ultimate being that is non-being can Wagnerian merging finally occur.

That is why Wagner's opera is so different in form as well as content from any of the *Tristans* that preceded it. In Wagner, love denies the goodness of the ordinary world, and does so within a ritual that precludes the possibility of tragedy. Wagnerian love *grows*; it does not struggle or engage in moral conflict. *Tristan and Isolde* has very little action, just a thematic focus in each of its three parts, since nothing on earth is worth acting against. The overall narrative line is not dramatic but evolutionary within a single progression (as conveyed by the wave motifs).

Pitting love against honor and feudal duty, the medieval legend is indeed dramatic. It shows glorified love contending with elements of society that are equally idealized; neither system of values triumphs to the extent that passion does in Wagner. In the medieval, but not the Wagnerian, version adultery is a misfortune that prevents the lovers from living in a world they have every reason to enjoy. The medieval Tristan and Iseult suffer because they cannot have both love and life in their society. Wagner's protagonists suffer as a way of proving the worthlessness of everything that ignores the metaphysical grandeur of Romantic love. There is value only in their yearning for each other, and that must be satisfied beyond the world as we know it to be. Love such as this does not, cannot, exist in any conceivable reality.

Conclusion
Beyond Romantic Love

THE DIFFERENCES BETWEEN COURTLY
and Romantic attitudes are evident by the time we reach Wagner,
but the passage from one to the other dominates much of the
intervening philosophy and literature that we have studied in this
book. In the Renaissance the new patterns of romanticism begin to
emerge; in Shakespeare the development from courtly to Romantic
is well established, as well as the realist opposition to both. Hamlet is
a kind of transitional Tristan. Like courtly and Romantic Tristans,
he is a dispossessed prince who is expected to serve his uncle the king
but cannot do so because of his relationship to the queen. He tries to
convince her that she cannot truly love her present husband, that
she ought to remain faithful to the man with whom Hamlet desperately wishes to identify himself—his own father. Towards Ophelia,
the daughter of what in the medieval legend would be a felon
knight, Hamlet feels at times a Romantic type of love that exceeds all
bounds and shows no interest in accommodating itself to the practical necessities of its society. The play is neither courtly nor yet
Romantic but an intermediate mixture of elements of both. Since
the queen is Hamlet's mother, it is impossible for the courtly theme
to be realized fully; since Hamlet still believes in an objective reality
that underlies his sense of obligation (the duty to avenge his father
and reestablish lawful authority in the state), he cannot abandon
everything for the sake of Romantic love. He is therefore stymied,
frozen between two idealistic tropes, and that defines his drama.

Romeo and Juliet also contains a mixture of courtly and Romantic, but in that play an early form of Romantic love has been given a better opportunity to work itself out. In *Hamlet,* each type of love undercuts the other and neither is allowed to reach fruition—though the fact that by the end all the heads of state have died may indicate the direction in which Shakespeare was tending. In *Romeo and Juliet* the lovers die together, virtually in each other's arms, and they leave behind a society that has shown itself to be utterly corrupt and vicious. In reuniting their people by means of their death, Romeo and Juliet do not attain the salvation that Wagner idealized; but they, like Antony and Cleopatra, become the models for Romantic love that cannot survive the evils of this world.

At the same time, Shakespeare anticipates the benign as well as the pessimistic aspects of romanticism. His optimistic side reappears in operas by Berlioz, Verdi, and others who used his plays to show how love between man and woman overcomes impediments to its joyful consummation on earth, in the midst of nature. This approach to Romantic love derives from some of the types of courtly love that we have been discussing, and like them it generates humanistic ideals of oneness between the sexes. In our search for a valid love of persons, we in the twentieth century must always return to the tradition that eventuated in thinkers like Shelley, Stendhal, Schlegel, Hume, and even Hegel. They show us what must be done in philosophy; and to some extent, they give us the tools for doing it.

In the sequel to this volume, I shall reconsider the concepts of courtly and Romantic love in order to determine why it was necessary for modern man not only to perpetuate them but also to go beyond them. With respect to several problems related to the love of persons, I shall argue that both forms of idealism are highly deficient. Some of the difficulties were recognized in the nineteenth century by latter-day figures like Kierkegaard, Tolstoy, and Nietzsche. In their writings the ambiguity between optimistic and pessimistic aspects of romanticism turns into paradox, which then becomes a structural element that helps each of these three to develop his own post-Romantic conception of love. Kierkegaard, Tolstoy, and Nietzsche were tortured human beings—in a way that neither Hegel nor Schopenhauer was—and much of the turmoil in their troubled souls can be traced to a conflict between the optimistic, healthy-minded perspective that they partly accepted and disabilities in themselves that made pessimism seem more defensible to them. But though they would not espouse ideas about love that were foreign to their experience, they were too honest to make their own experience definitive of human possibilities. The tensions in each of them are never resolved; but, as I shall try to show, this irresolution itself enables them to function as transitional figures in modern thought.

From their different points of view Kierkegaard, Tolstoy, and Nietzsche (particularly in his defense of naturalistic values, what Feuerbach called "the great health") provide an introduction to the twentieth century. Despite the fact that their thinking about love is limited in scope, Ralph Waldo Emerson and John Stuart Mill do the same. In a journal entry dated 1840, Emerson remarks that he has been transcribing for publication his essay on love but that he already sees its "inadequateness": "I, cold because I am hot,—cold at the surface only as a sort of guard and compensation for the fluid tenderness of the core,—have much more experience than I have written there, more than I will, more than I can write." Emerson's sense of inadequacy must be shared by everyone who writes about love; but what strikes me as particularly prophetic of the following century is the realization that hidden, unconscious forces—however hot or fluid they may be—may reach the surface of our experience only as a cold and armored appearance to the world. In their exhaustive analyses of love, both Freud and Proust will develop this idea at very great length.

Emerson's essay on love combines Hegelian, Neoplatonic, and Christian elements in a way that reveals why each of these is so unsatisfactory from our contemporary perspective. Assuming in nature an "over-soul" of which we are but manifestations, Emerson defines true love as something that takes us beyond a love of persons. He sees interpersonal love as merely the "training for a love which knows not sex, nor person, nor partiality, but which seeks virtue and wisdom everywhere." Elsewhere he criticizes the mystic Swedenborg for having proclaimed that in heaven men and women will find each other in spiritual marriages that compensate for the "false marriages on earth." Since God is the proper bride or bridegroom for each soul, Emersonian heaven is "not the pairing of two, but the communion of all souls. . . . So far from there being anything divine in the low and proprietary sense of *Do you love me?* it is only when you leave and lose me by casting yourself on a sentiment which is higher than both of us, that I draw near and find myself at your side; and I am repelled if you fix your eye on me and demand love."

In twentieth-century philosophers such as Peirce, McTaggart, and Bergson we can find a similar conception of cosmic love; and Santayana acknowledged his indebtedness to that much of Emerson which is Neoplatonic. This approach, pervasive as it was at the beginning of our century, lost most of its appeal in later years. I myself consider it far less promising than utilitarian and post-utilitarian theory which finds in Mill a major source of inspiration. While cultivating the scientific attitude that realism respects, Mill incorporates into his thinking much of benign romanticism. Since he says nothing about sexual love and is too precise a logician to entertain the idea of merging, it would be inaccurate to list him among the advocates of Romantic love. But in his autobiography he documents the beneficial influence that Romantics such as Coleridge and the German poets exercised upon him in a period of emotional crisis. Telling us very little about the psychodynamics of his nervous breakdown, Mill dates it from his sudden realization that even if he were able to attain the utilitarian goals for which he was striving, this desirable outcome would not affect him deeply. He saw no reason to believe that success in achieving the greatest happiness of the greatest number would bring about his own happiness. In other words, his crisis was based upon the recognition that he did not really care about other people, that he felt no spontaneous love for them, although as a moral philosopher he could and did use his intellect to promote their well-being.

Apart from saying that Romantic poetry helped cure him of his psychological disorder, Mill scarcely explains how the therapeutic process took effect. One of its by-products, however, was the recurrence throughout his later writings of ideas he must have encountered in the Romantics. Writing about the nature of poetry, he defines all art as the expression of strong feelings that might not have found an outlet otherwise; and when he discusses "the ultimate sanction of the principle of utility," he identifies it as the "powerful natural sentiment" of what he calls "the contagion of sympathy." Sounding at times like Shelley, he argues that a "firm foundation" for morality is to be found in "the desire to be in unity with our fellow creatures." He speaks of the feeling in many persons "that the interests of others are their own interests." It is a "feeling of unity" with other people that leads a man "to identify his *feelings* more and more with their good."

The many problems within utilitarianism have dominated English and American moral theory in the last hundred years; but questions about the nature of sexual love have generally been neglected by Anglo-Saxon philosophers in our century, most of whom chose to relegate such matters to the psychologists. To see how psychology has affected the history of thinking about love, we must study the entire sweep of psychiatric theory from Freud to the present. Its details need to be examined within their historical context, arising from the Romantic and post-Romantic speculations of philosophers like Schopenhauer and Nietzsche, evolving throughout Freud's lifetime, and contributing to contemporary schools of revisionist and existential psychoanalysis. Freud himself wished to create a unified doctrine that would be as rigorous as the sciences of physics or chemistry. His dream has never been realized, but it renews itself in the efforts of current psychobiologists while the content of psychoanalytic theory serves as a frequent point of departure for ethology, sociobiology, and other behavioral studies of human affect.

These different branches within the life sciences, seeking empirical solutions to questions about love and sexuality and devoted to ideals of health and harmonious functioning in nature, belong to a new ideology that offers great hope for the future. But the importance of the scientific venture cannot be appreciated in isolation from the work of humanists both literary and philosophical. We cannot understand either the ideals or the realities of the twentieth century without analyzing concepts of love in thinkers such as

Proust, D. H. Lawrence, Santayana, Sartre, and Buber. Much of my final volume will be addressed to them.

Towards the beginning of the twentieth century many thinkers attacked the idealistic bases of courtly and Romantic love. In turning to the science or scientific philosophy of their day, they foresaw a realistic attitude superior to any that had been possible in previous centuries. As we approach the end of the twentieth century, we realize how much more must still be done. In our present condition, we may well lament the fact that empirical science has given us few glittering conceptions comparable to those of the past. But the work is still in progress: the contemporary synthesis of realism and idealism, of verifiable truth and meaningful aspiration, remains as an unfinished cathedral in the mind. Thus far, little more than the groundwork has been laid. Coming generations may someday marvel when they see what was being built.

Notes

p. x *l.27* Denis de Rougemont, *Love in the Western World*, trans. Montgomery Belgion, revised and augmented ed. (Princeton: Princeton University Press, 1983); *Love Declared: Essays on the Myths of Love*, trans. Richard Howard (Boston: Beacon Press, 1964).

p. xi *l.33* *Collected Essays of Aldous Huxley* (New York: Bantam Books, 1960), p. 74.

p. xiii *l.15* For an encyclopedic approach to writings about love, see Robert G. Hazo, *The Idea of Love* (New York: F. A. Praeger, 1967).

p. 2 *l.13* Review of Henry T. Finck, *Romantic Love and Personal Beauty*, in *The Nation* 45 (September 22, 1887):237–38.

p. 8 *l.4* Act V, scene 3.

p. 8 *l.19* *The Symposium*, trans. W. Hamilton (New York: Penguin Books, 1951), pp. 63–64.

p. 11 *l.32* The caritas-synthesis, as well as the two types of mysticism previously mentioned, are discussed in *The Nature of Love: Plato to Luther*.

p. 19 *l.21* D. W. Robertson, Jr., "The Concept of Courtly Love as an Impediment to the Understanding of Medieval Texts," in *The Meaning of Courtly Love*, ed. Francis X. Newman (Albany: State University of New York Press, 1968), p. 1. For relevant statements by Gaston Paris, see his "Etudes sur les romans de la table ronde: Lancelot du Lac," *Romania* 12 (1883):459–534. See also his *Mélanges de Littérature Française du Moyen Age* (Paris: Champion, 1912), and *Poèmes et Légendes du Moyen-Age* (Paris: Société d'Edition Artistique, n.d.).

p. 20 *l.17* J. Huizinga, *The Waning of the Middle Ages* (New York: Anchor Books, 1954), particularly chaps. 2–5, 8, 9.

p. 21 *l.25* C. S. Lewis, *The Allegory of Love* (New York: Oxford University Press, 1936), p. 3.

p. 21 *l.35* Cf. an excellent article by John C. Moore, " 'Courtly Love': A Problem of Terminology," *Journal of the History of Ideas* (October–December 1979), as well as his *Love in Twelfth-Century France* (Philadelphia: University of Pennsylvania Press, 1972). See also Roger Boase, *The Origin and Meaning of Courtly Love: A Critical Study of European Scholarship* (Totowa: Rowman and Littlefield, 1977), and Henry Ansgar Kelly, *Love and Marriage in the Age of Chaucer* (Ithaca: Cornell University Press, 1975), particularly pp. 19–26.

p. 24 *l.12* *De Doctrina Christiana*, III, 10.

p. 25 *l.32* Act I, scene 1.

p. 29 *l.27* On the compatibility of love and marriage in medieval literature, cf. Kelly, *Love and Marriage in the Age of Chaucer*, particularly pp. 31–67.

p. 31 *l.2* Brooks Otis, *Ovid as an Epic Poet* (Cambridge: Cambridge University Press, 1966), p. 266.

p. 31 *l.5* Cf. Kelly, *Love and Marriage in the Age of Chaucer*, pp. 71–100 and passim. Cf. also Edgar Finley Shannon, *Chaucer and the Roman Poets* (New York: Russell & Russell, 1964).

p. 32 *l.6* For recent discussions about love in Plato, see Donald Levy, "The Definition of Love in Plato's *Symposium*," *Journal of the History of Ideas* (April-June 1979); Gregory Vlastos, "The Individual as Object of Love in Plato," in *Platonic Studies* (Princeton: Princeton University Press, 1973); and J. M. E. Moravcsik, "Reason and Eros in the Ascent Passage of the *Symposium*," in *Essays in Ancient Greek Philosophy*, eds. J. P. Anton and G. L. Kustas (Albany: State University of New York Press, 1972).

p. 33 *l.8* On this, see my chapter, "The Sensuous and the Passionate," in *The Goals of Human Sexuality* (New York: W. W. Norton, 1973); reprinted in *Philosophy of Sex: Contemporary Readings*, ed. Alan Soble (Totowa: Littlefield, Adams, 1980).

p. 34 *l.19* Cf. Peter Dronke, *Medieval Latin and the Rise of European Love-Lyric* (Oxford: Clarendon Press, 1965), 1:9–11.

p. 38 *l.36* Plato, *The Symposium*, p. 87.

p. 39 *l.18* Ibid., p. 91.

p. 41 *l.3* Quoted in Thomas Austin Kirby, *Chaucer's Troilus: A Study in Courtly Love* (Gloucester: Peter Smith, 1958), p. 292.

p. 41 *l.14* Plato, *The Symposium*, p. 94.

p. 41 *l.24* Ibid., p. 111.

p. 41 *l.29* Ibid., p. 97.

p. 42 *l.9* Ibid., pp. 103 and 107.

p. 43 *l.23* Quoted in A. J. Denomy, "An Inquiry into the Origins of Courtly Love," *Mediaeval Studies* 6 (1944): 221. For the text itself, cf. Ibn Sina, "A Treatise on Love," trans. Emil L. Fackenheim, *Mediaeval Studies* 7 (1945): 208–28.

p. 44 *l.14* Ibid., p. 222.

p. 44 *l.30* Ibn Hazm, *The Ring of the Dove: A Treatise on the Art and Practice of Arab Love*, trans. A. J. Arberry (London: Luzac, 1953), p. 225.

p. 44 *l.35* Ibid., p. 23.

p. 45 *l.7* Ibid., p. 26.

p. 45 *l.29* Ibid., p. 28.

p. 45 *l.37* Ibid., p. 58.

p. 46 *l.18* Ibid., p. 68.

p. 46 *l.36* On this, cf. Denomy, "An Inquiry into the Origins of Courtly Love."

p. 48   *l.27*   Cf. Henry Adams, *Mont-Saint-Michel and Chartres* (New York: Anchor Books, 1959), chap. 11.

p. 50   *l.7*   Quoted in A. J. Denomy, "Fin' Amors: The Pure Love of the Troubadours, Its Amorality, and Possible Source," *Mediaeval Studies* 7 (1945): 177n.

p. 50   *l.9*   Quoted in Kirby, *Chaucer's Troilus*, p. 294.

p. 50   *l.12*   Ibid.

p. 50   *l.16*   Quoted in Denomy, "Fin' Amors," p. 150n.

p. 50   *l.18*   *Lyrics of the Troubadours and Trouvères: An Anthology and a History*, trans. Frederick Goldin (New York: Anchor Books, 1973), p. 45.

p. 50   *l.25*   Quoted in Denomy, "Fin' Amors," p. 176n.

p. 50   *l.29*   Quoted in Kirby, *Chaucer's Troilus*, p. 203.

p. 50   *l.31*   Quoted in Maurice Valency, *In Praise of Love* (New York: Macmillan, 1958), p. 158.

p. 50   *l.33*   Quoted in Denomy, "Fin' Amors," p. 155.

p. 51   *l.34*   Valency, *In Praise of Love*, p. 167.

p. 53   *l.1*   Quoted in Denomy, "Fin' Amors," p. 182.

p. 53   *l.6*   Ibid. On Richard of St. Victor, see my discussion in *The Nature of Love: Plato to Luther*.

p. 53   *l.18*   Act IV, scene 1. For the making of this juxtaposition, I am indebted to Valency, *In Praise of Love*, p. 188.

p. 53   *l.26*   Cf. Etienne Gilson, *The Mystical Theology of St. Bernard* (New York: Sheed and Ward, 1940), p. 194ff.

p. 54   *l.8*   "Quand erba vertz e fuelha par," in Harriet W. Preston, *Troubadours and Trouvères* (Boston: Robert Brothers, 1876), p. 183.

p. 54   *l.20*   "Quand vei la laudeta mover," ibid., p. 186.

p. 56   *l.15*   On this, see James J. Wilhelm, *Seven Troubadours: The Creators of Modern Verse* (University Park: Pennsylvania State University Press, 1970). On the lack of a "uniform ethic" among poets of the Middle Ages, see also Peter Dronke, *Medieval Latin and the Rise of European Love-Lyric*, 2nd ed. (Oxford: Clarendon Press, 1968), vol. 1, passim.

p. 56   *l.18*   Quoted in Sir Maurice Bowra, *Mediaeval Love-song* (London: The Athlone Press, 1961), p. 30.

p. 56   *l.32*   Goldin, *Lyrics of the Troubadours and Trouvères*, p. 129.

p. 57   *l.1*   Quoted in Peter Dronke, *The Medieval Lyric* (London: Cambridge University Press, 1977), p. 123.

p. 57   *l.28*   For an analysis of this sort, see Herbert Moller, "The Meaning of Courtly Love," *Journal of American Folklore* (73): 39–52.

p. 59   An earlier version of this chapter appeared in *MLN* (December 1973), pp. 1288–1315.

p. 60   *l.8*   Alexander Denomy, *The Heresy of Courtly Love* (New York: McMullen, 1947), p. 40.

p. 60   *l.33*   Andreas Capellanus, *The Art of Courtly Love*, trans. John Jay Parry (New York: W. W. Norton, 1969), p. 187.

p. 61   *l.35*   See D. W. Robertson, Jr., "The Subject of the *De Amore* of Andreas Capellanus," *Modern Philology* (February 1953): 145–61; John F. Benton, "Clio and Venus: An Historical View of Medieval Love," in *The Meaning of Courtly Love*, ed. F. X. Newman; E. Talbot Donaldson, "The Myth of Courtly Love," in *Speaking of Chaucer* (London: University of

London Press, 1970). See also W. T. H. Jackson, "The *De Amore* of Andreas Capellanus and the Practice of Love at Court," *The Romanic Review* 49 (1958): 244–51.

p. 62   *l.19*   Andreas Capellanus, *The Art of Courtly Love*, p. 28.
p. 63   *l.12*   Ibid., p. 29.
p. 63   *l.36*   Ibid., p. 31.
p. 64   *l.5*   Ibid.
p. 65   *l.8*   Ibid., p. 35.
p. 67   *l.13*   Ibid., p. 39.
p. 67   *l.25*   Ibid., pp. 40–41.
p. 68   *l.6*   Ibid., p. 42.
p. 70   *l.20*   Ibid., p. 88.
p. 71   *l.3*   Ibid., p. 90.
p. 71   *l.35*   Ibid., pp. 37–38.
p. 72   *l.7*   Ibid., p. 55.
p. 72   *l.11*   Ibid., p. 65.
p. 72   *l.15*   Ibid.
p. 74   *l.5*   Ibid., p. 134.
p. 74   *l.13*   Ibid., p. 156.
p. 74   *l.30*   Ibid., p. 100.
p. 75   *l.4*   Ibid., p. 102.
p. 76   *l.11*   Ibid., p. 22.
p. 76   *l.18*   Ibid., p. 200.
p. 76   *l.20*   Ibid., p. 208.
p. 76   *l.30*   Ibid., p. 201.
p. 77   *l.5*   Ibid., p. 209.
p. 77   *l.32*   Stendhal, *On Love*, trans. H. B. V. under the direction of C. K. Scott-Moncrieff (New York: Grosset and Dunlap, 1967), p. 349.
p. 78   *l.33*   Andreas Capellanus, *The Art of Courtly Love*, p. 49.
p. 79   *l.32*   Ibid., p. 53.
p. 80   *l.13*   Ibid., p. 107.
p. 81   *l.8*   Ibid., p. 102.
p. 81   *l.19*   Ibid., p. 107.
p. 81   *l.31*   Ibid., p. 171.
p. 82   *l.8*   Ibid., p. 185.
p. 82   *l.32*   Ibid., p. 122.
p. 83   *l.25*   Ibid., p. 167.
p. 84   *l.18*   Ibid., p. 187.
p. 84   *l.22*   Ibid., p. 102.
p. 84   *l.30*   Ibid., p. 103.
p. 86   *l.4*   Ibid., p. 111.
p. 86   *l.22*   Ibid., p. 142.
p. 88   *l.5*   In recent scholarship on Abelard and Heloise, see Peter Dronke, *Abelard and Heloise in Medieval Testimonies* (Glasgow: University of Glasgow Press, 1976), and D. W. Robertson, Jr., *Abelard and Heloise* (New York: Dial, 1972).
p. 90   *l.26*   Cf. Etienne Gilson, *Heloise and Abelard* (Ann Arbor: The University of Michigan Press, 1960).

p. 91   *l.11*   *The Letters of Abelard and Heloise*, trans. C. K. Scott-Moncrieff (London: Guy Chapman, 1925), p. 9. For a later translation, with a useful introduction, see *The Letters of Abelard and Heloise*, trans. Betty Radice (Harmondsworth: Penguin Books, 1974). Except where indicated differently, my quotations are all from the Scott-Moncrieff translation.

p. 91   *l.26*   Ibid., p. 85.

p. 93   *l.1*   Ibid., p. 9.

p. 93   *l.11*   Ibid., pp. 10–11.

p. 94   *l.12*   Ibid., p. 65.

p. 95   *l.35*   Cf. Gilson, *The Mystical Theology of St. Bernard*, pp. 162–65.

p. 96   *l.5*   Quoted in Gilson, *Heloise and Abelard*, p. 56.

p. 96   *l.33*   *The Letters of Abelard and Heloise*, p. 47.

p. 99   *l.13*   Gilson, *Heloise and Abelard*, p. 96.

p. 100   *l.5*   *The Letters of Abelard and Heloise* (New York: Cooper Square Publishers, 1974), p. 19.

p. 100   *l.11*   Ibid., p. 57.

p. 100   *l.22*   Henry Osborn Taylor, *The Medieval Mind: A History of the Development of Thought and Emotion in the Middle Ages* (New York: Macmillan, 1919), 2:34.

p. 101   *l.14*   Quoted in Peter Dronke, *The Medieval Lyric*, p. 54.

p. 102   *l.17*   See Joan M. Ferrante, *The Conflict of Love and Honor: The Medieval Tristan Legend in France, Germany, and Italy* (The Hague: Mouton, 1973), p. 20; see also Esther C. Quinn, "Beyond Courtly Love: Religious Elements in *Tristan* and *La Queste del Saint Graal*," in *In Pursuit of Perfection: Courtly Love in Medieval Literature*, ed. Joan M. Ferrante and George D. Economou (Port Washington: Kennikat Press, 1975), and W. T. H. Jackson, *The Anatomy of Love: The Tristan of Gottfried von Strassburg* (New York: Columbia University Press, 1971).

p. 104   *l.29*   Gottfried von Strassburg, *Tristan*, trans. A. T. Hatto (Harmondsworth: Penguin Books, 1960), p. 147.

p. 105   *l.35*   Ibid., p. 264.

p. 106   *l.19*   Ibid., p. 263.

p. 106   *l.33*   Ibid., pp. 267–68.

p. 108   *l.4*   Cf. Paull F. Baum, "The *Troilus* Epilogue," in *Chaucer: A Critical Appreciation* (Durham: Duke University Press, 1958), pp. 143–67. Cf. also Alex J. Denomy, "The Two Moralities of Chaucer's *Troilus and Criseyde*," in *Chaucer Criticism*, ed. Richard J. Schoeck and Jerome Taylor (Notre Dame: University of Notre Dame Press, 1961), 2:147–59.

p. 109   *l.3*   "Aucassin and Nicolette," in *The Ways of Love: Eleven Romances of Medieval France*, trans. Norma Lorre Goodrich (Boston: Beacon Press, 1964), pp. 222–23.

p. 109   *l.37*   Ibid., p. 185.

p. 110   *l.8*   Ibid., p. 197.

p. 110   *l.19*   "The Lay of the Little Bird," in *Aucassin and Nicolette and Other Mediaeval Romances and Legends*, trans. Eugene Mason (New York: Dutton, 1958), p. 77.

p. 112   *l.20*   *Lays of Marie de France and Other French Legends*, trans. Eugene Mason (New York: Dutton, 1964), contains both. See also *The Lays of Marie de France*, trans. Robert Hanning and Joan Ferrante (New York: Dutton, 1978).

p. 112 *l.28* *Lays of Marie de France and Other French Legends*, pp. 149–50.

p. 115 *l.8* *The Romance of Tristan and Iseult*, as retold by Joseph Bédier, trans. Hilaire Belloc and Paul Rosenfeld (New York: Vintage Books, 1965), pp. 46–47.

p. 115 *l.27* Both lays are in *Lays of Marie de France and Other French Legends*.

p. 117 *l.10* Erich Auerbach, *Mimesis: The Representation of Reality in Western Literature* (New York: Anchor Books, 1957), p. 122. For a more comprehensive account of medieval literature in general, see John Stevens, *Medieval Romance: Themes and Approaches* (New York: W. W. Norton, 1973), and W. T. H. Jackson, *The Literature of the Middle Ages* (New York: Columbia University Press, 1960).

p. 118 *l.6* Chrétien de Troyes, "Cligés," in *Arthurian Romances*, trans. W. W. Comfort (New York: Dutton, 1963), p. 132.

p. 119 *l.19* Charles Moorman, *A Knyght There Was: The Evolution of the Knight in Literature* (Lexington: University of Kentucky Press, 1967), p. 54.

p. 120 *l.35* W. T. H. Jackson argues for this interpretation in *The Anatomy of Love*.

p. 121 *l.32* Guillaume de Lorris and Jean de Meun, *The Romance of the Rose*, trans. Harry W. Robbins (New York: Dutton, 1962), p. 48.

p. 122 *l.11* I am indebted to Winthrop Wetherbee for this idea.

p. 122 *l.22* Adams, *Mont-Saint-Michel and Chartres*, p. 276.

p. 122 *l.26* Ernst Robert Curtius, *European Literature and the Latin Middle Ages* (New York: Pantheon, 1953), p. 126.

p. 123 *l.26* Lorris and Meun, *The Romance of the Rose*, p. 168.

p. 124 *l.23* Ibid., p. 447.

p. 124 *l.31* Ibid., p. 450.

p. 125 *l.17* Winthrop Wetherbee, *Platonism and Poetry in the Twelfth Century: The Literary Influence of the School of Chartres* (Princeton: Princeton University Press, 1972), p. 189. See also Peter Dronke's Introduction to Bernardus Silvestris, *Cosmographia* (Leiden: E. J. Brill, 1978), p. 47, and Wetherbee's Introduction to his translation of *The Cosmographia of Bernardus Silvestris* (New York: Columbia University Press, 1973), pp. 6–12.

p. 125 *l.16* Cf. M.-D. Chenu, "Nature and Man—The Renaissance of the Twelfth Century," in *Nature, Man, and Society in the Twelfth Century*, ed. and trans. Jerome Taylor and Lester K. Little (Chicago: University of Chicago Press, 1968), pp. 1–48.

p. 126 *l.4* Cf. George D. Economou, "The Two Venuses and Courtly Love," in *In Pursuit of Perfection*, ed. Ferrante and Economou, p. 29. See also Winthrop Wetherbee, *Platonism and Poetry in the Twelfth Century*, pp. 257–65.

p. 126 *l.17* Lewis, *The Allegory of Love*, pp. 154–55.

p. 132 *l.7* *Petrarch's Secret or the Soul's Conflict with Passion: Three Dialogues between Himself and S. Augustine*, trans. William H. Draper (London: Chatto and Windus, 1911), p. 114.

p. 132 *l.13* Ibid., pp. 124–25.

p. 132   *l.19*   Ibid., pp. 125–26.
p. 132   *l.35*   Ibid., pp. 131–36.
p. 134   *l.9*   Ibid., p. 84.
p. 135   *l.10*   Quoted in Herbert Moller, "The Meaning of Courtly Love," p. 47.
p. 135   *l.13*   Quoted in Morris Bishop, *Petrarch and His World* (Bloomington: Indiana University Press, 1963), p. 191.
p. 135   *l.29*   Quoted in Valency, *In Praise of Love*, p. 136.
p. 136   *l.13*   Quoted in Bishop, *Petrarch and His World*, p. 154.
p. 136   *l.16*   Ibid., p. 156.
p. 136   *l.32*   Ibid., p. 77.
p. 137   *l.3*   Quoted in Valency, *In Praise of Love*, p. 135.
p. 137   *l.7*   Ibid., p. 136.
p. 137   *l.10*   Guillaume de Lorris and Jean de Meun, *The Romance of the Rose*, p. 47.
p. 137   *l.19*   De Rougemont, *Love in the Western World*, p. 38.
p. 138   *l.9*   Quoted in Bishop, *Petrarch and His World*, p. 76.
p. 138   *l.11*   Ibid.
p. 139   *l.10*   Ibid., p. 154.
p. 139   *l.22*   William Dudley Foulke, *Some Love Songs of Petrarch* (London: Oxford University Press, 1915), p. 113.
p. 139   *l.24*   Henry Cochin, *La Chronique du Canzoniere de Pétrarque* (Paris: Bouillon, 1898), p. 139; quoted in Foulke, *Some Love Songs of Petrarch*.
p. 139   *l.34*   Petrarch, "Epistle to Posterity," quoted in Foulke, *Some Love Songs of Petrarch*, pp. 217–18.
p. 140   *l.10*   No. CXXXII, quoted in Bishop, *Petrarch and His World*, p. 154.
p. 140   *l.36*   Ibid., p. 298.
p. 141   *l.14*   Percy Bysshe Shelley, "A Defence of Poetry," in *Shelley's Prose or The Trumpet of a Prophecy*, ed. David Lee Clark (Albuquerque: University of New Mexico Press, 1954), p. 289.
p. 143   *l.1*   Giovanni Boccaccio, *The Decameron*, vi, 9, quoted in Jefferson Butler Fletcher, *The Religion of Beauty in Woman and Other Essays on Platonic Love in Poetry and Society* (New York: Macmillan, 1911), p. 76.
p. 143   *l.11*   *Dante and His Circle: With the Italian Poets Preceding Him, 1100–1200–1300, A Collection of Lyrics*, trans. Dante Gabriel Rossetti (London: Ellis and White, 1874), p. 5.
p. 143   *l.13*   Ibid., p. 15.
p. 143   *l.19*   "Cavalcanti," in *Literary Essays of Ezra Pound* (New York: New Directions, 1968), p. 159, where he also says: "One can . . . scarcely exaggerate the gulf between Guido's state of mind and that of Dante in the same epoch."
p. 144   *l.4*   *Marsilio Ficino's Commentary on Plato's Symposium*, trans. Sears Reynold Jayne (Columbia, Mo.: University of Missouri Press, 1944), p. 217.
p. 144   *l.16*   "Platonic Love in Some Italian Poets," in *Essays in Literary Criticism by George Santayana*, ed. Irving Singer (New York: Scribner's, 1956), pp. 97–98. Permission to reprint granted by Mrs Margot Cory and MIT Press.

p. 144   *l.36*   Ibid., p. 99.

p. 146   *l.22*   Sonetto XV, my translation.

p. 147   *l.21*   *The Romance of Tristan and Iseult*, pp. 124–25.

p. 148   *l.27*   Ballata IX, my translation.

p. 149   *l.1*   J. E. Shaw, *Guido Cavalcanti's Theory of Love: The Canzone d'Amore and Other Related Problems* (Toronto: University of Toronto Press, 1949), p. 118.

p. 152   *l.4*   Quoted in Ezra Pound, *The Spirit of Romance* (New York: New Directions, 1968), p. 96.

p. 153   *l.25*   *Three Philosophical Poets*, in *Essays in Literary Criticism*, p. 45.

p. 155   *l.27*   See Charles Singleton, *An Essay on the Vita Nuova* (Cambridge: Harvard University Press, 1949), pp. 69–71. On Guinizelli's influence on Dante, see Karl Vossler, *Medieval Culture: An Introduction to Dante and his Times* (New York: Frederick Ungar, 1958), 1:303.

p. 157   *l.23*   Cf. T. S. Eliot, "Dante," in *Selected Essays* (New York: Harcourt, Brace, 1950), p. 233.

p. 158   *l.6*   Cf. Maud Bodkin, *Archetypal Patterns in Poetry* (London: Oxford University Press, 1963), p. 190.

p. 160   *l.11*   Quoted in Introduction, *The Comedy of Dante Alighieri*, trans. Dorothy L. Sayers (Harmondsworth: Penguin Books, 1954), 1:52.

p. 161   *l.34*   Ibid., 3:347, *Paradiso*, Canto XXXIII.

p. 162   *l.9*   See Etienne Gilson, *Dante the Philosopher*, trans. David Moore (New York: Sheed and Ward, 1949). See also my discussion of Dante in relation to medieval theology in *The Nature of Love: Plato to Luther*; also Joseph Anthony Mazzeo, "Dante's Conception of Love," in *American Critical Essays on the Divine Comedy*, ed. Robert J. Clements (New York: New York University Press, 1967), pp. 140–57.

p. 162   *l.27*   On this, see William Anderson's Introduction to his translation of Dante, *The New Life: La Vita Nuova* (Harmondsworth: Penguin Books, 1964), p. 26.

p. 168   *l.36*   *Marsilio Ficino's Commentary on Plato's Symposium*, p. 140.

p. 170   *l.19*   Edgar Wind, *Pagan Mysteries in the Renaissance* (New Haven: Yale University Press, 1958), p. 69.

p. 170   *l.30*   *Marsilio Ficino's Commentary on Plato's Symposium*, p. 192.

p. 173   *l.14*   Pico della Mirandola, *A Platonick Discourse upon Love*, ed. Edmund G. Gardner (Boston: The Merrymount Press, 1914), p. 45.

p. 173   *l.37*   *Marsilio Ficino's Commentary on Plato's Symposium*, p. 213.

p. 175   *l.34*   On Ficino's ideas about agapē, see James A. Devereux, S.J., "The Object of Love in Ficino's Philosophy," *Journal of the History of Ideas* (April-June 1969): 161–70; see also Paul O. Kristeller, *The Philosophy of Marsilio Ficino* (New York: Columbia University Press, 1943), pp. 278n, 280n.

p. 176   *l.3*   *Marsilio Ficino's Commentary on Plato's Symposium*, p. 215.

p. 177   *l.30*   John Charles Nelson, *Renaissance Theory of Love: The Context of Giordano Bruno's Eroici Furori* (New York: Columbia University Press, 1958), p. 61.

p. 178   *l.34*   Pico della Mirandola, *Oration on the Dignity of Man*, in *The Renaissance Philosophy of Man*, ed. E. Cassirer et al. (Chicago: University of Chicago Press, 1948), pp. 95–96.

p. 179   *l.22*   Ibid., p. 97.

p. 179   *l.31*   Walter Pater, *The Renaissance* (London: Collins, 1961), p. 94.

p. 180   *l.18*   Nesca Robb, *Neoplatonism of the Italian Renaissance* (New York: Octagon Books, 1968), p. 245; see also Agnes Heller, *Renaissance Man* (London: Routledge and Kegan Paul, 1978), p. 255.

p. 180   *l.25*   Quoted in John Addington Symonds, *The Life of Michelangelo Buonarroti* (London: John C. Nimmo, 1899), 2:160–61.

p. 181   *l.17*   Michelangelo's drawing is reproduced in Robert J. Clements, *The Poetry of Michelangelo* (New York: New York University Press, 1966), p. 369.

p. 182   *l.20*   Robb, *Neoplatonism of the Italian Renaissance*, pp. 230–31.

p. 184   *l.12*   Quoted in Nelson, *Renaissance Theory of Love*, p. 46.

p. 185   *l.3*   Song from *Bacco ed Arianna*, my translation. Cf. Luigi Tonelli, *L'Amore nella poesia e nel pensiero del Rinascimento* (Florence: Sansoni, 1933), p. 30.

p. 185   *l.17*   Nelson, *Renaissance Theory of Love*, p. 119.

p. 187   *l.25*   Baldesar Castiglione, *The Book of the Courtier*, trans. Charles S. Singleton (New York: Anchor Books, 1959), pp. 339–40.

p. 188   *l.32*   Ibid., pp. 349–50.

p. 189   *l.4*   On Neoplatonic *trattati di amore*, see chapters in Robb, *Neoplatonism of the Italian Renaissance*, and Nelson, *Renaissance Theory of Love*. For an English translation of part of Leone Ebreo's *Dialogues on Love*, see *Renaissance Philosophy*, ed. Arthur B. Fallico and Herman Shapiro (New York: Modern Library, 1967), 1:172–228.

p. 189   *l.13*   Castiglione, *The Book of the Courtier*, p. 352.

p. 190   *l.11*   Machiavelli, *The Chief Works and Others*, trans. Allan Gilbert (Durham: Duke University Press, 1965), p. 805.

p. 190   *l.16*   Ibid., p. 819.

p. 191   *l.23*   On this and other parts of this chapter, see Jefferson Butler Fletcher, *Literature of the Italian Renaissance* (New York: Macmillan, 1934).

p. 191   *l.28*   Mario Equicola, *Libro di natura d'amore*, fols. 206^r–207^r, trans. and quoted in Donald L. Guss, *John Donne, Petrarchist: Italianate Conceits and Love Theory in the Songs and Sonets* (Detroit: Wayne State University Press, 1966), p. 143.

p. 192   *l.3*   Sperone Speroni, *Dialogi*, fols. a5^r–a7^r, trans. and quoted in Guss, *John Donne*, p. 144. See also Nelson, *Renaissance Theory of Love*, pp. 112–16 and 127–29.

p. 192   *l.9*   Mario Equicola, quoted in A. J. Smith, "The Metaphysic of Love," *Review of English Studies* 9, no. 36 (1958): 369.

p. 192   *l.20*   "Apology for Raymond Sebond," *The Complete Essays of Montaigne*, trans. Donald M. Frame (New York: Anchor Books, 1960), 2:137.

p. 192   *l.23*   "Of Experience," ibid., 3:368.

p. 192   *l.36*   "Of Friendship," ibid., 1:192.

p. 193   *l.17*   "On Some Verses of Virgil," ibid., 3:99.

p. 193   *l.24*   Ibid., 3:61.

p. 193   *l.37*   Ibid., p. 115.

p. 194   *l.4*   Ibid., pp. 76 and 92.

p. 194   *l.26*   Ibid., p. 108.

p. 194   *l.27*   Ibid., p. 119.

p. 195   *l.13*   Ibid., p. 116.

p. 196   *l.12*   Samuel Johnson, "The Metaphysical Poets," reprinted in *John Donne's Poetry*, ed. A. L. Clements (New York: Norton, 1966), p. 107. See also W. Jackson Bate, *Samuel Johnson* (New York: Harcourt Brace Jovanovich, 1977), pp. 540–41.

p. 196   *l.18*   Ibid., p. 108.

p. 197   *l.21*   "Community," ibid., p. 18.

p. 197   *l.25*   "A Valediction: Forbidding Mourning," ibid., p. 29.

p. 197   *l.34*   Ibid., p. 124.

p. 198   *l.1*   Samuel Taylor Coleridge, "Notes on Donne," ibid., p. 111.

p. 198   *l.5*   Cleanth Brooks, "The Language of Paradox," ibid., p. 184.

p. 198   *l.22*   Ibid., pp. 29–31.

p. 199   *l.27*   "The Good-Morrow," ibid., p. 1.

p. 199   *l.33*   "Lovers' Infiniteness," ibid., p. 8.

p. 200   *l.1*   "The Anniversary," ibid., p. 13.

p. 200   *l.10*   *Sermons*, 1:184–85.

p. 200   *l.15*   "The Canonization," *John Donne's Poetry*, p. 6.

p. 202   *l.13*   Clay Hunt, "Elegy 19: 'To His Mistress Going to Bed,' " ibid., p. 190.

p. 202   *l.24*   Wind, *Pagan Mysteries in the Renaissance*, pp. 121–28; Erwin Panofsky, *Studies in Iconology: Humanistic Themes in the Art of the Renaissance* (New York: Harper and Row, 1962), pp. 150–60.

p. 203   *l.34*   "Holy Sonnet XIV," *John Donne's Poetry*, p. 86.

p. 204   *l.15*   "Holy Sonnet XVII," ibid., p. 89.

p. 204   *l.28*   *The Poems of John Donne*, ed. Herbert J. C. Grierson (Oxford: Oxford University Press, 1958), 2:xlv.

p. 204   *l.31*   C. S. Lewis, "Donne and Love Poetry in the Seventeenth Century," *John Donne's Poetry*, p. 154.

p. 204   *l.36*   See Joan Bennett, "The Love Poetry of John Donne: A Reply to Mr. C. S. Lewis," ibid., pp. 160–77.

p. 205   *l.8*   See Smith, "The Metaphysic of Love."

p. 206   *l.5*   *Complete Poetry and Selected Prose of John Milton* (New York: Modern Library, 1950), pp. 691–92.

p. 209   I am indebted to the writings of many Shakespeare scholars, too numerous to mention here. Works specifically on the concept of love in Shakespeare include: Hugh M. Richmond, *Shakespeare's Sexual Comedy: A Mirror for Lovers* (Indianapolis: Bobbs-Merrill, 1971); Charles R. Lyons, *Shakespeare and the Ambiguity of Love's Triumph* (The Hague: Mouton, 1971); Juliet Dusinberre, *Shakespeare and the Nature of Women* (New York: Barnes and Noble, 1975); W. B. C. Watkins, *Shakespeare and Spenser* (Princeton: Princeton University Press, 1950); Herman Harrell Horne, *Shakespeare's Philosophy of Love* (Raleigh: Edwards and Broughton, 1945); John Vyvyan, *Shakespeare and Platonic Beauty* (London: Chatto and Windus, 1961); Stanley Cavell, "The Avoidance of Love: A Reading of *King Lear*," in *Must We Mean What We Say?* (Cambridge: Cambridge University Press, 1976); Norman Rabkin, *Shakespeare and the Common Understanding* (Chicago: University of Chicago Press, 1984).

p. 210   *l.3*   William Hazlitt, "On Shakespeare and Milton," in *The Norton Anthology of English Literature*, ed. M. H. Abrams (New York: W. W.

Norton, 1962), 2:534. For Santayana's ideas about Shakespeare, see his essays "The Absence of Religion in Shakespeare" and "Tragic Philosophy," in *Essays in Literary Criticism.*

p. 216   *l.22*   Act III, scene 3.
p. 217   *l.1*   Act III, scene 2.
p. 217   *l.23*   Act III, scene 1.
p. 217   *l.34*   Act II, scene 3.
p. 217   *l.37*   Act V, scene 2.
p. 219   *l.7*   Act II, scene 3.
p. 219   *l.10*   Act V, scene 4.
p. 219   *l.18*   Ibid.
p. 221   *l.5*   Act I, scene 5.
p. 221   *l.7*   Act II, scene 2.
p. 222   *l.37*   Cf. Maynard Mack's Introduction to *Antony and Cleopatra,* in *William Shakespeare: The Complete Works,* ed. Alfred Harbage (Baltimore: Penguin, 1969), pp. 1169–71.
p. 223   *l.37*   Plutarch, "Life of Antonius," in *The Lives of the Noble Grecians and Romans.*
p. 224   *l.8*   Act II, scene 2.
p. 225   *l.13*   On this, see my essay "Erotic Transformations in the Legend of Dido and Aeneas," *MLN* (December 1975), pp. 767–83.
p. 225   *l.21*   Act IV, scene 14.
p. 228   *l.3*   Act III, scene 2.
p. 228   *l.11*   Act V, scene 1.
p. 228   *l.15*   Act II, scene 4.
p. 228   *l.25*   Act IV, scene 1.
p. 228   *l.36*   Act V, scene 2.
p. 229   *l.5*   Act IV, scene 2.
p. 232   *l.15*   Act II, scene 7.
p. 232   *l.28*   Act III, scene 2.
p. 234   *l.7*   Act I, scene 2.
p. 235   *l.5*   Act V, scene 3.
p. 236   *l.2*   Act IV, scene 4.
p. 236   *l.19*   Act V, scene 4.
p. 236   *l.26*   Act V, scene 3.
p. 239   *l.3*   Act III, scene 3.
p. 239   *l.6*   Act I, scene 3.
p. 239   *l.23*   For a statement of this approach, see Stanley Cavell, *The Claim of Reason* (Oxford: Clarendon Press, 1979), pp. 486ff. Cf. also W. D. Adamson, "Unpinned or Undone? Desdemona's Critics and the Problem of Sexual Innocence," *Shakespeare Studies* 13 (1980): 169–86.
p. 239   *l.28*   Act I, scene 3.
p. 239   *l.34*   Ibid.
p. 240   *l.1*   Act IV, scene 1.
p. 240   *l.3*   Act IV, scene 2. On Othello's sexual pathology, see Stephen J. Greenblatt, "Improvisation and Power," in *Literature and Society,* ed. Edward W. Said (Baltimore: The Johns Hopkins University Press, 1980), particularly pp. 84–89.
p. 242   *l.36*   On this, see Jean H. Hagstrum, *Sex and Sensibility: Ideal and*

Notes

Erotic Love from Milton to Mozart (Chicago: University of Chicago Press, 1980), particularly pp. 24–49. On Puritan attitudes toward love and sexuality, see Dusinberre, *Shakespeare and the Nature of Women*, pp. 2–7 and passim; see also Edmund S. Morgan, *The Puritan Family: Religion and Domestic Relations in Seventeenth-Century New England* (New York: Harper and Row, 1966), pp. 29–64.

p. 243   *l.13*   8. 495–99.
p. 244   *l.1*   9. 952–59.
p. 246   *l.1*   8. 622–24.
p. 246   *l.9*   8. 471–73.
p. 247   *l.11*   8. 600–605.
p. 248   *l.1*   4. 296–301.
p. 248   *l.11*   Quoted in Edward LeComte, *Milton and Sex* (New York: Columbia University Press, 1978), p. 52.
p. 248   *l.14*   9. 1182–84.
p. 248   *l.24*   Quoted in Hagstrum, *Sex and Sensibility*, p. 36.
p. 248   *l.29*   9. 823–25.
p. 249   *l.10*   8. 383–85.
p. 249   *l.29*   St. Augustine, *The City of God*, trans. Marcus Dods (New York: Modern Library, 1950), book 14, p. 475.
p. 252   *l.9*   LeComte, *Milton and Sex*, p. 29.
p. 252   *l.18*   4. 748–53.
p. 252   *l.26*   4. 765–70.
p. 253   *l.27*   *CPW*, vol. 2, p. 258, quoted in LeComte, *Milton and Sex*, p. 30.
p. 255   *l.28*   12. 645–49.
p. 256   *l.11*   Martin Luther, *Table Talk* (London: George Bell & Sons, 1884), p. 307.
p. 256   *l.17*   10. 898–908.
p. 257   *l.22*   "On Some Verses of Virgil," *The Complete Essays of Montaigne*, 3:69.
p. 258   *l.20*   Ibid., pp. 68 and 72.
p. 258   *l.29*   "Letter to Chanut," in *Descartes: His Moral Philosophy and Psychology*, trans. John J. Blom (New York: New York University Press, 1978), p. 201. I am indebted to Harry Frankfurt for having called my attention to this book.
p. 259   *l.10*   "The Passions of the Soul," in *Essential Works of Descartes*, trans. Lowell Bair (New York: Bantam Books, 1961), pp. 150–51.
p. 261   *l.12*   Ibid., p. 147.
p. 261   *l.24*   *Descartes: His Moral Philosophy and Psychology*, p. 206.
p. 262   *l.18*   *Essential Works of Descartes*, p. 148.
p. 262   *l.29*   *Descartes: His Moral Philosophy and Psychology*, p. 210.
p. 264   *l.3*   Blaise Pascal, *Pensées* (New York: Modern Library, 1941), no. 323, p. 109. For a discussion of Pascal's argument, see *The Nature of Love: Plato to Luther*.
p. 264   *l.4*   *Pensées*, no. 162, p. 59.
p. 264   *l.36*   Part III, *The Ethics*, in *The Chief Works of Benedict de Spinoza*, trans. R. H. M. Elwes (New York: Dover, 1955), 2:175.
p. 265   *l.5*   Ibid., pt. III, p. 174.
p. 265   *l.34*   Ibid., pt. III, p. 156.

p. 266 *l.22* Ibid., pt. IV, pp. 201–2.
p. 267 *l.34* Ibid., pt. V, p. 258.
p. 269 *l.1* Ibid., pt. V, p. 264.
p. 269 *l.11* Benedict de Spinoza, *Ethics*, ed. James Gutmann (New York: Hafner, 1949), pt. IV, p. 222.
p. 273 *l.16* Quoted in de Rougemont, *Love in the Western World*, p. 198.
p. 274 *l.3* Madame de La Fayette, *The Princess of Clèves*, trans. Walter J. Cobb (New York: Signet, 1961), p. 23.
p. 275 *l.22* Quoted in Stirling Haig, *Madame de Lafayette* (New York: Twayne, 1970), p. 95.
p. 276 *l.9* *The Maxims of La Rochefoucauld*, trans. Louis Kronenberger (New York: Modern Library, 1959), no. 467, p. 118.
p. 276 *l.11* Ibid., no. 205, p. 70.
p. 276 *l.32* Ibid., no. 113, p. 53.
p. 277 *l.35* Ibid., no. 69, p. 46.
p. 278 *l.12* Ibid., no. 519, p. 131.
p. 278 *l.18* Ibid., no. 176, p. 65.
p. 278 *l.23* Ibid., no. 68, pp. 45–46.
p. 279 *l.9* On this and much else related to this chapter, see Louise K. Horowitz, *Love and Language: A Study of the Classical French Moralist Writers* (Columbus: Ohio State University Press, 1977).
p. 280 *l.15* For a more extended discussion of these matters, see two essays of mine: "The Shadow of Dom Juan in Molière," *MLN* (December 1970): 838–57; and "Molière's Dom Juan," *The Hudson Review* (Autumn 1971): 447–60.
p. 283 *l.5* Quoted in Franklin L. Baumer, "Romanticism (ca. 1780–ca.1830)," in *Dictionary of the History of Ideas: Studies of Selected Pivotal Ideas*, ed. Philip P. Wiener (New York: Charles Scribner's Sons, 1973), 4:198.
p. 283 *l.15* René Wellek, "Romanticism in Literature," in *Dictionary of the History of Ideas*, 4:195.
p. 283 *l.21* Cf. Morse Peckham, *The Triumph of Romanticism* (Columbia: University of South Carolina Press, 1970).
p. 286 *l.5* Quoted in Hagstrum, *Sex and Sensibility*, p. 179.
p. 286 *l.17* Quoted in Walter Jackson Bate, *From Classic to Romantic: Premises of Taste in Eighteenth-Century England* (New York: Harper and Row, 1961), p. 174.
p. 286 *l.26* William Wordsworth, "Preface to the Lyrical Ballads," quoted in Lilian R. Furst, *Romanticism in Perspective* (New York: Humanities Press, 1950), p. 229.
p. 286 *l.34* Quoted in Bate, *From Classic to Romantic*, p. 131.
p. 287 *l.13* Ibid., p. 134.
p. 287 *l.31* Quoted in James Engell, *The Creative Imagination: Enlightenment to Romanticism* (Cambridge: Harvard University Press, 1981), p. 247. Cf. also two essays by Jean H. Hagstrum: "Babylon Revisited, or the Story of Luvah and Vala," in *Blake's Sublime Allegory*, ed. Stuart Curran and Joseph Anthony Wittreich, Jr. (Madison: University of Wisconsin Press, 1973); and "Eros and Psyche: Some Versions of Romantic Love and Delicacy," *Critical Inquiry* (Spring 1977): 522–42.
p. 288 *l.21* Samuel Taylor Coleridge, *Shakespearean Criticism*, ed. Tho-

mas Middleton Raysor (London: Dent, 1960), 2:106. I am grateful to James Engell for advice about this source.

p. 288 *l.34* Ibid., p. 107.

p. 289 *l.20* Ibid.

p. 289 *l.32* Ibid., p. 108.

p. 290 *l.21* Quoted in Bate, *From Classic to Romantic*, p. 131.

p. 290 *l.22* Quoted in M. H. Abrams, *Natural Supernaturalism* (New York: Norton, 1971), p. 247.

p. 291 *l.12* *Epipsychidion*.

p. 291 *l.16* Emily Brontë, *Wuthering Heights*, chap. 9.

p. 294 *l.27* October 13, 1819, to Fanny Brawne, quoted in Gerald Enscoe, *Eros and the Romantics: Sexual Love as a Theme in Coleridge, Shelley and Keats* (The Hague: Mouton, 1967), p. 130.

p. 295 *l.4* Recently discovered letters from Wordsworth to his wife reveal a libidinal dimension in him that Shelley could not have surmised from his published work.

p. 296 *l.1* Irving Babbitt, *Rousseau and Romanticism* (New York: Meridian Books, 1955), p. 178.

p. 296 *l.5* Ibid., p. 179.

p. 297 *l.2* Jean-Jacques Rousseau, *Oeuvres Complètes* (Paris: Gallimard, 1964), 2:1224–31. My translation.

p. 298 *l.37* Babbitt, *Rousseau and Romanticism*, p. 184.

p. 301 *l.14* Quoted in Denis de Rougemont, "Love," in *Dictionary of the History of Ideas*, 3:96.

p. 302 *l.7* On this, see Lawrence Stone, *The Family, Sex and Marriage in England, 1500–1800* (New York: Harper and Row, 1977); see also Ian Watt, *The Rise of the Novel* (Berkeley: University of California Press, 1957).

p. 308 *l.27* For examples of, and discussion about, the different interpretations of *La Nouvelle Héloïse*, see Ronald Grimsley, *Jean-Jacques Rousseau: A Study in Self-Awareness* (Cardiff: University of Wales Press, 1961), particularly pp. 121–23, and M. B. Ellis, *Julie or La Nouvelle Héloïse: A Synthesis of Rousseau's Thought (1749–1759)*, (Toronto: University of Toronto Press, 1949), particularly pp. xxiii–xxvii.

p. 308 *l.34* Jean-Jacques Rousseau, *La Nouvelle Héloïse: Julie, or the New Eloise*, trans. Judith H. McDowell (University Park: Pennsylvania State University, 1968), p. 409.

p. 309 *l.17* Ibid., p. 393.

p. 310 *l.13* Ibid., p. 191.

p. 311 *l.1* *The Confessions of Jean-Jacques Rousseau*, trans. J. M. Cohen (Harmondsworth: Penguin Books, 1953), p. 37.

p. 311 *l.3* Ibid., p. 36.

p. 311 *l.27* Ibid., pp. 396–97.

p. 312 *l.29* Rousseau, *La Nouvelle Héloïse*, p. 124.

p. 313 *l.4* Voltaire, *Philosophical Dictionary*, in *The World of Love*, ed. Isidor Schneider (New York: Braziller, 1964), 1:73.

p. 313 *l.22* Denis Diderot, "Jouissance," *The Encyclopedia*, trans. Stephen J. Gendzier (New York: Harper and Row, 1967), p. 96.

p. 313 *l.33* Ibid., p. 97.

p. 314   *l.29*   Rousseau, *La Nouvelle Héloïse*, p. 194.

p. 315   *l.12*   Stendhal, *On Love*, p. 257.

p. 315   *l.26*   *CG*, xix, 243–44, quoted in Grimsley, *Jean-Jacques Rousseau: A Study in Self-Awareness*, p. 105.

p. 316   *l.9*   Jean-Jacques Rousseau, *Emile or On Education*, trans. Allan Bloom (New York: Basic Books, 1979), p. 214. Except where otherwise indicated, all quotations from *Emile* are taken from this translation.

p. 316   *l.16*   Ibid., pp. 15–16.

p. 317   *l.22*   Rousseau, *La Nouvelle Héloïse*, p. 163.

p. 317   *l.26*   Ibid., p. 319.

p. 321   *l.20*   Quoted in Paul Zweig, *The Heresy of Self-Love* (New York: Basic Books, 1968), p. 148.

p. 322   *l.26*   Diderot, "Jouissance," *The Encyclopedia*, p. 97.

p. 323   *l.8*   Rousseau, *Emile*, p. 214.

p. 323   *l.23*   Ibid.

p. 324   *l.28*   Jean-Jacques Rousseau, *Emile*, trans. Barbara Foxley (New York: Dutton, 1974), p. 48.

p. 326   *l.33*   Quoted in Lester G. Crocker, *Jean-Jacques Rousseau* (New York: Macmillan, 1973), 2:140.

p. 328   *l.5*   Rousseau, *Emile*, p. 220.

p. 330   *l.11*   Ibid., p. 479.

p. 333   *l.31*   Jean-Jacques Rousseau, *Politics and the Arts: Letter to M. D'Alembert on the Theatre*, trans. Allan Bloom (Ithaca: Cornell University Press, 1968), p. 135n.

p. 336   *l.14*   Cf. Elizabeth Rapaport, "On the Future of Love: Rousseau and the Radical Feminists," in *Philosophy of Sex: Contemporary Readings*, ed. Alan Soble (Totowa: Littlefield, Adams, 1980), pp. 369–88.

p. 337   *l.7*   Rousseau, *Emile*, p. 40.

p. 337   *l.25*   John Locke, *Of Civil Government*, chap. 8, no. 101.

p. 338   *l.31*   On this, see Ernst Cassirer, *The Question of Jean-Jacques Rousseau*, trans. Peter Gay (New York: Columbia University Press, 1954), p. 101.

p. 341   *l.19*   On this, see Jean Starobinski, *Jean-Jacques Rousseau: La Transparence et l'Obstacle* (Paris: Gallimard, 1971); see also Ronald Grimsley, "Rousseau and the Problem of Happiness," in *Hobbes and Rousseau: A Collection of Critical Essays*, ed. Maurice Cranston and Richard S. Peters (New York: Anchor Books, 1972), pp. 450–53.

p. 341   *l.22*   Rousseau, *Politics and the Arts*, p. 126.

p. 343   *l.1*   Jean-Jacques Rousseau, *The Reveries of the Solitary Walker*, trans. Charles E. Butterworth (New York: New York University Press, 1979), p. 141.

p. 343   *l.14*   *The Confessions of Jean-Jacques Rousseau*, p. 213.

p. 343   *l.16*   Rousseau, *The Reveries of the Solitary Walker*, p. 141.

p. 344   *l.4*   The Marquis de Sade, *Philosophy in the Bedroom and Other Writings*, trans. Richard Seaver and Austryn Wainhouse (New York: Grove Press, 1965), p. 134.

p. 345   *l.35*   Ibid., p. 285.

p. 346   *l.14*   Ibid.

p. 346   *l.31*   Ibid., p. 284.

p. 347   *l.30*   The Marquis de Sade, *The 120 Days of Sodom and Other Writings,* trans. Richard Seaver and Austryn Wainhouse (New York: Grove Press, 1966), p. 73.

p. 348   *l.7*   Quoted in Simone de Beauvoir, "Must We Burn Sade?" in ibid., p. 33.

p. 348   *l.16*   Ibid.

p. 349   *l.3*   Quoted in Maurice Blanchot, "Sade," in the Marquis de Sade, *Philosophy in the Bedroom and Other Writings,* p. 68.

p. 350   *l.33*   Ibid., p. 309.

p. 351   *l.24*   Stendhal, *On Love,* p. 3.

p. 358   *l.10*   Ibid., p. 267.

p. 354   *l.23*   For alternative views about vanity-love in Stendhal, see Victor Brombert, "Stendhal, Analyst or Amorist?" in *Stendhal: A Collection of Critical Essays,* ed. Victor Brombert (Englewood Cliffs: Prentice-Hall, 1962), p. 158; and also René Girard on "triangular desire" in Stendhal, in *Deceit, Desire, and the Novel* (Baltimore: The Johns Hopkins Press, 1965), pp. 1–53.

p. 354   *l.29*   Stendhal, *On Love,* p. 2.

p. 355   *l.10*   Ibid., p. 3.

p. 356   *l.35*   Ibid., p. 272.

p. 360   *l.5*   Ibid., p. 5.

p. 360   *l.14*   Ibid.

p. 360   *l.25*   Ibid., p. 6.

p. 363   *l.9*   Ibid., p. 363.

p. 364   *l.13*   Cf. José Ortega y Gasset, "Love in Stendhal," in *On Love: Aspects of a Single Theme,* trans. Toby Talbot (New York: New American Library, 1957). See also my essay, "Ortega on Love," *The Hudson Review* (Spring 1959): 145–54.

p. 364   *l.32*   Stendhal, *On Love,* p. 6.

p. 365   *l.10*   Ibid., p. 44.

p. 365   *l.26*   Cf. "Appraisal and Bestowal," in *The Nature of Love: Plato to Luther.* Cf. also the discussion of Stendhalian crystallization in Russell Vannoy, *Sex Without Love: A Philosophical Exploration* (Buffalo: Prometheus Books, 1980), pp. 157–58.

p. 366   *l.4*   Ortega y Gasset, *On Love,* p. 26.

p. 366   *l.25*   Ibid., p. 25.

p. 367   *l.31*   Stendhal, *On Love,* p. 146.

p. 367   *l.34*   Ibid., p. 112.

p. 369   *l.13*   Ibid., p. 11.

p. 370   *l.8*   Ibid., p. 192.

p. 370   *l.16*   Ibid., p. 318.

p. 370   *l.22*   Quoted in Emmet Kennedy, *Destutt de Tracy and the Origins of "Ideology": A Philosophe in the Age of Revolution* (Philadelphia: American Philosophical Society, 1978), p. 260.

p. 370   *l.31*   Tracy, *De l'amour,* ed. Gilbert Chinard (Paris: Société d'édition "Les Belles-lettres," 1926), p. 3. My translation.

p. 372   *l.2*   Stendhal, *On Love,* p. 243.

p. 372   *l.20*   *Commentaire*, p. 72, quoted in Kennedy, *Destutt de Tracy*, p. 267.

p. 373   *l.21*   *Stendhal: A Collection of Critical Essays*, ed. Victor Brombert, p. 164.

p. 373   *l.30*   Stendhal, *On Love*, p. 12.

p. 377   *l.32*   Immanuel Kant, *Lectures on Ethics*, trans. Louis Infield (New York: Harper and Row, 1963), p. 163.

p. 378   *l.5*   David Hume, "Of Polygamy and Divorces," in *Sexual Love and Western Morality*, ed. D. P. Verene (New York: Harper and Row, 1972), p. 153.

p. 378   *l.28*   Ibid., pp. 151–52.

p. 379   *l.22*   Immanuel Kant, *The Metaphysical Principles of Virtue* (Indianapolis: Bobbs-Merrill, 1964), p. 87.

p. 380   *l.33*   Kant, *Lectures on Ethics*, p. 167.

p. 381   *l.7*   Ibid.

p. 381   *l.17*   Ibid.

p. 382   *l.10*   Ibid., p. 163.

p. 382   *l.32*   For a contemporary argument similar to Kant's, see Bernard H. Baumrin, "Sexual Immorality Delineated," in *Philosophy and Sex*, ed. Robert Baker and Frederick Elliston (Buffalo: Prometheus Books, 1975), pp. 116–28; for a critique of Baumrin, see Vannoy, *Sex Without Love: A Philosophical Exploration*, pp. 101–7.

p. 384   *l.14*   W. Windelband, *A History of Philosophy* (New York: Macmillan, 1901), p. 603.

p. 385   *l.19*   Quoted in Robert M. Wernaer, *Romanticism and the Romantic School in Germany* (New York: Haskell House, 1966), p. 237.

p. 386   *l.18*   Friedrich Schlegel, *Lucinde and the Fragments*, trans. Peter Firchow (Minneapolis: University of Minnesota, 1971), p. 113.

p. 387   *l.5*   Ibid.

p. 387   *l.28*   Quoted in Engell, *The Creative Imagination*, p. 311.

p. 387   *l.36*   Ibid., p. 313.

p. 388   *l.37*   Schlegel, *Lucinde and the Fragments*, p. 60.

p. 389   *l.30*   Ibid., p. 125.

p. 390   *l.23*   Kant, *Lectures on Ethics*, p. 206.

p. 391   *l.4*   Schlegel, *Lucinde and the Fragments*, p. 65.

p. 391   *l.8*   Ibid., p. 66.

p. 393   *l.18*   Ibid., p. 48.

p. 394   *l.11*   Quoted in Walter Kaufmann, *Hegel: Reinterpretation, Texts, and Commentary* (Garden City: Doubleday, 1965), p. 74.

p. 400   *l.17*   Georg Wilhelm Friedrich Hegel, *Early Theological Writings*, trans. T. M. Knox (Chicago: University of Chicago Press, 1948), p. 305. Words in brackets added by the editor. On what the translator calls Hegel's "Pantheism of Love," see his Introduction, pp. 11–12. See also H. S. Harris, *Hegel's Development: Toward the Sunlight, 1770–1801* (London: Oxford University Press, 1972), pp. 305–9; and Gustav E. Mueller, *Hegel: The Man, His Vision, and Work* (New York: Pageant Press, 1968), pp. 122–26.

p. 402   *l.19*   Quoted in Jacques Choron, *Death and Western Thought* (New York: Collier Books, 1963), p. 155.

p. 402   *l.33*   Hegel, *Early Theological Writings*, p. 307.

p. 403   *l.5*   G. W. F. Hegel, *Aesthetics*: *Lectures on Fine Art*, trans. T. M. Knox (Oxford: Clarendon Press, 1975), p. 562. Translation modified slightly.

p. 404   *l.5*   Hegel, *Early Theological Writings*, p. 307.

p. 404   *l.16*   Ibid., p. 308.

p. 406   *l.1*   Hegel, *Aesthetics*, p. 567.

p. 406   *l.15*   Ibid., p. 568.

p. 410   *l.21*   *Philosophy of Mind*, no. 474. Quoted in W. T. Stace, *The Philosophy of Hegel*: *A Systematic Exposition* (New York: Dover, 1955), pp. 371–72.

p. 411   *l.23*   Quoted in Josiah Royce, *The Spirit of Modern Philosophy* (Boston: Houghton Mifflin, 1893), p. 226.

p. 412   *l.1*   Cf. T. S. Eliot, "Shelley and Keats," in *The Use of Poetry and the Use of Criticism* (London: Faber and Faber, 1968), pp. 87–102.

p. 415   *l.1*   *Shelley's Prose*, p. 220.

p. 415   *l.37*   Ibid., p. 170.

p. 417   *l.18*   Ibid.

p. 418   *l.38*   Cf. Herbert Read, "In Defence of Shelley," in *The True Voice of Feeling*: *Studies in English Romantic Poetry* (New York: Pantheon, 1953), pp. 212–87.

p. 419   *l.10*   *Shelley's Prose*, pp. 282–83..

p. 420   *l.2*   *Hymn to Intellectual Beauty*.

p. 420   *l.9*   *Shelley's Prose*, p. 220.

p. 422   *l.17*   George Santayana, "Shelley: or the Poetic Value of Revolutionary Principles," in *Essays in Literary Criticism*, p. 205.

p. 424   *l.2*   David Hume, *A Treatise of Human Nature* (Oxford: Clarendon Press, 1888), pp. 575–76.

p. 424   *l.24*   Ibid., p. 365.

p. 424   *l.29*   Ibid., p. 576.

p. 425   *l.10*   Ibid., p. 220.

p. 425   *l.28*   Ibid., p. 394.

p. 426   *l.2*   Ibid., p. 395.

p. 427   *l.14*   Cf. Charles E. Robinson, *Shelley and Byron*: *The Snake and Eagle Wreathed in Fight* (Baltimore: Johns Hopkins University Press, 1976).

p. 430   *l.12*   Byron, *Letters and Journals*, 1:52, quoted in Nathaniel Brown, *Sexuality and Feminism in Shelley* (Cambridge: Harvard University Press, 1979), p. 174.

p. 430   *l.29*   Quoted in Brown, *Sexuality and Feminism in Shelley*, p. 161.

p. 430   *l.32*   Bryon, *Letters and Journals*, 8:15, quoted in Brown, *Sexuality and Feminism in Shelley*, p. 175.

p. 433   *l.27*   Quoted in Brown, *Sexuality and Feminism in Shelley*, p. 41.

p. 435   *l.5*   On this, see Hans Eichner, *Friedrich Schlegel* (New York: Twayne, 1970), pp. 88 and 154–55.

p. 435 *l.33* Johann Wolfgang von Goethe, "Reflections on Werther," in *The Sorrows of Young Werther and Selected Writings* (New York: Signet Books, 1962), p. 136.

p. 436 *l.31* Letter of July 16, Johann Wolfgang von Goethe, *The Sorrows of Young Werther*, trans. Victor Lange (New York: Rinehart, 1958), p. 38.

p. 437 *l.23* Letter of August 18, ibid., pp. 54–55.

p. 438 *l.16* Quoted in Walter Kaufmann, *From Shakespeare to Existentialism* (New York: Anchor Books, 1960), p. 76.

p. 439 *l.9* Ibid., p. 61.

p. 441 *l.19* Wolfgang von Goethe, *Elective Affinities* (New York: P. F. Collier, n.d.), p. 384.

p. 442 *l.9* Quoted in Emil Lucka, *Eros: The Development of the Sex Relation Through the Ages* (New York: Putnam, 1915), p. 321.

p. 444 *l.29* Quoted in Choron, *Death and Western Thought*, p. 155.

p. 447 *l.11* Arthur Schopenhauer, *The World as Will and Representation*, trans. E. F. J. Payne (New York: Dover, 1966), 2:507.

p. 448 *l.22* Ibid., 2:533.

p. 448 *l.30* Schopenhauer misrepresents La Rochefoucauld's maxim. See my discussion on p. 277.

p. 451 *l.12* Schopenhauer, *The World as Will and Representation*, 2:535.

p. 451 *l.28* Ibid., p. 536.

p. 454 *l.12* Ibid., p. 557.

p. 455 *l.4* Ibid., p. 558.

p. 456 *l.20* Ibid., p. 548.

p. 457 *l.13* Arthur Schopenhauer, *Studies in Pessimism*, in *Complete Essays of Schopenhauer* (New York: Wiley, 1942), p. 79.

p. 457 *l.15* Quoted in Karl Stern, *The Flight from Woman* (New York: Noonday Press, 1968), p. 113.

p. 457 *l.27* Schopenhauer, *Studies in Pessimism*, in *Complete Essays of Schopenhauer*, p. 82.

p. 461 *l.24* Arthur Schopenhauer, *On the Basis of Morality*, trans. E.F.J. Payne (Indianapolis: Bobbs-Merrill, 1965), p. 144.

p. 464 *l.21* Schopenhauer, *The World as Will and Representation*, 2:626.

p. 465 *l.5* See Bertrand Russell, *A History of Western Philosophy* (New York: Simon and Schuster, 1945), pp. 753–59.

p. 468 *l.9* This section originally appeared in *Opera News* (December 24, 1983), pp. 11, 12, 14, 16, 17.

p. 468 *l.11* *Wagner on Music and Drama: A Compendium of Richard Wagner's Prose Writings*, ed. Albert Goldman and Evert Sprinchorn, trans. H. Ashton Ellis (New York: Dutton, 1964), p. 271.

p. 468 *l.17* Ibid., p. 272.

p. 469 *l.28* Cf. Thomas Mann, *Essays*, trans. H. T. Lowe-Porter (New York: Vintage Books, 1957), pp. 197–254.

p. 473 *l.14* *Wagner on Music and Drama*, p. 255.

p. 473 *l.17* Ibid., p. 258.

p. 473 *l.27* Ibid., p. 262.

p. 474 *l.12* Ibid., p. 273.

p. 474 *l.17* Ibid., p. 290.

p. 474 *l.22* Ibid., p. 291.

p. 475 *l.18* Quoted in Robert Raphael, *Richard Wagner* (New York: Twayne, 1969), p. 135.

p. 475 *l.28* P. 374.

p. 476 *l.14* For a somewhat different interpretation, see Bryan Magee, "Schopenhauer and Wagner," in *The Philosophy of Schopenhauer* (Oxford: Clarendon Press, 1983), particularly pp. 372–78.

p. 477 *l.31* Quoted in Mann, *Essays*, p. 203. These lines appear in a letter from Wagner to August Röckel. For a discussion of it, see George Bernard Shaw, *The Perfect Wagnerite: A Commentary on the Niblung's Ring* (New York: Dover, 1967), pp. 99–102.

p. 484 *l.17* *Selections from Ralph Waldo Emerson*, ed. Stephen E. Whicher (Boston: Houghton Mifflin, 1957), p. 141.

p. 484 *l.33* "Love," in *The Selected Writings of Ralph Waldo Emerson*, ed. Brooks Atkinson (New York: Modern Library, 1940), p. 220.

p. 485 *l.2* *Selections from Ralph Waldo Emerson*, p. 142. On Emerson's thinking about love, see Erik Ingvar Thurin, *Emerson as Priest of Pan: A Study in the Metaphysics of Sex* (Lawrence: The Regents Press of Kansas, 1981), particularly pp. 95–113.

p. 486 *l.2* "Utilitarianism," in *The Philosophy of John Stuart Mill*, ed. Marshall Cohen (New York: Modern Library, 1961), pp. 358–59.

Index

Index

Cavalcanti, 34, 130, 142–51, 159, 183, 184
Chamfort, Sébastien, 454
Chapman, George, 196
Chateaubriand, 286, 297
Châtelaine of Vergi, The, 98, 115
Chaucer, 107, 122, 130, 190, 205, 212, 225
Chrétien de Troyes, 20, 34, 99, 116–21, 136–37, 270
Cicero, 24, 100, 192
Cohen, Josh, xv
Coleridge, 197–98, 286, 288–90, 411, 414, 419, 485
Corneille, 270–73, 309
Croce, Benedetto, 141, 154
Cull, Michael, xv
Curtius, Ernst Robert, 122

Dante, 12, 34, 93, 122, 126, 130, 140–41, 143, 151–65, 178, 180–81, 183–84, 190–91, 197, 220–21
D'Arcy, M. C., x
Da Vinci, 181–82
De Musset, Alfred, 298–99
Denomy, Alexander, 60–61
De Rougemont, Denis, x–xi, 28, 77, 80, 114, 121, 135, 137, 295, 298–99, 301, 478
Descartes, 258–64, 266–67, 270, 285, 317
Destutt de Tracy, 370–72
Diderot, 304, 312–14, 322
Dilthey, Wilhelm, 384
Donaldson, E. Talbot, 61
Donne, xiv, 6, 189, 195–205, 206, 241
Dostoyevsky, 467

Ebreo, Leone, 189, 193, 195
Eckhart, 285, 293
Eilhart, 107, 116
Eliot, T. S., 157, 411–12, 421
Emerson, 484–85
Encyclopedists, 312, 317, 336, 353
Engelhardt, Herbert, xv
Equicola, Mario, 191–93, 195

Feuerbach, Ludwig, 472, 476
Fichte, 292, 383–84, 394, 396–97, 450–51
Ficino, xiii, 130, 143–44, 165–80, 183, 185–86, 188–89, 192–93, 199, 202, 211, 262, 381
Fielding, 286
Francis, St., 54–55
Freud, 5, 262, 347, 362, 412–13, 454, 478, 484, 486
Friendship, 175–77, 193, 207, 243, 260–61, 277, 301, 318, 323, 328, 330, 371, 378, 384, 388–90, 460–61
Fromm, Erich, 5

Gide, André, 354
Gilson, Etienne, 53, 90, 95–96, 162
Giotto, 55
Godwin, William, 423
Goethe, 184, 284, 315, 352, 394, 435–42, 444, 448, 474
Gottfried von Strassburg, 101–8, 110, 117, 221, 294, 473
Grierson, Herbert J. C., 204
Guillaume de Lorris, 121–23, 126, 137
Guillaume IX, 50, 52, 54–56, 130
Guinizelli, Guido, 130, 155, 159

Hagstrum, Jean H., xv
Hartmann von Aue, 57
Hazlitt, 210, 296
Hegel, 11, 116, 129, 290, 376, 383, 393–411, 422, 432–33, 438, 444, 449, 451, 459–60, 462, 468, 472, 483–84
Heine, Heinrich, 384, 473
Heloise, 88–101, 104, 122, 305, 313, 318, 378–79
Helvétius, 352, 356
Henry of Suso, 137
Hobbes, 303, 337, 345, 350, 418, 423
Hölderlin, 398, 400, 442
Hugh of St. Victor, 125
Huizinga, Johan, 20